A Companion to Herman Melville

Blackwell Companions to Literature and Culture

This series offers comprehensive, newly written surveys of key periods and movements and certain major authors, in English literary culture and history. Extensive volumes provide new perspectives and positions on contexts and on canonical and post-canonical texts, orientating the beginning student in new fields of study and providing the experienced undergraduate and new graduate with current and new directions, as pioneered and developed by leading scholars in the field.

A COMPANION TO

HERMAN MELVILLE

EDITED BY WYN KELLEY

Blackwell
Publishing

BLACKWELL PUBLISHING
350 Main Street, Malden, MA 02148-5020, USA
9600 Garsington Road, Oxford OX4 2DQ, UK
550 Swanston Street, Carlton, Victoria 3053, Australia

First published 2006 by Blackwell Publishing Ltd

1 2006

Library of Congress Cataloging-in-Publication Data

A companion to Herman Melville / edited by Wyn Kelley.
    p. cm. — (Blackwell companions to literature and culture; 41)
Includes bibliographical references and index.
ISBN-13: 978-1-4051-2231-3 (alk. paper)
ISBN-10: 1-4051-2231-5 (alk. paper)
1. Melville, Herman, 1819–1891.—Criticism and interpretation—Handbooks, manuals, etc.
I. Kelley, Wyn. II. Series.

PS2387.C66 2006
813'.3—dc22

2006003196

A catalogue record for this title is available from the British Library.

Set in 11 on 13pt Garamond
by SPI Publisher Services, Pondicherry, India
Printed and bound in Singapore
by Markono Print Media Pte Ltd

The publisher's policy is to use permanent paper from mills that operate a sustainable forestry policy, and which has been manufactured from pulp processed using acid-free and elementary chlorine-free practices. Furthermore, the publisher ensures that the text paper and cover board used have met acceptable environmental accreditation standards.

For further information on
Blackwell Publishing, visit our website:
www.blackwellpublishing.com

Herman Melville by Joseph O. Eaton, 1870. Reprinted by permission of the Houghton Library, Harvard University

For Dale Peterson

Contents

Illustrations

Notes on Contributors

Charlene Avallone writes as an independent scholar based in Kailua, Hawai'i, having served on the faculties of the universities of Notre Dame and Hawai'i. She sits on the editorial board of *Leviathan* and, with Carolyn Karcher, co-directed the Fourth International Melville Conference, *Melville and the Pacific*, on Maui in 2003. Her publications treat Margaret Fuller and Catharine Sedgwick in addition to Melville, as well as the gender and racial limitations of the American renaissance critical tradition. Her work in progress studies the feminization of conversation in the US (1770 to 1870). Forthcoming essays include "Elizabeth Palmer Peabody and the Discipline of Conversation" in *Reinventing the Peabody Sisters* (edited by Katharine Rodier, Julie Hall, and Monika Elbert).

Mary K. Bercaw Edwards is a past president of the Melville Society and an Associate Professor in the Department of English at the University of Connecticut. She teaches primarily for the Maritime Studies degree program. Bercaw Edwards is the author of *Melville's Sources* (1987) and the co-editor of Wilson Heflin's *Herman Melville's Whaling Years* (2004). In addition to teaching, Bercaw Edwards works at Mystic Seaport: The Museum of America and the Sea. She sets sails aboard the whaleship *Charles W. Morgan*, the only extant whaleship in the world, which was built in the same town as, and only six months after, Melville's first whaleship, the *Acushnet*.

Dennis Berthold is Professor of English at Texas A&M University, where he teaches nineteenth-century American literature and literature of the sea. His scholarship emphasizes the cultural politics of iconography, landscape, and the visual arts, and covers writers ranging from Charles Brockden Brown, Nathaniel Hawthorne, and Herman Melville to Mark Twain, Constance Fenimore Woolson, and Joshua Slocum. His articles have appeared in *William & Mary Quarterly*, *American Literary History*, *American Literature*, and *Nineteenth-Century Literature*, and he has contributed essays on Melville and Dutch genre painting to Christopher Sten's *Savage Eye: Melville and the Visual Arts* (1991), contemporary sea fiction to Haskell Springer's *America and the Sea* (1995), and maritime fiction to the forthcoming *Oxford Encyclopedia of Maritime History*. He has co-edited a book on Walt Whitman and one on Hawthorne and is completing a monograph on Melville and Italy.

Hester Blum is Assistant Professor of English at Pennsylvania State University; she received her Ph.D. from the University of Pennsylvania. She is currently completing a book entitled *The View from the Mast-Head: Antebellum American Sea Narratives and the Maritime Imagination*. The book describes sailors' broader participation in literary culture, and argues specifically that first-person narratives of working sailors propose a method for aligning labor and contemplation. Blum has written essays, forthcoming and in print, on Barbary captivity narratives, James Fenimore Cooper's sea fiction, Douglass's and Melville's narrative treatment of rape, and Pacific Island gravesites and burial at sea.

John Bryant, Professor of English at Hofstra University, has published *A Companion to Melville Studies* (Greenwood, 1986) and *Melville and Repose* (Oxford 1996), and editions of *Typee* (Penguin 1996, 2005) and *The Confidence-Man* (Random House, 2003), as well as *Melville's Tales, Poems, and Other Writings* (Random House, 2001). Editor of the Melville Society's periodical *Leviathan: A Journal of Melville Studies*, he is also General Editor of the *Pearson Custom Anthology of American Literature*. Bryant's work in textual scholarship includes *The Fluid Text: A Theory of Revision and Editing for Book and Screen* (Michigan, 2002). His study of the *Typee* manuscript, entitled *Melville Unfolding: Typee as Fluid Text* (University of Michigan Press), along with the electronic edition of the manuscript (University of Virginia Press), are forthcoming in 2006. Bryant and co-editor Haskell Springer are currently working on the Longman critical edition of *Moby-Dick*, due out in 2006.

Alex Calder teaches in the English Department at the University of Auckland, New Zealand. His research focuses on literature and the processes of cultural contact and settlement, particularly with regard to writings from New Zealand, the Pacific, and the United States. His most recent book is an edition of *Old New Zealand and Other Writings* by F. E. Maning – a writer who lived something of the life Melville might have done had he accompanied Tobias Greene to New Zealand and married into a Maori tribe. His current project, a book entitled the "The Settler's Plot," offers environmental and cross-cultural perspectives on New Zealand literature.

Christopher Castiglia is Professor of English at Loyola University Chicago. He is the author of *Bound and Determined: Captivity, Culture-Crossing, and White Womanhood from Mary Rowlandson to Patty Hearst* (Chicago, 1996) and *Interior States* (Duke, forthcoming), as well as co-editor of Walt Whitman's *Franklin Evans* (Duke University Press, forthcoming).

Carol Colatrella is Professor of Literature in the School of Literature, Communication, and Culture, and Co-director of the Georgia Tech Center for the Study of Women, Science, and Technology at Georgia Institute of Technology. She has published *Evolution, Sacrifice, and Narrative: Balzac, Zola, and Faulkner* (1990), *Literature and Moral Reform: Melville and the Discipline of Reading* (2002), and (with Joseph Alkana) *Cohesion and Dissent in America* (1994). She is currently working on a book analyzing representations in popular culture of women engaging with science and technology, to be titled *Toys and Tools in Pink: Cultural Narratives of Gender, Science, and Technology*.

Edgar A. Dryden, Professor of English at the University of Arizona and editor of the *Arizona Quarterly*, is the author of *Melville's Thematics of Form*, *Nathaniel Hawthorne: The Poetics of Enchantment*, *The Form of American Romance*, and *Monumental Melville*, as well as numerous essays and reviews.

Marvin Fisher, a past president of the Melville Society, has been writing on Melville topics since the mid-1960s. Two of his four published books also focus on Melville, and another on the cultural impact of early American industrialization. Aided by four Fulbright lecture-ships, he has ranged far from his home base at Arizona State University to teach American literature at universities in Greece, Norway, and Germany, as well as holding visiting positions at the University of Minnesota and the University of California at Davis.

Peter Gibian teaches in the English Department at McGill University in Montréal. His publications include *Mass Culture and Everyday Life* (Routledge, 1997) and *Oliver Wendell Holmes and the Culture of Conversation* (Cambridge University Press, 2001, awarded the Lois Rudnick Prize for Best Book in 2001 and 2002 by NEASA), as well as essays on Whitman, Poe, Twain, Justice Holmes, Wharton and James, and cosmopolitanism in nineteenth-century American literature. His new book (*American Talk*) explores the workings of a mid-nineteenth-century "culture of conversation" across the spectrum of talk modes and venues as it shaped the writings of a wide range of authors, and he is at work on a book on the emergence of a cosmopolitan tradition in American writing.

Robin Grey received her Ph.D. from the University of California at Los Angeles and is Associate Professor of English at the University of Illinois at Chicago. She is author of *The Complicity of Imagination: The American Renaissance, Contests of Authority, and Seventeenth-Century English Culture* (Cambridge University Press, 1997), and most recently she edited and contributed an essay to *Melville and Milton: An Edition and Analysis of Melville's Annotations on Milton* (Duquesne University Press, 2004). She has been a recipient of the Andrew W. Mellon Fellowship, as well as the Hennig Cohen Award from the Melville Society. She is currently working on two book projects: antebellum nineteenth-century alternative histories of the Civil War; and the American landscape in painting, politics, and literature: the quest for an American national identity.

Bruce A. Harvey, who received his Ph.D. in English from Stanford University, is an Associate Professor at Florida International University. He teaches a wide range of American literature and culture studies courses, designed to interweave US literary or cultural narratives with more world-embracing ones. In addition to articles in *American Quarterly* and elsewhere, he has published *American Geographics: U.S. National Narratives and the Representation of the Non-European World, 1830–1865*. Currently, he is completing an interdisciplinary study entitled "After Elvis After Cook: Pacific Island Identities, from Anthropology to Pop Culture."

Wyn Kelley, of the Literature Faculty at the Massachusetts Institute of Technology, is author of *Melville's City: Literary and Urban Form in Nineteenth-Century New York* (1996). Associate Editor of the Melville Society journal *Leviathan*, she has published in a number of journals and collections, including *Melville and Hawthorne*: *Writing Relationship*, *Ungraspable Phantom*: *Essays on* Moby-Dick, *Melville and Women*, *"Whole Oceans Away"*: *Melville in the Pacific*, and the *Cambridge Companion to Herman Melville*.

A. Robert Lee, formerly of the University of Kent at Canterbury, UK, since 1996 has been Professor of American Literature at Nihon University, Tokyo. His recent publications include *Multicultural American Literature: Comparative Black, Native, Latino/a and Asian American Fictions* (2003), which won an American Book Award, *Designs of Blackness: Mappings in the Literatures and Culture of Afro-America* (1998), and, with Gerald Vizenor, *Postindian Conversations* (1999). His longstanding Melville interests are reflected in Everyman editions of *Typee* (1993), *Moby-Dick* (1973, 1992, 1993) and *Billy Budd and Other Tales* (1993), and the essay collections *Herman Melville: Re-Assessments* (1984) and *Herman Melville: Critical Assessments* (2001).

Maurice S. Lee is an Assistant Professor of English at Boston University where he specializes in nineteenth-century American literature. He is particularly interested in how literature mediates intellectual and cultural histories; and his articles have appeared in *American Literature*, *PMLA*, *ESQ*, and *African American Review*. He has also recently published his first book, *Slavery, Philosophy, and American Literature, 1830–1860* (Cambridge University Press, 2005).

Caroline Levander is Associate Professor of English at Rice University. She is author of *Voices of the Nation: Women and Public Speech in Nineteenth-Century American Literature and Culture* (Cambridge University Press, 1998), and *Cradle of Liberty: Race, the Child, and National Belonging from Thomas Jefferson to W. E. B. Du Bois* (Duke University Press, forthcoming). She has published on nineteenth-century American literature and political cultures in *American Literature*, *American Literary History*, *Radical History Review*, and elsewhere.

Paul Lyons is Associate Professor of English at the University of Hawai'i-Manoa, where he specializes in US literatures, regional/settler literatures, and literary and cultural theory. Lyons is the author of three novels, most recently *Button Man*, and writes regular reviews and essays on cultural production in Oceania. His book on US involvement in Oceania, *American Pacifism: Oceania in the U.S. Imagination*, is forthcoming from Routledge.

R. D. Madison is Professor of English and Director of English Honors at the US Naval Academy. An Editorial Associate of the Northwestern–Newberry edition of *The Writings of Herman Melville* and a member of the editorial board of *The Writings of James Fenimore Cooper*, he has edited a variety of literary and historical works, including T. W. Higginson's *Army Life in a Black Regiment*, William Bligh and Edward Christian's *The Bounty Mutiny*, Jack London's *The Cruise of the Snark* and (with Michelle Allen) R. D. Blackmore's *Lorna Doone* for Penguin Classics. He is a prize-winning playwright and an avid motorcyclist and birdwatcher.

Sanford E. Marovitz is Professor Emeritus of English at Kent State University, where he taught from 1967 to 1996. He has also taught at the University of Athens and as a Visiting Professor at Shimane University (Japan). Author and co-author/editor of four books, he has published widely in journals and critical collections. With A. K. Christodoulou, he co-directed the first International Melville Conference in Volos, Greece (1997); the proceedings volume *Melville Among the Nations*, was published by Kent State University Press in 2001.

Hilton Obenzinger is author of *American Palestine: Melville, Twain and the Holy Land Mania*, along with articles on American literature, culture, and religion, including "Going to Tom's Hell in *Huckleberry Finn*" in Blackwell's *Companion to Mark Twain*. A poet and novelist, and a recipient of the American Book Award, his books include *A*hole, Cannibal Eliot and the Lost Histories of San Francisco*, and *New York on Fire*. He teaches advanced writing and American literature at Stanford University.

Samuel Otter, Associate Professor of English at the University of California, Berkeley, has published *Melville's Anatomies* (1999). He currently is working on a book about race, manners, violence, and freedom between the Constitution and the Civil War, entitled *Philadelphia Stories*. He has published essays recently in books about Philadelphia and on Stowe and race and has essays forthcoming on Melville and disability, American literary criticism, and fiction and fact in *Typee*. He is co-editing a volume of essays on Frederick Douglass and Herman Melville.

Rachela Permenter, Professor of English at Slippery Rock University of Pennsylvania, earned her MA at Kent State University and her Ph.D. at Northern Illinois University. She has published in the areas of Melville studies, film, and Native American literature. Her book, *Nondual Vision: Sighting Romantic Postmodernism*, is currently under review for publication.

Leland S. Person is Professor and Head of the English Department at the University of Cincinnati. He is the author of *Henry James and the Suspense of Masculinity* (2003), *Aesthetic Headaches: Women and a Masculine Poetics in Poe, Melville, and Hawthorne* (1988), and many articles on nineteenth-century American writers, especially Hawthorne, Poe, Melville, Henry James, and James Fenimore Cooper. He has recently edited a new Norton Critical Edition, *The Scarlet Letter and Other Writings*.

Basem L. Ra'ad is Professor and Chair of English at Al-Quds University in Jerusalem. Born in Jerusalem and educated in diaspora, he has a Ph.D. from the University of Toronto and has published on Herman Melville, John Updike, landscape aesthetics, linguistics, ancient place-names, travel writing, and other subjects. His recent research emphasizes ancient civilizations, identity politics, and the relationship of scholarship to public information.

Elizabeth Renker is the author of *Strike Through the Mask: Herman Melville and the Scene of Writing* (1996), as well as of numerous essays on Melville, on American literature and culture, on the history of higher education, and on the effective teaching of poetry. She is also the author of the introduction to the Signet Classic edition of *Moby-Dick* (1998). She has two books in progress. The first, *American Literature in the Higher Curriculum*, is a cultural history of how "American literature" became a field of knowledge in American colleges and universities between 1870 and 1950. The second, *The Lost Era in American Poetry, 1865–1910*, explores the phenomenon of realist poetry. She is Associate Professor of English at the Ohio State University.

Laurie Robertson-Lorant is the author of *Melville: A Biography* (1996) and *The Man Who Lived Among the Cannibals: Poems in the Voice of Herman Melville* (Spinner Publications, 2005). She has taught at Berkshire Community College, St. Mark's School, and MIT, and is currently a Full-Time Visiting Lecturer in the Education Department at the University of Massachusetts, Dartmouth. Her articles have been published in the US and abroad, and she has directed workshops for teachers on "Melville and Pacific History" for the Hawai'i Council for the Humanities, and National Endowment for the Humanities workshops on "Melville and Multiculturalism" and "Visions of Slavery and Freedom in the Writings of Lydia Maria Child, Frederick Douglass, Herman Melville, and Harriet Jacobs." Her poems have appeared in *Igitur, Leviathan, South Coast Poetry Journal*, the *American Voice*, the *North American Review*, the *Worcester Review*, and *October Mountain: An Anthology of Berkshire Writers*, edited by Paul Metcalf.

Geoffrey Sanborn is the author of *The Sign of the Cannibal: Melville and the Making of a Postcolonial Reader* (Duke University Press, 1998) and the editor of the New Riverside Edition of *Typee* (2003). He has contributed essays on Melville to *American Literature, Arizona Quarterly, Nineteenth-Century Literature*, and *ESQ*, and has published several studies of other writers, including Nathaniel Hawthorne, Edgar Allan Poe, Emily Dickinson, Sandra Cisneros, and Frances Harper. He is currently at work on a book called *Whip-scars and Tattoos: Tracing the Maori in* The Last of the Mohicans *and* Moby-Dick.

Elizabeth Schultz retired in 2001 from the University of Kansas, where she was the Chancellor's Club Teaching Professor in the English Department. The author of *Unpainted to the Last:* Moby-Dick *and Twentieth-Century American Art* (1995) and *Shoreline: Seasons at the Lake* (2001), she has published extensively in the fields of African American fiction and autobiography, nineteenth-century American fiction, American women's writing, and Japanese culture; she continues to publish poetry, short stories, and essays on nature. A founder of the Melville Society Cultural Project in New Bedford, Massachusetts, she has curated several exhibitions related to Melville and the arts, and has edited a collection of essays on Melville and women to be published in 2006.

John Stauffer is Professor of English and the History of American Civilization at Harvard University. He received his Ph.D. from Yale University in 1999, and has written and lectured widely on slavery, abolition, social protest, and photography. His first book, *The Black Hearts of Men: Radical Abolitionists and the Transformation of Race* (2002), received four major awards, including the Frederick Douglass Book Prize, the Avery Craven Book Prize, and the Lincoln Prize runner-up. Other publications include the Modern Library edition of Frederick Douglass's *My Bondage and My Freedom*, an anthology on John Brown, *Meteor of War: The John Brown Story*, and numerous essays in *21st: The Journal of Contemporary Photography*. He is completing a new book, *By the Love of Comrades: American Interracial Friendships in History and Myth*.

Christopher Sten is Professor of English and Director of Writing in the Disciplines at George Washington University. He has published two critical studies of Melville's fiction – *The Weaver-God, He Weaves* (1996) and *Sounding the Whale* (1996) – and edited a collection of essays on Melville's appropriation of the visual arts, titled *Savage Eye* (1991), all with Kent State University Press. He is currently co-editing a collection of essays on "Melville and the Pacific," and completing a history of American writers' involvement in national politics, to be titled *Washington, DC: The Politics of American Writing*. A former Senior Fulbright Lecturer in Würzburg, Germany, he is a past president and executive secretary of the Melville Society and currently serves as the Society's historian.

Gale Temple is Assistant Professor of English at the University of Alabama at Birmingham, where he specializes in early American literature and culture. He has published an article on Fanny Fern and has another forthcoming on Hawthorne's *Blithedale Romance*. His current projects include essays on Charles Brockden Brown and James Fenimore Cooper, and a book manuscript that focuses on connections between literature, economic change, and social reform in antebellum America.

Robert K. Wallace is Regents Professor of Literature and Language at Northern Kentucky University. His most recent book is *Douglass and Melville* (2005). Earlier books include *Frank Stella's* Moby-Dick (2001), *Melville and Turner* (1992), *Emily Brontë and Beethoven* (1986), *Jane Austen and Mozart* (1983), and *A Century of Music-Making* (1976). Wallace has curated exhibitions on Douglass and Melville, Stella and Melville, Turner and Melville, Melville's print collection, and student art inspired by Melville's writing. He is a former president of the Melville Society and a founding member of the Melville Society Cultural Project in New Bedford, MA.

Ellen Weinauer is an Associate Professor in the Department of English at the University of Southern Mississippi. She is the author of articles on Hawthorne, Melville, Elizabeth Stoddard, and others, and the co-editor, along with Robert McClure Smith, of *American Culture, Canons, and the Case of Elizabeth Stoddard* (University of Alabama Press, 2003).

Cindy Weinstein is an Associate Professor of English at the California Institute of Technology. She is the author of *The Literature of Labor and the Labors of Literature: Allegory in Nineteenth-Century American Fiction* (Cambridge University Press, 1995) and *Family, Kinship, and Sympathy in Nineteenth-Century American Literature* (Cambridge University Press, 2004). She is also the editor of *The Cambridge Companion to Harriet Beecher Stowe* (Cambridge University Press, 2004). She has written essays for *The Cambridge Companion to*

Herman Melville (Cambridge University Press, 1998), *A Companion to American Fiction 1780–1865* (Blackwell, 2004), and *What Democracy Looks Like: A New Realism for a Post-Seattle World* (Rutgers, forthcoming).

John Wenke is Professor of English at Salisbury University, where he teaches American literature and writing. His books include *Melville's Muse: Literary Creation and the Forms of Philosophical Fiction* and *J. D. Salinger: A Study of the Short Fiction*. He has published numerous essays, short stories, and chapters. His earlier essays on *Billy Budd* have appeared in *Leviathan* and *New Essays on Billy Budd*.

Acknowledgments

My utmost gratitude goes to the authors in this book, who taught me the pleasures of collaboration on a grand scale. I owe many thanks to Andrew McNeillie for inviting me into the project, and to Emma Bennett, Karen Wilson, Jenny Hunt, and Glynis Baguley for their wise guidance through its different stages. Wai Chee Dimock, Diana Henderson, and Timothy Marr offered invaluable advice during the planning phase. I am immensely grateful to John Bryant and Robert S. Levine for their generous readings of the proposal. Members of the Melville Society Cultural Project – Jill Barnum, Mary K. Bercaw-Edwards, Elizabeth Schultz, Christopher Sten, and Robert K. Wallace – lent unfailingly kind support throughout. Millicent C. Kelley's courage continues to inspire my work, Britt and Bayne Peterson sustain it with their joy and creativity, and Dale Peterson is the staunch companion who makes it all worthwhile.

Texts and Abbreviations

Unless otherwise noted by individual authors, all references to Melville's works are to *The Writings of Herman Melville*, ed. Harrison Hayford, Hershel Parker, and G. Thomas Tanselle in 13 vols. (Evanston and Chicago: Northwestern University Press and the Newberry Library, 1968–). The only exceptions are *Collected Poems of Herman Melville*, ed. Howard P. Vincent (Chicago: Hendricks House, 1947); and *Billy Budd, Sailor*, ed. Harrison Hayford and Merton M. Sealts, Jr. (Chicago: University of Chicago Press, 1962). Abbreviations for these texts are as follows:

T	*Typee*
O	*Omoo*
M	*Mardi*
R	*Redburn*
WJ	*White-Jacket*
MD	*Moby-Dick*
P	*Pierre*
PT	*The Piazza Tales and Uncollected Prose*
IP	*Israel Potter*
CM	*The Confidence-Man*
L	*Correspondence*
J	*Journals*
CP	*Collected Poems*
C	*Clarel*
BB	*Billy Budd*

Other works to which authors may refer by author's last name (and in the cases of Leyda and Parker, volume number) are as follows:

Bercaw, Mary K. *Melville's Sources*. Evanston, IL: Northwestern University Press, 1987.
Leyda, Jay. *The Melville Log: A Documentary Life of Herman Melville, 1819–1891*. New York: Gordian Press, 1950. In two volumes.

Parker, Hershel. *Herman Melville: A Biography. Vol. 1, 1819–1851. Vol. 2, 1851–1891.* Baltimore and London: Johns Hopkins University Press, 1996, 2002.

Robertson-Lorant, Laurie. *Melville: A Biography.* New York: Clarkson Potter, 1996; Boston and Amherst: University of Massachusetts Press, 1998.

Sealts, Merton M., Jr., *Melville's Reading.* Revised and enlarged edition. Columbia, SC: University of South Carolina Press, 1988.

Note   Spellings of certain words – Hawaii/Hawai'i, Nukuhiva/Nuku Hiva, Typee/Taipi – differ from chapter to chapter, depending on authors' sources and preferences.

Preface

Wyn Kelley

Although Herman Melville (1819–91) longed for appreciative readers, he might have viewed with skepticism any attempt to inspect his writing too closely: as he remarked in his article, "Hawthorne and His Mosses" (1850), "on a personal interview no great author has ever come up to the idea of his reader" (*PT* 240). Indeed, even his essay on Hawthorne begins with an attentive study of the book's mossy-green cover, and in reviews of works by James Fenimore Cooper, J. Ross Browne, and Francis Parkman, Melville tended to comment on the books' showy bindings and titles as much as on their contents, as if to advertise his disdain for more invasive forms of criticism. His conclusion to a review of Cooper's *The Red Rover*, "A Thought on Book-Binding," reminds us that Melville was an avid reader before he was ever a writer: "at the present day we deem any elaborate criticism of Cooper's Red Rover quite unnecessary and uncalled-for. Long ago, and far inland, we read it in our uncritical days, and enjoyed it as much as thousands of the rising generation will when supplied with such an entertaining volume in such agreeable type" (*PT* 238). His own novels, stories, and poems, however, have inspired considerably more penetrating analysis over the more than 150 years since his career began, and not just on their covers and typefaces either. For many a contemporary newcomer to Melville, however, the weight of that criticism may bear down forbiddingly, suggesting that one can no longer encounter him freshly as his first readers did, or without scholarly aids. Many new readers approach Melville's works with trepidation; not realizing that Melville was for much of his life an outsider in the nineteenth-century literary establishment, they see him as an example of elite literary status and hence a somewhat forbidding challenge.

This volume attempts to head off some of this apprehension by offering, not a comprehensive guide to or theory of his works, but rather a companion, such as what Melville himself was looking for in his readers. If Melville's view is any indication, literary companionship on his terms might be pleasurable indeed. Take, for example, Melville's description of the narrator's friend Jack Chase in *White-Jacket* (1850), his novel about the US navy. When listening to the poet-sailor Lemsford recite his verses, Chase, captain of the foretop, extends the kindest of responses: "Taking the liberty of a well-wisher, he would sometimes gently criticize the piece, suggesting a few immaterial alterations. And upon my word, noble Jack, with his native-born good sense, taste, and humanity, was not ill qualified to play the true part of a *Quarterly Review*; – which is, to give quarter at last, however severe the critique" (*WJ* 41). Jack Chase is as generous on the subject of authorship as he is as critic, arguing that literary value inheres in men's hearts, not always on the printed page: "'I've that here, White-Jacket' – touching his forehead – 'which, under happier skies – perhaps in yon solitary star there, peeping down from those clouds – might have made a Homer of me. But Fate is Fate, White-Jacket; and we Homers who happen to be captains of tops must write our odes in our hearts, and publish them in our heads'" (271). With Jack Chase for literary companion, Melville suggests, one can spin yarns, reel off lines of poetry, or listen to storied adventures with ease and pleasure.

Another inspiring literary companion was Nathaniel Hawthorne, whom Melville addresses in one of his letters as an ideal reader of *Moby-Dick*: "A sense of unspeakable security is in me this moment, on account of your having understood the book." The communion he imagines between them grows from Hawthorne's heartfelt acceptance of what Melville wrote: "But, now and then as you read, you understood the pervading thought that impelled the book – and that you praised. Was it not so? You were archangel enough to despise the imperfect body, and embrace the soul." The companionship Melville envisions is not without conflict or strain – "when the big hearts strike together, the concussion is a little stunning" – but nevertheless provides an almost unearthly satisfaction: "with you for a passenger, I am content and can be happy." Uplifted by Hawthorne's friendship, Melville plans to "write a thousand – a million – billion thoughts, all under the form of a letter to you. The divine magnet is on you, and my magnet responds" (Nov. 17?, 1851; *L* 212–13).

As these brief extracts suggest, the spirit of Melville's ideal of literary companionship is expansive, inclusive, and exuberant. The alternative appears far less appealing, as in his vision of authors like Lombardo in *Mardi* (1848), who despises his projected readers – "Critics? – Asses!" (*M* 599) – or his protagonist in *Pierre* (1852), who "felt the pyramidical scorn of the genuine loftiness for the whole infinite company of infinitesimal critics" (*P* 339). These authors are companionless, writing in a spiritual and social void apart from the world of readers. Yet they have been taken as autobiographical portraits of Melville's own literary solitude and elitism. Much has been made, in fact, of Melville's bookish isolation in the long years that followed his early recognition and success. It has become axiomatic to think of Melville as someone who found his real audience only midway through the twentieth century, long after such appreciative responses could do him any good.

But Lombardo and Pierre are satiric portraits of the kind of author Melville saw as a literary dead end. His descriptions of intense and cordial dialogue among characters in his long poem *Clarel* (1876) – a narrative of pilgrims and tourists in the Holy Land – and his portrayals of omnivorous book-lovers like Ishmael, even his thoughtful (if limited) readers, like the narrator of "Bartleby, the Scrivener" (1853) or Captain Vere in *Billy Budd, Sailor* (1891), or his genial raconteurs, like the Cosmopolitan in *The Confidence-Man* (1857) and "Bridegroom Dick" in *John Marr and Other Sailors* (1888), suggest that he imagined the relationship between author and reader as fluid, open, and embracing. A self-taught writer who famously proclaimed that "a whale-ship was my Yale College and my Harvard" (*MD* 112), Melville did not demand a reader equipped with any more degrees than he had – only the curiosity, passion, imagination, and openness to experience that sent him to sea and later to authorship.

This Companion, then, offers twenty-first-century readers a model of capacious appraisal along the lines of Jack Chase's or Hawthorne's receptive understandings of Melville's work. It aims to encourage as many different interpretations and potential readers as possible. And its sense of what constitutes a potential reader is informed by global technologies and economies which Melville could only faintly imagine but which deeply influence what texts get consumed today and in what ways. Melville labored in and critiqued the earliest phases of the United States' and Europe's attempts to establish a global economy, but he could not have anticipated that the descendants of Marquesans among whom he lived as a captive, or of Asian or South American or Azorean sailors he could have met on his voyages, might one day find their way to his books – on the internet. He could not have conceived of worldwide modes of dissemination of texts and ideas, nor of the branding that separates *Moby-Dick* as global icon from the book itself. As foreign to him as the academic societies and conferences devoted to his works would be the free-floating, oceanic tides of his reputation lapping the farthest shores of a world he described in *Moby-Dick* as "things remote" (7).

Ironically, however, that inter-network of words, people, ideas, nations, cultures, and identities provides the ground for a readership newly prepared to appreciate a writer of Melville's global reach. Whether his books are seen as examples of US cultural imperialism, precursors of Hollywood and Coca-Cola, or as protests against that cultural dominance, or, more accurately perhaps, as something in the rich and liminal space between, Melville speaks to a wider audience than ever. With the development of expanded technologies, media, and theoretical tools, the resources for considering Melville globally have become vastly more diverse and sophisticated. This confluence of new media and scholarship presents a superb opportunity for rethinking – and offering a new companion for – an author who has become the most global of America's writers.

This volume is organized according to the broadest possible categories, some of them quite traditional, for thinking of Melville's literary concerns, sources, and significances. Its six sections engage some of the many different domains of Melville's work and experience. The first, "Travels," offers various ways of thinking about the comprehensive span of Melville's voyaging life, culture, and reputation. As an introduction to themes developed elsewhere in the volume, it provides biographical, historical, and theoretical tools for considering Melville's place in what he called in *Redburn* (1849) "a moving world" (*R* 137). These essays also suggest that as much as Melville traveled the world, travel itself and the world he traveled through moved and changed, and they continue to change the way his works are perceived.

The next section, called "Geographies," explores some of the parts of the earth Melville journeyed through and studied. Melville's whaling years uprooted him from accustomed places and reoriented him toward ocean, earth, sky, deep time, planetary space, and antediluvian history. These essays examine the new nineteenth-century sciences of geography, natural history, and pre-evolutionary theory, the world of ships and the sea, Melville's experience of and thinking about nature, and his encounters with other cultures in the development of his *œuvre*. In looking more specifically at oceans, these essays also connect with issues of the economic and cultural exploitation of Africa for slaves and the Pacific islands for converts and resources. The chapter "Ancient Lands" considers Melville's exploration of the Mediterranean and the Holy Lands later in his life, when the oceans of his voyaging years seemed like distant paradises, and his inspiration came from, to him, new – and ancient – landscapes.

Melville was a citizen of one nation, the United States of America, but his writing concerned itself deeply with nations and themes of nationhood in the century of European and American empire building. The third section imagines the different "Nations" that occupied a space called the United States – nations of competing races, religions, genders, and classes. These essays look at the political and social issues that marked these concerns and show Melville as profoundly aware of and responsive to the contradictions of American democracy throughout his career. Although there is considerable disagreement over Melville's political positions and their significance, it is clear at the same time that his writing was energized by the national debates jostling the public space around him – debates over slavery, poverty, urbanization, the church and its institutions, gender and sexuality, and the public sphere of a troubled and contentious democracy.

In *Moby-Dick* Ishmael claims that he "swam through libraries" (136). Melville's reading ranged from popular to highbrow authors in a wide range of discourses: philosophy, history, poetry, fiction, science, maritime narrative and exploration literature, women's fiction and poetry, theology, and other realms. This volume's fourth section, "Libraries," examines his responses to literary predecessors like Shakespeare and Milton, Camoens and Scoresby, to contemporaries like Wordsworth, Emerson, Mme. de Staël, Richard Henry Dana, and Hawthorne, as well as to the popular publishing market and visual arts. These essays sketch the breadth of Melville's literary interests and some of the varieties of his reading experiences and aesthetic preferences. They give a sense of the productive ways he adapted, stole from, and reconfigured some artists and acknowledged his love and reverence for others.

We can think of Melville's "Texts," as the next section is called, as rising from his travels through the worlds of science, nature, politics, and philosophy, but a contemporary reader often encounters them simply as works of "literature." This section, then, samples Melville's writings and the ways they take up broad themes – social class, the spiritual quest, labor, race, capitalism, identity, gender, domesticity – as well as literary topics: uses of metaphor, theories of language, epic form, narrative point of view, poetics, style. In different ways these chapters reflect on Melville's concept of artists and their work, narrators and what they see, the possibilities and limits of language, the fluid boundaries between different genres and forms, or between poetry and prose.

This section, then, might address questions many contemporary readers have about Melville's achievement and might help to explain his prevailing impact as a literary artist. The study of Melville does not end with close reading of his books, however. As a cultural phenomenon, a symbol of the American literary canon, and still, remarkably, an enduringly popular author, Melville continues to generate strong responses and considerable controversy. The final section, "Meanings," considers the way Melville persists in "meaning" something to an ever-widening readership. This section surveys his critical reputation, with the dramatic "Melville Revival" of the twentieth century, his relationship with popular culture and visual media, and the new possibilities for reading his work with the tools of digital technology. It also signals that Melville's "meanings" are not grounded in scholarship and criticism alone but in the ever-generative work of those who continue to buy, read, spread, and talk about his books. The "weaver-god" (*MD* 450) of Melville's artistic inspiration continues to ply an elastic and fluid thread and to construct an expansive web.

What might Melville have made of his expanding circle of literary companions? A wry passage from *White-Jacket* suggests an answer:

> My book experiences on board of the frigate proved an example of a fact which every book-lover must have experienced before me, namely, that though public libraries have an imposing air, and doubtless contain invaluable volumes, yet, somehow, the books that prove most agreeable, grateful, and companionable, are those we pick up by chance here and there; those which seem put into our hands by Providence; those which pretend to little, but abound in much. (169)

It is hard for twenty-first-century readers to think of Melville, the towering creator of what many still consider America's greatest novel, as so modest a writer as the "companionable" authors he praises here. Dwelling in his company, however, as this volume invites one to do at leisure, may make him a good comrade – just what he might have wished.

Part I
Travels

1
A Traveling Life

Laurie Robertson-Lorant

By 1819, the year Herman Melville was born, New York, the "insular city of the Manhattoes, belted round by wharves as Indian isles by coral reefs" (*MD* 3), was a bustling seaport, a labyrinth of streets and alleyways where names like Canton, Guinea, Curaçao, Java, New Orleans, Papua, Calcutta, Maracaibo, and Marseilles rolled like poetry off the tongues of tattooed ruffians. A proverbial "forest of masts" swayed above the waterfront, and from the docks, great wooden cities of sail set forth carrying cotton, tobacco, spirits, furs, lumber, whale oil, cheese, livestock, potash, grains, and flours to the farthest reaches of the globe and returned with sugar and rum from the West Indies, spices and teas from India and Ceylon, porcelain and silk from China, Flemish lace and Belgian linens, bushels of cocoa beans, and slabs of rosewood, teak, and mahogany.

Melville was born at 6 Pearl Street, a stone's throw from the Battery, where a baby in a carriage on the promenade could inhale salt and spicy air from oceans half the world away. His earliest boyhood memories were of ships and sailors and strange languages. His mother and grandmother conversed in Dutch, his father and Uncle Thomas both spoke French, and, from an early age, the apple-cheeked boy dreamed of exploring exotic shores and distant seas.

Both of Melville's grandfathers were heroes of the American Revolution, which made the family's history coeval with the history of the new nation. Melville's maternal grandfather, the late Colonel Peter Gansevoort, had owned slaves, as many northern gentlemen did in those days, and he had cracked the heads of several Iroquois during the French and Indian Wars. His paternal grandfather, Major Thomas Melvill,[1] a Boston merchant and sometime customs inspector, kept a glass vial on his mantel filled with tea leaves from the Boston Tea Party that conjured images of himself and the other Sons of Liberty dressed up as Mohawk Indians, war-whooping their way to Boston Harbor to dump the British tea. A neighborhood fire warden in his old age, the eccentric patriot wore the knee-breeches, silk stockings, buckled pumps, and tricorn hat of the Revolutionary War until his dying day.

Melville's father was both an epitome and a victim of the era of good feeling that followed the War of 1812. By the time Allan Melvill met Maria Gansevoort at a ball honoring Admiral Oliver Hazard Perry in 1813, the confluence of military victory and economic prosperity had given rise to a fulsomely nationalistic rhetoric that conflated the Puritan vision of Boston as "a city on a hill" and English settlers as a Christian army in the heathen wilderness of the New World with the secular vision of America as an entrepreneurial Eden where hard-working people could get ahead — everyone, that is, except American Indians, enslaved Africans, immigrant laborers, and women, all of whom lacked property and voting rights.

The suave Allan, an importer of fancy dry goods from France, and the lovely Maria were married in Albany in 1814, and the following year Maria gave birth to a son whom they named Gansevoort. Although Maria preferred to remain near her family and friends, so many merchants were competing for shrinking markets in Albany that Allan decided to move his family to Boston, where his father would help him set up his business. Their first daughter, Helen Maria, was born there in 1817. The following year, with New York's trade with Europe and the Far East far outstripping that of both Boston and Philadelphia, Allan decided to move his family and his business there. Maria, who was certain her husband's enterprise and ambition would earn them a place among the city's fashionables, half-reluctantly agreed.

By the spring of 1818, thanks to loans from his father that enabled him to purchase luxury French dry goods, Allan sailed for France, stopping first in Edinburgh, where he hoped to establish the family's descent from Scottish nobility. In Paris, he purchased fine linen handkerchiefs, kid gloves, lace mantillas, Leghorn hats, merino shawls, ostrich feathers, Moroccan reticules, satin, taffeta and velvet ribbons and perfumes from Cologne and had them shipped home to America. He also dined with the Marquis de Lafayette and the French family of his brother Thomas's first wife.

Allan Melvill approached business with a kind of missionary zeal. He repeatedly expressed the conviction that religious piety guaranteed material success, and that commercial success was a sign of the favor of GOD, always capitalizing that name. The letters he wrote to his wife echo the Calvinism old Major Melvill repudiated when he left the Congregational Church to become a Unitarian. For Maria, a faithful communicant of the Dutch Reformed Church, Allan's piety was proof that he was destined to succeed.

Confident of his future success, Allan leased an elegant house at the opposite end of Pearl Street from his office and moved his family there, but by midsummer, business was absolutely stagnant. By the time the couple's third child, a robust boy, was born on a hot, muggy August 1, 1819, the first of the antebellum boom and bust cycles had forced twelve to thirteen thousand people in New York to go on relief. The baby was christened Herman, after his first ancestor in the New World, Harmen Harmense Gansevoort, a master brewer who emigrated from the Netherlands in 1656 and settled in Fort Orange (Albany), where he opened a brewery and taproom and, like other Dutch immigrants in the Hudson Valley, founded a dynasty.

Shortly after his first birthday, baby Herman was "entirely weaned" (Allan Melvill to Thomas Melvill, Jr., August 15, 1820, BA), and a year later his father was boasting that he was "rugged as a Bear" (Allan Melvill to Peter Gansevoort, November 3, 1821, Leyda 1: 9). Meanwhile, on August 24, 1821, he gained a younger sister named Augusta who, like her brother, developed a "literary thirst" (Augusta Melville to Fanny Melville, March 17, 1954, MFP). After Augusta was born, Maria suffered a postpartum depression that dragged on for months. It is not clear how well Maria understood the extent of her husband's mounting debts and incongruously grandiose schemes, but money worries did not prevent her from giving birth to a fifth child, a "noble boy" named Allan, after "hours of peril & anguish" (April 8, 1823, Leyda 1: 13). Three more children, Catherine, Frances Priscilla, and Thomas, followed in alternate years.

When Herman was six, his parents enrolled him in the Dutch Reformed Sunday School on Broome Street, where he was required to memorize the Calvinist catechism. Even that strict introduction to schooling did not prepare him for the rigors of the New-York Male High School, which was founded on the Lancastrian system of heavy punishments and light rewards. The school's masters and student monitors considered boys who asked questions dangerous free thinkers, and free thinkers, like boys who misbehaved in ordinary ways, were dealt with harshly. To avoid humiliating punishments such as being suspended from the ceiling in a sack, shackled in a corner, or forced to wear a log around his neck, Herman learned to blend in and observe – a skill that would later serve him well on whaleships and a man-of-war. He was so shy his parents thought him backward: "As far as he understands men & things [he is] both solid & profound, & of a docile & amiable disposition ... [but] very backward in speech & somewhat slow in comprehension," Allan Melvill warned his brother-in-law Peter Gansevoort before sending Herman to stay with him in Albany (AM to PG, August 10, 1826, Leyda 1: 5). More than likely, Melville, who was a sensitive child, was traumatized by the Male High School. Fortunately, his next school, Columbia Grammar School, was more liberal and humane.

Despite the fact that both parents favored the glib Gansevoort over the inarticulate dreamer, Herman had fond memories of his worldly father. Allan sometimes took his two older sons with him to the office, and as they walked down Pearl Street, Herman peered at the "old-fashioned coffeehouses" to see the "sunburnt sea-captains going in and out, smoking cigars, and talking about Havanna [*sic*], London, and Calcutta." Even shipping notices held "a strange, romantic charm" (*R* 4) for the imaginative boy.

Between the ages of eight and twelve, Herman spent three summers with his Boston grandparents and a summer with his Aunt Mary and Uncle John D'Wolf in Bristol, Rhode Island. Captain John D'Wolf had sailed to Archangel in Russia and crossed Siberia by dogsled from the Sea of Okhotsk to St. Petersburg with Georg H. Langsdorff, the naturalist who had accompanied the Krusenstern expedition. Visits with globe-trotting relatives put Herman in touch with the world of exploration and discovery.

Before Melville was ten years old, his parents moved three times to larger houses in better neighborhoods, first to Courtlandt Street, next to Bleecker Street, then to Broadway. One more move – to one of the marble mansions on Bond and Great Jones Street – would have meant Mr. and Mrs. Allan Melvill had "arrived," but that was not to be. As addicted to easy credit as a gambler to his dice, Allan borrowed constantly and fell deeper and deeper into debt. In desperation, he signed a promissory note for money he did not have and could not obtain when the note was called in. Forced to declare bankruptcy, he packed his family off to the Gansevoorts in Albany, liquidated his business, and left Manhattan in disgrace.

As difficult as it was to be uprooted, the move to Albany gave Melville the opportunity to attend Albany Academy – whose fine classical curriculum included Geography, Natural History, Greek, Roman, and English History, Jewish Antiquities, and Latin – and the Albany Classical School, where the boy developed a "love for English composition" that led to his first attempts at writing fiction (Stedman).

Although Allan rehabilitated himself to some extent in Albany, he was determined to re-establish himself in Manhattan. Tragically, as a result of exposure during an unsuccessful steamer trip to New York in sub-zero weather, he contracted lobar pneumonia and died in Albany in January, 1832, quoting the Bible and raving deliriously. The shock Herman suffered was profound: "never again can such blights be made good; they strike in too deep, and leave such a scar that the air of Paradise might not erase it," he would write in 1849 (*R* 53).

Left with eight children and dependent on her brother Peter to dole out funds from her late husband's estate, Maria relied on her oldest sons to contribute to the family bank account. Gansevoort took over his father's fur business, and Herman was forced to interrupt his schooling to work as a bank messenger. To escape, he spent several summers working on his Uncle Thomas's Berkshire farm. Like Major Melvill, Thomas Melvill, Jr. was a colorful character. Having lived in Paris for a number of years with a French wife, he fancied himself something of a *boulevardier*. He wore his Sunday clothes and took pinches of snuff while raking hay in the fields. Herman enjoyed both his uncle's foppish affectations and the rustic manners of his country cousins, especially Julia Maria, a bright girl who seems to have been a close friend.

In 1838, Melville's mother moved her household across the river to Lansingburgh, a planned community of Albany expatriates that included several friends and relatives. Far from being a sleepy backwater in the 1830s and 40s, Lansingburgh, the oldest incorporated village in the United States, was a hub of transportation and trade. Because of its accessibility from the river and good roads, Lansingburgh was the transfer point for mail that traveled by boat between Albany and New York and by stagecoach between Boston and the Berkshires. Village industries manufactured guns, scales, brushes, ink for United States currency, shirts and collars, furniture, and oilcloth linoleum, which was popular with working-class families who could not afford costly carpets; and the shipyards along the river built ocean-going merchant vessels to transport these local products around the world.

At age nineteen, Herman enrolled in Lansingburgh Academy, whose principal had a theology degree and a passion for zoological taxonomy that he shared with his students. Melville studied engineering and surveying on the theory that he would almost certainly find work on the Erie Canal. Unfortunately, the nation's economy had not fully recovered from the recession of 1837, so even technical training and his uncle Peter's help were not enough to land Herman work on the canal. With Gansevoort running the fur business, and younger brother Allan apprenticing in the law offices of Peter Gansevoort, Herman felt pressure to find employment. He tried teaching in a country school in the hills above Pittsfield but found that his job consisted more of trying to control obstreperous louts than of inspiring future scholars.

In his free time, he strolled beside the river reciting the poetry of Byron and Tennyson to various belles of Lansingburgh. Several anonymous love lyrics addressed to a girl named Mary Parmalee appeared in the local newspaper, and he wrote two melodramatic gothic sketches that appear to have been influenced by Edgar Allan Poe. Unfortunately, the satisfaction Herman derived from his studies, friendships, adolescent flirtations, early literary endeavors, and the attainment of his surveyor's license could not compete with the preference for working outdoors he had developed on his uncle's farm. He had little inclination to confine himself to a country school for the rest of his life, much less embrace the claustrophobic drudgery of office work or the roller-coaster of commercial life, and although he had a longstanding desire to go to sea, he had no wish to become a naval officer like his cousins Guert and Stanwix Gansevoort.

Melville made up his mind instead to sign on a whaleship bound for the South Seas – a decision of which the Gansevoorts disapproved. Whaling was a dangerous, dirty job fit for the lower classes, not gentlemen. In an effort to dissuade him, Leonard Gansevoort, who had gone whaling against his family's wishes, advised him to try a short voyage before signing on a "blubber-hunter" for a voyage that could last several years.

Thus, in June, 1839, Herman joined the crew of the *St. Lawrence*, a fast-sailing packet ship bound for Liverpool with thirty-two passengers and a cargo of cotton headed for England's "dark satanic mills" (William Blake, "Jerusalem"). In *Redburn* (1849), Melville notes that Liverpool's immense wealth came from the slave and cotton trades with the southern United States. Two of Melville's shipmates, the steward and the cook, were of African descent, and Melville's fictionalized account of his six-week summer voyage includes horrific allusions to the Atlantic slave trade and a daring reference to the sight of the ship's black steward walking arm in arm with a white English woman as a sign that in some things, other countries did a better job of carrying out the principles of the Declaration of Independence than the United States.

The voyage to Liverpool introduced Melville to the dark underside of Anglo-American civilization and whetted his appetite for travel. Returning home to find his mother living in comparatively genteel poverty, Melville took a teaching job in a village school east of Lansingburgh. The pupils in East Greenbush were much easier to teach than the farm boys at the Sykes District School, but halfway through the year, the school closed without paying the teachers their wages. Perhaps feeling his mother ought to be satisfied that he had at least tried to settle into a respectable profession, but more likely glad of an excuse to travel, he and his friend Eli James Murdock Fly headed west to Galena, Illinois, the lead-mining town where Thomas Melvill, Jr. had relocated his family after his Berkshire farm failed.

The trip west held out a promise of adventure to Melville, and he must have wondered what his life would have been like if he had been hired as a surveyor on the Erie Canal. A triumph of modern engineering, the canal spanned New York State from the Hudson River to Lake Erie, a gentle, meandering boat-boulevard forty feet wide and four feet deep with a series of aqueducts and locks. Travelers hiked along the towpaths, dodging the droppings of the mules who hauled the barges and the trotters who pulled the faster packet boats. The hard-drinking, tobacco-spitting young Canallers who hung out along the busy waterway resembled sailors in many respects, and the work songs and ballads they played on their banjos and harmonicas resembled the chanteys sailors sang at sea.

At the western terminus of the canal, Melville and Fly had a chance to see two of New York State's wonders, one natural and one man-made: Niagara Falls and the quintessential frontier city, Buffalo, where Indians in colorful blankets and buckskins strolled alongside German, Irish, French, and Scandinavian immigrants. They were, as he wrote in *The Confidence-Man: His Masquerade* (1857), "a piebald parliament, an Anacharsis Cloots congress of all kinds of that multiform pilgrim species, man" (9). In Melville's eyes, Buffalo epitomized "the dashing and all-fusing spirit of the West, whose type is the Mississippi itself, which, uniting the streams of the most distant and opposite zones, pours them along, helter-skelter, in one cosmopolitan and confident tide" (9).

Melville and Fly arrived in Illinois when the prairie flowers were in full bloom and stayed with Herman's family until the ripe, golden wheat was harvested and the corn husks had turned brown and brittle. Then they said their goodbyes and took the steamboat to Cairo, Illinois, passing the Mormon settlement at Nauvoo and stopping to explore the Indian mounds at St. Louis, before drifting downriver past towns like Herculaneum and Cape Girardeau, whose cliffs bore ominous names like Devil's Oven and the Devil's Anvil.

At the end of the summer, Melville came home to a mother oppressed by debt and illness and aggravated by her son's inability to get a job, so he and his friend Fly decided to look for work in New York City. They rented rooms in the city at $2.50 a week, and Fly found a job copying documents in a nearby office. Melville, however, preferred not to do routine copying; his fictional scrivener, Bartleby, stands as a monument to the acts of resistance he stored up in his soul.

He was reading James Fenimore Cooper's *The Red Rover*, whose pirate protagonist appealed to the rebellious young man, and Richard Henry Dana's bestseller *Two Years Before the Mast*, a book that stirred the salt water in his blood. He could not have been trying terribly hard to get a job, because he let his hair and beard grow until his "savage" appearance became "a great source of anxiety" to his brother Gansevoort, who urged Herman to get "his hair sheared & whiskers shaved" before going home again. By the time he saw his mother in Lansingburgh, he looked "more like a Christian than usual" (GM to AMjr., November 26, 1840, BA, and GM to MGM, November 26, 1840, BA), but he had made up his mind to go to sea.

To Herman, signing aboard a whaler meant a few years' steady employment as well as a chance to escape the pieties of the parlor by going native in the South Seas. Being a sailor was infinitely easier than mastering the complex tasks of young adulthood in a family where a young man had to tack around submerged emotional reefs and navigate the treacherous shoals of Victorian sexuality. Gansevoort, who took his role as paternal surrogate quite seriously, accompanied his younger brother to New Bedford, Massachusetts, the whaling capital of the world. On January 3, 1841, the *Acushnet*, under the command of Captain Valentine Pease II of Edgartown, cleared its mooring and sailed for the open ocean with Herman Melville aboard. Three months later, somewhere off the coast of Brazil, the future author of *Moby-Dick* experienced the thrill of his first hunt, and for the next ten months, the men succeeded in harvesting 720 barrels of oil on their way to the Marquesas.

A year and a half later, after stops in Rio, the Galapagos, and Santa, Peru, the *Acushnet* sailed into Taioa Bay, Nukuhiva. Not far from their anchorage they could see French warships that had brought four thousand soldiers to the island to prepare the way for colonization, and on shore were the remains of the "city" built by Protestant missionaries in 1833. No sooner had the ship dropped anchor than the men saw a flotilla of naked "whihinees" swimming out to welcome them. They held garlands of flowers above their heads as gifts for the sailors, who had already broken out the rum to celebrate the sexual favors the island women were about to bestow on them.

Eager as he might have been to experience the sexual freedom of the islands, Melville may have found the orgy that ensued when the island women boarded the ship as disgusting in reality as "Tommo" claims in *Typee*. Confined to the ship with a tyrannical captain and a crew of crude, uneducated men, Melville and his shipboard chum Richard Tobias Greene decided to jump ship and hide in the island's interior to escape capture and punishments as deserters.

In *Typee*, his fictionalized account of his four-week sojourn in Polynesia, Melville claimed he and "Toby" spent four months living among the Taipi, a tribe Captain David Porter and other westerners called cannibals. Melville, by contrast, found the islanders courteous and kindly, and their peaceful, prosperous society a contradiction to Porter's accounts of their savagery. Melville was attracted by the physical beauty of the tattooed islanders and fascinated by their androgynous style of dress – or undress, to be more precise. Intrigued by their casual enjoyment of sex as well as by their religious practices and social mores, Melville concluded that Christian missionaries were guilty of destroying a peaceful, utopian pagan culture. Re-examining his own society through the lens of an Edenic world, he found the "examples of civilized barbarity, the vices, cruelties and enormities of every kind that spring up in the tainted atmosphere of a feverish civilization" (*T* 125) to be far more abhorrent than the religious ritual of cannibalism which, for the missionaries, marked Oceanic peoples as "savages."

Despite the attractions of carefree island life, Melville could not quell his restlessness and anxiety. If the account he gives in *Typee* is at all accurate, Melville felt if he chose to stay in the islands, he would have to be tattooed – a practice that both attracted and repelled him. In any event, it would have marked his face indelibly, making it difficult, if not impossible, for him to go home again. Fearing their hosts might actually be cannibals, "Toby" had gone to the coast to get help for Melville, who had an infected leg, and although Toby was unable to return, he sent a boat to rescue his injured friend. To avoid capture, Melville signed on the Australian whaler *Lucy Ann* as an able seaman. Serving on the *Lucy Ann* was much more arduous than languishing in the Typee Valley. Badly captained and unlucky in the hunt, she had taken only two whales since leaving Sydney, and the crew finally struck, refusing to take orders from the captain.

For their part in this mutiny, Meville and his friend Dr. John B. Troy were taken ashore at Papeete and clapped in the "Calabooza Beretanee," a makeshift outdoor jail where prisoners were confined to stocks. Luckily for them, the jailer was a sympathetic chap who let them free during the day if they promised to spend their nights in jail. This leniency gave Melville a chance to see the effects of colonization on the Tahitians, who suffered from venereal diseases, alcoholism, and other ailments as a result of contact with westerners. Protestant missionaries condemned their sexual behavior, forced them to wear ill-fitting western clothes donated by church groups, and banned their native dances, games, festivals, and religious rituals. The result, Melville observed in *Omoo* (1847), was loss of cultural identity, depression, and despair.

Once the *Lucy Ann* left port, the jailer let his captives go, and to avoid detection, they sailed to Moorea and worked on a potato farm for nearly three weeks. In October, 1842, after a series of adventures, the two men went their separate ways, and Melville signed on as a boatsteerer aboard the *Charles & Henry*, a Nantucket whaler that had experienced bad luck all the way. By the time the ship reached the Hawaiian port Lahaina, an American colony ruled by missionaries since 1821, Melville had decided to spend some time in Honolulu. There, he evidently set pins in a bowling-alley before signing an indenture with an educated English merchant named Isaac Montgomery. On July 13, 1843, Melville began work as a clerk-bookkeeper at an annual salary of $150 to be paid quarterly, plus free board, lodging, and laundry. His duties consisted of measuring calico, waiting on customers, keeping the ledgers, and doing inventory.

Once again, his sense of social justice was offended by what he observed. Old men and boys, harnessed to carts, pulled the wives of missionaries to Sunday services, which for Melville perfectly epitomized the evils of colonialism: "Not until I visited Honolulu was I aware of the fact that the small remnant of the natives had been civilised into draught horses and evangelised into beasts of burden. But so it is. They have been literally broken into the traces, and are harnessed to the vehicles of their spiritual instructors like many dumb brutes!" he wrote in *Typee* (196). The missionaries had built schools and playgrounds for white children and then surrounded them with high fences "the more effectually to exclude the wicked little Hawaiians," he observed sarcastically in *Omoo* (188).

Melville witnessed first-hand the competition between Britain and America for control of the Sandwich Islands that paved the way for the brutal and shameful annexation of Hawai'i by the United States later in the century. For various reasons, not least among them the sight of Kamehameha III wearing western-style military uniforms and aping the affectations of the conquerors, Melville formed an intensely negative view of the Hawaiian people. Although in *Typee* and *Omoo* he dismissed the Hawaiians as lazy and ignorant, by 1859 he was supporting the right of Hawaiians to speak their native language in their schools and expressing his opposition to American annexation of the islands.

By August, he was ready to go home, and his boss Isaac Montgomery, who became a friend, released him from his indenture. Wary of signing on another whaleship whose captain might recognize him as a deserter, on August 17, 1843 he signed on the *USS United States*, a naval frigate bound for Boston.

He could not have chosen a more rigidly hierarchical, oppressive, undemocratic world to enter than that of a man-of-war. Once a month, the entire crew had to stand at attention on deck for the ritual reading of the Articles of War, with its solemn refrain, "SHALL SUFFER DEATH!" Almost every day, the ship's company was piped on deck to watch some poor fellow tied to the gratings and flogged with the cat-o'-nine-tails, that tore strips of bloody flesh from a sailor's back. In the six months Melville was stationed on the gun-deck of this floating hell, he was forced to watch 163 of his shipmates flogged, often by mercilessly sadistic officers.

On the positive side, the *United States* had a well-stocked library, and two or three members of the crew told stories and wrote poetry, skills that made them pleasant companions for Melville when they had time to relax and spin yarns or sing chanteys during their watches. In *White-Jacket* (1850), his bitterly satirical account of his six months' cruise in the Navy, he immortalized seagoing bards like Jack Chase, foreman of the maintop, who recited whole cantos of Portugal's epic poem, the *Lusiad*.

The frigate reached the shores of Massachusetts in mid-October, 1844, and Melville lingered in Boston before heading home to Lansingburgh, perhaps to reacquaint himself with Elizabeth Shaw, the daughter of his father's friend, Lemuel Shaw, Chief Justice of the Massachusetts Supreme Judicial Court. At home, he regaled his family and friends with such entertaining stories of his adventures in the South Seas that they urged him to write a book about his experiences. Measuring his own perceptions against those of travelers prejudiced against native cultures, he drew on European models of contact with "primitive" peoples to challenge American racial and ethnic stereotypes and to contradict prevailing assumptions about what constitutes "civilized" and "savage" societies. In addition to being a picturesque, suspenseful, and informative first book, *Typee* (1846) is a paean to Polynesian culture and a scathing critique of Christian imperialism. The book's sequel, *Omoo* (1847), takes the case against "snivelization" even farther by describing the disastrous effects of contact with "the white civilized man ... the most ferocious animal on the face of the earth" (*T* 125) on the Tahitians and Hawaiians.

By 1848, Melville was a successful author and a married man, having wooed and won Elizabeth Shaw while writing two popular travel narratives. Friends and family members referred to him affectionately as "Typee" and his new household as the "Happy Valley." His third book, *Mardi* (1849), a sprawling allegorical romance whose flights of philosophical fancy and political satire dismayed fans of *Typee* and *Omoo,* nearly destroyed his literary reputation. Heavily influenced by Melville's reading of eighteenth-century English and Continental authors, *Mardi* transforms the archipelagos of the Pacific into a metaphysical landscape not bound by space and time.

Mardi contains some of Melville's most beautiful descriptions of the sea and sea creatures as well as some of his wildest explorations of the mind and soul. Chapter 119, "Dreams," anticipates passages of *Moby-Dick* in which Melville starts from an identifiable object or place and soars above both earth and sea until earth, sea, sky, and stars become swirling galaxies. His dreamer is "like a frigate ... full with a thousand souls," scudding before the wind and nearly dashed against "shoals, like nebulous vapors, shoreing the white reef of the Milky Way, against which the wrecked worlds are dashed; strowing all the strand, with their Himmaleh keels and ribs" (*M* 367). The ambitious *Mardi* foreshadows *Moby-Dick* with its elaborate sentence structures and headlong metaphors, similes, allusions, and analogies linking the concrete and the cosmic, the physical and the metaphysical, the known and the unknown.

Unfortunately, readers were baffled by *Mardi,* and it garnered bad reviews, so Melville retaliated by writing two books he considered potboilers. Although *Redburn* was published in 1849, *White-Jacket, or the World in a Man-of-War* (1850) was so critical of the United States Navy that no American firm would publish it. Not one to give up easily, Melville said goodbye to his wife and infant son, Malcolm, who was teething while his father was writing *White-Jacket*, and sailed for England to sell his manuscript to Richard Bentley, a London publisher. On the voyage out, he made the acquaintance of several other passengers, notably a philosophy professor named George Adler, who became his traveling companion and friend. After a trip rich in impressions, at the beginning of February, 1850, Melville returned to the crowded New York townhouse he shared with his wife, his brother Allan and Allan's wife Sophia, two toddlers, his mother, and whichever of his sisters happened to be visiting. Although he soon began working on a book about the sperm-whale fishery that he referred to affectionately as his "Whale," he found it difficult to concentrate, and by July, he was so desperate to escape the heat that he packed up his wife Elizabeth and their infant son and went to stay with Aunt Mary Melville and her son Robert in the Berkshire Hills of Massachusetts.

By October, largely as a result of his meeting that August with Nathaniel Hawthorne, the darling of Boston's literary establishment, Melville's "Whale" had evolved into a mythopoeic epic of the sea, and Melville had purchased a farmhouse not far from his cousin's inn. Between visits to the red cottage overlooking Lake Mahkee-nac where Nathaniel Hawthorne lived with his wife Sophia, their son Julian, and their daughter Una, and philosophical discussions in the barn at Arrowhead with the author of dark tales of Puritan New England, he finished writing *Moby-Dick* (1851). Melville's oceanic cadences and cosmic images infuse *Moby-Dick* with magic and mysticism. From the magic of "the pool in the stream" Ishmael evokes in "Loomings" to the "mystical vibration" he says he felt when, during his maiden voyage, he realized he was out of sight of land, Ishmael puts before us "the image of the ungraspable phantom of life" (5) that drew Melville to the American West, the South Seas, Europe, the Holy Land, and, in 1860, California.

Ishmael speaks for the iconoclastic Melville when he boasts that he is "King of the Cannibals, and ready at any moment to rebel against him" (*MD* 270). Unfortunately, *Moby-Dick* was not popular in Melville's day, and his next book, an ambiguous psychosexual melodrama called *Pierre, or The Ambiguities* (1852), scandalized readers and panicked critics like the hysterical reviewer for New York's *Day Book*, who pronounced "HERMAN MELVILLE CRAZY" ("Historical Note," *P* 380).

Neither *Israel Potter* (1853), a picaresque novel whose hapless protagonist meets Benjamin Franklin, Ethan Allen, and John Paul Jones, nor the short stories and sketches published in *Putnam's Monthly Magazine* and *Harper's New Monthly Magazine* could rehabilitate Melville's reputation. While stories such as "Benito Cereno" and "The Encantadas" combine maritime lore and Melville's own experiences, others like "The Apple-Tree Table" and "Bartleby the Scrivener" draw on Melville's knowledge of folklore and urban legends prevalent in New England and New York. To modern readers, some of Melville's stories and sketches are masterpieces; others seem dated and comparatively slight. In any case, Melville managed to bridge the gap between the red and white chowder literary worlds. He even received decent remuneration for his short fiction, so it was a shock when *Putnam's* ceased publication in 1856. Financial worries, physical ailments, and marital stresses, plus a familial dependence on alcohol, drove Melville to the verge of a nervous breakdown. In the fall of 1856, a dispirited Melville sailed for Europe and the Holy Land.

Melville's *Journal 1856–57* is a much richer document than his 1849–50 *Journal* of the trip to London and the Continent. The sections describing his experiences in Egypt, Italy, and the Middle East approach the depth and intensity of his best prose fiction, and the emotional exhaustion and spiritual fervor of his entries undoubtedly reflect his precarious mental health.

Disembarking in Liverpool, Melville presented his passport to his old friend Nathaniel Hawthorne, who countersigned it and stamped it with his seal. Hawthorne had been awarded a consular post in Liverpool for writing the presidential campaign biography for Franklin Pierce, a Bowdoin classmate and friend. In his *English Notebooks*, Hawthorne noted that Melville looked "a little paler, and perhaps a little sadder" than before and still retained "his characteristic gravity and reserve of manner" (*J* 628ff.) At the Hawthornes' home in Southport, a seaside village twenty miles from

Liverpool, the two men conversed "on pretty much our former terms of sociability and confidence." The next day they took a long walk on the beach and sat down "in a hollow" out of the cold wind to smoke cigars and talk. Melville began "to reason of Providence and futurity, and of everything that lies beyond human ken, and informed me that he had pretty much made up his mind to be annihilated, but still he does not seem to rest in that anticipation; and, I think, will never rest until he gets hold of a definite belief," wrote Hawthorne. His poignant reminiscence of Melville continues:

> It is strange how he persists – and has persisted ever since I knew him, and probably long before – in wandering to and fro over these deserts, as dismal and monotonous as the sand hills amid which we were sitting. He can neither believe, nor be comfortable in his unbelief; and he is too honest and courageous not to try to do one or the other. If he were a religious man, he would be one of the most truly religious and reverential; he has a very high and noble nature, and better worth immortality than most of us. (*J* 628–9)

Melville's entry for November 12 is telegraphic and terse: "At Southport. An agreeable day. Took a long walk by the sea. Sand & grass. Wild & desolate. A strong wind. A good talk" (*J* 51).

If Melville had hoped to find renewed faith in the Holy Land, he must have been sorely disappointed. He was profoundly depressed by everything from the diseased and dirty street urchins to the vendors shrilly hawking cheap souvenirs at holy shrines. At the base of the Pyramids, he was gripped by "awe & terror" (*J* 75) at the concept of monotheism, and peering into passageways that led to burial chambers made him feel dizzy and faint. In his journal, he returns obsessively to the claustro-phobic Egyptian tombs and imagines the arid deserts, sacred to Christians, Moslems, and Jews, as symbols of spiritual death.

Given what we know about the disappointments and frustrations Melville had suffered in publishing, his failure to secure a comfortable government job, his physical ailments, and his wife's family's fears for his mental stability, it's not surprising to find Melville experiencing "a genuine Jonah-feeling" in Joppa, where he felt "emphatically alone" with the wind "rising and the swell of the sea increasing, & dashing in breakers upon the reef of rocks within a biscuit's toss of the sea-wall" (*J* 80–1).

Judea's "accumulation of stones" made him question whether "the desolation of the land" was "the result of the fatal embrace of the Diety" (*J* 91), and wandering in Jerusalem, a "city besieged by [an] army of the dead" (*J* 86), he began to feel like one "possessed with devels [*sic*]" (84). The "foam and beach & pebbles" on the shore of the Dead Sea looked "like the slaver of a mad dog" (*J* 83), and at Mount Zion he felt "the mind can not but be sadly & suggestively affected with the indifference of Nature & Man to all that makes the spot sacred to the Christian" (*J* 85).

In Italy, by contrast, Melville was rarely alone; most of the time, he was with other Americans he had met along the way. Individual paintings or sculptures such as the "touchingly maternal" Madonna by Raphael in Naples, the Giotto frescos in Padua, and the statues of the "beautiful" Antinous and the Dying Gladiator which showed "that humanity existed amid the barberousness [*sic*] of the Roman time" (*J* 106), impressed him so favorably that the first lecture he wrote for his lecture tour in 1858 was on "Statues in Rome." Although European cities did not arouse the same dread in Melville as the cities of the Near East, the obsessively morbid tenor of his entries points to a depressed state of mind.

More than mere exploration of Europe and the Near East, this trip was an exploration of his doubts and beliefs, an odyssey of psychic survival and painful self-discovery. In addition to *Clarel* (1876), the fruits of Melville's desperate pilgrimage include "Statues in Rome" and the poems about art, architecture, ancient history, and sexual identity that appear in the privately published volume *Timoleon* (1891).

"Statues in Rome" focuses on great works of art as "realizations of the soul" and "representations of the ideal. They are grand, beautiful, and true, and they speak with a voice that echoes through the ages" (*PT* 408). The lecture, however, was a complete flop with audiences who had come to hear "the man who lived among the cannibals" talk about his adventures; thus, for his next lecture tour, Melville wrote "The South Seas." Unfortunately, Melville focused not on retelling the adventures that had made him so popular as the author of *Typee*, but instead on using the lecture platform for romantic comparisons between utopian primitive cultures and the degraded modern world. Blaming Christian missionaries for turning "an earthly paradise into a pandemonium," he called on Christians to eschew contact with native cultures until they had created "a civilization morally, mentally, and physically higher than one which has culminated in almshouses, prisons, and hospitals" (*PT* 420). A reviewer in Pittsfield deemed the talk "redolent of the spicy odors of the South Seas, and sparkling with original thoughts" (*Berkshire Eagle*, December 17, 1858, Leyda 2: 597). Most people in the audience, however, felt let down by Melville, who eschewed the role of entertainer and wanted to make his listeners think.

In his third lecture, "Traveling: Its Pleasures, Pains, and Profits," he extolled travel as a way to "get rid of a *few* prejudices" (*PT* 422), but instead of relating personal experiences, he gave generalized illustrations of his ideas: "the stock-broker goes to Thessalonica and finds infidels more honest than Christians; the teetotaller finds a country in France where all drink and no one gets drunk; the prejudiced against color finds several hundred millions of people of all shades of color, and all degrees of intellect, rank, and social worth, generals, judges, priests, and kings, and learns to give up his foolish prejudices" (422). He made such obvious advantages as leaving home to experience new sensations and returning to the comfort of the "old hearthstone" sound much less exciting than "the persecutions and extortions of guides" (422) and endless battles with vicious bedbugs and fleas.

Although his pronouncement – "Travel to a large and generous nature is a new birth. Its legitimate tendency is to teach personal humility, while it enlarges the sphere of comprehensive benevolence till it includes the whole human race" (*PT* 423) – is a strong expression of his global vision, most listeners were disappointed. They preferred dramatic anecdotes and spicy stories to noble ideas. Worn out and feeling ill after this engagement, he stayed in Manhattan for a week reading Vasari's *Lives of the Painters*, visiting art galleries and museums, and stocking up on books, like a squirrel hoarding nuts for another winter.

By New Year's, 1860, Melville was reading and writing poetry. The trip to the Holy Land was the last Atlantic crossing Melville made. Later that year, he sailed to the West Coast with youngest brother Thomas, captain of the *Meteor*, a merchant ship bound for Manila and the Far East. After waiting in San Francisco for a shipment of goods for the Far East, Tom told Herman they might not be sailing for China after all; Melville, who by then was homesick anyway, went home via steamship and train across the Isthmus of Panama.

With government positions overseas still among the main sources of income for American writers and artists, Melville traveled to Washington to ask for Charles Sumner's help in securing a consular post soon after the election. Missing Lizzie and the children, he attended the inaugural reception and shook hands with Abraham Lincoln, but he failed to secure a diplomatic posting overseas.

Soon after the Civil War broke out in 1861, Melville began reading *The Rebellion Record*, a compendium of war dispatches followed by dozens of pages of conventional patriotic verse. Soon, he was writing his own poetry, some of it in response to the news, and some to memorialize the dead relatives of his friends. In 1862, badly shaken up in a carriage accident while driving with his friend Joseph E. A. Smith, editor of the *Berkshire Evening Eagle*, he sold Arrowhead to his brother Allan and moved his family to a brownstone at 104 East 26th Street in Manhattan. Walking in Manhattan, browsing through stacks of old books, prints, and engravings had a rejuvenating effect. In 1864, he felt spry enough to take the train to Washington for a visit to his cousin Colonel Henry Gansevoort in his camp and even rode out with a scouting party pursuing Mosby's Raiders.

When *Battle-Pieces and Aspects of the War* was published in 1866, it gained respectful reviews, but little understanding or appreciation of its anti-war attitudes and its innovative, proto-modernist style. Contemporary reviewers made no mention of the paternalistic prose supplement and the almost complete absence of persons of African descent, slave or free, in Melville's poems, despite their author's consistent opposition to slavery. Before the year was out, Melville took a job as a Customs Inspector for the New-York Port, earning $4 a day.

In May of 1867, his long-suffering but devoted wife Lizzie sought the advice of her pastor about divorcing her husband. Against the advice of her family, she decided not to leave, but tragedy followed, for reasons largely unfathomable, despite the abundance of rumor and innuendo. In October, the Melvilles' oldest son Malcolm shot himself in the head. In whatever free moments he could find at work, Melville coped with his son's tragic suicide and his own tumultuous and troubled psyche by focusing on poetry. In 1876, with a generous subvention from his uncle Peter, he published *Clarel: A Poem and Pilgrimage in the Holy Land*.

Malcolm's death and the illnesses and deaths of close friends and relatives combined with advancing age and intimations of his own mortality gradually mellowed Melville. In 1885, he retired from the Custom House, and a year later, 35-year-old Stanwix, the Melvilles' second son, died in San Francisco of tuberculosis, guilt, and grief. Their daughter Bessie, crippled by arthritis by the time she was 26, lived at home. Her sister Frances married happily and had four daughters who were the delight of their grandmother's old age.

In March, 1888, Melville made his last ocean voyage, to Bermuda, arriving back in New York to find the mountains of snow from the great blizzard of '88 piled up before his house. During the last three years of his life, Melville completed three volumes of poetry he had been working on for years, and with Lizzie's help he published them privately: *John Marr and Other Sailors* (1888), *Timoleon* (1891), and *Weeds and Wildings, with A Rose or Two* (1891).

On September 28, 1891, less than a month after he presented an inscribed copy of *Weeds and Wildings* to Lizzie, Melville died in his sleep of "an enlarged heart" (E. S. Melville's *Memoir* 171).

The posthumously published *Billy Budd, Sailor (An Inside Narrative)* poignantly expresses the sorrow and guilt that haunted Melville as he reflected on his losses and all the small, corrosive failures of his heart. He worked on this masterpiece until a few months before his death, focusing first on the innocent Billy, then on the malevolent Claggart, and finally on the rationalizing, murderous Captain Vere until he created a tragic portrait of the modern world at war that ceased to resemble its putative source, the 1842 mutiny aboard the brig *Somers*. Although to Lizzie and the children, Melville could seem heartless when his demons possessed him, in the end, he stood for the heart, condemning Captain Vere's Caesar-like dismissal of "the feminine in man" (*BB* 111). The result of Vere's cold casuistry was the sacrifice of a young sailor he knew to be innocent to "forms, measured forms" – in other words, to "military necessity" (128).

In his lecture "Traveling: Its Pleasures, Pains, and Profits," Melville asserted that "The sight of novel objects, the acquirement of novel ideas, the breaking up of old prejudices, the enlargement of heart and mind – are the proper fruit of rightly undertaken travel" (*PT* 423). Like his Quaker captains, he was a man of "greatly superior natural force, with a globular brain and a ponderous heart," who "by the stillness and seclusion of many long night-watches in the remotest waters, and beneath constellations never seen here at the north," was "led to think untraditionally and independently" (*MD* 73). A voracious reader, he traveled in books and in his imagination as well as in ships and carriages and trains and wrote more than one "mighty book" (*MD* 497) whose "bold and nervous lofty language" (*MD* 73) takes us through "the great flood-gates of the wonder-world" (*MD* 7). As Emily Dickinson observed, "There is no Frigate like a Book / to take us Lands away," and fortunately for us, Melville's books have survived to tell the story of his marvelous voyages of mind and spirit.

Note

1   Melville's mother added a final "e" to the family's name after her husband's death (Robertson-Lorant 622).

References and Further Reading

Primary Sources

The Berkshire Athenaeum, Pittsfield, Massachusetts (BA).

The Gansevoort–Lansing Collection, New York Public Library (GLC).

The Melville Family Papers, New York Public Library (MFP).

Melville, Elizabeth Shaw. *Memoir.* In Sealts, Merton M., Jr. *The Early Lives of Melville: Nineteenth Century Biographical Sketches and Their Authors.* Madison: University of Wisconsin Press, 1974.

Melville, Herman. *Weeds and Wildings, Chiefly; with a Rose or Two, by Herman Melville: Reading Text and Genetic Text*, ed. with an introduction by Robert Charles Ryan. Evanston, IL: Northwestern University Press, 1967.

Stedman, Arthur. "Marquesan Melville." *New York World* (October 11, 1891): 26. In Sealts, Merton

M., Jr. *The Early Lives of Melville: Nineteenth Century Biographical Sketches and Their Authors.* Madison: University of Wisconsin Press, 1974. 101.

Secondary Sources

Hawthorne, Nathaniel. *The English Notebooks by Nathaniel Hawthorne*, ed. Randall Stewart. New York: Russell and Russell, 1941, 1962.

Newman, Lea Bertani Vozar. "Marginalia as Revelation: Melville's 'Lost' Copy of Dante and a Private Purgatorial Note." *Melville Society Extracts* 92 (March, 1993): 4.

Robertson-Lorant, Laurie. *Melville: A Biography.* New York: Clarkson Potter, 1996; Boston and Amherst: University of Massachusetts Press, 1998.

2

Cosmopolitanism and Traveling Culture

Peter Gibian

Cosmopolitanism and American Literature

When people first hear the words "cosmopolitan" and "American Literature" in the same sentence, they tend to think of the early twentieth century. Two major waves of famous American writers went abroad in that era to put American writing at the forefront of international literary developments, forging an American literature centered on the "International Theme" and defining an international modernism fundamentally concerned with issues of cosmopolitanism in what was seen as a newly "cosmopolitan" world. Henry James was the first ambassador for this movement of expatriation, going to Europe to study from every possible angle the stories of "ambassador" figures who attempt to mediate between Europe and America, exploring the drama of identity formation provoked by the modern experience of cross-cultural encounter. T. S. Eliot and Ezra Pound (and Ernest Hemingway in a different way) then headed a large second wave of American writers who followed in James's footsteps, inspired by the pattern of his life and his work.

"I have lived too long in foreign parts" is the repeated refrain of Winterbourne, the archetypal lost cosmopolitan in James's early story "Daisy Miller" (206). Developed as James's self-critical portrait of one in his own situation as a member of the expatriate leisure class at the turn of the century, Winterbourne defined the bare bones of a story that was replayed in a number of James's later fictions – culminating most memorably in the complex study of Strether in *The Ambassadors* who, in a plot pattern that appears again and again, is transformed from a one-way position as univocal ambassador (representing one culture *to* another) to a more complex predicament as "ambassador at large," an ambassador *between* cultures (going back and forth as a translator, mediator, and advocate painfully involved with all sides). And Winterbourne also defined a life-pattern central to the explorations of later modernist writers, epitomizing a predicament characteristic of the modern male in this expatriate traveling culture. A deracinated intellectual paralyzed by

self-consciousness, Winterbourne clearly served as a model for Eliot's paradigmatic-
ally modern persona, J. Alfred Prufrock. The "Winterbourne type" in James's works
knows too much; his traveler's life may have begun in a mode of easy *flânerie*
involving purely externalized and aesthetic spectatorship of lives always neatly
distanced from his own roots and responsibilities, but it can develop into a deeply
pained empathy of witness that leaves him torn between the emotional involvements
and competing demands of different worlds, and so condemned to cosmopolitanism
as a homeless bachelor wanderer. The story of this early twentieth-century cosmopolitan figure then raises large questions about (to borrow a phrase from Homi
Bhabha) "the location of culture": the location of home and of home culture for
American writers who characteristically see themselves, after this move into the
realm of the international, as unable to go home again.

Indeed, in defining themselves as moderns and cosmopolitans, these early twentieth-century writers saw themselves as making a clear revolutionary break from
previous traditions of American writing that they had left behind – which were
seen to be (for good or ill) always resolutely national rather than international,
provincial rather than cosmopolitan. In James's view, for example, both the intense
power and the peculiar limitations of Nathaniel Hawthorne's work arose out of his
situation in a literary world that was fundamentally "local" (*Hawthorne*).

But is the story of the relation between twentieth- and nineteenth-century
American writing really the story of a relation between cosmopolitans and locals?
Is this really a case of a radical break from past traditions? If we look more closely at
a wide range of nineteenth-century American authors and writings, it becomes clear
that the emergence of cosmopolitan themes at the turn of the century was not a
radical rupture or a new beginning; rather, it should be seen more truly as
the emergence into full flowering of tendencies that had been developing since the
beginning of literary writing in the new nation. In fact, if we trace one long and
important alternative line of American writing as it develops through the nineteenth
century – drawing connections between works of Benjamin Franklin, Washington
Irving, Herman Melville, and Margaret Fuller as they lead to Edith Wharton and
Henry James – we find an ongoing, anxious debate about the powers and limits of
the cosmopolitan, about the American writer as a cosmopolitan figure, and about
America as a cosmopolitan culture. This line of nineteenth-century American writing
then gives us some of the clearest case studies we have of what anthropologist James
Clifford – questioning the conventional distinctions between cosmopolitans and
locals – describes as the vision of a "traveling culture."

Melville in the Age of Travel

Herman Melville would certainly stand as *the* key exhibit for this claim. Centering on
the intersections between watery travel and American writing, his work continually

focuses attention on the dynamics of cross-cultural encounter and the question of intercultural mediation, with each new novel, essay, or poem elaborating a new stage in the author's ambivalent, multivocal meditation on cosmopolitanism and the International Theme. Melville's accounts of his actual and imaginative mid-nineteenth-century voyages – often travels among non-European peoples, in the company of common, working seafarers from a wide range of cultures or nations – test and expose the limits of dominant conceptions about mid-nineteenth-century travel or travel-writing. And as his literary experiments in imaginative transport begin to suggest the conception of a personal or cultural identity grounded in intercultural travel, anticipating current visions of a "traveling culture," they bring to the fore unsettling challenges to an American identity seen to be anchored in a pure, singular, or static "home culture" – challenges in many ways more radical and more deeply cosmopolitan in their implications than anything in the "international" Henry James.

Melville's literary career coincided with a great age of American travel – an important transitional moment when continuing interest in an earlier mode of global exploration coincided with a widespread popular fascination with emerging forms of leisured touristic travel, and, within the latter category, the Grand Tour for the aristocratic few was evolving toward modern modes of mass tourism. Not surprisingly, then, this period also saw a huge boom in travel writing. Publishers found that American readers had a voracious appetite for classic written accounts by the famous British or European explorers – Captain Cook, Mungo Park, Alexander von Humboldt, and so on – that were reprinted in multiple US editions or excerpted in the many popular travel anthologies produced to meet this new interest, such as Charles Goodrich's *Universal Traveller* (1838) or Bayard Taylor's *Cyclopaedia of Modern Travel* (1856). And new additions to the literature of exploration were reviewed or summarized, and avidly followed, in most of the major monthly journals. At the same time, belletristic writing about touristic travel emerged as one of the prime forms for new work in American literature. Ever since Washington Irving, the country's first professional author, had in his *Sketchbook* (1819) identified American literature with the oceanic journey, introducing the influential image of the American writer as a bachelor traveler at sea, a central line of the nation's most popular authors – Richard Henry Dana, Jr., Henry Wadsworth Longfellow, Bayard Taylor, N. P. Willis, and John L. Stephens, among others – continued to figure the American writer as a traveler, each launching his career with an account of his own wide-ranging travels, and in many cases then making travel writing the center of his entire literary production.

While Melville's career as a writer was launched with the sudden, surprising popular success of his first travel-adventure accounts, *Typee* and *Omoo*, which thrilled a huge international readership with wild scenes of cannibalism, erotic temptation, strange religious rites, and full-body tattooing, even these less self-aware travel narratives test the limits of conventional generic patterns in the contemporary literature of travel. In *Imperial Eyes: Travel Writing and Transculturation*, Mary Louise Pratt shows how the literature of exploration played a crucial role in the ascendance of a Western cultural identity – an identity that had to be constructed from the outside in through contact with and contrasts to foreign, non-Western Others – at the same time that it was often itself a critical tool in the actual process of empire building, a vehicle for the imposition of Western imperial hegemony and the expansionist conquest of further territory. The standard explorer's account is generally seen, then, to reinforce or repeat the relations of dominance in the larger colonial situation – as the powerful home culture simply imposes its vision on a foreign world. Working along similar lines but in another register, touristic or literary narratives of leisured travel (such as those surveyed in Larzer Ziff's *Return Passages: Great American Travel Writing, 1780–1910*) are generally seen to operate through a movement of "return passage," presenting foreign travel as a test of the character of the home culture that is most important, finally, as it serves to bring out and define that native character and then to reinforce the narrator's sense of ties to that home.

In the early years of Melville criticism, he was often held up as a model traveler on this classic pattern. Carl Van Doren, for example, celebrated Melville's voyaging narrators as fine examples of the ability of Western culture to maintain its integrity in the face of challenges from "foreign" elements; in *Typee*, Tommo never abandons "civilization" for the temptations of primitive or exotic life, "never loses himself in it entirely as did later men, like Lafcadio Hearn and Pierre Loti, but remains always the shrewd and smiling Yankee" (Lauter 9). But most recent readings of Melville stress just the opposite tendency. Geoffrey Sanborn sees Melville's travel writings mounting a "world-altering challenge to colonial Truth-claims" (10); for Carolyn Porter, Ishmael's encounter with Queequeg "deviates markedly from the pattern set by earlier accounts of travel among savages, in which the encounter with alien people serves to reconfirm the boundaries of the civilized" (81).

If the narrators in some Melville works begin as one sort of more conventional ambassador from and for the West, they often end their travels by challenging or exploding the notion of an easy return passage. While many American authors, taking up the International Theme plot, tend to see travel through foreign cultures as a valuable test helping to bring out the innate and distinctive qualities of the American character, Melville can develop the same plot to explore the paradox of an American writerly identity that finds itself most fully in transnational situations, at the boundary between cultures.

Traveling Culture in the Pacific

In a fertile and influential essay entitled "Traveling Cultures," anthropologist James Clifford introduces a revisionary notion of culture itself as a fluid, mobile, transnational phenomenon – opening his essay with a anecdote about North American experience that he takes as the paradigm of this new perspective: he calls it the "Squanto effect," after the Indian, Squanto, who greeted the traveling Pilgrims landing on the shores at Plymouth, Massachusetts in 1620 – and was found to speak good English! The example of "this disconcertingly hybrid 'native' " met on

American shores leads Clifford (citing Appadurai) to challenge the idea of localism so cherished by classical anthropologists or by conventional travel writers: "Natives, people confined to and by the places to which they belong, groups unsullied by contact with a larger world, have probably never existed" (18–19, 24). As he continues to define his new vision, Clifford advocates renewed attention to travel and to the concept of the "cosmopolitan": "One needs to focus on hybrid, cosmopolitan experiences as much as on rooted, native ones . . . . The goal is not to *replace* the cultural figure 'native' with the intercultural figure 'traveler.' Rather, the task is to focus on concrete mediations of the two" (24). Along these lines, Clifford suggests a new way of conceiving of encounters between cultures: not as meetings between cosmopolitans and locals but as "mediations" between "discrepant cosmopolitanisms . . . interconnected cosmopolitanisms" (36, 27–8). Rethinking cultures on the model of the hotel, as "sites of dwelling *and* travel," Clifford then defines a new subject or topic that he hopes will redefine the field for future anthropological study: "encounters between people to some degree away from home," where the key question becomes "not so much 'Where are you from?' as 'Where are you between?' " (36–7).

Clifford's "Traveling Cultures" seems especially well suited to help us understand the cross-cultural encounters at the center of Melville's early travel writing. Melville's first novels trace a clearly defined progress along the lines of Clifford's analysis, as they move from the anxieties, confusions, and failures of *Typee* to the self-aware and self-conscious enactment of these themes in *Moby-Dick*. *Typee* turns on the failure of contact between its narrator and the foreign world he travels through, a failure based in the narrator's continued attachment to the conventional thinking of his home culture. Though he may at some moments want to use his experience of this exotic Other world as the ground for a radical critique of Western ways, even these critiques are clearly rooted in basic elements of the Western vision. No matter how far he seems to go in experiencing island exoticism, Tommo always remains firmly tied to the easy binaries of conventional travel: he is the "civilized" adventurer, while the Marquesans are primitive "savages"; he arrives as the worldly voyager full of the comparative knowledge gained from broad experience, while the islanders are celebrated or criticized as unsophisticated "locals." And Tommo's vision of culture is always monolithic; he wants to defend what he sees as the "purity" and simplicity of an undefiled, simple, innocent island culture that has not been corrupted by communication with Western influences, but then he finally also feels compelled to escape the island to defend the integrity of his own local identity when it seems to be threatened by too close an interchange with the Marquesans.

But there is a twist. Melville structures his presentation of Tommo's thought processes to expose key moments when this highly conventional vision breaks down – finally suggesting that the real innocent here is Tommo himself, who only falls back on these generic conventions as a means of self-protection, as a way of avoiding a more complete experience of or insight into this fearfully foreign world. First, Tommo's claims about the "innocence" of the Typee seem to be contradicted by the glimpses we get of the life outside his blinkered vision. It turns out the islanders do have constant wars between tribes and quarrels between individuals; they do have a social hierarchy defining unwritten boundaries in private and public space; they do have institutions of government. Though he remains admittedly baffled by it, the Typee also have a complex notion of beauty worked out in crafts and self-conscious arts (textile making, oratory, singing, tattooing), as well as a systematic theology expressed in elaborately defined religious rites. And although it cannot be deciphered by foreign visitors, the Typee follow a system of "taboo" rules that permeate every aspect of their life. In short, the Typee are not natural innocents but have a complex, conscious, and sophisticated culture.

Melville's work develops, then, through a series of scenes of reversal, where the tables are turned on Tommo to reveal the limits of his knowledge. Even at the outset, when he stood on the ridge and tried to re-enact what Pratt calls the "master-of-all-I-see" trope of classic travel writing, literally and figuratively "looking down" on the natives from an all-encompassing panoramic overview, we soon see that in fact this time the anti-heroic explorers are lost: they have no idea where they are or which tribe they are looking at. After months of immersion within the Typee's everyday life, Tommo still has to admit, "I saw everything, but could comprehend nothing" (177). And even the conclusion of his tale is a confession of the limits of his knowledge; he still has not been able to provide firm answers to his deepest questions: Are the Typee really cruel savages? Did they really mean to eat him?

But if *Typee* thus unfolds as the story of Tommo's blindness, it also seems to be a story of willful blindness. Tommo tells us several times – usually as a prelude to another of his disquisitions on Typee "innocence" – that his decision to seem to give himself over to enjoyment of the island life is strategic: he feels this is the best way for a captive to convince his captors that he is not trying to resist or escape. If he enters into these rosy visions of a lost paradise partly to deceive the Typee, though, it becomes clear that Tommo is also deceiving himself. When Tommo mounts an idealistic, anti-colonial defense of cannibalism while he suspects he is being fattened for slaughter, or when he joyfully details the preparations for a lavish ritual feast without mentioning his fear that he might end up as the main dish, his words seem to function more as a symptom of and screen for his own anxieties than as a mirror of the outside world; in fact they speak for an effort at self-censorship, working to repress consideration of darker possibilities here. The rhapsodies about swimming and sailing with Fayaway and her band of loving, naked mermaids, or about becoming literally immersed in the proffered bodily life of the Typee, are presented as naïve fantasy rather than reality – an attempt to evade a more complex and genuine encounter across a recognized cultural divide. Tommo does not want to consider the slight suspicion that even innocent Fayaway, like the breast-feeding African woman set up as a theatrical display by Babo to deflect Captain Delano's suspicions in the later "Benito Cereno," may be mobilizing her bodily charms as part of an artful scheme to play into his traveler's fantasies about primitive innocence and so distract him from awareness of his situation as a hostage or from dwelling on the disappearance of his friend Toby.

This sort of willful misprision is most clearly evident in Tommo's relations with Kory-Kory. In fascinating moments that anticipate Melville's more self-conscious play upon Delano's blinding "innocence" in "Benito Cereno," we begin to see here how Tommo's vision of native innocence serves mainly to guard his own innocence – and to block a more complex experience of cross-cultural interaction. When Delano jokes about what he perceives as the excessively close, almost marital, bond of friendship between Babo and Cereno, taking this as further evidence of the mindless docility and contentedness that make blacks a natural servant class, readers see that the American's prejudice keeps him from recognizing that the issue here is not only bonds but bondage: the seemingly conventional servitude that warms Delano's heart is in fact a subversive theatrical show stage-managed by an African who controls the scene with violent power, has a mind full of schemes and designs, has a breadth of cosmopolitan knowledge that allows him to play upon Western conventions, and is anything but content with conditions of bondage and servitude. Similarly, Tommo mocks what he sees as the "excess of deferential kindness" in his "man-servant" Kory-Kory (97). Noting how this simple native throws himself at him, feeding him, carrying him, sleeping next to him, seeming to offer a guilt-free entrance into same-sex bodily closeness as he makes himself a sort of parodic spouse, Tommo retreats into the myth of Marquesan generosity, simplicity, bodily ease, and natural subservience as a way of masking other unpleasant recognitions: it may be that this bond with Kory-Kory is also a form of bondage; perhaps this close friend never leaves his master because he is also a prison-guard, keeping the foreigner under constant surveillance. But to recognize that Kory-Kory's proffered love might be part of such a "perfidious design" (76) would be to recognize him as not only a body but a mind, not only a servant but a master, not only a naïve innocent but a conscious, artful performer – who, like the *tayo* "friends" encountered later in *Omoo*, begins to emerge as a potential mediator between worlds.

Marnoo is the most significant islander figure in this line – breaking the ground for the later appearance of Queequeg in *Moby-Dick*. He steals the central scene in *Typee* (and in fact then takes over the book), not as an object of erotic desire but as a model of an intellectual possibility. Although Marnoo is described as a semi-androgynous beauty, what attracts Tommo's fascinated gaze is not so much Marnoo's body as his mind; this boundary-crossing character stands out of the confusions of the *Typee* voyage as a figure not of polymorphous sexuality but of polymorphous nationality. A condescending rhetoric of "love" for the "body" of an innocent primitive – which prevented Tommo from full recognitions about the status and worldview of Fayaway and Kory-Kory – clearly has no place in this encounter. In fact, comically reversing the sexual dynamics of conventional travel plots, Marnoo finally leaves a flabbergasted Tommo in a passive, vulnerable, feminine position – feeling like a "belle of the season" who has been "cut" in public by her beau (136). Certainly Marnoo shows none of the obsequious deference of a Kory-Kory. When he stuns Tommo by suddenly turning to address him in perfect English (like a latter-day Squanto), he makes clear that he does so only when it suits him – not to cater or defer to the Westerner but as a strategic move to underline his mastery of the situation.

And Marnoo emerges in this meeting as a model, teacher, and guide for Tommo – pointing the way toward possibilities that the Westerner can only begin to imagine. Formed by experiences in Western culture as well as in various island tribes, and uncannily blurring distinctions between male and female, body and mind, nature and art, native and foreign, Marnoo dominates the attention of Tommo and other islanders not for his tribalist purity but as a model of hybrid identity, not as an epitome of the seamlessness of local culture but as a character arising out of the local who is able to travel between worlds. The encounter between Tommo and Marnoo then develops as a classic enactment of Clifford's vision: the sense of a potential intimacy in the interaction emerges not out of a knowing traveler's condescension to the local but rather out of a traveler's first tentative recognitions of kinship in a meeting between "discrepant cosmopolitanisms" (Clifford 36). And it is Marnoo, the non-Western voyager in this meeting, who most fully elaborates the vision of a "traveling culture" here. Tragically separated from his origin or home, condemned to a life of constant, solo voyaging, this "omoo" traveler nonetheless also comes to stand for Tommo as a key example of a voyager who is able to maintain his integrity of identity, his dignity and self-possession, despite his departure from the ground of a singular home culture. Marnoo also emerges here for Tommo as an alternative figure of the writer; his personal integrity and power as a cultural mediator seem to arise through his special combination of traveler's knowledge with verbal artistry. Speaking in multiple languages, idioms, and tones, and honing his formal orations into highly polished and strategic rhetorical performances, Marnoo demonstrates that the islanders are not only creatures of unconscious Nature but can be conscious producers of Art. But his special gifts give him a unique power to speak at the boundaries between tribes. Though in *Typee* Tommo fails as a cultural mediator himself, he comes to revere Marnoo as a model of the traveling writer whose "arts of the contact zone" (to use Pratt's phrase) make him a powerful communicator between worlds.

Melville's conception of the intercultural traveler with an expanded sense of collective belonging, then, is not founded in Western notions of the cosmopolitan "citizen of the world" so much as in this Marquesan model of the "Taboo kannaker," or sacred wanderer. Indeed his second book takes its name from an islanders' word – "Omoo" – referring to the special figures in their culture who, like Marnoo, are granted a privileged position as travelers between isolated islands or between warring tribes. While the narrator of *Omoo*, "Typee," and his new traveling companion, Doctor Long Ghost, may not live up to the full demands of the position of the Marquesan sacred wanderer, these free-spirited adventurers do engage in undirected travel that begins and ends at sea – and leaves them far from any home-feeling for their ship or for any national identity. After all of his experiences of wandering between worlds, and all of his meetings with other mobile, hybrid "rovers," "beachcombers," and "castaways," Typee can only joke at the book's end about the irrelevance of questions (posed by the questionable ship's captain) about his national affiliation or about his final passage home.

As a successor to these "Omoo" rovers, Melville's narrator in *Moby-Dick* is also a much more developed version of the type. Introducing himself with the famous line "Call me Ishmael," taking up the name of the famous biblical outcast, Ishmael immediately foregrounds his stance as an eternal wanderer, highlighting issues of cultural dislocation and questions of the boundaries between an exile and his cultural home. But the plot of Ishmael's relations with Queequeg – who emerges as the other full-fledged epitome of the Omoo figure – then brings out possibilities within this sacred wanderer role that were only latent in *Omoo*. Here the wanderer is not simply imagined as a permanently displaced figure living out a nomadic existence defined negatively as a movement away from home, but begins to suggest the outline of a newly positive function – as cross-cultural mediator. If travel in *Typee* raised searing questions about cultural allegiances, and *Omoo* then responded to that questioning by joining a world of voyagers without allegiances – a subculture of independent individuals, bachelor travelers whose only allegiance is to their own survival and continued mobility – in *Moby-Dick* we meet wanderer figures whose travels leave them with multiple allegiances.

Comparative Cosmopolitanism in *Moby-Dick*

Melville began to formulate his more ambitious plan for *Moby-Dick* when he was already a known writer, publishing out of New York City, and very much stimulated by debates in the many New York literary societies and Bohemian Clubs that had sprung up to promote various schools of American writing after Irving's day. The central subject for debate between each of these competing groups was: Should American writing develop along the lines of Irving's cosmopolitanism or along the lines of Young America nationalism? Melville's revisions to *Moby-Dick* emerged in a fervor of Young America nationalism (evident in the strident tones of the "Hawthorne and His Mosses" review from this period) but, perhaps surprisingly, the book then develops as a sharply divided study of the direction of this microcosmic ship of state (the *Pequod*), contrasting two central organizing visions about the ship's voyage – and the contrast here pits a strong centripetal urge to nationalist integration against the centrifugal tendencies of cosmopolitanism. Ahab, the whaling ship's captain, emerges as an archetypal figure of absolutist centralization as he stage-manages political rituals working to forge a monolithic social whole around his own charismatic and patho-logically obsessed subjectivity, making diverse sailors into a seamless unit by orient-ing them all towards the end of one self-destructive mission. But the global voyage of the *Pequod*'s markedly diverse and international crew raises severe challenges to such efforts at nationalist integration. And Ahab's story is narrated by Ishmael, a bachelor traveler amongst the working seamen whose impulses all tend in the opposite direction.

Ishmael develops as one of the most memorable case studies of the mid-nineteenth-century cosmopolitan type – in fact combining elements of Benjamin

Franklin and Irving to take them both in a new direction. In scenes playing off of the vision of young Franklin arriving in Philadelphia with almost nothing to make his way in the world, the lone Ishmael arrives guileless and almost penniless at the Spouter-Inn in New Bedford. But his direction from there is more strongly guided by his obvious relation to Irving's portrait of the American writer in "The Voyage." For this character is more literary/philosophical than practical, more a spectator than an actor, more airy than grounded, more prone to self-loss than to self-making. Giving us no details about his home, family, age, or even his real name, Melville's storyteller simply takes up the persona "Ishmael," alluding to the biblical wanderer to summarize his defining tendency: an urge to travel, to move away from origins, away from land to the sea, even away from himself. More clearly than Irving, Ishmael associates his fascination with oceanic whiteness with a tendency to dangerous self-loss. Ishmael's centrifugal tendencies make him a changeable, fluid, buoyant, flexible self – and in the end it may be this personal fluidity and buoyancy (or lack of solid integrity) that allows him to survive in the fluid environment of the sea: he is only one who lives to tell the tale of the *Pequod*'s destruction.

"I am tormented with an everlasting itch for things remote," Ishmael tells us in Chapter 1; "I love to sail forbidden seas, and land on barbarous coasts. Not ignoring what is good, I am quick to perceive a horror, and could still be social with it . . . since it is but well to be on friendly terms with all the inmates of the place one lodges in" (7). Here we see how broad is Ishmael's notion of home: for him, the non-familial, impermanent, hotel-like "place one lodges in" encompasses the entire world. And we soon see how far the fluid and flexible Ishmael might go in his urge to be "friendly" and "sociable" even with the "forbidden" elements encountered at sea, with what a more familiar moral code might call a "horror," when we see him waking up after his first night at the Spouter-Inn to find himself cuddling up in quasi-marital coziness with a huge, naked, dark-skinned, tattooed, idol-worshipping cannibal: Queequeg. If he has a few moments of culture shock and eruptions of prejudice and panic, Ishmael calms down surprisingly quickly and finds that his xenophilia and ability to be "social" with a "horror" guide him toward a fast friendship with this pagan savage. In fact, Ishmael is soon smoking the tomahawk peace pipe with Queequeg, learning the tricks of harpooning and knot-tying from him, and trying out Queequeg's idol worship in a classically cosmopolitan urge to religious tolerance, contrasting the broad church of the inn to the fundamentalist narrowness of organized temples: "When a man's religion becomes really frantic, . . . [it] makes this earth of ours an uncomfortable inn to lodge in" (85). He then launches into a tirade, telling one of Ahab's captains that "Queequeg here is a born member of the First Congregational Church . . . . the same ancient Catholic Church to which you and I, and Captain Peleg there, and Queequeg here, and all of us . . . belong; . . . we all belong to that; . . . in *that* we all join hands" (87–8). Along the same lines, he is soon holding his cannibal friend up as a model of kindness, civility, sobriety – values much more genuine than "hollow" Christian virtues. After just a few days as "bosom friend" of Queequeg, Ishmael pictures himself merging into almost complete, boundary-blurring identity with his savage comrade – or, more precisely, exchanges identities with him. A white man is nothing more than "a white-washed negro," he says, pronouncing himself an "idolator" and "savage," while Queequeg now appears not so foreign after all – instead emerging as a "George Washington cannibalistically developed" (60, 52, 50).

But here again the quasi-marital bosom friendship of male bedfellows is never simply a barely sublimated love affair; the love plot works for Ishmael (and for Melville) as a comic vehicle to bring to the fore the dynamics and difficulties of an attempt to achieve the unsettling and almost impossible cosmopolitan ideal: cross-cultural interchange. And indeed the unconventional pairing of Ishmael and Quee-queg departs significantly from the pattern of the classic travel story; this is not simply another meeting between a sympathetic and tolerant Western cosmopolitan and his resolutely local native informant. Rather, the interaction at the Spouter-Inn emerges as a perfect example of what Clifford describes as an encounter between "discrepant cosmopolitanisms" (36). For Queequeg is a sort of ideal Squanto, a Squanto who has retained his integrity. In fact, even more than Ishmael, and more than Marnoo, Queequeg is described in *Moby-Dick* as a finely balanced, model cosmopolitan. In some ways he is a mirror image of Ishmael. Born a prince in his native tribe, he left home out of an inexplicable urge to see the broader world, to learn from the Other, until he finds that he has become such a "queer" hybrid identity that he is unfitted for the throne of his "pure and undefiled" pagan world – he can't go home again (56). He tries hard to study Christian rites and Bibles, he speaks a creolized mix of diverse world languages, he incorporates some Western dress into his wild costumes to cut quite a figure amongst the working-class dandies developing cosmopolitan looks as they saunter around shipyard coffeehouses. And Queequeg is able to act in key situations upon cosmopolitan principles: after jumping into dangerous waters to save white sailors, he explains: "It's a mutual, joint-stock world, in all meridians. We cannibals must help these Christians" (62). But what distinguishes Queequeg is that, unlike Ishmael, he stands as a model of the possibility of retaining some personal and cultural integrity amidst all of this intermixing: "Here was a man some twenty thousand miles from home … thrown among people as strange to him as though he were in the planet Jupiter; and yet he seemed entirely at his ease; preserving the utmost serenity; content with his own companionship; always equal to himself" (50).

In contrast to this, Ishmael, with his tendency to disappear in idle speculation and self-loss, seems a case study of the limits as well as the powers of cosmopolitanism. But we cannot lose sight of the fact that Ishmael, in contrast to a monological truthsayer like Father Mapple or to an autocratic orator like Ahab or to his regionally and ideologically provincial shipmates, is able at least to begin to be social with the cultural Other, to the point that he does open up an intercultural conversation with this "savage" across the boundaries of race, religion, ideology, language, and class. In contrast to Ahab, with his monomaniacal obsession with unity, Ishmael emerges through the structuring of his encyclopedic narration as a writer-librarian-anatomist who is able to comprehend a multiplicity of perspectives on the doubloon, a variety of

approaches to the whale and to the world. The character who rises out of the
shipwreck to compose *Moby-Dick* tells his tale by setting the voices of a wide range
of opposed dogmas and ideologies in conversation – without, however, committing
himself to any one of these anthologized positions. Melville's greatest work, then, can
in some ways be read as an ambitious test of the possibilities for cross-cultural or
cosmopolitan conversation in an increasingly diverse and interdependent world.

The Cosmopolitan Muse: From *Moby-Dick* to James's Cosmopolitan World – and Beyond

After this high point of cosmopolitan vision in *Moby-Dick*, Melville continued to be
centrally concerned with exploration of the dynamics of cross-cultural travel, but,
especially in the dark years of the 1850s, the figure of the intercultural ambassador
seems to drop out of the picture – often remaining only as an implied ideal against
which narrators and characters and story elements can be measured and found
wanting. Like a withdrawn god, intercultural exchange itself becomes an unapproach-
able vision somehow not available within the storyworlds of many later poems,
fictions, or magazine pieces. But even through the periods of most bleak vision,
Melville remained a seeker, continuing to envision himself or his narrators as exiled
wanderers inspired by the dream of the cosmopolitan ideal as it had emerged in his
earliest writings. In an 1849 review of Francis Parkman's record of his journey on the
California and Oregon Trail, written just a few years before *Moby-Dick*, Melville
already evokes Ishmael's ideal of universal brotherhood to criticize the American
traveler's failure to imagine a relation to "savage" Indians outside of his home culture:
"We are all of us – Anglo-Saxons, Dyaks and Indians – sprung from one head and
made in one image. And if we reject this brotherhood now, we shall be forced to join
hands hereafter" (*PT* 231). A decade later, in his 1859 Lyceum lecture entitled
"Traveling," Melville is still primarily interested in a mode of travel that takes us
out of ourselves, opening us to a sort of world citizenship. "Every man's home is in a
certain sense a 'Hopper,' which however fair and sheltered, shuts him in from the
outer world," observes Melville in his opening remarks. But he then goes on to stress
that the goal of serious travel is to open out of such home-bound insulation. For while
he recognizes that there is a pleasure in "coming back to the old hearthstone" at the
end of a voyage, Melville's emphasis here is characteristically on the "pleasure of
leaving home," as the "breaking up of old prejudices" helps us to burst out of native
boundaries, making way for "a new birth" into an expansive, explicitly cosmopolitan
sense of global belonging: "[Travel] enlarges the sphere of comprehensive benevolence
till it includes the whole human race" (*PT* 421–3).

The glimmer of such a potential perspective animates even some of Melville's
darkest works. In "The Two Temples," one of his "diptych" stories of the mid-1850s,
for example, two paired sketches represent a polarized world lacking a larger vision
that might connect America and England, rich and poor, religion and art.

The traveling narrator, cast out from the narrow, exclusive church in New York, and then prevented (because of a sponsor's national and class prejudice) from continuing on the standard aristocratic tour of Europe, is condemned to the role of Ishmaelite drifter between these separate worlds, a homeless castaway, a lone rover without firm allegiances to any home or class. In his native scene, his ambiguous traveler's status makes him suspect; neither fully local nor alien, both "insider" and "outsider," all-seeing but himself "unseen," this "inside prowler" develops a comparative, ethnographical overview on his church's rites that makes him seem a potentially dangerous "disturber of the ... peace" (*PT* 305–6, 309). But this voyager is not by nature a bounded isolato: though of gentlemanly airs, he opens to the experience of the poor; his continued questing is clearly compelled by the search for some larger benevolence or charity in the "public worship" of a broad church; this urban *flâneur*, then, wandering like a "beggar" with a "prayer-book" under his arm, emerges as an ironic, minor-key version of the "sacred traveler" figure, seeking a form of spirituality associated with a generous, non-exclusive sense of community (309, 305, 303). And finally, wandering as a "stranger in a strange land," the forlorn Melvillean drifter meets his foreign, male muse – and an unexpected model of "genial humane assembly" (315, 311). Inspired by the "hospitality" of a ragged, working-class English boy, offering free mugs of ale "in all directions," and especially welcoming to a foreign Yankee (since the boy's own father's departure for America has given him a cosmopolitan sense of solidarity with other travelers), the narrator finds that this "glorious" boy's spirits revive his spirits – and his access to spirit (314). With rising emotion, he concludes in a celebration of the hybrid vision available through foreign travel, presenting the crowded British theater as a masthead-like site for a visionary experience of "perfect love" and social unity, reading the "mimic" motions of a stage show about Richelieu as a close translation of the experience of a true church, and finding a rare home feeling of belonging in a momentary encounter with foreigners in a strange land (314–15).

In another diptych, "The Paradise of Bachelors and the Tartarus of Maids," Melville develops a bitter travesty of two conventional modes of mid-century touristic travel writing (the Irvingesque gentleman's tour of a picturesque old London club, and the required visit to the most advanced of New England textile mills), raising uncomfortable questions about the ideological relations between these seemingly separate veins of popular vision. The problem raised by this diptych, then, is the failure of communication between these unnaturally separated story parts: men and women, capital and labor, consumption and production, England and America. In this allegory of technological, literary, and sexual production and reproduction – and, in the broadest sense, the division of labor – the separation between these spheres makes for sterility on all levels, and Melville's work calls out for an ambassador figure who might travel between these worlds, beginning to explain their relation and probe their contradictions, thus bringing them back into some fertile, productive connection. The journeying of the traveler-narrator here makes him the only figure who enters both story scenes, but the diptych narrative structure foregrounds his failure to develop the sort of traveler's knowledge that might make him an effective intercultural ambassador; a witness to horror, injustice, and folly, he does not know how to respond to or comment on what he encounters. The narrator's aggravating silence may, however, finally lead to one productive result – if it serves to prod some active readers who begin to speak from the gap between the two sketches, to try to make their own connections, and thus to fill the vacant role as traveling mediator figures in this divided world.

In *The Confidence-Man* (1857) American society is represented not as a seamless whole but as a traveling culture, a fragmented grouping of diverse isolatoes, each continually moving away from home on a modern pilgrimage with no known end. In this mobile, socially fluid world, any seeming "sacred traveler" selling a settled or fixed belief is clearly a devilish con-man, seeking only to take advantage of a vacancy on the *Fidèle*. In the series of enigmatical encounters between the solo pilgrims on this steamship, nothing is shared; when all relations are simply alienated market relations, no cultural or psychological interchange is possible; any figure, like the "Cosmopolitan," who seems to offer mediation or connection or the benevolent vision of "charity" simply performs a parodic travesty of true mediation or exchange, playing for profit upon vestigial desires for those lost ideals.

Like *The Confidence-Man*, the ambitious long poem *Clarel* (1876) explores a mid-century mode of voyaging defined mainly by its distance from earlier ideals of "sacred travel" – or from Melville's Omoo model of the "sacred traveler." Studying encounters among another group of diverse wanderers – this time an international group of tourists in the Near East – *Clarel* presents them as descendants of the *Canterbury Tales* pilgrims. Pilgrimage here, though, is not oriented toward a single spiritual home or goal but is set in the context of a modern, cosmopolitan world; this is a *Canterbury Tales* based in the vision of a "traveling culture." Always on the move away from home, these seekers are brought together to share stories of a global crisis of faith. *Clarel* suggests that what is most formative for these travelers is not their anchoring in a singular national or theological origin but their relation to the process of an ongoing collective voyage – a movement of continual geographical, ideological, and spiritual displacement and exploration that defines the shifting ground for a new, experimental, ethnographical, cross-cultural approach to meditation on the bases of human belief. But during this journey through a desiccated Holy Land, few productive connections are finally made between the tales of speakers who remain confined to their separate spheres; none of these lone, exiled wanderers emerges as the sort of "sacred traveler" who might open up a productive dialogue between isolated seekers; no ambassador figure emerges to inspire the bachelor American divinity student, Clarel, to enter into fertile or lasting interactions with his fellow travelers.

Through the last years of Melville's life, however, two presiding characters seemed to serve a special function as muse or "genius" figures for his writing – both epitomizing the cosmopolitan ideal of ambassadorship in its alliance with genial sociability. One of these figures, the Marquis de Grandvin, presented less as a real human character than as a mythic personification of the social spirit inspired by wine, defining a motivating ideal for the lone, despondent writer, was meant to be the "talismanic" central figure in an ambitious but unfinished book project, "The Burgundy Club," collecting works in poetry and prose begun in 1859 (on the inspiration of the author's 1856–7 trip to the Near East) and then revised from the 1870s on until Melville's death (Melville 412). Grandvin and his American "friend and disciple" Jack Gentian convene the international roster of speakers in two long poems, "At the Hostelry" and "Naples in the Time of Bomba," in which Melville continues to explore the possibilities of good fellowship and conviviality found through close friendships between bachelors at Irvingesque clubs and inns, and expressed in gay, multi-voiced, intellectually cosmopolitan symposia on travel, history, and art. Although the charmed circle of these imaginary club conversations seems to define a rarefied, elite, restricted scene, prose character sketches written to frame the Grandvin poems celebrate the Marquis primarily as the epitome of cosmopolitan inclusiveness and openness. While he is of French birth, Grandvin is truly multinational, a "genial foreigner" easily taken up by Americans and received "in the high circles of every European capital"; though male, he is recognized by all women as "a cordial friend"; though of patrician origins, "his cosmopolitan sympathies, transcending his class, go out to mankind"; he has troops of friends "on both sides of the water" and is revered by "divers parties in Church and State" (411). What makes the mysterious, polymorphous, mythic Grandvin such a successful mediator in conversation groups, and such a potent literary model for Melville's narrator, is his intellectual mobility. Here the Melvillean narrator encounters a fascinating, intoxicating, genial muse figure who evokes cosmopolitan possibilities he can only barely grasp. Like Tommo in his meeting with Marnoo, the narrator in the Grandvin portraits hails the Marquis as his complement, the embodiment of what he lacks: wine-like flow versus the narrator's clogged, static prose; travel versus immobility; sociability versus isolation; fecund abundance versus dry sterility; beauty and effervescent joy versus grave depression. Motivated to write by his experience of the "genial flood" of Grandvin's outpouring of spoken words in social conversation, Melville's abject narrator can only dream that in his "methodizing" written language he might incorporate some of his idol's cosmopolitan spirit and "dramatically put on his personality ... since he it is that kindles me, inspires me, usurps me" (414).

But the most resonant figure inspiring Melville's late work – the Handsome Sailor archetype introduced at the opening of *Billy Budd* – operates in a completely different social register. If Grandvin speaks for the later Melville's continued imaginative faith in a Western ideal of the cosmopolitan, the Handsome Sailor shows Melville at the same time further developing his fascinated meditation on non-Western traveler figures in the line of Marnoo and Queequeg. The defining instance of this seafaring archetype seems to step directly out of Melville's world of personal memory as, in an unusual narrative intrusion within this late work, the author turns to his own first-person voice to relive the scene of an epiphanic encounter with a majestic African sailor during his travels to Liverpool in 1839. This attractive working-class dandy wears a hybrid mixture of clothing (a "gay silk handkerchief" around his neck, "big hoops of gold" in his ears, and a Scotch "Highland bonnet with a tartan band" on his head) that speaks for his openness to international influences through a lifetime of global travel (*BB* 43). Though he stands out for his personal beauty, the narrator and his peers revere and respect the "intensely black" Handsome Sailor not for his erotic charms so much as for his social power – for the cultural work he does in creating community amongst an international group of world-wanderers: he is "the center of a company . . . made up of such an assortment of tribes and complexions as would have well fitted them to be marched up by Anacharsis Cloots before the bar of the first French Assembly as Representatives of the Human Race" (43). Unlike Ahab, the Handsome Sailor defines a generous social spirit that does not obliterate the personal or national integrity of others; unlike Billy Budd, he is able to serve (along the lines of a Marnoo) as articulate spokesman for his brothers, inspiring in them a sense of solidarity across cultures among traveling workers of the world. Though he stands outside of the story proper here, the colorful, talismanic folk figure of the Handsome Sailor defines the horizon of expectations in the tale to come – setting the ideal standard by which we understand and measure Billy Budd, and reaffirming Melville's commitment to his youthful dreams of international brotherhood.

In his final years, then, Melville was still centrally inspired as a writer and thinker by the potential of ambassador figures, continuing a lifelong exploration of the dynamics of intercultural travel that not only anticipates James's modernist cosmopolitanism of the early twentieth century but also leads beyond it. Opening to a diverse reach of non-Western cultures and challenging conventional notions of the relations between elite cosmopolitans and pure locals, Melville's travel-based, experimental writing can serve as a rich point of departure for thinking about the "global" world of the early twenty-first century.

REFERENCES AND FURTHER READING

Bhabha, Homi K. *The Location of Culture.* New York: Routledge, 1994.

Clifford, James. "Traveling Cultures." In *Routes: Travel and Translation in the Late Twentieth Century.* Cambridge, MA: Harvard University Press, 1997. 17–46.

James, Henry. *The Ambassadors.* Ed. Leon Edel. Boston: Houghton Mifflin, 1960.

—— "Daisy Miller: A Study." In *The Complete Tales of Henry James.* Ed. Leon Edel. London: Rupert Hart-Davis, 1962. 141–207.

—— . *Hawthorne.* London: Macmillan, 1879.

Lauter, Paul. "Melville Climbs the Canon." *American Literature*, 66.1 (March 1994): 1–24.

Melville, Herman. "The Burgundy Club." In *Herman Melville: Tales, Poems, and Other Writings.*

Ed. John Bryant. New York: Modern Library, 2001. 405–35.

Porter, Carolyn. "Call Me Ishmael, or How to Make Double-Talk Speak." In *New Essays on Moby-Dick.* Ed. Richard H. Brodhead. Cambridge: Cambridge University Press, 1986. 73–108.

Pratt, Mary Louise. *Imperial Eyes: Travel Writing and Transculturation.* London: Routledge, 1992. 1–27.

Sanborn, Geoffrey. *The Sign of the Cannibal: Melville and the Making of a Postcolonial Reader.* Durham, NC: Duke University Press, 1998.

Ziff, Larzer. *Return Passages: Great American Travel Writing, 1780–1910.* New Haven, CT: Yale University Press, 2000.

3
Melville's World Readers

A. Robert Lee

You cannot spill a drop of American blood without spilling the blood of the whole world ... We are not a narrow tribe of men ... No: our blood is as the flood of the Amazon, made up of a thousand noble currents all pouring into one ... Our ancestry is lost in the universal paternity, and Caesar and Alfred, St. Paul and Luther, Homer and Shakespeare are as much ours as Washington, who is as much the world's as our own. (*Redburn* 169)

Writer for the World

Wherever his present masthead, Melville might readily be imagined to bring all his wry caution to so encompassing a judgment as "writer for the world." Did he not once think that his early South Seas fictions would shadow him into posterity, the Yankee mariner-turned-penman whose reputation, as he wrote ruefully to Hawthorne on June 1, 1851, ran the risk of becoming that of the "man who lived among the cannibals" (Leyda 1: 413)? Did not the obituary in the *New York Daily Tribune*, after Melville's death on September 28, 1891, add its own twist in referring to his literary bow as an event once warmly greeted but long forgotten: "He won considerable fame as an author by the publication of a book in 1847 [*sic*] entitled 'Typee'" (Leyda 2: 837)? Yet, conspicuously, it is this same Melville, cannibal Melville indeed, and his "investigative poetics," in Anne Waldman's wonderfully apt phrase for *Moby-Dick* (121), who has come to rank as one of the great presiding voices of American literature.

For in the America of his Manhattan birth, early residence in Albany and Lansing-burgh, New York and Boston sailings-out, Pittsfield farm, and the East 26th Street house of the later years, and in locales and languages infinitely beyond, readerships leave little doubt. Melville has won an accepted place as a writer of Atlantic and Pacific sweep. Whether, too, one does or does not opt for Melville under modern protocols, new historicist or postcolonial, say, the effect of recent theory has been to confirm new-found layers of attractive complication in his work.

Lively and greatly revealing as are these approaches, Melville can still arouse criticism, even annoyance at his entanglements or supposed willful wrong turns. In the letter he wrote to Evert Duyckinck in March 1849, he himself supplied a key to the challenges of his own work, however unwittingly. On hearing Emerson lecture in Boston, he confesses to a reluctant surprise at easily understanding the New England sage. His account might point as much to his own eventual imaginative achievement as to that of Emerson:

> I had heard of him as full of transcendentalisms, myths & oracular gibberish . . . . To my surprise, I found him quite intelligible . . . I love all men who dive. Any fish can swim near the surface, but it takes a great whale to go down stairs five miles or more; . . . I'm not talking about Mr. Emerson now – but the whole corps of thought-divers, that have been diving & coming up with bloodshot eyes since the world began. (Leyda 1: 292)

Who better than Melville himself to qualify as also one of America's "thought-divers"? In middle age he would complain, quite literally, of weak eyes, but the metaphor of surfacing with "bloodshot" eyes gives powerful expression to his unyielding inner searches. Given its ocean widths and depths, *Moby-Dick* understandably has carried this imprimatur most of all, his own ocean book of "down stairs five miles or more."

"You must have plenty of sea-room to tell the truth in." So, in "Hawthorne and His Mosses," his masked, purposive review of *Mosses From An Old Manse* (1846) for the *Literary World* of August 17 and 21, 1850, runs another of Melville's self-references. From *Typee* to *The Confidence-Man*, *Battle Pieces* to *Clarel*, with *Billy Budd* as epilogue, one quickly gets a sense of what he means: diving, space, truth-telling. Nobody doubts he could write at a local, even miniaturist, pitch, as *The Piazza Tales* and other stories and many of his poems give evidence. But the note struck by "sea-room" hits the mark. Whether in the whaling epic of *Moby-Dick* or the Mississippi river carnival of *The Confidence-Man*, Melville's will to enquiry, his fierce, necessary probing of truth, is always elusively inter-folded or cross-layered.

Perhaps more than anything else it has been this boldness of mind, a very American kind of boldness, that has caught and held attention both in and beyond America. For there can be little question that since his death, itself too passingly noted at the time, an international Melville has won inexorable recognition. Readerships have increasingly better understood his diver-bloodshot imaginative daring: the buoyancy of mind, the textual self-fashioning and virtuosity, the dark humor, the claims made for him as modernist or postmodern, and much to immediate purposes, his extraordinary range of multicultural and transnational interests and sites.

American Melville

Global Melville, necessarily, has beginnings in American Melville, however much in his own century his side of the Atlantic felt the sway of British reviewers. Highlighting this American response, especially from fellow creative writers, helps locate the process whereby the national author emerges into the international author. Two early shows of interest, Melville as the season's find, give a point of departure. In an unsigned review of *Typee* for the New York *Tribune* of 4 April 1848, Margaret Fuller, Boston transcendental luminary and co-founder with Emerson of *The Dial*, was among the first to spot the larger resonance of this first book's "imaginary adventures." She likens its "hair-breadth 'scapes" to those told by and about Shakespeare's Othello (Lee *Assessments* I: 196). In a subsequent *Tribune* review for 10 May, 1849, George Ripley, also a luminary of New England's Unitarian-transcendental literary brethren, could vent his dismay at *Mardi* for its "shapeless rhapsody." Yet he too recognized the "graphic, poetical narration" and "dim, shadowy, spectral Mardian region of mystic speculation and wizard fancies" (Lee *Assessments* I: 253). Whatever their reservations, both writers sensed Melville's scale of ambition, along with his working ventriloquy.

Not inappropriately, Melville's admired Hawthorne best captured his energy of creative and intellectual appetite. Writing up their after-supper conversation over cigars at Lenox in his Journal for August 1, 1851, Hawthorne recalls how the two of them took to pondering "time and eternity, things of this world and of the next, and books, and publishers, and all possible and impossible matters" (Leyda 1: 419). The account, in line with his far better-known journal entry for November 12, 1856 – "He can neither believe, not be comfortable in his unbelief" – suggests the typical will to enquiry in Melville, his unceasing call to interior journey, as well as a wholly tantalizing moment in the Hawthorne–Melville relationship (Leyda 1: 529). At the same time it affords a pathway into the kinds of general-reader response Melville would increasingly elicit across the international spectrum.

That interest in Melville in the nineteenth century, with the exception of *Typee*, became increasingly rare gives yet sharper emphasis to those occasions when it did occur. Among early American contemporaries few responded to him more shrewdly than Sophia Hawthorne. Writing to her mother in September, 1850, she acknowledges herself drawn to the deep vitality in reserve of Melville's disposition – "a man with a true heart & a soul & an intellect – with life to his finger-tips." Evert Duyckinck, in his two-part review of *Moby-Dick* for the *Literary World* of 15 and 22 November, 1851, could censure the possible blasphemy ("this piratical running down of creeds and opinions") yet readily praise "a most remarkable sea-dish" (Leyda 1: 434, 437). The Irish-born and New York literary man, Fitz-James O'Brien, under the title of "Our Young Authors" in *Putnam's Monthly Magazine* for February, 1853, judges Melville's writing after *Typee* "a decided falling off" yet also seamed in "magnificent diction" (Leyda 1: 466–7).

Given Melville's ensuing fade from public view, the Customs Inspector years from 1866 to 1885, and his turn to poetry, the small circle of personal support he met with throughout the 1880s offered a degree of recompense. In the essayist and reviewer Richard Henry Stoddard, the poet-critic Edmund Stedman, and his son Arthur Stedman, he could look to a genuine vein of loyalty, even enthusiasm. The 1920s, famously, usher in the Melville revival, the rise toward canonical status. The touchstones are striking, whether Frank Jewett Mather's writing in the *Review* (1919), "most American writers look pale beside him" (Lee *Assessments* I: 512), Raymond Weaver's *Herman Melville: Mariner and Mystic* (1921), describing Melville as an "undoubted genius" and *Moby-Dick* as his "fabulous allegory" (Weaver 22), or Carl Van Doren in the New York *Bookman* for April 1924, "He writes with the energy of a man who is tirelessly alert" (Lee *Assessments* I: 550). Lewis Mumford in the 1920s, like Van Wyck Brooks in the 1940s, seeks to place Melville alongside Emerson, Hawthorne, Whitman, and Thoreau in a mid-nineteenth-century American literary efflorescence. The appearance in London of Constable's *The Works of Herman Melville* in 1922–4 added to the momentum, the look of *un oeuvre*, in the form of a sixteen-volume standard edition.

For the most part throughout this revival the focus centered on Melville's fiction, the novelist-romancer launched in *Typee*. With Willard Thorp's landmark *Herman Melville: Representative Selections* (1938), a more all-round Melville began to command attention, not only the fiction, but also the poetry, letters, logs, and reviews. In Thorp's wake arose, in F. O. Matthiessen's *American Renaissance* (1941) and Charles Olson's *Call Me Ishmael* (1947), "Shakespearean" Melville, the author who in *Moby-Dick* and "Hawthorne and His Mosses" strikingly refracts Shakespeare's plays into his own language of vision. Here was the Melville who apotheosizes a Shakespeare given to "short, quick probings at the very axis of reality," "flashings-forth of the intuitive Truth," in all "the profoundest of thinkers" (*PT* 244). To have located Melville himself within these terms marked a major ratchet forward in the enlarging of his reputation.

The busy decades of critique to follow have infinitely confirmed the regard for Melville's appetitive energy, the "keen perceptive power" and "animation" so winningly noted by Sophia Hawthorne. The span has been enormous. Folkloric Melville, the writer steeped in an America of vernacular local myth and word play, had its pioneer expression in Constance Rourke's *American Humor* (1931). Marxism can look to V. F. Calverton's Depression-era reading of *Moby-Dick* as an indictment of capitalist aggression and accumulation (1932) and, latterly, to Bruce Franklin's account of Melville as the prescient critic of America's military-industrial nuclear hegemony (1984) and a global imperialism from slavery to Vietnam (1997). For Richard Chase (1949) and Newton Arvin (1950), as for F. O. Matthiessen before them, Melville serves as the very incarnation of the liberal imagination, an exemplary figure of open ideology to be played against the time's Cold War ethos. With Leslie Fiedler in *Love and Death in the American Novel* (1966) the insistence becomes almost theatrically Freudian, Melville's fiction marked by its male bondings – Tommo–Toby, Redburn–Harry Bolton or Ishmael–Queequeg – in an intimate, adventuresome masculinity unfettered by the conventions of Victorian-American marriage or parlor domesticity.

Latterly, John Irwin (1980), operating under Derridean auspices, has opted for deconstruction of "hieroglyphic" Melville, *Moby-Dick* and the principal texts as given to hidden keys and conundrums. New Historicist thinking, amid the current Age of Theory, and notably from Jonathan Arac (1979), Wai-chee Dimock (1989) and

William V. Spanos (1995), explores Melville's emergence within a context of how canons are created and why "universal" texts find favor on the basis of a given time's cultural-political inclinations. A Melville of complex sexuality, dutiful husband-father but also overwhelmingly smitten by Hawthorne, androgynously drawn to the freed-up sailor worlds of ship and ocean, and given to portraiture of male beauty from Marnoo to Billy Budd, has had its outing, among others, in the work of Robert K. Martin (1986). Feminism finds a latest turn in Elizabeth Renker's work on text and misogyny (1996), Melville's blockages of penmanship as signs of his family outbursts and exploitation of wife and daughters. Recent African American interest has been greatly significant, whether in the novelist David Bradley writing on the in-crowd/out-crowd race implications of *Moby-Dick* (1997) or Sterling Stuckey on Melville's richly figurative uses of tambourine and ring-shout as ancestral black iconography (1998, 2002).

But if Melville is confirmed as a major American canonical voice, contrarily and at the same time he has often enough been a species of counter-voice. Few readers are not struck by his will, or, given the letters to Dana, Hawthorne, and Duyckinck, perhaps his compulsion, to challenge, against the grain, one or another orthodoxy or ruling illusion. Why otherwise have general readers, critics, and scholars been so taken up with the maverick qualities of Melville's mind and storytelling? However much they can seem standard adventure fare, dramas of first-person travel and encounter, do not works like *Mardi*, *Moby-Dick*, *Pierre*, "Benito Cereno" or, above all, *The Confidence-Man*, challenge, and even mock, these conventional storytelling genres?

Alongside the anti-conventional Melville, there has been American intertextual Melville. Time and again Melville gives rise to the residual allusion, the working echo. William Faulkner, writing in the *Books-Chicago Tribune* in 1927, alluded to *Moby-Dick*'s "Greek-like simplicity," together with its *symboliste* force of whiteness, as "a crash of massed trumpets" (Lee *Assessments* IV: 666). In novels like Paul Metcalf's *Genoa* (1965), hugely inventive in its use of family-biographical parallel, or Sena Jeter Naslund's *Ahab's Wife: Or, The Star-Gazer* (1999), with the fictive Una Spenser as the spouse of the *Pequod*'s captain, the Melville connection may be explicit but only as given new shapings of plot and viewpoint.

Melville exerts a more tacit, shadowy presence elsewhere, the connection one of metaphor or frame. In *The Naked and the Dead* (1948) Norman Mailer's scenario may be World War II Pacific combat rather than man against whale, but the will to power, to dominion, could not more suggest Ahabian hubris. Ralph Ellison's *Invisible Man* (1952), and posthumous *Juneteenth* (1999) feed a lifelong interest in Melville and his ambiguous figurations of black and white. *Invisible Man* actually opens with a key quotation from "Benito Cereno" ("what has cast such a shadow upon you?" (*PT* 116)). In Jack Kerouac's *On The Road* (1957) the Neal Cassady figure reincarnated as Dean Moriarty, the Denver-raised coast-to-coast highway speedster, is said to resemble "a mad Ahab at the wheel" (213). Thomas Pynchon several times has acknowledged a debt to Melville in *Gravity's Rainbow* (1973), be it in his scale or his encyclopedic impulse or his vision of a modern entropic universe. In the phenomenon of *Jaws*, whether the Peter

Benchley novel (1974) or Steven Spielberg film (1975), *Moby-Dick* becomes pop-cult New England ocean horror. Who could fail to be reminded of Melville's "The Encantadas" by Kurt Vonnegut's dark-humored *Galapagos* (1985) with its satiric reverse Darwinism? Thomas King's *Green Grass, Running Water* (1993) offers at once a Native American creation story envisioning benign "waters and floods" and an inspired trickster use of "Benito Cereno." Maxine Hong Kingston's *The Fifth Book of Peace* (2004), set at the time of the Oakland–Berkeley Hills Fire in 1991 and extending into the First Gulf War, weaves any number of war-and-peace Melville references into this most recent of her Chinese-American narratives.

Poetry affords few rarer, or richer, invocations of Melville than those to be found in Hart Crane's "At Melville's Tomb" (1926) with its symbolist allusions to "drowned men's bones" and "fabulous shadow," or Robert Lowell's "The Quaker Graveyard in Nantucket" (1946) with its memorable and haunting injunction "Sailor, can you hear / The Pequod's sea wings ...". John Updike, likewise, has given a working writer's tribute. In "Melville's Withdrawal" (1982), initially a *New Yorker* profile, and "The Appetite for Truth: On Melville's Shorter Fiction" (1997), a *Yale Review* contribution, he addresses the interplay of a unique sensibility with craft. This is the Melville who, even in the reduced scale of his *Piazza Tales* and story writing, "offers vast inklings and the resonance of cosmic concerns" (47). So multifarious a Melville also now has the benefit of the Northwestern–Newberry Edition (1968–), a benchmark in textual scholarship, though not without its critics.

If biography yields its own matching continuum, it has not led to some readily agreed single self. Raymond Weaver (1921) and John Freeman (1926) offer the early attempts at the Melville life-story, followed by Lewis Mumford (1929), William Gilman (1951), Leon Howard (1951), Jay Leyda (1951) and his cinema-influenced two-volume *Log*, Eleanor Melville Metcalf (1953), Edwin Haviland Miller (1975), Sheila Post-Lauria (1996), Laurie Robertson-Lorant (1996) and, most recently, Hershel Parker (1996, 2002). As the Melville archive has grown – letters, manuscripts, diaries, genealogies or hitherto unregarded notices and reviews – the picture has inevitably found fuller detail and texture. The cumulative effect of Melville biography, even so, points to a still elusive and not a little secretive figure, bachelor and paterfamilias, writer-debutant and writer-veteran. There will, and likely should, remain an unknown inner dynamic in Melville, his own always intractable version of the "Inmost Me" conjured up by Hawthorne in "The Custom House."

Visual Melville equally has played its part. Early cinema sought to transpose Melville "straight" to the screen, from John Barrymore's silent movie *The Sea Beast* (1926) and his Warner Brothers *Moby-Dick* (1930) through to John Houston's *Moby Dick* (1956) and, thereafter, the TV miniseries *Moby-Dick* (1978). But a counter Melville also appears in other popular culture representations, whether the art-work of Rockwell Kent, Frank Stella, Maurice Sendak, and Robert Del Tredici, or science fiction series like Ridley Scott's *Alien* (1979) and its successors – the initial interstellar vehicle named Starbuck, Star Trek's *The Wrath of Khan* (1982), George Lucas's *Star Wars* (1977), or the Australian-American *Farscape* (1999–2004) with its Galactic spacecraft called Moya.

To these can be added the Marvel and other comic-book strips, or all the multifarious bookstores, coffee houses, restaurants, and even pop groups, named for Melville references and ranging from Moby-Dick to Pequod to Bartleby.

British Melville

As a Britisher, and at that time a graduate student, I began my own first readings of Melville "abroad" in 1960s London, and have continued on the page and in university classrooms across the United Kingdom, Europe, America, and Japan. The notion of Melville as situated not on any single island but a global one, accordingly, could not hold a more personal appeal. To this end let me come at global Melville – a recent study by Edgar Dryden (2004) uses the term monumental – first as an Atlantic writer born of a literary heritage both American and British.

"British" Melville, on these shared grounds of history and language and early reception in London and elsewhere in the British Isles, plays a key contributing role in the rise of Melville's international reputation. There were, in the first instance, the reviews, a gallery of evolving critique in the *Spectator*, *The Times*, *John Bull*, the *Daily News*, the *Athenaeum*, *Blackwood's Edinburgh Magazine*, *Dublin University Magazine*, *Academy*, the *Scottish Art Review*, and the *Gentleman's Magazine*. He also won passing high regard from the poet James Thompson and the pre-Raphaelite circle of Dante Gabriel and William Michael Rossetti. Melville himself had his British correspondents, most notably James S. Billson, Leicester-born Oxford graduate who sent him books in the 1880s and spoke of the "rapidly increasing knot of 'Melville readers.' " Henry S. Salt, Eton schoolmaster and scholar of Thoreau, Shelley, and Tennyson, also corresponded with him, and in his essay "Herman Melville" for the *Scottish Art Review* of November, 1889 asserted the "epic grandeur and intensity" of *Moby-Dick* and, overall, Melville's "undoubted genius" (Lee *Assessments* I: 476).

A similar warmth of regard runs through "A Claim for American Literature" in the *North American Review* of February, 1892 by W. Clark Russell, prolific fellow sea-writer albeit of the British merchant fleet, who seizes upon Melville's "most startling and astonishing inventions" (Lee *Assessments* I: 478). In "The Best Sea Story Ever Told," in the *Queen's Quarterly* for October 1899, Archibald MacMechan, from British Canada, who also had exchanged letters with Melville, laments how *Moby-Dick*, as "at once the epic and the encyclopaedia of whaling," has become "a monument overgrown with the lichen of neglect" (Lee *Assessments* I: 489). Taken together, these accounts make for a slim but actually consequential body of appraisal, the transatlantic Melville of the coming revival.

But British views did not all go Melville's way. Joseph Conrad, Polish by birth and English by adoption, notoriously demurred. Asked by Humphrey Milford in 1907 to write the preface to an Oxford edition of *Moby-Dick*, he could hardly have sounded less enthusiastic: "It struck me as a rather strained rhapsody with whaling for a subject and not a single sincere line in the 3 vols of it" (Lee *Assessments* IV: 629). By contrast

D. H. Lawrence in *Studies in Classic American Literature* (1923), with his own visionary agenda of "blood consciousness," responded effusively, dramatically, whether seeing *Omoo* as "une bonne bouche" or *Moby-Dick* as a work which "commands a stillness in the soul, an awe" (Lee *Assessments* I: 538). E. M. Forster, whose *Aspects of The Novel* (1927) remains a benchmark, takes a yet different tack, alighting on *Moby-Dick* for its "prophetic song" and dialectical "contests" as modes of refracting the human condition (Lee *Assessments* V: 630).

Less consequential but important as a British "first" is John Freeman's *Herman Melville*, written by a minor Georgian versifier and belle-lettrist for the English Men of Letters series, synoptic, derivative of Raymond Weaver, and yet commendably early to address the poetry. Awareness of Melville, in fact, finds its way into any number of British authorial footfalls and eddies. Robert Louis Stevenson, in a letter of September 6, 1888 to his friend Charles Baxter, and having recently visited Nuku Hiva, recognizes him as a kindred Pacific spirit: "I shall have a fine book of travels, I feel sure; and will tell you more of the South Seas after very few months than any other writer has done – except Herman Melville, perhaps, who is a howling cheese." "Howling cheese," as memorable a bit of phrasing for Melville as exists, presumably is meant fondly yet wryly (Stevenson II, 136).

In an interview with John Cournos, John Masefield, Edwardian England's poet laureate yet in his youth another sailor runaway, speaks of Melville's "picturesqueness and directness" (New York *Independent*, 73 (September 5, 1912): 537). Bloomsbury, in turn, would have its say, whether through Alice Meynell, novelist, biographer, and editor of the influential World's Classics *Moby-Dick* (1921), who praised Melville's whaling saga as "a work of wonderful and wild imagination," or Leonard Woolf, who with a very British mix of censure and admiration denounced the "execrable prose" in *Moby-Dick* while emphasizing "Melville's immense fecundity of expression" (*The Nation and the Athenaeum*, 3, September, 1923). Frank Swinnerton, prolific novelist and author of studies of Gissing (1912) and Stevenson (1914), feared "the treasure of *Moby-Dick*," or at least its new lease on life, might be short-lived (*Bookman*, 53 (May 1921)), yet a year later T. E. Lawrence, writing to the editor Edward Garnet, saw its "sublimity" as inspiration for his *Seven Pillars of Wisdom* (1922).

Each, it has to be suspected, in some degree registers a response to Melville's expansive American openness to life as against the more circumscribed Britishness. Is there not, too, a hint of custodial anxiety, the sense of an end to Matthew Arnold's notion that all literature written in English was indeed "English literature"? Melville's name, moreover, recurs, and at times rather unexpectedly. In the title essay of George Orwell's *Inside The Whale* (1940), Melville supplies the source for the world-as-whale, a figuration of the broken nature of interwar European politics and culture, with Henry Miller, Paris expatriate, the expression of a historically uninhibited, open, and even daredevil American creative energy.

Other footfalls include: W. H. Auden's "Herman Melville" (1940), with its beguiling first line of "Towards the end he sailed into an extraordinary mildness" (*Collected Poetry*, 1940); Malcolm Lowry's *Under The Volcano* (1947), albeit about Lowry himself – "The identification, on my side ... was with Melville himself and his life" (*Selected Letters of Malcolm Lowry* [1965] 197) – more than Geoffrey Firmin as the despairing British consul in Mexico; Somerset Maugham's heady encomium to *Moby-Dick* published first in *Atlantic Monthly* as "Herman Melville and *Moby-Dick*" [1948, No.181] and then in his *Great Novelists and Their Novels* (1948) – "You must go to the Greek dramatists ... and to Shakespeare to find that terrible power" (Lee *Assessments* IV: 659); or "Moby Dick or the White Whale" by Brigid Brophy, Michael Levey and Charles Osborne, irreverent British whimsy with its talk of "Victorian-Gothic ... papier-mâché," "brutality to animals," and "the great white elephant" (*Fifty Works of English (and American) Literature We Could Do Without* [1967] 74).

In the Benjamin Britten opera (1951) of *Billy Budd*, with libretto by E. M. Forster and Eric Crozier, and the Peter Ustinov–Terence Stamp film (1962), two other kinds of "reading" give fresh nuance to the text, the former through its virtuoso score and the latter its scrupulous, if not brilliant, screen direction. Melville notably enters British postmodern literary ranks with the impact of *Pierre* upon John Fowles's *The French Lieutenant's Woman* (1969), two marital fictions with the one sited in the Manhattan of the nineteenth-century literary market-place and the other in the English southwest coastal town of Lyme Regis. Both overlap not only in their dramas of love and betrayal but as cannily self-mirroring fictions. Melville tells *Pierre* as the very story his title figure is trying to write. Fowles, for his part, writes a "double" novel at once modern and in the narrative guise of a Victorian melodrama. In "Imaginary Homeland" (1982), the seminal postcolonial title essay of his *Imaginary Homelands* (1991), Salman Rushdie gives a further witness to Melville's inspirational example as author-diver: "it is perhaps one of the more pleasant freedoms of the literary migrant to be able to choose his parents. My own – selected half consciously, half not – include Gogol, Cervantes, Kafka, Melville, Machado de Assis, a polyglot family tree, against which I measure myself, and to which I would be honoured to belong" (23).

British scholarly attention has likewise paid its dues, as notably as anywhere in Ronald Mason's attentive if unideological account in *The Spirit Above The Dust: A Study of Herman Melville* (1951). It may well be that a sense of meeting Melville from an ocean's distance, and of his own country's hesitation before a "global" Melville, lies within observations like "He arrived upon American literature at the moment of its most self-conscious expansion," and "He courted misunderstanding by his refusal, or even his inability, to limit his context" (19). Either way Mason, then a civil servant from outside academia, draws from a fund of sharp critical intelligence.

Times have moved on: the short but greatly alert studies of A. R. Humphreys (1962) and Brian Way (1978); Martin Green's would-be high judicious stance, with Melville held to disadvantage next to Dostoevski (1965); Q. D. Leavis's magisterial assessments of the stories (1978); Harold Beaver's Penguin editions of *Redburn* (1976), *Moby-Dick* (1987) and *Billy Budd* (1967) with their provocative commentaries and footnote suggestions of a pansexual Melville; and a line of UK-organized Everyman, Oxford, and like editions and scholarship of which the essay-collections by Faith

Pullin (1978) and A. Robert Lee (1984, 2001) can be thought representative. Melville, perhaps, still does not match Henry James in British eyes as transatlantic luminary, but he is wholly installed as a necessary figure, the presence so keenly anticipated by Billson, Salt, and Clark Russell and their early circle of readership.

Pacific and Caribbean Melville

The emphasis upon Anglo-American Melville, important as it is, in no way eclipses the yet wider anglophone response. Collections like those of Hershel Parker (1967) on Melville's recognition, and Watson Branch (1974) on the critical heritage, and the reception studies of Leland Phelps (1983) and Sanford Marovitz (1986), have done conscientious good service in issuing reminders of Melville's truly international reach. These collections helpfully underline, furthermore, not only Melville's impact upon the English-speaking world but also the interest Melville arouses when seen through the prisms of different languages and cultural assumptions. Melville under foreign purview has recurrently been celebrated as his own kind of nineteenth-century modern.

Anglophone allusion to Melville, assuredly, has found voice from Canada to India, or in the Pacific of Australia, as in the Chinese-heritaged Brian Castro's *Birds of Passage* (1982), a complex memory of settlement told through both nineteenth- and twentieth-century narrators, and *Drift* (1994), much of which is set upon an early whaling craft. One can look, too, to the related transnational authorship of Polynesia, not least in the Samoa–New Zealand writing of a major contemporary like Albert Wendt. In novels like *Leaves of The Banyan Tree* (1979), his epic of Western Samoan dynasty, and *Black Rainbow* (1992), an indictment of French nuclear testing in the Pacific, Melville clearly shares a shaping influence with Camus and Faulkner.

Rarely, however, has any anglophone writer interpreted Melville to more challenging effect than the Caribbean C. L. R. James in *Mariners, Renegades and Castaways: The Story of Herman Melville and the World We Live In* (1953). Written when the Trinidad-born James was detained on Ellis Island for an alleged passport violation, though more likely for his Marxist activism at a time of Cold War suspicion, it links *Moby-Dick* to the world-political situation as he sees it. Nazism and Soviet Communism he designates "totalitarian madness" (3) and, in the liberation of Africa and elsewhere, looks to the coming stir of "great mass labor movements and colonial revolts" (3). In this regard he invokes the intriguing interplay of two worlds, Ellis Island as a global island-in-small and the *Pequod* as global worker-factory.

James's reading of Melville will likely remain contentious, anchored as it is in the Trotskyist, pan-African, and Third World politics of its own time and place. He reads Melville as a voice of transnational fraternity, Ellis Island and the *Pequod* as sites of human solidarity in the face of nativist politics and industrial capitalism. But whether James can be said to have proved persuasive in all respects, his summary of Melville's vision in *Moby-Dick* is bracing, the call, nothing less, to a new human order:

In his great book the division and antagonisms of an outworn civilization are mercilessly dissected and cast aside. Nature, technology, the community of men, science and technology, literature and ideas are fused into a new humanism, opening a vast expansion of human capacity and human achievement. *Moby-Dick* will be universally burnt or be universally known in every language as the first comprehensive statement in the literature of the conditions and perspectives for the survival of Western Civilization. (89)

European Melville

"European" Melville has produced its own, and unslowing, stream of translations and editions. Who better, perhaps, to carry the banner than Cesare Pavese, poet, novelist, translator of *Moby-Dick* in 1932, with an accompanying string of essays on both Melville and other major American authorship? That Pavese took to Melville, even as he fought Mussolini's Fascism and served as a political prisoner as a consequence, adds a powerful historical resonance. Once again Melville's open modernism provides grounds for interest, Pavese's attention drawn to *Moby-Dick* and the best of his other texts for how they warn against unitary frames of authority, the one or another closed ideology. Pavese, moreover, heads a considerable body of Italian interest in Melville, including Gabriele Baldini's *Melville o le ambiguità* (1952) and Paolo Cabibbo's essay collection *Melvilliana* (1983), and which in university coursework and *studi americani* conference-gatherings have much drawn their inspiration from the homegrown semiotics and narratology of the theorist Umberto Eco.

Pavese's own preface to *Moby-Dick* is another call to arms: "To translate *Moby-Dick* is to put yourself in touch with the times." He applauds the resolve of American culture to find and secure its own terms, and gives Melville his due for an eclecticism which can draw both from bottom-of-the-rung forecastle life and from high literary authorship. He sees Melville, man and text, as embodying "investigations," a sense of renegotiation of the world across class or hierarchy or geography which, for Pavese, amounts to a wholly formidable achievement:

The fascinating list of references, fished for in 'the long Vaticans and street-stalls of the earth,' and the etymologies, from more than a dozen languages, which precede it, serve to bring the reader to that level of universality, to accustom him to that secularized atmosphere of learned discussion, which will be the structural basis, sometimes humorous and sometimes heroic, of all the future chapters. This is a curious thing in *Moby-Dick* and in Melville: although it is a work inspired by the experiences of a nearly barbarian life at the ends of the earth, Melville is never a clown who sets out to pretend that he too is a barbarian and a primitive, but dignified, courageous, he is not afraid to reelaborate that pristine life by means of all the knowledge of the world. (Lee *Assessments* II: 308)

All, however, is not paean. In Pavese's essay "Herman Melville" for *La Cultura* in 1932 he chastises "minor" Melville as he calls him. *Typee* and *Omoo*, much as they entertain as freewheeling picaresque, come under his hammer as "barbarian" adventure.

White-Jacket shows great documentary verve but suffers from the "deluge" of characters. *The Confidence-Man* fares yet worse, at once "wordy, obscure, and heavy-handed satire." But *Moby-Dick* holds redemptive pride of place, its "wealth of techniques and effects" put to the imaginative service of "life mysterious and swollen." (Lee *Assessments* IV: 635–44). For Pavese this assured combination of storytelling technique and the appetite for life in its every variety, signifies, quite precisely, a global Melville.

To turn from Italy to France is to encounter, amid another considerable body of interpretation, a matching prime name in Albert Camus. It is little surprise that so resolute an existentialist writer-philosopher, not least in *The Myth of Sisyphus* (1955), should have been drawn to Melville as a maker of world-myth. Writing in *Les Écrivains célèbres* (1952) he recognizes the author of *Moby-Dick* as a true fabulator and Ahab's gladiatorialism as among the most radical of all human metaphors:

> The story of captain Ahab ... can doubtless be read as the fatal passion of a character gone mad with grief and loneliness. But it can also be seen as one of the most overwhelming myths ever invented on the subject of man against evil, depicting the irresistible logic that finally leads the just man to take up arms against creation and creator, then against his fellows and against himself. Let us have no doubt about it: if it is true that talent recreates life, while genius has the additional gift of crowning it with myths, Melville is first and foremost a creator of myths. (Lee *Assessments* IV: 667–8)

Camus marks but one French voice. The range has been invitingly wide, from the exemplary pioneer reviews of Philarète Chasles in *Revue des deux mondes* (1849) – *Typee* and *Omoo* as "fictions adorned with all the details of verisimilitude" and *Mardi* as "symbolic Odyssey of the strangest nature" (Lee *Assessments* I: 256, 261) – through to Jean Simon's landmark *Herman Melville, marin, métaphysicien et poète* (1939), Jean Giono's speculative life, *Pour saluer Melville* (1941), and Jean-Jacques Mayoux's perceptively annotated text-and-image *Melville par lui-même* (1958).

The abundance to follow, whether journal special issues, conferences, or the Pléiade, Gallimard, and other editions, runs the interpretative gamut from Viola Sach's *Le Contre-Bible de Melville: Moby-Dick déchifré* (1975), with its putative numerological decodings, to Régis Durand's *Melville: Signes et métaphores* (1980), with its debts to Gilles Deleuze and Jacques Derrida on metaphoricity. In much French thinking Melville continues to occupy an almost apostate status as a canonical figure but also a cultural protestant. Seen from a Europe long institutionalized in its assumptions about history, belief, or art, Melville becomes all the more understandable as a maker of new signs, the literary sea-goer indeed *transatlantique* yet at the same time, and beckoningly, always *contre* the world's larger codes and schemes.

To emphasize this one selective roster of Western readerships is not to deny others their due. Melville is now to be found on bookshelves and in myriad translated versions across the European board. Germany's 1947 generation, seeking de-Nazification of their language and with the US as occupier, saw in Melville something of a beacon.

Gunther Grass's encyclopedic *The Flounder* (1987), a novel-as-anatomy in the mode of *Moby-Dick* or *The Confidence-Man*, offers one kind of subsequent trace. German and Austrian scholarship has exhibited its own range of interests, whether religio-philosophic and with an eye to Schopenhauer and Heidegger, or more literary with Kafka as a recurring point of comparison – typically "The Hunger Artist" with "Bartleby."

Critical interpretation from elsewhere in Europe includes Yuri Kovalev's Russian-written *Herman Melville and American Romanticism* (1972) and A. K. Christodoulou's dual-language Greek translation of *Moby-Dick* (1986) and his Melville art-work. To these should be added a Melville for whom the Middle East compelled his attention even as its cults and poverty alienated him. In *Melville, Twain and the Holy Land Mania* (1993) Hilton Obenzinger supplies focus and context, Melville as the American quester behind the posthumously published *Journal Up The Straits, October 11– May 6, 1857*, whose *Clarel: A Poem and a Pilgrimage to the Holy Land* ponders not only the broad general issues of belief and unbelief but the Holy Land itself as literal yet always emblematic landscape in the collective mind of the West.

South American Melville

Spanish-language Melville invokes the almost magical figure of Jorge Luis Borges. Spain's critics, understandably, have often compared Melville with the Cervantes of *Don Quixote*, just as Portuguese reaction has invoked Melville's own favorite, the Camões of *Os Lusíadas* (1512). A compendium like José de Onís's *Melville y el mundo hispánico (Nueve conferencias y un prólogo*, 1974), published in Puerto Rico, usefully spans Spain and the Americas. But the Argentinian Borges, the maker of fantastical, for many exquisite, adventure parables, or as he called them *ficciones,* and a Spanish-speaker with a bilingual grounding in anglophone literature, brings to bear other plies of interest. His account of Melville in *Introducción a la Literatura Norteamericana* (1967), summary as it may be, sets his writings within a context of greatly suggestive analogies:

> Melville's work consists of books about navigation and adventure, fantastic and satiric novels, poems, short stories, and the prodigious symbolic novel *Moby-Dick*. Among his stories we shall recall *Billy Budd*, whose essential theme is the conflict between justice and the law; "Benito Cereno," which in some ways foreshadows *The Nigger of the Narcissus* of Conrad, and "Bartleby, the Scrivener," the atmosphere of which is like the last books of Kafka. In the style of *Moby-Dick* there can be seen the influence of Carlyle and Shakespeare: there are chapters conceived like the scenes of a drama . . . . It is curious to note that the whale, as a symbol of the Demon, figures in an Anglo-Saxon bestiary of the ninth century and that the notion that white is horrible constitutes one of the themes of Poe's *Arthur Gordon Pym*. Melville, in the very text of the work, denies that it is an allegory; the truth is that we may read it on two planes: as the story of imaginary doings and as a symbolic tale. (29–30)

Asian Melville

"Asian" Melville has known no more avid a following than in Japan, a fact that to a degree, reflects US cultural influence dating as in Germany from World War II and occupation. But Melville's Japanese fortunes, in fact, began earlier. The contributing role played by the writer-critic Tomoji Abe cannot be overestimated, with initially his brief monograph *Herman Melville* (1934) and then his translation of *Moby-Dick* (1956), which remains, despite competition, the version most read. Abe early acknowledged that it was the English poet and critic Edmund Blunden who prompted his Melville interests, but he unquestionably made good on his own account. His was Melville the tragic outsider, one of America's Romantics.

This version has increasingly been challenged, notably by the Nobel novelist Kenzaburo Oe in his *The Day When the Whales Die Out* (1972). Melville, for him, serves as a figure of the world's necessary ambiguity, a condition he makes the heart of his *Japan, the Ambiguous, and Myself: The Nobel Prize Speech and Other Lectures* (1995) and which characterizes a Japan emerging from the Showa era's military but also literary-cultural nationalism. Interest in Melville's ambiguity, its semiotics and "translation," recurs in Japanese critical response, as reflected in many of the contributions to *Sky-Hawk*, the Meiji University house journal under the editorship of Arimichi Makino. Japan's own zen-conceived sense of time and space, its floating-world and color symbolism, lie within the now more than a dozen full-length studies of Melville: among them Hideyo Sengoku's deconstructive *Towards the Inside of The Whale – The World of Melville* (1990), Kenzaburo Ohashi's state-of-the-art essay compilation *Melville and Melville Studies in Japan* (1993), Kazuko Fukuoka's historicist *The Metamorphosis of the Text: The Novels of Herman Melville* (1995), and Arimichi Makino's *White Phantom Over The World – Melville and American Ideology* (1996), an examination of the coming of the "white" world to Japan with the landing of Commodore Perry in 1854 and the case for thinking it anticipated in Melville's white whale.

Global Melville

Melville has become as internationally read an American author as most, albeit, it has to be said, often on the basis of a select number of his works. Translation, notoriously, can go astray, most of all in *Moby-Dick*, given the density of its original English. How, furthermore, is the Chinese or Swahili, Korean or Arab reader, or one from Indo-Pakistan languages like Bengali, Hindi or Urdu, to tackle from a distance the American cultural specifics of "Bartleby" or *Israel Potter*? In other words, and as in the English-speaking world, "global" Melville needs a degree of qualification. That, even so, is not to deny Atlantic or Pacific Melville, postcolonial or multicultural Melville, the Melville of the city as of the sea, sexual Melville, self-referential Melville, or the war-poet Melville. But as important as these are, one other Melville especially applies for the global reader: the Melville who renews, even as he challenges, the assumptions not only of his own American culture but also, and quite as exhilaratingly, of the culture through which he is being read.

REFERENCES AND FURTHER READING

Abe, Tomoji. *Hakugei [Moby-Dick]*. Tokyo: Iwanami, 1956.

——— . *Herman Melville*. Tokyo: Kenkyusha, 1934.

Arac, Jonathan. *Commissioned Spirits: The Shaping of Social Motion in Dickens, Carlyle, Melville and Hawthorne*. New Brunswick, NJ: Rutgers University Press, 1979.

Arvin, Newton. *Herman Melville*. New York: Sloane Associates, 1950.

Benchley, Peter. *Jaws*. New York: Doubleday, 1974.

Borges, Jorge Luis. *Introducción a la Literatura Norteamericana/An Introduction to American Literature*. Buenos Aires: Editorial Columba, 1967.

Bradley, David. "Our Crowd, Their Crowd: Race, Reader, and *Moby-Dick*." *Melville's Evermoving Dawn: Centennial Essays*. Ed. John Bryant and Robert Milder. Kent, Ohio: Kent State University Press, 1997. 119–46.

Branch, Watson. *Melville: The Critical Heritage*. Boston: Routledge and Kegan Paul, 1974.

Brooks, Van Wyck. *The Times of Melville and Whitman*. New York: Dutton, 1947.

Calverton, V. F. *The Liberation of American Literature*. New York: Scribner's, 1932.

Camus, Albert. "Herman Melville." Trans. Ellen Conroy Kennedy. In *Lyrical and Critical Essays*. Ed. Philip Thody. New York: Alfred A. Knopf, 1968. 288–94.

Castro, Brian. *Birds of Passage*. North Sydney, NSW: Allen and Unwin, 1982.

——— . *Drift*. Port Melbourne, Victoria: Heinemann Australia, 1994.

Chase, Richard. *The American Novel and Its Tradition*. Garden City, NY: Doubleday, 1957.

——— . *Herman Melville: A Critical Study*. New York: Macmillan, 1949.

Dimock, Wai-chee. *Empire for Liberty: Melville and the Poetics of Individualism*. Princeton, NJ: Princeton University Press. 1989.

Dryden, Edgar. *Monumental Melville: The Formation of a Literary Career*. Stanford, CA: Stanford University Press, 2004.

Duran, Régis. *Melville: Signes et métaphores*. Lausanne: Éditions de l'Age de l'Homme, 1980.

Fiedler, Leslie. *Love and Death in the American Novel*. New York: Stein and Day, 1966.

Fowles, John. *The French Lieutenant's Woman*. London: Cape, 1969.

Franklin, H. Bruce. "From Empire to Empire: *Billy Budd, Sailor*." In *Herman Melville: Reassessments*. Ed. A. Robert Lee. London and Totowa, NJ: Vision Press, 1984. 199–216.

——— . "Slavery and Empire: Melville's 'Benito Cereno.' " In *Melville's Evermoving Dawn: Centennial Essays*. Ed. John Bryant and Robert Milder. Kent, Ohio: Kent State University Press, 1997. 147–61,

Freeman, John. *Herman Melville*. New York and London: Macmillan, 1926.

Fukuoko, Kazuko. *The Metamorphosis of the Text: The Novels of Herman Melville*. Tokyo: Eiha Sha, 1995.

Gilman, William H. *Melville's Early Life and* Redburn. New York: New York University Press, 1951.

Giono, Jean. *Pour saluer Melville*. Paris: Gallimard, 1941.

Green, Martin. *Re-Appraisals: Some Commonsense Readings in American Literature*. New York: W. W. Norton, 1965.

Howard, Leon. *Herman Melville: A Biography*. Berkeley, CA: University of California Press, 1951.

Humphreys, A. R. *Herman Melville*. Edinburgh: Oliver & Boyd, 1962.

Irwin, John. *American Hieroglyphics: The Symbol of Egyptian Hieroglyphics in the American Renaissance*. New Haven, CT: Yale University Press, 1980.

James, C. L. R. *Mariners, Renegades and Castaways: The Story of Herman Melville and the World We*

Live In. New York: C. L. R. James, 1953. Rpt. ed. Donald E. Pease. Hanover, NH, and London: University Press of New England, 2001.

Kerouac, Jack. *On The Road*. New York: Viking, 1957.

King, Thomas. *Green Grass, Running Water*. Boston: Houghton Mifflin, 1993.

Kingston, Maxine Hong. *The Fifth Book of Peace*. New York: Vintage, 2004.

Kovalev, Yuri. *Herman Melville and American Romanticism*. Leningrad: Xudozestvennaja Literatura, 1972.

Lawrence, D. H. *Studies in Classic American Literature*. New York: Doubleday, 1951.

Leavis, Q. D. "Melville: The 1853–6 Phase." In Faith Pullin (ed.). 197–228.

Lee, A. Robert (ed.). *Herman Melville: Critical Assessments*. 4 vols. Robertsbridge, Sussex: Helm Information Ltd., 2001.

—— (ed.) *Herman Melville: Re-Assessments*. London and Toyota, NJ: Vision Press, 1984.

Lowry, Malcolm. *Under The Volcano*. New York: Reynold & Hitchcock, and London: Jonathan Cape, 1947.

Mailer, Norman. *The Naked and the Dead*. New York: Rinehart, 1948.

Makino, Arimichi. *White Phantom Over the World – Melville and American Ideology*. Tokyo: Nanundo, 1996.

Marovitz, Sanford E. "Herman Melville: A Writer for the World." In *A Companion to Melville Studies*. Ed. John Bryant. New York: Greenwood Press, 1986. 741–80.

Martin, Robert K. *Hero, Captain, and Stranger: Male Friendships, Social Critique, and Literary Form in the Novels of Herman Melville*. Chapel Hill: University of North Carolina Press, 1986.

Mason, Ronald. *The Spirit above the Dust: A Study of Herman Melville*. London: John Lehmann, 1951.

Matthiessen, F. O. *American Renaissance: Art and Expression in the Age of Emerson and Whitman*. New York: Oxford University Press, 1941.

Metcalf, Eleanor Melville. *Herman Melville: Cycle and Epicycle*. Cambridge, MA: Harvard University Press, 1953.

Metcalf, Paul. *Genoa: A Telling of Wonders*. Millerton, NY: The Book Organization, 1965. Republished Albuquerque: University of New Mexico Press, 1991.

Miller, Edwin Haviland. *Herman Melville: A Biography*. New York: Braziller, 1975.

Mumford, Louis. *Herman Melville*. New York: Harcourt, Brace, 1929.

Obenzinger, Hilton. *American Palestine: Melville, Twain and the Holy Land Mania*. Princeton, NJ: Princeton University Press, 1999.

Naslund, Sena Jeter. *Ahab's Wife: Or, The Star-Gazer*. New York: William Morrow, 1999.

Oe, Kenzaburo. *The Day When the Whales Die Out*. Tokyo: Bungei Shunju, 1972.

——. *Japan, The Ambiguous, and Myself: The Nobel Prize Speech and Other Lectures*. Tokyo: Kodansha International, 1995.

Ohashi, Kenzaburo (ed.). *Whale and Text: Melville's World*. Tokyo: Kokusho-Kankokai. 1983.

Olson, Charles. *Call Me Ishmael*. New York: Reynal & Hitchcock, 1947.

Onís, José de. (ed.) *Melville y el mundo hispánico (Nueve conferencias y un prólogo)*. Editorial Universitaria: Universidad de Puerto Rico, 1974.

Orwell, George. *Inside The Whale, and Other Essays*. London: Gollancz, 1940.

Parker, Hershel (ed.). *The Recognition of Herman Melville*. Ann Arbor: University of Michigan Press, 1967.

Pavese, Cesare. *American Literature*. Trans. Edwin Fussell. Berkeley: University of California Press, 1970.

Phelps, Leland R. *Herman Melville's Foreign Reputation: A Research Guide*. Boston: G. K. Hall, 1983

Post-Lauria, Sheila. *Correspondent Colorings: Melville in the Marketplace*. Amherst: University of Massachusetts Press, 1996.

Pullin, Faith (ed.). *New Perspectives on Melville*. Edinburgh: Edinburgh University Press, 1978.

Pynchon, Thomas. *Gravity's Rainbow*. New York: Viking, 1973.

Renker, Elizabeth. *Strike Through the Mask: Herman Melville and the Scene of Writing*. Baltimore: Johns Hopkins University Press, 1996.

Rourke, Constance. *American Humor*. New York: Harcourt, Brace, 1931.

Rushdie, Salman. *Imaginary Homelands*. London: Grantham Books, 1991.

Sachs, Viola. *Le Contre-Bible de Melville: Moby-Dick déchifré*. Paris and The Hague: Mouton, 1975.

Sengoku, Hideyo. *Towards The Inside of The Whale – The World of Melville*. Tokyo: Nanundo, 1990.

Simon, Jean. *Herman Melville: marin, métaphysicien et poète*. Paris: Boivin, 1939.

Spanos, William V. *The Errant Art of Moby-Dick: The Canon, the Cold War, and the Struggle for American Studies*. Durham, NC: Duke University Press, 1995.

Stevenson, Robert Louis. *The Letters of Robert Louis Stevenson*. Ed. S. Colvin. 2 vols. New York: Charles Scribners, 1899.

Stuckey, Sterling. "Herman Melville, Paul Robeson, and Richard Wright on the Arts and African Culture." In *Literature on The Move: Comparing Diasporic Ethnicities in Europe and the Americas*. Ed. Dominique Marçais, Mark Niemeyer, Bernard Vincent, and Cathy Waegner. Heidelberg: C. Winter, 2002. 179–97.

——— . "The Tambourine in Glory: African Culture and Melville's Art." In *The Cambridge Companion to Herman Melville*. Ed. Robert S. Levine. New York: Cambridge University Press, 1998. 37–64.

Thorp, Willard (ed.) *Herman Melville: Representative Selections, with Introduction, Bibliography, and Notes*. New York: American Book Co., 1938.

Updike, John. "Melville's Withdrawal." In *Hugging The Shore*. New York: Alfred A. Knopf, 1983. 80–106.

——— . "The Appetite for Truth: On Melville's Shorter Fiction." *Yale Review* 4 (October 1997): 24–47.

Vonnegut, Kurt. *Galapagos*. New York: Delacorte Press/Seymour Lawrence, 1985.

Waldman, Anne. *Vow To Poetry: Essays, Interviews, and Manifestos*. Minneapolis: Coffee House Press, 2001.

Way, Brian. *Herman Melville: Moby-Dick*. London: Edward Arnold, 1978.

Weaver, Raymond. *Herman Melville: Mariner and Mystic*. New York: Doran, 1921.

Wendt, Albert. *Leaves of the Banyan Tree*. Auckland, New Zealand: Longman Paul, 1979.

——— . *Black Rainbow*. Auckland, New Zealand, and New York: Penguin Books, 1992.

Yeager, Henry. *La Fortune littéraire d'Herman Melville en France*. Liège: Presses Universitaires de Liège, 1970.

4

Global Melville

Paul Lyons

The distinct national colors of the imperialist map have merged and blended in the imperial global rainbow. (Hardt and Negri xiii)

Gone Global: Melville and the World "We" Live In

You sink your clan, down goes your nation; you speak a world's language, jovially jabbering in the Lingua-Franca of the forecastle. (*Mardi* 13)

Fifty years ago, C. L. R. James subtitled his *Mariners, Renegades, and Castaways* "Melville and the World We Live In." James recalls lecturing for several years on Melville and finding remarkable "the readiness of every type of audience to discuss him, and sometimes very heatedly, as if he were a contemporary writer." James's experiences on Ellis Island, which he saw as a *Pequod*-like "miniature of all the nations of the world and all sections of society," further convinced him that Melville had "painted a picture of the world in which we live, which is to this day unsurpassed" (Introduction). Melville's prescience lay in his precisely describing how the subjectivities produced by technological and economic development were incubated in a multicultural America. Because of conditions which massed laborers together from the ends of the earth, in America a looming crisis of modernity was registered "in every personality, in every social institution" (James 149, 194), from the captains of industry to the managerial classes to workers, whose forecastle Lingua Franca James "recoded into forms of emancipatory struggle" (Pease xiv). This sense of ruthless telos – with capitalism reinventing itself in dialectical relation to the "types" it produced, whose humanity, for different reasons, revolted – made the voyage of the *Pequod* into nothing less than "the voyage of modern civilization seeking its destiny" (James 18).

To consider the problem of theorizing a global Melville in the twenty-first century is to ask how Melville's texts can be recoded within an altered scene of reading to speak to the conditions we now live in. Whether considered as an extension of the voyage into modernity or of that into postmodernity, these conditions are what most would describe as *gone global*. In this state, goods, peoples, and information are irretrievably caught in a world-wide web of unruly flows that potentially erode the institutions that traditionally interpellated subjects. Consciousness at even the village level undergoes a transformation, experiences itself as linked up. The most "remote" or vernacular levels and strata of society register the threat or promise directed at them by technological advances and the transnationalization of capital. Within the body of "global theory" that attends to these uneven developments, the "local" generally figures as the site for negotiating globalism's impact, though "local" here might be considered less as small or inherently resistant than as that which responds to similar phenomena differently (Staheli 18) – not "anti"-globalization so much as "alter"-globalization. If today, to paraphrase Jacques Derrida, "Il n'est pas hors du mondialisation" (there is no outside globalization), such a truism provokes reflection on what globalism portends, or on how and on what terms "local" movements might counter globalism's destructive aspects.

What follows in this essay considers directions that theorizing a global Melville within scenes of reading that aspire to transnationalism might take. I attempt to read Melville reading globalization and to read global theory reading Melville, while positing coordinates within which Melville's theoretical usefulness in responding to globalism might be addressed. As one who approached human destiny as planetary and framed his questions accordingly, Melville, and his texts, have new resonances when read through the concerns of global theory. If he could not have imagined how advances in economic, communicative, and military technologies would reconfigure modern life – any more than he could have predicted the arms race, revolutionary movements, and gulags of James's day – he did anticipate that the processes by which peoples would spill over nation-state boundaries and commingle would be world-changing. The "Etymology" section that ushers in *Moby-Dick* suggests that the text aims to be global, to invoke all of the world's languages and traditions, to dust them with "a queer handkerchief, mockingly embellished with all the gay flags of the known nations of the world" (*MD* xv). The transnationalist James was visionary in recognizing this world-integrating emphasis in a Melville archive that Cold War Americanists insisted on reading through frames that validated their world-splitting national narrative.

The mode of close reading that foregrounded Melville's textual and philosophical ambiguities – and disregarded his socio-political approach to global issues – in this sense functioned as a cover story for the maintenance of a staunchly nationalist understanding of Melville. For powerful shapers of American Studies like F. O. Matthiessen and Richard Chase, Donald Pease argues, *Moby-Dick* was never "merely an object of analysis." Rather, "it provided the field itself with a frame narrative that included the norms and assumptions out of which the field was organized. The action that *Moby-Dick* narrated was made to predict the world-scale antagonism of the Cold War" (Pease xxiii). Given multivocal approaches to US literatures and the attention to contexts of production and consumption, no text of US literature can be read today as a self-contained narrative of national identity. Yet given Melville's iconic status – and a lingering sense that *Moby-Dick* is "the greatest and most eccentric work of literary art produced in the United States" (Said *Moby-Dick* 356) – the book and the Melville archive retain an indexical force. If *Moby-Dick* authorized the national self-understanding and reading practices of Cold War American Studies, in which a geopolitical area's boundaries were naturalized and policed by a cluster of disciplines (Pease xxix), what frames might it authorize for an American Studies Unbound, released from tightly nationalistic aims, gone global, that embodies at every junction the discourses that now deregulate its terms of circulation?

In the present moment, marked by shifts in the structure and cultural mission of the University, it seems that what provided coherence to Cold War and post-Civil Rights Americanist scholarship was a sense of the University as a means by which the nation discussed and reconstituted itself. However, in this age of accelerated globalization, as universities function more like transnational corporations, this sense of cultural mission has shifted from a promotion of "national culture" to the promotion of "excellence," quantitatively measured by its contributions to the market economy (Readings). Much as Michael Hardt and Antonio Negri see a supranational "Empire" as the possible frame for exploring contemporary subjectivities, Bill Readings considers the "ruins" of the national culture model as a promising place to reconceptualize intellectual work, to shift the period-style national framework of English Studies to globally articulated, interdisciplinary study. The challenge is to reconfigure disciplines in progressive ways that circumvent the economistic logic that drives and assesses them.

For many in English Studies, the shift away from national frames is not necessarily liberating. Masao Miyoshi argues that necessary processes of delinking literature from national narrative and the equally necessary move toward multiculturalism have been accompanied by the appropriation of difference by neoliberal transnationalists, diminishing the political touch and effectiveness of literature and criticism as instruments of progressive planetary change. Within an increasingly linked world, in which democracy is promoted as a "universal value" (Sen) which only the atavistic resist to their own detriment, Miyoshi decries the shift in focus from questions of economic oppression and political economy toward the socio-poetics of individual subjectivities. Like Miyoshi, those who object to global theory argue that it functions as an instrument of what it criticizes, while failing to articulate with insurgent social movements that effectively oppose inequality. On the other hand, for Readings and others, global consciousness has progressive political power, lines of flight and fight that might coalesce into a genuinely liberationist movement, or what Derrida describes as a "New International," linked in "affinity, suffering, and hope" (Derrida 85) and freed from the hegemonic narratives of nation-states. The fact that subjected peoples the world over continue to fight for nation-state status and cultural survival, and feel that, as Maori writer Linda Tuhiwai Smith puts it, "there can be no 'postmodernity' for us until we have settled some business of modernity" (Smith 34), is accommodated within such analyses into visions of coalition modeled on linkages among blocs with discrepant epistemologies and political agendas.

Within this reimagined scene of reading, radically thrown open for the global rearticulation of old texts along new lines of communication (technoscapes) and for new communities (ethnoscapes) and for new purposes (ideoscapes) – the terms are Arjun Appadurai's – aspects of Melville's boundary-breaking imagination appear as forms of sociocultural theorizing and practice. However, this simultaneous enunciation and demonstration of global theory is recodable in competing ways. On the one hand, Melville's deterritorializing, world-circling, mobile imagination, in which sailing is always a metaphor for a thinking that can "try all things" (*MD* 345), offers to the global imaginary reading models of liberatory freedom and fluid identitarian politics. Melville's works, Edward Said writes, "spill over national, aesthetic, and historical boundaries" (358). On the other hand, even as Melville engages globalization with philosophical restlessness and anarchic formal energy, his prose might be read as moving in alliance with aspects of globalization that dispense old human rights prescriptions in neoliberal bottles. While he promoted universalist principles that in theory protect deregulated flows from infringing on the rights of others, he recognized himself that in practice such processes were often destructive. And while he depicted an egalitarian multicultural mingling of the world's peoples, in which the citizen-sailor would sink the nation and speak a world's language, their common language was English.

In part because Melville's complex and often contradictory corpus will not yield fixed positions on the global processes that they describe and arguably reproduce, his texts are potentially productive sites for staging debates about concepts fundamental to globalism. In attempting to facilitate this discussion, I proceed in the second part of this essay by suggesting that Melville's ideas about globalism took shape within and against a nineteenth-century US discourse on globalism, concerned with the costs, benefits, and terms on which the world's peoples were to be linked; the section "Melville's 'Grand Principles' and America Among the Nations" below takes up the general problem of America among the nations, not simply as a problem to itself, but as the world's problem, and explores Melville's attempt within such considerations to delineate "grand principles" (*T* 201) on which human relations might be grounded; the final section elaborates on contemporary, transnationalist scenes of Americanist reading before returning to questions of what, within such altered frames, Melville's texts offer students of globalism.

"One Cosmopolitan and Confident Tide": Scenes of Globalization in Nineteenth-Century US Writing

Natives of all sorts, and foreigners . . . in short, a piebald parliament . . . of all kinds of that multiform pilgrim species, man. (*The Confidence-Man* 9)

However one chooses to historicize globalization – and one must believe that the telos of globalism is important if historical approaches are to deliver anything theoretically useful to the present – observations about globalization have a substantial history in American writing. Melville's views on globalism derive not only from his own experience in ports that were nodal points for the flow (import/export) of foreign goods, peoples, and ideas but from an emerging American discourse on globalism. The sense of the "blood" of the American as flowing from multiple sources to produce a new cosmopolitan pilgrim-refugee of European faction now rehabilitated by democratic conditions of production, so rapturously described by Crèvecoeur, is a constitutive feature of nineteenth-century US national narrative. This New Man finds expression in the encyclopedic catalogue rhetoric, which pulls the whole world into redemptive relation with America. It was in port cities, however, that catalogues of human diversity most strikingly included non-whites as peoples to whom Americans might be increasingly linked. What differentiates Melville from many contemporaries in describing these scenes is his attentiveness to race/class analysis, and a theoretical bent that diminishes the locational specificity of his analyses.

Most telling in nineteenth-century descriptions of multicultural scenes, generally presented with excitement and a sense of future shock, are the terms on which people meet. While there is something progressive in a scene like James Jarves's description of Honolulu streets in *Scenes and Scenery in the Sandwich Islands* (1844), it takes place in bigoted terms that the text naturalizes: "Frenchmen, Spaniards, Portuguese, Russians, in fact, representatives from almost every race under the sun, from the cannibal of New Zealand to his civilized prototype, the convict of New South Wales; – the dark Arab and ebony African. Amid such a medley every shade of civilization and barbarism, with their attendant virtues and vices, are to be seen. And this variety and novelty renders society here agreeable to the voyager, though not always so to the resident" (39). For Jarves, whom Hawaiians laughingly nicknamed *po kanaka*/skull man (literally "po'o"/head + "kanaka"/man) for having skulls exhumed to send to craniologists in Boston, that the putative "cannibal" shares social space with "civilized" Europeans suggests that the ends of the globe have been joined. If the resultant human medley presents itself as a touristic variety show, imagined as a nuisance for "the resident" (by which it is doubtful that Jarves means Hawaiians), it at least begins to imagine civil society as a social space shared by international citizens. However, that social-political space is "progressive" strictly in US proto-imperialist terms. It should be remembered that the refiguring of Jarves's Hawai'i by "residents" was part of a process that displaced Hawaiian values and rights and that cost Hawaiians their sovereignty. Whether this fact is a historical footnote or narratively central in the present, of course, depends upon where and how and for what one stands in relation to the global.

In contrast, in *Two Years Before the Mast* (1840), Richard Henry Dana presents an exhilarating scene of cultural interaction within a virtual free-zone, as perhaps possible only where no one is seen to be laying claim to the land:

We had now, out of forty or fifty, representatives from almost every nation under the sun: two Englishmen, three Yankees, two Scotchmen, two Welshmen, one Irishman, three Frenchmen (two of whom were Normans, and the third from Gascony,) one Dutchman, one Austrian, two or three Spaniards, (from old Spain,) half a dozen Spanish-Americans and half-breeds, two native Indians from Chili and the Island of Chiloe, one Negro, one Mulatto, about twenty Italians, from all parts of Italy, as many more Sandwich Islanders, one Otaheitan, and one Kanaka from the Marquesas Islands. (160)

In a scene set in the hide-tanning camps of California, which would not become a US state for another ten years, the "Digger" Indians seem simply part of the mix. Here languages circulate, with Spanish as the common ground, "for everyone knew more or less of that" (160). In the Hawaiian camp where he works, Dana describes Native Americans speaking Hawaiian, which he learns as well. The Marquesan kanaka was mingling European and non-European languages before Melville jumped ship in the Marquesas to experience what he later described, if polemically, as natives in a state of nature, or "wholly unchanged from their original primitive condition" (*T* 170).

Jarves, Dana, and Melville stressed scenes involving Pacific Islanders in part because the Islands allowed nineteenth-century US citizens to think about globalization without the anxieties and guilts of the black/white or Native-American/white paradigms: this time, "civilization" might get it more democratically right. That the remote islands – geographically and culturally as distant as possible from "civilized" Americans – were now sites of US commerce suggested that the globe was completely linked economically, and raised the question of how and on what terms it might be culturally integrated as well. Melville was struck by the notion, as so many theorists across the disciplines have been since, that "progress" in the islands indexed the nature of world-integration. His reports from the Pacific front lined up the Islands in terms of their degree of exposure to "civilization": Marquesas (state of nature), Tahiti (half-civilized), Hawai'i ("civilized into draught horses" [*T* 196]). He entreated home-audiences to audit the terms of cultural exchange: "Let the savages be civilized, but civilize them with benefits … let heathenism be destroyed, but not by destroying the heathen" (*T* 195), he wrote, without clarifying how it should be decided what aspects of "heathenism" should be destroyed, or evincing much faith in the "benefits" Islanders were receiving.

By *Moby-Dick*, however, Melville emphasized that one did not need to travel to the "South Seas" to see globalization at work. In New Bedford, where "actual cannibals stand chatting at street corners," the most comical sight is "green Vermonters and New Hampshire men." Such scenes are repeated in cities across the globe, where "live Yankees have often scared the natives" (31). Through such cosmopolitan streets, Queequeg and Ishmael walk arm in arm, the people more surprised at their intimacy than at the sight of Queequeg, "for they were used to seeing cannibals like him in the streets" (58). There were so many Islanders in New Bedford at this time that a section of town was known as New Guinea (Olson 22). At the same time, on board a ship the conditions of relation became manifest. Melville finds that, once quit of the land, whether on the *Pequod* or the *Fidèle*, representatives of all of the world's cultures are in the same boat, at times harmoniously, at times xenophobically, but always on structurally unequal terms.

While in *Two Years* Dana presented a pragmatic and localized scene in which learning about other cultures required him to move outside of his own languages, Melville never came to such a localized imagination. Melville supported the notion of "tribes" federated into a "mystic league" (*M* 536) that protected the rights of groups, but he did not seek the specificities of cultural locations so much as the principles of their organization. In *Typee*, he admits and performs his bafflement about Marquesan practices ("I saw everything, but could comprehend nothing" [177]). In *Omoo*, he presents Tahitian culture in the process of being debased (beginning to market itself). After these books, Melville tended to resolve the question of cultural difference by dissolving or insubstantializing it and by suggesting in a serio-comic Platonism that all knowledge that mattered was already "in our cores" (*M* 576). All cultures were to be absorbed into each other in ceaseless mixture, as the poetry of ideas ran together in the borderless world of the imagination. What Melville envisioned as a new cultural subject would face problems of modernity, brought into being by economic and technological forces that broke down the historic boundaries that previously separated peoples and "federated" them "along one keel" (*MD* 121).

In a series of "prophetic" passages that mock American political evangelism as they engage in it, Melville projects futures in which the new cultural subject will recognize the need to "take all Mardi for [their] home. Nations are but names; and continents but shifting sands" (*M* 638). Humanity will return to the period before continental drift as "a common continent of men" (*MD* 121); "the estranged children of Adam [shall be] restored" and "the curse of Babel [shall be] revoked" (*R* 169). If Melville's globalism is not ideologically that of the twenty-first century, in such passages it does and does not quite seem to be that of the nineteenth century either. This is to say that, unlike Jarves and Dana, Melville is more interested theoretically in intercultural relation and the implications of recombinations and circulation than in localized description. That the specificities of culture, history, and resistance of the catalogues of peoples invoked figure so little in Melville's euphoric scenes of globalism – and that Melville most frequently imagines postnationalism as the absorption of all nations into an American "ark of the liberties of the world" (*WJ* 151) – suggests the tendency of one Melville specter – cosmopolitanism – to collude with forces it criticizes.

There is no question, however, that Melville viewed globalization as an inevitable, world-transforming process. The exhilarated moment in his vision, if in hyperbolic, ironic, unsettling ways, *seems* to be summed up by the chapter "The Advocate" in *Moby-Dick*, in which Melville presents the whaler as a figure for the poetry of globalization. The whaler has links to the US state but is not identical with it: if the sea is the whaler's, "he owns it, as Emperors own empires" (*MD* 64). This "empire" is not land with boundaries but a mode of capitalism involving international labor and promoting free trade as world-integrating. "The cosmopolite philosopher," Melville writes, cannot point to any "peaceful influence" that has "operated more potentially upon the whole broad world" than "the business of whaling." Old World Empire, that of exploitative colonies, gives way to transnationally driven republicanism: "It was the whaleman who first broke through the jealous policy of the Spanish Crown, touching those colonies; and . . . it might be distinctly shown how from these whalemen at least eventuated the liberation of Peru, Chili, and Bolivia from the yoke of Old Spain, and the establishment of the eternal democracy in those parts" (109). Likewise, if "double-bolted Japan is ever to become hospitable it is the whale-ship alone to whom the credit will be due; for already she is on the threshold." It is whalers (globalizers), in other words, who create conditions, non-coercively and with mutual benefit, for the world's peoples to merge together, like "the streams of the most distant and opposite zones" merging in the Mississippi, into "one cosmopolitan and confident tide" (*CM* 9).

Of course, nothing could be more conventional than this seeming "advocacy" of whalers – whose "butcher sort of business" produces the world's oil (*MD* 108) – functioning as benevolent avatars of globalism. It is core American ideology of the Early Republic – in which the US sought partners and not colonial subjects abroad – that trade makes the world interdependent (thus more politically stable) and that it helps the world's peoples to feel their interests and cultures joined, while spreading values (industry, cultivation, cooperation) believed to be as salutary to nations as to individuals. Such a pollyanna vision could only be offered up by Melville serio-comically, in a moment of "advocacy" that appeals to landsmen to see the poetry of the seemingly grimy industrial enterprise Ishmael is engaged in. This is "The Pacific as sweatshop" (Olson 23) that lies behind the metafictional image of the Try-Works converting blubber into light. If the vision of "The Advocate" has the poetry of a particular historico-politico narrative behind it – based on the sublimation of the violence-to-others through which national narrative and later the notion of a global village emerge – for a writer concerned with the ethical "grand principles" undergirding global integration, the official vision raises questions more readily than it raises hopes.

Melville's "Grand Principles" and America Among the Nations

Settled by the people of all nations, all nations may claim her for their own. You can not spill a drop of American blood without spilling the blood of the whole world. . . . We are not a narrow tribe of men. . . . No: our blood is as the flood of the Amazon, made up of a thousand noble currents all pouring into one. We are not a nation, so much as a world. (*Redburn* 169)

In the face of institutional and intellectual calls to participate in "Globalizing Literary Studies," one measure of the perceived relevance of curricula, programs, or projects resides in their ability to redirect research toward the problems posed by globalism, including the problems of growing social inequalities, diaspora, and dislocation, the position of "America" within globalization, and the changing forms and responsibilities of global citizenship. To a large degree, as C. L. R. James suggests, Melville collapses these problems into each other through the vision of America as the first international nation-of-nations, the model for the globalized world-to-come, as well as the most aggressive agent within the world-linking process. That Melville presented the world of the *Pequod* as hierarchically arranged along racial lines, with the ironic image of white American officers "provid[ing] the brain, the rest of the world generously supplying the muscles" (*MD* 121), suggests a distinctly international understanding of the power imbalances among nations. (Were the spheres that Melville used for his demonstration more inclusive of women, as in "The Paradise of Bachelors and the Tartarus of Maids," perhaps this analysis would have extended more productively to the gendered distributions of labor, and would seem more contemporary.)

When in the course of Melville's work globalization and Americanization seem synonymous, the alignment often seems polemical, exhortatory, and directed at fellow Americans. As Rob Wilson describes it, Melville's "advocacy" of trade carries with it "a cautionary insight into national purpose and method, as economy precedes and installs the ideology of 'freedom' " – a freedom that in "interlocking disparate regions into a coherent space of American fantasy and design" (82–3) is fundamentally imperialistic. The most apparently jingoistic statements in Melville's work are destabilized by irony or explicitly undermined. In *White-Jacket*, for instance, Melville describes Americans as the "chosen people": "God has given to us, for a future inheritance, the broad domains of the political pagans, that shall come and lie down under the shade of our ark, without bloody hands being lifted" (151). Yet in relation to Native Americans he writes that an American frigate amounts to "blood red hands painted on [the] poor savage's blanket," and asks, "Are there no Moravians in the Moon, that not a missionary has yet visited this poor pagan planet of ours, to civilize civilization and christianize Christendom?" (267). The spirit of these contradictions, emphasizing (as Moravians did) the centrality of conduct, seems to be that of holding up an America-to-be, always in the dialectical process of creation and decreation, as a field of self-critique. This critique, as Derrida writes of a certain specter of Marx, "*wants itself* to be in principle and explicitly open to its own transformation, re-evaluation, self-reinterpretation" (88). As refugees flood into America seeking asylum, turning the nation outside-in, American institutions are, in theory, pressured to accommodate difference. That the aggression of the US and other imperial powers sets the process in motion and then claims that the movement of colonized people to the metropolis models a visionary pluralism is constitutive of the self-validating discourse. And yet from Melville to Hardt and Negri, the image of American democratic ideals, however rapaciously the US acts politically, is held up as the social model that the world must eventually adopt.

Melville approaches these issues, particularly that of an international democracy ushered in through trade, with a sense that their fraught contradictions are inherent to globalism. His critique of predatory American capitalism stems from a suspicion that trade corrupts higher ethics, whether among individuals or states. Trade assumes "trust" and depends on "confidence" about fairness among partners, while creating incentives for confidence to operate as a scam. Without genuine trust and regard for each other's wellbeing and commercial interest – which capitalism, in Melville's view, does not foster – only rigorously policed international law could stabilize exchange, and such international law itself requires "confidence," consensus, and intercultural understanding among participant nations. Furthermore, when a stronger nation can essentialize its own righteousness and mesmerize citizens to enact its will, nothing prevents it from ignoring or manipulating international law. For instance, according to the agreed-upon Western legal principles, in the nineteenth century land belonged to those who cultivated it; "developed" nations were those with assets cultivated and organized through infrastructure for trade. Less developed or "civilized" peoples, groups that followed alternative systems of governance, were by Western consensus "loose fish" or "fair game for anybody who can soonest catch" them, as Melville ironically put it (*MD* 396). In other words, if in theory spreading democratic capitalism to "savage" peoples and organizing them into "civilized" nations inter-linked through trade promises individual freedom to peoples subjected by commun-istic chiefs, in practice exporting civilization seems to Melville to be as exploitative abroad as American slavocracy or genocide against Native Americans is domestically. Capital-driven processes treat Native peoples and workers as instruments.

At the same time, as disgusted as Melville was at the sight of contaminated Islanders in *Typee* and *Omoo*, restoring Islanders to their "state of nature" seemed a denial of human relation and a philosophical cop-out. Historical questions of Islander agency in the matter – a genuine attention to the politics of the local – were to the side of this: Islander politicians only appear in Melville's texts as buffoonish mimics. The work of culture had to go forward, and Melville fundamentally accepts the West's developmental, temporal narrative, in which in Freudian/Marxist terms, peoples begin in a "state of nature" and gradually mature into increasingly repressed/alienated yet cultured states that prioritize individual rights. The crux of the problem of encounter between developed and undeveloped for Melville thus seems that of finding kinder, gentler means of bringing primitives into modernity than those by which civilization is imposed for profit motives (such as the US ventures to open routes through the Islands for the China trade). The terms of such an analysis, Melville's attribution of a developmental stage to Islanders, as opposed to recognizing alterna-tive cultural systems as viable, constitute an imperialistic stance. In the end, although he admires *Moby-Dick*, what Said says of Euroamerican universalizing discourses seems to apply to Melville: there is "incorporation" and "inclusion," but "there is only infrequently an acknowledgement that the colonized people should be heard from, their ideas known" (Said *Culture* 50).

Nonetheless, how to secure egalitarian relations, based on a securing of every human's individual rights, is a central theme of Melville's work. Whether he approaches it in terms of the engagement of imperial powers with "savages," or in terms of interpersonal topoi, a set of global questions underlines Melville's trajectory. It begins with the question of how non-coercively to bind the world's peoples while respecting different lifeways, continues with the critique of capitalism and centralized power formations as means of achieving this end, and concludes with the problem of establishing and protecting personal rights. Individual works engage related issues, such as the centrality of human dignity (*White-Jacket*) and the right to rebel against oppressive force, as well as the costs of doing so ("Benito Cereno"), the ethics of inaction and non-participation ("Bartleby"), the susceptibility of even just "law" to manipulation and abuse (*Billy Budd*), the division of domestic and public spheres before the law (*Pierre*), and the power of rhetoric (today advertising, media) to manufacture consent or manipulate reality (*Moby-Dick*, *The Confidence-Man*). What pins these together, from the assertion in *Typee* about a "universally diffused percep-tion of what is *just*" (201) to the conspicuously named ships in *Billy Budd* (*Rights of Man*, *Bellipotent*), is a sense that relations between individuals, grounded in "grand principles," provide the foundational model for undoing the surrounding regulatory forces that criss-cross and connect every life in "a Siamese connexion with a plurality of other mortals" (*MD* 320), many of whom are unaware of how their structural position subordinates others. Only laws premised on safeguarding the dignity of the foreigner irrespective of race and prior to knowledge could free humans from adjudi-cating for others through the language games of their own self-interest.

For this reason, the Queequeg/Ishmael marriage is at the heart of Melville's social vision, a compressed topos of worker relations under conditions of globalization based on non-materialistic ethics of fraternity. In Melville, from *Typee* on, the relation between two men, *pace* Greek philosophy, models a micropolitics. When Toby shakes hands with Tommo, for instance, it is a "ratification" that echoes the literal politics of Marquesan name-exchange, about which "ratify" is used as well (*T* 33, 72, 139). The Queequeg/Ishmael scene resolves in the sweetest terms the questions of hospitality and friendship that Derrida in a cluster of texts on friend-ship, hospitality, and cosmopolitanism brings to the study of contemporary prob-lems associated with globalization, such as the problem of how a "host" culture welcomes immigrants and refugees. This question of how to be hospitable to the new mobile citizen-worker is about how (on what or whose juridical principles) to open one's home (or institutions or nation) without oppressively legislating terms (forcing assimilation), while protecting one's institutions from the imposition of or corruption by a foreign system of values.

With Ishmael, the homeless outcast, and Queequeg-the-friendly-cannibal (who explores, with disappointment, the Christian world in search of knowledge "to make his people still ... better than they were" [*MD* 56]), no one is properly the host. This relationship seems the utopic key to Melville's dream of a non-materialistic "first congregation to which we all belong" (*MD* 83). As with Dana's topos of language circulation, egalitarian interculturalism is most imaginable among equally displaced persons, as if Crèvecoeur's American-as-"Western pilgrim"/refugee could only form against the "virgin land" imagined by Henry Nash Smith. In such

moments it is the planet that plays host. One is required only to be faithful to
principles of common humanity as one tries to be "on friendly terms with all the
inmates of the place one lodges in" (*MD* 7). Echoing the Pequot minister William
Apess, Ishmael assures readers that "a man can be honest in any sort of skin" (21), and
then recodes the Christian categorical imperative into a justification for worshipping
Queequeg's "Congo idol." Cultural specificity matters less in the image of this
composite Islander worshipping an African image and smoking a tomahawk than
the *idea* of embracing what is, from Ishmael's perspective, the humanity of someone
who is as culturally foreign to him as possible.

As the tone of the passages describing the formation of their friendship makes clear,
Ishmael's openness to Queequeg as "a human being just as I am" (24) is not exactly
cultural relativism and cosmopolitanism, though Melville does draw upon notions of
friendship derived from his admiration of Pacific Islander friendship ritual. What
matters most is Ishmael's willingness to *act* as if it is, Melville's insistence that
humanism is something practiced in the face of a materialistic, "wolfish world"
(51). Pivotal here is their recognition of each other as human beings, as embodied
confirmations of the belief, first formulated in *Typee*, that "The grand principles of
virtue and honor, however they may be distorted by arbitrary codes, are the same the
world over: and where these principles are concerned, the right or wrong of any action
appears the same to the uncultivated as to the enlightened mind" (201). By "arbitrary
codes" it seems that Melville means something like "culture," presented as a distort-
ing function, behind which there is, nonetheless, the inviolable "Republican Progressiveness" which he as an American author is bound "to carry into Literature, as well as
into life" (*PT* 245).

Melville and the Newest (Dis)Course of American Studies

Freedom is more social than political. And its real felicity is not to be shared. That is of
a man's own individual getting and holding. (*Mardi* 529)

As I have been suggesting, to theorize Melville as, like literary studies, gone global is
not so much to track Melville's "foreign" reception or the endless array of popular
cultural registers into which his works are *translated* internationally, so much as to
speculate about how within reconfigured scenes of reading Melville's textual spectres
might speak to the global present. The newly imagined, dispersed scenes of Americanist reading coincide with the "end" of decades of US decathection from the old
national cultural model. This involved what Robyn Weigman describes as a "struggle
to break apart the coherence of the field's object of study" (5) in the name of doing
justice to the plurality of America, along with a critique of American imperialism. As
American Studies shifted from unitary myth to competing rhetorics or regions,
the delinking of US identities from geography recovered roots/routes outside of the

borders of the US state, and in turn led to a recognition of the need for transnational, postnational, post-Americanist understandings of the fluidity of subjectivities within a world of disjunctive "scapes" and post/colonial borderlands. With the discursive borders open for free trade, critics like John Carlos Rowe call for a new internationalist comparativism, in which, say, the study of the Philippine–American or Vietnam Wars would require not simply Filipino/a and Vietnamese perspectives, but some sense of US culture as refigured by the encounter.

This new comparativism requires a recognition that American Studies is now, whether as the historic result of US imperialism or as an accelerating and uneven globalization, part of the cultural geography of many states and communities. What international Americanists and global theorists alike oppose, rhetorically at least, is the massive trade imbalance involved in this deregulation of borders, with a surplus of American culture being exported, while US institutions remain less hospitable (insufficiently infrastructured) to support forms of cultural exchange that would require US students to learn about or to be able to recognize "foreign" cultures in other than violent translation (Spivak 164). A scene of encounter imagined as the interface of the US with various local formations, in which every nation discerns its hyphenated-American reflection, and every nation reads through its political relation to the US, is less one of exchange than of dissemination. While the US is purportedly cleansed of exceptional status and turned inside out for critique, every junction where American Studies engages local formations becomes a further port of entry for the logic of a global theory that, like Melville's grand principles, follows a universalizing logic pursued in the name of a democracy-to-come and free markets, whether or not its flows exacerbate gaps between the "haves" and the "have-nots."

Within foreign American Studies institutions the institutional locus of interest gravitates toward transnational, cosmopolitan scholars and authors who can frame issues of globalization both for diasporic communities in the US and an international community, while suggesting that, as Homi Bhabha argues, the "truest eye may now belong to the migrant's double vision" (5). This development promises forms of analysis that cannot simply be reabsorbed into nationalist projects. Within this restructuring of Americanist scenes of reading, the study of US cultures seems to follow a dual line: on the one hand, there is a general resentment of US military and economic power and a concern with the effects of US-led policies. On the other hand, foreign Americanist institutions acknowledge compelling aspects of US culture – its pluralism and dynamism, its egalitarian ideals, and its pervasive popular cultural forms – while emphasizing the pragmatic value to their constituencies of learning English and understanding how US sociopolitics informs contemporary global practices.

Within these coordinates of international American Studies, Melville might well be given the appreciative reading that Edward Said gives *Moby-Dick*: "Melville's contribution is that he delivers the salutary effect as well as the destructiveness of the American world presence, and he also demonstrates its self-mesmerizing assumptions about its providential significance" (Said *Moby-Dick* 364). Melville's critique of racial hatred and exploitative capitalism, and his premonition that US failures were potentially cataclysmic, speak to that part of global theorizing that affirms the republican principles for defining human rights while lacking confidence in the integrity of the US to lead in achieving planetary egalitarianism. At the same time, Melville's works both critique and embody a central contradiction of globalism, its belief that trade will diminish the importance of nation-states, along with the suspicion that its driving agents, through imposing conditions on "less developed" nations, will appropriate their sovereignties into their own.

To the new mobile worker of Empire, however, Melville arguably speaks the language of accommodation to globalism. This is predicated on a separation of the emotive life and culture of the free mind from the realm of political economy and social community. That capitalism interferes with the free flow of human relations while trade drives people over borders in ways that wear away nation states is a conflict resolvable within global theory through the separation of interior life and material conditions. In the end, this separation rests on Melville's conviction that "freedom is more social than political," and ultimately that the culture that matters is "of a man's own individual getting and holding" (*M* 529). Internally, culture is polyphonic and metropolitan, a global village: "we are all fuller than a city" (*M* 594). As Slavoj Žižek serio-comically puts it about Western Buddhism as the fetish of late capitalism, this sense of the priority of internal culture "enables you to fully participate in the frantic pace of the capitalist game while sustaining the perception that you are not really in it .... that what really matters to you is the peace of the inner Self to which you know you can always withdraw" (15). It does not ultimately matter what job you have, Ishmael assures the reader: "Who ain't a slave?" Melville, that is, remains more committed to the dignity and mental culture of the worker than to questions of relieving structural inequality. He would never, James argues, endorse "any kind of a program" of concerted political action, least of all revolutionary socialism (James 20).

This apolitical political content finds expressive form in the wildness of Melville's swishing together of the styles and tropes of all traditions with utter disregard for the proprieties of those conventions, a style that pulls in the same direction as his dream of wearing away the alienating languages that make men "Isolatoes." For the imagination, no thing or place is inherently separate. Beyond the irony of the ways that Melville's relentless allusiveness and often convoluted sentences shut out and even anger readers (Melville wrote Hawthorne that, while a supporter of "ruthless democracy on all sides" [*L* 190] he believed in an aristocracy of the brain), antagonists of globalization or believers in traditional cultures – not as pure entities, but as the non-arbitrary ancestral knowledges that ground a people's collective subjectivity – would find Melville's dream of "sinking your own tribe and nation," or of being absorbed into one vast detribalized America-like pluralism, the height of neo-colonial arrogance. It is partly for this reason that, in Oceania, for instance, insofar as Melville is discussed at all, it is less as an anti-racist defender of human rights than as an author whose terms of critique of colonialism reinscribe its assumptions.

Along these lines, anti-colonial critics might hear global Melville as dismissive of traditional cultural values and priorities, despite his theoretical defense of every people's human right to traditional culture, or argue that, to the degree that Melville is concerned with culture as such, it is with the curious power of cultural scripts to delimit what the I/"eye" sees. Intellectually for Melville culture ultimately has no closeable borders, but ceaselessly absorbs and refigures what it comes into contact with. Thus rather than seeking interior knowledge of cultures, or feeling it important to represent them in some responsible anthropological sense, Melville emphasizes the viewer's response to difference, or parodies the prejudicial preconceptions of his readers, a device that arguably fails as pedagogy, since telling what something is not hardly explains what it is. This level of abstraction (exacerbated by his textual play and irony) in Melville's manner of posing questions of the global, especially in an age in which Melville texts and pop-Melvilleana circulate as made-in-the-USA commodities, consistently imbricates Melville in the world-integrating processes he critiques.

In other words, Global Melville circulates today not simply as a writer who critiqued the ontology of the American errand within processes recognized as globalization, and who deplored its costs to native peoples, its effects on the interior lives of workers, and the tendencies of globalism's imperial agents to warp weaker nations into ugly versions of themselves. Rather, Melville simultaneously circulates *as* a form of global theory and can be read as duplicating many of its assumptions. Tonally, his work offers a mix of cautionary rhetoric and wild excitement at the forms by which, in Homi Bhabha's terms, "newness enters the world." Sociopolitically, his text inclines toward the neoliberalism that neutralizes multiculturalism by assimilating difference, celebrating the endless play of differences in a mobile world in which subjects are unmoored from traditional or national cultures, and encouraged to rearticulate themselves as self-fashioning participants in a liberal-democratic world. This is a world, as Melville predicted, in which there is a surplus of possibility: "all that has been said but multiplies what remains to be said. It is not so much paucity as superabundance of material that seems to incapacitate modern authors" (*PT* 246).

It would be hard to place much revolutionary confidence in collective subjectivities formed within such flows, imagined as radically democratized and unregulated. The postmodernist poetry of transnational capitalism seems as self-mesmerizing as did the modernist poetry of transnational whaling. Rather, the new subjects of global culture seem to be joined primarily as fellow consumers, albeit with vastly different means at their disposal or degrees of access to technological participation. The aim, the promise of "Empire," Hardt and Negri argue, is precisely to incorporate everyone in ways blind to the old racist, chauvinist categories of difference (198). Difference in the new model, thoroughly amenable to global capital, is to be affirmed in order for it to be more effectively managed. This phenomenon raises the question of whether today one could make C. L. R. James's leap in imagining Melville's crew as redirected toward liberatory ends – engaged in pursuing cooperative alternatives to neoliberal capitalism – or whether one imagines the *Pequod*'s crew individually dreaming about where they would vacation if they raised the whale and cashed in proceeds from the Doubloon.

REFERENCES AND FURTHER READING

Appadurai, Arjun. *Modernity at Large: Cultural Dimensions of Globalization*. Minneapolis: University of Minnesota Press, 1997.

Bhabha, Homi. *The Location of Culture*. London: Routledge, 1994.

Dana, Richard Henry. *Two Years Before the Mast: A Personal Narrative of Life at Sea*. Ed. J. H. Kemble. Los Angeles: Ward Ritchie Press, 1964.

Derrida, Jacques. *Spectres of Marx: The State of the Debt, the Work of Mourning, and the New International*. Trans. Peggy Kamuf. London: Routledge, 1994.

Hardt, Michael and Antonio Negri. *Empire*. Cambridge, MA: Harvard University Press, 2000.

James, C. L. R. *Mariners, Renegades, and Castaways: The Story of Herman Melville and the World We Live In*. New York: C. L. R. James, 1953.

Jarves, James. *Scenes and Scenery in the Sandwich Islands*. London: Edward Moxon, 1844.

Miyoshi, Masao. "Turn to the Planet: Literature, Diversity, and Totality." *Comparative Literature* 53.4 (2001): 283–96.

Olson, Charles. *Call Me Ishmael*. New York: Reynal & Hitchcock, 1947.

Pease, Donald E. "C. L. R. James's *Mariners, Renegades, and Castaways* and the World We Live In." Introduction to *Mariners, Renegades and Castaways*. Ed. Donald E. Pease. Hanover, NH: University Press of New England, 2001.

Readings, Bill. *The University in Ruins*. Cambridge, MA: Harvard University Press, 1996.

Rowe, John Carlos. *The New American Studies*. Minneapolis: University of Minnesota Press, 2000.

Said, Edward. "Introduction to *Moby-Dick*." In *Reflections on Exile and Other Essays*. Cambridge, MA: Harvard University Press, 2000.

——— . *Culture and Imperialism*. New York: Knopf, 1993.

Sen, A. K. "Democracy as a Universal Value." *Journal of Democracy* 10.3 (1997): 3–17.

Smith, L. T. *Decolonizing Methodology: Research and Indigenous Peoples*. London: Zed Books, 1999.

Spivak, Gayatri C. *A Critique of Postcolonial Reason*. Cambridge, MA: Harvard University Press, 2001.

Staheli, U. "The Outside of the Global." *Centennial Review* 3.2 (2004): 1–22.

Sumida, Stephen H. "Where in the World is American Studies? Presidential Address to the American Studies Association, November 15, 2002." *American Quarterly* 55.3 (2003): 333–52.

Weigman, Robyn. "Introduction: The Futures of American Studies." *Cultural Critique* 40 (1998): 5–9.

Wilson, Rob. *Reimagining the American Pacific: From South Pacific to Bamboo Ridge and Beyond*, Durham, NC: Duke University Press, 2000.

Žižek, Slavoj. *On Belief*. London: Routledge, 2001.

Part II
Geographies

5

Science and the Earth

Bruce A. Harvey

That Melville's texts frequently allude to ocean phenomena, volcanic processes, fossilized organisms, lightning, astronomical data, and so forth tells us that he had a solid layman's acquaintance with what we today call the earth sciences (geology, geography, meteorology, zoology, and botany). Melville read widely in popular journals that reviewed major scientific treatises, and he learned much from narratives and official documents reporting on sea and land exploratory expeditions. His knowledge also came from his earlier sailor years, where he saw first hand exotic locales such as the Galapagos Islands or the Marquesas, whose difference naturalistically from the environs of New England led him to be acutely aware of how identity takes shape within and against a weighty, felt world. Of his literary contemporaries, perhaps only Henry David Thoreau responded with equal attentiveness to the raw immediacy of the physical-natural locale beyond the perceiving "I." Much more than Thoreau, however, Melville notes the tension between external concreteness and inward, probing perception. Melville's stories are always grounded in non-mental, palpable realms, and yet frequently his protagonists deny the separation of self from environment. In *Moby-Dick*, Ahab declares " 'O Nature, and O soul of man! How far beyond all utterance are your linked analogies! not the smallest atom stirs or lives on matter, but has its cunning duplicate in mind' " (312). Ahab, though, is not Melville, who as much as he longs to foist meaning on the world, also knew that the world in the end, both beautifully and horrifyingly, does not correspond to our soul.

Nature for Melville invites reflection because it both bedazzles and existentially alienates, as illustrated by a scene in *Moby-Dick* in which the African-American lad, Pip, is inadvertently abandoned in the swelling otherness of the Pacific:

Pip's ringed horizon began to expand around him miserably. By the merest chance the ship itself at last rescued him; but from that hour the little negro went about the deck an idiot; such, at least, they said he was. The sea had jeeringly kept his finite body up, but drowned the infinite of his soul. Not drowned entirely, though. Rather carried down alive to wondrous depths, where strange shapes of the unwarped primal world glided to and fro before his passive eyes; and the miser-merman, Wisdom, revealed his hoarded heaps; and among the joyous, heartless, ever-juvenile eternities, Pip saw the multitudinous, God-omnipresent, coral insects, that out of the firmament of waters heaved the colossal orbs. He saw God's foot upon the treadle of the loom. (414)

Melville here looks upon the sea's eerie subsurface realm as absolutely other and yet also as a metaphor for the soul turned toward its own fathomless depths. This subjectivism and drift from a natural landscape to a mental one is the hallmark of a Romantic sensibility, but the profusion of metaphor, analogy, and metaphysics derives as much from Melville's reading of British Renaissance authors – Shakespeare, Spenser, and Sir Thomas Browne – who saw the self and nature as being linked in microcosm/macrocosm patterns.

The interfusion of self and non-self, of metaphysics and earthly domains, resists eighteenth-century rationalism and positivism, which required that nature be objectified and placed at a distance so that it could be systematically studied. Michel Foucault, the renowned French intellectual historian, aptly comments on the shift of epistemological attitudes between the Renaissance and the nineteenth century: the "activity of the mind ... will therefore no longer consist in *drawing things together*, in setting out on a quest for everything that might reveal some sort of kinship, attraction, or secretly shared nature within them, but, on the contrary, in *discriminating*, that is, in establishing their identities ... [in comparative] successive degrees of a series" (55). Melville, heir both of Renaissance mysticism and Enlightenment rationalism, reads the world as simultaneously intimate to the mind and alien from it, and his personae, Ishmael especially, typically counterbalance a habit of cataloguing or indexing by "discriminating" at a distance (for example, the different species of whales in *Moby-Dick*) with more sensuously immediate contact.

The comprehension of nature as a mechanical system – although at first buttressing eighteenth-century deistic theology (the notion that nature's intricate designs required an originating, supernatural designer) – ultimately removed God from the world. The longstanding neo-Platonic medieval and Renaissance insistence on each life form's hierarchical aptness, its rightness of rank within a Great Chain of Being divinely authorized, lost its vertical rationale. Nature came to be perceived no longer as descending from God through humankind to noble creatures (lions, for instance) and then downward to more ignoble ones (turtles), to end with turnips, rocks, and finally – at the very nadir of being, infinitely removed from the Creator – to Satan and his realms of dark negation. Instead, comparative zoology and botany established a system of lateral gradations and affiliations based upon visual evidence rather than essentialist attributes, and in so doing desacralized the living world of species.

Nineteenth-century geological and astronomical theories in turn desacralized time, by opening up a temporal corridor into an indefinite past. Those who accepted the Bible literally would maintain that the Creation took place in approximately 4004 BC, the date earnestly calculated by Bishop Ussher (1581–1656) and thereafter taken as being definitive in nearly all schoolbook geographies and universal history textbooks as the beginning of time. But those who read the rocks, and saw, as did Melville, strata upon strata signifying incalculable past eons, had troubles discerning where in that now hugely extended timeline the story of Adam and Eve, as it were, might be pinpointed.

Geological-Cosmological Imaginings: or, Digging toward Eternity

Melville encountered geology at a moment when it was directly responsible for an intellectual-theological paradigm shift in the understanding of time and unrecorded history. Geological discoveries pushed the age of the earth backwards far before the traditional date of 4004 BC for the world's creation. The Scotsman James Hutton, in 1795, published *Theory of the Earth*, in which he proposed that land-mass change – from erosion, for example – took place uniformly throughout time. Unlike the more conventional "catastrophist" theory (that the earth took shape from a series of catastrophes, such as the biblical deluge), Hutton's presented a vista of slow geological effects that could accumulate only after many long epochs. Hutton's ideas were conveyed to the general public through such volumes as John Playfair's *Illustrations of the Huttonian Theory of Earth* (1802) and Charles Lyell's *The Principles of Geology* (1830–3). These works opened up the prospect of indefinitely remote pastness – what we now popularly name "deep time" – that could not be calibrated by traditional scales of, say, biblical genealogy and the recorded advancement of civilizations from pastoral tribes (as recounted in the Bible), to ancient Egypt, through antiquity, on through the Middle Ages to the nineteenth century, the age of progress. In the period of Melville's primary creativity, scientists and theologians valiantly joined hands to submerge qualms that the idea of unknown millennia of change through purely natural processes was discordant with the Biblical story of an intervening, designing deity. The US geologist-theologian Edward Hitchcock wrote in 1842, for example, that "geology proves Him to have been unchangeably the same, through the vast periods of past duration, which that science shows to have elapsed since the original formation of our earth.... Geology furnishes many peculiar proofs of the benevolence of the Deity" (quoted in Novak 56).

Melville responded to geological findings and speculation with both amused levity and somber reflection. In his early works of fiction, geology's processes and extended temporality are mostly viewed as items of curiosity. At one point, in *Typee*, Tommo the narrator pauses to explain the formation of coral reefs: "The origin of the island of Nukuheva cannot be imputed to the coral insect; for indefatigable as that wonderful creature is, it would be hardly muscular enough to pile rocks one upon the other more than three thousand feet above the level of the sea. That the land may have been thrown up by a submarine volcano is as possible as anything else" (155). Tommo's offhand comment refers to a variation of the uniformitarian/catastrophist debate: Neptunists argued that land forms emerged slowly from precipitated rock layers in the oceans, and Vulcanists (or Plutonists) maintained that the key molding process came from convulsive igneous flows, the volatility of the earth's crust, and slow erosion. Both theories pushed the age of the earth far back beyond known antiquity, and both had equal credibility; but here Melville implicitly mocks scientific bickering and is not seriously engaged with the philosophical or metaphysical implications of geological discovery.

The same may be said of *Mardi*, which even more explicitly mimics and satirizes geological theorizing. In the chapter "Babbalanja regales the Company with some Sandwiches," Babbalanja explains to a group of travelers on the "Isle of Fossils" that from the record of the rocks "we read how worlds are made; here [we] read the rise and fall of Nature's kingdoms . . . . These are the secret memoirs of times past" (415). The ensuing lecture seems intended to parody the squabble between the Neptunists and Vulcanists:

> "The coral wall which circumscribes the isles but continues upward the deep buried crater of the primal chaos. In the first times this crucible was charged with vapors nebulous, boiling over fires volcanic. Age by age, the fluid thickened; dropping, at long intervals, heavy sediment to the bottom; which layer on layer concreted, and at length, in crusts, rose toward the surface. Then, the vast volcano burst; rent the whole mass; upthrew the ancient rocks; which now in divers mountain tops tell tales of what existed ere [the realm of] Mardi was completely fashioned. Hence many fossils on the hills, whose kith and kin still lurk beneath the vales. Thus Nature works, at random warring, chaos a crater, and this world a shell." (417)

And then the alternative theory is given:

> "My lord, then take another theory – which you will – the celebrated sandwich System. Nature's first condition was a soup, wherein the agglomerating solids formed granitic dumplings, which, wearing down, deposited the primal stratum made up of series, sandwiching strange shapes of mollusks, and zoophytes; then snails, and periwinkles: – marmalade to sip, and nuts to crack, ere the substantials came." (417)

Babbalanja may be preposterous and clearly Melville intends comedy in the implausible metaphoric collisions ("granitic dumplings"), and yet the number of pages given to geological detail intimate that Melville was fascinated by it even as he poked fun. Even in these early works, earthly processes and odd creatures are a matter of delight or awe, the incipient prelude to the outsized wonders of the Whale and the sea in *Moby-Dick*.

In his mid-career fiction, geological processes are treated less satirically. Theories about the earth's age became part of Melville's imagistic vocabulary, and geological discovery provided him with naturalistic metaphors that deepened his sense of mystery. His interest, ultimately, was less in the Christian theological ramifications of deep time than in the rawer metaphysical proposition of unrecoverable primordialness. Thus, for instance, in the short story "I and My Chimney" the unnamed narrator fetishizes a massive chimney deeply rooted in his house's foundation in terms of a metaphoric geological dig into the antediluvian past:

Very often I go down into my cellar, and attentively survey that vast square of masonry. I stand long, and ponder over, and wonder at it. It has a druidical look, away down in the umbrageous cellar there whose numerous vaulted passages, and far glens of gloom, resemble the dark, damp depths of primeval woods . . . . I set to work, digging round the foundation, especially at the corners thereof, obscurely prompted by dreams of striking upon some old, earthen-worn memorial of that by-gone day, when, into all this gloom, the light of heaven entered . . . . (*PT* 357)

Another example of temporal deepening comes in Melville's most well-known short story, "Bartleby, the Scrivener," from the same creative period. Bartleby, impossibly intransigent, has been carted off to "The Tombs," the prison in New York City. Melville compares the massive blocks of concrete to Egyptian architecture, and the image of Bartleby incarcerated abruptly expands out into a vast temporality, at once dignifying us all in our existential nobility and yet also shaming us for our puniness: "The surrounding walls, of amazing thickness, kept off all sounds behind them. The Egyptian character of the masonry weighed upon me with its gloom. But a soft imprisoned turf grew under foot. The heart of the eternal pyramids, it seemed, wherein, by some strange magic, through the clefts, grass-seed, dropped by birds, had sprung" (*PT* 44). For Melville, Egyptian edifices – the "weigh[t]" of the past – and geology's unveiling of non-human-scaled time both conveyed a sense of sublimity beyond mundane comprehension. Similarly, but with antithetical emphasis, in *Pierre* the haunting notion of an abysm of geological stratification, of endless catastrophes receding in time, paradoxically leads Melville to see the earth's history as being "surface stratified on surface"; the geologist's art produces, Melville gloomily tells us, only "vacancy" and a world consisting of "nothing but superinduced superficies" (285).

The anxiety that long stretches of time diminished present meaning did not lead Melville to shirk the message of geology. Increasingly, he came to emphasize the existential resonance of geological findings. What he could not tolerate, early and late, was empirical reductionism. In his extended post-Civil War poem of spiritual longing and anomie, *Clarel*, a German geologist named Margoth strikes out with his pickaxe a cross marked on a stone by a pilgrim intending to signify the hope of Christ's redemptive powers even amidst the soulless vacancy of the Dead Sea. The "total tract" of "the plain" and "Lot's sea," he asserts, needs via "geological hammers" to be demythologized and put "on a par / With all things natural. . . . " (2:20, 46–57). The poem's satire of Margoth's tools and blasé positivism – which grant him knowledge of the scoriations of the earth but not of the psyche – reflects Melville's contempt for a smug empiricism blind to the depths of human grandeur and angst. Geological discoveries and debate made the comforting scale of traditional biblical time – the earth's creation, Adam and Eve's fall, Christ's redemptive martyrdom, an apocalyptic resurrection in a not-too-far-off future – untenable. But, simultaneously, Melville almost exulted in the grandeur of colossal spans of time not domesticated by biblical chronology. The problem with Margoth is not that he is a geologist, but that he is indifferent to what a truly aged earth means to human-oriented time scales.

Natural History and the Post-Biblical World of Ruins

In *Pierre*, the hero and narrator can find no solid ground or, put differently, all ground – interpreted geographically/geologically, psychologically, or metaphysically – becomes ruinous, the fragments that, chiaroscuro-fashion, hint at an unseen and unavailable numinosity. Initially, it was not so much the possibility that species mutated into novel forms, a theory which would invalidate the Mosaic account of singular original creation, that distressed Melville's contemporaries, at least not until the publication of Darwin's *On the Origin of Species* in 1859. Rather it was the incompatibility of a designing God with the evidence of prodigal wastefulness, and the eons of time filled with lifeforms living and dying that had absolutely nothing to do with human drama writ small (the individual life) or large (national destinies).

The evidence of nature's spendthrift ways emerged in the eighteenth century at the hands of European scientists. Yet it was precisely the systemizing of nature that, even as the notion of extinction became clearer, formed a psycho-cultural defense against unsettling thoughts. The comprehensive classification of plants and animals in such works as Carolus Linnaeus's *Systema Naturae* (1735) combined with theorizing from fossil evidence, especially in the work of Georges Cuvier, a French paleontologist and zoologist, to demonstrate that many lifeforms had become extinct. But these works – along with the effort of Count Buffon, another French scientist, to accumulate and categorize all naturalist knowledge in his massive 44-volume encyclopedia, *Histoire Naturelle* – gave the positivistic pleasure of control, as grids of textual knowledge radiated over the superabundance of the natural sphere.

Before Melville's vision substantially darkened, in his post-*Moby-Dick* works, he presents the positivistic obsession with classification in tongue-in-cheek form, most brilliantly in the elaborate parodies in the cetology chapters of *Moby-Dick*. Yet at the same time even these chapters less mock eighteenth- and nineteenth-century science than reflect a more archaic urge to gather together curiosities and odd natural specimens. Melville's catalogues and classifications are intended directly to satirize Cuvier and his lesser acolytes, but they also return us to the *Wunderkammern* or cabinets of curiosity of the sixteenth and seventeenth centuries, those quasi-museum collections that displayed the odd, curious, and aleatory. In his third novel, *Mardi*, the butt of Melville's humor is an all-too-enthusiastic antiquarian or curio-collector, scouring his domain for relics. Oh-Oh, as he is called, collects "precious antiques, and *curios*, and obsoletes," such as the "complete Skeleton of an immense Tiger-shark; the bones of a Pearl-shell-diver's leg inside. (Picked off the reef at low tide)" and "A curious Pouch, or Purse, formed from the skin of an Albatross' foot, and decorated with three sharp claws, naturally pertaining to it" (379–80). The satire, however, also is directed towards scientific peculiarity when it becomes too myopic:

> "By this instrument [his microscope], my masters," said he, "I have satisfied myself, that in the eye of a dragon-fly there are precisely twelve thousand five hundred and forty-one triangular lenses; and in the leg of a flea, scores on scores of distinct muscles.

Now, my masters, how far think you a flea may leap at one spring? Why, two hundred times its own length; I have often measured their leaps, with a small measure I use for scientific purposes." (381)

Those who see only empirically Melville deems lacking in a requisite angst or ambition. In the short story "The Lightning-Rod Man," published seven years after *Mardi*, a fear-mongering peddler of lightning rods fails to appeal to the unnamed householder, who taunts him: "you mere man who come here to put you and your pipestem between clay and sky, do you think that because you can strike a bit of green light from the Leyden jar, that you can thoroughly avert the supernal bolt?" (*PT* 124).

Melville routinely satirizes the naturalist who observes too closely, but when he considered humankind as subjected to the same passage of time that all other creatures suffer in mute silence his fiction takes on a darker perspective. *Typee*, for example, tells us much about the flora and fauna of Nukuheva Island, but what most strikes Melville, or his narrator, is how the natives, as they age, sink into animal-like stupor:

[On] four or five hideous old wretches ... time and tattooing seemed to have obliterated every trace of humanity.... [The] bodies of these men were of a uniform dull green color – the hue which the tattooing gradually assumes as the individual advances in age .... Their flesh, in parts, hung down upon them in huge folds, like the overlapping plaits on the flank of a rhinoceros .... These repulsive-looking creatures appeared to have lost the use of their lower limbs altogether; sitting upon the floor cross-legged in a state of torpor. (92–3)

More flesh than sentience, the tribal elders stagnate and slip into being, it would seem, part of a non-human animal realm, which as the earth itself knows no time, knows no sense of duration.

Melville's vision of the earth as antique and in ruin is conveyed perhaps most strongly in a series of sketches "The Encantadas or Enchanted Isles," published in *Putnam's Monthly Magazine* from March to May, 1854. The sketches were based on Melville's brief visit to the Galapagos Islands as a young man, and may usefully be compared to *The Voyage of the Beagle* (1845), Darwin's account of the voyage that was seminal for his development of the evolutionary theory which he unveiled in 1859 in *On the Origin of Species*. On the same islands Darwin took notes, with immense curiosity, about species differentiation from island to island; he marveled at nature's capacity to distribute varieties in what seemed an ordered sequence yet without evidence of a providential hand. Melville's text, however, sees environs of only decay and exhaustion: "Take five-and-twenty heaps of cinders dumped here and there in an outside city lot; imagine some of them magnified into mountains, and the vacant lot the sea; and you will have a fit idea of the general aspect of the Encantadas .... It is to be doubted whether any spot of earth can, in desolateness, furnish a parallel to this group" (*PT* 126). In the "Sketch Third" Melville morosely fixates on birds diving on baby turtles and insists upon a natural world of voracious appetite, cruelty, and predation, what in *Moby-Dick* he was to sum up as the "horrible vulturism of earth"

(308). William Howarth, from whom several of the previous points have been drawn, concludes that the two authors committed themselves to fathoming the natural environment, but whereas Darwin pursued the mystery of patterns of horizontal, non-metaphysical significance – the spread of variation from locale to locale – Melville could see nature's creatures only as contained within a "malevolent hierarchy" (Howarth 107) where the weak succumbed to the more powerful.

Aqueous Geographies: Fluidic Spaces and Ecofeminism

To view nature as negating human agendas is Manichean, and presupposes the material world as being a demonic antagonist; to view it as being cruel to its own is anthropomorphic. Both views are offered in *Moby-Dick*, but Melville's epic of men-at-sea also, at times, tries to describe the sea and its creatures in a non-philosophical fashion. The novel swamps us with naturalistic whale lore and fact, at once pointing to the incapacity of human science to reveal nature fully and to the sublimity of nature's realm as such. Eric Wilson argues that *Moby-Dick*, although published eight years before Darwin's *On the Origin of Species*, signals the "passing of pre-Darwinian, anthropocentric thought ... and the inauguration of a version of Darwin's more ecological evolution" ("Melville" 131); no longer would the earth and its creatures – to those who had eyes to see through the new geological/evolutionary time scale – be subordinated to biblical narrative or the traditional concept of a Great Chain of Being.

Technology and what we broadly call the scientific, rational attitude led in the eighteenth and nineteenth centuries to the external world being grasped in terms of instrumentality or the abstractions of categorization. The self seemed increasingly distant from the environment, and the capacity to make the world scientifically knowable conflicted with a spontaneous, sensuous appreciation of it. Hegel, the German philosopher writing a generation before Melville, nominated this analytical comprehension that categorizes the world but severs us from a lived entanglement with it *Verstand* (understanding).

Melville was highly sensitive to the trap of the narcissistic, solipsistic mentality, and that led him to want to bond with otherness as a way out of turmoiled selfhood or to chastise the egoistic vainglory that would refuse to see domains and beings beyond itself. It would be anachronistic to appraise Melville's fiction as manifesting ecological thinking – which entails not just an empathy for the otherness of nature, but a desire to preserve it and to agitate politically on nature's behalf. Yet the current blending of eco-political and literary-theoretical concerns into ecocriticism makes Melville's disenchantment with what Glen Love calls "Ahabian anthropocentricism" (562) of timely interest.

Melville's prose style – with its elliptical and metaphoric associations by which every natural artifact or phenomenon means more than itself – would seem to make a claim for his ecological or environmental awareness doubtful. The white whale, in

Moby-Dick, famously is never just a whale. Jamey Hecht argues that Ishmael's classificatory obsession serves to fend off the void beyond the self:

> All the detailed research of Ishmael-the-naturalist in chapters like "Cetology" and "Measurement of the Whale's Skeleton" serves him as insulation against the deadly knowledge which the whale bears within it, a knowledge that remains inherently beyond human space. Ishmael is willing to employ any strategy available to abbreviate the depth (but not the breadth) of his intellectual transaction with the whale. (123)

However, Melville was also struck by the sheer facticity of the given world, which is the point of the metaphysically dramatic scene in the novel in which Ishmael imagines the dreamy sailor, having succumbed to transcendental musings, plummeting into the very real swirls of the ocean.

The strongest evidence for Melville's environmental vision comes from such passages as when he, almost casually, considers the non-binocular, separate-visioned eyes of the sperm whale or, more intensely, the agony of a whale dying when harpooned. It is, though, the "Grand Armada" chapter that gets us most out of our species-specific skins by directing us to consider other modes of being and adopt what Lawrence Buell refers to as a "fellow-creaturely identification" (208).

> But far beneath this wondrous world upon the surface, another and still stranger world met our eyes as we gazed over the side. For, suspended in those watery vaults, floated the forms of the nursing mothers of the whales, and those that by their enormous girth seemed shortly to become mothers.... One of ... [the] little [whale] infants, that from certain queer tokens seemed hardly a day old, might have measured some fourteen feet in length, and some six feet in girth. He was a little frisky; though as yet his body seemed scarce yet recovered from that irksome position it had so lately occupied in the maternal reticule; where, tail to head, and all ready for the final spring, the unborn whale lies bent like a Tartar's bow. The delicate side-fins, and the palms of his flukes, still freshly retained the plaited crumpled appearance of a baby's ears newly arrived from foreign parts. (387–8)

Melville, through the persona of Ishmael, makes no explicit eco-political point here, and yet – even as all language must always fall short of capturing the otherness of non-human animals – he empathically attempts to realize a densely vital realm apart from the human. As Buell pointedly puts it, *Moby-Dick* may indeed at times be about "Whaleness as such" and not "whales as symbols" (207).

In the same year that *Moby-Dick* came out, 1851, Louis Agassiz, an immigrant Swiss who taught zoology at Harvard, published his *Principles of Zoology*, which promoted a sentimentally optimistic vision of humankind's destiny on the earth: "It is evident that there is a manifest progress in the succession of beings on the surface of the earth.... The Creator['s] ... aim, in forming the earth, in allowing it to undergo the successive changes which Geology has pointed out, and in creating successively all the different types of animals which have passed away, was to introduce Man upon the surface of the Globe" (quoted in Wilson "Melville" 134). Agassiz's sentiment characterizes what was known as natural theology, the effort to reconcile scripture and science that became normative at mid-century. Insofar as it casts "Man" as the supreme entity on the planet, it also enables Ahabian conceit. Ahab and Agassiz make an unlikely pairing, and yet both share a will-to-power in terms of epistemology that ecologically minded scientists and theorists currently largely resist. Ishmael makes a fetish of cataloguing whale lore in the hope of mastering the white whale's gargantuan profundity, but it is Ahab in his reckless disregard for anything beyond himself as "Man" through whom Melville presciently envisions what today we critique as ecological disaster, as Ahab and his crew with a factory-like mechanics and zeal labor to depopulate the oceans of sperm whales.

The Ahab/Ishmael dichotomy in the novel also points to Melville's intuition of the fluidic identities that contemporary, postmodernist feminists such as Donna Haraway have embraced as an antidote to rationalistic, ecologically disastrous politics and policies. Ahab's traumatic wound puts him in opposition to the material world, and he sees all other bodies and physical geographies as merely instrumental, as tools implementing his will against the white whale; for Ishmael, though (or Melville writing behind Ishmael), solace comes through empathic linking of the body's vulnerability to the vagaries, both bloody and exultant, of the corporeal world itself. In opposition to Ahab, whose aggressiveness represents the transcendental or rationalist habit of putting mind into what-is-not-mind, Ishmael would let nature be and, although recognizing physical jeopardy, would also make his peace with the necessity of being-in-the-world. Ishmael, unlike his captain, willingly would allow himself to be subsumed within a fluid, organic and interconnected mode of being that extends beyond himself. The famous episode in which he, squeezing globules of sperm with his whaler comrades, sinks into a reverie of nurturing, liquid association represents a maternal/feminine – or at least non-aggressive, non-phallic – form of knowing.

Conclusion: The Science of Charts and the Hubris of Representation

The nineteenth century was, of course, an age of exploration; another way of labeling it, though, would be to say it was the age of systematic charting and mapping. In Melville's young adulthood, between 1830 and the outbreak of the Civil War, surveying and mapping became a patriotic enterprise, and there was a rush to translate into print form – based on systematic, reliable geographic grids – observations about the newly acquired western territories as well as the coastlines and navigational routes of wherever US interests, or anticipated interests, might be held to lie. The federal government sponsored projects and funded institutes – such as the United States

Naval Observatory, founded in 1842 – to coordinate oceanic, meteorological, and geological data. The most renowned instance of cartographic and taxonomic zeal was the US Navy's Polar and Pacific Expedition, commanded by Lieutenant Charles Wilkes, which from 1832 to 1836 meticulously tracked sea lanes and coastlines, recorded nautical findings, and collected naturalist specimens throughout the South Pacific. Matthew Fontaine Maury, a decade and two later, achieved fame by producing a series of spectacularly learned and useful oceanographic and navigational volumes crucial to the rise of maritime trade: *A Wind and Current Chart of the North Atlantic* (1847), *Lanes for Steamers Crossing the Atlantic* (1853), and his classic *Physical Geography of the Sea* (1855).

These volumes and expeditions all advanced scientific knowledge and were pragmatic in intent, but they also manifest what Mary Louise Pratt characterizes as an imperial drive to master the world by representing it. The bestselling author of juvenile antebellum geography volumes, Samuel Goodrich (writing under the pseudonym Peter Parley) commented in 1845, not tongue-in-cheek, in his *The World and Its Inhabitants* (a volume from *Parley's Cabinet Library*) that "Whatever is known is recorded in so many forms, that no event, unless it be one which is coextensive with the surface of the world, and which blots out mankind from existence, can quench its light" (323). It is a running subject of critique in Melville's fiction that to reproduce the world – whether in curiosity-cabinet-styled museums (Oh-Oh's antiquities in *Mardi*) or in the fashion of a scientific or quasi-scientific index (the geological strata in *Mardi*) or in catalogues or digests (the Sub-Sub Librarian's "Extracts" that preface *Moby-Dick*) – is to lose touch with the world and hazard either insanity or irrelevance.

The lofty urge to scientifically understand and the less lofty urge to control often merge in Melville's stories and novels, a prime example being in the chapter "The Chart" in *Moby-Dick* in which we see Ahab – "who knew the sets of all tides and currents" – arrogantly believing that he could calculate "the driftings of the sperm whale's food" and thereby "arrive at reasonable surmises" (199) as to his nemesis's location. Ahab's pursuit of the whale and the disastrous sinking of the *Pequod* is also an elaborate trope for the fate of a country too assured of its peculiar manifest destiny, too exultant in its own national narrative in disregard of more planetary/ global contexts and stories. As Wai Chee Dimock excellently suggests, in the antebellum era national US time and world history/time had incommensurate trajectories: "Deep time is denationalized space" (760). Melville's sensibility expanded beyond the local or parochial – beyond smug, nationalistic New England conservative values – not only because he saw more of the world's cultures in his travels or encountered more diversity of peoples aboard ships he sailed upon, but also because he saw a vertical, planetary dimension, an immensity of scale, both figurative and geologically literal, that amplified even as it diminished the mystery of humanity itself.

REFERENCES AND FURTHER READING

Allen, Thomas M. "A Republic in Time: Temporality and Social Imagination in Nineteenth-Century America." Book manuscript.

Bohrer, Randall. "The Living Mirror: Melville's Vision of Universal Process." *Research Studies* 50.1 (1982): 46–61.

Buell, Lawrence. *Writing for an Endangered World: Literature, Culture, and Environment in the U.S. and Beyond.* Cambridge, MA: Harvard University Press, 2001.

Connery, Christopher L. "The Oceanic Feeling and the Regional Imaginary." In *Global/Local: Cultural Production and the Transnational Imaginary.* Ed. Rob Wilson and Wimal Dissanayake. Durham, NC: Duke University Press, 1996. 284–311.

Crawford, T. Hugh. "Networking the (Non) Human: *Moby-Dick*, Matthew Fontaine Maury, and Bruno Latour." *Configurations* 5.1 (1997): 1–21.

Dimock, Wai Chee. "Deep Time: American Literature and World History." *American Literary History* 13.4 (Winter 2001): 755–75.

Foster, Elizabeth S. "Melville and Geology." *American Literature* 17.1 (1945): 50–65.

Foucault, Michel. *The Order of Things: An Archaeology of the Human Sciences.* New York: Random House, 1970.

Franklin, H. Bruce. "The Island Worlds of Darwin and Melville." *The Centennial Review* 11 (1967): 353–70.

Haraway, Donna J. *Simians, Cyborgs, and Women: The Reinvention of Nature.* New York: Routledge, 1991.

Harvey, Bruce. *American Geographics: U.S. National Narratives and the Representation of the Non-European World, 1830–1865.* Palo Alto, CA: Stanford University Press, 2001.

Hecht, Jamey. "Scarcity and Compensation in *Moby-Dick*." *Massachusetts Review* 40.1 (Spring 1999): 111–30.

Howarth, William. "Earth Islands: Darwin and Melville in the Galapagos." *Iowa Review* 30.3 (2000): 95–113.

Love, Glen A. "Ecocriticism and Science: Toward Consilience?" *New Literary History* 30.3 (1999): 561–76.

Novak, Barbara. *Nature and Culture: American Landscape and Painting, 1825–1875.* New York: Oxford University Press, 1980.

Nye, Russel Blaine. *Society and Culture in America, 1830–1860.* New York: Harper and Row, 1974.

Pratt, Mary Louise. *Imperial Eyes: Travel Writing and Transculturation.* New York: Routledge, 1992.

Rossi, Paolo. *The Dark Abyss of Time: The History of the Earth and the History of Nations from Hooke to Vico.* Trans. Lydia G. Cochrane. Chicago: University of Chicago Press, 1984.

Schultz, Elizabeth. "Melville's Environmental Vision in *Moby-Dick*." *ISLE: Interdisciplinary Studies in Literature and Environment* 7.1 (2000 Winter): 97–113.

Smith, Richard Dean. *Melville's Science: "Devilish Tantalization of the Gods!"* New York: Garland Publishing, 1993.

Wilson, Eric. "Melville, Darwin, and the Great Chain of Being." *Studies in American Fiction* 28.2 (2000): 131–50.

——— . *Romantic Turbulence: Chaos, Ecology, and American Space.* New York: St. Martin's Press, 2000.

6
Ships, Whaling, and the Sea

Mary K. Bercaw Edwards

Authors make literary use of the sea for different reasons. William Shakespeare's *The Tempest* (1611), the most maritime of his plays, begins with a storm that precipitates a crisis of leadership. The boatswain, a petty officer, tells the nobles, his social superiors, "I pray now, keep below." Antonio, acting Duke of Milan, asks, "Where is the master [captain], boatswain?," and the Boatswain replies, "Do you not hear him? You mar our labour: keep your cabins: you do assist the storm." Gonzalo, a counselor, remonstrates, "Nay, good, be patient," to which the Boatswain irritably responds, "When the sea is. Hence! What care these roarers for the name of king? To cabin: silence! trouble us not" (I.i). Shakespeare replaces the raging tempest of the first scene with a world of tranquility and quiet in the second, in which Miranda falls asleep after hearing the story of her life from her father Prospero (I.ii). Unlike the insubordinate "roarers," Miranda submits willingly to her father's, and king's, command.

Shakespeare uses the sea to dramatize a political point. Herman Melville, too, uses the sea metaphorically, but unlike Shakespeare, Melville actually served at sea aboard ship. His experience, then, made it impossible to view the gales of nautical life with a literary sensibility alone. The physical and metaphysical storms and calms in Melville's writing draw on his actual experiences as well as on his imagination. Even more strikingly, though, they allow him to return to and resolve the tensions he experienced as a sailor laboring within shipboard hierarchies, for unlike leaders on land, ship captains enjoy a "dictatorship beyond which, while at sea, there was no earthly appeal" ("Benito Cereno" *PT* 53). In four years at sea, Herman Melville served under masters of varying levels of competence. Different captains led him to consider the qualities needed to command and direct with skill, fairness, and justice. He employs storms and more often calms to explore how a good leader rules and controls those under him.

When many readers think of Melville's seafaring years, those voyages may seem the most joyous, liberating, and adventurous times of his life. Only when he came to convert his actual experience of hard labor and servitude into fiction, however, did

Melville truly break free. To understand this process, we need first to know more about Melville's life in ships and at sea, then to understand how he incorporated his experiences as well as written sources in his writing, and finally to probe the larger questions posed in his works by the spectacle of absolute power holding sway over the confined space of a ship and its men set in the vastness of the sea. In his own fictional versions of *The Tempest*, Melville, more than any other nautical author of his time, exposed the unsuspected latitudes of human abuses of power.

Melville's Voyages

Melville's popular success began with his first book, *Typee* (1846), and continued with *Omoo* (1847). While financial rewards eluded him after these first two books, their reception by readers was a major influence on his continuing to write on maritime subjects. His time at sea inspired his next four books: *Mardi* (1849), *Redburn* (1849), *White-Jacket* (1850), and *Moby-Dick* (1851). Only *Pierre* (1852) is a complete departure from the sea: he returns to maritime subjects with "The Encantadas" (1854), the John Paul Jones section of *Israel Potter* (1854–5), and "Benito Cereno" (1855). *The Confidence-Man* (1857) is set on a steamboat, and many of Melville's United States Civil War poems in *Battle-Pieces* (1866) concern naval warfare. Late in his life, he published the poetry collection *John Marr and Other Sailors* (1888). *Billy Budd, Sailor* (1924), the short novel he was working on at the time of his death, again takes place entirely at sea.

Melville's maritime fiction draws from an unusually wide and varied experience of different kinds of seafaring. At age nineteen, Melville signed on to the merchant vessel *St. Lawrence* (1833), Oliver P. Brown, master. His first voyage took Melville from New York to Liverpool and back to New York. Melville's fourth book, *Redburn: His First Voyage*, subtitled *Being the Sailor-boy Confessions and Reminiscences of the Son-of-a-Gentleman, in the Merchant Service*, describes in a fictional manner what Melville encountered as he learned the skills of a sailor. As the son of a gentleman, Melville was unusual among the common sailors. Like Richard Henry Dana, Jr. (as recorded in his *Two Years Before the Mast* [1840]), Melville berthed with other common seamen "before the mast," in the forecastle (or fo'c's'le) at the vessel's forward end; the officers lived separate from the crew in the relative comfort of the officers' quarters aft, in the stern of the ship.

Melville's next major water passage came in 1840, when he traveled to Illinois by vessel with a friend, Eli James Murdock Fly. Their three-day journey by canal boat from Albany to Buffalo may have provided the description of the Erie Canal found in "The Town-Ho's Story," Chapter 54 of *Moby-Dick*. Melville and Fly crossed Lake Erie by steamboat. From Detroit, the pair booked passage on a Lake Huron and Lake Michigan steamboat to Chicago. From Chicago, Melville and Fly crossed the prairie to Galena, Illinois, where an uncle, Thomas Melvill, Jr., had a farm. It is unknown whether Melville actually went up the Mississippi River, since the source for his description of "The River" (meant to be a part of *The Confidence-Man*) is actually Timothy Flint's *A Condensed Geography and History of the Western States; or, The Mississippi Valley* (1828). However, Melville's time on inland waterways decidedly influenced his tenth book, *The Confidence-Man*, a bleak work of despair set on board the *Fidèle*, a Mississippi River steamboat.

With his family still in financial trouble, Melville embarked from New Bedford, Massachusetts, on January 3, 1841, for the most influential voyage of his life. He joined the crew of the whaleship *Acushnet* (1840), Valentine Pease, Jr., master, on its maiden voyage, sailing from Fairhaven, across the river from New Bedford. His time on the *Acushnet* is the basis for the whaling voyage in his classic and sixth book, *Moby-Dick*. But the vessel Melville creates in *Moby-Dick*, the *Pequod*, is a fantastical Nantucket ship, with belaying pins of sperm-whale teeth and a tiller made from the lower jaw of a sperm whale. Melville, at age twenty-one, shipped as a greenhand on the *Acushnet* – the same rank he had held on the *St. Lawrence*. However, before his whaling years were finished, Melville had worked his way up to bow oarsman, the position held by Ishmael in *Moby-Dick*, and then possibly to boatsteerer (harpooneer).

The *Acushnet* sailed around Cape Horn into the Pacific and spent months slowly cruising for whales. In November 1841 the vessel spent six days at anchor off Chatham Island in the Galápagos Islands. The Galápagos, the location of Melville's ten sketches entitled "The Encantadas, "were called enchanted because the baffling currents in nearby waters were," Melville writes, "so strong and irregular as to change a vessel's course against the helm, though sailing at the rate of four or five miles the hour" (*PT* 128). The *Acushnet* was to return to the waters of the Galápagos for the month of January the following year, but his initial encounter of six days at Chatham Island was the longest continuous period during which Melville may have had the possibility of going ashore. Surprisingly, Chatham Island is referred to only twice – and then in passing – in "The Encantadas."

When the *Acushnet* reached Nuku Hiva in the Marquesas Islands in July 1842, Melville and his shipmate Richard Tobias Greene, whom he called "Toby," deserted. The events of their desertion served as the factual basis for his first book, *Typee*. Melville hurt his leg and was forced to remain behind when Toby set out in search of medicine. Toby never returned, and Melville learned only years later that his co-deserter had left the island on another Fairhaven whaleship, the *London Packet*.

Melville left Nuku Hiva on the Australian whaleship *Lucy Ann* (1819), Henry Ventom, master. Although he had joined the *Acushnet* as a greenhand and had never served as an ordinary seamen, Melville signed on the *Lucy Ann* as an able seaman, the third and highest rank of seaman. The *Lucy Ann* was quite small, only 87 feet long. Aboard the *Lucy Ann*, Melville encountered a crew in severe crisis. He had joined a ship's company torn by dissent, with a sickly captain and a first mate, James German, who was prone to drink. Additionally, the vessel lacked officers. It carried four whaleboats, but had only one mate rather than the four needed to command the boats. Instead of the four boatsteerers needed to throw the harpoons, it had only three: two who were illiterate and one newly shipped, who soon turned against the captain. Captain Ventom became very ill, and Mate German headed for Tahiti, where the captain was put ashore. In an effort to prevent desertion while yet staying close to the captain, the *Lucy Ann* left port and sailed back and forth off the harbor of Papeete, Tahiti. Then, ten men refused duty. These men were held on the French frigate *La Reine Blanche*; later, they were taken to a Tahitian "calaboose" (jail). Although uncomfortable with the way the *Lucy Ann* was commanded, Melville at first had not been willing to commit himself to mutiny; however, when the mutineers were confined ashore, Melville stepped forward and joined them. During his time as a prisoner, Melville was under a doctor's care, and his injured leg, still ailing, was treated. Some three weeks later, in October 1842, Melville escaped to the neighboring island of Eimeo (now Moorea), in the Society Island group. Melville's passage on the *Lucy Ann*, the mutiny, and his imprisonment are treated in his second book, *Omoo*.

Melville wandered the island of Eimeo until November 1842, when he joined the Nantucket whaleship *Charles and Henry* (1832), John B. Coleman, Jr., master. Aboard this vessel Melville finally experienced a well-run ship. Melville respected Coleman for his just, kind treatment of his men. Apparently signed on as boatsteerer, Melville spent five months aboard the *Charles and Henry*, much less than the claim of "the author's own personal experience, of two years & more, as a harpooneer" which he made to his English publisher, Richard Bentley (letter of June 27, 1850; *L* 163). From his time on the *Charles and Henry*, Melville drew the beginning of his third book, *Mardi*.

Discharged at Lahaina, Maui, Hawaii, Melville traveled to Honolulu, Oahu, aboard the *Star*, Captain Burroughs, master. During Melville's stay in Honolulu, the *Acushnet* came into port, and on June 2, 1843, Valentine Pease, Jr. filed an affidavit taking notice of Melville's desertion, a federal offense, eleven months earlier. Six weeks later, Melville enlisted on the American naval frigate *United States* (1797), James Armstrong, master. The frigate sailed under the pennant of Commodore Thomas ap Catesby Jones. Melville was one of approximately 480 officers and men on board, and although he had served on the *Lucy Ann* as able seaman and on the *Charles and Henry* as boatsteerer, a petty officer, his rank on the *United States* was reduced to ordinary seaman. The respect he had for the master of the *Charles and Henry* did not hold for the officers of the naval frigate. Melville spent fourteen months on the *United States*, and in that time he witnessed 163 floggings. His absolute hatred of this form of corporal punishment resounds throughout his fifth book, *White-Jacket*, and in his final work, *Billy Budd, Sailor*.

Melville's longest period at sea ended on October 3, 1844, when the *United States* arrived at Boston. He sailed several more times, but never again as a seaman. In 1860, he rounded Cape Horn aboard the clipper ship *Meteor* (1852), on which his younger brother Thomas served as captain. Homesick and depressed, however, Melville took a steamer from San Francisco to Panama, crossed the isthmus, and then returned to New York on the steamer *North Star*.

Whaling

Many readers turn to Melville to understand the hunting and processing of whales. In writing *Moby-Dick*, however, Melville did not rely only on his first-hand knowledge of whaling. Like all his writings, *Moby-Dick* draws heavily from his reading. "I have swam through libraries," he tells us in "Cetology" (136). Melville consumed books and was consumed by them. As he read, he argued with them, laughed and cried over them, and became fiercely angry. His books are filled with notes and jottings done with slashing pen marks and furious periods. An alchemist of words, Melville transformed his often mundane sources. For example, although the information in "Cetology," Chapter 32 of *Moby-Dick*, is borrowed nearly verbatim from the "Whales" entry in Volume 27 of *The Penny Cyclopaedia of the Society for the Diffusion of Useful Knowledge* (1843), Melville infused the dry information with his own humor and philosophical ponderings, transforming it into literature of the highest order.

The major whaling sources for *Moby-Dick* – Thomas Beale, *The Natural History of the Sperm Whale* (second edition, 1839), J. Ross Browne, *Etchings of a Whaling Cruise* (1846), William Scoresby, *An Account of the Arctic Regions* (1820), and Owen Chase, *Narrative of the Most Extraordinary and Distressing Shipwreck of the Whale-Ship Essex* (1821)[1] – lack this literary alchemy. In a review of Browne's book in the *Literary World* (March 6, 1847), Melville notes sadly, "the poetry of salt water is very much on the wane" and finds Browne's work "a book of unvarnished facts" (*PT* 205). He acknowledges that Browne "presents a faithful picture of the life led by the 20 thousand seamen employed in the 700 whaling vessels … under the American flag" (205), but takes him to task for writing of the whale's roaring: "We can imagine the veteran Coffins and Colemans and Maceys of old Nantucket elevating their brows at the bare announcement of such a thing. Now the creature in question is as dumb as a shad, or any other of the finny tribes" (*NN* 206). William Scoresby and his *Account of the Arctic Regions* received still rougher treatment from Melville's pen. Even as Melville borrowed from Scoresby in *Moby-Dick*, he poked fun at him, calling him one of the "most famous" of the Esquimaux doctors, Zogranda (298), an expert on smells named Fogo Von Slack (409), and Dr. Snodhead, a "professor of Low Dutch and High German in the college of Santa Claus and St. Pott's" (405).

But Melville was a whaleman as well as a close reader during America's whaling boom. He departed from Fairhaven, across the river from New Bedford, in 1841; by 1846, the peak year of American whaling, ships sailing under the flag of the United States accounted for over 90 percent of the international whaling fleet. Of the more than 700 American whaleships, over 400 sailed from greater New Bedford. As Charles Roberts Anderson notes, the *Acushnet*'s crew was "normal in all respects save that in addition to mortal harpoons it carried an immortal pen" (*South Seas* 35).

By the time Melville sailed, New Bedford had superseded Nantucket as the major whaling port. Nantucket had fallen behind because the sand bar across the entrance to the harbor allowed only smaller-draft vessels to enter, because men and supplies for the ships had to be transported to the island and whale oil transported back to the mainland, and, finally, because the great fire of 1846 destroyed much of the water-front, including the oil warehouses. Melville looks backward in time when he has Ishmael sail from Nantucket. Ishmael admits as much: "[T]hough New Bedford has of late been gradually monopolizing the business of whaling, and though in this matter poor old Nantucket is now much behind her, yet Nantucket was her great original – the Tyre of this Carthage" (8). Intriguingly, Melville did not visit Nantucket until July 1852, *after* the publication of *Moby-Dick*. His information about the island is based on his reading of Obed Macy, *The History of Nantucket* (1835).

Both Melville's reading and his experience made one thing forcefully clear: whaling was a brutal, nasty business. The average whaling voyage lasted two to five years. Vessels increasingly had to make their way down around Cape Horn and up into the Pacific, drawn by the number of sperm whales to be found there. Oil from sperm whales generally brought twice as much per gallon as oil from right and other whales. Sperm whales are found in all oceans of the world, but they are most plentiful in the Pacific. A vessel could go months without even sighting a whale. Even then, the chances of catching the whale were small.

In order to sight the whales, men stood on planks of wood called spreaders near the top of the masts. Later, masthoops that encircled the men's waists were added, but in Melville's day, the men had only the mast to hold on to. Once whales were sighted, the officer on deck would determine how many and which whaleboats to lower. The boats were steered from the back by an officer while five men rowed. When the boat approached the whale, the officer would call to the boatsteerer (harpooneer), who would plunge a harpoon into the whale. In Melville's day, the head of the harpoon was generally double-edged, in the shape of an arrowhead, and it pulled out quite easily. More whales were lost than were caught with this "double-flued iron." Not until 1848 was the more effective toggle iron perfected in New Bedford by African-American shipsmith Lewis Temple.

After the whale was harpooned, it would react in one of three ways. It might turn around and smash the boat: whales have powerful tails and jaws and could easily snap the boat in two. However, such events rarely occurred. The whale could also sound or dive straight down, a problem since each whaleboat usually carried only 2,000 feet of line. Most often, the whale swam quickly across the surface of the water, towing the whaleboat behind, in what whalemen called a "Nantucket sleigh ride," lasting anywhere from twenty minutes to over twenty-four hours. During the sleigh ride, the officer at the back of the boat, who initially manned the steering oar, exchanged positions with the boatsteerer, who planted the harpoon. As the whale tired, the boat would draw alongside and the officer thrust the lance, generally into the lungs. When the whale began to spout blood instead of the normal white mist out of its blowhole, the fight was nearly over. At death, the whale would lose its equilibrium and roll on its side with its pectoral fin in the air in a position called "fin out" by whalemen.

Then began the arduous work of towing the whale back to the ship. Whalemen averaged only one mile per hour towing a whale, in contrast to the six miles per hour they rowed while in pursuit. Whales weighed an average of 40–60 tons and produced 40–60 barrels of oil (a barrel of whale oil is a unit of measurement containing $31\frac{1}{2}$ gallons; the amount could vary depending on the substance carried). Once the sailors reached the ship, the bloody, exhausting, and dangerous work of stripping the blubber began. The blubber was cut into portions and rendered into oil in the try-works on the deck of the ship. The blubber had to be stripped quickly in order to prevent it from going rancid and in order to keep the sharks from tearing it to pieces. Melville tells us that the smoke from the burning blubber "has an unspeakable, wild, Hindoo odor about it . . . . It smells like the left wing of the day of judgment; it is an argument for the pit" (*MD* 422).

This, then, was whaling: hours or days of perilous and backbreaking work set off against perhaps months of boredom, during which the whaleship slowly sailed back and forth over vast stretches of water looking for whales. During the year in which *Moby-Dick* takes place, eleven whales are killed: ten sperm whales and one right whale. It took an average whaleship, one the size of the *Acushnet*, two to five years to catch an average of sixty whales.

Adding to the rigors of whaling were the oppressive and rigid living conditions. In *Moby-Dick*, Melville succeeds brilliantly in giving a sense of the hierarchically organized space on board ship. The higher the rank, the greater the privacy. Captain Ahab lives aft on the *Pequod*, in a cabin that few dare enter. The men are packed into the small fo'c's'le forward. The fo'c's'le is where Queequeg lies dying – one of the odd errors in Melville's work, for a boatsteerer such as Queequeg would be berthed aft, just forward of the captain's cabin. First mate Starbuck considers literally breeching the hierarchy of the *Pequod* by shooting a musket through the cabin wall and thus murdering Ahab. He murmurs to himself, "On this level, Ahab's hammock swings within; his head this way. A touch, and Starbuck may survive to hug his wife and child again" (515). Starbuck questions, "[S]hall this crazed old man be tamely suffered to drag a whole ship's company down to doom with him? – Yes, it would make him the wilful murderer of thirty men and more" (514–15). Ultimately, Starbuck leaves Ahab unharmed, and the isolation and privilege of the captain's cabin remains. It is Pip, a small black boy, the lowliest member of the crew, who penetrates the literal and metaphorical barrier between captain and crew. Ahab tells Pip, "Do thou abide below here [in the cabin], where they shall serve thee, as if thou wert the captain" (534). Ahab ultimately leaves Pip in the cabin, for he finds him "too curing to my malady" (534); he must re-erect the barrier between them in order to maintain his focused leadership in the hunt for the white whale.

Storms and Calms

Melville's own life was tempestuous far more often than it was peaceful. However, his sea stories, surprisingly, are most often set in the midst of calms. He seems more interested in the interactions between men confined aboard ship than in their actions as they battle physical storms. Calms breed intensity that can lead to metaphysical storms; physical storms detract from that intensity.

Despite his interest in the intensity created by calms, Melville does include some storm scenes in his sea works. The *Pequod* encounters a typhoon in "The Candles," Chapter 119 of *Moby-Dick*. In darkness, the "sky and sea roared and split with the thunder, and blazed with the lightning," the masts are "disabled," and the sails are torn to "rags" (503). The static electricity generated by the storm causes corpusants, or "St. Elmo's fire," to appear on the tips of the yards, a sight that enchants and terrifies the crew. Other storms occur in Melville's works as well, although the fiercest tempest is probably that encountered by Tommo and Toby as they make their way along the ridges of Nuku Hiva – and this storm is set on land and not at sea.

Melville rounded the infamous Cape Horn twice, first *en route* to the Pacific aboard the whaleship *Acushnet* and finally homeward bound from the Pacific aboard the naval frigate *United States*. Unlike other maritime authors, however, Melville does not resort to using the fear evoked by Cape Horn for the climax of his story. Only the *Neversink*'s rounding of Cape Horn in *White-Jacket* is described; the *Pequod* doesn't even round Cape Horn but makes her way to the Pacific in *Moby-Dick* via the much calmer Cape of Good Hope transit. (The *Dolly*'s rounding of the "horrid headland," Cape Horn, in *Typee* is referred to [223], but not described.) The Cape of Good Hope lies at 34° South latitude, whereas Cape Horn lies at 57° South latitude – 23 degrees farther south. This dramatic difference, easily seen by looking at a map of the world, makes Cape Horn far more dangerous. The waters of the two great oceans, the Atlantic and the Pacific, are compressed into the narrow passage between Cape Horn and the continent of Antarctica, sometimes causing waves to build as high as a hundred feet. One of the best descriptions of Cape Horn appears in *White-Jacket*:

> Who has not heard of it? – Cape Horn, Cape Horn – a *horn* indeed, that has tossed many a good ship. Was the descent of Orpheus, Ulysses, or Dante into Hell one whit more hardy and sublime than the first navigator's weathering of that terrible Cape? ... You may approach it from this direction or that – in any way you please – from the East, or from the West; with the wind astern, or abeam, or on the quarter; and still Cape Horn is Cape Horn. Cape Horn it is that takes the conceit out of fresh-water sailors, and steeps in a still salter brine the saltest. (96)

Melville's own two passages around Cape Horn were stormy but less dramatic. The *Acushnet* made one of the fastest roundings of the Horn in 1841. The logbook of the *United States* describes first a calm off Cape Horn and then increasing squalls. The *United States* finally had to lay to under reduced sail for six hours (actually quite a short period for storms off the Cape) until the "wind abated and then shifted in our favour, and we were on our way once more" (Anderson, *Journal* 65).

Nonetheless, calms are far more prevalent than storms in Melville's works. Consider the waters off the island of St. Maria in "Benito Cereno." After Captain Delano boards the *San Dominick* and sends his whaleboat back to his own ship for supplies, "to the vexation of all, the wind entirely died away, and the tide turning, began drifting back the ship helplessly seaward" (*PT* 51). The *San Dominick* seems held in this enchanted calm through most of the story, much as Shakespeare's Italian nobles are held enchanted in *The Tempest*. And, as in *The Tempest*, the calm exacerbates the question of leadership in "Benito Cereno" as well. Who is in charge? What is going on? Delano is a man of action imprisoned by dim thoughts, fears, and wonderings. His thoughts speak a "sleepy language," just as Shakespeare's Antonio, who has usurped the dukedom of Milan from his brother, does when he tries to induce Sebastian to steal the throne of Naples from his brother. Sebastian tells him, "[S]urely / It is a sleepy language and thou speak'st / Out of thy sleep" (II.i). Delano does not understand the sleepy language of usurpation he hears aboard the *San Dominick*. Sleepwalking through the story, he misses the usurpation that occurred not only when Babo took power from Cereno but also when the Africans were enslaved in their native country.

Melville also uses calms and physical enchantment explicitly in "The Encantadas," the Enchanted Isles, as Melville calls the Galápagos. The currents surrounding the islands were so strong and irregular and the winds so light and variable that early navigators became confused as to the exact location of the group. "[T]his apparent fleetingness and unreality," Melville writes, " . . . was most probably one reason for the Spaniards calling them the Encantada, or Enchanted Group" (*PT* 128). As in "Benito Cereno," stillness increases intensity. "[C]hange never comes" (126) to the Galápagos; they are eternally desolate, hot, and solitary. *Billy Budd*, too, occurs in a world of stultifying calm. The sense of physical movement across the ocean is removed, and the psychological drama aboard the *Bellipotent* is thus intensified. The film "Billy Budd" (1962), directed by Peter Ustinov, adds a naval fight scene at the end to relieve tension – tension that Melville leaves unresolved in the original work.

Storms are exciting, vibrant, passionate, alive. But in ordinary sailing, days of wind and days of calm are far more common. Melville, who perhaps better than any other sea-writer except Joseph Conrad has captured a true sense of life at sea, chronicles these common days. Oddly the very ordinariness of *White-Jacket* makes the story all the more powerful. The nearly 500 men crushed together on the *Neversink* do not see battle. Instead, they contend with lack of sleep, lack of privacy, bitter cold, harsh discipline, hunger, and enervating boredom. These ordinary deprivations of sailors produce a numbing inhumanity. The men of the *Neversink* stand watch and watch; they are on duty for four hours and then off for four hours. But they must stow their hammocks at eight o'clock in the morning, and thus those who stand watch from eight in the evening until midnight and again from four in the morning until eight have less than four hours' sleep in their hammocks. There is no other place to sleep, even when they are off duty; they are constantly sleep-deprived. Each morning, the men are required to scrub the deck: barefoot, on their knees, in the bitter cold, dragging the heavy "holy stones" back and forth across the wooden planking. The three meals of the day all occur between eight in the morning and four in the afternoon: the men go without food for the remaining sixteen hours. Thus, even before he reaches his four searing chapters on punishment – "A Flogging," "Some of the Evil Effects of Flogging," "Flogging not Lawful," and "Flogging not Necessary" (Chapters 33–6) – Melville in *White-Jacket* reveals the inhumanity produced by the rigid protocols of naval life.

An understanding of what it means to be continuously at sea, completely cut off from the land, is difficult for non-sailors to comprehend. Such isolation *can* lead to happiness. Joseph Conrad writes in *The Nigger of the* Narcissus (1897): "The men working about the deck were healthy and contented – as most seamen are, when once well out to sea. The true peace of God begins at any spot a thousand miles from the nearest land" (Chapter 2). Melville asks in *Moby-Dick*: "Why upon your first voyage as a passenger, did you yourself feel such a mystic vibration, when first told that you and your ship were now out of sight of land?" (5). The thought of being out of sight of land can be alluring, but Melville generally sees the tyranny that can come with such isolation, for which the nineteenth-century sailor had little or no legal recourse. The captain and officers held sway aboard ship, and consuls and courts on land favored those same officers if a case actually did make it to court. Melville asks in *Typee*: "To whom could we apply for redress? We had left both law and equity on the other side of the Cape" (21). Richard Henry Dana, Jr.'s *Two Years Before the Mast* (1840) powerfully presents an example of such lawlessness. After flogging a sailor without just cause, Captain Thompson states: "If you want to know what I flog you for, I'll tell you. It's because I like to do it! because I like to do it! It suits me! That's what I do it for!" The sailor cries out in pain, "O Jesus Christ! O Jesus Christ!" The captain responds, "Don't call on Jesus Christ . . . . *He can't help you. Call on Frank Thompson!* He's the man! He can help you! Jesus Christ can't help you now!" (Chapter 15; emphasis in original).

Melville's Whaling Captains

Melville's first captain, Valentine Pease, Jr., master of the whaleship *Acushnet*, has often been regarded by literary scholars as a tyrant, driving Melville to desert in the Marquesas. Drawing on the research of whaling scholar Briton Cooper Busch, however, maritime historian Glenn Grasso has argued persuasively that Captain Pease was no more nor less brutal than any other whaling captain:

> Overall, the whaling industry in the mid-nineteenth century was rife with desertion. Certainly, men deserted due to poor living and working conditions, but they also deserted out of boredom or the desire to try another occupation. . . . They might fall victim to crimps ashore and be placed on board other vessels. . . . In addition, desertion was often looked upon by experienced sailors as a rite of passage in the industry, often having nothing to do with the commander or usage on board a particular vessel. . . . One captain, in 1859, felt that desertion was inevitable and commented in frustration that "if the ship were bound for heaven and should stop at Hell for wood and water[,] some

of the crew would run away" [Busch, 104] .... the *Acushnet* sailed near the peak years of the American whaling industry. Any sailor who jumped ship would have plenty of options for finding another vessel and subsequent passage home. (Grasso 8)

While there certainly were brutal captains and reasons for desertion such as severe discipline, inadequate food, and unsound ships, Grasso's argument that Pease's treatment of Melville was in no way atypical is sound and supported by other studies of desertion.

Against the backdrop of whaling – its dangers and boredom, storms and calms, and rigorous hierarchy – can be drawn a portrait of Pease as captain. Six deserters from the *Houqua*, a vessel under Pease's command on a voyage earlier than Melville's, were questioned by the acting English counsel in Tahiti in 1833. They testified that they deserted because Pease had lowered only three whaleboats on a four-boat ship, that one man had quarreled with him, that another was forced to work with frostbitten feet, and that a third was afraid of the whale, but their greatest complaint was lack of food. Inadequate food is the most common complaint of deserters from whaleships in the nineteenth century. From the historic record, then, Pease appears to be an average captain, neither uncommonly humane nor outstandingly cruel.

Although Pease was the whaling captain under whom Melville sailed the longest, it is not at all certain that Pease was the model for Ahab. Ahab has the arbitrary and apparently limitless power of a captain at sea. He cries to Starbuck, "There is one God that is Lord over the earth, and one Captain that is lord over the Pequod" (474). He can subvert the *Pequod*'s mission from the catching of whales to the catching of Moby Dick. Ahab's use of power more closely resembles that of Thomas ap Catesby Jones, commodore of the Pacific Fleet, under whose pennant Melville sailed aboard the naval frigate *United States*, than that of Pease. The character most like Pease is Peleg, former captain and part-owner of the *Pequod*. Peleg offers some insight into the characters of Ahab, Bildad (another part-owner and former captain), and himself: "Oh! he [Ahab] ain't Captain Bildad; no, and he ain't Captain Peleg; *he's Ahab*, boy; ... I know Captain Ahab well; I've sailed with him as mate years ago; I know what he is – a good man – not a pious, good man, like Bildad, but a swearing good man – something like me – only there's a good deal more of him" (79). Peleg's own profanity is certainly apparent in Chapter 22, "Merry Christmas," when he orders the capstan manned with a quick "Blood and thunder!" (103) and then when he kicks Ishmael, calling him a "sheep-head" (104). Valentine Pease's nephew, Alexander Pease, reflected on his uncle for a 1929 article published in the *Vineyard Gazette* from Martha's Vineyard, Massachusetts, USA. When asked about Valentine's reputation as a tyrannical captain, he said, "I don't recall that Uncle Val was a harsh man." Alexander then reflected for a moment and added, "I should say he was an upright man, but at times quite profane." In other words, he was a "swearing good man."

Captain Henry Ventom of the *Lucy Ann*, in contrast to Pease, was a remarkably poor master. Five months out, the *Lucy Ann* called at Tahuata in the Marquesas. There, nine men deserted, including the second mate and two of the four illiterate boatsteerers.

Many of those who remained revolted, and Ventom had to rely on the French authorities to mount an armed guard aboard the vessel each night for protection for himself and his officers. The *Lucy Ann* finally made its way to Nuku Hiva, where more men deserted and where Melville joined the crew. The *Lucy Ann* left Nuku Hiva on a cruise for sperm whales. A day or two out from port, Ventom became painfully afflicted with a severe infection in his groin region and was soon confined to his cabin. James German, the first mate, thus had to serve not only as the sole remaining mate, but also as acting master and as nurse to his ailing captain. German turned the *Lucy Ann* toward Tahiti, where the captain, now dangerously ill, was taken ashore. Despite his illness, despite the lack of officers on his ship, and despite the recent revolts and desertions that had occurred, Ventom ordered the ship to sea under German. Rather than face such a cruise, ten men refused duty. They were later joined by Melville, making a final total of eleven revolters.

In *Omoo*, Melville translates Ventom's incompetence into a landsman's lack of seamanship:

> The captain was a young cockney, who, a few years before, had emigrated to Australia, and, by some favoritism or other, had procured the command of the vessel, though in no wise competent. He was essentially a landsman, and though a man of education, no more meant for the sea than a hair-dresser. Hence every body made fun of him. They called him "The Cabin Boy," "Paper Jack," and half a dozen other undignified names. In truth, the men made no secret of the derision in which they held him. (10)

Throughout the first part of *Omoo*, Melville explores the problem of leadership through the incompetence of Captain Guy, the courage, seamanship, and natural aptitude of the mate, John Jermin, marred by his insatiable thirst for alcohol, and the wildness of Bembo, the New Zealand Maori boatsteerer thrust into power by the sick captain and the mate who accompanied him ashore. Melville writes: "Guy's thus leaving the ship in the men's hands, contrary to the mate's advice, was another evidence of his simplicity; for at this particular juncture, had neither the doctor [Doctor Long Ghost] nor myself been aboard, there is no telling what they might have done" (70). By the time he was imprisoned, Melville had not yet served under a leader for whom he felt deep respect.

That situation changed with Captain John B. Coleman, Jr., of the *Charles and Henry*. Melville joined the Nantucket whaleship in the Society Islands and sailed aboard her to Lahaina, Maui, Hawaii. Coleman cared about his men, even to the extent of giving them their dinners before lowering for whales. The logbook of his earlier command records: November 11, 1832: "got our diiners [*sic*] and lowred [*sic*] 4 boats and chased them"; July 30, 1834: "got our dinners and lowred [*sic*] Again" (Logbook of the *Zenas Coffin*). The respect that Coleman's leadership engendered is evident in Joseph Castro, who joined the *Charles and Henry* with Melville. Castro had earlier deserted the whaleship *John Adams*, but he served aboard the *Charles and Henry* to the end of this voyage and on the next. Coleman is Melville's model for the master of the *Leviathan* in *Omoo* – "a sailor, and no tyrant" (312) – and for the captain of the *Arcturion* in *Mardi*, whom Melville describes as a master who "himself was a trump; stood upon no quarter-deck dignity; and had a tongue for a sailor" (5). Coleman made a luckless voyage aboard the *Charles and Henry*, but this did not embitter him, and he continued to treat his men with fairness and humanity.

Melville, then, sailed under three whaling captains, one average, one kind and humane, and one utterly incompetent. Yet even Coleman, the ship's master for whom Melville had the most respect, was inadequate: though he treated his men well, he could not find whales, and the profits of the *Charles and Henry* were the lowest for all whaleships then sailing from Nantucket. Melville makes literary use of all his whaling captains, but the questions raised by Ahab's uncompromising, monomaniacal leader-ship, as suggested above, are probably more closely grounded in Melville's experience of naval hierarchy.

Melville's Naval Leaders

Fairness, humanity, and competence are lacking in Melville's portrayal of leadership aboard the naval frigate *Neversink* in *White-Jacket*. Melville has fun with his portrait of Captain Claret – "Captain Claret was a portly gentleman, with a crimson face, whose father had fought at the battle of the Brandywine, and whose brother had commanded the well-known frigate named in honor of that engagement" (153) – but Melville disparages Claret's lack of skill and leadership. In the storm the vessel encounters off Cape Horn, Claret bursts from his cabin in his night-dress, shouting "Hard *up* the helm!" (106; emphasis in original). This is the worst possible command under the circumstances. Mad Jack, the lieutenant, countermands his order, crying: "Damn you! . . . hard *down* – hard *down*, I say, and be damned to you!" (106; emphasis in original). Had it not been for Mad Jack, the vessel would have foundered off Cape Horn. Claret's appearance in his night-dress emphasizes his incompetence. Instead of being fully clothed and on deck during the passage around Cape Horn, he shows by his dress that he was below decks drinking.

Claret's lack of fair play and inhumanity are shown shortly afterwards when he has four men flogged for fighting. John, a brutal bully, is the "real author of the disturbance" (136). Nevertheless, all four men are flogged. The flogging turns nineteen-year-old Peter, one of the punished sailors, from a competent mariner, a great favorite with the crew, into an embittered man. He vows, "I don't care what happens to me now! . . . I have been flogged once, and they may do it again, if they will. Let them look out for me now!" (138). Melville suggests that a leader who degrades the quality of the individuals under his command and the morale of his subordinates in order to flatter his own vanity is counterproductive and self-involved.

Melville sailed under Captain James Armstrong on the *United States* in 1843–4, but the frigate itself sailed under the pennant of Commodore Thomas ap Catesby Jones. Catesby Jones was a controversial figure who is best known for his mistaken seizure of

Monterey, California, from Mexico in 1842. The occupation lasted only a few days; Catesby Jones shamefacedly returned the town when he learned that the United States was not at war with Mexico. This action caused a crisis in the relations between Mexico and the United States. Catesby Jones was court-martialed in 1850 for fraud against the United States, libel, neglect of duty, and oppression. He was found guilty. Catesby Jones's cavalier attitude toward other countries and his rigid authority over his own crews as well as the 163 floggings in his fourteen months aboard the *United States* did not arouse respect for naval leadership in Melville. "[A]re there incompetent officers in the gallant American navy?" (112), Melville asks in *White-Jacket*, and then evades answering his own question. But his whole book is an answer, crying out from almost every chapter: yes, yes, there are.

Another naval captain appears in *Billy Budd, Sailor* in the character of Captain Vere. Faced with the death of Claggart at the hands of Billy Budd, he cries out, "Struck dead by an angel of God! Yet the angel must hang!" (101) and remains firm that Billy must die despite the questions asked of him by his officers. Vere lays the burden of his decision upon the military law. "Our vowed responsibility is in this: That however pitilessly that law may operate in any instances, we nevertheless adhere to it and administer it" (111). Vere's stance is unequivocal, but Melville's is not. *Billy Budd* leaves ambiguous the question of the rightness or wrongness of Vere's decision.

Melville's first cousin Guert Gansevoort was serving as first lieutenant aboard the United States training brig *Somers* (1842) under the command of Captain Alexander Slidell Mackenzie when three men, including the son of the Secretary of War, were hanged for planning a mutiny in December of 1842. Mackenzie was court-martialed after questions arose regarding whether a mutiny had actually been planned. Some claimed that Mackenzie should have waited until the *Somers* reached St. Thomas, Virgin Islands, a mere two days away, to try the men in a formal military court. Mackenzie was acquitted, but uncertainties remained. Fifty years later, Melville, still troubled by an incident so closely tied to his family, worked and reworked *Billy Budd*, with its many similarities to the *Somers* incident, including a suspected mutiny, a "drumhead court" or officers' council controlled by the commanding officer, punishment by hanging, and unresolved questions about the commander's decision.

Conclusion

The isolation of the sea grants absolute power to masters of ships. What they do with that power is one of Melville's central concerns. Does absolute power corrupt absolutely? Does might make right? Melville transmuted his own experience of shipmasters into fiction. Unlike Shakespeare at the beginning of *The Tempest*, however, Melville chooses to explore questions of leadership and power more often in calms than storms. The reader is not blinded by the passion and heroic action precipitated by a gale, but must examine instead the role of leader. Guy, Claret, Ahab, Delano, Cereno, Vere – all are scrutinized. And all are finally richer, deeper, more complex than simply a fictional rendering of the men under whom Melville sailed. Ahab's blasphemy is more tragic and more transcendent than the incompetence of Captain Ventom of the whaleship *Lucy Ann* or even than the arrogance of Thomas ap Catesby Jones, commodore of the Pacific Fleet. In fictional calms, Melville faced and resolved the storms of his seagoing life.

NOTE

1   When known, I have included the date of the edition that Melville used rather than the date of the first edition. These dates are confirmed in Bercaw, *Melville's Sources*.

REFERENCES AND FURTHER READING

Abstract Log of the *Acushnet*. Matthew Fontaine Maury Collection of Abstract Logs of Ships, Weather Bureau Records, Dept. of Agriculture Section, National Archives. Record Group 27, M1160.

Anderson, Charles Roberts, ed. *Journal of a Cruise to the Pacific Ocean, 1842–1844, in the Frigate United States*. Durham, NC: Duke University Press, 1937.

——. *Melville in the South Seas*. New York: Columbia University Press, 1939.

Bercaw, Mary K. *Melville's Sources*. Evanston, IL: Northwestern University Press, 1987.

British Consular Papers, Tahiti. Vol. 8. Mitchell Library, State Library of New South Wales, Sydney, Australia.

Gilman, William H. *Melville's Early Life and Redburn*. New York: New York University Press, 1951.

Grasso, Glenn. "Valentine Pease, Jr. and Melville's Literary Captains." Paper delivered at the Second International Melville Conference, "Melville and the Sea," Mystic, CT. 18 June, 1999.

Hayford, Harrison. "Unnecessary Duplicates: A Key to the Writing of *Moby-Dick*." *New Perspectives on Melville*. Ed. Faith Pullin. Kent, Ohio: Kent State University Press, 1978. 128–61.

Hayford, Harrison and Merton M. Sealts, Jr. "Editors' Introduction." In *Billy Budd, Sailor*. By Herman Melville. Chicago: University of Chicago Press, 1962. 1–39.

Heflin, Wilson. *Herman Melville's Whaling Years*. Ed. Mary K. Bercaw Edwards and Thomas Farel Heffernan. Nashville, TN: Vanderbilt University Press, 2004.

Hough, Henry Beetle. "Melville's Captain Was a Vineyarder." *Vineyard Gazette*. 2 July 1929. 8.

Logbook of the *Zenas Coffin*. Kendall Institute, New Bedford Whaling Museum, New Bedford, MA.

Lucy Ann Papers. Mitchell Library, State Library of New South Wales, Sydney, Australia. Reprinted as "Revolt Documents." In Herman Melville. *Omoo*. Ed. Harrison Hayford. New York: Hendricks House, 1969. 309–39.

7

Pacific Paradises

Alex Calder

"Paradise" comes from an old Persian word meaning a walled garden, an enclosed pleasure ground. Make the wall a coral reef and the garden a lush palm-fronded island, and you might almost hear the fabled Bali Ha'i,

> whispering in the wind of the sea,
> Here am I, your special island!
> Come to me, come to me! (*South Pacific*)

But if you go to the Polynesian Islands of the actual South Pacific, where people trade, as they still must, on the call of Bloody Mary's siren song, you will find that a rule applies: the crummier the hotel, the more likely it will be called something like "Pacific Paradise" – a cliché that has long since come to rest on the bottom shelf of indifference to any incongruity between name and environment. Then again, the place that looks like a shack is probably local and might well be closer to heaven than the international resorts monopolizing the beachfront like scavenging starfish that leave the reef barren and dead. Viewed either way, the idea that an earthly paradise has been punctured, that happy valley is no longer what it is cracked up to be, is an old one, and not so much a corrective to idealizations of the Pacific as their obverse side. Any so-called "hell-hole" of the Pacific is part of the same discursive formation as its Edenic counterpart.

In the years before Melville was writing, strangers generally represented the peoples and places of the Pacific in the light of one of two loosely defined sets of cultural expectations. Some, influenced by Rousseau's ideal of the noble savage whose natural humanity is uncorrupted by civilization, would regard Tahiti or the Marquesas as a secular Eden; there was no poverty, no work, no crime, no artificiality in these islands of sexual freedom and Arcadian civility. Others, influenced by Christian ideas of original sin, would expect to find the consequences of Adam and Eve's fall writ large in debauchery, superstition, and idolatry. Both groups believed the "primitive" peoples of Polynesia were closer to nature than "civilized" Europeans, but each placed a different value on those associations. If the motto for the enlightened do-gooder was "Educating Nature's Children," its missionary counterpart might be "Liberating Satan's Slaves"; these catchphrases are chapter titles in T. Walter Herbert's *Marquesan Encounters,* which examines the contrasting perspectives of two early visitors – the naval officer, David Porter, and the missionary, Charles Stewart – alongside Melville's response to Pacific Island cultures. Herbert's study is a masterpiece of ethnographic "thick description," but his target is not so much the culture of the Polynesians as the visitors themselves who, in their diverse encounters with the Marquesans, stage a debate over what it means to be civilized.

A generation before Herbert, Charles Roberts Anderson, in *Melville in the South Seas* (1939) first demonstrated what a thoroughly bookish place Melville's Pacific was. Not only had Melville fictionalized his own experiences in the Pacific – he had first-hand knowledge of ports in Peru and Chile, of the Galapagos Islands, and of the Marquesas, Society, Austral and Hawaiian Islands – but he had also relied more heavily than he acknowledged on a library of prior writings about the Pacific. The relationship between the larger discursive paradigms through which nineteenth-century Europeans and Americans understood "primitive" peoples, the particular archive Melville had at his fingertips, his imaginative transformation of those sources and of his personal experience in far-flung places – between all that and what we might term Pacific actualities, is bound to be complex; and bound also to raise questions about the extent to which we can really know other cultures and other times. Edward Said offers one analogy for this relationship. Suppose an explorer encounters a fierce lion and writes a book about it.

> A book on how to handle a fierce lion might . . . cause a series of books to be produced on such subjects as the fierceness of lions, the origins of fierceness, and so forth. Similarly, as the focus of the text centers more narrowly on the subject – no longer lions but their fierceness – we might expect that the ways by which it is recommended that a lion's fierceness be handled will actually *increase* its fierceness, force it to be fierce since that is what it is, and that is what in essence we know or can *only* know about it. A text purporting to contain knowledge about something actual, and arising out of circumstances similar to the ones I have just described, is not easily dismissed. Expertise is attributed to it . . . . Most important, such texts can create not only knowledge but also the very reality they appear to describe. (Said 94)

In the Pacific, there are many sundry notions we could substitute for the fierceness of lions: some of them, such as the friendliness of Polynesians, relate to notions of the Pacific as paradise, others, such as their cannibalism, to its infernal opposite.

The apparent stakes are summed up in *Typee*, in Tommo's stark alternative, "Typee or Happar?," cannibal or friend, but the novel that Melville wrote is now generally thought to unravel the binary. Neither version of Polynesia is at all adequate to the reality of Tommo's experience, but where does the traveler's deconstruction of the frames of Eurocentric interpretation leave the interpreter? Perhaps the best one can say is that we will never have positive knowledge of Melville's Pacific paradises, that beyond the limits of our own interpretive schemes we reach a kind of cautionary lesson in the final predicament of Tommo, who flees, in a moment of violence and desperation, from a culture he has come to regard as inscrutable, that could never be home, that has intolerable designs on him.

Against this view, which has Tommo/Melville as an outsider visiting the islands of the Pacific, I would like to develop an island perspective that is well used to receiving visitors. The model is no longer that of a misconceiving Westerner encountering a misconceived Polynesia, but of "crossing the beach," Greg Dening's term for the pattern of mutually transformative exchanges that has characterized the human settlement of Oceania. "Every living thing on an island has been a traveler," Dening writes, and "in crossing the beach every voyager has brought something old and made something new" (Dening *Islands* 31). Over several millennia, in a series of island-hopping migrations, the ancestors of today's Polynesians discovered and settled every island group in the immense ocean triangle that extends from Hawaii to Rapanui (Easter Island) to Aotearoa (New Zealand). They took plants and animals with them on these voyages; each new arrival would adapt (or not) to an environment that would never be the same again. The stories, values, customs, and technologies they brought with them would also change in the new home, becoming acclimatized, as it were, but keeping a family resemblance with Pacific cultures developing in relative isolation elsewhere. When strangers from Europe first came from beyond the sky, the rate of interactive accommodation between old and new accelerated, but it was essentially the same process. To the people of the land, those aliens who rowed ashore backwards, as if they had eyes in the back of their heads, were *atua:* gods, but not the kind of God an Englishman like Captain Cook took himself to be when he was treated as one in Hawaii, or his fictional offshoot Taji, that "gentleman from the sun," who is deified in *Mardi;* but nor were the new arrivals – to continue the Hawaiian example – fully identical with usurping god-chiefs like Lono, however much they acted like "sharks walking upon the land" (Dening *Performances* 64) in their arrogance, rashness, and sense of superiority to "simple" natives. For islander and stranger, the meaning of what a god/*atua* could be crossed the beach and was extended and modified as it did so. In this two-way process of effective mistranslation, "Things come across the beach partially, without their fuller meanings" (Dening *Islands* 34). In *Omoo*, for example, Dr. Long Ghost and the narrator are shown a royal apartment in which "superb writing desks of rose-wood ...; decanters and goblets of cut glass; embossed volumes of plates; gilded candelabras; ... were strewn about among greasy calabashes half filled with '*poee*,' rolls of old tappa and matting, paddles and fish-spears, and the ordinary furniture of a Tahitian dwelling" (310). The European objects in this lumber-room have lost the value they once had as presents from foreign dignitaries; items from the bargain basement of empire – ironware, fishhooks, nails, muskets – would be worth far more. The consequences of people, ideas, and objects crossing the beach are in large measure unpredictable. They might on occasion give rise to a joyful hybridization, they might at times constitute a "fatal embrace" (*T* 26), they very often produce violence, but the surest thing one can say is that they give rise to island histories that resemble each other in patterns that emerge through the cumulative effects of trivialities.

Melville is among the best eyewitness historians and analysts of these transformations. His qualifications so far as personal experience are concerned are far less impressive than, say, those of William Pascoe Crook, the idealistic young missionary who spent two years alongside the people of the land and wrote an unpublished ethnographic "Account of the Marquesas Islands" on his return to London in 1799; or of Edward Robarts, the young sailor who jumped from the very ship that would later rescue Crook. Robarts hoped for a life of tropical ease, but when the breadfruit crop failed, he starved, and watched two-thirds of the population die in the famine. Unlike Tommo, Robarts agreed to be tattooed and settled down with a Nukuhivan woman; after many adventures, he too wrote a journal of his years as a Pacific rover. With genuine beachcomber accounts like these, one must read between the lines of threadbare statements of fact and literary and religious cliché to develop a glimmering sense of what it would have been like to be there. Melville had rather less experience to draw on, but he wrote about his adventures vividly and imaginatively, often embroidering fact to showcase the dramatic significance of his material. One would not look first to *Typee* or *Omoo* in search of a native understanding of Fenua'enata (the Marquesas) or Tahiti in the 1840s, but they are no less records of the actualities of encounter for that.

Readers of *Typee*, like Tommo himself, are presented with a number of mysteries. Why do these people want him to stay? What on earth can we make of taboo? Are they cannibals? It sometimes seems that he would need to read their minds to come up with answers. In a telling scene, the narrator recalls being on the receiving end of a look he cannot begin to fathom.

> [Mehevi] placed himself directly facing me, looking at me with a rigidity of aspect under which I absolutely quailed. He never once opened his lips, but maintained his severe expression of countenance, without turning his face aside for a single moment. Never before had I been subjected to so strange and steady a glance: it revealed nothing of the mind of the savage, but it appeared to be reading my own. (71)

We are often told what ethnographers, staring ever so intently at their subjects, make of indigenous peoples, but Tommo is uncomfortable in being stared at. It makes him feel all too visible and, moments later, he uses mimicry – copying what Mehevi says – to quench the spotlight of that gaze. Whenever Tommo tries to find a mind-reader's answer to the enigmatic behavior of the Taipi, he runs into blank walls of contradiction and paradox. Whenever he tells us how he got along, or made himself agreeable, he shows, often without intending to convey any knowledge of this sort, how the murk of cultural difference clarifies whenever people cross the beach.

Although Tommo finds his captivity perplexing, Marnoo explains the situation with admirable clarity.

Kannaka no let you go no where . . . you taboo. Why you no like to stay? Plenty moee-moee (sleep) – plenty ki-ki (eat) – plenty whihenee (young girls) – Oh, very good place Typee! Suppose you no like this bay, why you come? You no hear about Typee? All white men afraid of Typee, so no white men come. (241)

There were many reasons why a white sailor earning a fraction of a lay on a whaling ship was a person of import ashore. In Taiohae, a captured deserter could be ransomed back to a captain desperate for men, but around the bay in Taipivai a runaway was worth binding fast with every silken rope the people of the valley could offer: leisure befitting a lord, the best food, an attractive partner for sex. All through the Pacific, European tools and weaponry had crossed the beach inequitably; someone always got them first, and the tribe so favored generally used their advantage to develop a surplus of goods for trade, obtaining in return muskets that were used for traditional ends in wars of conquest with their competitors. Pomare in Tahiti, Hongi Hika in the north of New Zealand, Kamehameha in Hawaii, all had their own missionaries and traders, and through them their own special relationship with visiting ships.

The would-be Napoleon of all Nukuhiva was Temoana – Melville's Mowanna – *haka'aki* (chief) of Taiohae. He had already journeyed to the other side of the beach, running away to sea in 1834, and visiting New Zealand, Sydney, London, and Bona-parte's tomb on St. Helena before returning in 1839. The French, in a competition for *mana* (power, authority, prestige) with their neighboring tribes in Europe, were by this time keen to acquire Pacific territories of their own. On May 31, 1842, Admiral du Petit-Thouars, with seven ships and a force of over two thousand men, arrived at Taiohae and quickly formed an alliance with the local chief. In return for a base, they gave Temoana 1800 francs, cases of champagne, a colonel's red coat and a white stallion, and promised a royal pension if he would agree to be King of the island. Melville's analysis is exact: "On some flimsy pretext or other, . . . the king of Nukuheva . . . has been set up as the rightful sovereign of the entire island, – the alleged ruler by prescription of various clans who for ages perhaps have treated with each other as separate nations" (18).

For the Taipi, it must have seemed that history was about to repeat itself. In 1813, Captain David Porter, also landing at Taiohae, took possession of the islands in the name of America, and was goaded by the Teii into making war against the Taipi. Porter threw up fortifications and put cannons ashore, but failed to appreciate the capacity of an apparently "primitive" people to neutralize his overwhelming advan-tage in firepower. When an invasion force landed in Taipivai, the warriors of Taipi routed the Americans in a sharp skirmish and then vanished into the jungle; in return, Porter torched all the houses in the valley and set fire to their crops. Any "enemy" he could find, he killed, but the Taipi's doughty resistance earned them a reputation for ferocity and kept visitors away.

There were no other Europeans in Taipivai when Herman Melville and Tobias Greene arrived overland from Taiohae. They were immediately grilled about "the recent movements of the French" (75), but the effort to semaphore complex intelligence across the language barrier was fruitless. It would be unfortunate all round if the wanderers were to move on and face a similar interview on a French warship, but if the young men were genuine deserters, if, as their recent movements indicated was most likely the case, they wished only to have a good time in Taipivai, then they could be plucked for all sorts of other information. Yet when Tommo is shown a sick musket and it becomes plain no cure would be forthcoming, he recalls Mehevi regarding him, "as if he was some inferior sort of white man, who after all did not know much more than a Typee" (185). Practical knowledge ought to have been his beachcomber's calling card, but one suspects Melville was lackluster in this respect. He still had potential value as a resident who, with care and proper training, could become like Jimmy Fitch – the Irishman who managed ship-to-shore relations to the Teii's advantage in Taiohae, and who would soon be sent packing by the French; in the meantime, the young American sailor was as good as television. The invention of the pop-gun, the pugilistic demonstrations with an invisible opponent, the singing (so-called), his generosity with old shoes, his geniality and willingness to enter into the spirit of things, all marked Melville as the sort of white man it would be good to have if you could not get one of the more practical, entrepreneurial ones.

Some of the time, though, during those "midnight reflections," all this kindness and hospitality made Melville feel rather like Hansel being fattened up in his cage. Ever since the publication of Cook's journals, the one thing every traveler knew about the peoples of the Pacific was that they were cannibals. From a local perspective, the ongoing Western fascination with this topic is overwrought. The practice occurred throughout the islands of the Pacific, and in my own country (New Zealand) it is celebrated in legend, genealogy, and *waiata* (song). The significance and frequency of cannibalism is not the same in all parts of the Pacific, but it was never a dark satanic appetite for human flesh, nor was it a dietician's improvement on fare otherwise deficient in protein; yet people were eaten, and there is a kind of reverse ethnocentrism in the postcolonial inclination to save indigenous people in our part of the world from a terrible slur, as if there were nothing more to cannibalism than the European discourse about it.

Melville makes the apparent mystery of cannibalism a matter of epistemological suspense in *Typee*. From comic conviction – "a baked baby, by the soul of Captain Cook!" (95) – to shoulder-shrugging relativism, suspicions are tested and theories are entertained only to dissolve in the face of an obscure moment of revelation.

> In passing along the piazza ... I observed a curiously carved vessel of wood, of considerable size, with a cover placed over it, of the same material, and which resembled in shape a small canoe. It was surrounded by a low railing of bamboos, the top of which was scarcely a foot from the ground. As the vessel had been placed in its present position since my last visit, I at once concluded that it must have some connection with the recent festival; and, prompted by a curiosity I could not repress, in passing it I raised one end of the cover; at the same moment the chiefs, perceiving my design, loudly ejaculated, "Taboo! taboo!" But the slight glimpse sufficed; my eyes fell upon the disordered members of a human skeleton, the bones still fresh with moisture, and with particles of flesh clinging to them here and there! (238)

Finding bones is one thing – relating them to a correct context is another. Two days earlier, Tommo had seen the palm-wrapped bodies of three enemy warriors carried on poles in triumph to the *Tai* (Melville's Ti) – a *tapu* house reserved for the use of men, at one end of the *tohua* (a raised dancing platform, about a hundred yards long) that Melville refers to variously as the "pi-pi" *(paepae)* or "hoolah-hoolah grounds" (he calls the whole complex, which also includes the chief's house, the "Taboo Groves"). As his attempts to investigate the blood-stained bundles were thwarted, he admits, in an ostentatiously scrupulous sentence, that "thick coverings prevented [his] actually detecting the form of a human body" (236). On the following day, a *koina* (feast) for senior men of the tribe took place; Tommo knows "the whole tribe were never present at these cannibal banquets" (237), knows too, that he is expressly not invited; any attempt to so much as look in the direction of the building is greeted with cries of "Taboo, taboo!" At this point, his suspicions about the "inhuman feast" taking place amount "almost to a certainty" (237). In the novel, these background details stack the deck for the next day's discovery, but they actually derive from Captain Porter's journal:

> On my way to the square, . . . I could hear them beating their drums and chanting their war-songs. I soon discovered five or six hundred of them assembled about the dead bodies, which were lying on the ground, still attached to the poles with which they had been brought from the scene of the action . . . . Ah! said Wilson, they are now making their infernal feast on the bodies of the dead. At this moment my approach was discovered. They were all thrown into the utmost confusion; the dead bodies were in an instant snatched from the place where they lay, and hurried to a distance among the bushes, and shouting and hallooing evinced the utmost consternation. I now believed the truth of Wilson's declaration, and my blood recoiled with horror at the spectacle I was on the point of witnessing. I directed them in an authoritative manner to return the bodies . . . With much reluctance they brought them back; two of them carefully covered with branches . . . I immediately caused them all to be exposed to my view, and to my great surprise found them unmutilated . . . . I told them that I was apprehensive that they intended to eat them, and expressed, with the strongest marks of horror, my detestation of the practice. They all assured me that they had no intention of eating them . . . but entreated I would indulge them with the bodies a day or two longer to sing over and to perform their ceremonies, and that I would grant them two to offer as a sacrifice to the manes of their priests, who had been slain; requesting, at the same time, that I would send a person to attend the ceremony and witness their burial; assuring me that they would bury them any depth I should wish. (Porter 2: 44–5).

Porter believes he has gotten to the bottom of a misunderstanding, that the Islanders did not in fact practice cannibalism, and merely used the bodies of slain enemies for ritualistic purposes. Yet the practice of *e ika*, fishing for men, is well documented. It produced *heana*, victims, predominantly female commoners snatched from another tribe, who were killed and eaten. Even a beachcomber might be used as food if the man was worthless or a transgression was serious enough: in 1835, Pakoko (a future resistance leader later executed by the French) killed and ritually ate a beachcomber who had stolen and eaten his *tapu* pigs. But we must be careful not to equate Marquesan cannibalism with the cartoon "cooking-pot" version. "It is not even possible to say with certainty that *heana* were cooked," concludes Dening in an authoritative discussion. "More likely they were merely singed with a candlenut torch. There was no feasting on the body. Its parts belonged to a few ... *tapu* men" (Dening *Islands* 249).

Melville drew selectively on Porter's description and ignored the Captain's own inferences, presumably in preparation for the subsequent discovery scene. But when he came to write the climactic episode, Melville also took care *not* to make the find one of those fresh-from-the-oven horrors that are a staple of colonial romance in the Pacific, and he also included a number of suggestive details whose significance may have escaped him. Tommo discovers "the disordered members of a human skeleton" inside a "curiously carved vessel of wood, of considerable size, with a cover placed over it, and which resembled in shape a small canoe." All containers dug from tree trunks will resemble canoes, but if human remains are found in them, they are almost certainly coffins rather than lunchboxes. Porter writes:

> Their coffins are dug out of a solid piece of white wood, in the manner of a trough; the size is just sufficient to cram the body in ... When a person dies, the body is deposited in a coffin, and a stage erected, either in a house vacated for the purpose, in which the coffin is placed, or a small house of sufficient size to contain the coffin is built in front of a *tabbooed* house, on the platform of stones, in which the coffin is deposited .... When the flesh is mouldered from the bones, they are, as I have been informed, carefully cleansed: some are kept for relics, and some are deposited in the morais. (Porter 2: 123).

Melville has carefully constructed a set of circumstances and suspicions that, viewed from one side of the beach, seem to point to the European idea of a cannibal feast. There is perhaps just enough evidence to reconstruct how things might have looked from the other side: the canoe is a coffin, the corpse placed in it has been allowed to rot, and it is now time to scrape and clean the bones for distribution as relics or deposition at the *Me'ae* (ceremonial ground).

Taboo is an integral component of the discovery scene, too. The "low railing of bamboos" that surround the coffin mark a *tapu* object, and Tommo's efforts to see inside the container, like his efforts to gain access to the feast the day before, are greeted with loud exclamations of "Taboo! Taboo!" Of all the Polynesian signs that crossed the beaches of the Pacific, *tapu* was perhaps the most conspicuous and the most complex. It very quickly became an English word for something forbidden to certain persons, but its meanings, as Dening reminds us, crossed the beach partially, and lost their sense as a positive and transferable sacred quality related to concepts like *mana* and *utu* (balance) as they did so. The word was well adapted to become part of the cross-cultural pidgin of the Pacific, and as soon as captains began "tabooing" their ships and Islanders began making allowances for the ignorance of their visitors, the traditional understandings and uses of the terms were caught up in a rapid process of change. Among early commentators "taboo" often became a higher-order term for the puzzle of cultural difference in the Pacific. It seemed like an organic whole: overarching, interfused, greater than the sum of its parts. If an interpreter could crack *tapu*'s code, everything ought to become clear, but its patterns of use were so variable and inconsistent no all-encompassing solution could ever be accepted. Conversely, if an interpreter could not understand something, it was probably because "taboo" was at the heart of it – in its own way, a variation on the tautological explanations that continue to characterize our use of words like "culture." Melville tries out many speculations about taboo in *Typee*: his most notable oversight is a failure to appreciate *tapu* as a socially differentiating force separating chiefly ranks from commoners, men from women, sacred from profane; his best insight is to link the mysteries of "taboo" to general problems of translation in a language where "one brisk, lively little word is obliged, like a servant in a poor family, to perform all sorts of duties; for instance, one particular combination of syllables expresses the idea of sleep, rest, reclining, sitting, leaning, and all other things anywise analogous thereto, the particular meaning being shown chiefly by a variety of gestures and the eloquent expression of the countenance" (224–5).

Melville is superb at describing what it is like to be on the receiving end of "eloquent expressions of the countenance." If one is in search of the Pacific actualities underlying a work like *Typee*, the various occasions when Tommo has to modify his behavior in the light of something he cannot understand seem to me the most central. In the interview scene and the discovery scene, in throwaway details like the circlet of leaves that marks Tommo with the personal *tapu* of Mehevi (222), in the sundry occasions when he is "called to order" (221) without the least clue as to what constitutes his offense, we have exemplary instances of someone crossing the beach. As his behavior tests limits and maps lines of permission and constraint, he inevitably works with the expectations he brings to the moment of encounter, but his sense of himself in a location where he is all too visible is defined rather more by the Taipi perception of him than by his perception of them. The beachcomber's traditional response to standing out awkwardly in one's surroundings is to "go native": to accommodate oneself to one's surroundings, to be personable, and to become a fluent and inexhaustible relater of meanings back and forth across the beach. Melville is the beachcomber as novelist. I have always thought efforts to finally separate fact and fiction in *Typee* founder on this point. When information crosses the beach, it is altered; something actual takes on the quality of fable, something imagined seems true to life – the compounded strands cannot be unpicked, and the necessity of their interrelation is a condition and resource of the beachcombing style. Even so, there are tall stories in *Typee*, and the tallest of all is the sustained impression readers receive (and which withstands obvious contradiction in the novel itself) that this is a story of very early contact, that the people of the valley have had little truck with "civilization." It is the case that Taipivai has been less of a cross-cultural crossroads than Taiohae, and that fewer ships have touched the islands of the Marquesas than Tahiti or

Hawaii. By 1842, the welcome to visiting ships was not the sportive capture by graceful nudes that Melville teasingly describes, but an uglier, workaday prostitution. In the previous twelve months, as many as forty other ships, almost one a week, had sailed into the bay. Many lost crew: Melville was one of eighteen sailors to jump ship at Taiohae that year. Back home, the writer exaggerated the contrast between a supposedly unspoiled valley and the progressively more sordid worlds of Taiohae, Tahiti, and Hawaii, in order to pursue an interrogation of the consequences of Western colonial expansion into the Pacific – and in his own backyard, too, for the fate of Polynesians and Native Americans seemed comparable. His attitudes toward all this were ambivalent and sometimes contradictory. *Typee* ends with an Appendix consisting of reckless generalizations about the degraded character of the Hawaiians and their "imbecile" monarch – opinions tempered, if that is the word, by a withering attack on the "junto of ignorant and designing Methodist elders" and buccaneering merchants holding effective power (255). *Omoo* is a more considered examination of the later consequences of contact. By 1815, Pomare II and his allies in the London Missionary Society mission had unified Tahiti in the name of Jehovah. Within a few years, most Tahitians regarded themselves as Christians; within a decade, the first syncretic religion, *Mamaia*, appeared in opposition to the prevailing theocracy. A generation later, what did all these civilizing influences and "backslidings" amount to? Was it possible to reconcile a beachcomber's pleasure in the experience of encounter with the likelihood that crossing the beach might ultimately amount to destroying it?

If *Typee* is a travel experience we can no longer have – an adventure of "pure" cultural difference – *Omoo* is more like travel as we know it. Unlike Tommo, who meets a people apparently very different from himself, the narrator of *Omoo* meets a people who only used to be different from himself. What they once were is the subject of legend, but Tahiti is not paradise now, and a flattening out of difference promotes cynicism all round. Call this an experience of impure or "fallen" cultural difference. Even so, the narrator hopes the real thing might still be available, away from Western influences, if only he knew where to look. His worst fear in crossing the beach is that he will be snagged by officials or cheated by folk who befriend him, but he has the good luck to be treated with genuine warmth and hospitality time and time again. If there is a downside, it is that he too confidently supposes signs like "closed" or "keep out" do not apply to him; but alas, they most certainly do. All things considered, the adventurer has a great time in a place not too different from home, not too different from anywhere else these days. When *Typee*'s narrator-as-anthropologist becomes *Omoo*'s narrator-as-tourist, the problem is no longer "too many signs I can't read" but "so many signs that seem familiar."

The word familiar is used twice in the Preface to *Omoo*. We learn that the author proposes "a *familiar* account of the present condition of the converted Polynesians" (xiii) – the emphasis is Melville's, and several connotations of that word apply. Most obviously, the author claims to be thoroughly acquainted with his subject, to know it at first hand. We might also suppose a familiar account to be one that concerns itself with ordinary and everyday experience. Yet the choice of phrasing cannot but raise the ghost of a rather different sort of account: one based on second-hand knowledge, one that may be familiar to a reader who has read stories like this before. *Omoo* is a familiar account in all of these senses. It records Melville's actual and rather commonplace experiences in Tahiti, but it is padded out from William Ellis's *Polynesian Researches* and other works in a manner that the Preface's comments about the benefit of "collateral information" (xiv) only partly acknowledge. Melville's Preface then goes on to say that *Omoo* makes "no pretensions to philosophical research" but "in a familiar way," merely describes what its author has seen (xv). Familiar, in this sense, means informal, unfussy, affable. It is a means of approach and a quality of style. The familiar style, it seems to me, is fundamental to the problems of the familiar account, for by it Melville converts the already read into an original, the expected into the unanticipated, and mere description into another kind of performance altogether.

Another word of importance touched on in the Preface to *Omoo* is "converted." One of the objects of the Tahitian sections of the book is to investigate the effectiveness and consequences of the conversion of the Polynesians to Christianity – a subject on which Melville was always prone to editorialize. Suffice it to say that missionaries are a bad lot, and Melville is never more pleased than when revealing their hypocrisy and lack of efficacy. But the missionaries are by no means the central agents of conversion in *Omoo*. They are off-stage, although their effective or ineffective "conversion" of the Tahitians poses a first layer of interpretive problems. In their place, there are two raffish beachcombers who go under the apostolic aliases of Peter and Paul, and the *mikonaree* who minister to them. What kind of conversion or counter-conversion might those encounters amount to?

At first, the narrator finds, and largely expects to find, that the malign influence of Christianity is everywhere pervasive. In describing the Church of the Cocoanuts at Papeetee, for example, Melville converts details from Ellis's description of a quite different church to precisely this end. In the midst of a section describing the roof, the rafters, the matting, fringes and tassels, Ellis notes that: "The pulpit ... was hexagonal, and supported by six pillars of the beautiful wood of the pua, ... which resembles, in its grain and colour, the finest stain wood" (Ellis II: 85). Melville, in the midst of a section describing the roof, the rafters, the matting, fringes and tassels, departs from Ellis to observe: "the pulpit, made of a dark and lustrous wood ... is by far the most striking object. It is preposterously lofty; indeed, a capital bird's eye view of the congregation ought to be had from its summit" (169). In the next chapter, a Hawaiian sailor translates the missionary's sermon from mount Pulpit into the language of the forecastle, comically revealing the bombast and greed of the loftier discourse. These, and many other details, are part of a larger picture of a church ruled by the obnoxious discipline of the "Kanakippers" for the aggrandizement of chiefs and the material benefit of the missionaries.

But this all-too-familiar perspective is countered by another: the Tahitians are not really Christians at all. When Paul asks a young woman if she is *mikonaree*, the response is pleasingly qualified:

Mickonaree *ena* (church member *here*) exclaimed she, laying her hand upon her mouth, and a strong emphasis on the adverb.... This done, her whole air changed in an instant; and she gave me to understand, by unmistakeable gestures, that in certain other respects she was not exactly a "mickonaree." In short, Ideea was "A sad good Christian at the heart – A very heathen in the carnal part." (178)

Again, this detail combines with many others to suggest a selective immunity to Christianity that the narrator wholly approves of. Yet the realization that converted Polynesians are not necessarily Christians needs to be associated with another form of negative discovery: they are not true Polynesians either. Many historically accurate details in the chapter "Tahiti As It Is" point to an all-encompassing pattern of decline and fall: the population has collapsed, congenital syphilis is endemic, the people are idle and demoralized, even the benign custom of *tayo*, once of mutual benefit to sailors and islanders, has degenerated into insincerity and self-interest. But of the many signs of a "lost" Tahiti, one that interests me particularly is the old Cathedral of Papoar, built by Pomare II. The actual building was over 700 feet long; it had three pulpits, from which three sermons might be simultaneously preached; it was erected – or woven – in three weeks with no iron tools and, most striking of all, had a stream running through it. Melville owes these details to Ellis, but where the missionary rolls his eyes at a folly, Melville delights in the incongruity and exorbitance of a church in the Tahitian style. And he converts Ellis's account to his own purposes when he says that the "sides of the edifice were open" (168). The Cathedral of Papoar is a temple of nature, and its open sides are in keeping with everything that contrasts with the present-day Church of the Cocoanuts, with its plain chapel style, closed wooden walls, and single panoptic pulpit.

However, this counter-perspective – not Christian, thank heavens, but alas, no longer Tahitian – is in turn overthrown toward the end of the novel when the narrator and Dr. Long Ghost travel round the island of Imeeo (Moorea) to sojourn in the household of Ereemear Po-Po. "Jeremiah" is a deacon in the church, but I doubt there is a more open-hearted and generous character in all of Melville. This contradiction is as important to the novel as similar contradictions are to *Typee*. The narrator's explanation for this is plausible but by no means satisfactory: "Po-po was, in truth, a Christian, the only one, [his wife] excepted, whom I personally knew to be such, among all the natives of Polynesia" (280).

There are a number of reasons why this assessment is out of line with Pacific actualities. The first once again has to do with Melville's conversion of his sources in Ellis. In this instance, he draws on passages in which the missionary laments the state of housing in old Tahiti: the houses are "little adapted to promote domestic comfort," grass scattered on the floor becomes "a resort for vermin" (Ellis II: 66), meals lead to spillages, spillages lead to dampness, dampness promotes rotting. Point by point, Melville rebuts Ellis in his description of a meal at Po-Po's house. The easily renewable grass is freshly laid; reclining at their ease, the guests enjoy a delicious meal; if there is a whiff of anything unsanitary, it comes from the bedraggled apostles of "civilization" who are pointed in the direction of a bath. Ellis then goes on to deplore the sleeping arrangements: "there was no division or screen between the sleeping places ... what the state of morals must necessarily be ... it is unnecessary to shew" (Ellis II: 67), and remarks that he makes a point of admonishing converts who do not have European-style cottages to "partition bedrooms in their present dwellings" (Ellis II: 68). In Melville's Partoowye, more than twenty years after Ellis described the deplorable conditions at Fa-re, there are European houses, but they are derelict. In his commodious and pleasant house, thatched in the Polynesian style, not only does Deacon Po-Po have no bedrooms, but also there is no untoward behavior, except possibly on the part of Dr. Long Ghost, but the daughter of the house is well equipped to deflate amorous overtures from him.

Po-Po's family attend church at Taloo; unlike the New England frame house mission chapel in Papeetee, it is made of coral. Melville mostly chooses not to touch up his sources on this occasion – all agree it is "one of the best constructed and handsomest chapels in the south seas" – except to note that, on a first impression, "the tall spectre of a pulpit look[ed] anything but cheerful" (297). But this autochthonous building offers, if only for afternoon service on a weekday, a discernibly indigenous form of service. The missionary begins with a short prayer, a hymn is sung, and then the Tahitians take over:

> Communicants rise in their places, and exhort in pure Tahitian, and with wonderful tone and gesture. And among them all, Deacon Po-Po, though he talked most, was the one you would have liked best to hear. Much would I have given to have understood some of his impassioned bursts; when he tossed his arms overhead, stamped, scowled, and glared, till he looked like the very Angel of Vengeance. (298)

Po Po is *mickonaree* but he is no less Tahitian for that. Many tourists visiting the South Pacific today find scenes like this hard to take. "The singing is lovely," one hears, "but the churches are so lavish and the people so poor ... " What Melville describes, yet may not himself fully see, is that Christianity is nonetheless a way of continuing to be profoundly Polynesian. We do not overhear the deacon's sermon, but it is likely to be more radically syncretic than Melville imagines, for the author sides with Dr. Long Ghost's demurral: "Deluded man!" sighed the doctor, ... "I fear he takes the fanatical view of the subject" (298). But the "stamping, scowling and glaring" he saw and described are still discernible features of traditional Polynesian oratory, and it is by no means impossible that the theological point in question might have concerned whose ancestor first prophesied the coming of the missionaries, or some other accommodation of the new to the old as surprising and extravagant as the decayed temple of Pomare.

If beachcombing characterizes Melville's practice in writing *Typee*, the more appropriate term for that familiar, genial, and freebooting style in *Omoo* would have to be conversion. It is another "crossing the beach" word, and has to do with the turning of a familiar form to an unfamiliar purpose, or an unfamiliar form to a familiar purpose.

In the Pacific, it is closer to the conversion of currencies than the conversion of heathens, and has a whiff of the improper about it, as the cheeky conversion of another's property is a specialty of Dr. Long Ghost, not to mention the semi-plagiarizing author. And conversion certainly has a future in Melville's work. In *Moby-Dick*, Pomare's woven temple is the precursor of the visionary "Bower of the Arsicades," where the beached skeleton of a sperm whale is surrounded by a living temple of vines and flowers in a manner that suggests that the very pulse of the universe is to weave this into that. In Melville's early Pacific novels, ambiguity is fundamentally a quality of objects – cannibals, Christians, whales. In our effort to know them, it may seem they have something to hide, and that their inmost truth either becomes decipherable through an ethnocentric reduction or hovers beyond our interrogative reach. The beachcomber, by contrast, acts in the absence of any mastering perspective, turning this to that, making do with imperfect translations and partial knowledge, forming the creole of the beach. Conversion is a flexible and pragmatic principle of style where rightness means fitting in, means blending with the environment – means, Tommo is alarmed to discover, becoming tattooed. It is not a principle to rely on. Either Dr. Long Ghost's charm gets him into Queen Pomare's Palace or his cheek gets him thrown out. He won't know in advance. But he will need what a later book calls confidence, and those he encounters will need what that later book calls trust. What I have called conversion is largely a principle of light and sweetness in Melville's "Pacific paradise" novels, but perhaps the reason it would become dark and malign on the *Fidèle* and on the *San Dominick* may be read in the Bower of Arsicades, where ambiguity ceases to be a simply a property of objects in nature or behavior in culture but is woven into the material of signification itself.

REFERENCES AND FURTHER READING

Anderson, Charles Roberts. *Melville in the South Seas.* New York: Columbia University Press, 1939.

Borofsky, Robert, ed. *Remembrance of Pacific Pasts.* Honolulu: University of Hawai'i Press, 2000.

Calder, Alex. "The Temptations of William Pascoe Crook: An Experience of Cultural Difference in the Marquesas, 1796–98." *Journal of Pacific History* 31.2 (1996): 144–61.

——. "Melville's *Typee* and the Perception of Culture." *Representations* 67 (1999): 27–43.

Dening, Greg. *Beach Crossings.* Melbourne: Miegunyah Press, 2004.

——. *Islands and Beaches.* Honolulu: University of Hawai'i Press, 1980.

——. *Performances.* Melbourne: Melbourne University Press, 1996.

Ellis, William. *Polynesian Researches.* 2 vols. 1829 Rpt. London: Dawsons, 1967.

Herbert, T. Walter. *Marquesan Encounters.* Cambridge, MA: Harvard University Press, 1980.

Howe, K. R. *Where the Waves Fall.* Honolulu: University of Hawai'i Press, 1991.

Porter, David. *Journal of a Cruise Made to the Pacific Ocean.* 2 vols. 1822. Rpt. Upper Saddle River, NJ: Gregg Press, 1970.

Robarts, Edward. *The Marquesan Journal of Edward Robarts*. Ed. Greg Dening. Canberra: Australian National University Press, 1974.

Rodgers, Richard and Oscar Hammerstein. *South Pacific*. New York: Williamson Music, 1949.

Said, Edward. *Orientalism*. Harmondsworth: Penguin, 1991.

Samson, John. *White Lies: Melville's Narrative of Facts*. Ithaca, NY: Cornell University Press, 1989.

Stewart, C. S. *A Visit to the South Seas in the U.S. Ship* Vincennes, *During the Years 1829 and 1830*. New York: Praeger Publishers, 1970.

8

Atlantic Trade

Hester Blum

In an arresting moment in *Moby-Dick*, the crew of the *Pequod* is described as an "Anacharsis Clootz deputation from all the isles of the sea, and all the ends of the earth" (121). Clootz (or, more commonly, Cloots) was a figure of some interest to Melville. A Prussian baron who fancied himself the "Orator of the Human Race" and ardently supported the French Revolution, Cloots (1755–94) was best known for marshaling before the French National Assembly a group of people who represented multiple nationalities and ethnicities. His aim was to demonstrate the heterogeneous group's shared humanity in support of the cause of a Universal Republic. The playful comparison of Ahab's sailors to Cloots's "deputation" of humanity therefore suggests the serious notion that the varied crew of the *Pequod* is a model of collectivity – both socially and politically – much as the word "crew" itself is a singular noun that represents plurality. Melville invokes Cloots on two other occasions in his writing, in both instances using the figure to stand for a variegated collection of human types. A party of sailors in *Billy Budd*, for one, comprises "such an assortment of tribes and complexions as would have well fitted them to be marched up by Anacharsis Cloots before the bar of the first French Assembly as representatives of the human race" (43). In *The Confidence-Man* the "piebald parliament" or "Anacharsis Cloots congress" that is the ship's passenger manifest includes, in small part, "Northern speculators and Eastern philosophers; English, Irish, German, Scotch, Danes; ... slaves, black, mulatto, quadroon; modish young Spanish Creoles, and old-fashioned French Jews; Mormons and Papists ..." (9).

In each of these literary works Melville's own "Anacharsis Cloots deputation" is assembled aboard a ship, rather than before a national congress. This is striking for several reasons. For one, in Melville's time seamen were commonly thought to be profane, licentious, and at variance with the ideals of humanity, and of humanism in particular. As such, Melville's association of sailors with the Universal Republicans of Cloots's vision serves to elevate them to participatory citizenship, a status not automatically associated with working seamen until the American reform movements of the mid-nineteenth century made sailors into figures of sympathetic interest. Further, the Cloots comparison makes the ship analogous to the world – or a microcosm of the world, as many critics have observed of the *Pequod* (as well as of the *Neversink* in *White-Jacket; or, The World in a Man-of-War*, among other ships in Melville's fiction). The most important implication of the comparison of ships' crews to Cloots's delegation, though, arises from Melville's recognition of the unusual diversity of races, ethnicities, and nationalities aboard ships in the eighteenth- and nineteenth-century Atlantic world. On the *Pequod*, for example, the crew includes Tashtego, a Gay-Head Indian; Daggoo, an African; Queequeg, a Pacific Islander; as well as briefly noted French, Lascar, Tahitian, Spanish, Dutch, Sicilian, Malaysian, Maltese, and Icelandic sailors. Variation characterizes the crews in Melville's other nautical fiction, and even though the attention in *The Confidence-Man* is directed towards the passengers of the *Fidèle* rather than the crew, the general heterogeneity of the Mississippi waterway is best suggested by the Confidence Man himself, whose various personae include a black beggar, a white herb doctor, and a "cosmopolitan."

Melville's sharp focus on the racial and ethnic variety of mariners on late eighteenth- and nineteenth-century ships makes visible how much maritime labor differed from contemporary sites of wage labor on land. At sea, in spite of the putatively homogeneous national ranks of merchant and military service, the widespread operation of piracy and press gangs routinely produced heterogeneous crews. Thus, for example, Melville's Israel Potter, after complaining that as an American he has been unfairly "kidnapped into the [British] naval service" through impressment, can be told "[t]here's no Englishmen in the English fleet. All foreigners. You may take their own word for it" (*IP* 84). To "take their own word," presumably, would mean listening to a Babel of foreign accents. Further, rapid turnover of labor while in port, whether due to desertion, ill treatment, or caprice, meant that few ships returned home with the crew that inaugurated a given voyage. Why did the maritime labor force present such a miscellaneous face to the world? The answer is crucial to understanding both Melville's invocation of Cloots's vision of universal brotherhood, and, more broadly, the state of Atlantic trade in the aftermath of the Age of Revolution. Much of the trade in the Atlantic was legitimate, as merchant and colonial enterprises (both private and state-sponsored) enjoyed robust success in the eighteenth and nineteenth centuries. Yet Melville's interests, and thus the interests of this essay, are directed more toward the distasteful and illegal aspects of this commerce, which in their own way also experienced robust success. The Atlantic trade of the late eighteenth and nineteenth centuries was a vigorous marketplace of oppositional freedoms and fetters: it included the Middle Passage, or reverse terms slave trade; impressment, or forced naval servitude; privateering, or state-sponsored piracy; renegade piracy; and North African Barbary piracy. This sprawling global trade created unprecedented opportunities for movement, but slaves and, to a lesser extent, sailors experienced the often brutal (and brutally paradoxical) fact of repressive confinement while engaged in an expansive enterprise.

And at a time when Enlightenment and Revolution were making possible the rise of nationalism (or the participation in what Benedict Anderson has memorably called "imagined communities"), as well as a radical reconfiguration of the categories of "human" and "citizen," slaves and sailors were subjected routinely to the punitive laws of nations, without being granted their protection.

In Melville's fiction these tensions are made manifest primarily in three works: *Israel Potter*, "Benito Cereno," and *Billy Budd*. These works are set, provocatively, in the last decades of the eighteenth century. Critics who have taken note of this temporal shift to the eighteenth century have argued that Melville displaces his fiction to earlier historical moments in order to provide commentary on contemporary problems (see, in particular, Gilje; Sundquist). Perhaps the most striking example of such displacement is "Benito Cereno," a story adapted from the real-life American captain Amasa Delano's *Narrative of Voyages and Travels, in the Northern and Southern Hemispheres* (1817). As many critics have argued, notably Eric Sundquist in *To Wake the Nations*, Melville's reimagination of the details of Delano's encounter with a troubled ship transforms the narrative into a warning about the consequences of slavery and revolt in the New World. Sundquist points out that Melville's version of Delano's story is moved back in time to the Age of Revolution, and writes that Melville's interest in Babo's revolutionary consciousness "would surely have reminded readers of mounting anxiety not only over expansion alone but over the risk that present Caribbean nations would be the cradle for revolutions aimed at the United States and its southern slave economy" (Sundquist 172).

Yet to date there has been little if any attention to how the broader world of the Atlantic, and the Atlantic trades, might have guided Melville's literary impulses beyond "Benito Cereno." The same can no longer be said of the Pacific sphere. Compelling scholarship on the South Seas has recently reinvigorated the field of Melville studies – and the study of nineteenth-century America more generally – in its discussions of cultural encounter, ecology, globalism, and colonialism in the Pacific. In the wake of these studies, renewed attention to the Atlantic world would offer much to scholars and other readers of Melville. In fact, the larger circumstance of the extraordinary diversity of the Atlantic trades has been a source of enormous critical interest recently, particularly in the growing literary and historical fields of Atlantic or transatlantic studies, as well as the geographical and theoretical space that Paul Gilroy has named the Black Atlantic. The work of historians such as Marcus Rediker, Peter Linebaugh, Linda Colley, David Armitage, Bernard Bailyn, and C. L. R. James has been especially foundational to this field. In the American literary imagination of the late eighteenth and nineteenth centuries, the Atlantic world offered various degrees of freedom, opportunity, and alternatives to chattel slavery. Both Atlantic and Black Atlantic scholarship therefore seeks to redress the national limitations of histories that neglect the broader contexts of the maritime world that shaped those nations. In turn, this scholarship enlarges the definition of "transatlanticism," which has usually referred to Anglo-American relations. Melville's fictions address these issues directly and powerfully, although Atlantic and Black Atlantic scholars have yet to deal with his work substantively. The time is ripe for a return passage, as it were, to the Atlantic of Melville's fiction.

What follows therefore suggests how much Melville's writing has to offer to scholarship on the Atlantic world, and how much Melville's own readers would, in turn, benefit from an expansive understanding of the Atlantic trades. While his relationship to the relatively local events of his lifetime – the fallout from the Mexican War, abolition and the Civil War, financial panic, Indian removal – has earned critical notice in recent years, Melville's literary attention to the volatile late eighteenth century transatlantic world has been overlooked. This essay aims to redress this oversight, offering close readings of *Israel Potter*, "Benito Cereno," and *Billy Budd* within the context of Atlantic trade. *Redburn*, the novel most explicitly about legitimate Atlantic trade, merits attention as well. Understanding Melville's interest in Atlantic trade in the Age of Revolution enables new readings not only of texts whose setting fits neatly into the late eighteenth century, but of Melville's work more generally. For example, the image offered in *Moby-Dick* of laboring sailors as "Isolatoes" who are nevertheless "federated along one keel" (121) has a different resonance when placed in dialogue with the eighteenth-century rise of nations, and of nationalism, described in the work of Benedict Anderson and others. Seamen have always been international figures. Yet certain conditions of the maritime world in the late eighteenth century – specifically, the slave trade, piracy, impressment, and the rise of nationalism – sorely tested sailors' ability to move freely throughout the Atlantic world.

Israel Potter and the Tides of the Atlantic

Slighted by most readers and teachers of Melville, *Israel Potter: His Fifty Years of Exile* (serialized 1854–5; book edition 1855) is a brisk narrative of the life of a pauper who, Zelig-like, is present for many of the signal moments in the Age of Revolution. He fights at Bunker Hill, meets Benjamin Franklin in Paris, and falls victim to press gangs. In Melville's version of the biography, Potter meets King George III, John Paul Jones, and Ethan Allen, too. The historical Israel Potter was a sailor and marksman from Massachusetts who fought on land and at sea, in both the Revolution and the War of 1812, and on the sides of both the United States (willingly) and Britain (unwillingly). Impoverished and debilitated from a long "exile" from America, Potter produced a narrative of his life, which was published in 1824 as *Life and Remarkable Adventures of Israel R. Potter*. Melville, who claims to have recovered a "tattered copy" of the original narrative, "forlornly published on sleazy gray paper," revises and elaborates upon Potter's life in a work published serially in *Putnam's Monthly Magazine* (IP vii).

The lively incidents and encounters that Melville inserts into Potter's original history all reinforce the problem of national identification – and affiliation – that marks his late eighteenth-century world. Potter's narrative is a story of the vicissitudes of Atlantic life and trade, and their effect on a man of lowly status whose life would never register in the "volumes of Sparks" (viii) (i.e., the hagiographies of Founding Fathers penned by *North American Review* editor Jared Sparks). As an American citizen unable to claim the "protection" of his nation, whether at sea or on foreign shores, Potter discovers that his rights are neither inalienable nor independent of the will of sovereign states. *Israel Potter* thus curiously makes the experience of a common man both conditional on his status as American, and exempt from any of the political or commercial protection such national affiliation would provide.

The son of a farmer in western Massachusetts, Melville's Potter takes advantage of the opportunities offered by the Atlantic trades in order to secure his independence from an inflexible father and an unfaithful sweetheart. Israel goes to sea, "the asylum for the generous distressed," where, writes Melville, "man's private grief is lost like a drop" in a "watery immensity of terror." The course of Israel's travels immediately upon shipping illustrates the volatility of the Atlantic world. His sloop is bound from Providence to the West Indies, carrying lime. When the lime ignites and destroys the ship, Israel and the crew are rescued by a Dutch ship, bound from Eustacia to Holland. Before Israel has time to wonder what awaits him in Europe, an American brig appears and agrees to convey him to Antigua. From there Israel goes to Puerto Rico; after "[o]ther rovings" he goes whaling from Nantucket to Africa and the Western Islands (10–11). This experience predates his contributions as a marksman at Bunker Hill – marksmanship he unwittingly prepared for as a harpooneer on a whaleship and as a hunter in Canada. Israel's role in service of the American revolution, it can be argued, was made possible by his role in the broader Atlantic trades. For in light of his sailing experience, Israel is quick to volunteer for naval duty after Bunker Hill, and this volunteerism leads to incarceration on a British prison ship and encounters with English renegades. All of this action takes place in two early chapters of Potter's narrative, and the variable nature of his experience only increases over the course of the fifty years of his refugee life. Melville highlights throughout what Paul Gilje calls "the adaptability of the common sailor" (260).

For the mobility of Potter's Atlantic experience does not derive from personal agency: rather, Israel's sovereign identity is in thrall to the capriciousness of both nature and nations. This instability is characteristic of maritime life. If sailors were lucky enough to avoid wreckage or other loss due to weather, they faced the more dire threats of impressment or piracy. More significantly, eighteenth- and early nineteenth-century American seamen were issued "protections," government documents that testified to their citizenship (figure 8.1). These documents were supposed to keep the individual seaman free from forcible impressment (usually into the British Navy), and were thought to offer some small degree of security from privateers or pirates. In practice, however, protections were often useless. They were easily forged, and even more easily *accused* of being forged by sailors desperate to claim national shelter. Narratives written by sailors during this period frequently remark upon the flexibility of the protections, usually with sardonic humor. When Israel Potter, for example, tries to claim protection from an English press gang by advertising his American citizenship, he is told, "There's no Englishmen in the English fleet. All foreigners. You may take their own word for it"

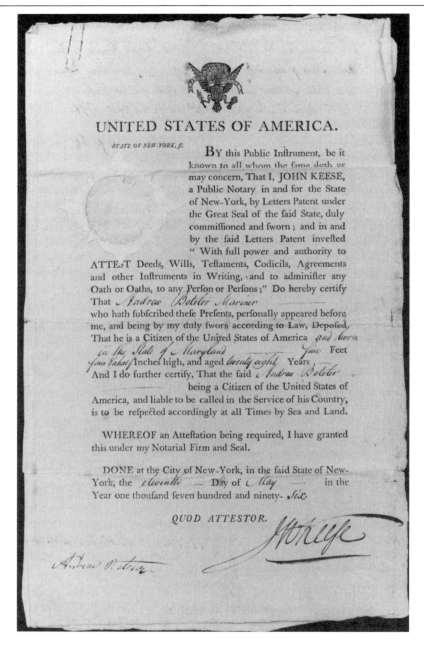

Figure 8.1 Notary Protection Certificate, issued to mariner Andrew Boteler by New York State, May 17, 1796. Like other Seamen's Protections, this document was designed to affirm the citizenship of an American sailor, although in practice many protections went unhonored. Image courtesy of the G. W. Blunt White Library, Mystic Seaport, Mystic, CT.

(84). The press gang member's impertinent reply to Israel's appeal underscores how little value American protection holds in the Atlantic world.

Even though America neither claims nor protects Israel Potter in his fifty years of impoverished wandering abroad, Melville ironically emphasizes that Potter himself asserts a peculiarly American identity, one that by definition is multiethnic or transnational in its implications. Of particular interest is the expedient (if odd) association of Potter and his fellow Revolutionary actors with New World Natives. Melville's invocation of this autochthonous privilege can be seen in Israel Potter's sense that he is a "trespassing Pequod Indian" while in England, longing to return to his native soil (164). This quality is on best display, however, in the person of the Revolutionary naval hero John Paul Jones (himself a native Scotsman). Described as "like an Iroquois," or a "disinherited Indian Chief in European clothes," Jones has a "rustic, barbaric jauntiness" to match his "tawny" complexion (56). Like any transatlantic sailor, Jones has shared his hammock with a Cloots deputation's worth of fellow seamen, including a "full-blooded Congo" (62). Strikingly, Melville describes America as the "Paul Jones of nations": "intrepid, unprincipled, reckless, predatory, with boundless ambition, civilized in externals but a savage at heart" (120). Ethan Allen, another Revolutionary hero whom Melville inserts into Potter's narrative, shares these extra-national qualities: he is "frank; bluff; companionable as a Pagan; convivial; a Roman; hearty as a harvest. His spirit was essentially western" (149).

For all the outlandishness of these exemplary American heroes, they prove wonderfully adaptable. That is, the qualities of jaunty rowdiness that mark John Paul Jones and Ethan Allen as special also aid Israel Potter, the anonymous common sailor. One of the more memorable scenes in *Israel Potter* enacts this circumstance. When a freak accident at sea lands Potter improbably aboard a British man-of-war, he must blend in with the crew or face punitive measures. Israel wanders from mess to mess, boldly affecting a pseudonym and the status of a member of the maintop, and is initially dismissed by all. But when he proves his cheerful and able seamanship in the maintop, the officer of the deck notes with surprise that he does "seem to belong to the main-top, after all." Never relinquishing his spirit nor his flexibility of identity, Israel, now "Peter Perkins," responds, " 'I always told you so, sir, . . . though at first, you remember, sir, you would not believe it" (141). Potter's mobility is both a geographical and a constitutional fact, but in this case mobility does not mean freedom, *per se*. The sailor's career, Melville writes,

> signally illustrates the idea, that since all human affairs are subject to organic disorder; since they are created in, and sustained by, a sort of half-disciplined chaos; hence, he who in great things seeks success, must never wait for smooth water; which never was, and never will be; but with what straggling method he can, dash with all his derangements at his object, leaving the rest to Fortune. (114)

The conditions of the Atlantic world in the late eighteenth and early nineteenth centuries created the opportunity for such fluidity of identity and affiliation, but sailors seldom had the chance to take advantage of this fluidity through sovereign action. In making sailors emblematic of a certain kind of flexible citizenship, but disallowing them from enjoying its benefits, Melville remarks on the conflict between the promise of any declaration of independence, and the "half-disciplined chaos" that arrests such efforts.

"Benito Cereno" and the Specter of the Atlantic

If *Israel Potter* shows the difficulties faced by free white sailors in securing a sovereign identity in the late eighteenth-century Atlantic world, then "Benito Cereno" illustrates the ghastly conditions for African slaves. Slavery, in turn, reconfigured the hierarchical expectations of every other actor in the Atlantic trades. For while "Benito Cereno" is set off the Pacific coast of Chile, the world of the Atlantic is fundamental to the action of the story, as well as to the American captain Amasa Delano's abject failure to recognize the slave revolt that has occurred on the Spanish ship he encounters. The transatlantic slave trade quietly governs the story. This trade was still legally practiced by both Spain and the United States in 1799, the year in which "Benito Cereno" is set. Although forms of slavery had existed for thousands of years, the enslavement of Africans by Europeans beginning in the fifteenth century had an enormity – and a lasting effect on Africa, Europe, and the Americas – that can hardly be calculated. Millions of African slaves, outnumbering European immigrants, permanently altered the face of the New World; further, slavery initiated the rise of capitalism in the Americas, the ravages of colonialism in Africa, and the moral and political movement known as abolitionism. The economic circuit of slavery throughout the Atlantic involved virtually every world industry, and every facet of production, consumption, service and transportation.

In "Benito Cereno," references to the slave trades, and to the piratical activity that was a byproduct of the Atlantic trades, range broadly to cover the first moment of European contact with the Americas, through to the issues contemporary with Melville's 1855 composition of the story. The course that Babo (the Senegalese slave who orchestrates the uprising) wishes to follow in planning his slave revolt is traced dimly throughout the story, and its negative inspiration – arrestingly, the voyages of Christopher Columbus – provides a most trenchant reflection on the Atlantic slave trade and its facilitation of colonialism. Columbus, who initiated New World colonization and slavery, is the Ur-figure of Atlantic trade. His importance to "Benito Cereno" is suggested throughout the story in the revisions that Melville makes to the historical Delano's account, as many critics have noted. For one, Melville changes the date of the story to 1799; this date more closely allies "Benito Cereno" with the famous Haitian Revolution, which began as a slave revolt led by Toussaint L'Ouverture, and led to the first free black republic in the New World. (The historical Delano's *Narrative of Voyages and Travels* describes the incident as taking place in 1805.) At the time of the revolt, Haiti was known as

St. Domingue (an allusion Melville makes in changing the name of the Spanish ship from *Tryal* to *San Dominick*), a name given by the French colonial rule. Yet the island was also called by its Spanish colonial name, Santo Domingo – and was thought to be one of the first landing places of Christopher Columbus in the New World. Columbus, of course, sailed under the flag of Spain (see Sundquist; Franklin; Karcher; and Emery).

The most dramatic signal of Columbus's importance to "Benito Cereno," though, is the story's repeated invocation of the injunction "FOLLOW YOUR LEADER." The phrase first appears painted on the side of the *San Dominick*, under the ship's figurehead, which itself is shrouded. Only in the deposition is it revealed that the original figurehead, Columbus, has been replaced by the cannibalized skeleton of the Spanish ship- and slave-owner, who was killed in the initial revolt. Therefore the phrase "FOLLOW YOUR LEADER," inscribed under the figurehead by Babo, serves as a warning to those who would resist the slaves' rebellion. And yet, the absent Columbus – replaced by a skeletonized slave trader – still serves as a spectral "leader" that the American captain, and by extension all Americans, may choose to follow. In extrapolating the figurative meaning of Columbus's New World colonialism to its dramatically violent termination, Melville invites scrutiny of the lasting effects of the Atlantic slave trade on mid-century America. This problem informs the final invocation of the phrase "FOLLOW YOUR LEADER," which occurs after the mastermind of the slave revolt, Babo, has been decapitated. His piked head, "that hive of subtlety," stands watch over Benito Cereno who – three months after Babo's execution – "borne on the bier, did, indeed, follow his leader" (*PT* 117). Cereno's seeming authority has in fact been the "ghost" of command, and Melville suggests that *any* authority in the colonial Atlantic world is artificially propped up by the mass of African slaves who, like Babo, were thought to be bodies without heads.

Babo's ritualistic shaving of Cereno best conveys this sham of power; the shaving scene is a "juggling play" whose meaning Delano is incapable of conning. Indeed, the scene's invocation of seminal events of the Atlantic world in the Age of Revolution is particularly tantalizing: the Spanish Inquisition, the Terror of the French Revolution, Catholic insurrection in England, and American chattel slavery are all invoked directly or indirectly. The settees upon which Cereno sits appear as "inquisitor's racks," and the armchair Babo uses for his work seems like a "grotesque engine of torment." Delano's liberal faith is almost shaken during the scene when he temporarily fancies that "in the black he saw a headsman, and in the white a man at the block." Cereno, bloodied by the razor, appears to Delano as terrified as "James the First of England," whose authority was threatened by the Catholic terror plot of Guy Fawkes. Finally, Delano's paternalistic enjoyment of the spectacle of Babo in the "natural" role of the barber – "singularly pleasing to behold" – evokes for him his "old weakness for negroes." We are told that when at leisure at home, Delano takes a "rare satisfaction in sitting at his door, watching some free man of color at his work or play" (82–8). The implication is that to Delano, all actions performed by blacks, whether enslaved or free, are for the general comfort and pleasure of whites. But whereas critics have read this scene's explicit evocations of the "revolutionary paradigm[s]" of "Jacobin terror, the Inquisition, and slave vengeance" as direct commentary on contemporary events informing Melville's composition of the tale (Sundquist 159), it may be productive to think of these references as decoys for national, religious, and racial identification. That is, the confidence that Delano places in his blind notions of expected behavior is betrayed doubly: by the individual actions of Babo, and by a broader Atlantic world which by definition is hostile to any fixed notions of national or racial identity.

Melville underscores the Atlantic presence by alluding to the Middle Passage, though in submerged and ironically inverted terms. After the revolt, Babo commanded that the ship be taken to "any negro countries" on the Pacific coast of South America, but as there are none, he insists on a "return" to Senegal. What is striking here is that Babo and the rest of the cargo of slaves were not imported directly from Africa – not the "raw" Africans of Delano's imagination – but instead were in the process of being transported from one colonial South American port to another, from Valparaiso, Chile, to Callao, Peru. The *San Dominick*'s voyage never included a Cape Horn passage, as Delano had been told. Babo's aim, in fact, is to retrace the Middle Passage in a return home. Yet despite his desire to subtract his Atlantic Middle Passage from his experience, Babo is judged, and executed, in a colonial South American court, far from both Senegal and his initial Atlantic passage. Melville suggests, then, the failure of African agency even in as bold a figure as Babo.

Another activity in "Benito Cereno" likewise illustrates the failure of sovereign authority: specifically, piracy shapes the expectations that Delano, and by extension his American readers, bring to the situation aboard the *San Dominick*. Piracy is a constant in the maritime world, and it is strongly affiliated with the slave trade in several ways. For one, the *de jure* abolition of the slave trade by many nations in the early nineteenth century meant that the *de facto* continuation of the trade was piratical or extra-legal activity. Delano, in fact, entertains suspicions of piracy from the moment he spots the Spanish ship, which enters a harbor without flying a national flag. Given the "lawlessness and loneliness of the spot," Melville writes, "and the sort of stories, *at that day*, associated with those seas," Delano should have felt uneasy (47; my emphasis). By specifying the temporal remove of "that day," Melville alludes to the late eighteenth century as a time of heightened threat of piracy, especially in uninhabited coastal bays such as the one in which "Benito Cereno" takes place.

Yet while the American captain fears encountering pirates when his ship first enters the bay, it is Delano himself who, provocatively, most successfully practices piracy. Delano's "design" after finally catching on to the slave uprising is to seize the Spanish ship from the control of the rebels, whom Delano sees in "ferocious piratical revolt." In this case, his judgment of the slaves as "piratical" reflects his sense that their behavior is illegal and malicious. But Delano expertly practices a mode of piratical leadership himself when, "the more to encourage the sailors," he tells them that "[the ship] and her cargo, including some gold and silver, were worth upwards of ten thousand doubloons." He promises his sailors that if they successfully take the ship, "no small part should be theirs" (101–2). By inspiring his men with the promise of booty, and by promising to share the wealth, Delano enacts the brutal yet relatively democratic structures of power that Marcus Rediker has identified in pirate captains of the eighteenth-century Atlantic.

To see "Benito Cereno," then, as a story about the broader Atlantic world rather than the more specific tensions between America, the Caribbean, and Old World Europe, is to dissolve the racial strictures and frameworks of power that cause Delano's misrecognition in the first place into a grander transnational scheme. In turn, the precariousness of national and individual sovereignty in the Atlantic world suggests that the Atlantic can be a specter present even on the Pacific shores of South America. And this conflation is ultimately mandated by Melville's story itself: when the "mask" is finally torn away from the faces of all three main actors in the story, "past, present, and future seemed one" (98). The conditions of the Atlantic trade can collapse both temporal and national identification, and "Benito Cereno" demonstrates the dangers of clinging too familiarly to such rigid perspectives.

Billy Budd and the Rights of Man

Melville returned to the world of the Atlantic in the Age of Revolution in his final fiction, *Billy Budd*. A twenty-one-year-old sailor on an inward-bound English merchant ship, Billy Budd is impressed into service in the British Navy. The time is "the close of the last decade of the eighteenth century," when the British Navy is engaged in the conflicts against France that would soon develop into the Napoleonic Wars. Billy Budd is described as the prototypical "Handsome Sailor," a man whose "strength and beauty," "comeliness and power," were evident in both his physical and moral natures (43–4). He has one physical flaw, however: he stutters when under duress. Once aboard the naval ship, Billy is targeted by the sinister master-at-arms, Claggart, and is accused of plotting mutiny. When he is unable to refute the charges verbally, Billy reflexively strikes Claggart a mortal blow. Despite the sympathies of the upright Captain Vere, Billy is convicted by a drumhead court and is hanged. The story has been read by critics primarily in three ways. First, it has been seen as a Christian allegory, in which a redemptive Billy is a martyr to the stern law of the Father (Coffler). Other scholars have seen the novella as a meditation on the justice of Vere's decision to obey the letter of a human law, rather than the spirit of natural law (Sten). The third dominant strain of criticism, which addresses sexuality in *Billy Budd*, has been sparked by Eve Kosofsky Sedgwick's pioneering work in the field of queer theory: Sedgwick exposes how the murder of Claggart reveals a homosexual panic within the homosocial world of the ship (see Martin as well).

Yet the lingering attention paid to Billy Budd's body and its spontaneous conduct must also be understood in the context of the novella's evocative first line: it is "the time before steamships" (43). The advent of steam reduced to a significant extent the demand for a laboring class of sailors; in the time before steamships, Budd's body, and those of his fellow crew members, were the engines that propelled the sailing ships and the global economy. Theirs was a fleet "wholly under canvas," Melville wrote, "no steam-power, its innumerable sails and thousands of cannon, everything in short, worked by muscle alone" (59). Impressment was the foul derivative of an industry that demanded extraordinary bodily sacrifice. In the mid-seventeenth century the British Royal Navy acquired the power to press sailors into service; when naval vessels were short-handed, bands known as press gangs would scour port taverns and merchant ships in order forcibly to recruit sailors into naval service. Nor was the press confined to British citizens, for foreign nationals and British colonials faced impressment well into the nineteenth century. Such sailors had little recourse – although most protested violently – and the Navy continued to struggle to attract willing sailors. Conditions on naval ships were wretched, with inadequate food, violent disciplinary and labor requirements, and low wages. Until the 1797 Spithead uprising, for example, naval wages had not been raised for a century. Sailors' own narratives affirm the oft-cited observation of Samuel Johnson, that

> no man will be a sailor who has contrivance enough to get himself into a jail; for being in a ship is being in jail with the chance of being drowned.... A man in jail has more room, better food, and commonly better company. (Quoted in Rediker 258)

Billy Budd is himself likened to a jailed bird when impressed; he offers no objection, for "any demur would have been as idle as the protest of a goldfinch popped into a cage" (45).

The analogy to imprisonment is important, since impressment calls into question the very categories of "citizen" and "free" that were brought into public debate in the Age of Revolution. *Billy Budd* makes this debate hard to avoid, as its studied references make clear. Budd is impressed onto a seventy-four-gun ship called *Bellipotent*, or "mighty in war"; he is taken off a merchant ship pointedly named the *Rights-of-Man*. The shipowner, an admirer of Thomas Paine, is likened to the Philadelphia magnate Stephen Girard, who named his ships after Voltaire and Diderot; both merchants christen their vessels in the best spirit of transatlantic humanism. Billy Budd's short passage to the *Bellipotent* is punctuated by his dramatic "good-bye" to the *Rights-of-Man*, an act that the recruiting lieutenant takes as a "sly slur at impressment in general." Even though the reader is told that Budd, like Delano in "Benito Cereno," is incapable of dealing in "double meanings and insinuations of any sort," the message is clear (49).

The possibility or threat of covert action takes on a special significance given the historical context of the story. Melville sets the novella in 1797, in the immediate aftermath of two momentous actions taken by sailors of the British Navy: the uprisings at Spithead and the Nore. The first, at Spithead (a roadstead in the English Channel), occurred when thousands of sailors struck for better wages and sailing conditions, as well as the elimination of impressment. The Admiralty, fearing catastrophe, capitulated to many of these demands (although the press was retained) in a gesture of leniency toward a crime – mutiny – usually punished by death. One month later, at the Nore near the Thames estuary, masses of sailors struck again, and this time the British Navy was not so conciliatory. The "Great Mutiny," which Melville describes as "more menacing to England than the contemporary manifestoes and conquering and proselyting armies of the French Directory," was swiftly punished, its ringleader, Richard Parker, hanged from a yardarm. In the aftermath of Spithead and the Nore, a lingering fear of mutiny governs the action of the officers and seamen aboard the *Bellipotent*. Melville is careful to highlight the trans-Channel impulse of the Nore mutiny: it was "ignited into irrational combustion as by live cinders blown across the Channel from France in flames" (54–5).

Hershel Parker has found Melville to be hostile to revolutionary action in *Billy Budd*; he argues that Melville's point of view is that of a "traditionalist, a deeply conservative man apprehensive at the thought that insurrection might shake England" (Parker 109.) Yet *Billy Budd* does not blankly condemn the uprisings, and like much of Melville's fiction, it slyly invites a countervailing view. C. L. R. James, notably, has endorsed this revolutionary viewpoint, recognizing that Melville's fiction represents a "long defense of sailors as a class of workers" (James 91). This sympathy with what has come to be called history "from the ground up" is especially visible in Melville's discussion of the fact that the Spithead and Nore mutinies have been excised from "the libraries" of British naval history. Melville mentions that the British naval historian William James would have preferred to "pass [the mutinies] over did not 'impartiality forbid fastidiousness' " (*BB* 55). But what is lost in "abridg[ing]" such a history of labor uprisings becomes clear in Hayford's and Sealts's commentary to their authoritative 1962 edition of *Billy Budd*. Hayford and Sealts usefully chronicle how Melville used his own (slightly misquoted) notes from the historical source. But Hayford and Sealts record, without comment, the fact that Melville's quotation of James in *Billy Budd* elides a significant part of the original discussion of the mutinies in James's 1860 *Naval History of Great Britain*: "the subject not being an international one, ... we may, consistently with our plan, abridge the account" (quoted in *BB* 146). This line, in which William James refuses to recognize any international importance to the mutinies, is recorded by Melville in his notes, but he does not, significantly, honor it in the text of the novella. In fact, Melville stresses that a trans-Channel current fans the flames of mutiny, a fact of international consequence.

For a "nation" to "abridge" such a story of rebellious uprising would be "natural" and "discreet," Melville writes, just as a *well-constituted individual* refrains from blazoning aught amiss or calamitous in his family" (*BB* 55; my emphasis). The language here is striking, and tricky. It is understandable that one might want to keep family secrets private; but Melville stresses that this urge paradoxically arises from someone "well-constituted." The language of constitutionally guaranteed individual sovereignty is impossible to ignore, and turns the meaning of the observation upside down. It is therefore difficult to read Melville as complicit with the silencing of certain histories, ones which "national pride along with views of policy would fain shade off into the historical background" (55). Neither the domestic limitations of the family, nor the nation, can be fully defended.

In a similar fashion, the story of Billy's execution cannot be contained within the ship that witnessed it, nor the fleet in which it sailed. The narrative of Billy Budd circulates more broadly within the Atlantic world in various formats and genres; these form the "ragged edges" that Melville finds in "[t]ruth uncompromisingly told." Significantly, the random accounts all serve to broaden the Atlantic context of the story far beyond the Royal Navy. For one, a naval chronicle reporting "News from the Mediterranean" gives an account of the affair that finds Billy stabbing Claggart, and reveals that Budd "was no Englishman, but one of those aliens adopting English cognomens whom the present extraordinary necessities of the service have caused to be admitted into it in considerable numbers" (128, 130). Impressment, here, is the "present necessity" that dare not speak its name. Or, while the chronicle account may be false to the narrative that had preceded it, it speaks the truth of an alternative history of forcible servitude in His Majesty's navy during the Age of Revolution. The character of "Billy Budd" found in the naval newspaper was nominally an Englishman while he was laboring for the crown, but could enjoy no national protection or citizenship in death.

Two other versions of Billy Budd's story continue to travel in the maritime world. For one, the spar from which Billy is hanged, "venerated" as if a "piece of the Cross," is tracked by sailors in its wide movement "from dockyard to ship, still pursuing it even when at last reduced to a mere dockyard boom." This relic tells one portion of the narrative, and is the evidence of Budd's sentence. The other account of Budd's story is told in "Billy in the Darbies," a ballad, which was a common genre for seamen's literary production. A poetic "tarry hand" crafts lines that first "circulate among the shipboard crews for a while"; only later is the poem "rudely printed at Portsmouth as a ballad" (131–2). Billy's narrative continues to circulate – and, appropriately, to mutate – in oral and print culture throughout the Atlantic world.

Coda: *Redburn* and the Wealth of Nations

Although *Redburn* (1849) is set in the relatively stable mid-nineteenth century of Melville's own youthful sailing experience, rather than the volatile turn-of-the-century Age of Revolution, it merits brief notice here as a coda to the discussion above. Going to sea in the wake of family disappointments, Wellingborough Redburn finds that the Atlantic offers him no expansive opportunity; his story is a *Bildungsroman* in reverse, for Redburn ends his transatlantic voyage with less money and less knowledge than he began with. Redburn fails to succeed as a sailor, arguably because he is incapable of reinventing himself in the manner demanded by the maritime world. In fact, stasis and fixity are Redburn's first experience of maritime life: he is obsessed with a glass model of a ship that his transatlantic-traveling father had brought home from France by way of Hamburg. The illusion of activity and menace presented by the model ship entrances him, but not until he is "older" does he realize that the glass ship "was not in the slightest danger in the world." Tellingly, the only real motion the glass ship experiences is its symbolic fracture on the very day that Redburn goes to sea, when the "figure-head" falls into the trough of the model's frozen "calamitous sea" (9).

Redburn is a poor reader both of his new circumstances, and of the actual texts at sailors' disposal. He is shocked to discover that instead of pious tracts his shipmates read *The Newgate Calendar* (the infamous annual crime report) and *The Pirate's Own Book*, while others consult mystical "Dream Books" of sham navigation. Redburn has himself brought Adam Smith's tome *The Wealth of Nations*; however, he finds it soporific – there are no *"wages and profits {for his} labor"* – and converts it to an exemplary pillow (87; original emphasis). The guidebook for Liverpool which Redburn's father had assembled in the previous generation proves equally worthless to him, with its radically outdated maps. The lesson Redburn learns from the failure of his father's guidebook, however, has a lasting resonance, and can serve as the best lesson in fluidity offered by the Atlantic trades:

> For the cope-stone of to-day is the corner-stone of to-morrow; and as St. Peter's church was built in great part of the ruins of old Rome, so in all our erections, however imposing, we but form quarries and supply ignoble materials for the grander domes of posterity. (149)

The impermanence of the record offered by guidebooks – and in this instance, Melville clearly means written texts in general – invites a participatory redrafting of the foundational documents of national and individual citizenship.

Whereas his fictions set in the late eighteenth century lament the Atlantic sailor's lack of autonomy, even his victimhood, Melville suggests in *Redburn* that fluidity might be turned to a seaman's advantage in the mid-nineteenth-century maritime world, when sailors had more opportunities for individual agency. Ultimately, Melville's response to the conditions of the Atlantic world in the Age of Revolution finds him substituting linguistic play and interpretive puzzles for the fixity of monuments. Such monuments – whether revolutionary declarations, cenotaphs for unknown soldiers, or legal judgments – have little stable meaning in the maritime world. In the Atlantic trades, individual sovereignty becomes the work of collective exchange.

References and Further Reading

Anderson, Benedict. *Imagined Communities: Reflections on the Origin and Spread of Nationalism.* London: Verso, 1991.

Armitage, David and Michael J. Braddick. *The British Atlantic World, 1500–1800.* Basingstoke: Palgrave Macmillan, 2002.

Bailyn, Bernard. *Atlantic History: Concept and Contours.* Cambridge, MA: Harvard University Press, 2005.

Bolster, W. Jeffrey. *Black Jacks: African American Seamen in the Age of Sail.* Cambridge, MA: Harvard University Press, 1997.

Casarino, Cesare. *Modernity at Sea: Melville, Marx, Conrad in Crisis.* Minneapolis: University of Minnesota Press, 2002.

Coffler, Gail. "Religion, Myth, and Meaning in the Art of *Billy Budd, Sailor*." In *New Essays on*

Billy Budd. Ed. Donald Yannella. Cambridge: Cambridge University Press, 2002. 49–82.

Colley, Linda. *Captives: Britain, Empire, and the World 1600–1850*. London: Pimlico, 2003.

Emery, Allan Moore. " 'Benito Cereno' and Manifest Destiny." *Nineteenth-Century Fiction* 39.1 (1984): 48–68.

Fabian, Ann. *The Unvarnished Truth: Personal Narratives in Nineteenth-Century America*. Berkeley: University of California Press, 2000.

Franklin, H. Bruce. " 'Apparent Symbol of Despotic Command': Melville's *Benito Cereno*." *New England Quarterly* 34.4 (1961): 462–77.

Gilje, Paul A. *Liberty on the Waterfront: American Maritime Culture in the Age of Revolution*. Philadelphia: University of Pennsylvania Press, 2004.

Gilroy, Paul. *The Black Atlantic: Modernity and Double Consciousness*. Cambridge, MA: Harvard University Press, 1995.

James, C. L. R. *Mariners, Renegades, and Castaways: The Story of Herman Melville and the World We Live In*. New York: Schocken Books, 1985.

Karcher, Carolyn L. *Shadow over the Promised Land: Slavery, Race, and Violence in Melville's America*. Baton Rouge: Louisiana State University Press, 1980.

Lemisch, Jesse. *Jack Tar vs. John Bull: The Role of New York's Seamen in Precipitating the Revolution*. New York: Garland, 1997.

Linebaugh, Peter, and Marcus Buford Rediker. *The Many-Headed Hydra: The Hidden History of the Revolutionary Atlantic*. Boston: Beacon Press, 2000.

Martin, Robert K. "Melville and Sexuality." In *The Cambridge Companion to Herman Melville*. Ed. Robert S. Levine. Cambridge: Cambridge University Press, 1998. 186–201.

Parker, Hershel. *Reading* Billy Budd. Evanston, IL: Northwestern University Press, 1990.

Post-Lauria, Sheila. *Correspondent Colorings: Melville in the Marketplace*. Amherst: University of Massachusetts Press, 1996.

Rediker, Marcus. *Between the Devil and the Deep Blue Sea: Merchant Seamen, Pirates, and the Anglo-American Maritime World, 1700–1750*. Cambridge: Cambridge University Press, 1987.

Sedgwick, Eve Kosofsky. *The Epistemology of the Closet*. Berkeley: University of California Press, 1990.

Sten, Christopher W. "Vere's Use of the 'Forms': Means and Ends in *Billy Budd*." *American Literature* 47.1 (1975): 37–51.

Sundquist, Eric J. *To Wake the Nations: Race in the Making of American Literature*. Cambridge, MA: Harvard University Press, 1993.

9

Ancient Lands

Basem L. Ra'ad

A flowery landscape you must come out of to behold. (*Mardi*, Chapter 64)

And yet is the God the native of these bleak rocks. (Emerson, "Experience")

"Look round. Are not here met
Books and that truth no type shall set?" (*Clarel* 2.32.62–3)

Introduction

To appreciate Herman Melville's complex aesthetics, readers who love his seascapes must turn to solid land – and also to the difficult terrain of *Clarel: A Poem and Pilgrimage in the Holy Land* (1876), a verse novel that took more than a decade to complete. Weaving together strands of nature imagery and character types that appear in work after previous work, Melville refashioned them in a final desert setting, so that iconographic objects (Bower, Palm, Spout, Wilderness, Grass, Sand, Stone, Skeleton, Rock, Island, Mountain, Pyramid) are reinterpreted in a suggestive environment, acting as referents, protagonists, or cosmic symbols. The result represents the author's life-summing position on nature and creed. For Melville, paradoxically, beliefs become a product of barrenness, rather than the comforting myths of greenness.

This Melville aesthetic finds its new/old home in the "Holy Land" (that is, Palestine and its environs) because, as the "source" of Western religious traditions, it is the place to negotiate issues of faith. Since its beginnings in the early seventeenth century, the US used the "Holy Land" or "Canaan" as a model to build and image itself, its founders adopting biblical typologies to explain their errand of establishing a "new Israel" or "New Jerusalem" in a "promised land" whose native people, or Canaanites, are unworthy pagans and enemies of God. In the nineteenth century, simultaneously with intensified exploration worldwide and increased travel to the Eastern Mediterranean, emerged a phenomenon called sacred geography, a type of travel writing intended to verify scriptural accounts in response to the debilitating impact of science on religious certainties. In culture and art, the US re-reflected itself in actual travel accounts, in visual and moral – even imperial – assumptions about the ancient world. (See Davis; Obenzinger; Ra'ad "Review"; and Long.) Mark Twain's *Innocents Abroad, or The New Pilgrims' Progress* (1869) presents a comic perspective on this obsessive and serviceable identification. *Clarel* is a serious epic treatment of matters related to American identity, to belief and doubt, to faith and science, and other controversies in Western thought. Rather than being an isolated product of Melville's mind, the poem represents a summative landscape: the most mature, perhaps definitive, expression of his religious, political, existential, and aesthetic views.

How do the landscapes visited in his various works relate to each other? Melville's interest in the Eastern Mediterranean and Levant (Palestine and Egypt specifically), like his attraction to Polynesia as a model idyllic green state, comes from his early questions about America – and his conclusion that the hope America offered has been "squandered" (*C* 4.21.156; cf. *M* 512), contrary to the pervasive optimism that celebrated the ax and the railroad. In contrast to grey Europe, Polynesia stood for a lost paradise, or an easy unconscious mythology, America for the promise of a fresh start and an essentiality in landscape and meaning, both eventually desolated by human deeds. Melville goes to the Old World to search the barrenness that gave rise to its belief system. In the process, he redefines traditional typology, its formative meaning of "desolation," by inverting it: the desolation is not, as previously thought, nature-inherent, but is human-generated and human-hearted. Natural blankness or barrenness is the primal, original condition on which verdure grows. So, by way of his American search, Melville also probes the myth-making mentality – in its variety of forms from the naïve to the obsessive – that tries to lend greenness to barrenness.

Two Hieroglyphic Scenes

Dotted throughout Melville's works are natural scenes of greenness and aridity that are particularly intriguing and pregnant with suggestions: the amphitheater of "universal," "perpetual verdure" in *Typee* (49,194), in both places dazzlingly contrasted to the "white thatch"; *Mardi*'s "Center of many Circumferences" (Chapter 79); the Arsacides bower in *Moby-Dick* (Chapter 102); "this American Enceladus" in *Pierre* (346); "Yon rock" in *Clarel* (2.30–2.31); the "solitary Date Palm mid-way in preci-pice" identified in 1857 (*J* 84), which first appears as "the solitary trunk of a palm" in *Mardi* (126), then fixates the famishing traveler George Lloyd Stephens in *Redburn*, and finally becomes a central emblem in *Clarel* (3.25–3.30); the spar from which Billy Budd is hanged that sailors turn into a "monument." These are concentrated physical and mental landscapes, foci of attention, invested with representational and referential values – acting as "doubloons" or, I hesitate to say religiously, "relics."

Here are two such expressive sites, one from Polynesia and the other from the "Holy Land."

In "A Bower in the Arsacides," Ishmael explains how he gained his "exact knowledge" of the leviathan's bone structure by viewing the skeleton of a great sperm whale in King Tranquo's Pupella glen. The image of a whale found "dead and stranded, with his head against a cocoa-nut tree, whose plumage-like, tufted droopings seemed his verdant jet" (449) merges two primal objects – a green, symmetrical palm tree and a blanched, ribbed skeleton – whose matter is botanical and zoological but whose signification is architectural and mythological. The details demand a larger interpretive context, especially since the scene is repeated in other works, as in *Mardi*: "All the past a dim blank? Think of the time when we [Taji and Yillah] ran up and down in our arbor, where the green vines grew over the great ribs of the stranded whale" (143). Similarly, Lucy's easel stripped of "vines" or "green heart-strings" leaving behind "the cold skeleton of the sweet arbor wherein she once nestled" expresses Pierre's final disillusionment and distraction (318). Once the bleached whale skeleton is moved from sand beach to glen, it grows into a human temple embellished with multicolored intertwining vegetation: earth's "green, life-restless loom" of vines and ferns and grasses covers "the mighty idler [who] seemed the cunning weaver ... assuming greener, fresher verdure; but himself a skeleton" (450). It is turned into a historical monument where annals of "strange hieroglyphics" are carved; it acquires godly status. "A Bower in the Arsacides" is Ishmael's explanation of a process that creates mythology, symbolically portrayed in constant weaving of "unwearied verdure" onto a naked skeleton, though (as the episode's ending shows) once established and recorded it degenerates into organized religion and priestly theological quarrels.

The other scene comes from the "Wilderness" cantos (2.28 to 2.39) in *Clarel*, on the Dead Sea shore:

> The legend round a Grecian urn,
> The sylvan legend, though decay
> Have wormed the garland all away,
> And fire have left its Vandal burn;
> Yet beauty inextinct may charm
> In outline of the vessel's form.
> Much so with Sodom, shore and sea.
> Fair Como would like Sodom be
> Should horror overrun the scene
> And calcine all that makes it green,
> Yet haply sparing to impeach

> The contour of its larger reach.
> In graceful lines the hills advance,
> The valley's sweep repays the glance,
> And wavy curves of winding beach;
> But all is charred or crunched or riven,
> Scarce seems of earth whereon we dwell;
> Though framed within the lines of heaven
> The picture intimates a hell. (2.29.1–19)

This is a passage rich in images and allusions that reverberate in works by Melville and others, among them Keats's "Ode on a Grecian Urn," Shelley's "Mont Blanc" (in lines 16–17), Ruskin's redefinition of beauty in *Modern Painters*, Dante's Paradise and Inferno, classical Tartarus ("Pluto's park," whatever green it has, is "Stygean" in hue, 2.28.1–6). Its direct source is Melville's January 1857 journal entry: "Ride over mouldy plain to Dead Sea – Mountains on tother [*sic*] side – Lake George ["Como" inserted above] – all but verdure" (*J* 83, 429). Located here is a type, or "mould" (2.36.100), in "outline" or "contour," of supreme truth that is real enough in nature, though it may appear unreal and difficult to reproduce in art or writing. As painterly picturesque representations, quiet lakes and forested mountains produce a mild and easy effect on the eye and so control perception. But the barren upper regions of Mont Blanc, like this view, echo emptiness and generate multiple uncertainties and inexplicable profundities in the mind.

For Melville, absence of green cover makes the Dead Sea region not less but more meaningful as an absolute landscape. The interplay of shore and sea, "wave and waste" (2.32.57), in this skeletal landscape captures the elusiveness and fluidity of truth – in opposition to efforts to limit and settle it in arcades of fresh green, to find pleasing, reassuring comfort. In sketching a perfect panorama, Melville does not mean it to be idyllic. The journal's three words "all but verdure" point to conscious formulation of an archetypal, essential scene. It is much like the Greek archipelago, where arid islands still recall old myths and "retain in outline" the "grace of form" of earth new and "primal": "'Tis Polynesia reft of palms" ("The Archipelago," *CP* 249).

Melville's observation in Egypt in 1857 at the border of sand and sown provides an analogy to the myth-making disposition: "*The Sphynx.* back to desert & face to verdure" (*J* 76). Melville brings the recognition of this duality – desert and greenness – to the analysis of belief systems worldwide, as in Polynesia or in Greece. But he finds its essence in that part of the Old World where Judeo-Christian mythologies and theologies originated. The Dead Sea region constitutes a landscape of bare essentials. Its lack of a green prospect, its all-but-verdure, its sullenness and absence of paradisiacal escape express awareness of present historical realities and artistic perception of them. The all-but-verdure condition is a primary and appropriate antecedent to any mythological creation, and now a preventative to acts of protective avoidance or self-imposition.

Iconographies

Drawing the line between verdure and barrenness, the tree line in "Mont Blanc," written in 1817, is a defining but unrecognized aesthetic moment. The "naked countenance of the earth" or "desart" in Shelley's poem can "repeal / Large codes of fraud and woe" and teach the "adverting mind" (231, 232). Emerson writes in "Experience": "It is very unhappy, but too late to be helped, the discovery that we have made, that we exist. That discovery is called the Fall of Man" (261). The Fall brings consciousness; a constant sense of "wickedness" or "evil" is Sodom; our essence is the Desert. "'Man sprang from deserts'" (C 2.16.106). Into this terrain, Melville brings the natural iconography of his earlier works to fashion his aesthetic anew.

Although the landscape was new, however, the metaphysical and aesthetic consciousness arose from earlier works. In *Moby-Dick* the "indefiniteness" of whiteness is akin to sea or waste: it "shadows forth the heartless voids and immensities of the universe, and thus stabs us from behind with the thought of annihilation ... a dumb blankness, full of meaning, in a wide landscape of snows – a colorless, all-color of atheism from which we shrink." Consider the terrors and mysteries beneath the sea's surface, "then turn to this green, gentle, and most docile earth; consider them both, the sea and the land; and do you not find a strange analogy to something in yourself? For as this appalling ocean surrounds the verdant land, so in the soul of man there lies one insular Tahiti, full of peace and joy, but encompassed by all the horrors of the half known life" (195, 274). Nomad and artist face the waste unabashed, plunge into seas, storm skies, while most humans remain fearful and land-contained. Consciousness alone can brave myth-generating sites, now uncovered, unobstructed, ungreened.

From the ingredients of that land, whether verdant or waste, out of natural botanical and geological architecture, outward cover and solid elements, shapes and colors, Melville constructs iconic forms to represent conditions, beliefs, and states of being. This natural iconography has multitudinous sources: a combination of the traditional and the improvised. We find origins and echoes from Spenser, Shakespeare, Milton, Bunyan, Herbert, and Marvell. Other writers and artists, Romantics and post-Romantics like Blake, Goethe, Shelley, Emerson, Carlyle, and Turner influenced Melville's landscape iconography too. Blake's figurative inversions, Shelley's mountain desert, Carlyle's clothes metaphor, and Turner's abstract paintings were new expressions appropriate for Melville's cultural moment. Even if we do not know whether Melville read Goethe's non-literary works, his *Metamorphosis of Plants* and *Theory of Colours*, the latter translated by Charles Lock Eastlake, whose books on the arts Melville borrowed, we should not discount that they may have proved useful. (Sealts; Kier. As sample studies in influence, see Norberg, and Ra'ad "Uneasiness.")

Melville's knowledge of science also informs his aesthetics. He employs descriptive details from zoology, botany, geology, physics, and other sciences (see Hillway, Foster, and Richard Dean Smith), though such details are insufficient to explain his position. Scientific discoveries and biblical criticism undermined traditional religious beliefs, forcing Melville's grudging admission that they have "robbed us of the bloom" (*J* 97).

For him science is limited and incomplete, its knowledge never final or absolute; it is mutable; there are alternative, less material sources of truth. Thus, while Melville uses scientific sources, he subverts them to his aesthetic purpose and to metaphysical applications.

Color theory is a good example of how science and aesthetics, physics and metaphysics combine and diverge in ways useful for Melville's iconography. Newton's optics was considered authoritative, but counter theories propounded by Goethe (controversial then, though some of his ideas have gained credibility in the light of recent science) lent themselves to aesthetic and metaphysical applications that were attractive to writers like Coleridge and Emerson because of their emphasis on the eye and the impact of colors on the mind (see Sepper, Amrine et al., Shepard, and Novak). Goethe studied the function of light in perception and its production of color in the visible world. He recorded experiments in optics and produced a "wheel" to classify mental qualities and "moral associations" of hues. For Goethe, that the mixture of all colors produces white is an absurdity, artistically a mess. Rather, everything living tends to local and specific color, to opaqueness, while everything in which life is extinct approximates to white, to "the abstract, the general state, to clearness, to transparence": "Not only are elementary earths in their natural states white, but vegetable and animal substances can be reduced to a white state without disturbing their texture" (sections 586, 594). Goethe's statement that color, "in its infinite variety, exhibits itself on the surface of living beings" (section 735) is a likely source for "that other theory of the natural philosophers" Ishmael cites in "The Whiteness of the Whale" to explain how earthly hues "are but subtile deceits, not actually inherent in substances" (195).

More essential than the spectrum is Goethe's division of the visible and invisible worlds according to light and darkness, the chromatic and achromatic. "Light, in its full force, appears purely white" (section 81). Chromatically, this basic division is controlled by the two elemental opposites yellow and blue: yellow is closest to light, earth, sun, force, warmth, proximity, repulsion, and action; blue is linked to darkness, sea, sky, weakness, coldness, distance, attraction, and passiveness. Equal mixture of yellow and blue makes green, where the opposites do not destroy each other but produce a harmony: green being easy on the eye, or in the words of Goethe a "simple" color that the eye and the mind experience with a "distinctly grateful impression" whereby the "beholder has neither the wish nor the power to imagine a state beyond it" (section 802).

Botany, zoology, and geology combine with color to shape Melville's aesthetic perspective. Melville uses the visible earth and its cover to construct a symbolic scheme relating to human life and its progress. Grass is the basic unit of the vegetable world, botanically simple, and a sign of productiveness; the human parallel to the "blades of grass" (*P* 9) are the masses of people that inhabit the earth's surface. Other plants of fertile cover have varied significance: moss is related to age and accumulation on rocks or possibly decay on old structures. In his essay on Hawthorne, Melville seems obsessed with the "perennial green" of mosses, though mosses could acquire somewhat negative associations ("And present Nature as a moss doth show / On the ruins of the Nature of the aeons of long ago" ["Pontoosuce" *CP* 396; *PT* 240–1, 243, 246]). Vines, usually human-created, also cover buildings and lend an impression of age along with qualities of design and life movement ("Vines overrunning ruins. Ruins here take the place of rocks" [*J* 104]; the "cloistral vine" ["Monody," *CP* 229]). These are indications Melville was working with formulations that are now called "refuge," "hazard," and "prospect" symbolism in landscape aesthetics (as used, for example, in Appleton 74–104).

Flowers traditionally connote beauty and temporality – as Emerson says "so strictly belong to youth" (324) – while weeds are distractive and tenacious and so not merely crowd but replace flowers (even "man's – a weed" ["A Dirge for McPherson," *CP* 82]). In Melville's work the competition of flowers with weeds suggests individual life's progress; it is a comment on historical, humanistic, and environmental decline in values. Trees, on the other hand, have a substantial form and structure and represent posture and states of mind. A strong, upright tree might show a youthful stance, a symmetrical tree symbolizes a vision of order or harmony, while a sturdy tree, such as the oak, connotes ancestry or perseverance. A contorted or misshapen tree can be seen as a grotesque chaos, or it otherwise has its special beauty or truth. Trees are also classified according to their climate, so the pine being geometrically "pyramidical" is a northern sort of palm that suggests stateliness and symmetry (*P* 41; "Pontoosuce," *CP* 396), while the northerly apple is akin to the more southerly olive tree in its associations with agony and grotesque appearance. The cypress is meaningful in Melville's aesthetic design, as its unique form and dark green are reminiscent of passion and pent-up sadness ("love's cypress tree"; "Cypress-moss that drapes the palm" ["The Enviable Isles," "Iris," *CP* 204, 278]; "The Cyprus [*sic*] a green minaret, & blends with the stone one," *J* 65).

The palm is the primal "Tree of Life" in primitive Polynesia. Its botanical characteristics evoke its symbolic meanings, as shown in Melville's fascination with the palm's shaft and tuft (*O* Chapter 69 "The Cocoa-Palm"). In a political allegory of America as a potential escape from cyclical history and decadence, the thirty states of the union in 1849 are represented as "a lofty structure, planted upon a bold hill, and supported by thirty pillars of palms; four quite green; as if recently added" (*M* 514). Like the date palm in drier climes, the tropical palm's dignified figure, its perfect shape, versatility, and fragile hardiness led Melville to place it (as Linnaeus did, classifying it as a grass though a tree) at the top of the vegetable hierarchy. Indicating a "palmology" as developed as his cetology, Melville associates the palm's tuft with the whale's waterspout in Polynesian, ocean, and desert settings.

Along with particular features like color and vegetation, Melville's landscapes derive meaning from history and time, specifically by opposing human architecture to the natural architecture of the earth. Buildings and other human efforts are transitory and relatively insignificant in his scheme, whereas botanical and zoological phenomena, being changeable and cyclical, are metaphors for potential renewal. This view turns America's newness into an advantage that seemed to disentangle it from the traps of history, arguing that constant value is supplied by time, and permanent natural features do not require historical association or legends and myths to give them legitimacy (Ra'ad, "Melville's Art"). The American Indian burial mounds, that William Cullen Bryant's "Prairies" appropriates and ascribes to a vanished race, for Melville are primal features. Inasmuch as geological features are solid and continuous, they represent eternal time, permanence, and essence. Instead of seeing history as the provenience of values and knowledge, Melville finds in it sources of decay. Thus, in *Israel Potter*, the narrator contrasts an American landscape invested with mythological powers and such "purple" depth that even its decay is "original" to both the "funereal" appearance of London as the City of Dis with "no speck of any green thing" and an American landscape fifty years later in 1826 that shows all signs of normal decay (4–5, 159, 168).

For Melville, then, earthly architecture, the power of barren landscape, derives its sublimity from time, but also from its simple and essential materials. Earthly substances in Melville range from the minutest dust to the highest mountain. Sands "[i]mpart the oceanic sense" (*C* 2.11.37) – as the element on earth closest to the sea's fluidity. Sandy deserts are pure barrenness. In contrast, solid deserts evoke a sense of desolation, whether they are high dry areas, islands, prairies, "Idumea or the Pole," or "frosted desolateness" (*C* "Of Deserts," "The High Desert"; "The Encantadas" *PT* 126; *MD* 194). Rocks are also inscrutable essence, solid essentiality, more ancient by far than any historical accumulations, bare in an ultimate sense. Stones, being broken friable rock, are remnants or quarries of life, symbols of hardness, meaninglessness, deadness, and fragmentation. In a short passage (*J* 90) Melville uses variations on "stone" and "stony" twenty-nine times. Melville thus distinguishes between pure wilderness and decayed aridity (the original condition and its mythic remnants) as well as between solid rock and fragmented stone (stolid reality and human construction).

For Melville human architecture is most powerful when it derives from primal architectural forms, particularly the circle, the dome or visible section of a buried sphere, and pyramid shapes. The dome of St. Sophia in Istanbul is described as "[s]uspended from above like fully blossomed tulip from its stem," its interior "a positive appropriation of space," and its "peculiar form" suggests an immense temple "yet to be disinterred" (*J* 158, 67). For Melville, the mosque is "a sort of marble marquee," the minarets like the stakes of a tent, an edifice that reproduces the Ishmaelite fluid form of habitation (*J* 60). Mountains are objects of sublimity and mystery, and the pyramids gain their situational meaning at the border between verdure and desert in their stylized encapsulation of mountain form, solidity ("Pyramids from a distance purple like mountains," *J* 75). The whale's head is pyramidal. Pierre moves from the condition of green bliss, of pastoral harmony and sheltered mansions, into the increasing levels of consciousness allegorized as the "charred landscape" of burning forests and mountain gloom within his soul, arriving at last at the moss-turbaned brow of a pyramid-like rock on the stark Mount of Titans, hoping to extract meaning from it, to "flog this stubborn rock as Moses his, and force even aridity itself to quench his painful thirst" (3, 35, 86, 345–6).

In the face of natural grandeur, Melville suggests that human efforts are insignificant, transient, and half-blind, even when the product astonishes us by "what a worm [that is, the human being] can do" ("Venice," *CP* 239). The Encantadas and a later version "The Island" (*C* 4.3), though uninhabited by humans, image the cultural world: the parched rocks are inexplicably "much worn down / Like to some old, old kneeling-stone / Before a shrine." Within this seemingly human architecture, the tortoise suggests humanity, its encrusted arch history. Humanity keeps blindly, stupidly attempting to "solve the world" by persistent creation of alternative systems and structures: "Of huge humped arch, the ancient shell / Is trenched with seams where lichens dwell, / Or some adhesive growth and sere ... / Searching, he creeps with laboring neck, / Each crevice tries, and long may seek" (*C* 4.3.32–4, 112, 62–4, 75–6).

Desert Mythology: Architecture of Belief and Unbelief

The "Holy Land" as a representative landscape of aridity negates the need for opposites in describing existential realities. Here is the perfect site for illustrating past and present. Aridity, barrenness, and inscrutability drive the human creation of myth, providing the symbols of human loss of belief and its desolation. The "Holy Land" is the landscape of both belief and unbelief. Primitive hope is gone forever, not only because native societies are destroyed but also because of the damaging actions of "civilization" and of our awareness. It is particularly so for America since "America," as Melville had hoped for its realization as a fresh human start, a new model for human history, lapsed instead into amplified models of the Old World.

Melville found Christ's message to be inconsistent with what is signified by a barren environment and its mythological products, as well as with the world's blunt realities. Thus, Christ-like characters like Bartleby, Celio, and Billy Budd contain pain and incompatibility. "J.C. should have appeared in Taheiti. – Land of palms. – Palm Sunday," as he noted in his journal and *Clarel* (*J* 154; *C* 4.18.36–44). Christ in Tahiti, pre-colonial Tahiti, would have been in harmony with New Testament concepts of love, benignity, worldly humility, and eternal life beyond. But the accepting relationship represented by native Polynesians and Christ is threatened to extinction by the "vindictiveness" of "feverish civilization," the colonial "hive," and blinded self-centeredness of puritanical missionaries (*T* 125, 195). This conflict is painful because it is not merely religious; it relates to life attitudes and ways of being.

In his Polynesian adventures, as in *Journals* and *Clarel*, Melville does not merely propound anti-missionary and anti-colonial sentiments: his purpose is to undercut Christian self-privileging by drawing comparisons between native scenes and biblical narratives, as well as parallels to Western-appropriated Greek and Roman traditions. His editors, however, were keen to delete any obvious parallels, lest readers think he is saying: "No belief system owns the truth, and these pagans are not much different from characters we associate with our own monotheistic and classical traditions." Three among other instances indicate less than benign editorial coercion: an un-Melvillean preface to *Typee*'s American Revised Edition, almost surely written by others; in a comparison, also from *Typee*, of native carriers to the biblical spies carrying grape-evidence, editing out a phrase "the fatness of the Caananitish [Canaanitish] lands" that might have suggested a less than holy mission (see Bryant's manuscript transcription, xxix, 275, 306); and removal of a more explicit comparison between Christ and the Chola widow in "The Encantadas" (Ra'ad " 'The Encantadas' "). These details suggest Melville's persistent struggle to express his skepticism about religions, which are exploited for self-interest and cloak barren truths in beguiling verdure.

Indeed, most discussion of Melville's religion fails to fathom the depth of his perceptions: on the one hand, his recognition of the unconscious human need for mythic protection; on the other hand, his distrust of the self-deceptive obsessions that the religious mind creates. Instead, the literary criticism, though sometimes informative, is strangely divided between seeing Melville as a traditionalist and as a subversive. An assumption persists from the time of William Braswell, Nathalia Wright, and Lawrance Thompson that Melville's religious responses were immature, allegorical, biblically-reactive-imitative, or angry – in short, stuck in a Calvinistic tradition without quite realizing it. The recent rise in fundamentalism has generated banal attempts to show Melville as a believer in the Old Testament God. Others, like H. Bruce Franklin, have demonstrated Melville's diverse uses of comparative mythology, though Franklin admits skirting *Clarel*. Melville engaged in something more profound than making "comparative" points: he systematically explored various mythological systems, including the beliefs of Judaism and Christianity. This awareness is available in James Baird's *Ishmael* (1956) and Dorothée Finkelstein's *Melville's Orienda* (1961), the latter admitting "Melville's despair at the decadence of Christianity and the sterility of biblical Judaism, which lay behind it": "Christianity, too, is a myth" (Finkelstein 279). An essay by Jenny Franchot, rhetorically impressive in its use of the travel trope and "anthropological gaze" as yielding "renewed substance for an ideologically depleted Christianity" (161, 169), reasserts Baird's thesis about Melville as "a supreme example of the artistic creator engaged in the act of making new symbols to replace the 'lost' symbols of Protestant Christianity" (xv).

Melville understood that myth produces an environment that is comfortable for human perception, as the Arsacides episode intimates. Symbolically, the comfort comes from a mind that averts its attention from essential barrenness (skeleton, sand, sea, rock, or desert) and enshrines itself in a protective bower (by adding vines, green, or structure). That notion is entwined also with the understanding of Christ, whose charitable message becomes a consoling myth, incompatible with Christian practices, Old Testament models, and worldly rapaciousness.

So the question is: Can mythic creation result from elemental barrenness itself? Melville develops fairly comprehensive hypotheses about Judeo-Christian beliefs as landscape constructs: a god emerging in a pyramidal enclosure that rises in the midst of impenetrable, incomprehensible desert flux, followed by theological dogma resulting from interaction with arid landscape (a landscape unusually called "that unchristened earth" in "The High Desert," *C* 3.5.183). Such ideas appear throughout Melville's texts but not put all together into a coherent whole. Journal remarks about the pyramids, various poems, and cantos in *Clarel* leave little doubt, however, that Melville theorized about how the Mosaic God or Jehovah/Yahweh ("the transcendent conception of a God") originated in Egypt: "It was in these pyramids that was conceived the idea of Jehovah. Terrible mixture of the cunning and awful. Moses learned in all the lore of the Egyptians. The idea of Jehovah born here. . . . Line of desert & verdure, plain as line between good & evil. An instant collision of two elements" (*J* 78, 75–6). This notion of a typal structure at the edge of desert and vegetation, at the junction of death and life, the unknown and known lies behind the human need for assertion of self. Thus, in an echo of Yahweh's answer in Exodus, shaping the formless into stony form "bade this dumb I AM to start, / Imposing him" ("The Great Pyramid," *CP* 255).

Melville had less evidence to question biblical historicity than is available today, except early textual scholarship and a few archaeological discoveries. His analysis therefore depends primarily on analogies based on primitive response to natural environment. A clear case is "Of Desert" in *Clarel*, a canto premised on human responses to waste places (deserts, seas, solid barren tracts), responses of fear and love, terror and sublimity. Mount Sinai, for example, was "renown" for the terror that wraps its summit before it engendered "the thundered Law" (2.11.48–54). In explaining the theological byproducts of arid land, Melville draws on his journal, where he notes the "peculiar" landscape: "As the sight of haunted Haddon Hall suggested to Mrs Radcliffe her curdling romances, so I have little doubt, the diabolical landscapes great part of Judea must have suggested to the Jewish prophets, their ghastly theology" (*J* 89, 574). The vocabulary Melville employs ("awe" and "horror," "ghastly" and "terrible," both "faith" and "doubt" as inherent responses) derives partly from Shelley's "naked countenance of earth" or "desart" wilderness.

"Of Deserts" quotes Darwin agreeing with Shelley. Other sources are more difficult to pin down, though it is possible to trace a line of thinking to eighteenth-century philosophy, including David Hume's "Natural History of Religion." For Hume, there is little distinction between polytheism and monotheism: both exhibit "ignorance" and use gods as national tools. The primary source of religious concepts is people's "anxious fear of future events": "A panic having once seized the mind, the active fancy still farther multiplies the objects of terror; while that profound darkness, or, what is worse, that glimmering light, with which we are invironed, represents the specters of divinity under the most dreadful appearances imaginable" (94). Frank Manuel discusses rationalist views about Christianity and Judaism as among other "survivals from the mythic age of mankind" that share with all religions "a common source in terror-stricken humanity" (305). The impact of the desert on religious notions is suggested in Alexander Kinglake's 1844 *Eothen* during the Sinai crossing from Palestine to Egypt. Melville probably read reports of an 1872 lecture by George Smith, whose book *The Chaldean Account of Genesis, Containing the Description of the Creation, the Fall of Man, the Deluge, the Tower of Babel, the Times of the Patriarchs, and Nimrod* in 1876 recorded what were then astounding Mesopotamian and Assyrian antecedents to biblical narratives. Earlier, there were available insights from the decipherment of the Rosetta Stone, David Friedrich Strauss's 1835 *Das Leben Jesu* on the gospels as messianic construction, and the narratives of Buddhism and Hinduism (which influenced Emerson, among others; see "Of Rama" in *Clarel*). In reference to the dualistic nature of Old and New Testaments, the incongruous figures of Yahweh/ Jehovah and Christ, expressed in Gnostic doctrine and earlier mythological types, Melville concludes that "The two-fold Testaments become / Transmitters of Chaldaic thought / By implication" (*C* 3.5.48–50).

Advances in science and in biblical analysis mushroomed in the nineteenth century, concomitant with a virulent fundamentalist reaction, making it sound striking that eighteenth-century thinkers held more enlightened views. Melville formulated his theories well in advance of more concrete breakthroughs that unearthed connections between mythological systems in the ancient Eastern Medi-terranean region and affinities between monotheistic and polytheistic religions. Compared to later discoveries of Canaanite, Ugaritic, and Babylonian religious influences on Bible narratives, the Egyptian connections pursued in *Journals* are relatively minor in the light of today's scholarship. That Melville latches onto "Chaldaic thought," or in "Of Deserts" draws a parallel between Jove's and Jehovah's thunderbolts, therefore, is serendipitous – this long before we discover that Jove/ Zeus is directly derived from the Canaanite thunder and fertility God Ba'al, that Kronos is the same as Ba'al's father, the pantheon chief El, and that Yahweh/Jehovah is one of El's sons and a member of the pantheon. Nor did Melville have definite indications that Judeo-Christian places were arbitrarily allocated in the fourth century, mainly to supplant pagan sites, though he is aware in *Clarel* (1.31.206– 30) that Christ's story has close antecedents in regional "pagan" savior-figures such as Osiris. (See, for example, Gabel et al.; Ra'ad "Primal Scenes"; Mark S. Smith; Deut. 32.8–9 in *The Complete Parallel Bible*; entries in Metzger and Coogan; Robertson; Harpur; and Hunt.)

The challenges to nineteenth-century religious fundamentalism were real, however, and Melville distills them in "Nathan" (1.17), the longest canto in *Clarel* and one that rewards careful reading. The canto is a sweeping review of Western religious devel-opments and the particular temper of American religious experience. It tells the story of Nathan's confronting the raw powers of nature, which leads him into stages of response and belief: he is subjected to awe and fear of terror-invested natural calam-ities; he feels the impact of vast space and in that space the sight of three pyramidal "Indian mounds" appearing dimly "across the prairie green"; he undergoes an experi-ence reminiscent of the Arsacides episode:

> Hard by, as chanced, he once beheld
> Bones like sea corals; one bleached skull
> A vase vined round and beautiful
> With flowers; felt, with bated breath
> The floral revelry over death.(1.17, 56, 58, 67–71)

Nathan is brought by these encounters with naked nature, and then by reading and by events, to the varieties of deism, pantheism, and agnosticism, but the inner storms finally drive him to long for certainty and concrete belief. His conversion to Judaism occurs through marriage, but it also recreates America's wilderness "errand" by imagining biblical history and landscape in America: "for rear-ward shows / Far behind Rome and Luther – what? / The crag of Sinai. Here then plant / Thyself secure: 'tis adamant." Nathan's conversion is not inconsistent with the prototypal experience of the Puritans, who depended heavily on Old Testament laws and narratives: "'Twas passion. But the Puritan – / Mixed latent in his blood – a strain / How evident, of Hebrew source; / 'Twas that, diverted here in force, / Which biased – hardly might do less" (1.17.215–19, 227–31). Nathan's "northern nature" transfers this Puritanism, its attitudes to nature and native people, its associations and justifications, into a colonizing zeal in Palestine as the "Holy" or "Promised" Land, against his wife's and daughter's wishes and cautions. It leads to death and destructiveness not unlike the fate of Ahab and the ship. Perhaps Melville suggests, through this inversion of locale, something about the dangerous effects of imprinting one's theology on the land. For the Puritans, the land that could have been green paradise was instead seen as a "desert wilderness," to be traveled through or subdued on the way to some unseen heaven. The desolation Melville sees in nineteenth-century America forms a shadow of that perceptual barrenness which created its imported religion.

For Melville, it was a natural step to invert sacred topography as a way to uncover its workings: it is not in green land and human life that religion is manifested and substantiated. Rather, highlighting the barren parts of Palestine (his winter visit helped in this impression), Melville saw religion generated by human response to harsh and empty aridity, motivated by escape and need for certainty, thus reversing a mode of typological thinking that runs from Bradford to Nathan. The field of sacred geography and its obsessive literal applications are now open for Melville, not to retrace the Bible in the Land – be it Sinai, Canaan, Palestine, New England, or Utah (as was, still is, the habit of many a pious traveler) – but rather to reconstruct how land itself produced its mythology and subsequent theology. As Dorothée Finkelstein shows, Melville used travel accounts written by nineteenth-century clergymen like William Thomson and Arthur Stanley. But, clearly, Melville inverts traditional sacred topography by making the land not a tool for confirming religious narratives but an originating source of religious ideas and dogma.

Consciousness: Landscape as Protagonist

Melville's fictional and aesthetic designs explore not only religious systems but also degrees of consciousness in the human mind. His plots revolve around observations of how human beings interact with the landscapes around them, how they may be either blissfully unconscious or obsessively unaware and self-deceptive, or painfully or resignedly conscious. These individual states of mind are expressed in botanical and geological metaphors, in acts and narrative outcomes where landscape often becomes a protagonist. Taji's quest, Ishmael's survival, Pierre's search and despair, the Palm cantos, and six deaths in *Clarel* are expressed in terms of landscape as a factor of consciousness.

A cluster of twelve narrative and digressive cantos, *Clarel* 2.28 to 2.39, exemplifies Melville's fictional strategy, drawing one rounded segment into an argumentative circumference compassed by the entire work (Ra'ad "Death"). It shows human beings responding to a significant locale and landscape as a sign of their character or an instrument in their fate, in this case Nehemiah's death, for which there has been much presentiment. Melville positions his characters in relation to an ominously hanging rock near the Dead Sea, to reflect gradations of consciousness or self-deception. This peculiar waste-shored rock, personified with a "brow," is both the mysterious Rock of Impenetrability and the material Rock of Science, against which delusions are questioned and shattered. Nehemiah, on the lowest ring of consciousness, is "in sleep embraced" under the "'crag's impending block,'" oblivious to his imminent death (2.31.8–13, 83–7; 2.30.73); Derwent's responses exhibit duplicitous and facile religious optimism and ostrich-like necrophobia (2.39.42–5, 96–100 ; 3.21); the "Slanting Cross" inscription presumably etched by Mortmain, a modern seer who drinks the brine undeterred, is placed on "the tablet high"; below it is Margoth's erasable note (2.31); Vine sits pained and collected on another rock silently watching the waves. It is Vine who discovers Nehemiah's body washed up on the shore of the Dead Sea of Reality and pronounces softly: "Here is balm: / Repose is snowed upon repose – / Sleep upon sleep" (2.39.31–3). Nehemiah is buried in a sandy grave scooped out with camel ribs (from the same source as Mortmain's skull-stool), under the instrumental gaze of Margoth, for whom " 'All's mere geology, you know'" (2.33.47); Rolfe remembers the dreamer's Book or Bible and consigns it to the grave along with Nehemiah's other "relics" (2.39.122–30).

In a similar episode, up in the wilderness ("The High Desert"), inside the convent of Mar Saba, stands another isolated icon – a solitary palm midway up a precipice. This palm becomes another occasion for observations, with characters positioned relative to it on the stone stairs indicating rank on a consciousness scale. Vine is "Reclined aloof upon a stone / High up," Mortmain "dropped upon the under stone," definitely "under Vine"; Rolfe is "lowermost" of the three. The Celibate, Derwent, and Clarel are all lower, though Clarel, "Midpoised," is distinguished as recognizing Vine is highest (3.26.7–8; 3.28.68, 95; 3.29.24–5; 3.30.23, 134–40). Civilized unconsciousness, or self-deception, is unlike the native unawareness represented by the calm of Djalea the Druze or the Bedouin nomad. Vine, a variation on primitive repose, combines the ideal stance and acute conscious mind, reminiscent of the "original" in *The Confidence-Man*, the "Master Genius" in "Hawthorne and His Mosses," and Rama (1.32), reserved and distinct, retaining simplicity yet consciousness of self. Vine embodies, as his Christ-associated name suggests, an intertwining of vines and marble, of blood and rock, of human and god, of verdure and deadness, of light and shadow (e.g., 2.27 and 2.22.143–9). He is akin to Petra's architecture, which is created out of barren and inscrutable rock: "Mid such a scene / Of Nature's terror, how serene / That ordered form. Nor less 'tis cut / Out of that terror – does abut / Thereon: there's Art" (2.30.40–4).

The "ideal" posture imitates the "perfect" landscape. In the end, the nakedness Melville first perceived to be a positive American quality for renewal, whose acceptance he associates with primitive modes of life, which tolerated now becomes a measure of consciousness, is finally translated into art for a modernist barren condition.

Transformed Icons

In the works of the 1850s and later poetry, Melville expressed cultural decline in terms of receding and besieged natural symbols. The same "imprisoned verdure" in "London deserts" appeared as "imprisoned turf" in New York, its "Wall-street [is] deserted as Petra" (*IP* 164; "Bartleby," *PT* 27, 44), a token and painful reminder. "The weed exiles the flower" and its "coronation," in place of the rose, is at hand ("The Ravaged Villa," "The Rose Farmer," *CP* 222, 305). Even more drastically, as barrenness dominates the landscape, the greenness abundant in earlier fiction not only disappears but now appears an implausible comfort in the desert of existence.

The frontispiece in Henry Hawkins's *Partheneia Sacra* (1633) shows the prelapsarian and fallen worlds as two gardens, a palm in the first, in the other an apple tree. Rather than associating these trees conventionally, however, the palm with paradise and the apple with sin, Melville employs the two trees as aesthetic emblems to interpret individual experience and human history, pitching the palm's primal simplicity and timelessness against the apple's cultivated complexity and temporality. In "Hawthorne and His Mosses" (significant since *Mosses* contains "The New Adam and Eve"), those "twisted[,] and contorted old trees" symbolize tortured psychological complexity and experiential grotesqueness (*PT* 241). In "The Apple-Tree Table," the polished surface of present civilization contains the core of its own repeatable corruption, the constant ticks resisting attempts at "domesticating the table" (*PT* 381). In existential and aesthetic terms, the grotesque apple is a sign of our despair, an expression of complex abstraction. Likewise, along the Dead Sea waste, the palms of Polynesian verdure and of hope in Christ are salted and shriveled: at Vine's feet on the sandy shore lies half-buried a "branchless tree": "Of form complete – / Half fossilized – could this have been, / In ages back, a palm-shaft green?" (2.33.14–16). The solitary palm does not stay simply as part of an external landscape of associations or even of communicative symbol making. In a pervasive state of arid culture, the imagination turns the palm inward, converts it into an inner landscape – "The palm at the end of the mind" as Wallace Stevens calls it in his last poem. It is alive and extinct, permanent and anachronistic, a paradox – like the archetypal Christ or the imprisoned memory of wilderness.

Whether pessimistically romantic or fortuitously modernist, Melville's aesthetic is a precursor of the modern wasteland. All verdure is finally excrescence. " 'In nature point, in life, in art / Where the essential thing appears' " ("At the Hostelry," *CP* 318). This aesthetic appears in one ultimate instance in Vine's building of a crude cairn, Vine who is compared to a humanized rock tinted like Petra with veins of blood. The cairn is an appropriate artistic comment on the human condition and environment: it is one of the few structures really possible and meaningful in our new desolation. Constructed out of the fragmentary medium of stone into a pointed pyramidal shape, it is "yes, / A monument to barrenness" (*C* 3.7.75–85). Though it contains a yearning for lost verdurous opportunities, yet it is an eventual recognition that, since in a human-evolved earth greenery acquires the strangeness of inconsistency, both perception and creation of form must reproduce the state of aridity.

NOTES

I remove unnecessary commas used in the NN edition for the *Mardi* epigraph and on p. 139 restore Melville's final word choice of "ghastly" in *Journals* (89, 574). Line numbers in Walter Bezanson's edition of *Clarel* (New York: Hendricks, 1960) may differ slightly from the NN edition quoted here.

I thank Nina Butska for suggestions on the final draft and the Department of English at the University of Toronto for facilitating library access.

REFERENCES

Amrine, Frederick, Francis J. Zucker and Harvey Wheeler, eds. *Goethe and the Sciences: A Reappraisal*. Dordrecht: D. Reidel, 1987.

Appleton, Jay. *The Experience of Landscape*. Chichester: Wiley, 1996.

Baird, James. *Ishmael*. Baltimore: Johns Hopkins University Press, 1956.

Braswell, William. *Melville's Religious Thought: An Essay in Interpretation*. Durham, NC: Duke University Press, 1943.

Complete Parallel Bible, The. New York: Oxford University Press, 1993.

Davis, John. *The Landscape of Belief: Encountering the Holy Land in Nineteenth-Century American Art and Culture*. Princeton, NJ: Princeton University Press, 1996.

Emerson, Ralph Waldo. *The Essays of Ralph Waldo Emerson*. 1841, 1844. Cambridge, MA: Harvard University Press, 1987.

Finkelstein, Dorothée Metlinsky. *Melville's Orienda*. New Haven, CT: Yale University Press, 1961.

Foster, Elizabeth. "Melville and Geology." *American Literature* 17 (1945): 50–65.

———. "Another Note on Melville and Geology." *American Literature* 22 (1951): 479–87.

Franchot, Jenny. "Melville's Traveling God." In *The Cambridge Companion to Herman Melville*. Ed. Robert S. Levine. Cambridge: Cambridge University Press, 1998. 157–85.

Franklin, H. Bruce. *The Wake of the Gods: Melville's Mythology*. Stanford, CA: Stanford University Press, 1963.

Gabel, John B., Charles B Wheeler, and Anthony D. York *The Bible as Literature: An Introduction*. 4th ed. New York: Oxford University Press, 2000.

Goethe, Johann Wolfgang von. *Theory of Colours*. Trans. Charles Lock Eastlake. London: John Murray, 1840.

Harpur, Tom. *The Pagan Christ: Recovering the Lost Light*. Toronto: Thomas Allen, 2004.

Hillway, Tyrus. "Melville as Amateur Zoologist." *Modern Language Quarterly* 12 (1951): 159–64.

———. "Melville's Education in Science." *Texas Studies in Literature and Language* 16 (1971): 411–25.

———. "Melville's Geological Knowledge." *American Literature* 21 (1949): 232–37.

Hume, David. 1757. "Natural History of Religion." *Four Dissertations*. Bristol: Thoemmes, 1995.

Hunt, E. D. *Holy Land Pilgrimage in the Late Roman Empire AD 312–460*. Oxford: Clarendon Press, 1982.

Kier, Kathleen E. *A Melville Encyclopedia: The Novels*. Troy, NY: Whitston, 1990.

Long, Burke O. *Imagining the Holy Land: Maps, Models, and Fantasy Travels*. Bloomington: Indiana University Press, 2002.

Manuel, Frank E. *The Eighteenth Century Confronts the Gods*. Cambridge, MA: Harvard University Press, 1959.

Melville, Herman. *Typee: A Peep at Polynesian Life*. Ed. John Bryant. New York: Penguin, 1996.

Metzger, Bruce M. and Michael D. Coogan. *The Oxford Companion to the Bible*. New York: Oxford University Press, 1993.

Norberg, Peter. "Finding an Audience for *Clarel* in Matthew Arnold's *Essays in Criticism*." *Leviathan: A Journal of Melville Studies* 6 (March 2004): 35–54.

Novak, Barbara. *Nature and Culture: American Landscape and Painting, 1825–1875*. New York: Oxford University Press, 1980.

Obenzinger, Hilton. *American Palestine: Melville, Twain, and the Holy Land Mania*. Princeton, NJ: Princeton University Press, 1999.

Ra'ad, Basem L. "The Death Plot in Melville's *Clarel*." *ESQ* 27 (1981): 14–27.

———. " 'The Encantadas' and 'The Isle of the Cross': Melvillean Dubieties, 1853–54." *American Literature* 63 (1991): 316–23.

———. "Melville's Art: Overtures from the Journal of 1856–57." In *Savage Eye: Melville and the Visual Arts*. Ed. Christopher Sten. Kent, OH: Kent State University Press, 1991. 200–17.

———. "Primal Scenes of Globalization: Legacies of Canaan and Etruria." *PMLA* 116.1 (January 2001): 89–110.

———. Review of *American Palestine* by Hilton Obenzinger. *Leviathan: A Journal of Melville Studies* 5.1 (March 2003): 94–8.

———. "Uneasiness in 'Bartleby': Melville and Lockean Philosophy." In *Melville "Among the Nations": Proceedings of an International Conference, Volos, Greece, July 2–6, 1997*. Ed. Sanford E. Marovitz and A. C. Christodoulou. Kent, OH: Kent State University Press, 2001. 175–87.

Robertson, J. M. *Pagan Christs*. 1903. New York: Dorset, 1987.

Sepper, Dennis L. *Goethe Contra Newton: Polemics and the Project for a New Science of Color*. Cambridge: Cambridge University Press, 1988.

Shelley, Percy Bysshe. "Mont Blanc." In *The Complete Works of Percy Bysshe Shelley*. Ed. Roger Ingpen and Walter E. Peck. 10 vols. New York: Gordian Press. 1965. 1: 229–33.

Shepard, Paul. *Man in the Landscape: A Historic View of the Esthetics of Nature*. New York: Knopf, 1967.

Smith, Mark S. *The Origins of Biblical Monotheism: Israel's Polytheistic Background and the Ugaritic Texts*. New York: Oxford University Press, 2001.

Smith, Richard Dean. *Melville's Science*. New York: Garland, 1993.

Thompson, Lawrance. *Melville's Quarrel with God*. Princeton, NJ: Princeton University Press, 1952.

Wright, Nathalia. *Melville's Use of the Bible*. Durham, NC: Duke University Press, 1949.

Part III
Nations

10

Democracy and its Discontents

Dennis Berthold

Because Melville's greatest work, *Moby-Dick*, portrays the working classes so fully and sympathetically, many critics have viewed Melville as a champion of democracy, an advocate for the "kingly commons," the noble, ordinary workers who embody "that democratic dignity which, on all hands, radiates without end from God; Himself!" (*MD* 117). In 1941 F. O. Matthiessen counted Melville as one of five American writers devoted to "the possibilities of democracy" (Matthiessen ix), a choice that influenced Richard Chase, Newton Arvin, C. L. R. James, John Bernstein, Edward Grejda, H. Bruce Franklin, Carolyn L. Karcher, Larzer Ziff, David Reynolds, and Nancy Fredricks, all scholars who value Melville for his portrayals of our common humanity and individual worth. Unquestionably, Ishmael believes in a "just Spirit of Equality" (117) that demands toleration and respect for people of all races, nationalities, creeds, and classes, from the *Pequod*'s black cabin-boy Pip through its Polynesian, Native American, and African harpooners to its multi-lingual, international crew and even Captain Ahab himself, who for all his tragic grandeur is only "a poor old whale-hunter" (148). This great democratic theme runs throughout Melville's novels, from *Typee*, with its tolerant regard for Marquesan customs, through *Israel Potter*, the tale of a resourceful American ensnared in the destruction of the Revolutionary War, to the "uninstructed honor" of the young foretopman impressed from the *Rights of Man*, Billy Budd (*BB* 106). Melville's short stories portray the alienated employee Bartleby, offer enormous sympathy for exploited working girls in "The Tartarus of Maids," ironically attack racism and slavery in "Benito Cereno," and poignantly dramatize the debilitating effects of poverty in "Cock-A-Doodle-Doo," "Poor Man's Pudding and Rich Man's Crumbs," and "The Piazza." Melville's poetry, too, expresses sympathy for the common person, particularly in *Battle-Pieces*, which laments the young collegians, North and South, slain in the Civil War (*CP* 103–5). Another poem in this volume, "Formerly a Slave," ennobles the selfless patience of an old woman emancipated from slavery too late to help her but in time to let her "children's children ... know / The good withheld from her" (*CP* 101). Even *Clarel*, Melville's

18,000 line-poem examining religious doubt, addresses the conflict between Calvinism and democracy, the one premised on notions of human depravity and divine omnipotence and the other on Enlightenment ideals of individual worth and personal liberty. Along with Walt Whitman, Harriet Beecher Stowe, and Margaret Fuller, Melville was deeply sensitive to the social, racial, and economic inequities of his time.

When writing about an abstract concept such as democracy, however, some distinctions are in order. Democracy is primarily a political concept, subject to many different interpretations. Its practice and meaning vary considerably, even in the short history of the United States. Political democracy, most liberally defined in the contemporary formula "one person, one vote," does not necessarily insure social or economic democracy. And as we know from American history, racism, sexism, injustice, and intolerance coexist readily with a widespread franchise. Three principles help define Melville's view of democracy: first, focusing on political democracy, the right to vote; second, approaching democracy from the perspective of Melville's own time, the politically tumultuous mid-nineteenth century; third, seeking Melville's views across the spectrum of his life and works, including both fiction and poetry. James Duban, Wai-chee Dimock, Larry J. Reynolds, Carolyn L. Karcher, Stanton Garner, Sheila Post-Lauria, Laurie Robertson-Lorant, and Hershel Parker, among others, have embedded Melville's politics within the culture of his own era and illustrated its diverse definitions of democracy. Alan Heimert, Marvin Fisher, Michael Paul Rogin, John P. McWilliams, and Julian Markels, again with many others, have stressed the artistic complexity of Melville's political vision, and shown how he uses images, symbols, allegory, and allusions to express his subtle and shifting attitudes toward democracy. Most of these scholars agree that Melville became more conservative as he grew older, and some of them (notably Dimock, Duban, and Larry Reynolds) find a mix of democratic and anti-democratic attitudes running throughout his works. This more complex view enriches our sense of Melville's intellectual scope and political independence and intertwines his art more tightly with his thought. Less doctrinaire than Whitman, less abstract than Henry David Thoreau, yet more detached and elusive than Stowe or Frederick Douglass, Melville stands as one of early America's frankest commentators on the hopes and failures of democracy.

Melville came of age in a period generally known as "the golden age of democracy" in the United States. The franchise was considerably extended among white males during the first half of the nineteenth century, as most states abolished laws requiring voters to own property and pay property taxes. Participation increased in every presidential election, leading to lively campaigns during the 1830s and 1840s. Andrew Jackson, elected president on the Democratic ticket in 1828 and 1832, proved that common, uneducated men could rise to rule the state. Galvanized by his example, thousands of Americans rallied to the banner of Jacksonian Democracy. One of these was Herman's older brother Gansevoort, who became famous as a Democratic politician in New York City by ardently supporting the laborers, mechanics, small farmers, and backwoodsmen who made up the bulk of the Democratic Party. Herman reveals his own partisan sympathies when Ishmael credits God for lifting Andrew Jackson "from the pebbles," placing him "upon a war-horse," and thundering him "higher than a throne" (*MD* 117), a triumph for both political democracy and the Democratic party.

At the same time, however, women's suffrage gained few supporters, and voting restrictions based on race, residency, and nationality actually increased. Fewer states allowed African-Americans to vote in 1850 than in 1810, and some states, including Melville's native New York, employed literacy tests, registration and residency requirements, and highly selective naturalization laws to limit the voting population. Martin Van Buren, who followed Jackson in the presidency and staunchly supported Jacksonian democracy, openly opposed universal suffrage (Keyssar 68–9), a position that many Americans approved. Even though the presidential vote almost doubled between 1836 and 1840, it still represented less than twenty percent of the adult population and hovered around that figure until 1920, when the nineteenth amendment gave nationwide suffrage to women. In Melville's time, eligible voters were nearly all white males and hardly represented the general populace. Increased immigration, especially of Irish Catholics, fueled the rise of parties advocating waiting periods of up to twenty-one years before citizens could vote. The most successful party advocating such requirements was the "Know-Nothing" or American Party, which in 1854 gained all but two seats in the legislature of Massachusetts, Melville's home from 1850 to 1863. According to Alexander Keyssar, by 1855 only five states gave blacks the same voting privileges as whites, and many groups had lost political rights they possessed fifty years earlier (Keyssar 54–60). This trend continued after the Civil War, as newly emancipated slaves saw their rights increase during Reconstruction, then severely diminish for nearly a century afterwards. Additionally, the postwar flood of Asian and South European immigrants faced numerous hurdles designed to keep them from the ballot. If Melville had been a strong proponent of multiethnic democracy, he might have addressed such issues as did Mark Twain and William Dean Howells. Yet in his most explicit comments on minority voting rights, he sided with the conservatives. The prose "Supplement" to *Battle-Pieces* argues against enfranchising former slaves too quickly, for they are "in their infant pupilage to freedom," and the natural sympathy we have for them "should not be allowed to exclude kindliness to communities who stand nearer to us in nature," that is, white Southerners (*CP* 464–5). Ishmael's "great democratic God" (*MD* 117) might hurl Andrew Jackson into the presidency, but he would be well advised to take it slow with Southern blacks.

Democracy was an unstable, ill-defined, contested concept during Melville's lifetime, and his works reflect the ebb and flow of democratic ideals in the nineteenth century. Nevertheless, the great question "Who shall rule?," so central to *Moby-Dick*, was important not only for Ahab, Starbuck, and the sometimes mutinous crew of the *Pequod*, but also for American society at large. Of course, Americans agreed that "the people" should rule; but for most of the country's history before 1920, that meant white, Protestant, middle- and upper-class men. As the population began shifting during the 1840s to cities composed of immigrants, Catholics, and unskilled laborers speaking foreign tongues, definitions of "the people" required rethinking. The problem of a rising industrialized working class extended overseas as well, where monarchs still ruled Europe and extreme economic inequities bred class hatred. Revolutions rocked France, Italy, Germany, Hungary, and other countries throughout the century, most notably in 1848 when continental Europe rose against its kings. Americans were keenly aware of these revolutionary movements. Some in Melville's circle, such as Evert Duyckinck's brother George, actually witnessed the street fighting in Paris, while Margaret Fuller provided New Yorkers with detailed dispatches from Rome. Melville alludes frequently to political conflicts at home and abroad, and generally sympathizes with impoverished citizens even while he condemns excessive violence. He enjoyed debating political theory, and argued pleasurably the conventional question, "which was best, a Monarchy or a republic?," with a ship's captain in 1849 (Leyda 1: 323). He returned to this and other fundamental political issues time and again, almost always with an acute regard for the varied circumstances and conditions that dictated a response. Like Stowe and Whitman, he remained a philosophical humanitarian all his life, sympathetic to the suffering of the lower classes and tolerant of racial, religious, national, and ideological differences. Yet humanitarianism is not democracy. Tolerating, even sympathizing with others is one thing, but empowering them at the ballot box is quite another, as Melville made clear in the "Supplement" to *Battle-Pieces*.

The standard account of Melville's political beliefs, articulated most fully by Michael Rogin, stresses the ideological conflict between his aristocratic family and his working-class career, a conflict that led him from a liberal youth to a conservative old age. The grandson of prosperous Revolutionary War heroes on both his mother's and his father's side, Melville seemed destined for a career in business or the professions. But his father suffered several business reversals, and after his untimely death in 1832 the family's fortunes diminished. At age twelve Herman began the first of several jobs as clerk, and at nineteen he made his first cruise as an ordinary seaman on an Atlantic trading vessel. From 1840 to 1844 he voyaged among "meanest mariners, and renegades and castaways," as Ishmael terms them (*MD* 117), experiencing harsh working conditions and living daily among the laboring classes. He returned home and reclaimed some of his earlier status by becoming a writer. He moved quickly into New York's literary elite, particularly the circle that hovered around Evert Duyckinck, an ambitious young editor and critic. Under the general rubric of "Young America," the Duyckinck circle happily combined literature and politics. Through magazines such as *Arcturus*, the *United States Magazine and Democratic Review*, the *Literary World*, and *Putnam's Monthly Magazine*, Young Americans promoted a broadly nationalistic and Jacksonian political agenda, including Manifest Destiny, compromise with slavery, states' rights, and republican government. Yet they also had cosmopolitan tastes in art and enjoyed opera, Shakespeare, and Dante, along with the latest English novels and poetry. Young Americans were too diffuse to form a political party, but their publications were sufficiently popular to garner a wide audience. Melville's most enthusiastic comments about democracy come from the period of his greatest involvement with the Duyckinck circle, 1847–51, and fore-shadow late twentieth-century toleration for racial and religious differences and multicultural values.

In 1850, perhaps disenchanted with the feverish politics of New York, Melville left the city for the rural tranquility of Pittsfield, Massachusetts. Here he gained distance on Young American ideas and even satirized them in *Pierre*; yet he also began publishing his most socially aware stories in *Putnam's Monthly Magazine*, a practice that continued until 1856. In these tales, Marvin Fisher argues, Melville perfected a "subversive" literary style that covertly addressed political issues, couching social criticism in irony, image, symbol, or deceptively optimistic plots. Conservative readers could enjoy the tales on the surface, while liberal readers could discern deeper, more radical themes. "Benito Cereno," for example, seems to support Captain Dela-no's genial view of slavery, yet a closer reading reveals its true anti-slavery ideology. Laurie Robertson-Lorant finds hidden abolitionist views in "I and My Chimney," and suggests that Melville masked his true opinions in order to avoid offending his father-in-law, Chief Justice of the Massachusetts Supreme Court Lemuel Shaw, who sided with slaveowners in the case of the fugitive slave Anthony Burns (351–4). Whatever Melville's inner feelings, he became increasingly disillusioned with the prospects for democracy as the decade wound down. Mob violence and resistance to law increased among both abolitionists and pro-slavery forces, and Americans seemed less capable of peaceful self-government than ever before. In *Israel Potter* Melville's working-class soldier-hero ends up defeated and impoverished, and in *The Confidence-Man* the fools aboard the Mississippi steamboat *Fidèle* become victims of their own greed and gullibility. Melville's turn to poetry toward the end of the 1850s revealed his increased regard for tradition and authority in art as well as politics, and signaled a more skeptical view of democracy.

Melville moved back to New York City in 1863 and three years later took a routine government job as an inspector of customs, working six days a week on the docks. He was a staunch Unionist, but commiserated with the South's sufferings and postwar difficulties, and in *Battle-Pieces* wrote poems celebrating the Confederate heroes Stonewall Jackson, Robert E. Lee, and John Singleton Mosby, as well as numerous Union officers. He wrote nothing about his life as a customs inspector, and focused instead on *Clarel*, a poem based on his travels in the Holy Land. He also composed numerous short poems and prose sketches about a fictitious group of aristocratic gentlemen called the "Burgundy Club" and wrote several nostalgic poems about seafaring and his marriage. In *Billy Budd*, his final work, he left America's political problems behind by setting his story aboard an English man-of-war in 1799. When Captain Vere warns the drumhead court to ignore conscience and follow "duty and law" (113), many scholars feel that he describes Melville's final position on politics, a position decidedly at odds with Ishmael's bumptious Jacksonian democracy of forty years earlier.

This is a compelling overview of Melville's political development, and one can hardly disagree with the general movement from liberal to conservative that marks his writing. The danger of this account, however, is that it suggests a consistent movement in Melville's life and art toward greater conservatism, when in fact his social ideas oscillated throughout his life, even as they did in the country as a whole. Melville dramatized his political views as debates among competing personae rather than as a philosophically consistent ideology. He used this dramatic device extensively in his third novel, *Mardi*, developed it in his short stories and in *The Confidence-Man*, and perfected it in *Clarel*, which is structured around a series of debates on religion and politics. The same can be said for *Billy Budd*, which has provoked the most polarized interpretations of any work in the Melville canon. Many critics insist that readers must choose between Billy and Vere, and have constructed ingenious arguments demonstrating that one or the other is right. The story's true significance, however, lies in its power to make readers think more critically about social justice and individual morality, precisely the ethical conflict that democracy stimulates. Its English setting foregrounds class distinctions and imperialism, issues increasingly evident in late nineteenth-century America. At the same time, its historical setting of 1799 distances it from Melville's time, the 1890s, and encourages a more detached, philosophical reading. Melville's genius in *Billy Budd*, as elsewhere, is to construct a story that provokes radically differing interpretations while realistically engaging political, social, ethical, legal, and personal issues from a multiplicity of perspectives. Such diversity of opinion is the hallmark of democratic debate, and by encouraging it *Billy Budd* enacts the process of democracy itself. As David Reynolds observes, Melville's writing captures "the spirit but not the political content of working-class protest" (278). His art, in short, is more democratic than his ideology.

Because more people today read *Moby-Dick* than read *Mardi*, published only two years earlier, we neglect early evidence of Melville's competing vision of democratic possibilities. Yet if we compare sections of these novels, we see *Mardi's* political skepticism alongside Ishmael's social idealism and recognize that Melville, like American society at large, wrestled with the meaning and value of democracy throughout his career. *Mardi*, Chapters 145–69, contains Melville's most extended political allegory, a journey through South Sea islands analogous to Europe and the United States. The chapters explain the various customs and political systems of each island, and criticize monarchies and republics alike. Melville satirizes Dominora (England) for imperialism and class consciousness, and attacks Vivenza (the United States) for slavery and Manifest Destiny. Mirroring the revolutions of 1848, Franko (France) erupts in volcanic revolt, leading all of Porpheero (Europe) into conflagration. When the section concludes in Vivenza, a young person reads a scroll that compares Vivenza to the Roman empire and argues for a cyclical rather than a progressive view of history:

> though crimson republics may rise in constellations, like fiery Aldebarans, speeding to their culminations; yet, down must they sink at last, and leave the old sultan-sun in the sky; in time, again to be deposed. (527)

Most likely written by King Media, a sympathetic figure whose name indicates his mediatory views, the scroll presents one of Melville's most nuanced analyses of democracy, one at odds with much Young American thinking:

> Thus, freedom is more social than political. And its real felicity is not to be shared. *That* is of a man's own individual getting and holding. It is not, who rules the state, but who rules me. Better be secure under one king, than exposed to violence from twenty millions of monarchs, though oneself be of the number. (528–9)

In his vast sympathy for human variety, Melville understands the appeal of monarchy and the dangers of democracy, and unequivocally endorses neither.

Less than three years later, Melville finished *Moby-Dick*, and along with his celebration of Andrew Jackson's presidency he included a fervent chapter extolling human brotherhood, "A Squeeze of the Hand" (Chapter 94). Ishmael describes the process of squeezing lumps out of spermaceti, the waxy substance extracted from the sperm whale's massive head. The sailors gather around tubs filled with spermaceti and, as they knead the viscous material, they inadvertently squeeze each other's hands. This inspires in Ishmael such an "abounding, affectionate, friendly, loving feeling" that he wonders:

> why should we longer cherish any social acerbities, or know the slightest ill-humor or envy! Come; let us squeeze hands all round; nay, let us all squeeze ourselves into each other; let us squeeze ourselves universally into the very milk and sperm of kindness. (416)

Among the major writers of Melville's day, only Whitman imagined such a literal fulfillment of the American motto, *e pluribus unum* (one out of many), a democratic concept that equalizes individuals and links them with instinctive bonds of common humanity. Although the *Pequod*'s crew endures Ahab's tyranny, the perils of whaling, and conflicts among its own diverse individuals, for one rare moment it images an idealized, self-generated democratic community.

Taken together, Media's scroll and Ishmael's spermaceti tub construct a dramatic dialogue among contrasting personae that extends political debate into different times and environments. Readers must consider who voices a particular political opinion as well as the specific circumstances in which it is uttered in order to assess its merit. Melville is wary of universal truths, and knows that what is appropriate on shipboard may not apply on land. Such relativism makes irony a constant possibility, and many of Melville's narrators and characters make political statements clearly opposite to the author's personal views. Perhaps the most famous obtuse observer is Amasa Delano in "Benito Cereno." His outrageous statements about black slaves – he even offers to buy one – expose the racism at the core of American sensibilities. Even more obvious is "The 'Gees," a short sketch about Portuguese sailors that compares the flavor of their flesh to venison, effectively turning the narrator into a cannibal. Readers of Melville's day understood and appreciated such satire, as Sheila Post-Lauria's study of *Harper's*

New Monthly Magazine and *Putnam's Monthly Magazine* has shown. In fact, Melville's first foray into political writing, "Anecdotes of Old Zack" (1847), was a series of comic sketches of General Zachary Taylor, good-humored tales that even the General enjoyed reading.

In alternately criticizing and celebrating democracy, Melville was hardly alone. Edgar Allan Poe and James Fenimore Cooper attacked Jacksonian democracy, Ralph Waldo Emerson and Thoreau advocated unchecked individualism, Whitman sang the virtues of common men and women, Fanny Fern condemned restrictions on women's legal rights, and Frederick Douglass argued passionately for racial equality. These writers lived in the most tumultuous time in the young nation's history, when democracy underwent numerous difficult challenges: continuing legislative compromises over slavery, the volatile economics of early capitalism, rapid population growth and demographic shifts, enormous geographical expansion after the Mexican War, and ultimately the Civil War itself. Melville was born into a political "Era of Good Feelings" during the 1820s, when party politics were muted in favor of national unity. By the 1850s, however, both major political parties, Whigs and Democrats, were deeply divided over slavery and other issues, and split into new factions and parties with every election. Americans debated the most fundamental issues of nationhood and human rights, including whether the United States should continue as a single country and whether slaves were citizens with Constitutional rights. It was natural for a young novelist who had crossed class lines and attained a global cultural perspective to create characters who participated in such heady debates. Melville often elaborated his ideas as he wrote, taking different positions and experimenting with varied ideologies in order to reach his own conclusions. He was, in one apt formulation, at once "a refractory conformist and a reluctant rebel" (Karcher *Shadow* 3).

In this turbulent atmosphere, Melville remained distant from the agenda of any single party. Yet, despite such political instability, he followed his fellow writers in seeking government appointments to insure a steady income. Such appointments depended largely on party affiliation and were distributed at the beginning of each new federal administration in a practice known as the "spoils system" – to the winner belong the spoils of political victory. If a new party came into power, the winners dismissed the losers' appointees and replaced them with their own party faithful. Some writers were quite successful. Nathaniel Hawthorne, for a time a good friend of Melville's, remained a loyal Democrat his whole life and held three different government posts. In 1853, after writing a campaign biography of Franklin Pierce, the fourteenth president, Hawthorne was rewarded with a remunerative consulship in Liverpool, a position that allowed him to amass considerable wealth and spend over a year in Italy. Melville was much less successful. He approached both Democratic and Republican senators several times, but his attempts foundered because of his indifference to party politics. He finally succeeded in 1866 when he was appointed Inspector of Customs at the Port of New York, a post he maintained for nineteen years. Hawthorne lost all of his posts when administrations changed, but Melville's continuance suggests that he stayed aloof from party matters, precisely the independence one would expect of a writer who could create both King Media and Ishmael.

Although Melville's politics are often invoked in the name of one movement or another, Melville was, compared to his literary peers, decidedly apolitical. Hawthorne gained notoriety for his biography of Pierce, a pro-slavery Democrat, and wrote an unflattering portrait of Abraham Lincoln in a late essay, "Chiefly About War Matters." Cooper became famous for his attacks on American democracy in "The American Democrat" and for a trilogy of novels condemning the populist anti-Rent wars in New York state. Poe regularly railed about the Jacksonian populism that he and other conservatives saw as democracy run amok, and employed racist stereotypes in his fiction. On the liberal side, Stowe and John Greenleaf Whittier grounded entire careers on abolitionism, and Fuller, Fern, Douglass, and Lydia Maria Child argued repeatedly for the rights of women, Native Americans, workers, and African-Americans. Thoreau both practiced and preached civil disobedience, serving one night in jail and later lecturing in defense of John Brown, the radical abolitionist executed for attacking the United States arsenal at Harper's Ferry in 1859. In contrast, Melville seldom entered the sphere of public politics. On the one occasion when he did sign a public petition, he joined New York's Whig elite to condemn workingmen's protests at the Astor Place Opera House against the English actor William Charles Macready in May, 1849. The next night the National Guard was mustered to suppress the protesters, killing twenty-two citizens and injuring thirty-eight in one of the worst riots the city had ever seen. Melville, perhaps unwittingly, had sided with New York's cultural conservatives. Many articles in *Putnam's Monthly Magazine* were more overtly liberal than "Bartleby, the Scrivener" or "Benito Cereno," indicating that Melville wrote subversively not because he had to, but because he wanted to. When he made the lecture circuit in the winters of 1857–59, he chose to speak on Roman statuary, traveling, and the South Seas, popular and uncontroversial topics remote from the pressing political issues of the day. And when he did address a divisive issue such as John Brown's execution, he did so through an enigmatic poem on Brown's mysterious inner self, a gnomic verse that neither supports nor attacks Brown's actions. The second stanza of this terse, two-stanza poem indicates Melville's empathy for frustrated idealists, along with his recognition of the unpredictability of all human endeavor:

> Hidden in the cap
>   Is the anguish none can draw;
> So your future veils its face,
>   Shenandoah!
> But the streaming beard is shown
>   (Weird John Brown),
> The meteor of the war. ("The Portent," *CP* 3)

Among democracy's many discontented voices, Melville the man remained comparatively quiet, taking almost no public stands and leaving his political meditations to debates among his fictional characters. And even in his fiction, he is virtually silent on such leading issues as women's rights, abolition, the extension of slavery into the territories, workingmen's organizations, and other movements associated with democratic values. White-Jacket's famous opposition to flogging in the United States Navy is often cited as an example of Melville's outspoken support for progressive views. But the practice was dying out even before Melville wrote the novel, and proposals were already on the floor of Congress to outlaw it. Critics who valorize Melville for his liberalism ignore the even more liberal views of writers such as Child and Douglass, thus narrowing the political spectrum in order to place Melville further left than he actually was. Moreover, they often ignore his poetry, where he voices more conservative political opinions than in his fiction. In her comparison of Child's and Melville's views on the Civil War and Reconstruction, Karcher has shown how *Battle-Pieces* retreats from Melville's earlier egalitarian and interracial ideals into an accommodating conservatism that relegates blacks to a lesser status. Karcher suggests that Andrew Johnson, the conservative Democratic Vice-President who assumed the presidency after Lincoln's assassination, may have appointed Melville to the New York Custom House precisely because of the conservative cultural politics evident in *Battle-Pieces* and its famously reactionary "Supplement" (Karcher "The Moderate and the Radical" 231–2). Such temporizing on matters that seemed important to Melville earlier, especially racial equality, can hardly be attributed to the constraints of family, as Robertson-Lorant and others have argued. Judge Shaw, who had tried to avoid war by compromising with the South, died in 1861, five years before Melville published his most conservative opinions on racial politics. On the other hand, as Hershel Parker has pointed out, at least one member of Melville's family, his brother-in-law John Hoadley, advocated harsh restrictions on the political rights of former Confederate officers and continuing Union occupation of the South in order to guarantee the rights of former slaves, two positions that Melville directly questions in his "Supplement" (Parker 2: 810–11). Judge Shaw, like Melville, had once been fiercely anti-slavery, but when it came to a question of Union or civil rights, both men chose Union (see Rogin *passim*, especially 281–2). Melville's moderate, even conservative views on the Civil War and Reconstruction, the most important national event in his lifetime, may indicate more about his general political principles than any of his characters' specific effusions about democracy, equal rights, and the poor.

In *Clarel*, a work Melville wrote with little regard for sales or popularity, he composed his strongest critique of democracy. Ungar, a Confederate veteran of the Civil War, and Mortmain, once a republican agitator in the European Revolutions of 1848, are two failed rebels against authority. Embittered by defeat, each now believes that people are too selfish to merit the freedom democracy confers. "Man's vicious: snaffle him with kings" (2.3.180), growls Mortmain, while Ungar, a Roman Catholic, argues that secular reform is meaningless without religion: "Woe / To us; without a God, 'tis woe!" (4.20.132–3). Ungar, a profound conservative, is Melville's most anti-democratic figure. He specifically condemns Enlightenment idealism, human equality, universal suffrage, and democracy's disregard for tradition: "Ay, Democracy / Lops, lops; but where's her planted bed?" (4.19.126–7). Of course, neither man speaks unequivocally for the author. Melville undercuts Mortmain's reactionary politics by giving him a name which means "dead hand," and subverts Ungar's Christian conservatism by associating him with racism and xenophobia. In one especially revealing passage, Ungar denounces Asian immigration into the American West, an extreme position more like that of the Know-Nothings than anything reminiscent of Melville: "An Anglo-Saxon China, see, / May on your vast plains shame the race / In the Dark Ages of Democracy" (4.21.137–9). Mortmain and Ungar poignantly express Melville's disappointment with America's postwar turn toward an industrialized, corporate, utilitarian, and impersonal society fixated on material progress at the expense of spiritual fulfillment. Their anti-democratic diatribes, however, go beyond the political gradualism of *Battle-Pieces* toward an authoritarian ethic even King Media would have questioned. Melville's works all more or less agree, from Tommo's idealization of the "noble savage" in *Typee* through the compassion Vere and his drumhead court feel for Billy Budd, that magnanimity and tolerance, both lacking in Ungar and Mortmain, are key human values. Melville's humanitarian impulses remained strong throughout his life, and are perhaps his greatest social legacy. For example, few today can read Billy's story without regretting his death, even though they may condemn his act of killing a superior officer.

Nineteenth-century American democracy did have a decidedly dark side, not necessarily the one that troubles Ungar, but one that troubled many thoughtful and otherwise liberal Americans, including Melville. From colonial days through the early twentieth century, mob violence was commonplace in American life. Hawthorne's allegory of American politics, "My Kinsman, Major Molineux," depicts a pre-revolutionary mob that tars and feathers an aristocratic official appointed by the crown. The story shows how the noble impulse for republican self-governance can degenerate into anarchy and violence and uproot the very values of civility and toleration necessary for democracy to function. Hawthorne, like other American writers who portray mobs in their fiction, was responding to a historical reality far more present in his time than ours. In 1835, 147 riots occurred, 109 of them from July to October (Grimsted 4). Disputes over slavery motivated many mobs, but economic, religious, and class conflicts also played a role. In 1837 a pro-slavery mob killed the abolitionist editor Elijah P. Lovejoy in Alton, Illinois; another Illinois mob killed Joseph Smith, the founder of the Mormon Church, in 1844; a mob in Boston burned a Roman Catholic convent in 1834, the first of many attacks on Catholic institutions; and during the Panic of 1837, a severe economic depression, over 5,000 hungry workingmen and -women broke into flour warehouses in New York and were repulsed only when the mayor called out the state militia (Burrows and Wallace 609–11).

As Melville's personal experience with the Astor Place riots showed, New York was particularly susceptible to mob violence. Clashes between rival street gangs terrified middle-class citizens during the 1830s and 1840s. Strikes and their accompanying violence became increasingly common as workingmen began organizing labor unions (Wilentz). Ethnic and religious conflict surged in 1871, just as Melville was beginning *Clarel*, when Irish Catholics attacked a parade of Orangemen (Irish Protestants) and the militia suppressed them by killing over sixty protestors (Burrows and Wallace 1005–8). The parade was only three long blocks from Melville's house. But the worst riot in New York's history occurred in July 1863, at the height of the Civil War, with Union troops fighting desperately to repulse the Confederates at Gettysburg. Thousands of men and women, most of them poor Irish, violently protested a new draft law that allowed wealthy men to purchase exemptions. For four days, crowds of angry workers wandered the streets, attacking African-Americans, Republicans, the wealthy, and anyone who tried to protect them. They burned the Colored Orphan Asylum, hanged blacks and mutilated their bodies, barricaded streets, stoned commuter trains, and destroyed mansions, stores, and government offices. Troops had to be recalled from Gettysburg to suppress the riot, and before it was over 119 people had died. For the next several months, 10,000 Federal soldiers remained stationed in the city (Burrows and Wallace 884–95). Melville lived in Pittsfield at the time, but in *Battle-Pieces* he included one of his most profound meditations on democracy, "The House-top: A Night Piece (July, 1863)." The Draft Riots made some citizens think that the bloody, class-based French revolutions had finally arrived on America's shores. Melville's poem encourages such fears, as the narrator hears the "Atheist roar of riot" amid the baleful glare of "red Arson," images associated with French "Red Republicanism" (*CP* 57). He compares the rioters to "ship-rats / And rats of the wharves," and even digs at Irish Catholics when he laments the failure of "priestly spells" to maintain order. The Federal troops under "wise Draco," an allusion to a notoriously harsh Roman lawgiver, redeem the city with "black artillery," repressive measures that corroborate "Calvin's creed / And cynic tyrannies of honest kings," just the kind of authoritarian rule that democracy supposedly denies. Stanton Garner, who has thoroughly examined Melville's Civil War years, argues for an ironic reading of this poem (255–7). But within the wider context of Melville's consistent criticism of mobs and revolutions, any irony in the poem seems directed at those law-abiding citizens who ignore the implications of the riots and continue to believe in "the Republic's faith" that human beings are essentially good.

Mobs, riots, mutinies, revolutions, and violent protests, all democratic excesses that undermine the people's moral authority, pepper Melville's fiction. Some are humorous, as in the round-robin protest against Captain Guy in *Omoo* (73–7). Some are heroic, as in Steelkilt's mutiny in "The Town-Ho's Story" in *Moby-Dick*, a rebellion in which the ringleader shows more humanity toward his captain than the captain does toward him (242–59). Some are brutal, such as the slave rebellion in "Benito Cereno," where slaves strip the flesh from the bones of their owner and throw Spanish sailors overboard (*PT* 107). When Captain Delano restores order, the Spanish sailors take revenge by mutilating bound slaves, continuing a multiracial cycle of violence inherent in the inhumanity of slavery itself. *White-Jacket*, Melville's fifth and most straightforwardly political novel, portrays numerous conflicts between authority and rebellion on an American man-of-war, yet falls short of justifying violent rebellion. After condemning flogging, arbitrary orders, poor living conditions, impressment, and other naval abuses, the novel describes an incident when Captain Claret orders the men to cut off their beards. At first they refuse, and threaten to stop working. But the most respected officer aboard, Mad Jack, "jumped right down among the mob, and fearlessly mingling with them, exclaimed, 'What do you mean, men? don't be fools! This is no way to get what you want' " (358). The men promptly obey, and following the wise example of Jack Chase, the sailors' natural leader, they shave their beards. John Ushant, however, the oldest sailor on the ship, refuses to comply, and accepts twelve lashes and imprisonment rather than lose his beard. In a good example of Melvillean compromise, the narrator praises both Jack Chase's pragmatism and John Ushant's individualism. Moreover, the narrator even excuses Captain Claret, blaming the "usages of the Navy" rather than the man himself (367). Dissent that avoids violence and hearkens to reason is a tolerable feature of democracy. Indeed, the lone figure of Ushant suggests that, if one is willing to accept the consequences of peaceful disobedience, he may be deemed a hero. Violence, whether of the state or the mob, is Melville's true target in *White-Jacket*, as his conclusion suggests: "whatever befall us, let us never train our murderous guns inboard; let us not mutiny with bloody pikes in our hands" (400). Neither of the two "us," government or the people, should resort to violence to resolve social problems.

As Melville indicated in a letter to Hawthorne, political difficulties are more likely to erupt when we lose sight of the individual: "It seems an inconsistency to assert unconditional democracy in all things, and yet confess a dislike to all mankind – in the mass. But not so. – But it's an endless sermon, – no more of it" (*L* 191). "In the mass" mankind is a mob, submerging its individuality in faceless ideologies that deny personal freedom. Jack Chase, *White-Jacket*'s noble foretopman, accepts this distinction in language foreign to us today, but common in the nineteenth century: "The public and the people! Ay, ay, my lads, let us hate the one and cleave to the other" (192). The public represents human beings "in the mass," social animals conforming to dominant values; the people are independent, self-reliant, freethinking individuals who deserve to participate in the democratic political process. Ishmael makes a similar distinction when he observes whales mating among a huge group of their kin. In the human world, this would be taboo, a conflict between private and public behaviors. He finds in this event, however, a metaphor for a democratic society: "But even so, amid the tornadoed Atlantic of my being, do I myself still for ever centrally disport in mute calm; and while ponderous planets of unwaning woe revolve round me, deep down and deep inland there I still bathe me in eternal mildness of joy" (389). This is that "insular Tahiti" of the soul (274) that democracy should nourish. It is the balance between self and society that Emerson and other Transcendental thinkers sought, a balance that could be threatened by too much democracy as well as too little.

In Melville's fiction, democracy requires morally responsible leaders, an "aristocracy of the brain" as Melville called them in the same letter to Hawthorne quoted above (*L* 190). Given human shortcomings, what Melville called "that Calvinistic sense of Innate Depravity and Original Sin" (*PT* 243), such people are hard to find. Ahab falls short as a leader because he places personal revenge above his responsibility to his crew and the *Pequod*'s owners, traducing the rights of both labor and capital. As Starbuck says of his captain, "Who's over him, he cries; – aye, he would be a democrat to all above; look, how he lords it over all below!" (169). Captain Delano of "Benito Cereno" quells a slave rebellion and restores order, but fails to recognize his own moral corruption. "Ah, this slavery breeds ugly passions in man" (*PT* 88), he observes of Cereno, the Spanish captain, exempting himself from his complicity in the very institution he condemns.

Ahab's tyranny and Delano's hypocrisy are the reverse side of mobs, as several of Melville's short stories reveal, and one invariably begets the other. In Sketch Seventh of "The Encantadas," "Charles' Isle and the Dog-King," a Creole soldier declares himself a monarch and invites eighty men and women to become his subjects. A disorderly lot, the subjects soon drive their king to proclaim martial law and protect himself with a pack of ferocious dogs. After a bloody revolt and the Creole's exile, the insurgents break open the liquor casks and establish a Republic. Ignoring history, tradition, and common sense, they create "a democracy neither Grecian, Roman, nor American. Nay, it was no democracy at all, but a permanent *Riotocracy*, which gloried in having no law but lawlessness" (*PT* 149). The island soon becomes an asylum for deserters and "all sorts of desperadoes, who in the name of liberty did just what they pleased" (*PT* 150). Charles's Isle symbolizes democracy perverted by irresponsibility, disrespect for tradition, and license mistaken for liberty. In "Rich Man's Crumbs," an American visitor to London witnesses the annual Guildhall Charity, when the city's poor are invited to consume the leftovers from the aristocrats' banquet the night before. A huge, starving crowd rushes in and so greedily devours the scraps that it reminds the narrator of "the anarchic sack of Versailles" (*PT* 298), one of Melville's many allusions to the excesses of the French Revolution. In less than half an hour, the mob has eaten every bite. Still hungry, the people turn violent and raise a "fierce yell" that "filled the air with a reek as from sewers" (*PT* 301), an image comparable to "The House-top's" vision of a town taken by its rats. The narrator fights his way out through a side door and returns home, "bruised and battered," relieved at having escaped from "the noble charities of London" (*PT* 302). The Guildhall mob, which Melville compares to beasts, cannibals, and Dante's damned in Hell, is the most ferocious and terrifying in Melville's fiction. Like the corrupt democracy of Charles's Isle, it too is a creature of tyranny, here the well-intended but demeaning benevolence of wealthy English aristocrats. People treated this way cannot be expected to perform democratic duties, and as long as charity is used to justify class divisions, democracy will remain an impossible ideal. Both king and subject, rich and poor, master and man delude themselves that any political system – by itself – will resolve centuries of inequality and indifference to individual rights.

Democracy alone, Melville recognized, cannot engender a better society. Increasingly, he believed that more was needed, whether from religion, philosophy, education, economics, perhaps art itself. Hastening social progress with democratic rant, mob action, war, or enforced equality would avail little. Billy Budd's prescient phrase, "And good-bye to you too, old *Rights-of-Man*" (49), uttered in 1799 but premonitory of 1891, when Melville wrote it, embodies Melville's lifelong skepticism of democracy, and echoes the political pessimism that many American writers such as Twain, Howells, and Henry Adams expressed at the end of the nineteenth century. Democracy had not failed, but neither had it succeeded, and America's bold efforts in self-governance remained an experiment, still to be tested in the crucible of the century ahead.

References and Further Reading

Berthold, Dennis. "Class Acts: The Astor Place Riots and Melville's 'The Two Temples.' " *American Literature* 71 (1999): 429–61.

Burrows, Edwin G. and Mike Wallace. *Gotham: A History of New York City to 1898*. New York: Oxford University Press, 1999.

Dimock, Wai-chee. *Empire for Liberty: Melville and the Poetics of Individualism*. Princeton, NJ: Princeton University Press, 1989.

Duban, James. *Melville's Major Fiction: Politics, Theology, and Imagination*. De Kalb: Northern Illinois University Press, 1983.

Fisher, Marvin. *Going Under: Melville's Short Fiction and the American 1850s*. Baton Rouge: Louisiana State University Press, 1977.

Fredricks, Nancy. *Melville's Art of Democracy*. Athens: University of Georgia Press, 1995.

Garner, Stanton. *The Civil War World of Herman Melville*. Lawrence: University Press of Kansas, 1993.

Grimsted, David. *American Mobbing, 1828–1861: Toward Civil War*. New York: Oxford University Press, 1998.

Heimert, Alan. "*Moby-Dick* and American Political Symbolism." *American Quarterly* 15 (1963): 498–534.

Karcher, Carolyn L. "The Moderate and the Radical: Melville and Child on the Civil War and Reconstruction." *ESQ: A Journal of the American Renaissance* 45 (1999): 187–257.

——— . *Shadow Over the Promised Land: Slavery, Race, and Violence in Melville's America*. Baton Rouge: Louisiana State University Press, 1980.

Keyssar, Alexander. *The Right to Vote: The Contested History of Democracy in the United States*. New York: Basic Books, 2000.

Markels, Julian. *Melville and the Politics of Identity: From King Lear to Moby-Dick*. Urbana: University of Illinois Press, 1993.

Matthiessen, F. O. *American Renaissance: Art and Expression in the Age of Emerson and Whitman*. New York: Oxford University Press, 1941.

McWilliams, John P., Jr. *Hawthorne, Melville, and the American Character: A Looking-Glass Business*. Cambridge: Cambridge University Press, 1984.

Post-Lauria, Sheila. *Correspondent Colorings: Melville in the Marketplace*. Amherst: University of Massachusetts Press, 1996.

Reynolds, David S. *Beneath the American Renaissance: The Subversive Imagination in the Age of Emerson and Melville*. Cambridge, MA: Harvard University Press, 1989.

Reynolds, Larry J. *European Revolutions and the American Literary Renaissance*. New Haven: Yale University Press, 1988.

Rogin, Michael Paul. *Subversive Genealogy: The Politics and Art of Herman Melville*. New York: Knopf, 1983.

Scorza, Thomas J. *In the Time Before Steamships: Billy Budd, the Limits of Politics and Modernity.* De Kalb: Northern Illinois University Press, 1979.

Stafford, John. *The Literary Criticism of "Young America": A Study in the Relationship of Politics and Literature, 1837–1850.* Berkeley: University of California Press, 1952.

Trimpi, Helen P. *Melville's Confidence Men and American Politics in the 1850s.* Hamden, CT: Archon Books, 1987.

Widmer, Edward L. *Young America: The Flowering of Democracy in New York City.* New York: Oxford University Press, 1998.

Wilentz, Sean. *Chants Democratic: New York City and the Rise of the American Working Class, 1788–1850.* New York: Oxford University Press, 1984.

11

Urbanization, Class Struggle, and Reform

Carol Colatrella

A longtime resident of Manhattan, Melville traveled to many other cities in the US and around the world, so it is not surprising that a number of his works are set in urban environments and speak to urban social problems and reform solutions. He wrote during the heyday of realist urban novels by writers like Honoré de Balzac and Charles Dickens, who were celebrated for examining social processes at work among groups inhabiting their literary worlds. Melville's stories, novels, and poetry, however, are less directly concerned than are the works of his European contemporaries with describing rich historical detail, elaborate urban social hierarchies, or the city as a place of intersecting social worlds. Melville instead used suggestive images to represent social alienation and economic inequity that evoke reader sympathy for particular individuals in distressing circumstances. In Melville's fictions, cities promote class divisions and inhibit social mobility, despite the efforts of reformers to ameliorate class tensions and the suffering of the impoverished and/or socially marginalized.

Indeed, rather than describing characters moving up through hierarchical social systems, as many realist novels do, Melville's texts identify the downward pressure of social and cultural constraints on his characters. Alluding to complicated pathways of social success and failure, his fictions indicate that while social mechanisms and modes of mobility are obscure in their workings, they are inevitably rigged against the poor, foreign, female, or young. His protagonists maneuver through complex urban and rural spaces, encounter corrupt features of market capitalism and failed reform efforts, and eventually become resigned to their downward mobility, often without observing others' success.

Even characters and plots in Melville's narratives set on exotic islands or ships at sea allude to class, gender, and racial or ethnic inequalities arising from urbanization. In particular, *Typee*, *Omoo*, and *Mardi* demonstrate how some Polynesian cultures lacked social hierarchies until Western Europeans introduced inequities into their communities. Accordingly, Melville's works note the need for social and economic remedies for a variety of individuals and groups – South Seas islanders subject to colonial authorities, the urban and rural poor, single women, immigrants, sailors, prisoners, and others.

In reconfiguring urban images popularized in contemporary newspapers and other narratives, many of Melville's novels and short stories explore how sociopolitical ideologies constrain and enable financial prospects, social mobility, and criminal and social transgressions for individuals from different classes. His fictions also evaluate the psychological and ethical shortcomings of clergy, politicians, and philanthropists and comment on the mixed outcomes of their urban reform projects. Whereas in his South Seas novels such reforms appear as hypocritical European demands promoted by libidinous, bibulous authorities who seek to constrain the pleasures of the islanders, later works like *Redburn, Pierre, Israel Potter*, and *The Confidence-Man* see social systems as corrupt or insufficient in protecting the urban poor, immigrants, and even, ironically, the charitably inclined. In fact, Melville's fictions link reforms to confidence schemes, thus suggesting the unsettled nature of urban industrial life. In coping with difficult economic circumstances, characters and narrators in his fictions experience, without resolving, ambiguities affecting their socioeconomic prospects. Melville's works thus demonstrate how urbanization, class struggle, and reform shape city life in ways that often work against the economic and social prospects of ordinary people (Kelley).

Urbanization

Historical accounts of urbanization in early nineteenth-century Europe and America connect several interrelated developments: technical innovations in industrial manufacturing and the concomitant growth of urban commercial centers, population migrations and expansions, waves of evangelism, increasing respect for science and an emerging scientific method, support for public education, and civic interest in building infrastructural systems to enhance cities (see Noble; Bailyn; Schultz; Melosi). In the antebellum United States, dramatic increases in urban populations in Philadelphia, Boston, and New York and the creation of new cities such as Washington, D.C. were matched by the significant expansion of the United States through territorial acquisitions. Urban development and westward migration offered individuals some degree of social and economic mobility in both Eastern cities and Western outposts.

Technological improvements in the mid-nineteenth-century United States were not limited to the manufacturing of goods, as advances in printing presses encouraged the interrelated development of mass media and urban culture (Leps). Philadelphia, Boston, and New York published newspapers, journals, and books in the early nineteenth century, producing a new national literature competitive with British and European traditions. The creation of mass media was affected by urban growth in that the continuing expansion of cities helped form an American reading public (Zboray). The widespread availability of newspapers and journals played a role in influencing cultural perceptions of national, urban, and Western experiences in salient ways (Tucher, Kolodny). Newspaper and fiction writers in the 1840s and 1850s elaborated the dangers of cities – immigration, crime, alcohol, poverty, prostitution, and exploitative labor (Reynolds) – while encouraging optimism concerning reforms aimed at these evils. Temperance fictions, domestic sentimental novels, city crime stories, and freedom narratives written by former slaves shared an interest in documenting social ills and promoting potential solutions to improve urban environments blighted by poverty, unemployment, and labor exploitation.

Journalistic, historical, and fictional perspectives on urbanization, class, and reform efforts provide a context for Melville's ambivalent representations of the problems and prospects of urban life. While the Puritan John Winthrop's characterization of America as a "city on a hill" emphasized ideals of community inspiring social and political reformers of successive generations, many prominent figures acknowledged anxieties concerning degenerative features of urban environments. For example, in a letter of September 23, 1800, to Dr. Benjamin Rush who treated the disease's victims, Thomas Jefferson remarked that, "The yellow fever will discourage the growth of great cities in our nation, & I view great cities as pestilential to the morals, the health and the liberties of man" (1081). This formulation of disease, poverty, and criminality as features of city life remained critical for many citizens concerned that urban life threatened democracy. As Alexis de Tocqueville remarked in a footnote to *Democracy in America* (1835, 1850), social inequalities of class, ethnicity, and race in "certain American cities" posed a "real danger" for the "future security of democratic republics of the New World" (278). Pessimistic about the prospects of cities to eliminate discrimination, Jefferson and Tocqueville understood that the metropolis would define America's future whether its problems were solved or not.

Reforming Cities

In the first half of the nineteenth century, fears of diseases associated with immigrants, the poor, and the intemperate and anxieties regarding social disorder prompted individuals and religious groups in US cities to work toward the prevention and elimination of urban problems (Smith-Rosenberg; Rothman *Conscience*; and Rothman *Discovery*). Factories located in cities attracted immigrant and native working classes who often lived at subsistence levels (Jackson and Schultz). Often correlating ethnicity, poverty, and lack of hygiene with deviance, reformers promoted employment, decent housing, and education. They worked to protect laborers, improve penal institutions, assist released convicts, raise literacy rates, promote temperance, and care for neglected and orphaned children (Smith-Rosenberg).

Newspapers, religious journals, and sentimental fictions supported various urban solutions, including improvements in hygiene, public works, religious and literacy instruction, public schooling, and employment. Although forms of rehabilitation suggested for men and women differed according to stereotypes of appropriate masculine and feminine behaviors, charitable individuals and agencies worked to eliminate problematic behaviors affecting social interactions, health, and family life, including drinking, common-law marriage, adulterous and promiscuous sex, gambling, and carousing (Stansell 33).

The overcrowding of the working classes, predominantly immigrants, in dense, closely packed tenements without adequate utilities motivated early nineteenth-century philanthropists to improve living environments and enhance public spaces in several cities. Northeastern reformers inspired by Enlightenment philosophy and evangelical religions developed institutional solutions to such social problems in New York, Boston, and Philadelphia. Individuals and groups created institutions (asylums, prisons, workhouses, and schools), established security systems (police forces, fire brigades), undertook sanitary studies, and built urban infrastructure (water, sewage, and power utilities; streets, sidewalks, and parks) (Monkkonen; Melosi). Reform-minded philanthropists and activists, including Mathew Carey in Philadelphia, Charles Loring Brace in New York, and Charles Spear in Boston, worked on behalf of the poor, orphans, and convicts and pressed cities to adopt solutions to protect these vulnerable populations (Smith-Rosenberg; Bender; Colatrella). Although not strictly linked to cities, movements promoting abolition of slavery, women's suffrage, and debt reform advocated these changes, along with infrastructural enhancements to sewers, parks, and security forces to improve cities for all residents (Melosi; Monkkonen).

Also hopeful about urban problems and prospects, Frederick Law Olmsted collaborated with Calvert Vaux to convince the city of New York to implement the 1857 Greensward Plan, which provided park space where citizens of all classes could meet (Kelley). As Olmsted argued around 1877, enhanced city environments improved the nation: "Our country has entered upon a stage of progress in which its welfare is to depend on the convenience, safety, order and economy of life in its great cities. It cannot prosper independently of them; cannot gain in virtue, wisdom, comfort, except as they also advance" (quoted in Bender 13). Other reformers agreed that developing infrastructural systems to support the increasingly dense, diverse populations in nineteenth-century cities would save souls and motivate social progress for a great number of Americans.

Melville's writings address the social dynamics of urbanization, class differences, and charitable reform in broad and detailed ways. He presented Romantic images of individualism, rebellion, and corruption in almost all of his works. His fictions typically depict the experiences of a young man making his way in the world and observing how many around him fail to thrive in rough urban environments or on board ships. And indeed, Melville identifies ships as sharing certain defining cultural characteristics with cities, for both social arrangements depend on hierarchical organizations ruled by an elite corps whose class exempts them from the harsh realities of daily life. Social inequalities – between children and adults, women and men, ordinary seamen and officers, poor immigrants and intimidating "natives" – emerge in cities and on ships. That such tensions between members of different groups – frequently identified as distinct and impermeable economic classes – appear in many of Melville's narratives suggests that the social marginalization he associated with urban class hierarchies reflected similar dynamic processes working across cultures.

Tropical Versions of Urban Problems

In his early South Seas fictions and in his short stories of the 1850s, Melville sketches an ideal world where one would find rural charm rather than decadent urban society, sentimental feminine feelings instead of masculine ambition and ego, and tolerant cosmopolitanism over parochial regionalism. Set on islands or on ships traveling among islands, his first three novels nevertheless evoke urban reform issues in considering social inequalities and ethnic, gender, and class tensions. Although differing generically and stylistically, *Typee*, *Omoo*, and *Mardi* share an interest in comparing and contrasting cultural values of US, European, and Polynesian societies and in judging the evil done in the name of civilization (Lehan 173). The American narrator of each text criticizes foreign influences and constraints imposed on islanders, suggesting that American and European authorities have behaved unethically, irresponsibly, and out of self-interest in imposing moral rehabilitation and other Western ideologies on these populations.

Colonized islands and beaches appear in *Typee*, *Omoo*, and *Mardi* as sites of social oppression and captivity, where British and French authorities impose moral prohibitions and social conventions on sailors and natives. The critique of corrupt authority and suspicion of philanthropists in the South Seas novels also indirectly comments on reforms taking place in the United States, including relocation of Native American tribes, harsh treatment of slaves and freed slaves, and exploitation of urban working classes. In the islands, as in cities, rehabilitation efforts are directed at improving the islanders' literacy, increasing their prospects for employment, and encouraging their temperance, religiosity, and good hygiene. Both European authorities in the South Seas and urban philanthropists sought to tame wild, primitive impulses by promoting civilized forms of behavior. Cleanliness, godliness, and a strong work ethic are depicted as desirable outcomes of a society (colonized or urban) restructured around commercial, entrepreneurial activities. Simplicity, creative expression, cultural rituals, and social equity, on the other hand, were values associated with native cultures, which wane in the new economy Melville described in his South Seas fictions.

As a romantic, somewhat ironic travelogue, *Typee* considers Tommo's enforced stay among the natives on a Polynesian island as a mostly idyllic captivity permitting the narrator's observation and analysis of and participation in a culture where harmonious social relationships and community matter more than money. The centerpiece of comparative cultural criticism in *Typee* occurs in Chapter 17 where the narrator indicates that the lack of money is a benefit for island society because "There were none of those thousand sources of irritation that the ingenuity of civilized man has created to mar his own felicity" (126). Tommo provides details associated with urban life that attest to the validity of this claim, arguing that no money in Typee also means no debts, no poor relations, no duns, no starving children, no beggars, no debtors' prisons, and "no proud and hard-hearted nabobs in Typee" (126). The likely mix of money, poverty, philanthropy, rehabilitation, and corruption found in urban areas provokes the narrator's catalogue of problems related to capitalism, despite the absence of these problems in Typee.

Also referencing negative accounts of how urbanization encouraged factory production as opposed to individual craftsmen producing and vending their wares, *Omoo* criticizes the way international development eliminated native crafts and thereby threatened island folk culture. Ordinary sailors and natives are similarly exploited by naval authorities in *Omoo*, which depicts the failures of the narrator Typee and his companion Dr. Long Ghost, whether the desired goal is romance, employment, freedom, or protection from unjust authorities. Although the island settings of *Omoo* appear paradises to the abused sailors, the effects of colonization and the excessive authority held by the ships' captains imprison the characters either on ships or in the island's seaport communities. Melville contrasts the disciplinary practices used on the ships with the loose informal arrangements of the island jail (Calabooza Beretanee) in ways that forecast the ironic depictions of city versus country life in his diptychs and the representation of city settings as prison-like in his later novels *Pierre* and *Israel Potter* (Colatrella).

Although the sailors in *Omoo* are unable to promote their own employment prospects or to enter into romantic liaisons with the islanders, they indulge in colonialist fantasies of improving the natives through Western intercessions. Typee shows this philanthropic tendency when he describes and comments on Dr. Long Ghost's dream of "improving" Polynesian society. Long Ghost plans to impose his Western values on the natives: "I'll put up a banana-leaf as a physician from London – teach English in five lessons of one hour each – establish power-looms for the manufacture of tappa – lay out a public park in the middle of the village, and found a festival in honor of Captain Cook!" Typee wryly adds, "The doctor's projects, to be sure, were of a rather visionary cast" (245). Melville hereby concisely frames the concerns of urban reformers – good health, literacy in English, improved manufacturing, and redesigned public spaces, connecting these interrelated urban projects with Dr. Long Ghost's dream of celebrating the colonizer Cook. Of course, associating Long Ghost with imperialist reform undermines any positive resonance his plans might have.

Melville too structures *Mardi* as political commentary clothed in fantastic travelogue. The extended conversations of Media, Babbalanja, Mohi, and Yoomy study the model governments of the islands and consider more perfect versions; these accounts suggest the author's interest in reconfiguring communities to incorporate more individual freedom and less hierarchical authority. While *Omoo* points to labor exploitation in ships and island economies, *Mardi* takes a broader social view in describing how hierarchical political systems abuse serfs and others in the lower classes so that rulers can enjoy their privileges. Although the characters' discussions take place on tropical islands, these arguments could just as easily apply to urban communities in the US and Europe, a view encouraged by Melville's use of invented mythic names for islands (Vivenza, Dominora).

Melville's critique of class differences on the tropical islands indicates that even apparently civilized governments are republics in name only. Such societies offer rhetorical praise for freedom while hypocritically oppressing certain groups. As *Omoo* shows, sometimes an individual exercises social mobility in crossing cultures; for example, Lem Hardy deserts an English ship and the prospect of poverty in Britain. He prefers to live among the islanders as a minor ruler married to a princess even though he looks like a savage, demonstrating how cross-cultural interactions do not always preserve social hierarchies. The tropical versions of social inequality depicted in *Typee*, *Omoo*, and *Mardi* exemplify how class depends on economic difference in any society based on an entrepreneurial economy, whether it resides in the islands or in European and American cities.

Cities, Ships, and Jails

Melville's narratives are not straightforward in offering either sentimental bromides or radical criticism concerning urbanization, class struggle, or reform. Instead, his works describe the insufficiencies of capitalism and Christianity as systems ensuring social and economic equity, especially in environments exhibiting rigid hierarchies with little prospect for mobility. The sociologist Erving Goffman's term "total institution" applies to Melville's depictions of cities, ships, jails, and other settings in which individuals are unable to escape from or even resist the constraints set upon them by authorities (Goffman). Such environments exhibit outright selfishness, reckless ambition, and lack of sympathy for those suffering.

In *Redburn*, the young Wellington Redburn barely scrapes through urban adventures in New York, London, and Liverpool as well as some difficult scenes on his ship, where he gradually comes to understand that no one, not even the seemingly paternal captain, will help him or anyone else. Sailors live narrow, constrained lives and are subject to physical abuse by anyone of greater rank, a situation that causes one Larry to complain that it would be better to live on an uncivilized island than on an American ship. Secondary characters heap particular scorn on effeminate boys, immigrants, and unmarried women, as Redburn learns that his compassion cannot protect his friend Harry Bolton, the Irish immigrants on the ship, or the mother and child dying of hunger in the poor Liverpool neighborhood of Launcelott's-Hey.

Redburn's despair at this family's demise amidst a thriving commercial center prompts his complaint that humanity is inhumane, a theme that appears in many of Melville's works:

Ah! What are our creeds, and how do we hope to be saved? Tell me, oh Bible, that story
of Lazarus again, that I may find comfort in my heart for the poor and forlorn.
Surrounded as we are by the wants and woes of our fellow-men, and yet given to follow
our own pleasures, regardless of their pains, are we not like people sitting up with a
corpse, and making merry in the house of the dead? (184)

Such inhumanity characterizes fortunate urban residents who find it preferable, and
perhaps necessary, to ignore those in need: the lawyer who fires Bartleby, Jimmy
Rose's wealthy friends, the blithe bachelors who carelessly waste what the maids have
produced. Yet Redburn eventually abandons his friend Harry, rationalizing this
betrayal as necessary for his own survival.

Although he has looked forward to exploring exciting foreign cities, Redburn returns
to New York disappointed with dreams he has formed in reading his father's guidebook
of Liverpool or from hearing Harry's tales. *White-Jacket* similarly speaks to the disappointing realities and physical anxieties of being a seaman, while characterizing the
world of the ship as a small city. For some characters in *White-Jacket*, the ship is an oasis,
where the afterguardsmen enjoy "comparatively light and easy" duties, permitting
them to "lounge," read, and chat about amorous adventures ashore (10). For the most
part, though, the sailors toil while, beneath them, the Waisters, stationed on the grog
deck, care for livestock and other foodstuff aboard, and the Troglodites mysteriously live
under deck and appear only during storms when all hands are called to help.

The highly disciplined hierarchy of shipboard life is also represented as a far worse
prison than those ashore (Levine), as scenes of physical punishment and death
demonstrate in several of Melville's works. Ishmael recognizes that to be a sailor is
to be enslaved, but "who ain't a slave?", he asks the workers of the world in *Moby-Dick*
(6). Ahab famously holds his crew in thrall to his revenge scheme, symbolized by his
nailing of a gold doubloon to the mast, but this potential reward for sighting Moby
Dick and the captain's indomitable, charismatic authority trouble more reasonable
characters such as Starbuck. The first mate will not mutiny even to save himself and
others, although he recognizes that Ahab disregards all reason and business commitments in seeking to murder his attacker.

Sometimes the prison-like ship appears a comparative refuge from urban despair. In
the same way that a sojourn in the South Seas conjures up Tommo's thoughts of living
in an urban environment without money, debt, and poor relations, White-Jacket
records how his shipmate Shakings dreams of his old life in the well-guarded Sing
Sing as a peaceful respite from "house-breakers" (175). Finding a prison preferable to
life on the man-of-war or even to ordinary urban existence, Shakings's dream ironically introduces readers to the anxieties about safety shared by the working classes with
their aristocratic counterparts.

Freely adapting conventions of cities as they appear in fictional and non-fictional
narratives, Melville's depictions of urban environments in *Redburn* and later novels
image the city as a panorama revealing intermingled social groups, as a labyrinth of
possible deceit, and as a mecca for idealistic pilgrims (Kelley). Also represented in

paintings, etchings, fictions, and newspaper accounts, these versions of the city retain significance as expressions of anxieties about urban life. Panoramic views open up the city to spectators who might be overwhelmed by burgeoning populations and who struggle to remain comfortable and secure. Wending one's way through the labyrinthine twists and turns of an urban environment increasingly populated with immigrants, criminals, and paupers is an occupation familiar to more than one of Melville's narrative protagonists. Cities are imaged in such fictions as industrial and commercial centers of failed opportunity. Melville's urban settings exemplify the great risks inherent in speculation in that they permit the naïve narrator to presume safety without ever encountering it.

In several fictions written in the 1840s and 50s, Melville illustrates how complicated mechanisms of city life crush individuals who are incapable of combating economic hardship and concomitant social disgrace. Melville's short stories set out case studies of the various ways city denizens fail and how they are abandoned by others. His depictions of urban environments reveal that class interests divide individuals and groups, perhaps most explicitly in "Bartleby the Scrivener," where the lawyer employer remains baffled by his eponymous enigmatic clerk.

Bartleby changes from a hardworking employee who sleeps in the office to a vagrant, and finally a criminal in the Tombs; this transformation takes place in the matter of a few pages as his deteriorating eyesight makes him unable to work and therefore of no interest to anyone. Closer to city mysteries and urban journalism than to sentimental novels, Melville's novels and short stories resist optimistic resolutions in favor of illustrating the chronic mistreatment meted out to the poor and unprotected in cities. Yet such diatribes conclude with somewhat cryptic exclamations and questions about man's inhumanity to others, as in the lawyer's ending to "Bartleby the Scrivener": "Ah Bartleby! Ah humanity!" (*PT* 45). A similar direct appeal to readers appears in Lydia Maria Child's *Letters from New-York* where the journalist recounts her 1842 visit to the New York city prison on Blackwell's Island, a visit undertaken and discussed with a companion: "God forgive me. If He deals with us, as we deal with our brother, who could stand before him?" (201). Child's question, like Melville's exclamation, provokes the reader to consider whether injustice can be eliminated by individual intervention based on compassion and sympathy.

Sometimes Melville implies that some must suffer for the sake of others' good fortunes. Jimmy Rose, another eponymous protagonist, endures economic hard times and therefore loses his friends, who apparently cared for him only when he had money. In the three diptych stories, which describe pairs of related scenes in mostly urban environments, the narrator shows how the luxury enjoyed by bachelor lawyers in London comes as the expense of the single women working in New England paper factories ("The Paradise of Bachelors and the Tartarus of Maids"), that churchgoers are less tolerant and generous than theatre audiences ("The Two Temples"), and that the rich are no different from the poor, except that they have material means that only occasionally trickle down in uncomfortably meager ways to the indigent ("Poor Man's Pudding and Rich Man's Crumbs").

Writing Reform

Economic difficulties for ordinary workers and the poor, especially women, are raised in diverse ways in fictions and essays by many women writers of the period, including Lydia Maria Child, Fanny Fern, and Catharine Maria Sedgwick. In her *Letters from New-York* (1845), Child advocated for prisoners and paupers who were judged by standards that would have been deemed harsh for upper-class individuals. Fern's *Ruth Hall* (1855) demonstrated how establishment forces made it nearly impossible for an honest woman to earn her own living in the city. Sedgwick examined in a number of novels such as *Live and Let Live* (1837) how urban employers exploited domestic servants. Individual and institutional responses to the needs of the poor and working classes appear sporadic and largely insufficient in these fictions, although the narratives offer some optimism that solutions might be found to resolve urban problems.

Like his contemporaries, Melville probed how socioeconomic inequalities defined the experience of urbanization, but he was more pessimistic about the prospect of eliminating problems in cities. In particular, by suggesting that such reform interventions could be misguided and dangerous, *Pierre* responded to the question of whether an individual might effectively improve the lives of others. Melville described *Pierre* to Sophia Hawthorne as "a rural bowl of milk" compared with *Moby-Dick's* "bowl of sea water," in this way promising a romance rather than an adventure story (*L*, 219). But although the opening of *Pierre* forecasts a romance, the plot in the last third of the novel takes place in a dark, insidiously drawn Manhattan marked by poverty, crime, and violence.

The engagement of the golden couple of Saddle Meadows, Pierre Glendinning and Lucy Tartan, is broken when Pierre decides he must take Isabel, who claims to be his father's daughter, and her friend, the seduced and abandoned Delly Ulver, to New York city as a means of escaping the disapprobation of their rural community. Because Isabel is orphaned, poor, and longing for connection with her half-brother, and because he feels sorry for her and Delly, Pierre concocts a plan to claim Isabel as family by pretending to marry her. He leaves behind his mother, his home, and any hopes of a legacy in Saddle Meadows to set up a new household in Manhattan where their fake marriage might protect them. The narrator hints that Pierre's motives for running away with these women might be at least partially affected by his strange attraction to the mysterious, rather seductive Isabel as much as by his filial and fraternal desire to honor "family" responsibilities.

The group's entrance into New York marks this city as an infernal prison where they hear "the locking, bolting, and barring of windows and doors" (230). After fighting with a suspicious, unfriendly coachman, Pierre temporarily safeguards Isabel and Delly at the Watch House and goes off to find the honeymoon accommodations originally promised by his cousin Glen Stanly to him and Lucy. Pierre bursts in to see Glen, who has refused to recognize his cousin. Being "disowned" enrages Pierre, who threatens Glen and suffers being removed by servants. Returning to the Watch House, Pierre finds a confused disorderly crowd of foreigners and likely criminals harassing Isabel and Delly, who have not been protected by the police officer as promised. Pierre asks a hackman to drive him and the women to some respectable hotel, ignoring the driver's "ambiguous and rudely merry rejoinder" (242). At the hotel, Pierre confronts still another suspicious and bold city resident in discussing his group's sleeping arrangements with the desk clerk.

Although Saddle Meadows was insufficiently welcoming for Pierre and his charges, the narrator emphasizes the group's degenerating fortunes by noting a shift from sunshine to shadow as they move from a rural tranquil setting to an urban environment marked by suspicion, hostility, and vice. Each interaction Pierre has on his first night in Manhattan indicates that the city is not a hospitable environment and that his protective actions will be distrusted and rebuked. Furthermore, the city's dark, dangerous atmosphere, its residents' suspicious, confrontational attitudes, and Pierre's angry, assertive responses combine to suggest that his escape from rural hypocrisy and his attempts to set up an independent household will be difficult. Pierre's intentions are at odds with his circumstances, and his experiences in navigating the city emphasize his similarities with the numerous other immigrants at the Watch House (Burrows and Wallace).

At the suggestion of his friend Charlie Millthorpe, another emigrant from Saddle Meadows, Pierre, Isabel, and Delly take up residence in a building popularly known as the Apostles. It has previously served as a church before being transformed into lawyers' offices, with upper floors used as residences. The other residents of the Apostles, followers of the philosopher Plotinus Plinlimmon, appear somewhat on the wrong side of the law in being kept under observation by the police. The vaguely subversive nature of their activities resembles Pierre's odd mixture of erratic actions and good intentions in appearing ambiguous rather than straightforwardly good or evil (Bercovitch). According to the narrator, he lives as a prisoner of his choices and situation.

Pierre's days of writing to earn enough money to support his household are challenging. He must work in a small apartment that is barely heated while Isabel and Delly, and later Lucy, who joins their small community, also work at home in separate rooms. The narrator playfully describes Pierre as "a poor be-inked galley-slave" (260) who writes in a "solitary closet" (297), a "most miserable room" in which he works "at that most miserable of all the pursuits of a man" (302). The household's disciplined schedule, their assigned rooms (where each member works and sleeps), and the group's isolated existence describe urban living as a form of penitentiary sentence (Colatrella).

Despite his moving to a city famous for its publishing operations, Pierre's professional prospects diminish as a result of his personal choices. Indeed, as the narrator recounts in two chapters describing the shift in Pierre's literary fortunes, while the aristocratic Glendinning was lauded for even his minor juvenile efforts, Pierre the reformer in the city finds it difficult to live up to these expectations. Reviews of Pierre's early literary efforts emphasized his morality and social status. Publishers and graphic designers approach Pierre to ask him about releasing his collected works and sending them cash advances. Editors request his daguerreotype and biography.

Admirers ask for his autograph and portrait. Before he needed to earn a living, Pierre abjured such vanities, but when he hopes to cash in on this praise he fails to earn money from his writing because his morality appears suspect.

The culmination of the novel's plot has Pierre receiving two letters in an episode that resembles a tabloid news story. One letter from his publishers calls him "a swindler" for sending them "sheets of blasphemous rhapsody" instead of the promised novel (356). The other is a joint effort from Glen Stanly, by now Lucy's aggrieved fiancé, and Fred Tartan, Lucy's brother, who call Pierre "a villainous and perjured liar" for taking her in (356). Pierre reacts quickly, stealing two pistols belonging to an Apostle and then meeting Glen and Fred. Publicly assaulted and insulted by Glen, Pierre shoots his cousin and kills him. The final scene of the novel describes the aftermath of Pierre's arrest: his and Isabel's suicides in the Tombs, as witnessed by Millthorpe and Fred Tartan.

During the course of the novel, Pierre moves from hypocritical, elitist Saddle Meadows to dangerous, suspicious Manhattan, and, finally, to the dark, dank Tombs. Each environment Pierre experiences is characterized as a type of captivity, but his last home, a prison, makes explicit what was subtly expressed in other environments, that searching for justice has no place in an urban economy and that radical reform efforts aiming to subvert the class system will fail. While elements of Pierre's situation appear unique in that few men would initiate a false marriage to adopt a sibling, he and members of his household face urban circumstances that many immigrants and other transplants to the city also confronted, including the high cost and deplorable conditions of housing, limited prospects for employment, and proximity to criminal enterprises (Smith-Rosenberg; Anbinder; Sante). By the late 1830s, poor city residents, like the members of Pierre's Manhattan household, were often deemed moral threats in that they exemplified deviance and could infect others (Smith-Rosenberg, Katz). Reform movements, many linked to evangelists, promoted moral solutions to resolve urban dilemmas, but the poor were also castigated for bringing their problems on themselves (Bender).

The City and the Country

Some American writers represent living in the country as providing the possibility for entrepreneurial innovation that builds nationhood. In *The Poor Rich Man and the Rich Poor Man*, Catharine Maria Sedgwick depicts how a hardworking family has a better chance of success by living frugally in the country than living beyond their means in the city. The story of how wilderness can be transformed into a village, a town, and then a city is embedded in the serial plots of many American fictions, from James Fenimore Cooper's Leatherstocking tales to William Faulkner's Yoknopatawpha novels.

While fictional representations of the country denote economic possibility, sincerity of human relations, and healthy living, portraits of the city indicate that urban environments are more likely to entrap individuals. Sensational fictions by George

Thompson and George Lippard paint cities as homes of numerous mechanisms and opportunities for corrupting innocence. Edgar Allan Poe's "Man of the Crowd" notes how anonymous the individual appears in the city. Nineteenth-century newspapers explicated murders such as those of Helen Jewett and Mary Rogers, effectively offering "interpretation[s] of city violence" (Davis 264).

Although the narrator of *Pierre* resists offering social commentary in recounting Pierre's move from country to city, the novel points to the power of social standing and hereditary money as forces aiding already fortunate individuals. Disowned by the Glendinnings and forfeiting his inheritance propel Pierre into urban poverty, for his chances of making his way in country or city depend upon his receiving such supports. Melville's descriptions of rural and urban landscapes in his fictions suggest that both environments present obstacles to social mobility, including limited employment opportunities, the high likelihood that one's economic individual interests conflict with the interests of others, and physical constraints on movement. For Melville, transgression against social norms, marginalization of particular groups or individuals, and despair for those at the lower end of socioeconomic hierarchies are not particularly linked to rural or urban landscapes, but appear to be endemic to the human condition.

Like Pierre, Israel Potter, the eponymous protagonist of Melville's only historical novel, moves through a variety of settings as a prisoner of circumstances. Despite his heroism as a soldier and enduring captivity as a prisoner of war, Potter remains alienated throughout his lifetime, whether as a captive, marginal, or silent historical actor; yet each setting documents his ingenuity in the face of difficult circumstances. Using only his own wits, he must pretend to be what he is not – beggar, spy, sailor, squire, scarecrow – in order to survive in the cities and countryside of England. His fate and fame are contrasted with those of more famous Americans Benjamin Franklin, John Paul Jones, and Ethan Allen, whose appearances in the novel belie their reputations as heroes.

Israel's opportunities do not differ much in the countryside, in cities, or on board ships. His masquerades protect him, but they do not help him succeed. Every situation documents how he is constrained by circumstances and by his modesty even as his ingenuity allows him to survive in old age, albeit in straitened financial circumstances as a mender of chairs in London. At the end of the novel, Israel manages to return from his exile abroad to his native Massachusetts, but he scarcely recognizes his surroundings. His decision to enlist and defend the Revolution initiated a sequence of adventures in which Israel barely manages to escape. Since he might have prospered as a farmer if he had not volunteered, his elderly years living as an urban pauper in a foreign city appear especially poignant.

Melville's next novel, *The Confidence-Man*, takes up the predicament that Israel exemplifies: the difficulties of trusting anyone in an economy where deception reigns under the pretense of improvement. The novel suggests that fraud is the inevitable outcome of investing in Wall Street stocks, reform-minded charities, and fiction, all identified with dynamic processes of urbanization, reform, and social inequality. The narrative is both a generic parable of human behavior and a pointed political allegory in its satiric representation of a variety of contemporary historical and political figures, including Transcendentalists (Trimpi).

The confidence man works his schemes on a riverboat that functions as a small city where residents exhibit varying degrees of individual self-interest, charitable and civic concern, and tendencies to fictionalize for personal gain and/or social improvement, which are difficult to distinguish from one another. The confidence man shifts disguises within a procession of vignettes describing his interactions with passengers and crew; such interactions appear similar to interactions of urban residents who meet by chance or in conversations based on financial exchanges (Bryant). The novel represents these exchanges as efforts of the confidence man to gain the trust of his interlocutor, who is asked to purchase an item, to invest in a financial prospect, to donate to a charity, or to appreciate a story. Some exchanges highlight the deceptive nature of charitable ventures such as the World Charity or suggest that even well-intentioned ventures have "dark" side effects, such as the Philosophical Intelligence Office man's persuasion of Pitch to pay for another boy's passage (Kelley).

The narrative connects the confidence man's continuing attempts to find investors/contributors to interpolated tales emphasizing themes of greed, selfishness, and exploited trust. One story tells of the unfortunate man married to Goneril, who bankrupts her husband and takes away their children. Another describes the formerly rich Charlemont, who, like Jimmy Rose, absents himself from friends likely to cut him because of his poverty. The story of China Aster describes how friendship is destroyed by greed when an unwanted loan results in misfortune. Marriage, friendship, and the legal system, which serve as tools for greed and self-interest, appear in these stories as corrupt institutions bedeviling unfortunates who are innocently caught up in schemes by others.

While some tales in *The Confidence-Man* concentrate on providing timeless moral commentary concerning human nature, others reflect and refract nineteenth-century political issues concerning cities. Stories about Thomas Frye, the innocent man unjustly sent to prison and punished for another's crime, and the Indian-hater John Moredock suggest specific historical criticisms, of penitentiary reform and Indian removal respectively. But both stories incorporate features of urban life, including Frye's description of the mob scene that permits an anonymous murderer to escape while Frye is arrested and incarcerated in the Tombs for the crime and Moredock's racial hatred of Indians that fuels his revenge and reform, for he eliminates those who killed his family in the name of "civilizing" the frontier (Lehan 181). These interpolated tales tell us that murder, racial hatred, and exploitation of innocence become the social foundations of building a city and a nation. The city is built and depends on reforms, "civilizing" experiences that are seldom as effective or ethical as their innovators claim.

Throughout his career, Melville produced fictions set in cities and beyond that offered tropical versions of urban problems and marginalized perspectives on urban life. His works depict individuals constantly in conflict with others, struggling to survive economically and to defend themselves against the schemes of criminals and urban reformers. As *The Confidence-Man* and other fictions establish, it is often difficult for characters and readers to determine who is who, whom to trust, and how to navigate social systems. Melville's last fiction, *Billy Budd*, provides another angle on the narrative problem he examined in "Benito Cereno," how to represent a case where some know, others do not, and those roles are interchangeable depending on the reader's investment and bias. For Melville, understanding the truth of any particular situation becomes a philosophical, generalized narrative account that can be undermined by different perspectives or new evidence. Such possibilities are familiar to city residents and travelers as they encounter at every turn new people, places, and things that might invert previously conceived ideas and theories. Indeed, as Melville's fictions confirm, urban experience of class divisions celebrates the discovery of difference, while at the same time acknowledging the limitations of reforms aimed at eliminating the worst effects of social inequality.

REFERENCES AND FURTHER READING

Anbinder, Tyler. *Five Points: The 19th-Century New York City Neighborhood That Invented Tap Dance, Stole Elections, and Became the World's Most Notorious Slum*. New York: Penguin, 2000.

Bailyn, Bernard. *Education in the Forming of American Society*. New York: Norton, 1960.

Bender, Thomas. *Toward an Urban Vision: Ideas and Institutions in Nineteenth-Century America*. Louisville: University Press of Kentucky, 1975.

Bercovitch, Sacvan. *The Rites of Assent*. London and New York: Routledge, 1993.

Burrows, Edward G. and Mike Wallace. *Gotham: A History of New York City to 1898*. New York: Oxford University Press, 1999.

Bryant, John. "*The Confidence-Man*: Melville's Problem Novel." In *A Companion to Melville Studies*. Ed. John Bryant. Westport, CT: Greenwood Press, 1986. 315–50.

Child, Lydia Maria. *Letters from New-York*. 1845. Rpt. Freeport, NY: Books for Libraries, 1970.

Colatrella, Carol. *Literature and Moral Reform: Melville and the Discipline of Reading*. Gainesville: University Press of Florida, 2002.

Davis, David Brion. *Homicide in American Fiction, 1798–1860*. Ithaca, NY: Cornell University Press, 1957.

Goffman, Erving. *Asylums: Essays on the Social Situations of Mental Patients and Other Inmates*. New York: Doubleday, 1961.

Jackson, Kenneth T. and Stanley Schultz, eds. *Cities in American History*. New York: Knopf, 1972.

Jefferson, Thomas. Letter to Dr. Benjamin Rush. September 23, 1800. *Writings*. New York: Library of America, 1984. 1080–2.

Katz, Michael. *Improving Poor People: The Welfare State, the "Underclass," and Urban Schools as History*. Princeton, NJ: Princeton University Press, 1995.

Kelley, Wyn. *Melville's City*. Cambridge: Cambridge University Press, 1996.

Kolodny, Annette. *The Land Before Her: Fantasy and Experience of the American Frontiers, 1630–1860*. Chapel Hill: University of North Carolina Press, 1984.

Lehan, Richard. *The City in Literature: An Intellectual and Cultural History*. Berkeley: University of California Press, 1998.

Leps, Marie-Christine. *Apprehending the Criminal: The Production of Deviance in Nineteenth-Century Discourse*. Durham, NC: Duke University Press, 1992.

Levine, Robert. "Fiction and Reform I." In *The Columbia Literary History of the American Novel*. Ed. Emory Elliott. New York: Columbia University Press, 1991. 130–55.

Melosi, Martin. *The Sanitary City: Urban Infrastructure in America from Colonial Times to the Present*. Baltimore: Johns Hopkins University Press, 2000.

Monkkonen, Eric. *American Becomes Urban: The Development of U.S. Cities and Towns*. Berkeley: University of California Press, 1988.

Noble, David. *A World without Women: The Christian Clerical Culture of Western Science*. New York: Oxford University Press, 1992.

Reynolds, David. *Beneath the American Renaissance: The Subversive Imagination in the Age of Emerson and Melville*. Cambridge, MA: Harvard University Press, 1989.

Rothman, David J. *Conscience and Convenience: The Asylum and its Alternatives in Progressive America*. Boston: Little, Brown, 1980.

——— . *The Discovery of the Asylum: Social Order and Disorder in the New Republic*. Rev. ed. Boston: Little, Brown, 1990.

Sante, Luc. *Low Life: Lures and Snares of New York*. New York: Farrar Straus Giroux, 1991.

Schultz, Stanley. *The Culture Factory: Boston Public Schools, 1789–1860*. New York: Oxford University Press, 1973.

Smith-Rosenberg, Carroll. *Religion and the Rise of the American City: The New York Mission Movement, 1812–1870*. Ithaca, NY: Cornell University Press, 1971.

Stansell, Christine. *City of Women: Sex and Class in New York, 1789–1860*. Urbana: University of Illinois Press, 1987.

Tocqueville, Alexis de. *Democracy in America*. Ed. J. P. Mayer. Trans. George Lawrence. New York: Doubleday, 1969.

Trimpi, Helen. *Melville's Confidence Men and American Politics in the 1850s*. Hamden, CT: Archon Books, 1987.

Tucher, Andie. *Froth and Scum: Truth, Beauty, Goodness, and the Ax-Murder in America's First Mass Medium*. Chapel Hill: University of North Carolina Press, 1994.

Zboray, Ronald J. *A Fictive People: Antebellum Economic Development and the American Reading Public*. New York: Oxford University Press, 1993.

12

Wicked Books: Melville and Religion

Hilton Obenzinger

I have written a wicked book, and feel spotless as the lamb. (To Nathaniel Hawthorne, 17 November, 1851 [*L* 212])

"Oh, devilish tantalization of the gods" (*MD* 481), Ahab exclaims at the indecipherable carvings on Queequeg's coffin; and the reader may often exclaim precisely the same in the face of Melville's books. In much of his work, Melville forces the reader to contemplate the Absolute suddenly placed in what appears to be the ordinary contingencies of life, and then to consider the consequences: a preternatural white whale hunted by an almost equally preternatural monomaniac; a Wall Street clerk whose passive refusal is both baffling and total; a metaphysical scamp who, as devil or godlike trickster, exposes hypocrisies and the inadequacies of both reason and faith; a rocky, barren Holy Land that refuses to yield answers to seekers on a pilgrimage quest. In each of these, the narratives set up speculative situations with some creature, person, process, idea, or place that cannot easily be digested or explained or contained. The reader then contemplates the possibilities and impossibilities of these situations, and the inadequacies of all perception and representation, while the narrative pushes the reader to dive even deeper into self-reflective thought despite constant uncertainty and doubt. These narratives radiate multiple ambiguities, mysteries, and contradictory interpretations, emanating from a profoundly religious – yet highly unorthodox – sensibility.

The skeptical, questioning attitude toward life has long been part of religious experience, as much as revelation, submission, faith, and devotion, even when, in Melville's case, it is often couched in layered ironies and with great humor. In many respects, Melville is a wisdom writer, in the tradition of Solomon's *Ecclesiastes* ("The truest of all men was the Man of Sorrows, and the truest of all books is Solomon's, and Ecclesiastes is the fine hammered steel of woe" [*MD* 424]), Marcus Aurelius's *Meditations*, Chuang Tzu's *Writings*, and other classic wisdom texts – even though he is no king, emperor, or sage, and his narrative meditations can verge on madness ("There is a wisdom that is woe; but there is a woe that is madness" [*MD* 425]). This is not to dismiss Melville's rich dissections of class, race, and other social dynamics, his meditations on philosophical and ethical dilemmas, his symposia on specific doctrines, his comic disruptions of commonplace assumptions, his hymns and criticisms of democracy, or his jeremiads on Empire. I am highlighting only the dominant religious sensibility of much of Melville's writing.

Melville shared the anxieties about challenges facing orthodox Christian belief in the late nineteenth century that are collectively known as the Victorian "faith–doubt crisis." Through the course of the century, scientific discoveries and radical departures in philosophy disrupted long-held paradigms of biblical authority and revealed religion: Darwin and the theory of evolution; Lyell and the discoveries of geology; and biblical scholars and the "higher criticism" which allowed the Bible to be interpreted as a historical and literary text rather than as divine revelation. All this – along with Enlightenment rationalism, German philosophy, materialist social theories, and the literary humanism of Shakespeare, Milton, Cervantes, Rabelais, and more – formed much of the ground for Melville's explorations.

At the same time, Melville writes within specifically American contours of religious experience, particularly in the profound way the King James Version of the Bible shapes his religious as well as literary universe. He writes deeply influenced by the conservative traditions of his mother's Dutch Reformed Church, particularly the Calvinist-derived sense of innate sin, and, later in life, in response to his wife's commitment to Unitarianism. While steeped in a sense of human depravity, he is also influenced by the more optimistic worldview of Christian perfectibility and covenantal providence that helped to form the ideology of America as a settler-colonial society.

Much American religious sensibility bespeaks a special, divine plan for American expansion, even when that outlook develops unchurched or takes secular, civil forms such as the concept of Manifest Destiny. "We Americans are the peculiar, chosen people, the Israel of our time," says the narrator of *White-Jacket*, invoking the covenantal identity; but then he continues with its secularized extension: "we bear the ark of the liberties of the world" (151). Such a sense of covenantal identity was so deeply embedded in an expanding, colonizing culture that even deists, doubters, and unbelievers adhered to a sense of America's special destiny.

American religious history is often viewed as a succession of Great Awakenings, but it may more accurately be regarded as an ocean of relentless tumult, constant ferment, ebbing and flowing at various times but always alive, unpredictable, and even violent. A proliferation of revelations and sects flowed out of the great creativity and sometimes grotesque contradictions of this religious turbulence. Melville was familiar with Adventist Millerites and Shakers alike: Gabriel of the *Jeroboam* in *Moby-Dick*, "originally nurtured among the crazy society of Neskyeuna Shakers" (314), is not an impossible character, particularly when the white whale seems to confirm his prophetic calling by behaving as "the Shaker God" (316). Melville was also well aware of traditions of skepticism, radical deism, and agnosticism, such as those embodied in the careers of Tom Paine and, after the Civil War, Colonel Robert Ingersoll, the celebrated Republican advocate of free thought.

One major feature of this religious turbulence was the urge to create specifically American texts of a new New-World revelation. Emerson had called for an entirely new vision as part of a spiritualized literary mission, but the eruption of new or purportedly rediscovered religious narratives poured out new revelatory texts as well. Joseph Smith responded to such a calling, even locating a second Holy Land in North America, as did Mary Baker Eddy, and other less successful prophets. Walt Whitman, Emily Dickinson, and many others also provided new religious texts, even new revelations, in their very different ways, and Melville was drawn by the same impulse.

Three books from very different periods of Melville's career illustrate the development of these concerns: *Typee: A Peep at Polynesian Life*, *Moby-Dick, or The Whale*, and *Clarel: A Poem and Pilgrimage in the Holy Land*. Each of these books embraces a different primary genre — captivity tale, romance novel, and the long narrative poem — as well as different modes of religious experience and literary expression: captivity, conversion, and ambivalent return in *Typee*; an epic quest for unsanctioned wisdom sought through Gnostic-like, prophetic blasphemy in *Moby-Dick*; and extended agon as pilgrimage ordeal in *Clarel*. I will end with a brief examination of Melville's final text, *Billy Budd*, as Melville's valedictory.

Typee: "Elasticity of Mind"

In *Typee*, Tommo shows up in Nuka Hiva just at the classic colonial moment of first contact. He becomes witness as well to the destruction of indigenous Pacific societies when the French begin their conquest, and witness to the depredations of the Americans and the British. It is a rare interlude: by the time *Typee* appeared in print, the pre-colonial society on Nuka Hiva that Melville describes had already begun to disappear. Tommo's narration arises out of the uneasy, violent relationship between conquering European and resisting native. Such first encounters are mythic moments in the formation of American settler culture, and Melville employs one of the classic modes of such experiences, the captivity tale.

While the book crosses several genres, such as fictionalized autobiography, travel book, novel, fantasy, ethnography, explorer's study, at its core *Typee* is a captive's narrative. Melville's "peep" at another culture falls within the tradition of earlier accounts of capture by Indians, such as Mary Rowlandson's famous narrative, albeit with radical departures. For one, the book actually relates not just one but three captivity tales, since it also includes Tommo's captivity on the whaling ship, as well as a less physical captivity, the ongoing account of how the Western self is a prisoner of civilization's own presumptuous self-regard and moral failures.

As in many travel accounts, Tommo's observations of alien society provide him the means to satirize his own. At the same time, he rejects the way the missionaries and other detractors inaccurately regard the indigenous society, describing the islanders with great sympathy along with broad irony: "[A] more humane, gentlemanly, and amiable set of epicures do not probably exist in the Pacific" (97), he jokingly observes of his savages, and he marvels at how they seem to thrive in a Happy Valley with no state and no advanced technology – and no Christianity. He discounts rumors of cannibalism, observing that the missionaries "had exaggerated the evils of Paganism, in order to enhance the merit of their own disinterested labors" (169), finding himself increasingly attracted to his captors and their ways.

Most notably, he begins "to experience an elasticity of mind" (123); his view of social life and consciousness literally expands. In comparison to the cruel failures of his own society, the alternative social, sexual, and of course religious sensibilities of the islanders allow him "that all-pervading sensation which Rousseau has told us he at one time experienced, the mere buoyant sense of a healthful physical existence" (127). Tommo links the ideal of the noble savage to sentiment, particularly to the sovereignty of the inner life. Health contrasts with the missionaries' repression and their smug sense of supremacy. His bitter commentaries on the activities of the missionaries (mostly expurgated from the American edition) – of how, for example, the natives of the Sandwich Islands "had been civilized into draught horses, and evangelized into beasts of burden" (196) – attack hypocrisy. Although Melville is careful to differentiate the "practice" of the missionaries from their intent, he also questions the entire civilizing mission's rationale:

> The fiend-like skill we display in the invention of all manner of death-dealing engines, the vindictiveness with which we carry on our wars, and the misery and desolation that follow in their train, are enough of themselves to distinguish the white civilized man as the most ferocious animal on the face of the earth. (125)

Melville's readers would expect that his "elasticity of mind" would have its limits, though, and that he would resist crossing over or conversion to the "other." Besides death, conversion is the greatest fear expressed in captivity tales, although "going native" or "turning Turk" also held their allures despite the colonizer's dread of losing his identity. Tommo's sojourn does test his faith in the solidity of his cultural values, and with questionable results. Although there are attractions to crossing the line, Tommo does not complete the conversion. Despite his doubts about the virtues of civilization, he panics at eating human flesh and displaying a permanent tattoo across his face. The tattoo and the eating of human flesh could be regarded as a type of circumcision and a communion, and they would mark him as a convert, making him a permanent outcast to his own people.

In the end, Tommo can only argue for his return in terms of "Mother" and "Home," invoking sentimental domesticity as the only plausible rationale for leaving his idyll. Perhaps Melville is striking a popular chord by calling upon the woman's sphere for his rescue, but his account has exhausted all the male rationales for return, although the violence of Tommo's escape – his attack on Mow-Mow – also makes Tommo complicit in the colonial savagery he condemns. He has made his sojourn in Eden, and now he would be cast from the garden as a killer.

Tommo is quite aware that conversion in the Pacific flows almost entirely in one direction, but his comparison of the "relative wickedness" of both societies leads to a remarkable "elasticity" in his sense of social being:

> The term "Savage" is, I conceive, often misapplied, and indeed when I consider the vices, cruelties, and enormities of every kind that spring up in the tainted atmosphere of a feverish civilization, I am inclined to think that so far as the relative wickedness of the parties is concerned, four or five Marquesan Islanders sent to the United States as Missionaries might be quite as useful as an equal number of Americans despatched to the Islands in a similar capacity. (125–6)

Through all the satiric comparisons between the two societies, Tommo invites the reader to join him in the realization of contingency and relativism. Tommo has become a Marquesan missionary of sorts: his tattoo is invisible but evident, even though he remains thoroughly ignorant of the deeper dynamics of the Typees' society and religious practices. Nonetheless, he carries back to Home and Mother a new, hybrid consciousness – one that does not assume the solidity of frontiers. "Tommo's loathing of the familiar West but fear of the unfamiliar heart of darkness," observes John Bryant, "can compound into one, then dissolve, and then give birth to a broader cosmopolitan acceptance" (ix).

Melville would come to regret that *Typee*'s enduring success meant that he would be always known as the "man who lived among the cannibals" (*L* 193). But his captivity/conversion tale documented a revelatory experience that haunted the colonial encounter, the possibility that the colonizer/colonized dyad, like others, could be disrupted, redrawn, or even erased. Most readers in the nineteenth century would turn to the book mainly for its adventure and exotic sexuality. The book allowed for nostalgia, masculine fantasies, dread, even guilt; but readers would also experience another dimension, willingly or not. *Typee* invites readers to entertain that "elasticity of mind," to experience an expanded consciousness of the world and its mysteries, a "broader cosmopolitan acceptance" of radical difference. The book proposes that all of our categories may be inadequate, our knowledge starkly limited, our absolutes less certain than we presume. Melville returned neither a Christian nor a Pagan missionary, but he did come back with the invisible tattoo of cultural ambivalence and doubt.

Moby-Dick: "Wicked Book"

In *Moby-Dick*, Melville poses ultimate questions of meaning, knowing and purpose on an even more expansive scale: "And some certain significance lurks in all things, else all things are little worth, and the round world itself but an empty cipher..." (430). In the quest for significance, the romance exhausts the pursuit of knowledge expressed in multiple texts – whales as books, the hieroglyphics on the whale itself, the dimensions of the whale tattooed on Ishmael's arm, "veritable gospel cetology" (xvii), paintings of whales, the tantalizing marks on Queequeg's body, the carvings on his coffin, dreams, omens, prophecies, and more. But as the book proceeds, the dizzying array of texts is revealed each to be inadequate and incomplete, even the Bible. The mincer, "invested in the full canonicals of his calling," the skin of the whale's penis, drops the minced blubber into the tub as "fast as the sheets from a rapt orator's desk. Arrayed in decent black; occupying a conspicuous pulpit; intent on bible leaves" (420). With ribald, scatological zest, Melville satirically dispenses even with the authority of scripture as one more flesh-bound symbolic system.

In *Moby-Dick*, one either does not know enough or seeks to know too much. Ishmael's meditations on the texts of cetology end up ultimately revealing the impossibility of knowing the whale, while Pip's vision of "God's foot upon the treadle of the loom" (414) reveals too much of the innards of creation and drives him mad. The search for knowledge is dangerous. Ishmael discourses on the whale's spout, but when he describes the dangers of an exploding blow-hole he advises, as he does in Chapter 55, that "you had best not be too fastidious in your curiosity touching this Leviathan" (264). In the end, "[the] wisest thing the investigator can do then, it seems to me, is to let this deadly spout alone" (373). The quest for knowledge is engaged always with the awareness that life itself is tenuous: "All men live enveloped in whale-lines. All are born with halters round their necks, but it is only when caught in the swift, sudden turn of death, that mortals realize the silent, subtle, ever-present perils of life" (281). The constant presence of death frames the search for meaning; we all stare into the void, and the true seeker knows that death can arrive at any moment.

Melville uses romance to construct a fantastic symbolic world, with a dense field of scriptural quotations and biblical allusions, including evocative characters such as the castaway son Ishmael and the wicked King Ahab. References to hymns, sermons, and other Christian works are joined to other religious sources (such as Bishop Ussher's account of the age of the world), and to other religions, including folklore, Hinduism, Islam, and, above all, Queequeg's Pacific animism. Along with this rich symbolic world, Melville creates a factual depiction of the whale industry – the facts of the commercial enterprise along with the organization of production on board the ship – and the naturalist examination of the whale itself, so that the pastiche of religions (including parodies of their forms, such as sermons) and metaphysics collides with the discourse of natural science, maritime engineering, social observation, and commerce. This creates a hybrid, unique language that mixes different realms and concepts freely, and allows for ironic combinations of the lofty and mundane: "Oh, Time, Strength, Cash, and Patience!" (145).

But the "message" of the symbolism and of the over-determined plot is never precise; we are given palpable intimations of doom, meditations on knowledge and action, on "invisible spheres...formed in fright" 195), but the overall "significa-tion" seems as indefinite as "the ungraspable phantom of life" (5). All the soliloquies the various characters perform before the doubloon nailed to the mast dramatize the various ways interpretations shape personalities and vice versa, and all are dispensed with by Pip's crazy reduction: "I look, you look, he looks; we look, ye look, they look" (434). The interpretations are real – "There's another rendering now; but still one text" (434) – but they are nonetheless all phantoms of the subjectivity inherent in language.

Seriousness is played against a counterpoint of a series of jokes and ironic render-ings. Ishmael observes the grand joke: "There are certain queer times and occasions in this strange mixed affair we call life when a man takes this whole universe for a vast practical joke, though the wit thereof he but dimly discerns, and more than suspects that the joke is at nobody's expense but his own" (226). But this cosmic practical joke takes a variety of literary forms in the book, starting in the "Etymology" (discover all the possibilities of symbolic meanings if you do pull the "h" from whale, as the passage from Hackluyt cautions, by looking up "wale" in the *OED*), and extending through all of the digressions. Any serious or somber meditation is qualified or questioned or undermined by humor. In "The Doubloon," Ishmael asserts that "some certain significance lurks in all things," otherwise nothing has value; but he goes on to qualify that all Earth would be worthless, "except to sell by the cartload, as they do hills about Boston, to fill up some morass in the Milky Way" (430). The only use for the universe would be to turn it into Back Bay landfill (for Boston's well-to-do): the grand thought is mocked at the same time that it is made more vivid, more cosmic by the incongruity, while the uneasy possibility remains that human striving may, indeed, be worthless.

Even the classic practical joke in the book, the landlord's bedding of Ishmael with Queequeg, goes beyond the usual mariner's tall-tale frame of the greenhorn's initi-ation. The landlord's prank plays out as planned; Ishmael is thrown into a panic when he discovers that he's sleeping with a savage. But there is an even more surprising incongruity when an unexpected bond develops between islander and Ishmael. The deeper joke appears in how easily Ishmael can accept Queequeg's animism, and in how shocked New Bedford society is to see the two walking together as equals: the landlord has been outdone.

Like the narrator in *Typee*, Ishmael can take on the pose of an ethnographer, a witness, an observer, even detached guest among the "meanest mariners, and rene-gades and castaways" (117). The romance is once again a captivity tale – with Ahab's mania creating the alien culture to which the entire crew, even Ishmael, ultimately converts. But it is Ahab himself, the captivating force, that throws the religious mode into another realm altogether. Melville had few friends among the missionary and evangelical press, so the equanimity with which Ishmael embraces Queequeg's reli-gion would only provoke more of the same ire. But when Ahab and his mania enter, *Moby-Dick* takes on the quality of a blasphemous prophetic epic. "I have written a wicked book, and feel spotless as the lamb," Melville commented in a letter to

Hawthorne (*L* 212). The missionary press would readily agree to the first part of that evaluation, but the idea that that book would also act as a Christ-like purification would escape them.

Ahab transforms the romance into a wicked/divine book with his monumental personality, the "certain sultanism of his brain" (147), and the heroic quality of his mania presents a forbidden challenge to God. When Ahab enters, the language shifts to iambic pentameter or becomes operatic or oratorical, more lofty and formal; while Ishmael's more vernacular digressions and musings on philosophy and cetology drop to the background. Stubb dreams he is kicked by a pyramid – the example for the human sublime, as described from at least Kant on; "you were kicked by a great man" (132), Stubb tells himself. Even Starbuck's Christian worldview is overpowered by Ahab. Through the personality of this domineering, impenetrable character, Melville voices unorthodox, even heretical, Gnostic-like ideas: he allows himself even greater "elasticity of mind" to cross over into unsanctioned thoughts. Ahab voices the possibility that mysteries can be understood through rage and action, through opposition and not submission: "That inscrutable thing is chiefly what I hate" (164). Through Ahab, Melville can speculate that an over-God may wait behind the pasteboard mask of reality; that God may be not just indifferent but malevolent; that we can gain access to secret realms of knowledge; that "man's insanity" may be "heaven's sense" (414); that humans can dare to challenge and conquer nature; that the force of one man's will can actually change reality.

Ahab is a creation of America's maritime frontier. His prophetic blasphemies are declaimed within a colonial context raised to a mythic level, with the natural world as the site of domination (and the crew of "isolatoes" as a part of nature as well as instrument). Even with his profound intellect, Ahab bears certain similarities to other "tall tale" characters of the continental frontier, such as Mike Fink and Davy Crockett, a wild man who is also godlike. Such a character can exterminate the demonic creatures who threaten settlement or, in this case, human control of the sea, a character who develops "an ecstasy of power and control" (Albanese 96) to extend his realm. Ahab is no Crockett, of course. He is a blasphemous prophet and not a comic, dialect figure – he speaks in high literary prose in contrast to the vernacular of the crew and the personal meditations of Ishmael – but Ahab is excessive and outrageous, very much in the mold of a Crockett.

However, it would be wise not to reduce *Moby-Dick* to Ahab's monomania. Ahab is only one, albeit a grand and grandiose, personality in response to the universe. Melville presents a wide range of human responses to various forms of captivity, and there are intimations of redemption offered throughout the romance. Ishmael, in particular, presents his ironic attempts to walk the middle path, asserting insufficiency, incompleteness, and contingency. "For whatever is truly wondrous and fearful in man, never yet was put into words or books" (477), he claims in his "draught of a draught" (145). "And the drawing near of Death, which alike levels all, alike impresses all with a last revelation, which only an author from the dead could adequately tell" (477). Ishmael is actually an "author from the dead," the one who "only am escaped alone to tell thee" (573), and Melville has him narrate this "last revelation." The Epilogue has Ishmael floating on the inscrutable "coffin life-buoy" of island people, surrounded by biblical and classical invocations (Job, the Fates, Rachel, the reference to Noah, when "the great shroud of the sea rolled on as it rolled five thousand years ago" [572–3]), and a strangely pacific sea – all written in a style that maintains the mixture of humorous irony ("coffin life-buoy"), heightened symbolism, and high drama. Ishmael is then thrust back to the beginning of the book, as if a witness in Job, to tell his tale of destruction "to thee." The reader has become implicated, has become a character, a stand-in for Job, and we can now differentiate between two readers, as we can between two Ishmaels: the Ishmael we read for the first time and the second Ishmael we reread, knowing the full import of his ultimate questions, along with the first reader who has not been given a "last revelation" and the second reader who has.

Ishmael returns to floating on the "coffin life-buoy" as an emblem of human love. The ironic oxymoron embodies the "marriage" between civilized Ishmael and savage Queequeg across all lines of race, culture, and power. If Ahab were to smash through the "pasteboard mask" (164) of the empty coffin, it would sink, but the mystery of its inscriptions and its buoyant vacancy remains and keeps Ishmael afloat, and that emptiness is an act of compassion. Throughout the novel, commonality of suffering and compassion present themselves as alternatives to the harsh cannibalism of the sea and the seamen. "Who aint a slave?" Ishmael rhetorically asks, and that sense of common abjection (even the masters are slaves to higher forces) unites all, while "the universal thump" is joined to how "all hands should rub each other's shoulder-blades, and be content" (6). In "A Squeeze of the Hand," Ishmael even jokes with notions of affection – "let us all squeeze ourselves into each other; let us squeeze ourselves universally into the very milk and sperm of kindness" (416) – but the moments of kindness and solidarity, of Queequeg's kindness, even Ahab's "humanities," stand out as delusions worth squeezing.

Ishmael seeks to write a "true" book, and he does. The ironies, parodies, sly essays, and jokes work to undermine the seriousness of the book – much as Father Mapple's sermon seems part parody through its excessive rhetoric – yet the hodgepodge of literary styles creates a new sense of lofty, even sacred, narrative. As Lawrence Buell has pointed out, "*Moby-Dick* becomes a sort of modern Book of Revelation, yet also a book that casts doubt on the possibility of revelation," while at the same time it "remains in some measure faithful to a biblical sense of God's elusiveness of human conception" (55). The mock epic-revelation actually transcends itself; the book becomes, in fact, a true epic of a new kind, one that reveals the phantoms of the world and our attachments to them. "To be true," Geoffrey Sanborn explains,

> is to realize the vanity of experience, the inevitable hollowness of everything we grasp, without giving ourselves up to the "woe that is madness" ... What makes *Moby-Dick* a true book, in Melville's terms, is that it drives us in the direction of this doubled realization. By asking us to see that it is necessary both to fill out our emptiness with

desire and to realize that our desire masks an emptiness, Melville means to drive us *against* our inclination to stop short, to end before the end ... (168)

In order to avoid ending before the end, we are returned to the beginning of the book, back to the revelation before death, there again to experience emptiness, delusion, and inscrutability, and what it means to live with mystery through compassion – what Sanborn calls "the ethics of looseness," after Melville's chapter on fast-fish and loose-fish – even as we are again made fast by Ahab's grandly blasphemous heroic crazy quest.

Moby-Dick is a cautionary tale that does not dispel the appeal of the danger from which it attempts to warn us. The reader seeks to escape Ahab (the way Tommo seeks to escape Nuka Hiva) but the allure is intoxicating; readers may break away, but we are left to contemplate an epic of the urge for enlightenment in relation to "the invisible spheres ... formed in fright" (195). Ahab may lead us to doom, but his desire for knowledge and his prophetic blasphemy remain appealing – even as we come to understand that the Absolute cannot be known.

Clarel: Jerusalem's "Blank, Blank Towers"

As a spiritual exercise *Clarel: A Poem and Pilgrimage in the Holy Land* demands an even more challenging reading practice than *Moby-Dick*. Based on nearly three weeks Melville spent in Ottoman Palestine in 1857 – after he abandoned his unsuccessful career as a novelist – and nineteen years of wide-ranging reading in Holy Land travel books, philosophy, Dante, Shakespeare, and more, the book was published in the country's centennial year of 1876. Most of it was written while Melville worked in the New York Customs House, and its composition was painstaking. "Dollars damn me" (*L* 191) no longer – and no longer writing fiction – he worked steadily at his day job, which allowed him to write without any compromise. Writing the poem, as Robert Penn Warren observes, was "a refuge, the 'other life,' the real life into which he might enter at night after the ignominy of the Customs House" (35), and its writing was a type of pilgrimage ordeal itself.

Clarel is Melville's only book to explicitly announce itself as religious: it is, as the subtitle indicates, both poem and pilgrimage, with the poem itself serving as a pilgrimage journey, and not an easy one. *Moby-Dick* entices the reader to return to the novel's beginning with its revelation from the dead, but *Clarel* insists that the reader repeatedly return to the beginnings of passages and whole cantos to understand subtle religious and philosophical dialogues in dense iambic tetrameter verse threaded with archaisms, New World lingo, maritime terminology, and wide-ranging cultural allusions. The poem-pilgrimage is highly dissonant, the plot and dialogues densely compressed, its four parts filled with constantly resonating ironies and clashing diction, and populated with a wide range of obsessed interlocutors in spiritual crisis.

More than most books, *Clarel* must be reread if it is to be read at all; it is, Melville would accurately note, "eminently adapted for unpopularity" (*L* 483).

The poem is structured around the quest of Clarel, a young American divinity student, for spiritual certainty among the "blank, blank towers" (1.1.61) of Jerusalem. In the Holy City, he meets Ruth, the daughter of Nathan, an American convert to Judaism, and falls in love. Nathan decides to build a settlement to hasten the restoration of the Jews, but he is attacked and killed by Arabs. Clarel is forbidden to see Ruth during the mourning period, and he goes off with a representative group of seekers to a journey to the Dead Sea and back by way of the Mar Saba monastery and Bethlehem. On this pilgrimage-within-a-pilgrimage, he engages in a wide range of discussions and observations involving the Abrahamic religions of the Holy Land, along with reflections on Hinduism, Buddhism, and secular doctrines, such as Darwinism, positivism, the communism of the Paris Communards, New World democracy, and more. Upon his return, he finds that Ruth and her mother Agar have died of grief, he curses the Jews and the ban that had kept him away, and he is left to join the march of suffering humanity in the procession down Via Crucis on Whitsun-tide.

Melville presents a broad range of ideas embodied in a wide variety of vivid personalities obsessed with different characteristic responses to the suffering and mystery of existence. The poem is a Menippean satire, a journey of expansive dialogues on all the ultimate questions set in a nether region of rich, albeit desolate, meanings. All religions are explored with a clear sense of their underlying unity, that in their essence they all attempt to address the same ultimate questions, recognize the common bond of suffering, and worship the divine: "The intersympathy of creeds, / Alien or hostile tho' they seem" (1.5.207–8). Such a sense of "intersympathy of creeds" was not too difficult for someone who has had the "elasticity of mind" first exercised among the cannibals, and it was a developing cosmopolitan outlook in the nineteenth century: all religions are, at root, the same. However, the poem does not find that any one faith, including Christianity, can resolve uncertainty, relieve the burden of doubt. The spiritual exercise of considering each one – as rich and beautiful as the dialogues may be – ends with no revelation. The poem, as Charles Olson observes, is a "rosary of doubt" (99).

The landscape of the Holy Land, "Terra Damnata," is a key character in the poem, particularly its stones. Clarel attempts to read these stones as texts, to become a "just interpreter / Of Palestine," despite the fact that "Our New World's worldly wit so shrewd / Lacks the Semitic reverent mood" (1.1.92–6). "But Palestine," Clarel asks a hedonistic, dissembling Jew from Lyons who does not share his quest, "do you not / Concede some strangeness to her lot?" (4.26.140–2). That "strangeness" is the way spiritual meanings reside in those stones, the fact that so many pilgrims and Protestant travelers have come seeking proof-texts in the rocky landscape. Yet Clarel fails, and the symbolic towers of Jerusalem remain blank, inscrutable. He resigns himself to his failure after the death of Ruth, as he joins the procession on

Whitsun-tide, commemorating the Pentecost, the day the Apostles received divine
tongues of fire, but no word from his dead love and no revelation comes to him:

> Wending, he murmurs in low tone:
> "They wire the world – far under sea
> They talk; but never comes to me
> A message from beneath the stone."
>   (4.34.50–3)

Despite this sense of *Deus abscondus*, Clarel and the narrator regard heartfelt
believers with great respect, no matter the tradition: Abdon, the black Jew from
India, Djalea, the stoic Druze guide, and Catholic priests and Mar Saba monks are all
comfortable and at peace in their faiths. But the other seekers are more troubled or
troubling. Derwent, the liberal Protestant, is too rationalist and wears his faith like
"an over-easy glove" (2.22.142), despite his feelings of compassion; Nehemiah is so
entranced by his millennialist beliefs that he sleepwalks into the Dead Sea to die; and
Celio, a Catholic hunchback from Rome, concludes that "This world clean fails me,"
and seeks "Some other world to find. But where? / In creed? I do not find it there"
(1.12.95–8). These believers are accompanied by those who have rejected orthodoxy
or religion with the same emphatic energy, such as Mortmain, a Swede who had
joined the revolutionary movement in Paris but now has lost faith in humanity, and
Margoth, a "Hegelized" Jew, an irreligious geologist who chips away at the landscape
with his hammer and dreams of materialist progress, that the walls of Jerusalem
would be flattened to let in fresh air so "That folk no more may sicken there! / Wake
up the dead; and let there be / Rails, wires, from Olivet to the sea, / With station in
Gethsemane" (2.20.89–94). Each argument – and each personality – is marked by a
different response to insufficiency and failure or to self-delusion.

   The poem is structured around several representative Jews who appear throughout
the divinity student's spiritual quest, and who because of Judaism's relationship to
Christianity are emblematic of a wide range of attitudes toward faith and modernism
that invoke both philo- and anti-Judaic stances. In particular, Melville presents
Nathan's journey from Protestantism to Judaism as an emblem of American religious extremism, and it is no accident that his mania is pivotal to what little
narrative structure there is in the poem-pilgrimage. But Nathan's story is also a
critique of the prevailing American fascination with Jews as God's people in need of
restoration, particularly in relation to America's sense of itself as the New Israel
which finds its own, figurative restoration in its settler mission. Nathan is a "strange
pervert" (1.16.198), the Puritan Zionist who links American aspirations materially
and not just typologically to the ancient landscape. In his journal of his visit to
Palestine 1857, Melville records many observations of Jews in the Holy City, and of
the missionaries trying to convert them as part of their "preposterous Jew mania" of
Jewish restoration: "Passages, presages he knew: / Zion restore, convert the Jew; /
Reseat him here, the waste bedew; / Then Christ returneth; so it ran" (1.8.26–9).

But to Melville, Jews are also fascinating because they are both the most ancient and most failed, and the mania about their restoration is a hopeless "Quixoticism" that appeals to his sense of absurdity. He is particularly fascinated by how the Chosen People labor under a curse reflected in the desolate landscape: "Is the desolation of the land the result of the fatal embrace of the Deity? Hapless are the favorites of heaven" (*J* 91).

This "fatal embrace" is paired to Melville's contemplation of a covenantal America, the other Holy Land, as yet another cursed favorite of heaven doomed to failure: "To Terminus build fanes! / Columbus ended earth's romance: / No New World to mankind remains!" (4.21.157–9). The critique of American optimism – and American culture's sense of special providential destiny – is embodied in the character of Ungar, a part-American-Indian, disillusioned veteran of the Confederacy who fought out of loyalty and not to defend slavery and who has now become a mercenary for the Sultan. No destiny is "manifest" to Ungar; he mocks Anglo-Saxons as "Mammonite freebooters, / Who in the name of Christ and Trade ... / Deflower the world's last sylvan glade!" (4.9.122–5), and he regards America's democracy of diverse communities and the prospect of universal suffrage with revulsion: "One demagogue can trouble much: / How of a hundred thousand such?" (4.21.110–11); and the "Dark Ages of Democracy" (4.21.139) provide only "New confirmation of the fall / Of Adam" (4.21.124–5). Ungar is yet one more obsessed character, and like the other obsessed characters, he takes a train of thought to its extreme conclusion. Yet his radical and rarely heard critique of the New World settler-colonial covenant, voiced during the centennial year of the republic, is as blasphemous as Ahab's Gnostic-like tirades.

Despite whatever elements of truth in all the views Clarel encounters, the poem elaborates what William Potter has called "the tempered heart" theme entwined within all the religious traditions. The "tempered heart" involves the idea that "the soul achieves a devout patience through its experience and endurance of the world's tribulations" (94), that whatever the various doctrines or rational excursions of the head, feelings of the heart for suffering beings underscore all beliefs, "the intersympathy of creeds."

And so, Clarel joins the procession of Christians, Jews, "Turk soldiers ... / Strangers and exiles," even animals – "Sour camels humped by heaven and man ... / Or man or animal, 'tis one" (4.34.26–42) – slowly making their way along the Via Dolorosa during Pentecost. The final vision of multiplicity and unity deepens Clarel's understanding of the common bond of suffering. Those he watches passing by, man or animal, become "Cross-bearers all" (4.34.43), and he too joins the procession, despite the fact that the stones of Jerusalem remain blank.

In the Epilogue, the narrator does offer some hope. In a looser rhyming pentameter, he consoles the divinity student (and the reader) for persistence of doubt in that none of the arguments of the poem have been resolved, that the anxieties of belief and unbelief, along with hope for "the spirit above the dust," remain, despite the challenges of modernity:

If Luther's day expand to Darwin's year,
Shall that exclude the hope – foreclose the fear?
. . .
   Yea, ape and angel, strife and old debate –
The harps of heaven and dreary gongs of hell;
Science the feud can only aggravate –
No umpire she betwixt the chimes and knell:
The running battle of the star and clod
Shall run forever – if there be no God.
                   (4.35.1–2, 12–17)

The mystery of death and suffering remains, but as long as life continues, so does the quest. This is as close to a calming apodicticity, that religious sense of certain truth, as can be achieved in the poem. Despite the attendant uncertainties, however, there are greater possibilities. "The light is greater, hence the shadow more," as the seeker goes through "life's pilgrimage," and we may even discover new realities at life's end: "Even death may prove unreal at last, / And stoics be astounded into heaven" (4.35–18–26). The narrator ends with buoyant, verdant images, encouraging Clarel to turn to his heart, "the issues there but mind," and to keep his head above water: "Emerge thou mayst from the last whelming sea, / And prove that death but routs life into victory" (4.35.28–34).

Coda: "To-and-Fro"

In the works examined here, Melville displays remarkable consistency, despite the different stages of his own literary and intellectual development. In each, there is "elasticity of mind": the ability to cross over and entertain forbidden arguments, identities, and states of being; the persistence to ask ultimate questions; the compassion to reach out to fellow slaves, savages, renegades, isolatoes, common sailors, "Cross-bearers all" who feel "the universal thump." All this as Melville creates literary works that become themselves spiritual exercises in belief and unbelief. When Melville visited Hawthorne in Liverpool on his way to Palestine, the older author wrote in his journal the most perceptive intellectual portrait of the agonistic spiritual life of his friend. Noting his persistent "wandering to-and fro over these deserts" of spiritual uncertainty, Hawthorne concludes that Melville "will never rest until he gets hold of a definite belief.... He can neither believe, nor be comfortable in his unbelief; and he is too honest and courageous not to try to do one or the other" (quoted in "Editorial Appendix," *J* 628). With great literary power, Melville invites readers to join him in his pilgrimage to the "to-and fro" of thought, and though we may not be "astounded into heaven" by the revelation, we may certainly be astonished into a deeper sense of life by reading a "true" book.

But Melville would experiment one more time with the notion of writing a spiritual or even sacred text almost as a coda or valedictory to the "to-and-fro" questions haunting him. In his last novel, *Billy Budd*, he actually writes a sacred text of sorts in the final poem "Billy in the Darbies," and then provides "an inside narrative" to explain its origins and the possibilities of the human perception of the divine.

Everything in the novel is prelude to the poem: The confrontation between the innate good of the Handsome Sailor and the "Natural Depravity" (75) of Claggart as presided over by the too bookish, too human Captain Vere is steeped in biblical references and moments of apparent supernatural significance. The "phenomenal effect" of Billy's surprising cry before his death, "God bless Captain Vere," causes the sailors to repeat Billy's words as if mesmerized; Billy is hanged, while the sailors are stunned into silence and then produce a "strange human murmur," the early cry of rebellion (123, 127). After the execution, the reader is provided with evidences of the profane world's disdain: the purser and the surgeon cavalierly discuss the fact that, when hanged, Billy did not jerk in ejaculatory spasms (a virgin death if not a birth), while the naval newspaper produces a distorted, official account that is cruelly self-serving, a blatant lie demonstrating the role of the state in crushing the truth, even the divine.

Meanwhile, the common sailors come to realize that they have witnessed something extraordinary, even sacred, in the execution of the Handsome Sailor – even Vere, at his death, testifies to this realization – and the sailors spontaneously begin cult practices as humble followers: the spar from which Billy was suspended is "kept trace of by the bluejackets"; and to them, "a chip of it was as a piece of the Cross" (131). Veneration for Billy produces a song "rudely printed at Portsmouth as a ballad" (131), and the story ends with that sacred text itself, "Billy in the Darbies."

The poem is direct and folkloric, eerie and evocative, filled with images of death and resurrection, the monologue of a simple soul who faces the absolute of death. But we also know the "inside narrative" of the ballad of the Handsome Sailor – or at least the "inside" story of the narrator's conflicted testimony. This gives the ballad added, even approaching divine, poignancy as a psalm, although primarily one that seeks comfort in his fellow sailors and not in God: "Ay, ay, all is up; and I must up too / Early in the morning, aloft from alow ... / But Donald he has promised to stand by the plank / So I'll shake a friendly hand ere I sink" (132). In *Clarel*, we are caught between "star and clod" (4.35.16), and with Billy we are suspended between "all is up" and the "oozy weeds" below, caught in the "to-and-fro" of ultimate questions expressed in the mixed voice of a sailor's ballad and a literary elegy.

Melville does not go on to describe the incorporation of the sacred text into the cultic practices of a new religion; but he does allow the reader to imagine such possibilities – or absurdities – as another dimension of the pathos and paradoxes of Billy's execution, as with other allusions to Jesus. At the same time, the idea that any text, whether song or gospel or novel, can present a clear, comprehensive sense of all the complex moral and philosophical issues involved in Billy's execution has been spun into doubt.

Of course, *Billy Budd* invokes far more than the production of a sacred text. The novel dramatizes problematic tensions between reason and feeling, the innocent and the worldly, father and son, the individual and the state, capital punishment and justice, freedom and duty, and more – dynamics that are delineated but left largely to the reader to puzzle through. Could there even be such absolutes of good and "the mystery of iniquity" as embodied by Billy and Claggart? *Billy Budd* exists today as an unfinished manuscript, so readers can argue that Melville, if he could have drawn his final draft, would have been more precise or have limited the evocations and allusions.

But the novel achieves effects in ways similar to many of Melville's works: the sacred text at its end is yet one more demonstration of reality moving far beyond accurate representation or signification, much less complete comprehension, while the expressions of the common sailors are as weighty as those of philosophers, and are capable of containing apparently contradictory feelings. The novel can be seen as a literary star pulsating with inherently multiple, ambiguous, ambivalent, haunting, troubling meanings – with the narrative's inscrutability, the tale's paradoxical, unresolved elusiveness (and allusiveness), the poem's simplicity and complexity, all provoking the reader to ever deeper meditations. Once again, the reader is asked to join Melville in the great "to-and-fro" of spiritual mysteries, daring to travel, as he writes in *Clarel*, even to "The perilous outpost of the sane" (3.19.98).

References and Further Reading

Albanese, Catherine L. "Davy Crockett and the Wild Man; Or, The Metaphysics of the *Longue Duree.*" In *Davy Crockett: The Man, The Legend, The Legacy, 1786–1986.* Ed. Michael A. Lofaro. Knoxville: University of Tennessee Press, 1985. 46–79.

Bryant, John. "Introduction." In *Typee: A Peep at Polynesian Life.* By Herman Melville. Ed. John Bryant. New York: Penguin Books, 1996.

Buell, Lawrence. "Moby-Dick *as Sacred Text.* In *New Essays on* Moby-Dick or, The Whale." Ed. Richard Brodhead. Cambridge: Cambridge University Press, 1986.

Obenzinger, Hilton. *American Palestine: Melville, Twain, and the Holy Land Mania.* Princeton, NJ: Princeton University Press, 1999.

Olson, Charles. *Call Me Ishmael: A Study of Melville.* San Francisco, CA: City Lights Books, 1947.

Potter, William. *Melville's* Clarel *and the Intersympathy of Creeds.* Kent, OH: Kent State University Press, 2004.

Sanborn, Geoffrey. *The Sign of the Cannibal: Melville and the Making of a Postcolonial Reader.* Durham, NC: Duke University Press, 1998.

Warren, Robert Penn. "Introduction." *Selected Poems of Herman Melville: A Reader's Edition.* New York: Random House, 1970.

13

Pierre's Bad Associations: Public Life in the Institutional Nation

Christopher Castiglia

Objecting to the Massachusetts Supreme Judicial Court's 2003 ruling that gays and lesbians may legally marry, US President George W. Bush asserted, "Marriage is a sacred institution between a man and a woman." He might have said, "a sacred *bond* between a man and a woman," but, as Malcolm Gladwell reasons, Bush had to say "institution" because "nobody imagines that the court's decision will actually jeopardize the personal bond between any particular man and any particular woman" (Gladwell 35). The remark expresses something important about institutionalism's role in cultural politics, however. While Gladwell describes institutions as "place[s] to hide when we can't find our principles" (35), it's more accurate to say that our participation in institutions like "marriage," by redirecting our agency into "private" matters, erodes our capacity for principled "public" action.

But why should debates about institutions arise in the specific context of *queer* intimacy? Institutions, Gladwell notes, offer citizens the impression that "there is some abstract thing out there ... that is bigger than them and will long outlive them all, and that it needs to be nourished and protected with socially approved behavior" (Gladwell 35). Promising futurity (they will outlive any constitutive member), institutions assume social responsibility and distribute socially accepted behavior (good "character"). Attributing these qualities to institutions requires, however, locating their opposing traits somewhere else. If we take those other traits to be an interest in present gratification and a disregard for "normal" social principles, we can see how queer people, who reportedly surrender a self-regulating (and self-sacrificing) commitment to social and biological reproduction in favor of an unprincipled hedonism, become institutionalism's other.

The final question we can ask of Bush's "misspeak" is how gay marriage led seamlessly to panic over institutional security or, to ask the question differently, why gay marriage debates flair up alongside concerns over global terror? Marriage is, I would argue, the privatized theater in which dramas of national security are made comprehensible to a radically de-publicized citizenry. Paradoxical claims that gay entitlement has gone so far as to lead to the outrageous demand for normalcy localizes the spread of global rage across the purportedly impenetrable (at least for the US) borders of the nation, forcing the government to resuscitate a failing nationalism in the name of "domestic institutions" (the not-quite-nationalism of the "homeland"). Here's Sandy Rios, president of Concerned Women for America, calling for a Constitutional Amendment to prohibit gay marriages: "If you don't do something about this, then you cannot [complain] in 20 years – when you see the American public disintegrating and you see our enemies overtaking us because we have no moral will" (see Lithwick). Rios links the futures of generational reproduction, civic responsibility, and social normality in opposition to not only the enemy without, but also the more potent one within, sexuality, which requires continual self-scrutiny and self-management, privatized anti-terrorism.

Before dismissing Rios's absurd equation of foreign enemies and gay domesticity, however, note her subtle assertion of a public sphere where citizens are free to "do something." Even as Rios asserts the possibility of action in such a sphere, however, the twin assertions underlying the gay marriage controversy – that private life (marriage) is equivalent to public life (and hence that privacy is, virtually, public), and that the public is threatened by reimaginings of what social affinity might comprise *in the present* (not in twenty years) – require properly patriotic citizens to defend institutions by remaining private and normatively immobile. Rios's proposition – that citizens can "do something" in "public" – is thus a trace fantasy supplementing the erosion of civic agency by the very normative institutions she wishes citizens patriotically to defend. Change and stasis, progress and permanence, choreographed in this unsteady promise, are seemingly stabilized through a belief in a paradoxical futurity I call *institutionality*: an abstract structure that apparently guarantees order despite the changes occurring across time and through the global circulations of bodies, commodities, and emotion (rage, terror, compassion). What allows us to believe, evidence to the contrary, that biological reproduction will correspond to social reproduction (that our children's children will *want* "our" way of life) or across borders (that "our" ways of life will best serve *all* cultures and nations) is our belief in institutions supposedly free from the vicissitudes of will or whimsy.

Institutionalism arose in the early nineteenth-century United States as a response to the paradoxes brought about by global expansion. As more immigrants moved to the US, upsetting the notion of a unified national or religious heritage, and as the United States increased its aggressive territorial appropriations in the West, institutions became the surest way to guarantee the perpetuation of supposedly "national" ways of life that, paradoxically, could spread beyond both the established borders of the nation-state and the temporal horizons of present democratic action. In his 1835 *A Plea for the West*, for example, the influential theologian and educator Lyman Beecher warned readers that "the conflict which is to decide the destiny of the West will be a conflict of institutions for the education of her sons, for purposes of superstition or evangelical light, of despotism, or liberty" (Beecher 12). The nature of the civic institutions responsible for the settlement of the West was, however, up for grabs. Dangerous institutions are brought to the West, Beecher contends, by "foreign emigrants ... unaccustomed to self-government, inaccessible to education, and easily accessible to prepossession, and inveterate credulity, and intrigue, and easily embodied and wielded by sinister design" (51). Beecher lumps together this hodgepodge of credulous, embodied, intriguing behaviors as "superstition": Old-World beliefs passed by word of mouth among those denied formal education. Beecher subtly transforms immigrants' geographic displacement (from one nation-state to another) into temporal displacement (from the past to a more modern present), and therefore renders competing cultural beliefs always already lost, hardly worth defending. In contrast to the backward-looking superstitions, home-grown "evangelical" institutions are forward-looking, tied by Beecher's appeal on behalf of "our sons" to the (always deferred) generational future.

While Beecher may well have imagined institutions as being for the people, then, he certainly didn't conceive them as being *of* the people. For Beecher, institutions prevent the danger that "our intelligence and virtue will falter and fall back into a dark minded, vicious populace – a poor, uneducated, reckless mass of infuriated animalism" (39). Not surprisingly, then, Beecher saw institutions, not "universal suffrage," as the safeguard of democracy: only when "republican institutions" have brought about "the education of the head and heart of the nation," imbuing them "with intelligence and virtue" (42), can people be trusted to rule themselves.

If the unschooled masses cannot be trusted with democracy, neither can their education be entrusted to the nation-state, which operates at too great a distance from the citizens' everyday lives. Civic institutions, touching "heads and hearts" (38), more effectively guarantee social order without appearing to violate the voluntary participation necessary to a democracy. In the same way, institutions carry out the work of empire without the military violence associated with European colonization. With the growth of institutions, Beecher assures readers, the "government of force will cease, and that of intelligence and virtue will take its place; and nation after nation cheered by our example will follow in our footsteps till the whole earth is free" (38); institutions, in short, generate "the power to evangelize the world" (10). To achieve such benevolent institutionalism, however, Beecher must project a disciplined conformity of opinion that apparently bridges the geographic distance brought about by territorial expansion. "And so various are the opinions and habits," Beecher laments, "and so recent and imperfect is the acquaintance, and so sparse are the settlements of the West, that no homogenous public sentiment can be formed to legislate immediately into being, the requisite institutions" (16). Institutions, Beecher imagines, will turn multiple populations with diverse belief systems into a single entity, "the public," capable of abstracting and hence supplanting those systems. Begging the question of whose authority (whose definition of virtuous sentiment) will establish such institutions, Beecher offers a paradox: the people will call forth institutions, which in turn will ensure (not coercively, but through the benevolence of the passive voice) that public sentiment is to "be formed" (38).

Freed from the embodied agency of constitutive members, institutions also seemingly become immune to the vicissitudes of history, becoming instead a realm of pure – if opaque – futurity: institutions, in other words, run by "a perpetual self-preserving energy" (42). For Beecher, institutions ensure that the future, not the past, will be America's glory, which comes not "by anniversary resolutions and fourth of July orations, but by well systematized voluntary associations" (43). In return for their "voluntary" participation, citizens are credited with interiority, an "inner" and often unruly domain, which they are responsible for managing, which is why institutionality appears in discussions of intimacy and relationship where it plays no obvious role. It is also why, to this day, heated contestation often arises at such moments, as efforts to abstract association into institutional (and managed) knowledge conflict with lived, various practices that diverge from and contradict institutionalized knowledge.

Institutionalism underlies the immense popularity in the antebellum period of social reform. Building on the liberalization of the Protestant churches in antebellum America, which encouraged free will and self-improvement, reform societies formed to disseminate bibles, religious tracts, and missionaries within the US and abroad. Alongside these religious reforms, national associations formed to abolish slavery, to encourage temperance, to ease the condition of the urban poor, to renovate education, to establish the vote for women. Conventional home life was challenged, both by "free love" reformers and by domestic reformers who attempted to make housework more productive and rewarding for women. These reformers saw structural inequalities within traditional American institutions, owing to the coercion of labor, the unequal distributions of profit and opportunity, the legal alienation of classes of citizens from civic participation, and the stultifying imaginative aridity of conventional domesticity. In response, they called for the overthrow of economic, political, and social structures, and sought to establish more just ways of life. At the same time, reform itself generated new institutions – vast national networks of temperance or abolition societies, held together by newspapers and national conventions. These organizations gave institutions their benevolent social face, while making membership in such institutions synonymous with public activism on behalf of equality and justice. The objects of these reform organizations were often the urban, immigrant poor – the ignorant and superstitious Beecher worries over – who were not consulted as to the "best" course for their own betterment, and whose cultural traits – competing social arrangements, different relations to the body and its pleasures, the after-effects of often degrading labor – became, through reform, synonymous with addiction and "bad character." Not just persons, that is, but whole ways of life were the objects of reform, which, in its institutional life, increasingly characterized its object in ways I have described above as queer: self-satisfying, pleasure-driven, collective, non-reproductive, persistently public, and heedless of self-sacrifice on behalf of an abstract "future."

But the most potent challenge to antebellum institutionalism arose, ironically, from the organization perceived to be itself the ur-institution: the Catholic Church. Beecher distinguishes between Protestant ministers, "chosen by the people who have been educated as freemen," and the "Catholic system," "adverse to liberty" (60–1). Not content to control Europe, Beecher reports, the Pope and other "foreigners opposed to the principles of our government" (61) send "accumulating thousands to the polls to lay their inexperienced hand upon the helm of our power" (54). As a result of Catholic immigration, "ignorance and prejudice, and passion and irreligion, and crime are wielded by desperate political ambition and a corrupting foreign influence" (75). In Beecher's paranoid nationalism, Catholic Americans become, not just a threatening force from without (Rome), but from within ("passion") as well, requiring of patriotic Protestants "keener vigilance and a more active resistance" (63; for a fuller account of Beecher's anti-Catholicism, see Franchot 99–125).

The problem with "vigilance," however, is that Catholicism, like most rhetorically effective national "enemies," is hidden, always only imminent. Calling Catholicism "the most powerful secret organization that ever existed" (Lieber 163), Francis Lieber, one of nineteenth-century America's most eloquent institutional advocates, represents Catholic priests, particularly Jesuits, working "in full organization, silent, systematized, unwatched, and unresisted action among us, to try the dexterity of its movements, and the potency of its power upon unsuspecting, charitable, credulous republicans" (148). As opposed to the "open" democracy practiced by Protestant Americans, the Jesuits, Lieber warns, "are essentially injurious to all liberty," as they "are, as all secret societies must inherently be, submissive to secret superior will and decision, – a great danger in politics, – and unjust to the rest of fellow-citizens, by deciding on public measures and men without the trial of public discussion, and by bringing to bear a secretly united body on the decision or election" (138).

The most powerful weapon in the Pope's secret arsenal, as Jenny Franchot has noted, was the confessional (Franchot 100). While Protestant ministers never "dare to attempt to regulate the votes of their people," Beecher asserts, Catholic priests "at the confessional learn all the private concerns of their people, and have almost unlimited power over the conscience as it respects the performance of every civil or social duty" (60). Despite his claim that priests were telling parishioners how to vote, Beecher shows their power arising from effective *listening*. Hearing "all the private concerns of the people," priests, maintaining local contact with those they represent, become paradoxically *anti*-institutional. Beecher can avoid this conclusion only by referring to Catholicism as a "system," depersonalized and abstracted as the government priestcraft threatens to subvert. The priests' familiarity with "private concerns" becomes particularly threatening to Beecher as it generates bonds of loyalty and affection that compete with "all such alliance of affection as might supplant the control of the priesthood" (127–8). "Nothing is more easy," Beecher laments, "than the perversion of associated mind; or difficult, than its recovery to society and a healthful self-government" (131–2).

Rome's conspiracy against democracy sounds oddly like Protestant institutionalism, however. While the Pope seeks to cohere various Catholic populations in America into a single voting-block, so institutions orchestrate various social "alliances" into a unified "public sentiment" echoing the teachings of the Protestant elite. While Rome works surreptitiously to make its dictates appear as the will of individual Catholics, so Protestant institutions exert an invisible influence through the educational and health mores (the norms of "good character" and "healthy lifestyles") they generate and publicize. But if the Roman "system" was so similar to the institutionalism sought by men like Beecher and Lieber, why the virulent anti-Catholicism? Although anti-Catholic sentiment may be attributed to the xenophobic class and cultural anxieties occasioned by dramatic increase in Irish and Italian immigration during the three decades before the Civil War, immigration does not explain the lengths to which Beecher goes to distinguish individual Catholics, who are blameless, from the "system" that manipulates those individuals, nor does it account for the outbreaks of anti-Catholicism in England (in the Gordon Riots, for instance), where immigration was not an issue.

While antebellum anti-Catholicism possibly deflected attention from the less desirable aspects of institutionalism (with a "foreign" devil like the Pope threatening Americans with surveillance, intangible control, and the loss of citizen autonomy, who could worry that domestic institutions might be enacting the same sorry effects?), the differences between Catholic and Protestant institutions, as Beecher depicts them, are just as telling. While Protestant institutions operate through "publicity" – especially print forms like newspapers and pamphlets, increasing the distance between authors and consumers – priests maintain verbal give-and-take with their parishioners. While Protestant institutions are figured as metonyms of the nation-state, securing national identity (even while expanding the nation, in Beecher's case, into Western territories), Catholicism's global reach wreaks havoc with the notion of national autonomy. If, as Beecher claims, Catholicism "perverts" all "alliance[s] of affection" (127), one of those "alliances" is surely citizens' patriotic ties to the nation-state itself. Catholicism may have functioned, then, as institutionalism's troubled conscience, an archive of alternative social arrangements, modes of communication, and cultural forms that institutionalism, while presenting itself simply as the outgrowth of the people's will, nevertheless sought to eradicate in favor of sanctioned models of public order and private virtue.

While Herman Melville's 1852 romance, *Pierre, or The Ambiguities*, might appear to have little to do with institutionalism, anti-Catholicism, or reform, I want to argue that these issues come together in Melville's fiction in ways that shed disturbing light on the consequences of all three for the social possibilities open to citizens in the antebellum United States. I would go as far as to argue that many of the "peculiarities" readers find in *Pierre* – its obsession with incest, its abrupt shift to New York, its Brechtian disruptions of narrative "realism" – may be best understood as arising from the novel's confluence of institutionalism, privacy, and Catholicism. *Pierre* allows us to see, moreover, and to trouble the ways institutionalism organizes (and often conceals) the relation between sameness and difference that, in works like Beecher's, takes the form of a binary about domestic and alien, national and global. *Pierre* may thus be more closely allied with Melville's earlier works (*Moby-Dick*, for instance) than criticism of it as a domestic-novel-gone-wrong usually supposes.

At the start of *Pierre*, for instance, Melville offers a manifesto on the relationships between families and futurity, sociality and sameness, cosmopolitanism and exceptionalism. "The monarchical world," Melville begins,

> very generally imagines, that in demagoguical America the sacred Past hath no fixed statues erected to it, but all things irreverently seethe and boil in the vulgar caldron of an everlasting uncrystalizing Present. This conceit would seem peculiarly applicable to the social condition. With no chartered aristocracy, and no law of entail, how can any family in America imposingly perpetuate itself? (8)

Melville establishes a tense opposition between fixity and futurity (the ability of families to "perpetuate" themselves) on the one hand and, on the other, the seething "social condition" that apparently topples "fixed statues." Fixity is particularly countered, Melville notes, in cities, where the democratic intermingling of cultures, classes, and bodies challenges the "sameness" purportedly represented by family names.

> Certainly that common saying among us, which declares, that be a family conspicuous as it may, a single half-century shall see it abased; that maxim undoubtedly holds true with the commonalty. In our cities families rise and burst like bubbles in a vat. For indeed the democratic element operates as a subtile acid among us; forever producing new things by corroding the old; as in the south of France verdigris, the primitive material of one kind of green paint, is produced by grape-vinegar poured upon copper plates. (8–9)

The passage shifts at this point from lamenting (on behalf of the "monarchical world") families' inability to preserve their conspicuous pre-eminence to endorsing the "art" of democratic "erosion."

> Now in general nothing can be more significant of decay than the idea of corrosion; yet on the other hand, nothing can more vividly suggest luxuriance of life, than the idea of green as a color; for green is the peculiar signet of all-fertile Nature itself. Herein by apt analogy we behold the marked anomalousness of America; whose character abroad, we need not be surprised, is misconceived, when we consider how strangely she contradicts all prior notions of human things; and how wonderfully to her, Death itself becomes transmuted into Life. (9)

While Melville seems to praise the exceptionally democratic "nature" of American newness, his introduction of this national trait raises some unsettling contradictions: the art that characterizes American exceptionalism is not indigenous, but French. The need to assert a distinctive quality for the United States, moreover, arises from the transatlantic circulation of its reputation, demonstrating the US participation in a global traffic in "character" (much less bodies and commodities) that *precedes* its "anomalous" self-definition. In the face of these contradictions, Melville introduces a mediating entity – *institutions* – to seemingly stabilize the tense relationships between nationalism and globalism.

> So that political institutions, which in other lands seem above all things intensely artificial, with America seem to possess the divine virtue of a natural law; for the most mighty of nature's laws is this, that out of Death she brings Life. (9)

If, for Melville, political institutions separate the United States from its Old-World predecessors, once again his language belies the nation-state's distinctiveness: American institutions, after all, only *seem* natural. The status of that "seeming," furthermore, is at best ambiguous: America's institutions apparently have their origins, to borrow Oscar Wilde's pun, in a terminus. How can autonomy be built on global traffic? What kind of future can be made out of death? And if, through his subtle chain of analogies, political institutions find their privatized twin in the perpetuity of families, what kinds of reproduction – generational or social–can come from a state of what Russ Castronovo calls necro-citizenship, "a posthumous existence that is post-historical to the extent that the material conditions that produce political difference, alienation, and unfreedom fail to signify" (Castronovo 12)?

To avoid such questions (but not to avoid them at all, since *Pierre* raises them with a vengeance), Melville deploys the naturalizing language of generational reproduction, paradoxically, to suspend nature, which shows itself cyclically allied with the difference-producing movements of time.

> Still, are there things in the visible world, over which ever-shifting Nature hath not so unbounded a sway. The grass is annually changed; but the limbs of the oak, for a long term of years, defy that annual decree. And if in America the vast mass of families be as the blades of grass, yet some few there are that stand as the oak; which, instead of decaying, annually puts forth new branches; whereby Time, instead of subtracting, is made to capitulate into a multiple virtue. (9)

Here, as throughout *Pierre*, metaphors give up in exhaustion. For what does it mean to invest one's future in generational reproduction, to naturalize *social reproduction* in metaphors of flourishing renewal, in a novel in which *no* family manages to "branch out," in which daughters surrender to chaste suicide and sons become either self-involved dandies or self-destructive misanthropes? While we might explain the bleak outcomes of *Pierre* in terms of Melville's biography – his financial and emotional setbacks upon the publication of *Moby-Dick* or the heartache over his dissolving friendship with Hawthorne – readers should not miss the important clue Melville offers in the analogy that launches the novel: the fate of American families is intrinsically connected to the fate of the nation's institutions. As long as both seek a self-perpetuating future by asserting an autonomous sameness that denies difference, even while profiting from the labor, the property, and the cultural mixings made possible by *international* conquest and commerce, the fate of both, Melville's plot suggests, seems bleak.

The opening of *Pierre* poses the question: can a family, an institution, or a nation with a scandalous origin project a glorious future? As Wyn Kelley has argued, *Pierre* "reveals the fault lines of the American family" (110); in doing so, Melville notes how America's bourgeois families, like his fictional Glendinnings, attempt to "make out a good general case with England in this short little matter of large estates, and long pedigrees," but Melville wryly concludes, "pedigrees, I mean, wherein is no flaw" (11). There *are* flaws in the Glendinning pedigree, however, brought about by the *imperial* genesis of *national* lands, wealth, and identity. Pierre's paternal grandsire, for instance, was a slaveholder and an Indian-killer (29). Pierre's father appears to have impregnated a poor refugee under the pretense of bringing her family relief. Far from indexing national glories, the Glendinning family "pedigree" registers the nation's engagement in and profit from political disruption abroad, international trade in bodies and commodities, and violent imperialism.

The Glendinning wealth's global underpinnings are obscured – for the innocent young Pierre, if not for Melville – by the appearance of an uninterrupted transmission across time of a seemingly stable and glorious essence, the mystification, Melville shows, of power and profit. Mary Glendinning, Pierre's mother, "long stood still in her beauty, heedless of the passing years" (5), the embodiment of the "hills and swales [that] seemed as sanctified through their very long uninterrupted possession by his race" (8). The ability to mask the violent disruptions of capital's historical movements with the apparently harmonious time*lessness* of domestic tranquility enables Pierre to project his affective satisfaction, imperialistically, onto the land and its inhabitants: "Pierre deemed all that part of the earth a love-token," Melville writes, "so that his very horizon was to him as a memorial ring" (8).

Pierre's "ring," however, seems in perpetual danger of memorializing, not love, but disappointment, betrayal, and impotence. Despite his phallic dream of "capping the fame-column, whose tall shaft had been erected by his noble sires" (8), Pierre manages only "a crumbling, uncompleted shaft" (8) whose stones are continually eroded by Time: "the proud stone that should have stood among the clouds, Time left abased beneath the soil" (8). "Oh, what quenchless feud is this," Melville mocks, "that Time hath with the sons of Men!" (8). Pierre's impotence is ultimately the nation's: if national rhetoric promises "equality" in ways that don't allow for difference, much less power, the imperial project of the nation-state requires the perpetual generation of difference in hierarchical relationships that permit power's violent excesses. But given that the nation-state was an imperial project to begin with (as Melville makes clear in tracing the Glendinning genealogy, the United States was founded as a colony, on lands stolen from other nations, and with an economy built on a transatlantic slave trade), the national rhetoric of "equality" masks a violent history of conquest, theft, and murder. If, as Amy Kaplan has argued, domestic rhetorics naturalized and nominally stabilized the imperial expansion of the nation-state, it stands to reason that as Melville troubles US imperialism, the supposedly "private" institutions of home and family, too, would come undone.

The "undoing" of the Glendinning family comes about through an almost parodic series of misnamed relations: mothers and sons pose as brothers and sisters, brothers and sisters pose as husbands and wives, fiancés pose as cousins, and so on. In each of these cases, a relationship built on inequalities of power (parents over children, the wealthy over the poor, husbands over wives) is reimagined as a relationship built on equality (sibling equality, affectionate unions). These reworkings of power relations into ties of mutuality and equality are dangerous, Melville suggests, because they disguise the often violent operations of force and theft as affection and consent (when Pierre decides to present his supposed half-sister, Isabel, as his wife, a plan he conceives and carries out without her knowledge, he tells the poor girl, " 'I call to thee now, Isabel, from the depth of a foregone act, to ratify it, backwards, by thy consent' " [191]). More dangerously, these misnamings collapse all social relations into domestic ones, thereby denying social differences in favor of a family model predicated on self-perpetuating sameness. Pierre interacts with few people who are not relations, and when he does, he either absorbs them into the family (making them a sister or a wife), or, as with Charles Millthorpe, grows to ignore them. The private relations of domesticity, marriage, and family thus apparently work to stabilize the inconsistencies, contradictions, and mixings – the epistemological challenges – occasioned by the global traffic that enables those families and homes in the first place. Even within the context of the "national family," these domesticating formations neutralize the very social conditions that Melville credits with democratic erosion. Yet the ridiculous reiteration of Pierre's strategy of collapsing "others" into his familial "same" in itself suggests that something continually exceeds privacy's imperial grasp: when an obviously unequal relationship between mother and son (" 'I will manage you yet' " [60], Mary mutters to Pierre) gets turned into a supposedly "equal" relation between brother and sister; for instance, the dramatically *unequal* relationship between the siblings, Pierre and Isabel, betrays the dark unconscious of Mary and Pierre's "game," and so Pierre turns his "sister" into his "wife." But we have already seen, in Pierre's relation to Lucy, that men and women in romantic relations are not equal (Pierre dumps Lucy unceremoniously for his new "wife" Isabel), so Lucy gets turned from a jilted lover into a "cousin." And then again, there's the troubling relationship between Pierre and his cousin Glen Stanly, suggesting that cousins are not always democratic peers. And on it goes. Power, it seems, cannot simply be renamed equality, nor can lack of options be called consent. If the failure of the Glendinning family to learn this lesson ensures its ultimate destruction, such will also be the fate, Melville suggests, of the national family, which habitually engages in similar misnaming at the expense of any claims to or of difference.

Pierre fails to learn his lessons – as, indeed, does the nation – because the work of misnaming is carried out at the level of neither the individual will nor governmental jurisdiction, but in intermediary institutions. Such institutions frame the relations between the past and the future (occluding the present, where history occurs), the private and the public (occluding the complex middling spaces where most of everyday life transpires), and familial and national autonomy (occluding the global movements underpinning both). Above all, institutions respond to the mortality of individual bodies, generating an abstract agency that reportedly suspends time in order to envision a better future ("We lived before, and shall live again," Melville writes, expressing succinctly the promise of institutionality, "and as we hope for a fairer world than this to come; so we come from one less fine" [32]). The problem becomes that, without recognition of the differences produced by global exchange, without a space for "private" individuals to interact and a present moment in which such meetings can occur, the possibility of developing ethical – Melville would say "principled" – "fairness" is greatly diminished. Ethical agency, in other words, is ceded to institutions, but if institutions are predicated on the "sameness" of participants and the deferral of outcomes, institutional principles, like the growth of the Glendinning family, will be severely stunted. "From each successive world," Melville observes, "the demon Principle is more and more dislodged; he is the accursed clog from chaos, and thither, by every new translation, we drive him further and further back again" (32–3). Such illusory banishments of "chaos" enable a jingoistic pride ("Hosannahs to this world! So beautiful itself, and the vestibule to more" [33]), but do not erase the material effects of differences, particularly, as Melville's analogy demonstrates, those produced by global migration: "Out of some past Egypt, we have come to this new Canaan," Melville writes, "and from this new Canaan, we press on to some Circassia. Though still the villains, Want and Woe, followed us out of Egypt, and now beg in Canaan's streets; yet Circassia's gate shall not admit them; they, with their sire, the demon Principle, must back to chaos, whence they came" (33).

Pierre can ignore want and woe because, among his other riches, he "inherited the docile homage to a venerable Father" (7). Believing that an unshakable identification with the Father will produce an institutional relationship between them – that the agency of the father will pass, despite the death of his body, to the son, and so on into an endlessly receding future – Pierre surrenders his capacity for action based on his own principles and becomes paralyzed by what his mother calls "sweet docility" (20). While Mary notes the "'most strange inconsistency'" of Pierre's desires, docility hardly befitting a patriarchal "'general's badge'" (20), she subordinates her insight so as to gain from the inconsistent relation between veneration and agency (her ability to "manage" Pierre's docility to achieve her own ends). Pierre also profits (ambivalently) from institutionality, through the inheritance of property, and, as an author, from "invitations to lecture before Lyceums, Young Men's Associations, and other Literary and Scientific Societies" (251).

While literary associations seem innocent enough, Melville shows the more serious consequences of institutionalism when he turns to social reform. The Miss Pennies, a pair of spinsters who cannot encounter the "needy" without putting their proverbial two cents in, have organized "a regular society" (44) to sew for the poor, most of the work apparently being done by the poor themselves, who, as "the less notable of the rural company," are "voluntarily retired into their humble banishment" (46) at a distance from their wealthier neighbors. The systematic segregation of the classes is rendered benevolent by its location within the purported benevolence of reform. Melville challenges such kindness, however, when Isabel, one of the sewing poor, shrieks and faints at the first sight of Pierre; the company "reminded not the girl of what had passed; noted her scarcely at all" (45). The ability of benevolent reformers to aid the poor while scarcely noting their embodied condition (indeed, while denying them a history – a memory of "what had passed" – that might kindle their sense of having been wronged) takes on a more sinister cast when Melville provides the story of Isabel's conception. When a group of destitute French refugees settles near Saddle Meadows, Pierre's father, "with many other humane gentlemen of the city, provided for the wants of the strangers, for they were very poor" (76). The gentlemen apparently "provided" more than food and clothing, for one of the Frenchwomen, unmarried and reportedly pregnant, hastily returned to France, where her daughter – if Isabel's account can be believed – is abandoned in another "benevolent" institution, an insane asylum.

Such moments of reform seem, on the surface, ethically superior to the scornful behavior of Mary Glendinning and her minister, who conspire to drive unwed and pregnant Delly Ulster from the community. Unlike his cruel mother, never "had the generous Pierre cherished the heathenish conceit, that even in the general world, Sin is a fair object to be stretched on the cruelest racks by self-complacent Virtue, that self-complacent Virtue may feed her lily-liveredness on the pallor of Sin's anguish" (177). If "Love is the world's great redeemer and reformer" (34), if, that is, benevolence tempered by love (either the particular love Pierre's father may have felt for the French refugee or the more abstract love the Pennies feel for the unclothed poor) seemingly excuses reform's less desirable consequences, however, Melville shows us, in Isabel's pregnant and abandoned mother and her ignored and mistreated daughter, that sometimes "love" is as cruel and lily-livered as contempt, and while contempt at least lets its object know who is the source of her hardship, "love," in its institutional forms, leaves its object at a double loss: abandoned and degraded, but seemingly without any legitimate grounds of complaint.

If "public" institutions – such as reform organizations or the more austere asylum – leave something to be desired, "private" institutions – marriage and family – come in for particular criticism in *Pierre*, as they produce what Melville describes as "the dreary heart-vacancies of the conventional life" (90). Conventional life becomes dreary, Melville suggests, precisely because its institutions generate the illusion of "privacy" that lets citizens (at least middle-class, white ones) believe they live in (never quite) securely self-contained units of "sameness" (the family and the home) that supposedly contain the *qualities* of social life (handbooks throughout this period instructed parents on how to raise children to be "good citizens" by being obedient, self-disciplined family members) while, in fact, isolating inhabitants from interaction with the differences that make social negotiations necessary. Such arrangements are naturalized and disseminated by rhetorics of "love" ("No Propagandist like to Love" [34], Melville writes), which ensure that institutional privacy, rather than seeming drearily isolating, appears as the most important site for exercising consent and deepening one's "inner" life: the ever-loving Pierre, for instance, achieves both interiority and consent when he offers his mother "the voluntary allegiance of his affectionate soul" (15). Producing consent by turning difference into sameness, love, for Melville, has an imperial grasp: "All this Earth is Love's affianced; vainly the demon Principle howls to stay the banns" (34). "For every wedding where true lovers wed," Melville wryly notes, "helps on the march of universal Love." Little wonder that Melville describes Mrs. Tartan, who in her own intentions conflates the domestic, the national, and the global, as "trying to promote the general felicity of the world" (27) by serving as "match-maker to the nation" (28).

In particular, love orients citizens toward futurity, transforming sons into (potential) fathers, and therefore reorienting attention from the past (always burdened with the threat of recognizable injustice and misrepresentation), to the future, a place of utopian possibility. "But Love has more to do with his own possible and probable posterities than with the once living but now impossible ancestries in the past," Melville writes; "So Pierre's glow of family pride quickly gave place to a deeper hue, when Lucy bade love's banner blush out from his cheek" (32). The shift from past to future seems loaded with promise, and indeed, culturally, we use the celebrations generated by institutions of privacy – engagements, marriages, anniversaries, baby showers – to reaffirm our commitments to futurity, to invest capital today (all of the events above are gift-giving occasions) in anticipation of future satisfaction. But when does satisfaction come; when, that is, does the future become the present? Perhaps reducing the broad – even the global – sphere of social interaction and experience to the significantly narrower spheres of "privacy" is what makes people less eager to ask that question, turning them to "jailors all; jailors of themselves; and in Opinion's world ignorantly hold their noblest part a captive to their vilest" (91).

To hold one's "noblest part" captive is not, however, to extinguish it. If his inability to encounter people without turning them into family or lovers leaves Pierre with a "strange feeling of loneliness" (7), it is not because there are no other models of sociality open to him. On the contrary, *Pierre* suggests "that the divinest of these emotions, which are incident to the sweetest season of love, is capable of an indefinite translation into many of the less signal relations of our many chequered life" (16). *Pierre* is crammed with such "translations," which rival, in the intense satisfactions and communicative freedoms they provide their participants, the institutional relationships that structure the "major" plots of the novel. Melville no sooner introduces the love story of Pierre and Lucy Tartan, for instance, than he offers readers the tale of Pierre's grandfather's attachment to his horse, a bond so strong that the horse died days after the grandsire's demise. Not long thereafter, Melville introduces Ralph Winwood, with whom Pierre's father "was rather intimate at times" (74). Among his other "curious whimsies" (79), Ralph "much liked to paint his friends, and hang their faces on his walls" (75), a practice that seemingly enables "the ever-elastic regions of evanescent invention" (82). Most dramatically, Isabel, left alone save for her mother's guitar, " 'made a loving friend of it; a heart friend of it. It sings to me as I do to it. Love is not all on one side with my guitar.

All the wonders that are imaginable and unspeakable; all these wonders are translated in the mysterious melodiousness of the guitar. It knows all my past history' "
(125). These "relationships" are, on some level, unsatisfying as viable social models,
even comically so, precisely because, made with objects or animals, they suspend the
"social" altogether. Melville shields from ridicule, however, these archives of subtly
competing models of sociality: a horse and its owner can be loyal without demanding sameness; an artist's painted "friends" are companionable without requiring
mutual knowledge (as Melville repeatedly asks, what can we learn from a portrait?);
one can have intimacies that affirm one's "history," rather than demanding an
amnesic orientation toward futurity.

While these relationships suggest intimacy's commodification, they also hold
open the possibility that people's desires for other modes of intimacy have not
been entirely supplanted, that one's affective alliances can still find strange, unpredictable channels. Despite these characters' alienation from family and romance, they
maintain the capacity "to respond," which, Melville attests, "is a suspension of all
isolation" (291) and an affirmation of "the imaginativeness of the supposed solidest
principle of human association" (142). Perhaps the institutions of privacy need such
alternative intimacies, for apparently fleeting, incomplete, even incoherent experiences make the permanence reportedly provided by institutions seem valuable ("all
sweet recollections become marbleized," Melville writes; "so that things which in
themselves were evanescent, thus become unchangeable and eternal" [68]). Nevertheless, intimacy retains some of its "sweetness" in *Pierre*, providing "that mysterious
thing in the soul, which seems to acknowledge no human jurisdiction" (7). Such
lawless imaginings are not always pleasant – Melville tells us they often take the
forms of "horrid dreams" and "unmentionable thoughts" (71) – but it is precisely
their unsettling qualities that undo our current categorizations and make new –
perhaps more just – arrangements thinkable. The intimacies lived at the margins of
Pierre suggest that "the strongest and fiercest emotions of life defy all analysis" (67),
and as long as such emotions are kept vibrant, there is hope that, in Melville's
cautiously optimistic words, "one single, intensified memory's spark shall suffice to
enkindle such a blaze of evidence, that all the corners of conviction are as suddenly
lighted up as a midnight city by a burning building, which on every side whirls its
reddened brands" (71).

Melville's gothic metaphor of a burning building lighting up an urban sky
might seem too dramatic to capture the intersection of memory, intimacy, and anti-
institutionality. The metaphor recalls, however, the 1834 Charlestown, Massachusetts, burning of an Ursuline convent, during which a mob of sixty disguised
workingmen drove twelve nuns and forty-seven female pupils into hiding, robbed
the Convent, and reduced it to ashes. The attack haunted American political rhetoric
for decades. To take two familiar examples: in 1835, Lyman Beecher invoked the
Charlestown mob to denounce "lawless force" as the enemy of "argument and free-
inquiry" (64–5), while Francis Lieber, reviving rumors that the Charlestown nuns
kept inmates hostage in the Convent, asserted the sacredness of private property in

opposition to proposed laws to assure "that certain offices should have the right to enter nunneries, from eight A.M. to eight o'clock P.M., provided there was strong suspicion that an inmate was retained against her will" (63–4).

Beyond these echoes, the Charlestown burning might have been part of Melville's family lore, as his father-in-law, Lemuel Shaw, was the presiding judge who acquitted the men accused of the attack (Franchot 140). There are no nuns in *Pierre*, but the cloistered life of Catholicism makes an important appearance as the Church of the Apostles, where Isabel and Pierre take refuge after fleeing Saddle Meadows for New York City, and where, as Kelley argues, Pierre found "a community congenial to his newly conceived revolt against house and home" (106). No longer used for religious services, the upper floors of the former church are occupied by men dubbed by their neighbors "the Apostles", "mostly artists of various sorts; painters, or sculptors, or indigent students, or teachers of languages, or poets, or fugitive French politicians, or German philosophers" (267), as well as "well-known Teleological Theorists and Social Reformers, and political propagandists of all manner of heterodoxical tenets" (268). The "heterodoxies" espoused by the Apostles are, on one level, ineffectual, for, despite the Apostles' revolutionary rhetoric, "yet, to say the truth, was the place, to all appearances, a very quiet and decorous one, and its occupants a company of harmless people" (269). The Apostles nevertheless are an important alternative to their neighbors, the new middle-class service providers. As religious orders abandoned the Church, Melville tells us, "the building could no longer be devoted to its primitive purpose," but "must be divided into stores; cut into offices; and given as a roost to the gregarious lawyers" (266), men with "full purses and empty heads" (267). If business displaces faith and law divides human collectivity, such aspects of life do not simply vanish, but move upstairs where, like the archival memory whose burning illuminates the corners of conviction, they recall *other* forms of social life, other intimate arrangements, and other collective values than those represented by the culture's new street-level social institutions.

Preserving alternative and arguably more generous social values (when Pierre is abandoned, the Apostles take him in; when he is attacked the Apostles protect him), the Apostles become one of the first literary examples of functional *subculture* in the new American cityscape: "finding themselves thus clannishly and not altogether infelicitously entitled," Melville writes,

> the occupants of the venerable church began to come together out of their various dens, in more social communion; attracted toward each other by a title common to all. By-and-by, from this, they went further, and insensibly, at last became organized in a peculiar society, which, though exceedingly inconspicuous, and hardly perceptible in its public demonstrations, was still secretly suspected to have some mysterious ulterior object, vaguely connected with the absolute overturning of church and State, and the hasty and premature advance of some unknown great political and religious Millennium. (269)

Like queer subculture today, the Apostles turn a shaming appellation into a principle of social organization, one that, like queer culture, often moves unnoticed – obliquely marked yet powerfully flexible – in and around the monumental institutions of public life and the intimacies they sanction. Like modern-day queers, the Apostles generate unpredictable alliances across lines of class or social experience, and therefore compete (and not only comically, as Melville suggests) with the intimacies sanctioned by Church and State (sounding quite queer indeed, Charles Millthorpe, Pierre's link to the Apostles, declares, "'By marriage, I might contribute to the population of men, but not to the census of mind. The great men are all bachelors'" [281]). It is significant, furthermore, that anti-institutional sociality arises in a Church, for Catholicism, as I have suggested, was perceived as being *too* powerful and utterly vulnerable, impossible to pin down yet ubiquitous, that is, as both *too* institutional and not *institutional* at all, even *counter*-institutional. Queers occupy precisely these paradoxical positions today (powerful enough to topple institutions like marriage yet not powerful enough to pass basic rights legislation; lurking in every daycare center and schoolyard, yet impossible to locate or define; living among "our" families, churches, and workplaces, yet utterly, even exotically, "other").

The Apostles teach Pierre important lessons about how to build community in ways that do not surrender difference ("heterodoxies") or romanticize it in ways that disable its agents' ability to speak of social – not aesthetic – injustice. Through his childhood friendship with Charles, for instance, Pierre has "some inkling of what it might be, to be old, and poor, and worn, and rheumatic, with shivering death drawing nigh, and present life itself but a dull and a chill!" (277). Ultimately, however, Pierre cannot build on that "inkling," as he remains subject to "his own private and individual affection" (49), another captive of privacy. Critics have often taken the failures of Pierre the character for those of *Pierre* the novel, however, whereas I see them as symptoms of broader failures in the American social imaginary, brought about by institutionalism's colonization of the public sphere. Leaving citizens isolated and privatized, managing (or trying to manage) home(land) institutions in the face of the nation's violent and global exchanges, institutionalism, *Pierre* shows, obscured – but not entirely – the catholic differences that made public life exhilarating in the first place.

REFERENCES AND FURTHER READING

Beecher, Lyman. *A Plea for the West*. 2nd ed. Cincinnati: Truman & Smith, 1853.

Castronovo, Russ. *Necro Citizenship: Death, Eroticism, and the Public Sphere in the Nineteenth-Century United States*. Durham, NC: Duke University Press, 1991.

Franchot, Jenny. *Roads to Rome: The Antebellum Protestant Encounter with Catholicism*. Berkeley: University of California Press, 1994.

Gladwell, Malcolm. "Institutional Health." *The New Yorker* (December 1, 2003): 35, 38.

Kaplan, Amy. "Manifest Domesticity." In *No More Separate Spheres! A Special Issue of* American Literature. Ed. Cathy N. Davison. Durham, NC: Duke University Press, 1998. 581–606.

Kelley, Wyn. "*Pierre's* Domestic Ambiguities." In *The Cambridge Companion to Herman Melville*. Ed. Robert S. Levine. Cambridge: Cambridge University Press, 1998. 91–113.

Lieber, Francis. *On Civil Liberty and Self-Government*. Philadelphia: J. B. Lippincott, 1859.

Lithwick, Dahlia. "Holy Matrimony: What's Really Undermining the Sanctity of Marriage." *Slate* 2004. http://slate.msn.com/id/2091475.

14

Melville, Slavery, and the American Dilemma

John Stauffer

And though all evils may be assuaged; all evils can not be done away. For evil is the chronic malady of the universe; and checked in one place, breaks forth in another. (*Mardi* [528, 529])

Slavery and the American Dilemma

In 1819, the year of Melville's birth, the Missouri crisis erupted "like a firebell in the night," as Thomas Jefferson noted, prompting his friend and fellow Virginian James Madison to write an allegorical story on the history, progress, and present condition of America (Jefferson 698). Madison's story, which remained unpublished during his life, not only responds to the national crisis over Missouri entering the Union as a slave state; it also maps out the basic debates over slavery that would lead to civil war. The story also addresses some of the central themes in Melville's writings: the limits of freedom; the problems associated with ending slavery and evil; and the dangers of utopian and perfectionist visions. In fact, in *Typee*, *Moby-Dick*, "The Happy Failure," and *Benito Cereno*, it is as though Melville responds directly to Madison's story and the cultural tensions that came to a head at the time of his birth and transformed his adult world.

Madison's story concerns Jonathan Bull (the North) and Mary Bull (the South), who were descendents of old John Bull, the personification of England. As Jonathan and Mary "grew up and became well acquainted," they acquired many of the same common interests and considered a "matrimonial connection" that would combine "their two estates under a common superintendence" (Madison, 77–8). But the old man and guardian, John Bull had "always found the means of breaking off the match, which he regarded as a fatal obstacle to his secret design of getting the whole property into his own hands" (78).

After some squabbles and skirmishes, John and Mary Bull defied the authority of their guardian, and eloped. Their marriage "was not a barren one" (78). Every year or two "a new member of the family" was added (78). A portion of land was set aside for each child once he or she attained adulthood, and in the meantime these lands were rapidly settled by tenants coming from the estates of Jonathan or Mary – from the North or South – or sometimes both.

Eventually a crisis ensued. After twenty-two children had reached adulthood – corresponding to the eleven free states and eleven slave states at the time of the Missouri crisis – Jonathan became "possessed with a notion" that all future lands be settled and cultivated by tenants from his estates alone and not from Mary's (79). Jonathan's prejudice stemmed from "a certain African dye" that had stained Mary's left arm in her youth, making it "perfectly black and somewhat weaker than the other arm" (79). The misfortune "arose from a ship from Africa loaded with the article which had been permitted to enter a river running thro[ugh] her estate"; and a part of the "noxious cargo" had been "disposed" onto her property, leaving a permanent stain (79).

Mary's stain was well known to Jonathan at the time of their marriage. But Jonathan had "made no objection whatever to [the] Union" (81). Indeed the "fatal African dye" "had found its way" onto Jonathan's body as well; when they married, "spots & specks" were "scattered over" his body that were as "black as the skin on [Mary's] arm" (81). It was only by "certain abrasions and other applications" that Jonathan had been able to remove his black spots and specks; yet there were still "visible remains" of the "noxious" stain (81). Nevertheless, Jonathan now demanded that if the color could not be taken out of Mary's black arm, then she should "either tear off the skin from the flesh or cut off the limb" (80). It was Jonathan's "fixed determination that one or [the] other should be done, or he w[oul]d sue [for] a divorce, and there should be an end of all connection between them and their Estates" (80). "White as I am all over," Jonathan told Mary, "I can no longer consort with one marked with such a deformity as the blot on your person" (80).

Mary was absolutely "stunned" by this language from her spouse (80). Although she was "generous and placable" in temper, she had a "proud sensibility," and "was almost choked with the anger and indignation swelling in her bosom" (80). But she regained her composure and good sense, "and changed her tone to that of sober reasoning and affectionate expostulation" in addressing Jonathan's fears and threats of divorce (80). "You know as well as I do," Mary said, "that I am not to be blamed for the origin of the sad mishap, that I am as anxious as you [are] to get rid of it" as soon as a "safe and feasible" plan can be worked out; and "that I have done everything I could to mitigate an evil that cannot as yet be removed" (81–2). Jonathan's prescription for removing the evil, she quickly added, would be disastrous. According to the "most skillful surgeons," tearing off her black skin or cutting off the unfortunate limb would only be followed by "a mortification or a bleeding to death" (82). She reminded Jonathan of their many mutual interests and of how important her lands and wealth were to the material and economic prosperity of their partnership.

Now, Jonathan "had a good heart as well as [a] sound head and steady temper," and he "was touched with this tender and considerate language" (85). He ended his bickering and quarrelling and their relationship returned to one of "affection and confidence" (85).

Madison's story reveals three major themes that over the course of the next forty years would shape national identity and Melville's consciousness. First, it reflects the tacit agreement that existed between the North and the South from the framing of the Constitution until the Missouri crisis. The agreement stipulated that the North would not interfere with slavery in Southern states, much as Jonathan was supposed to accept Mary's "blackened arm"; and the South would recognize slavery as an evil that should be discouraged and eventually abolished whenever it was safe and feasible to do so, much as Mary was anxious to rid herself of the stain.

Second, Madison's story illuminates the symbolic importance of race in America. The imagery of blackness in Madison's story underscores the widespread belief among Madison's generation that slavery was a sin. Indeed Madison called slavery America's "original sin" (Mellon 158). Slavery was the obstacle to white Americans' pretensions to perfection, the barrier blocking their path to the millennium, according to David Brion Davis (*Challenging* 32). The road would be clear, the new age in sight, were it not for the presence of blacks. Such beliefs affected many white and even a few black abolitionist writings and lay at the heart of the many proposals for colonizing blacks outside the United States. Hence, African Americans, the victims of slavery, became in the mind of whites "the embodiment of sin" (*Challenging* 33).

In Madison's story, sin and blacks are intertwined. After all, a "noxious" African dye has been disposed onto Mary's unstained property, and abrasions are required to remove Jonathan's specks and spots; even then, there are visible remains that make his skin not wholly white. For most whites during Madison's era, both slavery and blacks were seen as stains on the fabric of American identity and character.

And finally, Madison's story points to signs of a new era, a shift in the ways that national boundaries were defined (Davis *Challenging* 35–59). These reinterpretations of boundaries took many forms: the emergence of a national market economy; rapid westward expansion, which became the battleground of slavery; the belief that the United States was destined to control the continent; and a blurring of God's law and national law. During the Missouri crisis, the New York reformer Rufus King was the first politician to apply a "higher law" to slavery; he stated that any law upholding slavery was "absolutely void, because [it is] contrary to the law of nature, which is the law of God" (Davis *Challenging* 41–2). The higher law thesis would become a central rhetorical weapon in the writings of a later generation of black and white abolitionists.

The year of Melville's birth marked, in short, a moment in which Americans became increasingly unwilling to compromise with sin and to accept limits, the rule of law, and traditional boundaries in their quest to realize visions of a new age. This newfound sense of urgency manifests itself in Madison's story when Jonathan suddenly becomes *intolerant* of Mary's stained and impure limb. In the historical parallel, the tacit agreement between the North and South became, after the Missouri Compromise, untenable. Over the course of the 1820s Southerners affirmed pro-slavery ideology, repudiated the belief, shared by most of their Southern forefathers, that slavery was a sin, and began to envision an empire of slavery. At the same time the North witnessed the rise of "modern" or immediate abolitionism, as it was called by both blacks and whites, which distinguished itself from the first generation of abolitionists in its refusal to compromise with sin. Immediate abolitionists advocated an immediate end to all evil, and they saw slavery as the bolt around which all other evils swung.

In the broadest sense, then, the national rite of passage that occurred in 1819 reflected a move away from "gradualism" and toward "immediatism." This shift was linked to signs that the old Republic, defined by Enlightenment beliefs, was disappearing. Gradualism was closely linked to Enlightenment thought, and was torn between two ideals: the autonomous individual, which was antithetical to slavery; and a progressive, rational, and efficient social order, which feared the chaos that would result from ending slavery too quickly. From the Revolution through the first decade of the nineteenth century, there were few recorded instances in the United States of blacks or whites advocating an immediate end to all sin and thus immediate and universal emancipation. The first abolition societies refused to accept African Americans as members; and Quakers, the first white abolitionists, did not welcome free blacks into their churches and homes. Black gradualists advocated practical and patient measures for ending slavery, and accepted the authority of law and government. This was smart politics, for having witnessed the passage of gradual abolition laws throughout the North, blacks had good reason to believe that slavery would gradually and eventually end throughout the nation.

Gradual abolitionism also reflected the *newness* of anti-slavery thought and the desire for an orderly transition from slavery to freedom. Throughout history, few people have accepted their condition as slaves without rebelling in some way; but until the Age of Revolution, rebels sought to invert the master–slave hierarchy instead of advocating universal freedom. The St. Domingue rebellion of 1791 marks a major shift in the rise of anti-slavery thought and the strategy of rebellion; it was the first instance that we know of in which slave rebels also advocated universal freedom, and it can thus be seen as the first instance of immediatism, in which rebels sought not only to free themselves, but also to bring to an immediate end the institution of slavery.

Immediate abolition represented both a shift in strategy and a change in outlook. Immediatists, both blacks and whites, advocated a total and swift transformation of society. Early white immediatists emphasized moral suasion and non-violence, while blacks embraced political action and the use of force if necessary. But immediatism also reflected a shift from an Enlightenment to a Romantic worldview, from a "detached, rationalistic perspective on history and progress, to a personal commitment to make no compromise with sin" (Davis "Emergence" 255). Immediatism was an expression of inner freedom and triumph over worldly conventions; it reflected an eschatological leap, a sharp break from linear notions of progress and history, and assumed that a new age was dawning. It was thus an appropriate doctrine for a Romantic age.

Immediatism brought blacks and whites together as allies and friends in ways that had not occurred before. Abolitionists advocated racial equality and a few of them sought to realize those ideals. And there was a moral certainty to their outlook, which was absent among gradual abolitionists. While gradualists were willing to compromise with sin, immediatists believed that the nation would soon become all one thing or all the other, to paraphrase Lincoln, and so one needed to do the right thing right now. With such moral certainty came an acceptance of social chaos and violence, as in the example of John Brown and Radical Political Abolitionists, the party with which he was affiliated in the 1850s. They understood that moral certainty could more easily lead to chaos and bloodshed than order. Yet they also believed that slavery itself represented a state of war. Vanquishing slavery immediately, using violent means if necessary, would end the civil war that stemmed from slavery and preserve the peace.

Melville and Slavery

Over the course of his career Melville critiqued these efforts to redefine boundaries, realize perfectionist or utopian visions, and abolish sin. In effect he explored the tensions between gradualism and immediatism. He hated slavery, but could not countenance immediate abolitionism, for he understood, and continually emphasized, the costs of trying to realize one's utopian vision.

Melville was horrified by the idea of chaos and bloodshed, and in his desire for a peaceful and gradual end to slavery, he resembled his father-in-law Lemuel Shaw, the Chief Justice of the Massachusetts Supreme Court. In 1820, at the same time Madison wrote his short story, Shaw published a long essay on "Slavery and the Missouri Question," in which he argued that the proper course of action on slavery was central to the security of the nation. Sounding a lot like Madison, Shaw said that slavery "should be approached with great calmness and good temper," in which "the eager pursuit of a desirable end will not blindly overlook the only practicable means in arriving at it" (138). He was horrified by the idea of immediate abolition: a "sudden, violent, or general emancipation" would "shake if not subvert the foundations of society," and bring ruin to the nation and misery to blacks (143). Moreover, the abolition of slavery was "exclusively a question of local jurisdiction," a matter for individual states to decide (141). Yet Shaw coupled his plea for moderation by emphasizing that "a large proportion of human beings are utterly deprived of all their rights" (138). Slavery was a necessary evil; but because it was evil, it should be prevented from spreading. Prohibiting the spread of slavery was a constitutional right, and his defense of the non-extension of slavery anticipated that of Lincoln. Yet he still clung to his hope, implicit in the tacit agreement between North and South, that the South would work gradually and congenially to end the evil. And his basic attitudes toward slavery never much varied from those outlined in 1820 (Levy 59–71).

Melville differed from his father-in-law primarily in his understanding and treatment of blacks. Here he went farther than many abolitionists, who tended to treat blacks paternalistically and as symbols rather than as humans and equals. In his writings, Melville approached the perspective of John Brown, who, more than virtually every other white on the historical record, was able to burst free of cultural beliefs and break down the dichotomy of black and white.

Yet while Melville often empathized with slaves and other social outsiders, and envisioned a radical notion of racial equality, he could never endorse the kind of immediate abolitionism and millennialist faith of a John Brown or a Frederick Douglass. Douglass, Brown, and other Radical Political Abolitionists treated the Declaration of Independence, Constitution, and the Bible as sacred texts that needed to be realized on earth. They saw themselves as prophets, instruments in God's hands whose mission was to pave the way to millennium. They embraced sacred self-sovereignty, believing that the kingdom of God was at hand in America rather than in another realm. And they defined the millennium in nationalist terms. Frederick Douglass captured this sentiment when he argued that the principles of the Declaration of Independence, if fulfilled, "would release every slave in the world and prepare the earth for a millennium of righteousness and peace," adding: "I believe in the millennium" (Douglass 529, 552). For Melville, such millennialist or utopian visions were dangerous illusions, for they ignored the permanence of sin in the world. Dystopia was the dark twin of utopia, the result of what happened when people sought to realize their perfectionist visions.

Melville acknowledged the permanence of sin in his famous essay, "Hawthorne and His Mosses" (1850). He loved Hawthorne's writings partly because of the latter's emphasis on sin, or "darkness":

> For spite of all the Indian-summer sunlight on the hither side of Hawthorne's soul, the other side – like the dark half of the physical sphere – is shrouded in a blackness, ten times black. But this blackness gives more effect to the ever-moving dawn, that forever advances through it, and circumnavigates the world. (*PT* 243)

The power of blackness stemmed from an acknowledgment of the permanence of original sin:

> this great power of blackness in him [Hawthorne] derives its force from its appeals to that Calvinistic sense of Innate Depravity and Original Sin, from whose visitations, in some shape or other, no deeply thinking mind is always free. For, in certain moods, no man can weigh this world, without throwing in something, somehow like Original Sin, to strike the uneven balance. (243)

Most abolitionists believed that a heaven on earth, free from sin, was at hand. Melville's and Hawthorne's emphases on blackness offered a counterbalance to such rhetoric.

Melville sought to break down the dichotomy between black and white, slave and free, without fueling sectional tensions. In "Hawthorne and His Mosses" he poses as "a Virginian Spending July in Vermont" (239). Politically he was a Democrat, the party most closely affiliated with slaveowners. Unlike all abolitionists and most Northern Whigs, he supported the Mexican War, which was perpetrated by President James K. Polk, a Southern slaveowner, and his Democratic sympathizers in order to acquire more slave territory (*L* 40–1). Two factors help explain his support of the Mexican War: his brother Ganesvoort Melville was a Democratic party insider who worked tirelessly to elect Polk as president; and he continued to hope, as did Lemuel Shaw and a few other Democrats, that Southern states would come to their senses, reaffirm the tacit agreement between the two regions, and voluntarily agree to gradual emancipation at some future date (Widmer, 17, 86–9).

While Melville endorsed the Mexican War, he also championed egalitarian democracy, and denied that there was "an aristocracy of the brain," as he put it in an 1851 letter to Hawthorne (*L* 190). It "is true that there have been those who, while earnest in behalf of political equality, still accept the intellectual estates," meaning innate intellectual differences among certain groups (190). But he embraced a "ruthless democracy on all sides," as he told Hawthorne (190); no man was less than another man, and he went so far as to suggest that "a thief in jail is as honorable a personage as Gen. George Washington" (190–1). In *Moby-Dick*, which he was then finishing, he likens another social outsider – the dark-skinned, cannibalistic Queequeg – to Washington:

> It may seem ridiculous, but [Queequeg's head] reminded me of General Washington's head, as seen in the popular busts of him.... Queequeg was George Washington cannibalistically developed. (50)

Elsewhere Melville likened *himself* to Queequeg by signing a letter with "his X mark," as Queequeg does (*L* 200; *MD* 89). And in another letter he signed off as "Tawney," a colloquial term for Indian or light-skinned black (*L* 23). In his 1851 letter to Hawthorne, he said that comparing a thief to Washington was "ludicrous," but so was Truth: "Truth is the silliest thing under the sun" (191). In his quest for truth, Melville identified with reformers; they, too, were "bottomed [or bent] upon the truth, more or less" (191). And like him, they were outsiders – "almost universally laughing-stocks," since "Truth is ridiculous to men" (191). He lauded reformers' efforts to expose present truths about slavery and racial prejudice; but he distanced himself from their future utopian visions.

The Problem of Utopia

Melville explored the possibility of utopia – and thus implicitly of immediate abolition and the quest for perfection – in his first book, *Typee* (1846), which he dedicated to

Lemuel Shaw. The narrator Tommo places us inside the utopia of Typeean society, and uncovers the mystery that shrouds utopias from the uninitiated. *Typee* is set in an Edenic paradise: the inhabitants are the most beautiful Tommo has ever seen; the food is exquisite and bountiful; and the most grueling labor consists of lighting a fire and masturbating, two acts that become one in his symbolic description. "The penalty of the Fall [original sin] presses very lightly upon the valley of the Typee," Tommo concludes; "for, with the one solitary exception of striking a light, I scarcely saw any piece of work performed there which caused the sweat to stand upon a single brow" (195). Since there is no money in Typee, "that 'root of all evil' was not to be found in the valley" (126). In the absence of original sin and money, people do not have to sweat for their bread. "As for digging and delving for a livelihood, the thing is unknown" (195). While Tommo equates the Fall (original sin) with civilization, savagery becomes his dark Eden. And in almost every instance of comparison between savagery and civilization, savagery comes out looking better. Indeed, for a number of Melville's reform-minded readers, *Typee* was "a modern *Paradise Found*" (Parker 1: 460).

But Tommo has many problems with utopia. He fears that if he remains in this Typeean utopia, he will become a victim of cannibalism, even though there is no clear evidence for such fears. And he is afraid of being tattooed, a racialized rite of passage for becoming Typeean. "I now felt convinced that in some luckless hour I should be disfigured in such a manner as never more to have the *face* to return to my countrymen, even should an opportunity offer" (219). If he is tattooed, Tommo will lose face in multiple ways, as Samuel Otter has noted. His face will be horribly disfigured; his identity as a white and civilized man will be effaced; and he will lose his former self (Otter 12–24). In fact Tommo characterizes tattooing as a religious ritual: "The whole system of tattooing was, I found, connected with their religion; and it was evident, therefore, that they were resolved to make a convert of me" (220). Being tattooed was tantamount to a conversion experience, in which the former self gave way to a new "dark" self. No matter how attractive "dark" savagery appears in relation to "white" civilization, Tommo cannot countenance abolishing his whiteness as a marker of identity.

Tommo's problem with utopia resembles Melville's problem with radical abolitionists. Tommo is an outsider to the utopian community of Typee, much as Melville stood outside the ranks of abolitionists. Most whites who became abolitionists underwent a conversion experience; they were born again, cleansed of original sin, and totally devoted to their sacred vocation. They believed that one needed to purify the self before eradicating sin in society; they considered alcohol and tobacco sins and, unlike Melville, abstained from them. The path of purity flowed outward from self to society. Tommo has the opportunity to achieve such purity and live in paradise. But in order to become a utopian insider and a member of this dark Eden, he must relinquish entirely his past identity, and become born anew as a dark-skinned self. The most radical of white abolitionists, such as John Brown, Gerrit Smith, and James Redpath, sought to achieve such identity. Gerrit Smith continually sought to "make myself a colored man," as he put it, and so did Brown and Redpath (Stauffer 15; Redpath 6–7).

In renouncing his dark Eden, Tommo also relinquishes the possibility of freedom. His problem with freedom relates to Melville's problem with utopian and immediatist thought. Throughout the narrative, Tommo is in search of freedom but never finds it. The entire narrative is driven by Tommo's desire to escape captivity. After escaping servitude on board the ship, he becomes captive to his own body, and symbolically to sin. His leg swells and causes so much pain that he "half suspected I had been bitten by some venomous reptile" (48). Yet he notes that the Polynesian islands were "free from the presence of any vipers," or serpents that induce sin (48). Then he first glimpses the Edenic nature of Typee: "Had a glimpse of the gardens of Paradise been revealed to me I could scarcely have been more ravished with the sight" (49). At the moment when Tommo sees a world free from sin, he finds that he is captive to original sin. The postlapsarian man has glimpsed a prelapsarian world. He tries to baptize the wound and purify the sin by bathing it, and the Typee try to heal it by prayers, but to no avail. His leg begins to heal only after he realizes that he is a captive in Typee.

Tommo's freedom is thus thwarted by sin and whiteness. He can become truly free only by converting to a dark-skinned savage and embracing a paradise on earth. Individual freedom and self-sovereignty depended upon the denial of original sin, as David Brion Davis has shown: "The essence of both sin and slavery was a denial of self-sovereignty" (*Problem* 292). Neither Tommo nor Melville can burst free from his bondage to sin or the laws of white society. Tommo affirms the civil codes of his white society, which he foregrounds in his dedication to Shaw: he defines his affection for Shaw not as a friend or a future father-in-law, but in legal and civil terms, calling him "Chief Justice of the Commonwealth of Massachusetts" (vii). Melville, like Tommo, accepts the laws of a white slave republic instead of converting to perfectionism and championing a dark Edenic paradise.

Monomania and Immediatism

Moby-Dick (1851) similarly explores the failure of utopia and immediatist visions. Of all Melville's books, it is the fullest expression of the possibilities of an interracial utopia and the sharpest critique of American society. Ishmael places us inside the utopia of the *Pequod*, which is by turns "a parliament, a guildhall, a fortress, and, perhaps most notably, a factory," according to Tony Tanner (65). In teaching us the culture of whaling, Ishmael uncovers the mystery that shrouds utopias from the ignorant. Ahab is the charismatic leader – a central feature of all utopias – who exerts enormous control and prevents factions and dissent. Queequeg is the embodiment of utopia: he is a native of Kokovoko, an island "far away to the West and South," which is "not down in any map; true places never are" (55). He comes from no place, the literal meaning of utopia. Even the ship's name, *Pequod*, suggests utopia: it was once "the name of a celebrated tribe of Massachusetts Indians," but is "now extinct as the ancient Medes" and thus signifies a non-existent place (69).

Ahab is the great utopian, anti-democratic leader who seeks to realize his vision at all costs. He perverts the purpose of whaling and sacrifices his entire society in his quest to vanquish the white whale, the symbol of all evil in his mind. His efforts to realize his perfectionist vision make him one of the great monomaniacs in literature. Monomania clinically meant a form of insanity in which one or more faculties of the brain were "deranged." It was characterized by obsessive behavior, as though a person were "possessed" with one idea or a specific desire or objective. Eventually, the term gave way to the designations of manic-depressive (or bipolar) illness and schizophrenia, depending on specific conditions (Stauffer 43).

But monomania was also a popular epithet when Melville wrote *Moby-Dick*. The term was widely used to characterize utopian visionaries in both the North and South. In the Congressional debates over the Mexican War, Southern Congressmen publicly accused John Quincy Adams of being a monomaniac for sympathizing with "people as dark as Mexicans" or darker (Miller 423). Abolitionists were widely referred to as monomaniacs (Stauffer 42–4). But so were pro-slavery visionaries. In 1847 Northern Democrats and Whigs called John C. Calhoun and his followers monomaniacs:

> It is a strange monomania that possesses such minds as that of John C. Calhoun, which leads them to believe it possible to keep up a balance of power between the free and the slaveholding States of this Union, by nursing the sickly institution of slavery, and endeavoring to promote its extension over half of this great western hemisphere which is destined to be peopled by the liberty-loving and slavery-abominating spirits of the Anglo-Saxon race. ("Extinction")

In 1849 Kentuckians called South Carolina politicians monomaniacs:

> [Slavery] is all that the people of [South Carolina] exhibit any regard for.... It is the only thing they live for – it is the only thing they would die for – it is the only thing which would render Paradise itself attractive to them. Such monomania is fearful. ("South Carolina")

In his analysis of *Moby-Dick*, Alan Heimert referred to the political currency of "monomania" when Melville wrote the novel, but argued that the term was equated primarily with Southerners; and he identifies Ahab with Calhoun, Moby Dick with Daniel Webster (Heimert 513). But such allegorical readings limit Melville's "political imagination," as Michael Rogin observed (Rogin 108). Those accused of monomania were just as inclined to equate paradise with slavery as with immediate abolition or other utopian schemes.

The term "monomania" was pervasive in the North and South and remained a favorite epithet throughout the 1850s. The *National Era*, where Stowe first published *Uncle Tom's Cabin*, called President Franklin Pierce a monomaniac in 1856 for inciting Southern fears about the spread of abolitionist sentiment ("Troubles"). And soon after Lincoln was elected President, the *New York Herald*, a Democratic paper, called abolitionists monomaniacs for referring to Mrs. Lincoln as one, owing to her "political ambitions":

> To be an abolitionist "one-mind" must be so distorted, warped and obscured that it is no wonder if it often breaks entirely. An abolitionist cannot be practicable, for abolitionism is impractical. He must confuse right with wrong, and believe that slavery is wrong even to the extent of denying the existence of God, because he reasons that a God would not permit slavery. ("Mrs. Lincoln")

These are precisely the views of Ahab, according to Marius Bewley (210). Ahab confuses right with wrong and pursues Moby Dick even to the extent of denying God. Like abolitionists who embraced violent means for ending slavery, or Southerners who called slavery a positive good, Ahab subverts the polarity between good and evil and confuses God's sovereignty with his own.

The United States was, in short, a monomaniacal nation when Melville wrote *Moby-Dick*, a society delicately balancing irreconcilable utopian visions. The Compromise of 1850 sought to avert civil war, but it had the opposite effect. Americans *refused* to compromise or to accept limits and the rule of law, especially the Fugitive Slave Law. And of course Ahab highlights the costs of denying limits, ignoring rules, and seeking to vanquish all opposing, unknown forces in life. When he destroys the quadrant, he symbolically destroys the instrument of knowledge that should determine his place in the cosmos. Like Ahab pursuing the whale, Americans everywhere found in pro-slavery and abolitionist visions, as well other monomaniacal pursuits, the means to strike through the pasteboard masks of visible objects and seek to realize their utopian visions (Stauffer 43).

Some of the contemporary reviews of *Moby-Dick* suggest a literary-political reading of the novel. The black physician and abolitionist James McCune Smith explicitly does so. In a March 1856 essay entitled "Horoscope," which was addressed to Frederick Douglass and published in *Frederick Douglass' Paper*, Smith likened the *Pequod* to the ship of state in American politics. Horace Greeley, the influential editor and Republican party leader, was a "boatsteerer" much like Stubb. On the eve of an election, Greeley "shrieks out" to his party "like Stubb in Moby Dick" after spotting a whale: " 'Start her, start her my men! ... start her like grim death and grinning devils, and raise the buried dead perpendicular out of their graves, boys – that's all. Start her' " (Smith). For Smith, who was quoting from chapter 61, those in charge of the *Pequod* and the American ship of state were in pursuit of the wrong thing: the white whale on the one hand, whiteness and respect for white laws on the other. They were sacrificing "the one thing needful" – "HUMAN BROTHERHOOD" – and the "belief that all men are by nature free and equal" (McCune Smith; Stauffer 66). Greeley, William Seward, and other leaders of state had "avowed" their "belief in the inferiority of the negro to the white man," and their "disgust at the idea of social commingling with his black brother" (McCune Smith). They compromised their nation's ideals, and were not "morally fitted to advance the cause of Human Freedom." As a result, any hopes for the nation were "doomed to be blasted" (Smith). Like Melville, McCune Smith embraced human brotherhood and attacked the idea of whiteness as a sign of superiority. But he differed from Melville in *wanting* someone with Ahab's monomaniacal, immediatist vision. For McCune Smith, by ignoring the multiracial makeup of their country, American leaders were following the plight of the *Pequod* and heading toward destruction. His horoscope was more accurate than he knew.

Moby-Dick thus updates, in one sense, Madison's story of America's dilemma. Ishmael critiques the moral certainty and immediatist vision of Ahab, but is unwilling or unable to interfere. Instead of peaceful resolution to the conflict, as Madison would have it, which would preserve a white nation and the hope of national salvation, Ahab has his way, and the story ends in interracial apocalypse. Ishmael can be seen as part of Melville's efforts to resist the temptation to follow Ahab, a temptation that was quite powerful for him. He reflects Melville's (and Madison's) respect for limits, laws, natural order.

Melville suggests two alternatives to his dystopic ending. The first is in "The Town-Ho's Story," where the Christ-like Steelkit plans a mutiny, uproots society on board the ship, and finds freedom. But it is God rather than Steelkit who, by means of Moby Dick, wreaks vengeance on the evil leaders. The story portrays "the retributive justice of the whale," as Sherman Paul notes, suggesting "the glimmer of relief from the overwhelming sense of evil that engulfs Ahab" (Paul 41).

Starbuck offers the second alternative to the dystopic ending. From the outset he alone dissents from Ahab's monomaniacal pursuit of the whale. And he contemplates retributive justice against Ahab, and thus a form of national redemption. If the *Pequod* is destroyed, Starbuck notes, Ahab will be the "wilful murderer of thirty men and more," which corresponds to the nation's thirty states when Melville wrote the novel, with "more" states to come (515). Starbuck picks up a loaded pistol, and as Ahab sleeps, levels it at him. But he suffers a crisis of conscience: "The yet levelled musket shook like a drunkard's arm against the panel; Starbuck seemed wrestling with an angel," and he places the pistol back in its rack (515). The scene highlights Starbuck's weakness: he cannot withstand "spiritual terrors" (117). He chooses the "lawful way" over playing God and committing murder in the hopes of redeeming the ship of state (515). His restraint is the right thing to do, the narrator suggests. For while individual men are filled with "democratic dignity" and "divine equality," they are often "detestable" as "joint-stock companies and nations" (117). Not even the "great democratic God" can prevent evil; He might "pick up Andrew Jackson from the pebbles," and raise him "higher than a throne"; but Jackson, one of Ishmael's heroes, advanced on the backs of slaves (117). Moral man lives in an immoral society; when he seeks utopia or retributive justice in the name of nation, or social advancement, he becomes immoral.

The Problem of Progress

One of Melville's little-known stories, "The Happy Failure," suggests that he continued to hope slavery would die a natural, gradual, and lawful death. Published in *Harper's New Monthly Magazine* in May 1854 (the same month the Kansas–Nebraska

Act passed, which opened Northern territories to slavery), the story satirizes artificial and "immediatist" forms of progress, as well as grandiose schemes for transforming the national landscape. At the center of the story is a relatively benign master–slave relationship, which resembles that of Aggy and Judge Templeton in James Fenimore Cooper's *The Pioneers*, Legrand and his black servant Jupiter in Edgar Allan Poe's "The Gold-Bug," and the black–white relationships in Washington Irving's tales and *Diedrich Knickerbocker's History of New York*.

The narrator, a young man, helps his elderly unnamed uncle and his uncle's elderly slave Yorpy test a new invention on the Hudson River in upstate New York. Having worked on it for ten years, the uncle bombastically calls his new machine "the Great Hydraulic-Hydrostatic Apparatus" (*PT* 255). It consists of a "sphinx-like," "oblong box, hermetically sealed," that appears as a "mystery" to the narrator, even after he peers inside and sees "convoluted metal pipes and syringes of all sorts and varieties" (254, 258). This utopian contraption is designed to drain swamps "at the rate of one acre [per] hour"; and the uncle hopes it will bring immediate fertility to the landscape and immediate fame to him (255). The narrator and Yorpy help him row the contraption upstream to an island on the Hudson for testing. "Glory is not to be gained, youngster, without pulling hard for it – against the stream, too, as we do now," the uncle tells his nephew. "The natural tendency of man, in the mass, is to go down with the universal current into oblivion" (256). While the patriarchal uncle badgers and instructs his nephew, he denigrates Yorpy, calling him a "dunderheaded black" at one point, at another telling him to "take your black hoof from under the box!" (255, 259).

Of course the machine fails. When it does, the uncle initially collapses from despair, but then recovers and tells his nephew, "Boy, take my advice, and never try to invent any thing but – happiness" (260). "I'm glad I've failed," he concludes. "Praise be to God for the failure" (260). With his failure, he begins treating Yorpy with kindness, calling him "faithful," to which Yorpy responds: "Dear massa! Dear old massa! Dat be very fust time in de ten long 'ear yoo hab mention kindly old Yorpy. I tank yoo, dear old massa; I tank yoo so kindly. Yoo is yorself agin in de ten long 'ear" (260).

Despite the story's humor and sarcasm, the moral of the story seems clear. Traveling naturally down the "universal current" leads not "toward utter oblivion," but to kindness and happiness (256, 260). After his failure, the uncle's face "kindled with a strange, rapt earnestness" (261). The narrator never forgets "that look," and his story, born of failure, brings immortality to his uncle (261). Rowing ambitiously upstream, however, in search of fame and fortune, yields petulance and despair. Moreover, benevolent relations between master and servant stem from natural and organic, rather than ambitious and artificial, forms of progress.

It is also significant that the setting of the story is not dated, and so we do not know the legal status of Yorpy. New York State passed a gradual emancipation act in 1799, and freed its remaining slaves in 1827, much later than in the New England states. There is a quaintness in the description of the uncle and Yorpy, which suggests that Yorpy could legally be a slave. He is described as "a sort of Dutch African" and speaks with a Dutch accent; but such accents persisted well into the antebellum era (*PT* 255; Kaplan 189, 197). Yorpy's uncertain status means that, from the context of the story, it makes little difference whether he is slave or servant. It is as though the slave will gradually and organically become a servant. Though Yorpy will always remain subservient to his master, he has a name and a voice, and his identity is thus preserved for posterity, which is more than the unnamed uncle and narrator enjoy. The acceptance of gradual, linear progress ensures the peaceful transition from slave to employee and prevents despair and disaster.

The Costs of Freedom

"Benito Cereno" (1855), which was published one year after "The Happy Failure," is the fullest expression of Melville's fears of immediate abolitionism. This novella of a slave mutiny is dystopian from beginning to end. Philip Fisher perceptively characterizes society in the novella as a "police state" or totalitarian regime (94). No work gets done and the people resemble figures "met by Dante in Purgatory" (93). And as Fisher notes, the story itself resembles a dream: "The events on Melville's ship are exactly like the contents of a dream because dreams are the self-adjusting, self-describing, and self-regulating condition of the mind" (95). It is as though Melville tried to imagine immediate emancipation, and the result was a nightmare, a gothic horror of ruin and death that goes far beyond the threat of dismemberment in James Madison's vision of immediatism.

"Benito Cereno" is based on the historical account of Captain Amasa Delano, who in 1817 published his *Narrative of Voyages and Travels in the Northern and Southern Hemispheres*. Delano's travelogue describes an attempted slave mutiny and his encounter with the ship's captain, Benito Cereno, in 1805. The mutinous slaves take over the ship and re-enact their own enslavement in order to receive needed supplies and prevent Delano from suppressing the rebellion. Melville, too, re-enacts the masquerade, concealing from his readers for much of the narrative the mutinous conditions on board the ship.

Melville transforms the historical account in a number of ways. He turns Delano's picturesque adventure story into a gothic tale that highlights the ruin and horror of revolution, the untenable nature of equality in such a setting, and the ways in which the sins of the past haunt the present and destroy any attempt to "begin anew" (Edmundson 63, 71, 131). Melville also changes the name of Cereno's ship from the *Tryal* to the *San Dominick*, and the date of the mutiny from 1805, when it occurred, to 1799. These changes are crucial, for they link Melville's story to the Age of Revolution, specifically the St. Domingue rebellion, as Eric Sundquist has noted (Sundquist 140). Dominick was the name of Columbus's father, and so the name San Dominick yokes together the European "discoverer" of the New World and the setting of the world's first black republic. The date of 1799 reflects a moment in which St. Domingue slaves had achieved *temporary* freedom through revolution. Slaves on the island revolted in 1791, and three years later France temporarily abolished slavery in the French colonies and extended the rights of citizenship to all men regardless of color, in an attempt to win black allegiance in its colonial wars with England. St. Domingue finally achieved independence from France in 1804, and Haiti's new constitution prohibited slavery forever. Melville's novella explores this first instance of immediate emancipation in Western culture; but he begins his tale at a time when freedom, on St. Domingue and the *San Dominick*, hung in the balance.

One additional change from the historical account reflects Melville's horror of immediate emancipation and disdain for utopian thinking. In Delano's narrative, the dead body of Don Alexandro Aranda, the slaves' owner, is thrown overboard. In Melville's gothic rendering, the body of Aranda is stripped of its flesh (possibly through cannibalization), and the skeleton is "substituted for the ship's proper figure-head, the image of Christopher Colon [Columbus], the discoverer of the New World" (*PT* 107). Melville makes it hard to sympathize with blacks who dehumanize another human in such a way.

Don Alexandro Aranda's bones highlight the irony of New World settlement. The New World had long been synonymous with America. It suggested a utopia in which to create societies from abstract principles. The utopian idea of America led Sir Thomas More, in *Utopia* (1516), to locate his perfect society in the western hemisphere. Melville explodes the idea of the New World as utopia. Columbus first landed at Hispaniola, which became Haiti after blacks achieved their independence. For Melville, Columbus discovered not utopia but dystopia, the site of the most profitable slave labor and the largest slave insurrection in the New World. One man's utopia is the next man's dystopia, and the *San Dominick* fits all the characteristics of dystopia: a place with clearly demarcated boundaries that is shrouded in mystery to the uninitiated; a desire for order and control; and a charismatic and brilliant leader – in this case the slave Babo. In Melville's rendering, the figure-head of Columbus, "discoverer" of the New World, becomes the figure-head of death and dystopia – the whitening bones of a white man, a "chalky comment on the chalked words below, '*Follow your leader*,'" that appear on the side of the ship (99).

"Follow your leader" becomes a kind of refrain in the novella. It is repeated four times, and forces questions about who the leader is on a ship of a revolutionary state. The first time it is mentioned, leadership is uncertain, much as the nature of the ship's figure-head "was not quite certain, owing to canvas wrapped about that part" where the figure-head was located (49). In the second instance, immediately following the exposure of the masquerade, we realize that "follow your leader" appears alongside Aranda's bones, suggesting that the white leader is dead (99). "Follow your leader" occurs for the third time in the deposition, and here the leader refers to Babo, who tells Benito Cereno: "Keep faith with the blacks from here to Senegal, or you shall in spirit, as now in body, follow your leader," and he then points to Aranda's bones (107). The final instance is, significantly, the last line of the story, when Benito Cereno dies, and again the meaning is unclear: "borne on the bier, [he] did, indeed, follow his leader" (117). His leader could be God, the monastery, Babo, or all three.

The problem of leadership relates to the problem of slavery and of immediate abolition. According to Hegel's famous master–slave dialectic, the slave gains autonomy and the master becomes dependent through the slave's work. In Melville's account, the slave gains power and the master powerlessness (and death), through resistance. In a slave society no one is free, Melville seems to be saying. But neither is anyone free in a state of revolution, immediate emancipation, or utopia. In such societies there is a "rage for order," resulting in a police state (Kateb).

"Benito Cereno" thus exposes the problem of slavery as well as the problem of immediatism. Here again, Melville is anti-slavery but not abolitionist, not an immediatist. He accurately prophesies what will happen if slavery is abolished immediately: social revolution, chaos, and death. He understands the costs of freedom, but seems to prefer slavery to revolution. While he casts Babo as the dystopian leader and a very shrewd character, he never explores Babo's perspective in the kind of depth he does Captain Ahab's. For Babo and other slaves, slavery itself represents a state of revolution and war. *Making* war, *creating* revolution, is the solution. From Babo's perspective, bloodshed is the necessary cost of freedom. From the point of view of Melville, Shaw, Madison, and other gradualists who hoped for long-term solutions to the problem, slavery is the temporary cost of peace and order. While Melville's solution to slavery, and his narrative, are richly indeterminate, Bates and other abolitionists have a clearly defined, absolute goal: immediate freedom.

References and Further Reading

Bewley, Marius. *The Eccentric Design: Form in the Classic American Novel*. New York: Columbia University Press, 1963.

Davis, David Brion. *Challenging the Boundaries of Slavery*. Cambridge, MA: Harvard University Press, 2003.

——. "The Emergence of Immediatism in Antislavery Thought." In *From Homicide to Slavery: Studies in American Culture*. New York: Oxford University Press, 1986.

——. *The Problem of Slavery in Western Culture*. New York: Oxford University Press, 1966.

Douglass, Frederick. *The Frederick Douglass Papers, Series One: Speeches, Debates, and Interviews; Volume 3: 1855–63*. Ed. John Blassingame. New Haven, CT and London: Yale University Press, 1985.

Edmundson, Mark. *Nightmare on Main Street: Angels, Sadomasochism, and the Culture of Gothic*. Cambridge, MA: Harvard University Press, 1997.

"Extinction of Slavery." *Buffalo Daily Republic* (NY). Reprinted in *The National Era* (May 27, 1847).

Fisher, Philip. *Still the New World: American Literature in a Culture of Creative Destruction*. Cambridge, MA: Harvard University Press, 1999.

Heimert, Alan. "*Moby-Dick* and American Political Symbolism. *American Quarterly* 15.4 (Winter 1963): 498–534.

Jefferson, Thomas. *The Life and Selected Writings of Thomas Jefferson*. Ed. Adrienne Koch and William Peden. New York: Modern Library, 1944.

Kaplan, Sidney. *American Studies in Black and White: Selected Essays*. Ed. Allan D. Austin. Amherst: The University of Massachusetts Press, 1991.

Kateb, George. *Utopia and its Enemies*. 1963. Rpt. New York: Schocken Books, 1972.

Levy, Leonard W. *The Law of the Commonwealth and Chief Justice Shaw*. New York: Oxford University Press, 1957.

Madison, James. "Jonathan Bull & Mary Bull." In *The Writings of James Madison*. Vol. IX (1819–1836). Ed. Gaillard Hunt. New York: G. P. Putnam's Sons, 1910.

Mellon, Matthew T. *Early American Views on Negro Slavery*. Boston: Meador Publishing, 1934.

Miller, William Lee. *Arguing About Slavery: The Great Battle in the United States Congress*. New York: Alfred A. Knopf, 1996.

"Mrs. Lincoln and Social Abolitionism." *New York Herald* (November 11, 1861).

Otter, Samuel. " 'Race' in *Typee* and *White-Jacket*." In *The Cambridge Companion to Herman Melville*. Ed. Robert S. Levine. Cambridge: Cambridge University Press, 1998.

Paul, Sherman. "Melville's 'The Town-Ho's Story.' " In *On Melville: The Best from American Literature*. Ed. Louis J. Budd and Edwin H. Cady. Durham, NC: Duke University Press, 1988.

Redpath, James. *Echoes of Harper's Ferry*. 1860. New York: Arno Press and New York Times, 1969.

Rogin, Michael Paul. *Subversive Genealogy: The Politics and Art of Herman Melville*. 1979. Berkeley: University of California Press, 1983.

Shaw, Lemuel. "Slavery and the Missouri Question." *The North American Review* X (January, 1820): 137–68.

Smith, James McCune. "Horoscope." *Frederick Douglass' Paper* (March 7, 1856).

"South Carolina – The Curse of Slavery." *North Star* (November 16, 1849).

Stauffer, John. *The Black Hearts of Men: Radical Abolitionists and the Transformation of Race*. Cambridge, MA: Harvard University Press, 2002.

Sundquist, Eric J. *To Wake the Nations: Race in the Making of American Literature*. Cambridge, MA: Harvard University Press, 1993.

Tanner, Tony. *The American Mystery: American Literature from Emerson to DeLillo*. Cambridge: Cambridge University Press, 2000.

"Troubles in the South." *National Era* (December 18, 1856).

Widmer, Edward L. *Young America: The Flowering of Democracy in New York City*. New York: Oxford University Press, 1999.

15

Gender and Sexuality

Leland S. Person

I squeezed that sperm till a strange sort of insanity came over me; and I found myself unwittingly squeezing my co-laborer's hands in it, mistaking their hands for the gentle globules. Such an abounding, affectionate, friendly, loving feeling did this avocation beget; that at last I was continually squeezing their hands, and looking up into their eyes sentimentally; as much as to say, – Oh! My dear fellow beings, why should we longer cherish any social acerbities, or know the slightest ill-humor or envy? Come; let us squeeze hands all round. (*Moby-Dick*, 416)

Melville's writing has not inspired as many studies of gender and sexuality as the work of most nineteenth-century American male writers. With a few exceptions, such as Ann Douglas, Joyce Warren, and Judith Fryer, feminist scholars of the 1970s and 1980s ignored Melville. Warren expressed a common view in her claim that he "hardly portrays women at all" and "surpasses even Cooper in his failure to grant personhood to women." "When women do appear in his works," she argued, "they are either little more than animated memories – traditional images of femininity as conceived by men – or overpowering nightmare figures who threaten the autonomy of the male self" (115). In a provocative recent study, Elizabeth Renker updates feminist approaches by considering Melville an abusive husband and misogynist who probably beat his wife. Renker's view of Melville dovetails with Ann Douglas's earlier portrait of an embattled writer who detested the feminizing tendencies of nineteenth-century American culture, defined "genuine masculinity" in opposition to gentility, sentimentality, and conventional morality (355), and attacked femininity with a "narcissistic rage" (357).

Melville's preference for sea-going tales and nearly all-male casts of characters has made him a good subject for recent men's studies approaches, as well as for gay and queer theorists. As feminist scholarship spun off into men's, gay, and queer studies and critical interest in men could be undertaken without apology, Melville's focus on men and even all-male communities suddenly held new critical promise. Edwin Haviland Miller's characterization of the Hawthorne–Melville relationship in his 1975 biography, Robert K. Martin's groundbreaking analysis of male friendship in the sea novels (*Hero*), and James Creech's provocative reading of *Pierre* as a "gay" text have radically changed the way we think of Melville's engagement with issues of gender and sexuality.

Melville and Heterosexuality

Rather than criticizing Melville's omission of women from his fiction or his reliance on female stereotypes, it remains worthwhile to examine those works in which he does portray women and male–female relationships. Several of Melville's novels – most notably, *Typee*, *Mardi*, and *Pierre* – depict male relationships with women that have the potential for inspiring male creativity. Characters such as Fayaway, Hautia, and Isabel, I have argued, "are identified with the kind of art that Melville most wanted to create: spontaneous, fluid, self-creative and self-propelling, the product of deep 'diving' and an imaginative openness to experience" (Person *Headaches* 50). This is not to claim that Melville secretly idealized male–female relationships or should be situated within a sentimental tradition of domestic order and marriage. Insofar as he depicted male–female relationships, he emphasized their vexing nature – almost always from a male point of view – but he did portray more complex women characters and more complex male–female relationships than many scholars have recognized.

The novel in which Melville most seriously engages heterosexual relationships is *Pierre*. Not only does he give female characters (Lucy Tartan and Isabel Banford) central roles but also he fleshes out the light–dark woman dichotomy he had used allegorically in *Mardi* into a triangle involving the young Pierre Glendinning, who begins the novel engaged to the "heavenly" Lucy Tartan (36) before getting seduced, at least in his own mind, by the dark and mysterious Isabel. Isabel represents ambiguity and beckons Pierre into a fluid world of "invisible agencies" and "things [he has] no name for" (37).

By making Pierre an artist, Melville also explores the challenges that women pose for male writers – foregrounding the very problems of representation and relationship for which feminist critics such as Fryer and Douglas have criticized him. "Thy hand is the caster's ladle" that "holds me entirely fluid," Isabel tells Pierre. "Into thy forms and slightest moods of thought, thou pourest me; and I there solidify to that form, and take it on, and thenceforth wear it, till once more thou moldest me anew" (324). Although Fryer considers Isabel a "symbol, not a woman" (54), Isabel challenges Pierre to the depths of his being, provoking a revolution in his mind and feelings, as well as in his conception of himself as a writer. Throughout the novel Melville uses aesthetic metaphors to describe Isabel's effect on Pierre and even represents his career as a fictional text and Isabel as a hidden meaning inscribed within it – as in the following observation: "so perfect to Pierre had long seemed the illuminated scroll of his life ... that only one hiatus was discovered by him in that sweetly-writ manuscript. A sister had been omitted from the text" (7). Isabel even introduces herself to Pierre in a letter, immediately testing his ability to "read." A chemical reaction between tears and ink has made the letter appear to be written in blood, and Pierre thinks of it as the "scroll of a torn, as well as bleeding heart" (65). Empowering Isabel to write a letter in blood from her heart runs counter to the tendency in Melville's other works to abstract and allegorize female characters. Despite the often melodramatic qualities of the plot, he makes a serious effort in *Pierre* to represent and give voice to a woman's subjectivity.

Although Douglas termed *Pierre* a "savage study of the conspiratorial interaction between genteel religion, feminine morality, and polite literature against the interests of genuine masculinity" (355), Pierre's complex relationship with Isabel cannot be reduced to such simple terms. The novel affirms that the achievement of a "genuine masculinity" – a genuine *heterosexual* masculinity – requires a creative relationship to women. Melville privileges Isabel's creative powers and challenges Pierre to "read" her correctly in the process of developing his own creative ability. Isabel's voice, for example, transcends language and "speaks" directly to the heart, and her guitar playing suggests the sort of symbolic art that Melville most prized: "All the wonders that are unimaginable and unspeakable . . . rapturous pulsations of legendary delights eternally unexperienced and unknown" (125).

Melville registers Pierre's failure as a writer, moreover, by his alienation from Isabel. Instead of maintaining imaginative communication with his sister, Pierre withdraws from her – writing, for example, behind the closed door of his frigid room. While Isabel wants to keep the "connecting door" open, so that the "heat of the room might bodily go into his" (297), Pierre walls himself off from her imaginative and sexual "heat." Sarah Wilson connects this separation to problems associated with male writing. The absence of a writing space within the domestic sphere reflects the relative lack of status that writing – as a male profession – enjoyed (77–8). Pierre certainly does not become a *man* through his writing. He becomes a writing automaton, anticipating the mechanical paper production Melville would illustrate in "The Tartarus of Maids." He writes without inspiration, an amanuensis for a "stranger" that inhabits him (340). In exploring the relational possibilities of creativity, Melville broke new ground in his fiction. Pierre's final failure as a writer derives from his failure to maintain a productive, self-creative relationship with a woman. Moreover, suggesting the effect that this sort of alienation has on his gender identity, Melville notes that in estranging himself from both Lucy and Isabel, Pierre feels "neuter now" (360).

Robyn Wiegman has called "The Paradise of Bachelors and the Tartarus of Maids" a "diptych of segregated spheres of gender relations" (736), and the story follows logically from *Pierre* in its pessimism about the possibility of mutually creative male–female relationships. The bachelors of Paradise have no connection to women; the maids of Tartarus have no fruitful connection to men. "Tartarus," moreover, can be read as a proto-naturalist critique of the "neutering" effect that the factory has on its female workers or, from a male-identified point of view, as an elaborate sexual allegory – one of Melville's most successful efforts to slip sexual content past the censorious radar of readers who had, for the most part, spurned his fiction. Like "Bartleby, the Scrivener," which it resembles in its depiction of deadening, mechanical activity, "The Tartarus of Maids" features alienation of the sexes and the desexualization of human beings. While it is fun for modern readers to get Melville's sexual jokes and to work out the elaborate sexual allegory he builds into the story, we should not forget that sexuality and birth are rendered exaggeratedly mechanical and inhuman. The tale features an assembly line of mechanical sex, conception, gestation, and birth.

In the womb-like building where the paper is manufactured, a gigantic machine stamps a wreath of roses on "rose-hued note-paper." With its "vertical thing like a piston periodically rising and falling" (*PT* 328) upon sheets of paper, this "iron animal" reduces male sexuality and creativity phallocentrically to the driving thrusts of a mechanical "pen." Women both feed the machine and, symbolically, are associated with the raw material. They are "blank-looking" (328) and "sheet-white" (330) – like paper – objects rather than subjects; for their voices are "banished" (328). If the "iron animal" that embosses the paper is phallocentrically male, the "great machine" that makes the paper is unmistakably female. Located in a room "stifling with a strange, blood-like, abdominal heat," the machine is fed its supply of pulp by two large vats – gigantic ovaries "full of a white, wet, woolly-looking stuff" that resembles the "albuminous part of an egg" (331). Production – reproduction – takes only nine minutes, the narrator discovers, when he drops a slip of paper, on which he has written his guide's name (Cupid), into the pulp and watches its birth, signaled by a "scissory sound" as of "some cord being snapped." But the "child" of this process is only foolscap, and the word Cupid is already "half faded" when the paper appears from the machine (332). Love, like the human voice, has been banished. Given the analogy Melville draws throughout the tale between the factory and the writing process, "The Tartarus of Maids" comments pessimistically on what the creative process had become for him. But the story also comments astutely on the deadening, or neutering, effect of nineteenth-century ideologies of gender and sexuality. It portrays not only the estrangement of men and women from one another – their relegation to separate spheres – but the alienation of both genders from their own vital energies, including sexual energies.

Melville and Masculinity

Many critics have asserted that *Moby-Dick* is a man's book that inscribes a patriarchal, anti-female ideology and reinforces nineteenth-century separatism. Ann Douglas claimed the book was "written for men, or at least from a self-consciously masculine viewpoint" (367, 368). Richard Brodhead called it "so outrageously masculine that we scarcely allow ourselves to do justice to the full scope of its masculinism" (9). Neal L. Tolchin and David Leverenz, on the other hand, point out that Melville attributes female behavior to Ahab, who can be seen as a female mourner (Tolchin) or a female hysteric (Leverenz). Focusing on the role of homoeroticism in the novel, especially in the relationship between Ishmael and Queequeg, Robert Martin finds Melville contesting the "power of the patriarchy" with the "radical social potential" of homosexual relationships (*Hero* 70). Without emphasizing homoeroticism, Joseph Allen Boone considers the novel a "powerful critique of the male ethos ruling American society" (250).

In a 1994 article, I tried to reconcile some of the differences among these critics by arguing that Melville "both explores and challenges a traditional, essentially phallocentric masculinity (individualistic, instrumental, projective, competitive)" ("Melville's Cassock," 2). Many critics, notably Robert Shulman, T. Walter Herbert, and Herbert Schneider and Homer Pettey, have analyzed Melville's deft use of phallic and homosexual puns in *Moby-Dick*. I took my cue from the chapter "The Cassock", in which the mincer turns the foreskin of the whale's severed penis inside out in order to put it on for a protective covering, and suggested that Melville "puts on" masculinity in another sense – that is, satirizes male efforts to inhabit the phallus as the primary signifier of their masculinity. Destabilizing masculinity in this fashion enables Melville to open the possibility of multiple male identities and roles.

In the bawdy section of "The Tail" (Chapter 86), for example, Melville celebrates and deconstructs this obvious phallic symbol, emphasizing its masculine and feminine qualities. The "confluent measureless force of the whole whale seems concentrated to a point" in the tail (376), he notes, but the tail also becomes a site of "daintiness," "delicacy," "tenderness," and even "maidenly gentleness" (377). Ishmael and Queequeg, too, seem to divide and share gender roles. Ishmael awakens in Queequeg's "bridegroom clasp" in the Spouter Inn bedroom (26), but Queequeg plays "midwife" when he rescues Tashtego from the Whale's head (344). Even Ahab, the apotheosis of aggressive masculinity, celebrates his "queenly personality" in "The Candles" (Chapter 119) and acts maternally toward Pip, to whom he feels bound umbilically "by cords woven of [his] heart strings" (522). Sarah Wilson has recently pointed out, moreover, that Melville blurs the lines between male and female work in *Moby-Dick* and thus in the gender identities associated with that work (63).

Despite the instrumental priorities of vengeance that govern the *Pequod*'s manic voyage, very few of the values, ideas, or motives that Melville puts in play remain stable. Gender and sexuality are no exceptions. Melville celebrates the possibilities of homosocial and homoerotic communion between men in the bedroom scene in the Spouter Inn, as well as in "The Squeeze of the Hand," where spermaceti becomes a fluid medium in which bodily boundaries dissolve and men find themselves squeezing each other's hands in ecstatic joy. Melville positions conventional heterosexual marriage in the background of the novel – in Ahab's momentary nostalgia for the wife in whose marriage pillow he has left only a single "dent" (544) and in Starbuck's "far-away domestic memories of his young Cape wife and child" – memories that open him "to those latent influences which, in some honest-hearted men, restrain the gush of dare-devil daring" (116). Doing so, as Robert K. Martin argues, enables Melville to foreground and contrast two types of masculinity, "two kinds of phallicism": Ahab's desexualized, aggressive phallocentrism, which Martin terms a "hierarchical eros expressed in social forms of male power," and Queequeg's "polysemous phallicism," which sponsors a "democratic eros" that finds its "highest expression in male friendship" and in "masturbatory sexuality reflecting the celebration of a generalized seminal power not directed toward control or production" (*Hero* 4). David Leverenz connects Ahab's fatal phallicism with an emerging middle-class ideology of entrepreneurial manhood – driven to exploit natural resources and weaker men (288) – and considers *Moby-Dick* the "most extravagant projection of male penis envy in our literature" (294). *Moby-Dick* both apotheosizes and critiques nineteenth-century models of manhood – aggressive, competitive, self-centered, phallocentric. It also explores alternative constructs, especially in the marriage between Ishmael and Queequeg.

Several of the tales Melville wrote at Pittsfield in the 1850s reinforce the phallo-centric critique I have noted in *Moby-Dick*. Philip Young groups "The Lightning-Rod Man," "I and My Chimney," "Cock-A-Doodle-Doo!" and "The Tartarus of Maids" – stories with "secret" sexual content that "slipped past the guardians of Victorian taste that ruled magazines that published him" (96). It does not require extraordinary imagination for the modern reader to get the joke Melville embodies in the lightning-rod man's walking stick – "a polished copper rod, four feet long, lengthwise attached to a neat wooden staff, by insertion into two balls of greenish glass" (*PT* 119) – although the simple identification of rod and phallus does not produce a very complex story. "I and My Chimney" is a more elaborate sexual allegory if one makes the chimney–phallus connection that Melville invites. Ann Douglas termed the chimney a "bastion of phallic, assertive, and aggressive masculinity" (384), but it is insufficient simply to point out the phallic joke implicit in the chimney or to dismiss the tale and its phallic humor, as Douglas does, for representing Melville's battle with femininity. Like so many of Melville's tales from the 1850s, "I and My Chimney" satirizes its male protagonist and in the process offers an extended critique of phallocentric definitions of male identity.

Projecting the chimney as a double from the opening line of the tale, the narrator goes on to develop an extended metaphor – a metonym – in which the chimney takes his place in the household as the "true host" (352), the "one great domineering object." In effect, Melville brings the exaggerating traditions of Western humor into a domestic sphere in which a gigantic phallic object figures as tyrannical god of hearth and home. "In brief," he observes, "my chimney is my superior; my superior by I know not how many heads and shoulders; my superior, too, in that humbly bowing over with shovel and tongs, I much minister to it; yet never does it minister, or incline over to me" (353). By the end of the story, the narrator's identification with the chimney is so complete and the two of them so embattled that he is dedicating himself to the chimney's protection – and will not leave the house. "Some say that I have become a sort of mossy old misanthrope," he admits, "while all the time the fact is, I am simply standing guard over my mossy old chimney; for it is resolved between me and my chimney, that I and my chimney will never surrender" (377). In that confession, masquerading as defiance, Melville reveals the cost of phallocentric identification – hermetic enclosure, misanthropy, and estrangement from others.

"Cock-A-Doodle-Doo!" features a similar conflict between the first-person male narrator and forces that compromise the autonomy and power he desires. Whereas "I and My Chimney" places its narrator primarily in conflict with women and the domestic sphere, "Cock-A-Doodle-Doo!" emphasizes its narrator's problems in negotiating the economic world outside the home. The melancholic narrator feels powerless in a world that he experiences as increasingly hostile and misanthropic. "What a slight mark, after all, does man make on this huge great earth," he thinks. "A miserable world! Who would take the trouble to make a fortune in it, when he knows not how long he can keep it" (*PT* 269). Ostensibly depressed because the newspapers have carried reports of several recent calamities – railroad and steamboat accidents in particular – the narrator reports that his "own private affairs were also full of despotisms, casualties, and knockings on the head" – causing a serious case of the "hypos" (268).

Even more than *Moby-Dick* or "I and My Chimney," "Cock-A-Doodle-Doo!" both examines and critiques phallocentrism – in the form of a comic quest to acquire an "enormous" cock and, with it, the power it embodies. As complex an allegory in gendered terms as "The Tartarus of Maids," the tale does for manhood what "Tartarus" does for womanhood. In both cases, Melville externalizes the gendered body – that is, the genital and gestational attributes that engender bodies – and thus interrogates the identificatory power of those attributes. By the time he finishes "putting on" his narrator's phallocentric obsession in "Cock-A-Doodle-Doo!" Melville has thoroughly deconstructed phallogocentric manhood. Is manliness a function of phallic possession – of size and beauty and lusty energy? Does the cock make the man? The narrator certainly thinks so. Melville clearly doesn't.

For one thing, "Cock-A-Doodle-Doo!" tests the relationship between manhood and socioeconomic class. The cock's owner, Merrymusk, is working-class, suggesting the common presumption that working men are more virile and masculine. The narrator, however, despite being deeply in debt, identifies manhood with money and gentility. Manhood, as embodied in the extraordinary cock, is something to buy, even if he must take out another mortgage on his property in order to make the investment. Melville disjoins manhood and gentility, however, by contrasting the narrator with the woodcutter Merrymusk, who "would stand and saw all day long in a driving snowstorm" and quaffs his mug of cider "like a man" (280). Merrymusk has an invalid wife and four sickly children, belying the equation of cock and successful manhood. He has not lost his sense of humor, however; for when the narrator asks him if he knows any "gentleman hereabouts who owns an extraordinary cock," Merrymusk answers with a "twinkle" in his eye that he knows "of no *gentleman*" who has "what might be called an extraordinary cock" (281).

When the narrator finally makes his way up the mountain to Merrymusk's shanty, he initially believes that his dream has come true, as right before him he sees "the most resplendent creature that ever blessed the sight of man":

A cock, more like a golden eagle than a cock. A cock, more like a Field-Marshal than a cock. A cock, more like Lord Nelson with all his glittering arms on, standing on the Vanguard's quarter-deck going into battle, than a cock. A cock, more like the Emperor Charlemagne in his robes at Aix la Chapelle, than a cock.

Such a cock!

He was of a haughty size, stood haughtily on his haughty legs. (282)

It is hard to imagine a passage in which the phallocentric terms of manhood are more on display – the cock as metonym for manhood. "That's the cock," the narrator observes, "a little embarrassed" (282). His embarrassment stems from his class bias. He has spontaneously named the cock "Signor Beneventano," after a character he has recently seen in an Italian opera – "a man of a tall, imposing person, clad in rich raiment, like to plumage, and with a most remarkable, majestic, scornful stride" (283) – in other words, the image of the haughty man the narrator would like to be. "Is that cock yours?" he asks Merrymusk, with obvious doubt that a man like Merrymusk could own such an extraordinary cock. "I raised it," Merrymusk replies, in a line that must have tickled Melville to write. Enchanted as he is by this "marvelous" and "magic" cock, the narrator offers Merrymusk fifty dollars, then a hundred dollars, and then five hundred dollars (283). But Merrymusk won't sell. The scene is telling, for the narrator continues to believe that manhood, in the form of a "marvelous cock," can be bought. He equates personal power with possession of the phallus and has faith in the fungible power of money – his power to exchange money for the phallus and phallocentric potency. The narrator emphasizes the contrast, for example, between Merrymusk and the cock. Whereas Merrymusk sits "on an old battered chest, in his old battered gray coat, with patches at his knees and elbows, and a deplorably bunged hat," the cock is a "Spanish grandee caught in a shower, and standing under some peasant's shed. . . . He irradiated the shanty; he glorified its meanness" (284). Disjoining Merrymusk from his cock even as he recognizes the cock's power to redeem the "peasant's" "meanness," the narrator means to concentrate all manly power in the cock so that he can possess it for himself.

As the narrator focuses his desire on the cock, however, it seems to absorb energy from the other characters and grow so powerful that it even frightens the narrator himself – "like some overpowering angel in the Apocalypse." Overpowering in stature, the cock stands in sharp contrast to Merrymusk's wife and children. Marked by her "wasted, but strangely cheerful human face" and "shrunken" body, Merrymusk's wife lies beside three of her sickly, pale-faced children (285). Sadly, they count on the cock, which Merrymusk names "Dr. Cock" (285), to restore their health. In effect, Merrymusk has vested all value in the cock, leaving his wife and children to waste away and providing an object lesson for the narrator, who would do the same thing. When the narrator calls Merrymusk a "poor man," for example, Merrymusk resists the characterization. "Why call *me* poor?" he retorts. "Don't the cock *I* own glorify this otherwise inglorious, lean, lantern-jawed land? Didn't *my* cock encourage *you*? And *I* give you all this gratification away gratis. I am a rich man – a very rich man, and a very happy one."

The narrator agrees. "Oh, noble cock! Oh, noble man!" he exclaims (286), demonstrating his emotional investment in a phallocentric manhood.

When Merrymusk dies shortly afterwards, the narrator of course wants the cock for himself. At the same time, he fears the cock, because it is so independent and so powerful. Liberated from its "owner," it runs amok around the shanty – a cock with its man cut off. Despite its potency and its ability to cheer the spirits of the woman and her children, however, the cock is powerless to save them. They all die, and after crowing one last, "supernatural" note, the cock dies, too. The tale comes quickly to its end, with the narrator's notation that the Merrymusk family gravestone bears an image of a "lusty cock in the act of crowing" and the passage (from I Corinthians), "Oh! death, where is thy sting? / Oh! grave, where is thy victory?" (288). The narrator himself has buried the family and erected the stone. Representing the extraordinary cock iconographically, he has himself become the cock; for he ends the narrative with the observation that he has never again "felt the doleful dumps." Instead, "under all circumstances," he crows "late and early with a continual crow" – "COCK-A-DOO-DLE-DOO!—OO!—OO!—OO!—OO!" (288).

Although William Dillingham argues that the story "reveals the narrator's "victory over sexual insecurity" and achievement of a "new virility" and "sexual self-confidence" (58), I agree with Marvin Fisher that, like "Bartleby," "Cock-A-Doodle-Doo!" is a "study in dementia" (163). As cultural and gender critique, the tale demonstrates the fallacy of phallocentric investiture – the fixation on an "extraordinary cock" as the measure of confident manhood. Despite the narrator's crowing, despite Merrymusk's claims of wealth through the cock's possession, male cockiness entails poverty and even death upon others, who suffer malnourishment at the hands of men who suffer delusions of masculine grandeur. The cock's last act, after all, is "crowing the souls of the children out of their wasted bodies" (288).

Melville and Homosexuality

Critics interested in exploring Melville's representation of homosocial or homosexual relationships often cite his brief relationship in the Berkshires with Nathaniel Hawthorne, including Melville's letters to Hawthorne, his review of Hawthorne's *Mosses from an Old Manse*, the apparent reference to loving Hawthorne in the poem "Monody," and the depiction of Hawthorne in the character of Vine in *Clarel*. The review, with its striking images of Hawthorne's "soft ravishments" spinning Melville "round about in a web of dreams" (*PT* 241), of Hawthorne dropping "germinous seeds" into Melville's soul and then shooting his "strong New-England roots" into the "hot soil" of Melville's "Southern soul" (250), has crystallized for many critics the homoerotic content in Melville's writing and led to many speculations about his relationship to Hawthorne himself. Most famously, Edwin Miller argued that an "advance" from Melville that Hawthorne experienced as an "assault" caused the two writers to become estranged in 1851 (249–50). Few other critics feel so confident about the biographical facts, even though nearly all acknowledge the passionate feelings Melville expressed. Hershel Parker calls Melville's review of *Mosses* a "passionate private message to his new friend," and he speculates that "writing so intimately about Hawthorne's power to arouse his literary aspirations had left him more than a little febrile – excited intellectually, emotionally, and sexually – sexual arousal being for Melville an integral part of such intensely creative phases" (1: 760). Robert Milder dismisses for lack of evidence Miller's suggestion that Melville made a homoerotic "advance," and he concludes that Melville's attraction to Hawthorne "does not seem the object-cathexis of a free-floating homosexual disposition but a reaction to an extraordinary individual" (4). Critics have often examined *Pierre; or, The Ambiguities* and Hawthorne's *The Blithedale Romance* for clues about what transpired between the two men in the Berkshires, because these are the books they published in the immediate aftermath of their experience. Monica Mueller has devoted an entire book to the subject, and in his provocative reading of Pierre as a "closeted" gay text, James Creech considers Hawthorne the "erotic model" for Isabel Banford, Pierre's half-sister (119).

This is not to say that Hawthorne brought Melville out of the closet or inspired a sudden outpouring of homoerotic writing. Several critics have emphasized homoerotic traces in Melville's early fiction. Robert K. Martin notes that in *Typee* Melville created a "work of released sexual pleasure, one in which the body could be celebrated and in which individuals could be free to explore their deeper natures," but he also notes that Melville was "not prepared to depict the world of exclusive male friendship and sexuality that would characterize his later works" (*Hero*, 36–7). *Redburn* includes one of Melville's most romantic and sentimental paeans to the attractions of women, but also one of his most desirable male characters, Harry Bolton. In fact, Melville juxtaposes the two. In Chapter 43 Redburn encounters "three adorable charmers" in the English countryside. Eating a dinner of buttered muffins with their family, he wishes he were a buttered muffin (ready for the eating) and can't "help thinking what a fine thing it would be to carry home a beautiful English wife" (214). That night he dreams of "red cheeks and roses" (215), but he awakens the next morning not to act upon his dream of heterosexual bliss, but to meet the feminine Harry Bolton: "one of those small, but perfectly formed beings, with curling hair, and silken muscles," whose "complexion was a mantling brunette, feminine as a girl's," whose eyes were "large, black, and womanly," and whose "voice was as the sound of a harp" (216). Harry is one of Melville's most feminine male characters – a "figure of the homosexual as that construction was emerging out of one of effeminacy in the mid-nineteenth century" (Martin "Melville and Sexuality," 191) – and Redburn falls in love with him. Martin calls Redburn's elegy for Harry in Chapter 50 "unambiguous and unperplexed in its loving memory of a man who has been destroyed for his otherness" (*Hero* 43), and there is something chilling about Bolton's victimization at the hands of the *Highlander*'s crew. They have been watching the "girlish youth" for days around the docks, and after he comes on board, they treat him mercilessly, probing for every weakness (e.g., his fear of heights) and subjecting him to a brutal initiation that could well include rape. "How they hunted you, Harry, my zebra!" Redburn recalls, "those ocean barbarians, those unimpressible, uncivilized sailors of ours! How they pursued you from bowsprit to mainmast, and started you out of your every retreat! (253). By the end of the chapter, it appears that Harry has become a "punk," a "hunted hare to the merciless crew" (257), a willing sex slave. How was it, Redburn wonders, "that Harry Bolton, who spite of his effeminacy of appearance, had evinced, in our London trip, such unmistakable flashes of a spirit not easily tamed – how was it, that he could now yield himself up to the almost passive reception of contumely and contempt?" (257–8). Homoerotic desire seems clearer in *Redburn* than in any novel before *Moby-Dick*, but it is also bracketed and ultimately unable to shape the plot; for Melville seems unable to imagine a relationship between Redburn and Harry on land.

Despite efforts to take seriously Melville's treatment of male–female relationships in *Pierre*, the best recent scholarship on gender and sexuality in the novel has emphasized non-normative subjectivities and various ways in which Melville subverts nineteenth-century taxonomies of both gender and sexuality. In a wide-ranging study of American bachelorhood, for example, Vincent Bertolini observes that Pierre's "unconsummated fake heterosexual marriage" to Isabel "realizes in structure and desensualizing effect the equation of sisters and wives in domestic ideology," and he goes on to label Pierre "neither a married nor a single man but a sad, neutered combination of both" (722). For Bertolini, *Pierre* illustrates the deadening influence of sentimental domestic ideology and its prescription of desexualized gender roles. Despite the emotional churning one senses in the novel, erotic energy does not translate into coherent identity formation or creative relationship.

The most provocative alternative reading of *Pierre* is Creech's, because where I and others see heterosexual relationships, Creech sees disguised homoerotic ones. The incestuous relationship between Pierre and Isabel, for example, masks a different sort of proscribed relationship; "converting homosexual desire into incestuous desire" allowed Melville to "preserve homoerotic feeling" and to express "transgressive feelings," but it also allowed him, through the novel's "tragic ending," to punish those feelings (122).

For evidence that Isabel represents the closeted or "transvested" form (119) that Pierre/Melville's homosexual longing (for his father, for Hawthorne) assumes, Creech analyzes Pierre's grief over his father's death, noting the displacement of father by sister in Pierre's imagination as a "direct transgender encoding" (118). He analyzes Pierre's "two circuits of desire" (126) and his two options for achieving mature manhood: becoming a man by "phallic competition" with Glen Stanly over Lucy Tartan or by following a homoeroticized desire for an "incestuous object" in Isabel (127). The transgressive forces that Melville releases early in the novel, Creech argues, are closed off by novel's end. Normalizing homosocial desire displaces transgressive homosexual desire when Glen Stanly returns to vie with Pierre for Lucy. Finding himself in a "sexual sandwich" between Lucy and Isabel (169), Pierre feels "stuck between two contradictory sexual desires" (177), which then fuse into a "single, murderous, suicidal hatred" (178) that resolves conflict by destroying its terms and its subjects.

A novel only sketchily examined for homoerotic content, *The Confidence-Man* in many ways offers one of Melville's most extended and transgressive analyses of nineteenth-century same-sex practices and possibilities. In Chapter 22 the con man, in the guise of Philosophical Intelligence Officer, tries to sell a boy to Pitch, the Missouri bachelor who has used up some thirty boys on his backwoods farm and now wants to replace boys with machines. "But suppose I did want a boy," the bachelor coyly asks, "what they jocosely call a good boy – how could your absurd office help me?" Do you "make good boys to order?" (114). Marked by discussion of points and beards and sprouts and buds and teeth and flowers and butterflies, this transaction seems designed to set us up for identification with pederastic desire. Who after all can resist a good boy?[1]

Timothy Gilfoyle documents a "nascent male homosexual subculture" in New York City as early as the 1840s (135), and George Chauncey notes that an "erotic system of wolves and punks" (aggressive men and sexually available boys) was "widespread" by the end of the century (88). Melville must have known as much about this subculture as Walt Whitman; for a discourse of male prostitution invades many male-to-male solicitations in *The Confidence-Man*. And the Melville who played so many sexual jokes on his readers – isn't he cruising the reader in Chapter 22, rubbing our noses, as it were, in the face of pederastic desire? Isn't the Missouri bachelor figure an insatiable "wolf," who has used up thirty-five boys, the "flowers of all nations," as he himself puts it – boys sent to him by "one who well knew [his] perplexities" (117)? And doesn't the con man persistently eroticize the boys he is trying to sell? After all, he promotes the virtues of a "lily-bud," with "such points" that are "not all that could be desired" but still "as palpable as those of an adult." Such a boy, he goes on, "like the bud of the lily," "contains concealed rudiments," "points at present invisible, with beauties at present dormant" (121). Melville is warming up for *Billy Budd*, as the con man eroticizes "downy-chinned" little boys who will "eventually rival the goat in a beard." "Can it now with fairness be denied," he asks, "that, in his beard, the man-child prospectively possesses an appendix, not less imposing than patriarchal?" (122). He even focuses on boys' teeth, those "tender little puttings-forth" that are quickly "blown out of his mouth" in favor of a permanent set. Boys "bud forth," he says, with "sound, even, beautiful, and permanent virtues" (123). Boys are to men, he concludes triumphantly, as caterpillars are to butterflies (124).

Carolyn Karcher notes that the "bawdy sexual imagery" pervading this episode establishes "an analogy between sexual and economic exploitation" (246), and for her the connection between sexuality and economics points to the "licentiousness bred by the southern slave system" (243). But the novel need not be about slavery for the vexing relationship between sex and money to work. In his study of male prostitution in late nineteenth-century England, Jeffrey Weeks cites a common reluctance to accept money for sex – a resistance, in other words, to identification as a male prostitute. He observes that the "exchange of money could create a host of different symbolic meanings for both parties, while the uncertainty of both could make the transaction itself very ambiguous" (204). Homosexual acts did not necessarily inscribe homosexual identities, but accepting money for sex carried a worse stigma than the sex itself. Melville's representation of male-to-male exchanges in *The Confidence-Man* inscribes similar ambiguities and confusions – testing the possibility of male–male "geniality" in a world dominated by competition and confidence. Melville focuses on a problematical nexus of competing desires – on the difficulty in a capitalist, market economy of preserving egalitarian, non-competitive relationships, including sexual relationships, with other men. As soon as a man asks for money, Melville suggests, the nature of the transaction and the identities of both participants change forever.

Chauncey notes that young male prostitutes were usually called "punks" or "lambs" (89), for example, and Melville puns on the latter in the role-playing exchange between Frank Goodman and Egbert in Chapter 39. Like "any grown man, boy though I was," the cosmopolitan tells Egbert, "I went into the market and chose me my mutton, not for its leanness, but its fatness" (205). "My reason for choosing you," he goes on,

> was solely with a view of preserving inviolate the delicacy of the connection. For – do but think of it – what more distressing to delicate friendship, formed early, than your friend's eventually, in manhood, dropping in of a rainy night for his little loan of five dollars or so? Can delicate friendship stand that? And, on the other side, would delicate friendship, so long as it retained its delicacy, do that? Would you not instinctively say of your dripping friend in the entry, "I have been deceived, fraudulently deceived, in this man; he is no true friend that, in platonic love to demand love-rites?" (205–6).

Rather than promising mutual satisfaction and pleasure, the sodomitic exchange imaged in the "dripping friend at the entry" provokes anxiety and fear as it supplants "platonic love" with homoeroticized "love-rites." "Call to mind the days we went nutting," Frank Goodman reminds Egbert, in language that recalls Melville's terms for his relationship with Hawthorne, "the times we walked in the woods, arms wreathed about each other, showing trunks invined like the trees: – oh, Charlie!" (206). Through Goodman Melville mourns the loss of a "delicate" male friendship liberated from economic and sexual demands – a perfect friendship, sex and tax exempt from transactions that would position its participants in powerful and powerless roles.

In the long episode involving Charlie Noble and Frank Goodman in Chapters 25–35, Melville thoroughly explores the vexed nature of male homosexual relationships. Unlike the bachelor, Charlie Noble seems anything but resistant to male–male intimacy – a man after the cosmopolitan's "own heart," who acts the aggressor in their initial encounter, readily holding Goodman's hand and inviting him for a drink. Surprisingly, Goodman himself seems resistant, although he explains in an outrageous, sodomitic pun that he has "met so many old friends, all free-hearted, convivial gentlemen" that he is "at bottom almost in the condition of a sailor who, stepping ashore after a long voyage, ere night reels with loving welcomes, his head of less capacity than his heart" (158). Read queerly, Goodman's punning complaint becomes coy negotiation – an offer to assume a passive, effeminate position in a sexual encounter. At this mention of other men, furthermore, Charlie Noble's face turns dejected, "as a jealous lover's might at hearing from his sweetheart of former ones" (158), but he recovers to woo the cosmopolitan with a song from Leigh Hunt's "Bacchus in Tuscany." The cosmopolitan dissolves in "surrender," insisting that while he can easily resist women's seductions, he cannot resist a good man's: "When mermaid songs move figure-heads, then may glory, gold, and women try their blandishments on me. But a good fellow, singing a good song, he woos forth my every spike, so that my whole hull, like a ship's, sailing by a magnetic rock, caves in with acquiescence. Enough: when one has a heart of a certain sort, it is in vain trying to be resolute" (159).

"Ours is friendship at first sight," Charlie Noble declares as they sit over a bottle of port. "It is," replies Goodman, lest we miss the point, "and the same may be said of friendship at first sight as of love at first sight: it is the only true one, the only noble one." Indeed, as they spontaneously define this budding relationship, Goodman insists that there is "nothing like preserving in manhood the fraternal familiarities of youth," for it "proves the heart a rosy boy to the last" (160). In terms that recall Ishmael's apostrophes to homosexual marriage after his night in bed with Queequeg or the ecstasy he feels while squeezing spermaceti, Frank and Charlie sing praises to "geniality everywhere" – a geniality that is "much on the increase in these days" (175). "Every heart is ice-bound till wine melts it," Charlie observes, "and reveals the tender grass and sweet herbage budding below, with every dear secret, hidden before like a dropped jewel in a snow-bank, lying there unsuspected through winter till spring" (177). The relationship sours almost as soon as bud turns to bloom, however, for just as Charlie expects Frank to demonstrate his "generous confidence" and to confide a secret he assumes to be a love affair, the cosmopolitan drops the other shoe. "I am in want, urgent want, of money," he finally confesses, revealing the mercenary motives that have prompted his feigned geniality (178).

The bachelor gets his boy at the end of Chapter 22, but Melville's representation of other male bonds in the novel suggests that they are consistently thwarted by market forces. Weeks observes that in a "world of sexual barter, particularly given the furtiveness, the need for caution, and the great disparities of wealth and social position among the participants, the cash nexus inevitably dominated" (202), and I think Melville describes a similar domination aboard his own nineteenth-century cruise ship. The male bond possesses the potential to subvert a capitalist economy (in which men have competitive, homosocial, management–labor relationships with one another), but *The Confidence-Man* consistently restores that market economy when, at the end of virtually every episode, the confidence man asks for money – ironically destroying the "confidence" on which a non-competitive, non-market-driven bond between men might be founded.

Robert K. Martin has asserted that the "adoption of a queer model that proposes contingency instead of certainty seems likely to offer the best future for the study of sexuality in Melville's texts" ("Melville and Sexuality," 200). Uncertainty is such a common feeling for Melville's readers and contingency such a common experience for Melville's characters, that a "queer model" of approach to just about any issue in Melville's writing makes good sense. From *Typee* forward, Melville experimented with alternative forms of gender and sexuality identity – representationally, not scientifically. One senses genuine imaginative openness to transgressive forms in the novels up through *Moby-Dick*. Ishmael's marriage to Queequeg remains one of the most remarkable scenes in nineteenth-century American literature for its utterly forthright celebration of a physical and emotional bond between men. In Melville's later fiction (and including *Moby-Dick*), deviance comes with an edge, as Melville seems increasingly determined to rebel against social norms. Employing a remarkable array of semantic and narrational tricks, he disguises sexuality and sexual transgressions in ways that co-opt his readers, most of whom, I think he is betting, will get his jokes and thereby reveal themselves to be in secret sympathy. Come; let us squeeze hands all round.

NOTE

1   The following section on *The Confidence-Man* originated in a paper that Robert K. Martin and I presented, as an epistolary dialogue, at the 1995 American Literature Association convention. It is a condensed version of my side of the dialogue – with many thanks to Robert Martin for inspiring me to work out my responses to this novel.

REFERENCES AND FURTHER READING

Bertolini, Vincent J. "Fireside Chastity: The Erotics of Sentimental Bachelorhood in the 1850s." *American Literature* 68 (1996): 707–37.

Boone, Joseph Allen. *Tradition Counter Tradition: Love and the Form of Fiction*. Chicago: University of Chicago Press, 1987.

Brodhead, Richard H. "Trying All Things: An Introduction to *Moby-Dick*." In *New Essays on Moby-Dick*. Ed. Richard H. Brodhead. New York: Cambridge University Press, 1986.

Chauncey, George. *Gay New York: Gender, Urban Culture, and the Making of the Gay Male World, 1890–1940*. New York: Basic Books, 1994.

Crain, Caleb. "Lovers of Human Flesh: Homosexuality and Cannibalism in Melville's Novels." *American Literature* 66 (1994): 25–53.

Creech, James. *Closet Writing/Gay Reading: The Case of Melville's* Pierre. Chicago: University of Chicago Press, 1993.

Dillingham, William B. *Melville's Short Fiction, 1853–1856*. Athens: University of Georgia Press, 1977.

Douglas, Ann. *The Feminization of American Culture*. New York: Alfred A. Knopf, 1977.

Fisher, Marvin. *Going Under: Melville's Short Fiction and the American 1850s*. Baton Rouge: Louisiana State University Press, 1977.

Fryer, Judith. *The Faces of Eve: Women in the Nineteenth-Century American Novel*. New York: Oxford University Press, 1976.

Gilfoyle, Timothy J. *City of Eros: New York City, Prostitution, and the Commercialization of Sex, 1790–1920*. New York: Norton, 1992.

Herbert, T. Walter, Jr. "Homosexuality and Spiritual Aspiration in *Moby-Dick*." *Canadian Review of American Studies* 6 (1975): 50–8.

Karcher, Carolyn. *Shadow over the Promised Land: Slavery, Race, and Violence in Melville's America*. Baton Rouge: Louisiana State University Press, 1980.

Leverenz, David. *Manhood and the American Renaissance*. Ithaca: Cornell University Press, 1989.

Martin, Robert K. *Hero, Captain, and Stranger: Male Friendship, Social Critique, and Literary Form in the Sea Novels of Herman Melville*. Chapel Hill: University of North Carolina Press, 1986.

——— . "Melville and Sexuality." In *The Cambridge Companion to Herman Melville*. Ed. Robert S. Levine. New York: Cambridge University Press, 1998. 186–201.

Milder, Robert. " 'The Ugly Socrates': Melville, Hawthorne, and Homoeroticism." *ESQ* 46 (2000): 1–49.

Miller, Edwin Haviland. *Melville*. New York: Persea, 1975.

Mueller, Monica. *"This Infinite Fraternity of Feeling": Gender, Genre, and Homoerotic Crisis in Hawthorne's* The Blithedale Romance *and Melville's* Pierre. Madison, NJ: Fairleigh Dickinson University Press, 1996.

Person, Leland S. *Aesthetic Headaches: Women and a Masculine Poetics in Poe, Melville, and Hawthorne*. Athens: University of Georgia Press, 1988.

——— . "Melville's Cassock: Putting on Masculinity in *Moby-Dick*." *ESQ* 40 (1994): 1–26.

——— and Robert K. Martin. "But suppose I did want a boy?": Homosexual Economies in *The Confidence-Man*." American Literature Association Convention. Baltimore. May 1995.

Renker, Elizabeth. *Strike Through the Mask: Herman Melville and the Scene of Writing*. Baltimore: Johns Hopkins University Press, 1996.

Schneider, Herbert N. and Homer B. Pettey. "Melville's Ichthyphallic God." *Studies in American Fiction* 26 (1998): 193–212.

Shulman, Robert. "The Serious Function of Melville's Phallic Jokes." *American Literature* 33 (1961): 179–94.

Tolchin, Neal L. *Mourning, Gender, and Creativity in the Art of Herman Melville*. New Haven: Yale University Press, 1988.

Warren, Joyce W. *The American Narcissus: Individualism and Women in Nineteenth-Century American Fiction*. New Brunswick, NJ: Rutgers University Press, 1984.

Weeks, Jeffrey. "Inverts, Perverts, and Mary-Annes: Male Prostitution and the Regulation of Homosexuality in England in the Nineteenth and Early Twentieth Centuries." In *Hidden from History: Reclaiming the Gay and Lesbian Past*. Ed. Martin Duberman, Martha Vicinus, and George Chauncey, Jr. New York: Meridian, 1989. 195–211.

Wiegman, Robyn. "Melville's Geography of Gender." *American Literary History* 1 (1989): 735–53.

Wilson, Sarah. "Melville and the Architecture of Antebellum Masculinity." *American Literature* 76 (2004): 59–87.

Young, Philip. *The Private Melville*. University Park: Pennsylvania State University Press, 1993.

Part IV
Libraries

16

The Legacy of Britain

Robin Grey

From English Renaissance to the "American Renaissance"

"In the four quarters of the globe who reads an American book? Or goes to an American play? Or looks at an American picture or statue?" (Smith 79). Posing this taunting question in the January, 1820 *Edinburgh Review*, Sydney Smith starkly revealed the complicated and vexed relationship between a young American nation in search of its own cultural identity, and Britain, its fiercest literary rival. In the absence of an international copyright law, American publishers all too easily obliged the public by simply reprinting, without paying royalties, such popular British novels as those by Charles Dickens, Sir Walter Scott, and their contemporaries. Likewise, newspaper and magazine editors frequently reprinted English poetry, stories, and serial installments of novels, as well as English and Scottish literary criticism. Among earlier English authors, Shakespeare was America's favorite playwright in the first half of the nineteenth century. American authors – among them Herman Melville, Edgar Allan Poe, and Nathaniel Hawthorne – were exasperated by this reverence for English literature, and even more by the difficulty of earning a living as a writer in America. For decades America failed to support her own writers. Melville complained: "You must believe in Shakespeare's unapproachability, or quit the country. But what sort of a belief is this for an American, a man who is bound to carry republican progressiveness into Literature, as well as into Life?" (*PT* 245).

In the 1840s and 1850s, American writers, magazine editors, and other "Young Americans" responded by waging a national campaign to promote American authors and to answer the charges of provincialism and lack of invention in American literary productions. In his 1850 review entitled "Hawthorne and His Mosses," Herman Melville insisted that Nathaniel Hawthorne was fully capable of approaching the achievements of Shakespeare and that "the day will come when you shall say; who reads a book by an Englishman that is a modern?" Melville adds that

> It is for the nation's sake, and not for her authors' sake, that I would have America be
> heedful of the increasing greatness of her writers, ... [for w]hile we are rapidly
> preparing for that political supremacy among the nations, which prophetically awaits
> us at the close of the present century; in a literary point of view, we are deplorably
> unprepared for it; and we seem studious to remain so. (*PT* 247, 248)

Despite the "Manifest Destiny" to expand the United States across the North American continent in the 1840s and 1850s, and despite the belief that democratic republicanism and American exceptionalism would lead to an unparalleled richness in cultural production, America inexplicably trailed behind England in its literary art. America might view itself as God's chosen nation, as evidenced by its political and economic success, but its literary weakness was an embarrassment. Melville's public response was a fiat: "Let us away with this Bostonian leaven of literary flunkyism towards England" (*PT* 248).

However, from lists of books owned or borrowed by Melville, scholars know that his private response was quite different. Starting in 1848, he spent more than two years intensively reading English authors of the early and late Renaissance, including Francis Beaumont and John Fletcher, Christopher Marlowe, William Shakespeare, Edmund Spenser, Richard Hakluyt and Samuel Purchas, James Harrington, Ben Jonson, John Webster, Andrew Marvell, Francis Bacon, Thomas Hobbes, Sir William D'Avenant, Robert Burton, Sir Thomas Browne, John Bunyan, and John Milton. Like other American writers, then, he thus found himself in the awkward position of sharing a mother tongue and cultural heritage with Great Britain, while feeling compelled to search for a freshly original way of writing that was distinctly American.

Some antebellum authors solved this problem by viewing English Renaissance authors as their legitimate precursors rather than their rivals, much the way James Fenimore Cooper suggested in his *Notions of the Americans* (1828). Cooper insisted that authors prior to "the revolution, are common property, and it is quite idle to say that the American has not just as good a right to claim Milton, and Shakespeare, and all the old masters of the language, for his countrymen, as an Englishman" (Cooper 2: 100). Sir Thomas Browne, perhaps the foremost among the "old masters of the language," also experienced a significant vogue, not only in England, where Samuel Taylor Coleridge and Charles Lamb celebrated his elegant, cadenced style, but also in America, where his prose style and originality were admired by many. These authors of the English Renaissance constituted what we might today call a counter-culture's literary icons, and were often chosen as models to emulate in preference to the neoclassical canon taught in American colleges and revered for their clear and direct style. In fact one reviewer, dismayed with Melville's prose style in *Mardi*, prescribed a remedy: "Let him diet himself for a year or two on Addison, and avoid Sir Thomas Browne, and there is little doubt but that he will make a notch on the American pine" (O'Brien 164). By contrast, authors and magazinists eager to support the program of "Young America" in promoting American writers instead esteemed English writers like Shakespeare, Milton, and Sir Thomas Browne for their "Anglo-Saxon," "libertarian," tolerationist, or "democratic tendencies," to which Americans were the true heirs. Among still other nineteenth-century American writers (e.g. Emerson and Thoreau), there was an alternative sense of a legitimately shared English tradition based upon the notion that the English were forerunners of an unorthodox and revolutionary temperament in the American strain. Upon analyzing American literary magazines, newspapers, and estate inventories of libraries, one is indeed struck by not only the breadth but also the depth of antebellum America's reading knowledge of the literature of both the Renaissance and the English Civil War periods.

Taking their cues from their nineteenth-century predecessors, a number of mid-twentieth-century scholars similarly championed American literature in the academy by pointing to its resemblance to English Renaissance literature. Whereas the glories of English literature had long been taught in the United States, American literature as a field worthy of academic study could only be legitimated, as recently as the 1940s and 50s, by demonstrating its "rich vein" of English styles, characters, literary forms, and even "ventriloquism" of writers such as Shakespeare, Donne, Herbert, Browne, and Milton. Indeed, the period in American literature leading up to the Civil War, widely viewed as the efflorescence of literary production in America, is even now commonly referred to by the title of that influential study by F. O. Matthiessen – the *American Renaissance* (1941). American literature ironically gained much of its legitimacy in both the nineteenth and the twentieth centuries through its resemblance to English literature. Matthiessen particularly noted the effect of Browne's aureate prose style on Melville's writing, as well as Melville's use of Shakespearean soliloquies in *Moby-Dick*. In *Call Me Ishmael* (1947), Charles Olson noted the resemblance between Ahab's and Pip's relationship and that of King Lear and the Fool. He was equally struck by the ideal "terms of democracy" visible in the *Pequod*'s crew but sacrificed to Ahab's quest ("They're Melville's addition to tragedy as he took it from Shakespeare" [Olson 69]). Both Charles Olson and C. L. R. James (in *Mariners, Renegades, and Castaways* [1953]) remarked upon the impulse toward empire building, modified from Shakespearean drama, and suggested its relation to the tragedy of America's reckless individualism and imperialism. And in *Milton and Melville* (1950), Henry F. Pommer identified sources for characters' soliloquies as more Miltonic than Shakespearean and noted the "influence of Satan" on a number of Melville's daring characters.

Melville's interests in early modern texts were varied, as revealed by the hundreds of markings in his reading copies, most notably in his copies of Shakespeare and Milton. From these, we see Melville's tastes ranging from topics like the nobility to which mankind could aspire to the poetic beauty of particular lines. He was amused by factual curiosities, but also took note of human deceit, malice, and corruption. Humanity's comic and tragic dimensions were frequently remarked upon; he noted, too, the vicissitudes of politics and the genial humor – or anguish – of those who coped with being in its cross hairs. He commented upon civil war, regicide, exile, and the marring intrusion of partisan politics in poetry (for example, in his comments on Milton's *Lycidas*). He registered the discrepancies between appearance and reality, human knowledge and divine will, and between chance and human agency, often doubting the efficacy of the latter.

Despite this breadth of topical interests, the nature and tenor of Melville's comments and the frequency of his markings near particularly ironic or poignant passages weight his responses toward a darker vision of human nature, as well as of divine intent or cosmic disposal. Melville's interests in early modern English authors, in fact, were darker than those of most of his contemporaries. Melville frequently projected onto these authors his own doubts, suspicions, perceptions of bitter irony, and awareness of evil – a tendency that has become increasingly apparent as more and more of his personally annotated copies of literary works have come to light. Notwithstanding the diversity of characters in Shakespeare's plays and despite the religious convictions of Milton and Browne, Melville associated each of these authors with a kind of daring authenticity and ruthless veracity that verged upon the skeptical, the cynical, and often, the heretical. Commenting upon the "blackness" of Shakespeare in his review of "Hawthorne and His Mosses," Melville revealed much about his own writing strategies, and his own characters, like Captain Ahab or Pierre:

> Through the mouths of the dark characters of Hamlet, Timon, Lear, and Iago, he [Shakespeare] craftily says, or sometimes insinuates the things, which we feel to be so terrifically true, that it were all but madness for any good man, in his own proper character, to utter, or even hint of them. (*PT* 244)

In annotations in his copy of Milton's poetry, Melville thought he discerned similar tactics for conveying unsettling truths. "This is one of the many profound atheistical hits of Milton," he remarked in the margins of *Paradise Lost* near one of Satan's observations, "A greater than Lucretius, since he [Milton] always teaches under a masque, and makes the Devil himself a Teacher & Messiah" (Grey *Melville* 158, *Complicity* 222). In the margins of *Paradise Regained*, Melville noted what he believed were distinctly heretical insinuations on Milton's part: "Put into Satan's mouth, but spoken with John Milton's tongue; – it conveys a strong controversial meaning" (Grey *Melville* 173, *Complicity* 224). Elsewhere in the margins, he insisted that "There was a *twist* in Milton" (Grey *Melville* 187, *Complicity* 219).

And with the devout doctor, scientist, and prose stylist Sir Thomas Browne, Melville felt a kinship, particularly with his desire to search out – among all the odd specimens and legends – the most anomalous and appalling truths, even to the extent of acknowledging the unknown and uncontainable world of spirit that defied human intelligibility. Melville, moreover, took an interest in the Browne who wrote of human fallibility, even before the disobedience of Adam and Eve entailed Original Sin, and of "the impeachment of his [God's] Justice" in that speech of Adam to God "as implying God the Author of sinne, and accusing his Maker of his transgression . . . . This was a bold and open accusation of God, making the fountaine of good the contriver of evil, and the forbidder of the crime an abetter of the fact prohibited" (Browne 1: 11). In the margins of *Paradise Lost*, Melville himself had drawn similar inferences about Milton's God as ultimately unjust and culpable. Melville remarked that,

> The fall of Adam did not so much prove him weak, as that God had made him so. From all that is gatherable from Milton's theology the Son was created. Now, had the Son been planted in the Garden (instead of Adam) he would have withstood the temptation; – Why then he & not Adam? – Because of his created superiority to Adam. ["Sophomoricus," added later.] (Grey *Melville* 160, *Complicity* 224)

Melville, I suggest, interprets each of these authors – Shakespeare, Milton, and Browne – as men who unflinchingly dared to question the very moral, natural, and theological paradigms that structured their worlds, and it is Melville's relationship to these three authors' writings which we shall now examine in more detail.

Shakespeare: Kingly Tragedy, the Drama of Human Nature, and the Politics of Empire

Melville's interest in Shakespeare has attracted the most scholarly attention, doubtless owing to the playwright's perennial appeal, his familiarity, and the more than half a century of scholarly access to Melville's annotated reading copy of Shakespeare (housed at the Houghton Library, Harvard). Scholars have noted the frequency of Melville's "borrowings" from an array of dramas. *Antony and Cleopatra* and *King Lear* were most heavily marked, but many comedies, romances, and histories were also marked, as for example *A Winter's Tale*, *A Midsummer Night's Dream*, *Much Ado About Nothing*, *The Tempest*, and *Richard II*. (See Julian Markels's *Melville and the Politics of Identity* for a comprehensive list of markings in all of Shakespeare's plays [Markels 151–2].) Critics have tended to focus upon *King Lear* and *Macbeth* in connection with *Moby-Dick*, *Hamlet* in *Pierre*, and *Timon of Athens* in *The Confidence-Man*. Broadly characterized, critics have remarked upon Melville's interest in Shakespeare's plays as they examine the nature of human suffering, the complexity of human morality, the danger of kings who misjudge their powers, the poignancy of being betrayed by friends, and the folly of relying on prophecy.

Since Melville immersed himself in Shakespeare's plays from 1849, a period when he was preparing and writing *Moby-Dick*, critics have most often studied that novel for the effect of Shakespeare on Melville. In the *American Renaissance* (1941), Matthiessen marshaled considerable evidence for Melville's use of Shakespeare, ranging from a superficial resemblance to contrived imitation or "unconscious" absorption, to eventual mastery – his "liberation in *Moby-Dick* through the agency of Shakespeare" to his fullest creative powers (Matthiessen 415–21). Matthiessen ascribed to Shakespeare's influence many features in *Moby-Dick,* including: the novel's list of *dramatis personae*; Ishmael's "Epilogue"; the explicit stage directions or dramatic speeches in "The Quarter-Deck," "Sunset," and "Midnight, Forecastle"; the Hamlet-like soliloquy to a skull in "The Sphinx"; the comic scenes of Stubb ("Queen Mab") and Fleece ("Stubb's Supper"); the Weird Sisters' prophecies echoed in those of Fedallah; the Lear-like madness of Ahab in "The Quarter-Deck" and "The Candles"; and the mad truths uttered by the Fool Pip to Ahab's misguided kingship in "The Castaway" and "The Cabin." Although Matthiessen also notes in the novel "the possibilities of democracy" in *Moby-Dick*, his interest is mainly focused – as, for example, in his scanning lines of *Moby-Dick* into blank verse – upon the aesthetic process of Shakespearean mentoring and Melvillean mastery.

In *Melville's Quarrel with God* (1952), Lawrance Thompson demonstrates further that the relationship between Ahab and Pip resembles that of Lear and his Fool, in order to show Melville's preoccupation with the indifference of God that Melville saw as tantamount to God's malice. Thompson, moreover, likens Ahab's desperate curses and oath that "right worship is defiance," amid the masthead flames on a storm-tossed sea, to a similar scene in the play. The raging Lear and anguished Gloucester voice comparable ideas about the gods amid reported eclipses and howling storms upon the heath (*MD* 507; *Lear* III.ii–iv, IV.vi.) Ahab strategically articulates what his author cannot, analogously to what Melville notes of Lear in relation to Shakespeare: "Tormented into desperation, Lear the frantic king, tears off the mask, and speaks the sane madness of vital truth" (*PT* 244). And like the Fool in *King Lear*, Pip, with his tambourine and his "pleasant, genial, jolly brightness," speaks mad truths with impunity to his master (*MD* 411). His "foolishness" is initiated by "the accuracy of his perception" of the "maliciousness of God's indifference" (Thompson 228). Thompson further notes Ahab's Lear-like acquired compassion for unfortunates like Pip, and cites Ahab's words in *Moby-Dick* which echo Lear's and Gloucester's on the callousness of the gods.

It was from Shakespeare that Melville learned "to approach tragedy in terms of the drama," according to Charles Olson in *Call Me Ishmael* (1947) (Olson 69). Dark, sinister characters like Edmund and Iago, as well as Shakespeare's anguished characters like King Lear, attracted Melville's attention and provided psychological and dramatic types for his own characters. "What moves Melville," remarks Olson, "is the stricken goodness of a Lear, a Gloucester, an Edgar, who in suffering feel and thus probe more closely to the truth. Melville is to put Ahab through this humbling" (50–1). King Lear misjudges his kingly powers by abdicating his kingship and dividing his kingdom between two of his selfish, greedy daughters. In so doing, he plunges not only himself but also his kingdom into chaos. Ahab's use of his own absolute, kingly powers also wreaks havoc upon himself and his crew. Along with the tragic hubris noted of Shakespearean and Melvillean characters, Olson focuses not upon the monomania of Ahab, but rather upon the injustice of the human condition ("stricken goodness") to which Melville was particularly sensitive. On the other hand, notes Olson, Melville could not abide (but thought important to represent) one who sought to resolve ambiguities by dogged "rightmindedness," that is, by denying the dark realities of the universe: "Albany is a Starbuck" (49). He observes not only Melville's interest in the psychological deterioration of Lear but also his increasing awareness of human nature's vulnerability and darkness amidst the malignity of the natural world. Olson also cites, but does not comment upon, Melville's unusual observation of the base, illegitimate Edmund in *King Lear*: "The infernal nature has a valor often denied to innocence" (quoted in Olson 48). Melville's comment seems to suggest a fascination with counter-intuitive responses emanating from vicious characters, as exemplified by Edmund's desire to defend his honor, and later in the play, to do some good before dying. Perhaps Melville felt that the injustice meted out to such characters in some way pushed them toward villainy, so that any "valor" they demonstrated was won by overcoming obstacles, a more impressive feat than "innocence," which may have lacked the circumstances of temptation. Olson does comment upon the fact that Melville checked the lines in the play declaring that Edmund was beloved, observing of Melville that "It is a twisting ambiguity like one of his own – Evil beloved" (48). Perhaps Melville's achievement might be viewed in terms of the many-layered complexity of characters like Ahab, who undergo devastating experiences and emerge as tragic figures through a complexity of suffering that is revealed by their self-conflicted, and often mutually discordant, responses to experience.

But Olson's Ahab was also a reckless, dangerous captain, and *Call Me Ishmael* offered an ideological critique of America, a nation which he said had that "Roman feeling about the world" (73). His criticism, however, was presented as a cautionary tale about the repetition of history in relation to empire-building and heedless captains of industry, with Ahab as the "American Timon" or Mark Antony. Whereas Olson believed that "History was ritual and repetition when Melville's imagination was at its own proper beat" (13), more recent scholarship has challenged the notion of a unitary moral or political vision operating in Shakespeare's plays that is then translated by Melville into an American mode. Julian Markels's New Historicist approach has shown competing ideologies and sites of dissension in such a play as *King Lear*, to which Melville was attracted, and from which he took up and completed "the unfinished ideological business" of *King Lear* (Markels 2). Working from Melville's annotated copy of Shakespeare, and borrowing from two New Historicists' analyses of Renaissance texts, Julian Markels has identified a vestigial "field of force" operating in *Lear* that competes with an emergent one. In Markels's account, a hierarchical, feudal society knit together by mutual fealty and duty (represented by Cordelia and Kent) contends with an emergent, competitive bourgeois system focused on individualism, represented by Edmund, Goneril, Regan, and Cornwall. The cultural antecedent of the former society is Richard Hooker's peaceable and stratified society depicted in his *Laws of Ecclesiastical Polity* (1593–7); the latter's clearest articulation is the ruthless and brutish world of Thomas Hobbes's *Leviathan* (1651). Markels contends that King Lear is father to both worlds (as Shakespeare was analogously witness to both), and beholds the transition with apprehension. The "unfinished ideological business" transacted in *Moby-Dick* is the negotiation of the competing paradigms of Ahab (aligned with Hobbesian, relentless individualism) and the alternative one of Ishmael, which synthesizes, as an ameliorative accomplishment, the vestigial mutuality represented by Cordelia with that of America's Lockean contractualism and liberal democracy.

Milton: Free Will, Satanic Revenge, and Civil War

With the mid-1980s discovery of Melville's marked and annotated two-volume 1836 edition of Milton's poetry (now housed at Princeton University Library), we have learned that he saw in Milton an independent thinker who was as skeptical of religious and civil institutions as he was. Neither he nor Milton had any illusions about the difficulty of maintaining independence of mind, or about the grimness of the civil wars each had witnessed in his own lifetime. Melville, in fact, found the depiction of the first civil war in Heaven in *Paradise Lost* a useful paradigm for his Civil War poems in *Battle-Pieces* (1866). But perhaps the most intriguing implications for his novels arising from his annotations (dated 1849, 1860, and 1868) are registered in his penchant to attribute to Milton a degree of theological skepticism that is distinctly Melvillean and not Miltonic. He comments in the margins of Milton's biography prefacing the edition he owned: "He who thinks for himself can never remain of the same mind. I doubt not that darker doubts crossed Milton's soul, than ever disturbed Voltair. And he was more of what is called an Infidel" (Grey *Melville* 121, *Complicity* 227). Melville "misdoubt[ed] his intent" as the poet of the theodicy *Paradise Lost*, for how could a man who lived in blindness and political defeat "justify the ways of God to men," as the poem purports to do (Grey *Melville* 122; *PL* I.26)? And so Melville went to great lengths to discover in Milton's poetry ironies, deflections, insinuations, and other strategies camouflaging what he believed were signs of Milton's disillusionment and unbelief after the failure of the English Civil War (Grey *Complicity* 214). Despite his incomprehension and sense of injustice at the outcome of the English Revolution, Milton in fact never contemplated unbelief. But Melville nevertheless had his suspicions – and most often it was God he blamed.

From Melville's marginal markings and annotations of *Paradise Lost* as well as of Milton's *Samson Agonistes*, we know that Melville was drawn to depictions of free will, sublime wrath, and bitter revenge, but not because of the traditional Romantic leanings formerly ascribed to him. Melville's marginalia suggest his commitment not to a Promethean hero, but rather to a justified revenge against a devastatingly inscrutable God, who seemed to have vexed either his creatures to exasperation, or abandoned them altogether (Grey *Complicity* 213–27). It may be worth noting here, in light of the similar nature of the annotations in *King Lear* already discussed, that Melville read Shakespeare and Milton in the same year, 1849. On the issue of being tested by God, one notices a remarkable degree of consistency in his comments regarding both *King Lear* and *Paradise Lost*. (It may also be worth noting, in view of the unrelenting darkness of *Lear*, that Melville wrote the famous oath spoken by Ahab – "*Ego non baptizo te in nomine patris et filii et spiritus sancti – sed in nomine diaboli*" [I do not baptize you in the name of the Father, Son and Holy Spirit, but in the name of the devil"] – upon the endpaper to his copy of Shakespeare's tragedies.) Elsewhere in my scholarship I have focused upon God's vexing inscrutability, but here I shall examine the toll his testing takes upon the individual – one that often ends in reckless revenge.

Melville studied Milton's arguments in support of free will in *Paradise Lost*, as he noted in his journal for 1849: "Fixed Fate, Free-will, fore-knowledge absolute" were the topics he discussed with philosopher George Adler; these are also the topics the fallen angels debated in *Paradise Lost* II.560. Melville, moreover, questions the possibility of free will in his annotation to Book X of *Paradise Lost*: "All Milton's strength & rhetoric suffice not to satisfy, concerning this matter – free-will. Doubtless, he must have felt it himself; & looked upon it as the one great unavoidable flaw in his work. But, indeed, God's alleged omnipotence & foreknowledge, are insuperable bars to his being made an actor in any drama, imagined" (Grey *Complicity* 225). Before he composed the conciliatory "Supplement" to *Battle-Pieces*, Melville also, I suggest, examined *Areopagitica* (1644), in which Milton argues for tolerance and against censorship during the English Revolution. The crucial issues for Melville in this text are both Milton's insistence upon reason as the basis of free will and his belief in the necessity of testing reason and discernment in order to make the choice of virtue meaningful. Milton asserts that "many there be that complain of divin Providence for suffering Adam to transgresse, foolish tongues! when God gave him reason, he gave him freedom to choose, *for reason is but choosing*; he had bin else a meer artificiall Adam, such an Adam as he is in the motions [puppet shows]" (*CPW* 527; italics added). And Milton insists that if virtue is to be worthwhile, it must be shaped through temptations and trials: "I cannot praise a fugitive and cloister'd vertue, unexercis'd & unbreath'd, that never sallies out and sees her adversary .... [T]hat which purifies us is triall, and triall is by what is contrary." When Melville comments in the margins of *King Lear* that "The infernal nature has a valor often denied to innocence," he may have had in mind Milton's further elaboration in *Areopagitica*: "That vertue therefore which is but a youngling in the contemplation of evil, and knows not the utmost that vice promises to her followers, and rejects it, is but a blank vertue, not a pure; her whiteness is but an excrementall [superficial] whiteness "(*CPW* 515–16). The lessons of Milton's *Paradise Lost* and *Areopagitica* are even more valuable when combined with the lessons from Shakespeare's *King Lear*. Rational choice, which demonstrates free will, may need to be tested in order to summon genuine virtue into existence, as Milton argues (and Melville marked) in *Paradise Lost*, as well as in *Areopagitica*. But as Shakespeare shows, reason can also be tried beyond its limit, as with Gloucester, Lear, Edmund (as well as Satan and Ahab). Human reason then can become so overwhelmed that it is no longer rational or unconstrained, for it is overruled by an irrational, emotional necessity made manifest in despair or the pursuit of revenge. Inordinate trials or excessive punishment tend to curtail, rather than preserve, free will.

Melville adapts the process by which Satan moves toward heedless revenge in interesting and unpredictable ways in his depictions of Captain Ahab in *Moby-Dick*, as well as his portrayal of the South in *Battle-Pieces*. In neither instance is Satan's example used solely, or even predominantly, in order to demonize. Rather, Melville seeks to make intelligible, ultimately tragic, and even noble the frantic state of the vanquished. Perhaps even more than the moral position defended, Melville values the struggle, in spite of the risk of its psychological, or mortal, consequences: "better is it to perish in that howling infinite, than be ingloriously dashed upon the lee, even if that were safety!" (*MD* 107). Melville learns from Milton's Satan that the frenzied pursuit of revenge, regardless of outcome, may well be Ahab's only effective antidote to despair. He learns too that recourse to a notion of fated destiny is a desirable substitute for an encumbered memory, one that painfully recollects its misused free will, and uses it further to rehearse again and again its dubious actions – and God's merciless responses. (Melville particularly noted God's cruel words in *Paradise Lost*: "my long sufferance and my day of grace / They who neglect and scorn shall never taste; / But hard be hardened, blind be blinded more / *That they may stumble on, and deeper fall*" [*PL* III.198–201; italics identify the line Melville marked]).

The complicated and conscience-bitten quality of Satan in Book IV, his most unguarded and most poignant moment in *Paradise Lost*, offers us a sense of reason pushed beyond its limits and may help to explain a turning point, the momentary hesitation of the tearful and haunted Ahab before the final chase. As they contemplate their prospective plans, both Satan and Ahab experience a sense of insufficient, indeed diminishing, power behind their bravura confidence, though Satan here appears more pensive, and Ahab more strident. In an acknowledgment of his own dimmed brightness, Satan invokes the sun while gazing upon its "full-blazing" light, atop Mount Niphates and overlooking Eden. "But with no friendly voice, . . . O sun, to tell thee how I hate thy beams / That bring to my remembrance from what state / I fell, how glorious once above thy sphere" (*PL* IV: 36–9). Ahab similarly engages in self-provoking, agitated thoughts in the "Quarter-Deck" chapter: "Talk not to me of blasphemy, man; I'd strike the sun if it insulted me. For could the sun do that, then could I do the other; since there is ever a sort of fair play herein, jealousy presiding over all creations . . . . Who's over me?" (164). Exiled from Heaven and about to tempt Adam and Eve, Satan reflects upon his condition and his choices in what seems to be a potential turning point (much as Ahab reflects upon his quest in "The Symphony" chapter). Despite the "Eden which now in his view / Lay pleasant," Satan "Saw undelighted all delight" and falls more deeply into despair. Ahab is similarly surrounded by the mildness and "Sweet childhood of air and sky!" yet "[How] oblivious were ye of old Ahab's close-coiled woe!" (*PL* IV: 27–8, 286; *MD* 543).

Of Satan we are told that, "horror and doubt distract / His troubled thoughts" and now "conscience wakes despair / That slumbered, wakes the bitter memory / Of what he was, what is, and what must be / Worse; of worse deeds worse sufferings must ensue (*PL* IV: 18–19, 23–6). Tortured by the memory of virtue, Satan constantly feels "how awful goodness is, and s[ees] / Virtue in her shape how lovely; s[ees] and pin[e]s / His loss" (*PL* IV: 847–9). The awakened sense of knowing evil by knowing good, of free will, and of conscience seems to push Satan to despair, and, so it seems, Ahab. Although Satan insists throughout the epic that his role is fated, here he acknowledges that he indeed has free will and that his burden of gratitude to God has not been too heavy. He contemplates what he has left behind and whether he might return to it. All the while, however, he recognizes that the memory of his shamefully, freely chosen misdeeds, his ambition, his humiliating subjection to God in a plea for mercy, his fear of a worse relapse, and greater fear of God's particular hard-heartedness toward him vitiate any meaningful return to his former state. Satan recognizes that his painful memories are tied to his acknowledgement of free will, and this realization elicits from him new depths of despair, which can only be muted by a renewed and even more reckless drive toward his "fate" of seeking revenge.

Converting Satan's soliloquy into a dialogue between Ahab and Starbuck in the chapter "The Symphony," Melville portrays an Ahab who remembers the woman he once married and has figuratively widowed, remembers all else he left behind, and imagines the consequences the final chase will have. He describes himself as "faint, bowed, and humped, as though I were Adam, staggering beneath the piled centuries since Paradise," that is, staggering beneath the weight (like both Adam and Satan) of the consequences entailed by his freely willed decision to sin (544). Ahab racks his brain for reasons why he has allowed himself to be driven to such a life, thus giving Starbuck hope that this is a turning point for a change of plans. But, in an allusion to Satan's fate at the end of *Paradise Lost*, Ahab's "glance was averted; like a blighted fruit tree he shook, and cast his last, cindered apple to the soil" (545). Satan's Mount Niphates scene in *Paradise Lost* shows Melville the nature of a memory so laden and anguished that it can be stopped, not through remorse, but only by annihilation. "Be then his love accursed, since love or hate, / To me alike, it deals eternal woe," Satan resignedly notes of his relation to God (*PL* IV.69–70).

In his *Battle-Pieces*, Melville turns again to Satan's plight to emphasize the South's perception of excessive punishment in General Sherman's scorched-earth policy, and of a particularly galling penalty in Lincoln's Emancipation Proclamation. He sees these from the Southern rebels' perspective as issuing, not in reconciliation or Reconstruction, but rather in their undying hatred and desire for revenge. In "Battle for Stone River, Tennessee (January 1863)" Melville emphasizes the necessity of proportionality in meting out justice. Satan concludes his Mount Niphates dramatic monologue with his resolve, that "never can true reconcilement grow / Where wounds of deadly hate have pierced so deep" (*PL* IV: 98–9). An Englishman reflecting upon the American Civil War similarly asks with skepticism (and with intensified cruelty in Melville's revision), "But where the sword has plunged so deep, / *And then been turned within the wound* / By deadly Hate ... / Shall North and South their rage deplore, and reunited thrive amain?" (*CP* 49, ll.31–3, 38–9; italics added). The date of January, 1863 in the poem's title gives us the clue that from the Southern perspective, the Emancipation Proclamation freeing slaves in those states that seceded was akin to turning the sword within the wound. The English observer doubts that Americans can heal from such wounds, unlike those scars from which England recovered after the fifteenth-century "fratricidal" Wars of the Roses.

As general, Satan rallies his troop of fallen angels in Hell in Book I of *Paradise Lost* (scored and annotated in the margins by Melville) by asking: "What though the field be lost? / All is not lost; the unconquerable will, / And study of revenge, immortal hate, / and courage never to submit or yield" (*PL* I: 105–8; Grey *Melville* 123). In his poem aptly titled "The Frenzy in the Wake: Sherman's Advance through the Carolinas (February, 1865)," Melville's rebel soldiers similarly demand in a rallying cry, "So strong to suffer, shall we be / Weak to contend, and break / The sinews of the Oppressor's knee/ That grinds upon the neck?" (*CP* 87, ll.1–4). Despite the fact that the Civil War is nearing its end in two months, they galvanize themselves by concluding, "Have we gamed and lost? but even despair / Shall never our hate rescind" (*CP* 88, ll. 31–2). Here the havoc wreaked by Sherman's March to the Sea provokes a further desire for revenge that even trumps despair. Gauging the impossibility of surrender and return to his former state, Satan further notes in lines marked by Melville: "But say I could repent and could obtain / By act of grace my former state; how soon / Would height recall high thoughts, how soon unsay / What feigned submission swore; ease would recant / Vows made in pain, as violent and void" (*PL* IV: 93–6). In his "Supplement" to *Battle-Pieces*, Melville, a staunch Unionist, counsels the North – in advice based upon the lessons he learns from Satan and the fallen angels – not to ask for "contrition hypocritical," for that would constrain free will, but rather to treat the South with toleration and charity ("Supplement," *CP* 461). Melville asks,"[s]hall censorious superiority assumed by one section provoke defiant self-assertion on the other?" (466). Exiled from his Arlington home like Satan from Eden, Robert E. Lee in "Lee in the Capitol" counsels the Joint Committee of Congress after the war: "Push not your triumph; do not urge / Submissiveness *beyond the verge*" (*CP* 150, ll. 135–6; italics added). Although Melville values being tested to elicit truths however intolerable, he also sees the possibility of being provoked by extraordinary pain and the accretions of memory into choosing evil instead of virtue.

Sir Thomas Browne's Marvelous Travel Narratives, Speculative Gamesmanship, and Acknowledgement of the Insurgent World of Spirit

Henry David Thoreau gives us perhaps the best clue to Melville's interest in Sir Thomas Browne's *Vulgar Errors* (*Pseudodoxia Epidemica; Or, Enquiries into Very Many Received Tenets, and Commonly Presumed Truths* [1646–72]). Thoreau remarked that Renaissance explorers and men of a then nascent science were "so sensitive and sympathetic to nature that they could be surprised by the ordinary events of life. . . . [G]orgons and flying dragons were not incredible to them. The greatest and saddest defect is not credulity, but our habitual forgetfulness that our science is ignorance" (quoted Matthiessen 117). Most appealing to Melville here – but for reasons very different from Thoreau's – would be the chastened perspective on nineteenth-century science and human reason, to which credulity was preferable because it did not exclude the marvelous or the extraordinary. Melville's *Mardi* and *Moby-Dick*, I suggest, can be seen as varieties of epistemological travel narratives, which explore the limits of not only creation but also human reason as it confronts the unknown physical world and the enigmatic spiritual realm. As he embarks on his adventures, the narrator of *Mardi* vows, "Be Sir Thomas Brown our ensample; who, while exploding 'Vulgar Errors,' heartily hugged all the mysteries in the Pentateuch" (39).

Melville turned to Browne for the latitude of his methodological procedures in *Vulgar Errors*, as Browne "[W]ander[ed] in the America and Untravelled parts of Truth" (Browne 1: 3). Browne's process of investigation allowed for the expansive category of "the possible" – that which is neither certain nor impossible – and thus accommodated as well as authorized the vast scope of the seaman's extraordinary experiences. Diagnosing one of the causes of ignorance, Browne noted, "as Credulity is the cause of Error, so incredulity often-times of not enjoying truth" (1: 29). Natural philosophers, including Browne in *Vulgar Errors*, did in fact consider whether a vast array of rarities and prodigies of nature existed, including unicorns, griffins, phoenixes, amphisbaena, and spermaceti. To this list Melville adds a compendium of whales that need to be comprehended, and for which an elaborate taxonomy needs to be constructed (e.g., the "Cetology" chapter in *Moby-Dick*).

Ostensibly Browne's task is to strip away from natural phenomena and historical records the accretion of popular myths (vulgar errors) and legends, both in writing and painting, based upon what he could demonstrate to be true from his study of specimens and the most reliable sources. Melville's effort is professedly to do the same for whales, and more particularly, one white whale. Browne's chapter, "Of the Pictures of Mermaids, Unicorns, and some others," in his section examining "Many Things Questionable as They are Commonly Described in Pictures" is mirrored in *Moby-Dick*, which features chapters called "Of the Monstrous Pictures of Whales," "Of the Less Erroneous Pictures of Whales," and "Of Whales in Paint, in Teeth, &c." Browne examines the veracity of "Historical tenets generally received, and some deduced from the history of Holy Scripture" regarding "Methuselah," and Melville contemplates the possible truths of "Jonah, Historically Regarded." Browne seeks to render the meaning of the "Blackness of Negroes," and Melville's Ishmael speculates upon the significance of "The Whiteness of the Whale." Browne concludes, "Thus of colours in generall, under whose *gloss and varnish all things are seen*, no man hath yet beheld the true nature; or *positively set down their incontroulable causes*. Which while some ascribe unto *the mixture of elements*, others *to the graduality of opacity and light*" (1: 507). Ishmael similarly questions whether whiteness is "the visible absence of color, and at the same time the concrete of all colors," or whether we should "consider that *other theory of the natural philosophers*, that all other earthly hues ... are but subtle deceits, *not actually inherent in substances, but only laid on from without; so that all deified Nature absolutely paints like the harlot*" by virtue of that "*mystical cosmetic which produces every one of her hues*, the great principle of light," which "for ever remains white or colorless in itself "(195; italics added). Browne's quest to know whether skin color is in any way meaningful ends in frustration: "they have left our endeavours to grope them out by twilight, and by darkness almost to discover that whose existence is evidenced by light" (1:507). Ishmael similarly contemplates "the dumb blankness, full of meaning," that seems to signal difference. He too ends in exasperation, noting the obliterative influence of whiteness upon the act of discernment of one who "gazes himself blind at the monumental white shroud that wraps all the prospect around him" (195). Thus Melville adapted Browne's encyclopedic and intensely analytic Renaissance "anatomy" genre (another example of which is Robert Burton's *Anatomy of Melancholy*) to structure both *Mardi* and *Moby-Dick*.

To be sure, Browne's frequent willingness to sanction the implausible gave Melville *carte blanch*e to pass off, tongue in cheek, the preposterous as true, and to engage in speculative gamesmanship, as he taunted critics' restrictive notions of verisimilitude in "fact" and "fiction." This he does most often in *Mardi* where Babbalanja engages in lunatic sophistry as the crew navigates around the Mardean archipelago. But he also does so in *Moby-Dick*, in such chapters as "The Honor and Glory of Whaling," "The Great Heidelburgh Tun," "The Nut," and "The Pequod Meets the Rose-bud," the last three of which comically employ whole passages and an epigraph from Browne's chapter on spermaceti and ambergris. Browne himself is not without humor, as when he contemplates why Adam and Eve were depicted as having navels, whether men have one rib less than women, whether lampreys have nine eyes, or whether elephants have knees. Browne's epistemological leniency is revealed in many of his verbal formulations, as for example, when he acquiesces to an opponent's position: "because he hath probable reasons for it, and I no infallible sense nor reason against it, I will not quarrell with his assertion" (1: 29). And within this pliable, concessive procedure, the category of the improbable could find a breadth of scope in Browne's world of "virtuosi" natural philosophers which was no longer available in Melville's empirically oriented America.

Despite his (deliberately) humorous moments, Browne nonetheless genuinely desired to reconstitute knowledge on a more stable foundation by according opinions and theories carefully discriminated degrees of probability, and by allowing for the interpenetration of the natural and supernatural. Although some scholars (Sealts, Wenke) have pointed to Browne's Platonism as most clearly adapted by Melville, I suggest that Browne's method and examples in *Vulgar Errors* offered Melville an imaginative inventory, which aided him in proliferating questions, probing the too easily resolved, and exploring that which was otherwise unthinkable. In *Mardi*, Melville adapts Browne's methods to render intelligible the limits of human reason in understanding the divine, drawing attention to the boundaries between human and divine creation, faith and knowledge, and between human temporality and divine eternity. But those human limitations are acknowledged with awe, and are compensated in part by a (capricious) faith that on occasion appears to enhance reason. In *Moby-Dick*, however, those limitations are cause for alarm and uneasiness. While stripping away falsehoods, Browne sought to preserve both natural and supernatural truths, though they might elude all classification and may not yet be rendered intelligible. Ever mistrustful of human institutions, ever aware of human fallibility, and ever uncertain about divine existence, much less divine intent, Melville is powerfully drawn to this aspect of Browne's work – his undaunted acknowledgment of the unintelligible or the incomprehensible.

Whereas Sir Thomas Browne's faith gave him assurances of a presumed order in the universe, though one he believed was intermittently perforated by miraculous events,

Melville's (and Ishmael's) disturbing experiences could not be banished by a faith like Browne's or Starbuck's. ("Tell me not of thy teeth-tiered sharks, and thy kidnapping cannibal ways," insisted Starbuck. "Let faith oust fact; let fancy oust memory; I look deep down and do believe" [492].) Unlike Browne's world, that of Melville's *Moby-Dick* is one where the eruption of anarchy and chaos seems ever imminent. Melville repeatedly turned to Browne for his resistance to certitude and easy resolutions, but then in his revisionary adaptation intensified the irresolution into a heightened sense of human fallibility and frailty and into a world of undreamt-of experiences. Melville's adaptation of *Hydriotaphia, Or Urn Burial*, Browne's meditation on death, the spirit world, and funerary rites, is just such a case in point.

In that meditation, Browne speculated copiously upon the vanity of human burial practices in perpetuating being, but ended with the celebration of oblivion in humanity's Christian reunion with God. Ishmael's meditation on cenotaphs in "The Chapel," by contrast, exploits Browne's examples, but highlights the inefficacy of funeral rites to contain or suppress the world of spirit. Browne's examples of futile human attempts at immortality are turned by Melville into a haunting Pandora's box of alarmed speculation, where "the living so strive to hush all the dead," where "a knocking in a tomb will terrify a whole city," and where even "Faith, like a jackal, feeds among the tombs" (*MD* 37). Melville would have read the eyewitness accounts of a witchcraft trial in the biography prefacing Browne's writings in the volumes he borrowed (Wilkin, lxxxii–lxxxiii). Browne was willing to testify to the existence of evil spirits and witches because making such a theological statement helped to preserve the ontological category of the unseen, of (supernatural) spirit. Melville, however, seized upon this openness to malign forces as something answerable to his own (and Ishmael's) seaman's experiences. I suggest that Ahab's power to induce the otherwise skeptical Ishmael to ascribe supernatural power to him and to Moby Dick, and to join in the hunt, has its plausible basis in Ishmael's earlier unsettling suspicions about the dead. Those suspicions suggest the problem of discerning the agent of such turbulent natural or supernatural forces lying beneath humanly constructed myths that obscure more than they explain. Browne sought out all unyielding natural prodigies and daunting material registers of spirit because they might become the means of renovating fallible human conceptual categories. Neither Ishmael nor Ahab has any such enduring optimism. Ishmael's chapel meditation hints at an insurgent world of spirit of which no system of human belief – myth, religion, superstition, or ritual – has taken adequate account and over which it exercises no power. Adopting Browne's typical refrain in *Urn-Burial*, "all these things are not without their meanings," at the end of his chapel meditation, Ishmael perhaps hopes to tutor his perceptions to a sufficient level of discrimination to distinguish genuine wonders from demonic delusions and those from human myths, doubts, prejudices, and deceits (37). But Melville reconceives Browne's notion of provisional indeterminacy into one of perpetual indeterminacy. As the action of *Moby-Dick* progresses, Ishmael, chastened by experience and the irresolution of his Brownean "essaying," resorts to destroying, along with Ahab, "all these things [that] are not without their meanings" as the final alternative to the comprehension that eluded him.

The legacy of Britain to Melville, particularly from the early modern texts of Shakespeare, Milton, and Sir Thomas Browne, was a significant one. In the tragedies of Shakespeare, he saw the implications of dark injustices and a malign world, as well as the titanic emotions and spirit-broken responses elicited by them. From Milton's poetry and prose, he learned the importance of free will as well as its liabilities, and surmised further the culpability of a God who exacts too much justice. From Sir Thomas Browne's works, he gained a sense of the limitations of human knowledge, but also a key to the world of prodigies and wonders – a Pandora's box to be opened only with care. In each, as I have suggested, he sees a mirrored image of himself and his world, dark though they may be. D. H. Lawrence once aptly remarked of him: "Melville is like a Viking going home to the sea, encumbered with age and memories, and a sort of accomplished despair, almost madness" (Lawrence 131).

References and Further Reading

Berthoff, Werner. *The Example of Herman Melville.* Princeton, NJ: Princeton University Press, 1962.

Browne, Sir Thomas. *Sir Thomas Browne's "Pseudodoxia Epidemia."* Ed. Robin Robbins. 2 vols. Oxford: Clarendon Press, 1981.

Cooper, James Fenimore. *Notions of the Americans, Picked up by a Travelling Bachelor.* Ed. Robert E. Spiller. New York: Frederick Ungar, 1963.

Foley, Brian. "Herman Melville and the Example of Sir Thomas Browne." *Modern Philology* 81 (1984): 265–77.

Giles, Paul. " 'Bewildering Entanglement': Melville's Engagement with British Culture." In *The Cambridge Companion to Herman Melville.* Ed. Robert S. Levine. Cambridge: Cambridge University Press, 1998. 224–49.

Grey, Robin. "Annotations on Civil War: Melville's *Battle-Pieces* and Milton's War in Heaven." In Grey, *Melville and Milton,* 47–66.

——. *The Complicity of Imagination: The American Renaissance, Contests of Authority, and Seventeenth-Century English Culture.* Cambridge: Cambridge University Press, 1997. Chapter 6, on Melville's annotations, is expanded from "Surmising the Infidel: Melville's Annotations on Milton's Poetry." *Milton Quarterly* 26.4 (1992).

——. *Melville and Milton: An Edition and Analysis of Melville's Annotations on Milton's Poetry.* Ed. Robin Grey. Pittsburgh, PA: Duquesne University Press, 2004. Rev. and expanded from *Leviathan: A Journal of Melville Studies.* 4.1 & 2 (March & October, 2002).

James, C. L. R. *Mariners, Renegades, and Castaways: The Story of Herman Melville and the World We Live In.* New York: C. L. R. James, 1953.

Lawrence, D. H. *Studies in Classic American Literature.* New York: Viking Press, 1923; rpt. 1972.

Markels, Julian. *Melville and the Politics of Identity: From* King Lear *to* Moby-Dick. Urbana and Chicago: University of Illinois Press, 1993.

Matthiessen, F. O. *American Renaissance: Art and Expression in the Age of Emerson and Whitman.* New York: Oxford University Press, 1941.

Milton, John. *Complete Prose Works of John Milton.* Ed. Ernest Sirluck. Volume 2. New Haven: Yale University Press, 1959.

——. *Paradise Lost.* Ed. Alastair Fowler. 2nd ed. London: Addison Wesley Longman Limited Second, 1988.

O'Brien, Fitz-James. "Our Young Authors – Melville." *Putnam's Monthly* 1 (1853): 156–64.

Olson, Charles. *Call Me Ishmael.* New York: Harcourt, Brace, & Co., 1947.

Pommer, Henry F. *Milton and Melville.* Pittsburgh, PA: University of Pittsburgh Press, 1950.

Sealts, Merton M., Jr. "Melville and the Platonic Tradition." In *Pursuing Melville, 1940–1980.* Madison: University of Wisconsin Press, 1982. 278–336.

Shakespeare, William. *The Riverside Shakespeare.* Boston: Houghton Mifflin, 1974.

Smith, Sydney. "Review." *Edinburgh Review* 33 (January 1820): 79.

Thompson, Lawrance. *Melville's Quarrel with God.* Princeton, NJ: Princeton University Press, 1952.

Weisbuch, Robert. *Atlantic Double-Cross: American Literature and British Influence in the Age of Emerson.* Chicago: University of Chicago Press, 1986.

Wenke, John. *Melville's Muse: Literary Creation and the Forms of Philosophical Fiction.* Kent, OH: Kent State University Press, 1995.

Wilkin, Simon. "Supplementary Memoir." In *Sir Thomas Browne's Works, Including His Life and Correspondence.* Ed. Simon Wilkin. 4 vols. London: William Pickering, 1836.

Ziff, Larzer. "Shakespeare and Melville's America." In *New Perspectives on Melville.* Ed. Faith Pullin. Kent, OH: Kent State University Press, 1978.

17

Romantic Philosophy, Transcendentalism, and Nature

Rachela Permenter

With a broad and deep knowledge of philosophy, literature, and political issues, Herman Melville was a quintessential writer of the Romantic minor key. Romanticism, a dynamic yet vague condition of revolt against mechanism and overarching mercantilism, continues as an unresolved subtext of modern and contemporary industrialized cultures. Especially since the eighteenth century, it repeatedly emerges in transient forms and recedes into the undertones from which it came. During certain eras and by certain writers, it is a clarion call to creative action against threats to personal freedom. In the 1760s, 1830s, 1890s, 1920s, and 1960s, it found large audiences and lasted in each case from ten to twenty years. In the context of American Transcendentalism, the summons to awaken was sustained in the active Romanticism of writers such as Ralph Waldo Emerson, Henry David Thoreau, Margaret Fuller, and Walt Whitman. Less exultant writers of that era, especially Melville, Nathaniel Hawthorne, and Edgar Allan Poe, were no less charismatic and reformative. Romantic resignation, acknowledging the inevitable failures and disappointments that accompany exhilaration, is part of Romanticism's method and milieu.

Many critics who have summarized Melville's quarrel with Romanticism have defined the term narrowly enough to create for Melville dark disagreement with transcendental idealism, but Romanticism is not Platonism, Hegel's Idealism, nor Berkeley's immaterialism. To the contrary, Melville's Romanticism reflects the writings of Goethe, Kant, Schelling, Schlegel, Emerson, Carlyle, and Coleridge in ways that accommodate the coexistence of dark and light, individual and totality. Depicting Romantics as somehow cheerful and Melville as appositionally dark is a bit odd even superficially when convention also codifies Romantic artists, particularly British poets and painters, as writhing in the experience of loss and melancholy, dying young, going insane, moaning about ungratified love, or fading into drug addiction. Setting up a classification of "negative," "dark," or "ironic" Romanticism is misleading, as it contrives a saccharine binary with positive Romanticism. John Bryant reminds us that Melville's "evermoving dawn" is "neither complete darkness nor complete sunlight but that in-between state of mind always moving out of despair and toward redemption" (10). It is helpful to keep in mind that all serious Romantic writers, including the Transcendentalists, fit this description and suggest epistemological doubt and ontological insecurity as they ultimately imply that we are all lost between two worlds. This nonduality is not only a characteristic of Romanticism, but of our own culture's move toward a Romantic postmodernism that mixes Eastern and indigenous modes of thought into the Western mainstream of modernity more vigorously than Melville could.

According to many scholars, Melville's writing was somehow in dialogue with Ralph Waldo Emerson much of the time. Emerson, after all, was the leading American intellectual of the period whose cry for American thinkers to have "an original relation with the universe" was a challenge that could not go unheard. In the most complete recent study of the Melville–Emerson connection, John B. Williams points out that in many ways Emerson reinforced for Melville what he already knew from his reading (23). Williams concludes that those who read Melville as purporting a counterpoise to Emersonian optimism "may have underestimated both the comprehensiveness of Emerson's view of man, which makes room for the skepticism of Montaigne, and the capacity of Melville to create in his divided world of the mind an image of almost perfect spirituality" (183). From the time-honored study *American Renaissance*, F. O. Matthiessen's contention that Melville was forced to add evil to Emerson's benevolent view of the universe has too often been reduced to a boorish simplification, which fails to acknowledge the philosophical subtlety found in both writers' works. In disparate ways, most American writers of the mid-nineteenth century brought Romantic contradictions from society's shadows into fugitive forms that marked the age. Melville's creations, much more fleeting and receding from his mainstream culture than those of his famous contemporaries, dealt powerfully with Romantic questions about humanity, nature, community, and the universe.

Romanticism's Contradictions and Nondualities

Because of its equivocal nature, straightforward definitions of Romanticism are reductive half-truths. Romanticism, although a term used for the art and philosophy of the eighteenth and nineteenth centuries, is more a perspective or worldview. René Wellek warns that "we can only point to what is romantic as we can point to the color red" (Frye 117). Romanticism is particularly resistant to classification because its central mode is paradox or nonduality, Nicolas of Cusa's *coincidentia oppositorum* of "the two and the one," a concept and a mode of perception that embrace both duality and oneness in one thought. (The term *nonduality* is taken from the Hindu word *advaita*, the "not two" that does not mean one.) When referring to Chaucer and Shakespeare,

Peter Elbow affirms that the Boethian counterpoise of saying opposite things at the same time is valuable and "one of the patterns of thought that makes wise people wise" (161), a mode that Melville was likely to have emulated, and certainly Romanticism's equivocal voice. William Empson reads Coleridge's *Ancient Mariner*, for example, to depict both "the love that should unite all creatures" and the "terror of being unable to sustain and meet the love" (Rosen 40). Schlegel speaks of Romanticism's "eternal oscillation of enthusiasm and irony" (de Mul 10). Schelling asserts the coexistence of boundaries and the infinite, and Kant's sublime is either untamable or untenable since reason might only advance our knowledge by seeking for a completeness that is not to be found.

Michael Löwy and Robert Sayre write, "Apparently an undecipherable enigma, the Romantic phenomenon seems to defy analysis ... especially because of its fabulously contradictory character" (1). Romanticism's contradictions, as explained by Löwy and Sayre, include the following: Described by many as formed out of the enthusiasm of the French Revolution, some Romantic writings forward radical revolutionary ideas, while others promote the unifying power of the status quo, and some do both. Romantic writings valorize individual freedom, but simultaneously promote the importance of community. Romantics see the self as the source of all value, yet make metaphysical propositions. The Romantic assertion of personal freedom is seen to be at the core of the most significant societal and political revolutions; its unifying reach toward wholeness, however, is also believed to be the inspirational worldview for Nazi ideologues. In addition, Romanticism is best recognized by some for its disillusionment and by others for its hope, explained by Georg Lukács in the conundrum "the soul [is] larger and wider than the destinies which life has to offer it" (Löwy and Sayre 19). Finally, the contradiction of most interest to Löwy and Sayre is their assertion that "Romanticism is essentially a reaction against the way of life in capitalist societies" and yet it is "coextensive with capitalism itself" (17); thus "the Romantic view constitutes modernity's self-criticism" (21). This is why Romantics are often homesick wanderers, looking toward a past, real or imagined, in which humans were free to be whole and were not calculations of cogs of production. These writers therefore perpetuate and create their dominant society as they try to escape it. Perhaps most importantly, as Romantics long for a return to nature or to past societies for lessons about how to take humanity into the future, they look to the present; in doing so, their writings inevitably alternate or blend exhilaration and despair.

One of the most discussed characteristics of Romanticism, however, which occasionally brings contradiction into counterpoise, is the use of symbol and myth to yoke nature with the human imagination as a means to connect the self and the world. This can be seen as a method of thought or art that concerns individuals within a whole, thus forcing unanswerable questions: Is individual freedom more important than community? Do we have free will and to what degree? Are we part of nature or separate from it? If we are part of nature and separate beings, how does this condition affect consciousness? How can we live personally *and* as societies, as material beings *and* as something more? Some describe these central Romantic questions in philosophical terms, as "part of the great endeavor to overcome the split between subject and object" (René Wellek in Frye 132).

M. H. Abrams emphasizes that Romantic artists simply turn to life over death-in-life. The connections among nature, humans, and the universe that Romantics reach for are succinctly illustrated by Wordsworth: "For the discerning intellect of Man / When wedded to this goodly universe / In love and holy passion, shall find these / A simple produce of the common day" (V: 3–5). For Wordsworth, the human mind finds "great consummation" with nature (the tangible aspects of the universe) in some kind of passionate energy. When the mind so moved blends natural and divine forces it can then create, can in fact find "the creation," or more plainly, can be alive. In this way Abrams sees many of Romanticism's contradictions resolved in finding the infinite in the natural world with the active or passionate mind (a central move of the Transcendentalists). He describes it as "the oxymoron of the humble-grand, the lofty-mean, the trivial-sublime" (Abrams 64). Individual consciousness is therefore a deep Romantic consideration as an attempt to rescue the self from its orphaned state in the mechanized Newtonian-Lockean-mercantile worldview, whether by art, love, God, or inexplicable universal forces. To this aim, the Romantic vision includes the imagination and nature, self and perception, uniqueness or rebelliousness in tandem with unity, and the inevitable failure/success of the endless voyage. It sounds chords of both salvation and futility.

The interconnectedness of parts within an inexplicable whole and the confounding of subject and object are two abiding philosophical interests of Melville and all Romantics. Literary symbolism can be used to recognize that each part of the universe, including each human, is particular and that at the same time all these parts can also stand for the whole of which they are a part. Wellek explains the Romantic move to bring eternity into time as Romantic writers "want[ing] to express their own concrete experiences, their own personal apprehension of human timelessness" (Frye 122). He describes the importance of nature symbolism to Romantics as "a withdrawal from reality to the center of the self, which serves as a starting point for a return to nature, combining outside and inside." He uses texts by Coleridge and Shelley as illustrations of "this back-and-forth movement of the mind" (122). The move, then, can be seen as blurring the distinction between humans and the natural world and overcoming the opposition of subject and object, always to return inevitably to our separate or alienated experiences. Each part of the whole can be a symbol for the relationship between internal and external reality.

Before Sacvan Bercovitch reacquainted scholars with the powerful homegrown influence of Puritan symbolism as evidence of God's immanence, Wellek traced the concept of symbolism as we know it today through the British Romantics to their German influences: "Coleridge picked it up from Goethe, the Schlegels, and Schelling; so did Carlyle; and their version of symbolism . . . became most important for Emerson and Poe" (Frye 139). Symbolism relies on the threshold between perceiver and perceived, between part and whole. Gail Coffler contends that Melville's *Billy Budd, Sailor,* for example, shows "how theodicy (or myth, one could say) works to change dark into light, misfortune into good, and loss into gain." In this way, "art expresses the most profound truth" without being literally true and consequently helps to create literal truth, thus reconciling language and reality (49, 82). As "king of Romantics," Goethe explains the symbol as "the thing itself, without being the thing, and yet the thing." Goethe's explanation of the true symbol reveals it as more than representative. It is "a living, instantaneous revelation of the inscrutable" (Van Cromphout 69). This is also a one-line description of *Moby-Dick* and its whale – a living instantaneous revelation of the inscrutable. It is presented by Ahab when he calls out, "O Nature, and O soul of man! How far beyond all utterance are your linked analogies!" (*MD* 312). Linked separateness experienced through the mind's perceptions suggests central Romantic (non)contradictions and the significance of nature as symbol.

One of the most compelling uses of a natural symbol is certainly the white whale itself, as explained in "Loomings," where Melville has taken the entirety of *Moby-Dick* and condensed it into its opening chapter. Ishmael introduces the sea as having both material and mystical powers, with both its hard-knock, salty and sensual actuality and its metaphorical role as the unknown, the unconscious, which bids us all to dive. Getting "just as nigh the water as they possibly can without falling in" is the human response to some "magnetic virtue" of the sea that makes most of us at some time or another want to be divers and philosophers, to try to learn what Truth and human *being* are. Yet, with chiding self-mockery, Ishmael makes it clear that actually going to sea (to find life) is as suicidal as a "pistol and ball" or "Cato's sword," for Truth and Being can be experienced, but not known (3). Instead of diving in and losing the self, as Pip does later, Ishmael remains in the boundaries in order to speak about both realms.

This introduction to the *Pequod*'s fatal voyage reveals that Melville's central concerns had not changed much since he had Babbalanja in *Mardi* speak about the truth of human *being* and the mysterious link/separation of body and soul: "Oh, Man, Man, Man! Thou art harder to solve, than the Integral Calculus – yet plain as a primer; ... soul and body glued together, firm as atom to atom, seamless as the vestment without joint, warp or woof – yet divided as by a river, spirit from flesh" (433). For Babbalanja, babbler of the Truth for which Ishmael searches, the truth is at the boundary that reveals no boundary; the seamless seam is in each of us, Ahab's seam as a "crown to sole" scar from either birth or the whale (124), the cracked or split human division between self and nature, human and universal. That seam is the place where outside and inside, human consciousness and all else, unite. Some Romantics describe it as the place to find the human soul in its divine capacity to be larger than something contained within the human body. Similar in spirit to Pip and precursor in some ways to Queequeg, Babbalanja speaks "heaven's sense" as "man's insanity." We are physical and are conscious of that physicality. We are also more than the physical because we can go outside the body and join with what we perceive – a condition made possible by that very act of perception. We are "twain – yet indivisible; all things – yet a poor unit at best" (433). If we lose separateness in joining, however, we lose the self and the nonduality. "Loomings" contains forewarnings of *Moby-Dick*'s major Romantic explorations as it introduces the "appalling" color-inclusive and color-exclusive whiteness of nonduality: Ishmael's "wild conceits" of whales are processing "two by two" before him, but in the center is the multifarious one – "one grand hooded phantom like a snow hill in the air" (7). For the Romantics, the human experience is beyond rational dualism, both two and one.

In her study of the narration of *Moby-Dick*, Carolyn Porter finds in "Loomings" Ishmael's "shifting from eccentricity to normality" as part of his establishment of "a pattern to be repeated and enveloped in the chapter as a whole" (73). It is a pattern "whereby boundaries are invoked in order to be crossed and finally blurred," an image that extends to the boundary between land and sea and between the familiar and the unknown that Ishmael "creates and expands by traversing it, over and over again" (80). This pattern is Wellek's Romantic "back-and-forth movement of the mind" (122) between subject and object, part and whole. This suggests the fluidity of what many now call *l'écriture féminine*, which undermines notions of representation. Porter goes on to assert, however, that "by the same token, Ishmael never kills the authority vested in the discourses he parodies"; rather, his stance on the boundary "not only enables him to blur it but to defend it against the total dissolution that would render him, like Pip, a mad mimic rather than a sane one" (106). Thus Ishmael's voice permits an apprehension of the nondual. Melville suggests that we are continually creating and crossing that boundary by his repeated placement of Ishmael in the space where "tiger heart" and "velvet paw," fact and fancy, sea and land "interpenetrate, and form one seamless whole" (*MD* 491–2). Goethe connects contradictions as nondualities in the statement, "Nothing is inside and nothing outside since what is within is without" (Van Cromphout 93). Emerson learned from Goethe that "reality is neither in the subject nor in the object but in the activity between" (Wilkinson and Willoughby 137). This is quite literally the Romantic movement.

Ignoring neither its contradictory history nor the influences outside of Western thought, Julie Ellison's touchstone for categorizing Romanticism includes most writings with the "habit of reference to forms of post-Kantian idealism" (ix). It must be repeated that Romanticism is not idealism; rather, its writers have "a habit of reference to forms of" idealism. This is a crucial distinction. Although Melville effectively derides the unearthly flights of his contemporary Transcendentalists, his works have a "habit of reference" to idealism and reflect an aspect of mysticism. Rather than suggesting its common usage, the term *mysticism* is succinct in its pairing with Romanticism only when meaning any nonconceptual apprehension of the domain of the unknown without the use of an intermediary. Many scholars see this characteristic of Romanticism as using the imagination as a means of re-enchanting the world during its fall into cold calculation. We are reminded of Emerson's daily miracle of the individual's apprehension of primary faith beyond the constraints of language in "The Divinity School Address" and *Nature*, as well as other Romantic and postmodern references to the creative and true in the interstices. This of course does not denigrate the rational mind for Romantic writers. With their nondual vision, Romantic writers do not deny the importance of reason as they emphasize the importance of the non-rational or paraconceptual; rather, they valorize the rational mind highly. The antagonist of the Romantic tradition is not reason, but the attempt to sacralize empiricism or the rational, which belittles the imagination and ignores the primary apprehension of intuition.

Two of Melville's warnings against an imbalance of reason and spirit are Ahab and Pip, "one daft with strength, the other daft with weakness" (*MD* 522). Ahab of course, as his description of "a complete man" reveals, has very nearly "no heart at all, brass forehead, and about a quarter of an acre of fine brains" (470). Pip, considered mad by the crew and "wandering from all mortal reason," can no longer function effectively in a separate condition, living in "that celestial thought, which, to reason, is absurd and frantic" (414). Drunk with spirit, having merged with the depths of the sea and with otherworldliness (after leaving the nondual boundary or seam), Pip knows truth only in its watery chaotic state and ceases to function effectively. At the other extreme, seized solely by the rational will, Ahab has no shaping spirit with which to temper his temporary pragmatic truths and cannot avoid self-destruction. When sensitive to his "humanities" and to the place where his heart once was, he is aware of his need to balance his separate, rational self with some connection. He has Pip move into his cabin, admitting, "Thou touchest my inmost centre, boy." In Pip's vacant eyes, Ahab recognizes an overflow of "heaven's sense" of which he is devoid, and he yells to the sailor who seizes Pip, "Hands off from that holiness!" (522).

Much narrative art is appreciated as a primary apprehension of reality. On this point Romantic literature has most likely helped inform contemporary theory. In dealing with "how to rethink the unrepresentable" in contemporary terms, Alice Jardine recognizes that postmodern writers, for example, seem to be writing *"between* the dialectic and mysticism . . . attempting to found new discursive spaces for the unspeakable" (143–4). Gerald Vizenor quotes Derrida's statement that "Between the too warm flesh of the literary event and the cold skin of the concept runs meaning" as he explains that one finds meaning "in the seam in between . . . where the energy lies" (112, 174). This is certainly the contemporary reweaving of a central Romantic thread. As Kant explains the relationship of idealism and mysticism, he argues that idealism always has a mystical tendency. Mysticism was certainly not part of Kant's intention for the solution of certain problems of philosophy; nor does his use of the concept suggest the sublime as absolute in Romanticism. More precisely, that "mystical tendency" as explained by Kant is *Vernunft*, a faculty of reason, dissatisfied with confinement to the ordering of sense experiences and constantly striving for completeness and totality (*focus imaginarius*).

A sustaining paradox in Romantic literature follows Kant and the German Romantics in their striving toward a Unity of Being as the creative force of human consciousness forming a bridge between chaos and order. Since it is in part a human creation, the Unity of Being always *is* and *is not*. Romantic striving, then, must be balanced by Being, a paradox presented by Goethe as the equipoise of Being/becoming, and sometimes suggested in fiction by the relaxed acceptance of an outside observer such as Ishmael. Striving toward Unity without *"Being* of the matter," as

Melville called it (*L* 186), is not Romanticism, but is suggested instead by the personalities of Ahab and Pierre, ludicrously willful misinterpreters of Romantic individualism who cannot keep their whale heads balanced on both sides of the ship. It is precisely such lopsided interpretations of Romanticism that could be taken to the horrific extremes of the Third Reich. Melville offers a Romantic accommodation to the nonduality of striving and Being, of individualism and unity, of reason and imagination. That balance is fatally missing in the central character of *Pierre: Or, the Ambiguities* and in Ahab, but present in his three primitive harpooners who help Ishmael survive in balance.

Like Ahab, Pierre fails because of his obsession with absolutes. In true Romantic form, Melville's narrator points to Pierre and admonishes, "Civilization, Philosophy, Ideal Virtue! Behold your victim" (*P* 302). Heavenly ideals are necessary for individual freedom, yet do not have substance of their own on earth and can instead lead to tyranny. Pierre, always drawn to nebulous extremes, cannot view good and evil, male and female, light and dark, Vice and Virtue, Fate and Necessity as merely labels given to a momentary mark on a sliding scale from a fleeting vantage point. He cannot see the space between the "Chronometricals and the Horologicals" (292) as the blurred boundary from which one creates a self. He is given many opportunities, but his vision fails him or he denies it. Standing before his father's portrait, for example, he recalls his mother's advice to "always think of [his] dear, perfect father" (19). Pierre senses that the perfection of his father is impossible, and Pierre's opportunity for maturation appears as he stands before the portrait. He permits himself for a moment to see meanings as snowflakes "in a soft, steady snow-storm," but he refuses to yield to ambiguity. Instead, he regains his father's rigid bipolar truths in "the assured element of consciously bidden and self-propelled thought." The swirl of snowflakes disappears, and Pierre "upbraid[s] himself for his self-indulgent infatuation" (84–5). He promises never again to allow such a revery and thereby condemns himself to an imbalance of reason devoid of the non-rational. Consequently, when he discovers the insubstantiality of virtue and vice, or good and evil, he tells Isabel that when he looks for one or the other, "it casts one shadow one way, and another the other way; and these two shadows cast from one nothing" (274). When he says "I am nothing," he has discovered that his terms of bipolarity cancel each other out and he is incapable of creating a self to replace them. He will "lift the lid of the sarcophagus" and find that "no body is there" (285).

Isabel, on the other hand, begins to form herself from her extreme, the watery world of the non-rational. (The non-rational, unfortunately labeled in archetypal tradition as "the feminine," can also be read as Kristeva's symbolic.) She makes a valiant attempt to lead Pierre to the boundary or "twilight" where he can be born in a self, but he refuses. He is attracted to Isabel because he needs the lost unity with his mother to balance the one-sidedness of the rational-mechanical-mercantile side of being human in the modern world. Melville's narrator forces the reader to conclude that if Pierre had perceived the area of gradation within himself which was his sister Isabel, which Jung brackets symbolically as the feminine side of his soul, he would have grown to find wholeness within his own psyche. Because of his failure to recognize the crack in the universe as the human scar that both divides and unites, he deprives himself of growth into wholeness.

Melville wrote *Pierre* after completing *Moby-Dick* and planned on it being a "kraken." The striking change in tone and plot development which wildly opens Book 17 causes problems for many readers. Brian Higgins and Hershel Parker, among others, find that the split at the seventeenth chapter of *Pierre* is the result of Melville's anger and despondency over negative reviews of *Moby-Dick* and over the large cut in payment for its publication. They view the split as an unredeemable flaw and evidence of Melville's genius having gone to waste (192–3). When read with a deeper understanding of Romanticism, however, the loud crack in *Pierre*, the seams of *Moby-Dick*, and the split in *The Confidence-Man* are at the same point of abrupt contradiction that reveals the ubiquitous human scar, a badge of courage, beautiful necessity, the borderland for creation, Romantic nonduality between self and all else.

As new readings of Melville's works suggest, Romanticism has not disappeared from the scene. Nor is it unusual to hear current scholars of European Romanticism suggest that there is little in postmodern thought which was not said more imaginatively by the Romantics. Charles Rosen writes, "Words will not sit still. . . . At no time did words become as slippery as at the opening of the period we sometimes call Romantic" (ix). Both Tilottama Rajan and Jos de Mul have argued in opposition to Paul de Man that Romanticism has always consciously inverted itself, that Romantic texts both reveal and falsify unity and human liberation. De Mul maintains that "the crisis of consciousness is already inherent to the Romantic project" (9). Blake, Emerson, Yeats, Lawrence, and Thoreau were aware of a wild chaos in tandem with their promotions of unity.

Melville's work embodies Romantic vitality and resignation. Goethe insisted that whales and language remain unpainted because whenever we speak "outside of poetry," we are "bound for the moment to become one-sided. There is no communication, no theory, without separation" (Wilkinson and Willoughby 143). This pronouncement explains why Romanticism is unavoidably ironic and why it has a distinct poststructuralist/postmodern familiarity. As Rajan explains, the "debate between organicist and deconstructionist critics over the nature of Romanticism was originally waged by the Romantics themselves and was not resolved in favor of either side" (19). Melville is certainly not unique in being "vexed" by Romanticism when in fact all Romantics were.

Transcendentalism

Beginning to come together before Melville was whaling and writing his sea novels, the American Transcendentalists were a small group of young intellectuals who, in or near Boston in the 1830s, spontaneously revolted against what Ralph Waldo Emerson called "the corpse-cold Unitarianism of Brattle Street and Harvard College" (Miller

Transcendentalists 7–8). Without dogma or doctrine, these individuals looked for new forms for expressing the human condition other than the didactic Protestantism that prevailed around them. Looking to literature and philosophy for ways to reawaken emotional and spirited dialogue into the dry rational conservatism they saw as their cultural norm, they found that Wordsworth, Coleridge, Carlyle, and Goethe spoke to their needs. When Emerson finally accepted the name in his 1842 lecture, "The Transcendentalist," he explained that the term came from Kant and that it was really idealism as it appeared in 1842. The Transcendentalists mostly knew Kant through Carlyle and Coleridge, and Emerson's use of the word "idealism" is a very general one that could include Plato and Puritanism as well as more subtle manifestations. Nevertheless, it is important to note that with Kant, as well as with Carlyle and Coleridge, idealism relies on materialism and the rational. Emerson's legacy as a central influence on the American pragmatism of John Dewey and William James is evidence enough of this point.

This active group of Bostonian writers, widely diverse in their interpretations and uses of Romantic idealism, included Margaret Fuller's feminist writings, Amos Bronson Alcott's and Elizabeth Palmer Peabody's ideas about education, Theodore Parker's Christian discourses, and the writings of Orestes A. Brownson, William Henry Channing, George Ripley, Jones Very, and of course Emerson, their intellectual father, and Henry David Thoreau, who took Emerson's philosophical suggestions and put them into practice with his experiment in the woods near Walden Pond. Later, New Yorker Walt Whitman, after hearing one of Emerson's lectures, took it upon himself to become the American poet whom Emerson called for in his famous lecture and essay "The Poet." According to Perry Miller, despite the shortcomings of many of the lesser-known writers of the group and the brevity of their force, "The Transcendental movement was the most energetic and extensive upsurge of the mind and spirit enacted in America until the intellectual crisis of the 1920's." He contends, "For those who would understand the character of this country, a firsthand knowledge of the ideas that generated and sustained the movement is important" ("Melville" 14–15).

The ideas that generated and sustained the American Transcendentalism movement are essentially Romantic in the line that runs from Goethe and Kant to the British Romantics, and they focus on the same contradictions and unities that describe Romanticism in the section above. The American Transcendentalists also read Eastern texts and were enamored with the classical Greeks and pre-Socratics. For the most part they used this literature to put forward the belief that the New Testament is evidence of a truth that can also be found, as Theodore Parker describes it, through "the oracle God places in the breast" (Miller "Melville" 273). Although Transcendentalism is usually described as both a religion and a philosophy, its center is religious and largely Christian, revealing the divinity as present in humanity and the natural world. Perhaps its greatest influence has been on literature and the arts as instruments of spiritual growth for social reform. Politically, however, the civil disobedience proposed by Henry David Thoreau was a significant influence on Mahatma Gandhi's leadership in the liberation of India in the 1940s and on Martin Luther King, Jr.'s role in the American

Civil Rights Movement of the 1950s and 1960s. It follows that if the divine is immanent in nature and therefore in each person, then individual intuition is to be trusted and self-reliance is a means to freedom from those societal laws that are immoral.

F. O. Matthiessen maintains that Melville "felt a strong attraction in the transcendental beliefs; he frequently underscored Emerson's lines with that heavily-freighted nineteenth-century word 'noble,' " but at the same time Melville struggled uncomfortably with Emersonian Transcendentalism (184). In the often quoted letter of 1849 to Evert Duyckinck, Melville wrote, "nay, I do not oscillate in Emerson's rainbow, but prefer to hang myself in mine own halter than swing in any other man's swing." Here Melville asserts his self-reliance in independent thought, the central exhortation of Emerson's life works and adds, "frankly, for the sake of the argument, let us call him a fool; – then had I rather be a fool than a wise man" (*L* 121). John B. Williams explains that Emerson's strategy in his lectures was "to stimulate people to think about their entrapment in the routines and conventions of society by taking a stand that was deliberately 'too ideal' " (12). The talks were therefore both highly intellectual and enthusiastic in content. Consequently, despite Emerson's stateliness, he was sometimes depicted as a bit of a fool in newspaper drawings that parodied his "transparent eyeball" and caricatured him as a doll-like figure swinging in a rainbow. Although Melville responded to this tendency to see the Emerson of the 1830s as starry-eyed, Melville knew that he was much more, and Williams demonstrates that "it was the Emerson of 1849 that impressed him most", the Emerson who had more clearly grounded his essay *Nature* with that of "Experience." Melville wrote in several places such statements as, "I have heard Emerson ... Say what they will, he's a great man" (*L* 119). Certainly Melville had mixed feelings about the public persona of Emerson, but both men dealt with the same Romantic vacillations. Although it was unlikely that the two men ever met, Williams also notes, as others have, that Melville attended at least one of Emerson's lectures in the 1840s. He points out that Emerson's writings, lectures, and reviews of his lectures reveal Melville's ability to take ideas from his contemporary culture as well as from his own extensive reading to develop his best work.

Williams relates that the most notable examples of ideas suggested by Emerson and further developed by Melville are "the crack in human nature" and the final dart of the rope around Ahab's neck in *Moby-Dick*. Emerson writes in "Compensation" in 1841:

> A man cannot speak but he judges himself. With his will or against his will he draws his portrait to the eye of his companions by every word. Every opinion reacts on him who utters it. It is a thread-ball thrown at a mark, but the other end remains in the thrower's bag. Or rather it is a harpoon hurled at the whale, unwinding as it flies, a coil of cord in the boat, and, if the harpoon is not good, or not well thrown it will be nigh to cut the steersman in twain or to sink the boat. (*Collected Works* II. 110 in Williams 53)

Here Emerson exhorts his audience to be conscious of using one's will to judge and attack others, as those attacks will come back in a deadly recoil. Whether or not it was an original image, he may have set the course somewhere in Melville's mind for the unforgettable ending to *Moby-Dick* and Ahab, where Ahab's lashing out of unbalanced hatred toward the evil he sees as the white whale comes back to hit him directly and to sink the *Pequod*.

Although *Nature* leads the reader to believe that Emerson could easily apprehend the spiritual in moments of epiphany in which the phenomenal dissolves, and although that essay leaves little doubt as to Emerson's emphasis on the superiority of the spiritual world as much like the Platonic Real, his later writings move toward a stronger articulation of the struggle with "rough and surly" nature as "no sentimentalist" and the difficulty of finding transcendental moments. Stephen Whicher points out that despite his "identifying his real self primarily with the divine Self within him and dismissing the rest as outer shell" in his early essays, Emerson "came to recognize that his real self was his whole contradictory nature, diving potentiality and mortal limits together" (103).

Whereas Melville certainly does not focus on transcendental moments and instead focuses on Goethe's belief in the "revelation of the inscrutable" as forever unfathomable, he does occasionally suggest the possibility of momentary nonconceptual apprehension, at least among the best of us. In trying to describe the greatness of Shakespeare and Hawthorne in "Hawthorne and His Mosses," for example, he refers to the "augustness of the nature within" that "our visible frame," the "dust of which our bodies are composed," cannot "fitly express." He suggests that "the names of all fine authors are fictitious ones" because the true author is "the mystical, ever-eluding Spirit of all Beauty" (*PT* 241). He quotes from Hawthorne's "The Artist of the Beautiful": "When the Artist rises high enough to achieve the Beautiful, the symbol by which he makes it perceptible to mortal senses becomes of little value in his eyes, while his spirit possesses itself in the enjoyment of the reality" (Hawthorne 177). Yet Melville also warns against what D. H. Lawrence would later call the monstrous and mechanical in the transcendentalist valorization of Oneness. The chapter of *Moby-Dick* titled "The Mast-Head" suggests a longing for those transcendental experiences. Melville's subtle humor in handling weighty topics is evidenced as the narrator alerts shipowners against putting meditative Platonists in the crow's nest. Ishmael admits that he had difficulty doing his job watching for whales "with the problem of the universe revolving in me ... at such a thought-engendering altitude" (158). At such heights of meditation, Ishmael warns that one "loses his identity; takes the mystic ocean at his feet for the visible image of that deep, blue, bottomless soul, pervading mankind and nature" and falls to his death in "this enchanted mood" where "thy spirit ebbs away to whence it came" (159). For if you "slip your hold at all" from that Oneness by the move of a foot or hand, "your identity comes back in horror" and "with one half-throttled shriek you drop through transparent air into the summer sea." Ishmael finally exhorts, "Heed it well, ye Pantheists!" (159).

For Melville, a merge with nature is clearly death for the individual. Nevertheless, he does suggest that he has an inclination to understand Goethe's and Emerson's transcendental moments. He writes to Hawthorne in a letter in 1851:

> In reading some of Goethe's sayings ... I came across this, *"Live in all."* ... what
> nonsense! ... This 'all feeling,' though there is some truth in it. You must often have
> felt it, lying on the grass on a warm summer's day. Our legs seem to send out shoots into
> the earth. Your hair feels like leaves on your head. This is the all feeling. (*L* 193–4)

Some scholars see this tendency toward the balance of separateness with oneness (or
"all feeling") in *Clarel*, Melville's book-length poem. John T. Shawcross, for example,
sees Clarel as coming "to represent the person, any person, who is capable of finding
the godhead within himself" (71). Not eclipsing that interpretation, most readers also
see Clarel as being left with incomprehension and an acceptance of a God who cannot
be heard. Emerson's writings suggest that God speaks in everything, but is revealed
only in the harmony of the self with what is outside the self, a stipulation which also
allows for God's silence.

Politics and the Individual

Historians mostly agree that Western artists after 1750 expressed dissatisfaction
with their contemporary society. The Romantic ideal of the individual differs from
the Enlightenment and modern views of individualism in that it reaches for a
balance (in fact a nonduality) between the individual and society, between the
oneness and plurality of democracy in rebellion against the subjugation of the
individual by society, not against the organic unity of the whole. Emerson and
Thoreau looked to nature not to escape from community, but to help form it. To
that end, the Transcendentalists still speak to a contemporary world grown cold
with commercial materialism. In this aspect as well, Melville's writings fit strongly
and comfortably in the Romantic tradition of literary rebellion against society's
status quo.

   At a time when it was dissident to do so, Melville made many veiled objections to
America's policies of slavery and the extermination of the country's tribal people.
"Benito Cereno" is the clearest example of his trickster-like subversion. William
Richardson explains how at one level Melville is "a good citizen poet" and does not
subvert public opinion, but "at the deeper level ... the opinions which are seemingly
advanced on the surface are seriously challenged by certain fundamental political
problems Melville is addressing" (ix). Samuel Otter reveals Melville's use of "intense
political, patriarchal, and sexual anxieties" in *Pierre*, where "the American boast is
turned inside out, and allusions proliferate to the struggles that mark the 'history' of
the American land." Melville refers to the dispossession of the Native Americans and
alludes to Andrew Jackson's empty promise to give them their land "so long as grass
grows and water runs" ("Eden" 56, 57; *P* 11). Similarly, *The Confidence-Man's* "Indian
Hating" chapter has been much discussed as a witty parody of accepted bigotry. *Typee*
refers to the atrocities committed by Europeans in the South Sea islands: "These
things are seldom proclaimed at home" (*T* 54). In *Moby-Dick*, the *Pequod* sails from

Nantucket, since "where else but from Nantucket did those aboriginal whalemen, the Red-Men, first sally out in canoes to give chase to the Leviathan?" (31). Yukiko Oshima argues that *Moby-Dick* "contains a veiled homage" to Native Americans in general as it memorializes the tribe Pequot, wiped out in one quick slaughter. She points out that in Melville's unusual review of Francis Parkman's *The Oregon Trail* (1849), Melville admonishes Parkman's negative comments about Indians. Melville writes, "Why should we con[demn] them? – Because we are better than they? Assuredly not . . . . We are all of us – Anglo-Saxon, Dyaks and Indians – sprung from one head and made in one image" ("Mr. Parkman's Tour" in Oshima 255). The civilization/savagery dichotomy implodes with Queequeg as sober cannibal preferred over drunken Christian. Ishmael explains, "Your true whale-hunter is as much a savage as an Iroquois. I myself am a savage" (358). The savagery in which Ishmael takes part, of course, is done through the workings of mercantile calculations.

Lucy Maddox's study of nineteenth-century American literature and Indian affairs includes provocative comments about the century's canonized writers. She writes,

> Of the seven, only Melville offers anything like a radical critique of the civilization-or-extinction argument. . . . He can offer his critique only by populating his texts with significantly silent presences who, by their silence, call attention to their exclusion from American public discourse. (12)

For Maddox, Melville consistently made present in his fiction "the very different silence of a population that was being deliberately muted" (52). Thus we have the mute at the opening of *The Confidence-Man*, we have Bartleby who prefers not to, Isabel in *Pierre*, Babo in "Benito Cereno," who speaks only in artificial slave-to-master discourse, and we have Moby Dick himself. According to Maddox, the narrator of "Bartleby" tries to explain the scrivener to try to contain him within the narrator's discourse, "but fails because the discourse he understands and needs to validate cannot accommodate the figure of Bartleby within any of its available structures of meaning" (55). In this way, Maddox argues, Melville tries to "address the lie of emptiness" of the American continent "both by acknowledging the silence and by attempting to incorporate it – as *silence* – into his revised version of the American story" (53). In *The Confidence-Man*, Charlie Noble points out that "the voice of the people is the voice of truth" (82). Maddox argues this truth is found "where the voices of the talkers merge in a version of truth that the silence of the other passengers – including the slaves and the Indians – covertly undermines for the reader" (82). Among the many historical documents Maddox uses to build her reading, she cites one that mentions that a Narragansett Indian named Queequegunent was killed by the British and had signed a treaty that mortgaged all of the Narragansett country to the state of Connecticut (64). In view of Maddox's research, it is clearer that Melville's savages, drawn from his brief acquaintance with South Sea natives, also allude to his Native American contemporaries on his home continent much more strongly than was previously thought.

Where better than in Bartleby's "I prefer not to" can we hear Melville's quiet disdain for reducing the human spirit to account books, possessions, receipts, and expenses? For Romantics, the negative side of modern industrialism and mercantilism is its "spirit of rational calculation" that encourages death in life and the "quantification of the world" (Löwy and Sayre 35). In this mode and mood, all Anglo-American Romantics were in some ways children of the French Revolution and its demand for individual freedom.

Melville's Romantic Legacy

Melville's work has a larger and perhaps more amenable audience than it ever did. His Romanticism meets with the contemporary at the intersection of human creativity and our confined circumstances. The Romantic "spirit," in the style of Rousseau and Blake, is the perennial drive to break free of mortal limitation in the face of our unavoidable death sentence. Quite simply, Romantic writers have imagined that it is possible to transcend the boundaries of our skin, to move out of the container, so to speak, to demonstrate in the most favourable moments (at the very least just by thought itself) that we can somehow be free even as we bemoan our inescapable imprisonment. When Charles Rosen describes early Romanticism, he writes, "These years between 1797 and 1805 were filled with the most daring experiments in literature. They were a time of despair after the failure of the French Revolution and of half-ironic, half-serious hope for a new spiritual rebirth, a transformation of the world through art." He further uses Schlegel's *Fragments* as a manifesto of German Romanticism which depicts Romanticism as "a literature of visionary imagination alongside the portrayal of even the most repellent aspects of modern life" (Rosen 17). Melville uses the whale, the confidence man, his "savages," and Pierre's women to let his readers see with both dual and nondual perception. Even if Melville sat uncomfortably in his disbelief, existentialism and idealism are not two sides of a debate about Melville's leanings; rather, in his works they are two sides of the same doubloon, both bemoaned and admitted by most Romantics and many postmoderns. Like Melville, we are all always full of contradictions, even when some alternative truths never speak at all.

REFERENCES AND FURTHER READING

Abrams, M. H. "English Romanticism: The Spirit of the Age." In *Romanticism Reconsidered*. Ed. Northrop Frye. New York: Columbia University Press, 1963. 26–72.

Bryant, John. "The Persistence of Melville: Representative Writer for a Multicultural Age." In *Melville's Evermoving Dawn: Centennial Essays*. Ed. John Bryant and Robert Milder. Kent, OH: Kent State University Press, 1997. 3–28.

Coffler, Gail. "Religion, Myth, and Meaning in the Art of *Billy Budd, Sailor*." In *New Essays on Billy Budd*. Ed. Donald Yannella. Cambridge: Cambridge University Press, 2002. 49–82.

De Mul, Jos. *Romantic Desire in (Post)Modern Art & Philosophy.* Albany, NY: SUNY Press, 1999.

Elbow, Peter. *Oppositions in Chaucer.* Middletown, CT: Wesleyan University Press, 1975.

Ellison, Julie. *Delicate Subjects: Romanticism, Gender, and the Ethics of Understanding.* Ithaca, NY: Cornell University Press, 1990.

Frye, Northrop, ed. *Romanticism Reconsidered.* New York: Columbia University Press, 1963.

Hawthorne, Nathaniel. "The Artist of the Beautiful." In *Nathaniel Hawthorne's Tales.* Ed. James MacIntosh. New York: W. W. Norton, 1987. 159–77.

Higgins, Brian and Hershel Parker. "The Flawed Grandeur of Melville's *Pierre.*" In *New Perspectives on Melville.* Ed. Faith Pullin. Kent, OH: Kent State University Press, 1978. 162–96.

Jardine, Alice A. *Gynesis: Configurations of Woman and Modernity.* Ithaca, NY: Cornell University Press, 1985.

Löwy, Michael and Robert Sayre. *Romanticism Against the Tide of Modernity.* Trans. Catherine Porter. Durham, NC: Duke University Press, 2001.

Maddox, Lucy. *Removals: Nineteenth-Century American Literature and the Politics of Indian Affairs.* Oxford: Oxford University Press, 1991.

Matthiessen, F. O. *American Renaissance: Art and Expression in the Age of Emerson and Whitman.* New York: Oxford University Press, 1941, 1968.

Miller, Perry. "Melville and Transcendentalism." *Virginia Quarterly Review* 29 (1953): 556–75.

——— . *The Transcendentalists: An Anthology.* Cambridge, MA: Harvard University Press, 1950.

Oshima, Yukiko. "The Red Flag of the *Pequod/Pequot:* Native American Presence in *Moby-Dick.*" In *Melville "Among the Nations."* Ed. Sanford E. Marovitz and A. C. Christodoulou. Kent, OH: Kent State University Press, 2001. 254–66.

Otter, Samuel. "The Eden of Saddle Meadows: Landscape and Ideology in *Pierre.*" *American Literature* 66.1 (1994): 55–81.

——— . *Melville's Anatomies.* Berkeley: University of California Press, 1999.

Porter, Carolyn. "Call Me Ishmael, or How to Make Double-Talk Speak." In *New Essays on Moby-Dick.* Ed. Richard Brodhead. Cambridge: Cambridge University Press, 1986. 73–108.

Rajan, Tilottama. *The Supplement of Reading: Figures of Understanding in Romantic Theory and Practice.* Ithaca, NY: Cornell University Press. 1990.

Richardson, William D. *Melville's "Benito Cereno."* Durham, NC: Carolina Academic Press, 1987.

Rosen, Charles. *Romantic Poets, Critics, and Other Madmen.* Cambridge, MA: Harvard University Press, 1998.

Shawcross, John T. "Too Intellectual a Poet Ever to Be Popular." *Leviathan* 4.1 (2002): 71–90.

Urban, David. " 'Rousing Motions' and the Silence of God." *Leviathan* 4.2 (2002): 91–111.

Van Cromphout, Gustaaf. *Emerson's Modernity and the Example of Goethe.* Columbia: University of Missouri Press, 1990.

Vizenor, Gerald. "Gerald Vizenor [Interview]." In *Winged Words: American Indian Writers Speak.* Ed. Laura Cotelli. Lincoln: University of Nebraska Press, 1992. 155–84.

Whicher, Stephen F. *Freedom and Fate: An Inner Life of Ralph Waldo Emerson.* 1953. Philadelphia: University of Pennsylvania Press, 1971.

Wilkinson, Elizabeth and L. A. Willoughby. *Goethe: Poet and Thinker.* London: Arnold Press, 1970.

Williams, John B. *White Fire: The Influence of Emerson on Melville.* Long Beach: California State University Press, 1991.

Wordsworth, William. *The Poetical Works.* Ed. Ernest De Selincourt and Helen Darbishire. 5 vols. Oxford University Press, 1940–9.

18

Literature of Exploration and the Sea

R. D. Madison

In Chapter 27 of *Moby-Dick*, Melville describes the crew of the *Pequod* as an "Anacharsis Clootz deputation from all the isles of the sea," after the French revolutionist who led a delegation of foreigners into the National Assembly in 1790 as a gesture of internationalism (121). A whaleship may have been not only Melville's Yale College and Harvard, as he claimed in Chapter 24, but also the most cosmopolitan place in Melville's experience, out-diversifying even Liverpool and London. With the exception of Polynesia, for his novel-writing career Melville experienced all foreign cultures out of context – in the forecastle or in a thirty-foot boat. His racialized portraits of the harpooners on the *Pequod* – an African, a South Sea Islander, a Native American, and a Malaysian – indicate global awareness, but despite his own Pacific travels in the 1840s and a trip to Asia Minor in 1856–7, Melville's geography was largely second-hand, European and Anglo-American. The Galapagos and the coast of South America came to Melville as the decayed remnants of European expansion rather than the fresh frontiers of a new world, and even the Levant, as the eastern Mediterranean was called, may have revealed itself to Melville largely through expectations derived from Murray's guidebooks. Despite his remarkable wanderings over the watery part of the world, the "man who lived among the cannibals," as Melville feared he would be known to posterity (*L* 193), filled out even his own autobiographical works with gleanings from other travel writers.

As in other areas of Melville scholarship, Melville's relationship with the sea literature of his day has been most comprehensively catalogued in Merton M. Sealts, Jr.'s *Melville's Reading* (1988, with ongoing additions by Stephen Olsen-Smith) and Mary K. Bercaw's *Melville's Sources* (1987). In general these works suggest that as a reader Melville was much more engaged with poetry and non-fiction prose than with sea fiction. Melville's reading underwent "growth spurts" – obvious in the case of whaling material while he was writing *Moby-Dick*, less obvious as he studied poetry around 1849, 1858, and 1862. Melville's book purchases show that however focused his research may have been for a particular book, he never limited his reading by genre. While it is useful in this essay to focus on works about ships, sailors, and the sea, and however much Melville may have adopted the learned-sailor persona during the years he lived at his farm Arrowhead and hobnobbed with the New York literati, Melville never saw himself as strictly a sea novelist or a sea poet. His readings in exploration, sea fiction, and sea poetry were only part of a lifelong process of self-education.

Exploration

... and Satan stay'd not to reply,
But glad that now his sea should find a shore,
With fresh alacrity and force renew'd
Springs upward, like a pyramid of fire,
Into the wild expanse ...
Paradise Lost, Book II, 1010–14 (1:77)

To the ever-evolving literary mind of Herman Melville, the two central narratives of exploration were Milton's *Paradise Lost* (Bercaw #499) and the *Lusiad* of Camoens (Bercaw #111). To illustrate the difficulty of isolating specific genres and speaking with certainty about what Melville actually read, it would be wise to remind ourselves that the first of these is entirely a work of imagination, while Melville may never have completely read the second. We can at least, however, talk with some confidence about many influences. From internal evidence of the influence of Milton on Melville, for instance, Henry Pommer was able to deduce what text of the *Poetical Works* Melville had before him, twenty-four years before Melville's own set was recovered. Most sensible critics, however, would strain at discussing *Paradise Lost* as a travel narrative, suggestive as Satan's quest to discover a new world might be. But Melville's fascination with Satan ought to remind us that, for the sailor-turned-novelist-turned-poet, the literary and imaginative value of any voyage was largely determined by the character of the explorer.

Whether Melville actually heard Jack Chase of *White-Jacket* (1850) recite Mickle's translation of Camoens, or Camoens in the original Portuguese, is a question we cannot at this time answer. But sometime before 1849 Melville matched the character of the sixteenth-century epic poem to the free and high spirit of his version of his shipmate. Melville clearly knew enough about Camoens at that time to distinguish among his translators: what else did he know?

The *Lusiad*, as translated by Mickle, is a self-conscious and insistent epic of discovery. With 150 pages of introduction and many more of commentary in the 1776 edition, the translation Melville cites is as much a product of Mickle as of Camoens. The work begins with Vasco da Gama having rounded the tip of Africa: at the port of Melinda the hero recounts his adventures to that point – including a long and difficult summary of Portuguese history and the brilliant description of the Spirit of the Cape (mentioned in *Billy Budd*). With the intervention of gods both Christian and classical, Gama's fleet arrives at Calicut in India and initiates Portugal's eastern empire. Gama opens the East to commerce; Camoens (with Mickle) opens the Christian West to Hindu culture. On the return voyage the men are carnally and spiritually rewarded at the Isle of Love, while Gama is given a vision of the future of Portugal.

Mickle's long introductory discussions are focused on the genre of epic, the meaning of discovery, and the nature of commerce – three areas of inquiry that make him especially interesting to twenty-first century critics as well as to a literary ex-sailor. Mickle is as much the champion of British expansion as Camoens was of the Portuguese conquest of the East. A friend of Dr. Johnson, Boswell, and Goldsmith, Mickle saw only a glorious future for a nation so obviously created by God to maintain an empire.

It is hard to believe that Melville could have been familiar with the entire *Lusiad* at the time he wrote *Typee*: had he read the account of the Isle of Love in Book IX he could hardly have failed to allude to it as he described the women of Nukuhiva. It's equally hard to imagine that Melville would not have made a connection between Mickle's celebration of commerce and the nine pages of epic by a "neglected Liverpool poet" which celebrates the Mersey's "docks, and ships, and warehouses, and bales, and anchors" in Chapter 30 of *Redburn* (*R* 147). The two quotations from the poem in Chapters 65 and 93 of *White-Jacket* nevertheless prove that by late 1849 Melville knew what he needed from the *Lusiad*. Small discrepancies between Melville's versions and the originals might even suggest that Melville was writing from memory – or that he was deliberately adapting freely. Whatever the case, his selection of passages from the very beginning and the very end (Books I and X) leaves room – eight books of it – for doubt about his familiarity with the whole poem.

But it was the character of Camoens as a wandering hero turned disfranchised poet that lasted with Melville – his epic (or tragic) life, rather than his epic poem. The Camoens Melville addresses in two late poems (that, appropriately enough for a neglected poet, remained unpublished at the time of Melville's death) typifies the youthful fire extinguished by neglect in the literary careers of both men. "Fate's knife hath ripped the chorded lyre" ("Camoens in the Hospital (After)," *CP* 380), Melville wrote, while Camoens himself had written,

> Enough, my Muse, thy wearied wing no more
> Must to the seat of Jove triumphant soar.
> Chill'd by my nation's cold neglect, thy fires
> Glow bold no more, and all thy rage expires.
> (Mickle's *Lusiad*, Book X [483])

The volume of Camoens that Melville owned by 1867 contained only a few stanzas of the *Lusiad*, but Lord Strangford's introduction would have reinforced Melville's sense of kinship with the poet himself: "Camoens sank beneath the pressure of penury and disease," Strangford wrote, "and died in an alms-house" (*Camoens* 21). Melville, who was fond of epitaphs, would have appreciated Camoens's:

> Here Lies Luis De Camoens:
> He Excelled all the Poets of his Time
> He lived Poor and Miserable;
> And He Died So.
>   MDLXXIX (*Camoens* 22)

It's hard to tell whether the enthusiasm for poetry Melville ascribes to the character Jack Chase is derived from Melville's real shipmate or is a projection of the author's own reading. "Jack," Melville writes in Chapter 4 of *White-Jacket*, "had read all the verses of Byron" (14). Years after, Melville owned a ten-volume set of Byron's works (Sealts #112), but he had clearly encountered Byron's work much earlier – especially Byron's longest serious poem, *Childe Harold's Pilgrimage*, which he parodied in Chapter 35 of *Moby-Dick*: "Ten thousand blubber-hunters sweep over thee in vain" (158). Byron's more or less autobiographical poem recounts, in four cantos, journeys through Portugal and Spain, Italy and Albania, Belgium, the Rhine, and the Alps, and Italy, time, and the ocean itself. Until its fourth canto, Melville may have found Byron's poem singularly unreflective compared to Wordsworth's *The Excursion* (in Sealts #563a), yet he remembered snatches of it years later when he adapted Byron's phrase, "Yet such the fix'd inveteracy" from stanza lxxvi of Canto IV (2.226), into one of the most chilling lines of American poetry in his poem "The Haglets": "The unvarying flight and fixed inveterate mood" (*CP* 191).

The Excursion, eclipsed by the publication of Wordsworth's *The Prelude* in 1850, is little read today, but Wordsworth's long examination of faith, hope, and suffering provided a powerful unifying context for the themes, tone, and characterization of Melville's writing from *The Piazza Tales* through *The Confidence-Man* to *Clarel*. Despite its title, its mental travelers, and its geographical grounding, however, Melville didn't turn to Wordsworth's poem the same way he plundered more mundane travel literature. Wordsworth may have traveled widely in the Lake District, and at one time Melville may have seen Wordsworth's landscape mirrored in his beloved Berkshires, but when he came to write his own examination of faith in *Clarel*, Melville chose the sterile nineteenth-century landscape of the Holy Land. The study of the relationship between Melville and Wordsworth remains one of the largest gaps in Melville criticism.

In an essay in *Characteristics of Literature*, Melville's friend and mentor Henry T. Tuckerman claimed that *Childe Harold* was "most emphatically the illustrative epic of the age" (208), and the introspective journeys of the Romantics Wordsworth and Byron may have always been more important to Melville than mere collections of voyages. Nevertheless, there was a more literal voyage literature that Melville read, enjoyed, and drew on, a tradition that yields more certainties than epic poetry.

The literature of exploration is usually marked by three themes in varying degrees: discovery, commerce, and war. The interconnectivity of these categories is all too obvious. Melville made most use of the discovery aspect of voyaging literature, but had to look for his material in accounts of varying intent. One of the earliest and most influential was David Porter's *Journal of a Cruise* (Bercaw #563). Ostensibly a narrative of war at sea, Porter's book focuses on commerce raiding in the British whale fishery and exploring the relatively unfamiliar physical and cultural landscapes of the Galapagos and the Marquesas islands. As the protagonist of his own book, Porter did not stimulate Melville's literary imagination the way, for instance, William Scoresby later did. But as a writer on the defensive, a man accused of lying and indecency by William Gifford in the *Quarterly Review*, Porter was an important psychological predecessor for any man who lived among cannibals and wrote about the experience more or less explicitly. Melville could have taken vicarious delight in Porter's scattering of his enemies in the introduction to the second edition, but he would also have shrugged at the inevitable: the revised edition took out most of the naughty bits (we don't know which edition Melville read).

Missionaries as well as warriors were likely to end up in strange places, and Melville's most fruitful literary encounter with the church abroad was William Ellis's *Polynesian Researches* (Bercaw #245). More than simply refreshing his memory, Porter and Ellis gave Melville the factual foundation from which he could depart on his own literary discoveries.

Shortly after the completion of *Redburn*, Richard Henry Dana, Jr., son of an important New England poet and author of the trend-setting *Two Years Before the Mast* (Bercaw #189) and *The Seaman's Friend* (Bercaw #188b), two books Melville had been influenced by (or had plundered) for his recent work, wrote to the young novelist to urge him to write about his experiences in the navy. Melville stalled his answer long enough to report to his "sea-brother" (L 141) that the work was already written. Despite Melville's delight at being noticed by the most famous living sea-writer (rivaled only by James Fenimore Cooper), he must have been nettled that Dana – only four years older – seemed to be paternalistically guiding Melville's career. When Dana did the same thing again the next spring, Melville may well have been at work on *Israel Potter*, the novel for which we know Melville consciously gathered materials during his trip to England that intervening winter. This time the suggestion was for a whaling book, which Melville may have thought he had already written in *Mardi*. Melville "heartily" responded that he was "half way in the work" (L 160, 162): nevertheless, there is no other evidence he was, and Melville – a seasoned author by now, who knew what kind of materials he needed to write a book – within days of receiving Dana's letter ordered his copy of Thomas Beale's *The Natural History of the Sperm Whale* (Bercaw #52) and borrowed William Scoresby's *An Account of the Arctic Regions* (Bercaw #615) from the New York Society Library, the two most essential works for fitting out a literary "whaling voyage."

Beale brought to his study the exact and appreciative eye of a scientist, while the amateur Scoresby exhibited a dry but unquenchable curiosity. Under the influence of Sterne (Bercaw #670) and Carlyle (Bercaw #119), in *Moby-Dick* Melville transformed Scoresby into the various authorities Zogranda, Fogo von Slack, Dr. Snodhead, and Captain Sleet. Probably drawn to Scoresby and Beale by the "Whale" article in the *Penny Cyclopedia* (Bercaw #544), Melville built the "cetological center" of *Moby-Dick* around commercial accounts of whales and whaling. Melville had read Frederick Debell Bennett's *Narrative of a Whaling Voyage* (Bercaw #60) and J. Ross Browne's *Etchings of a Whaling Cruise* (Bercaw #82) well before he began *Moby-Dick*: he had reviewed the latter in the *Literary World* in 1847. Melville knew of another whaling source he would like to have had before him, one whose central incident of a whaleship sunk by an enraged whale provided the catastrophe of Melville's own projected novel. But only late in the composition of his book was he able to procure a copy of Owen Chase's *Narrative of the Most Extraordinary and Distressing Shipwreck of the Whale-Ship Essex* (Bercaw #130). Likewise, Melville also seems to have consulted Henry T. Cheever's *The Whale and his Captors* (Bercaw #136) only very late in the process of composition, perhaps because he was in England when the book was published. It is not clear how Melville could have missed a work written by an acquaintance and prominently advertised in the *Literary World*, but he seems to have used Cheever's book directly only in the "Extracts" that head *Moby-Dick* and in footnotes.

The conception of Ahab's quest owed more to the authors of two of the purest works of exploration literature Melville encountered: Charles Wilkes's *United States Exploring Expedition* (Bercaw #759) and Matthew F. Maury's *Explanations and Sailing Directions* (Bercaw #493). The latter was not published in time for Melville to consult it, but he was familiar with Maury's quantification of the migration of whales and with the abstract logs Maury requested whalemen to fill out to assist with his research. Ironically, the only account of Melville's actual voyage in the *Acushnet* comes from one of these abstract logs. What Captain Cook (Bercaw #159–60) was to the British Romantic writers, Wilkes was to a generation of Americans: many writers were connected to the expedition literally or literarily, including Audubon, Cooper, Hawthorne, Poe, and Thoreau. Like Cook, Wilkes basically attempted to fill in all the blank spaces on the chart. By Melville's time of nearly mythological stature in the South Seas, Cook was perhaps the first to navigate the Antarctic Ocean, but is better known for establishing contact with the Sandwich Islands – and being murdered there, in what is now Hawaii. Wilkes, a luckier if less tactful explorer, largely established that Antarctica was a continent. David Jaffe has even suggested, in *The Stormy Petrel and the Whale* (1976), that Wilkes was a model for Ahab.

Another pure work of exploration Melville read was Darwin's *Journal of Researches* based on the voyage of the survey ship *Beagle* (Bercaw #191). Not surprisingly, this work contributed most directly to Melville's "Encantadas," which might be claimed as his own purest narrative of exploration. Darwin famously studied the Galapagos finches; Melville – at least in retrospect – studied metaphysical hierarchies. At about the same time, Melville turned to Amasa Delano's account of commercial voyaging, *A Narrative of Voyages and Travels* (Bercaw #200), for the story of the *Tryal* which would be only slightly – but masterfully – retouched into "Benito Cereno."

Under the heading of exploration might also be included such works of naval autobiography as Samuel Leech's *Thirty Years from Home* (Bercaw #440) and more expository works on naval reform such as William McNally's *Evils and Abuses in the Naval and Merchant Service Exposed* (Bercaw #497), two books which loom large in the development of *White-Jacket*. Melville knew R. C. Sands's *Life and Correspondence of John Paul Jones* (Bercaw #604) and James Fenimore Cooper's *History of the Navy* (Bercaw #163) by the time he wrote *Israel Potter*, and he knew Robert Southey's *Life of Nelson* (Bercaw #658) by the time he wrote *Billy Budd* – as did, perhaps, every literate sailor of the century.

A plunderer less and less after the 1850s, increasingly Melville read source books for context rather than text. When he turned to poetry after his relatively brief career as a novelist, his own voyaging as a writer rather than as a working sailor largely supplied him with the nautical images that would continue to punctuate his verse. The Mediterranean, rather than the Atlantic or Pacific, would disproportionately engage his imagination – its shores providing the Italy of hope, the Greece of memory, and the Palestine of despair.

Sea Fiction

[I]t was a sort of provocation to dispute the seamanship of the *Pirate*, a quality to which the book has certainly very little just pretension. (Cooper, on praise for Scott's nautical detail, in the Preface to the 1849 edition of *The Pilot* [5])

Sir Walter Scott's awkward description of townsmen assailing a stranded right whale with pitchforks in *The Pirate* (1821) was strictly based on Scott's own observation, albeit the victims were blackfish only a fraction of the size of the fictional animal. When the "American Scott" decided to correct the "Wizard of the North," he inadvertently invented a new genre of literature: at the height of the Romantic novel, Cooper introduced a standard of realism for the sea novel that has never disappeared.

The realistic basis for a sea story was already in place in the world of poetry: William Falconer's *The Shipwreck* (Bercaw #261) is filled with so much technical detail that it might at times seem more like a manual of seamanship, detail that certainly lies uneasily in the twenty-five hundred neoclassical lines of heroic couplets. But what would one expect from the author of the *Marine Dictionary* (1769)?

Maritime realism as practiced by Cooper and Melville is not based on an accumulation of salty language ("I hate maritime expressions," Melville's friend Tuckerman remarked in 1849 [50]). Nor does it extend to characterization or plot. In *The Pilot*

(1824) Cooper introduced the three primary types of conflict in the sea novel, each demanding a certain level of realism: man versus man, man versus the sea, man versus the creatures of the sea. In discrete chapters, Cooper defines these elements (in the order of the plot) in the chase of a right whale, in a battle between the schooner *Ariel* and cutter *Alacrity*, and in the wreck of the beautiful *Ariel*. To this mix of conflicts, Cooper also added the ship-as-character, so the vessels frequently become personified – an aspect of the sea novel that may have as much to do with maritime culture as with Cooper's imaginative process.

Of Cooper's dozen or so sea novels, Melville is suspected to have read at least half. He reviewed two, *The Sea Lions* (Bercaw #171) and *The Red Rover* (Bercaw #170) for the *Literary World*: Cooper's Antarctic book reminded him of a passage from *Measure for Measure*, which he remembered as "thrilling regions of rock-ribbed ice." Shakespeare had actually written "thrilling region of thick-ribbed ice," but Melville may have had in mind Camoens's couplet on the Spirit of the Cape in Book V of *The Lusiad*: "And Me the rock-ribb'd mother gave to fame, / Great Adamastor then my dreaded name" (222). Melville may not have reread *The Red Rover*, but he did claim that "Long ago, and far inland" he had read it in his "uncritical days." By 1850, Melville could refer to Cooper's work as a "lighter sort of craft" (*PT* 238, 237).

Several readers have pointed out similarities between Melville's early novels and Daniel Defoe's *Robinson Crusoe* (Bercaw #196), one of those books which it would be astonishing if Melville did *not* read – like John Bunyan's *The Pilgrim's Progress* (Bercaw #93) or Oliver Goldsmith's *The Vicar of Wakefield* (Sealts #232). Except when he was looking for specific background detail – the description of a Marquesan custom or a particular species of whale – Melville probably never discriminated in his reading between sea and land settings, nor is there much point in trying to separate their influence by geography.

The most pre-eminent sea novelist in Britain before the Crimean War was Captain Frederick Marryat. Written in the British picaresque tradition, his episodic sea novels smacked more of the drawing-room than the forecastle. Melville may have read several, but only *Peter Simple* (Bercaw #481) has been convincingly linked to his writing.

As long as *Moby-Dick* is considered a sea novel, it must also be considered *sui generis*. The scope of Melville's epic novel owes more to his recent reading of Dante (Bercaw #190), Homer (Bercaw #369), and James Macpherson's *Fingal* (Bercaw #467) – and probably Camoens – than to his revisiting of Cooper, despite the latter's formal leap to religious allegory in *The Sea Lions*. While we can trace many elements of fiction through Melville's writing, the structure of the sea novel is probably not one of them. *Redburn* seems related to Cooper's *Afloat and Ashore* (Bercaw #162), but only because both capitalize on a non-fiction form initiated by Dana. Even *White-Jacket* is not completely in the tradition of Smollett, whose *Roderick Random* (Bercaw #654) Melville borrowed during the composition of *Moby-Dick*. *Typee* probably owes more to *The Last of the Mohicans* (1826) than it does to *The Pilot*. And while *Typee* and *Omoo* did inspire imitations (the most famous, perhaps, being Jack London's *Cruise of the*

Snark [1911]), *Moby-Dick* remains a giant book stranded on the shores of literature. Not even Melville's friend William Clark Russell, whose pious and sentimental *The Wreck of the* Grosvenor (Bercaw #595) may have been the most popular sea novel of the second half of the century, could shake himself loose from the example of Cooper. Admiring each other enormously as artists and sea-brothers, neither Melville nor Russell really influenced the other in the form of the sea novel.

Melville died just before the decade that capped the Romantic Revival and gave rise to Literary Naturalism and Modernism in sea literature, and which produced Rudyard Kipling's *Captains Courageous* (1897), Joseph Conrad's *Lord Jim* (1900), Erskine Childers's *The Riddle of the Sands* (1903), and Jack London's *The Sea-Wolf* (1904). In his desk was the manuscript of *Billy Budd*.

Sea Lyrics

> Not here! the white North has thy bones; and thou,
>   Heroic sailor-soul,
> Art passing on thine happier voyage now
>   Toward no earthly pole.
> (Tennyson, "Sir John Franklin: On the Cenotaph in Westminster Abbey" (1880) [183])

>   Implacable I, the old implacable Sea:
>   Implacable most when most I smile serene –
> Pleased, not appeased, by myriad wrecks in me.
> (Melville, "Pebbles," V, *John Marr and Other Sailors* (1888) [CP 206])

In his review of "Gertrude of Wyoming" in *Critical and Miscellaneous Essays* (Sealts #359), Sir Walter Scott identified Thomas Campbell's war odes "The Mariners of England" and "The Battle of the Baltic" and the two ballads "Glenara" and "Lord Ullin's Daughter" as "models in their several styles of composition" (I: 211). Scott's next essay in this volume, a review of J. W. Croker's *The Battles of Talavera: a Poem*, insisted that the war poet may be "permitted to strip himself as to a combat, and to evince that 'brave neglect' of the forms of versification which express an imagination too much exalted, and a mind too much occupied by the subject itself, to regard punctiliously the arrangement of rhymes or the measurement of stanzas" (214). Scott recognized in Croker's poem the same "irregular Pindaric measure" (213) he had used in the description of the battle of Flodden in the sixth book of his own *Marmion* (1808).

Although no one would accuse Scott himself of being over-economical or theme-driven, his observations would have made Melville particularly receptive to some of the poetry written in response to the Crimean War. Consciously or unconsciously (we simply don't know) accepting Mickle's preference for rhyme rather than Milton's rejection of it, Melville followed the lead of poets like Richard D. Blackmore, some of whose poems in *Bugle of the Black Sea* (1855) are extraordinarily similar in form and theme to Melville's own. In his sea lyrics, Melville consistently created tension between narrative and conservative rhyme on one hand, and stark imagery and theme on the other. In the most powerful of these, "A Utilitarian View of the Monitor's Fight," as in Blackmore's "The Battle of Alma," narrative is reduced to implication, while Melville nearly abandons rhyme entirely amid imagery drawn (as several critics have pointed out) from Milton's note on the verse to *Paradise Lost*: "Rime being no necessary Adjunct or true Ornament of Poem of good Verse, in longer Works especially, but the Invention of a barbarous Age" (I: cxxxii). After rejecting "rhyme's barbaric cymbal," Melville seems to have shared a different trope and aural imagery with Blackmore, who wrote:

> What need to tell the tramp and clank
> The guns that stopped the way,
> The crowded wharf, the broken rank
> The hurry and delay.

Melville responded with his own "Needless to dwell; the story's known. / The ringing of those plates on plates . . . ." (*CP* 40).

Melville's best battle-pieces are unique among the most famous war-lyrics of his age in being naval. Melville would have been familiar with topical poetry of the Civil War, much of which was reprinted in the poetry sections of the volumes of Frank Moore's *Rebellion Record* (Bercaw #576), but on the whole neither his poetic vision of the sea nor his formal aesthetic seems to owe much to his American contemporaries. Only Henry Howard Brownell, whose *War-Lyrics and Other Poems* (1866) was dedicated to Admiral David Glasgow Farragut, offered Melville a contemporary native analogue for naval poetry (1–24, 82–4). Yet in the preface to his earlier volume *Lyrics of a Day* (reprinted in the 1866 volume), Brownell had referred to his newspaper verse as "spray, as it were, flung up by the strong Tide-Rip of Public Trouble" (335); neither poet thought himself particularly bound to maritime subjects or even to the theme of war.

Melville may have been a Romantic novelist, but he was emerging as a Victorian poet. As early as the late 1850s he had begun to immerse himself in poetical theory and biography. To Melville, becoming a poet was more important than the mere act of writing poetry: Melville transformed himself no less self-consciously than Walt Whitman did. Melville continued to read Tennyson and Matthew Arnold and to shape his own lyric poetry accordingly, but in his last published collection of sea poetry, *John Marr and Other Sailors*, one doesn't seem to find the same linear connection between sources and art found in the fiction or even in *Clarel*. After *Battle-Pieces*, memory largely displaced the published book in Melville's maritime imagination.

For this important period of Melville's development as a writer, the most significant sourcebook was his own journal of October 1856 through May 1857. Beginning with an encounter with the Crag of Ailsa, a geological feature he had written about two years before in *Israel Potter*, the journal records a complex interplay of memory, art, and imagination that not only reflected Melville's career as a novelist but foreshadowed – and in fact seeded – his future as a poet. We know Melville mined this journal for lyric poems in *John Marr* and *Timoleon* (poems in the section called "Fruits of Travel Long Ago" may have been composed for Melville's unpublished 1860 collection), while the transition from steamship to travel by land impressed Melville with an "unleavened nakedness of desolation" (as Melville referred to Judea specifically [*J* 83]) that provided the future poet with the literary landscape of *Clarel*.

Near the beginning of the journal (apparently with reference to a Glasgow hill), Melville mentions the Acropolis, a place he knew well through written descriptions and illustrations. Near the end of the journal is the isolated word "Parthenon." This time Melville was not simply comparing British architecture to a picture in a book: he had been there, and in two separate poems in *Timoleon* – "The Parthenon" and "The Apparition" – imagined the different skeptics Spinoza and Diogenes reflecting on this perfect example of ancient art. Of course, Melville himself was the third skeptic – seeking to find in art what he had not found in faith.

"In Ocean Sand": The Timoneer

"I am that I am."

(Yahweh)

"[D]on't be too sure what I am."

(*The Confidence-Man*, Chapter 42 [225])

The stony mountains of Judah are an unlikely setting for a study of Melville's synthesis of the elements of sea literature. But a reexamination of the character Agath from Melville's long philosophical poem *Clarel* (1876) will remind us that even among the shifting sands of the Holy Land Melville never wanders far from nautical images and characterization. Agath appears in "The Timoneer's Story" (3.12), three-fifths of the way through a work that chronicles the search for faith of the young student Clarel and his companions. Agath is identified by his "sea-gear" as a "pilgrim-timoneer" (3.12.30–1), that is, a helmsman (Smyth [1867]; with the *OED* citing Falconer II: 178 [Bercaw #261]). Now, there is no point in calling every sailor a helmsman unless he has some special relationship to steering – even an ordinary seaman had to be able to hand (furl a sail), reef (shorten a sail), and steer, as Melville well knew and as Melville's friend Dana had made absolutely clear in *The Seaman's Friend* (Bercaw #188b, 163). And every sailor normally took his trick at the wheel. Agath was, to use a more resonant synonym, a boatsteerer.

This ancient mariner, with "weird and weather-beaten face" (3.12.32), could fit into any number of Melville's groups of thematically related characters. Melville's emphasis on Agath's position as a boatsteerer and his bald head immediately link him physically with *Moby-Dick's* Queequeg, but it is Agath's "wrinkles of cabala text" (3.12.34) that hearken most strongly to Queequeg's "Cretan labyrinth of figure" (*MD* 25), described by Stubb in "The Doubloon" as looking "like the signs of the Zodiac himself" (434) and further glossed by Ishmael in "Queequeg in his Coffin":

> And this tattooing, had been the work of a departed prophet and seer of his island, who, by those hieroglyphic marks, had written out on his body a complete theory of the heavens and the earth, and a mystical treatise on the art of attaining truth; so that Queequeg in his own proper person was a riddle to unfold; a wondrous work in one volume; but whose mysteries not even himself could read. (480–1)

The reader is therefore not so surprised as the other pilgrims when the timoneer reveals that not only does he wear the cabala in his face, but like Queequeg he also bears a tattooed legacy the meaning of which he cannot decipher himself: "Look here," cries out Derwent, the Emerson/Wordsworth figure of the poem, at seeing the timoneer's arm, "A living fresco!" (4.2.47–8):

> And indeed,
> Upon the fore-arm did appear
> A thing of art, vermil and blue,
> A crucifixion in tattoo ...
>   Quoth the sea-sage: "Nay;
> Sketched out it was one Christmas day
> Off Java-Head ..."
>   "We seamen, when there's naught to do
> In calms, the straw for hats we plait,
> Or one another we tattoo
> With marks we copy from a mate,
> Which he has from his elders ta'en,
> And those from prior ones again;
> And few, if any, think or reck
> But so with pains their skin to deck."
>   (4.2.48–51, 72–4, 87–94)

Rolfe, himself a former sailor, explicates the riddle of the elaborate tattoo as not only the obvious crucifixion but also the "ensign" of Jerusalem, indicating one who "had kneeled at Calvary" (4.2.109):

> But see,
> From these mailed Templars now the sign,
> Losing the import and true key,
> Descends to boatswains of the brine.
>   (4.2.121–4)

In "The Timoneer's Story" this reluctant survivor rehearses the first version of a tale that Melville developed from a journal entry made during his 1857 trip and would later reshape into his poem "The Haglets." Himself at the helm during the episode he recounts, the timoneer is disoriented by poor visibility ("fitful stars" [3.12.99]) and the spinning compass – a compass affected by the mass of swords in a strong box stowed beneath it, a distant reminder of Ishmael's disorientation while at the helm of the *Pequod* in "The Try-Works" chapter of *Moby-Dick*.

But although the timoneer, as he says, is the "sole wight that 'scaped the sea" (3.12.119), he is a very different kind of wandering outcast from *Moby-Dick*'s Ishmael. He is a Greek sailor, and only after he tells his first tale do we learn his name: Agath (3.12.150). "Agath" is the Greek root for "good," but Melville would have associated the name with suffering and tragedy. The "Agatha" story (see Parker 2: 114–15), a tale of desertion Melville heard in 1852 and then retold to Nathaniel Hawthorne at the height of their literary acquaintance, may have loomed large in Melville's literary imagination long after he had transferred its theme of suffering to the "Chola Widow" section of "The Encantadas" (1854) and developed it alongside the resignation of the humble ass – that same animal that reappears in *Clarel* to carry first the evangelical Nehemiah and then Agath as a symbol of persistence amid resignation.

Melville also knew Agatho as one of the "Persons of the Dialogue" in Plato's "The Banquet. Or, on Love" in his Bohn edition of the *Works* (Bercaw #555): "When we were still children," says Appollodorus, "it was that Agatho won the prize with the first tragedy" (475). And indeed, Agath may have the oldest history of the tragic figures in the poem.

Agath has other names – "pilgrim Greek," "graybeard," and "salted one, / That pickled old sea-Solomon" (3.25.145–6, 150–1), "the mariner" (3.27.30), "timoneer sedate" and "him of salt romance" (4.1.116, 122), "salt one" (4.1.173), "ocean's wrinkled son" (4.2.39), "sea-sage," "sailor," and "shipmate"(4.2.72, 84, 85), "stellar friend" (with the double pun of being tattooed with stars and steering by them) and "tattooed man" (4.2.140, 4.2.142), "man of nature true" (4.2.192), "salt one" and "a sailor" (4.4.30, 40), "mild merman gray" and "salt seer" (4.5.5, 22), and "old man" (4.13.14) – all reinforcing an ancient association with the sea, one that has produced wisdom and woe, but stops just short of madness (unlike that of the dry-land wanderer Ungar, whose gunpowder-peppered face shows he has literally looked too long into the face of the fire).

Agath's second adventure (in the chronology of *Clarel* and the reader's knowledge of him, but not of his life) is succinctly told by the Lesbian merchant, a jovial character who supplies the friars of Mar Saba monastery. A "robber-brood" has fallen upon Agath outside the walls of Mar Saba: "Choking his call, / They beat and stripped him, drawing blood, / And left him prone" (3.12.155–8). Agath's third episode is also one of too-narrowly escaped misfortune – again told by the Lesbian merchant about him rather than by Agath himself: attacked by a bird while aloft at sea, Agath is driven from the yard and falls into the sea, the bird making off with his hat. A shark pursues, him, but he is hauled safely aboard by his shipmates, "Being water-logged with spongy lump / Of quilted patches on the shirt" (3.27.37–8) in an episode mirroring the preceding loss of Mortmain's hat in 3.25 and recalling both the loss of Ahab's hat in *Moby-Dick* (539) and White-Jacket's fall into the sea (392–3). As he regards the Moor whose strong box wrecked the *Peace of God*, Agath thinks the bird who attacked him was "the devil" (3.27.45).

Agath's next episode is brief, but his Elijah-like gesture and cry "Wreck, ho! the wreck – Jerusalem" (4.1.187) leads to the discovery of his elaborate tattoo. His behavior recalls Melville's other crazed prophet: compare Agath, "Forth did his leveled finger go ... For index now as he stretched forth / His loose-sleeved arm in sailor way" (4.1.183, 4.2.43–4), to Elijah, who "levelled his massive fore-finger ... drawing back his whole arm, and then rapidly shoving it straight out from him, with the fixed bayonet of his pointed finger darted full at the object" (*MD* 91).

It is in Agath's final narration that a symphony of sea images comes together from Melville's reading and memory. Vine, a character normally aloof in his aestheticism, is drawn out by Agath (in a way he had not been by Clarel himself): "In those far regions," Vine asks Agath,

> strange or rare,
> Where thou hast been, may aught compare
> With Judah here?"
> (4.2.201–3)

Agath replies that he has been musing over the similarity between stony Judah and "one far isle forever banned / I camped on in life's early days" (4.2.206–7). In the description that follows Melville's primary sources are his own "Encantadas," by extension that work's own sources (Porter and Colnett), and Melville's blurred memories of his own voyaging – now perhaps hopelessly mixed up with his imaginative reading and writing:

> I hear, I see; return those days
> Again – but 'tis through deepening haze:
> How like a flash that life is gone
> (4.2.219–21)

Agath sees his vessel's boats drawn up and flipped over on the beach (whaleboats or ship's boats? one would love to know); in a detail one would like to ascribe to Melville's own memories Agath describes the "harpy sea-hawk" snatching the "hissing meat" (4.2.213, 215) from the fire (in "Sketch First" of "The Encantadas" Melville had written "the chief sound of life here is a hiss" [*PT* 127]); he records the sailors' response, Ancient Mariner-like, of attempting to stone the bird. Although one would like to identify Melville's sea-hawk with something more glamorous, here he is probably referring only to the Dusky, or Galapagos, Gull, *Larus fulginosus*, whose behavior was described by Robert Cushman Murphy in 1936: "They were forever devouring the meat he had hung out to cure ... Of stones tossed toward them they took absolutely no notice unless they were actually hit" (1048). (Although Murphy was one of Melville's earliest readers in the twentieth century, it is highly unlikely he knew of Agath's description in *Clarel*.) In a later detail one hopes equally is first hand, Agath relates the sound of a tortoise collapsing (4.3.90–5), with a continuing comparison to shields and "concussions" that parallels that in "Sketch Second: Two Sides to a Tortoise" (131–2). Ironically, throughout "The Encantadas" Melville had used sustained imagery of a blasted Holy Land that he had visited only in imagination: "Hence, even the Dead Sea, along with whatever other emotions it may at times inspire, does not fail to touch in the pilgrim some of his less unpleasurable feelings," Melville had written in 1854 (126); in *Clarel*, the same Holy and unholy lands are revisited through the character of Agath. Melville almost seems to have had his own work open before him: "It burns by night – by day the cloud / Shows leaden all, and dull and sealed," Agath relates (4.3.1112); "The blacker that cloud by day," Melville had written in "Sketch Fourth: A Pisgah View from the Rock," "the more may you look for light by night" (141).

At the end of Agath's description of the Galapagos, the timoneer himself is implicitly compared to the Albemarle Tortoise or Nehemiah's humble mount:

> He ended, and how passive sate:
> Nature's own look, which might recall
> Dumb patience of mere animal,
> Which better may abide life's fate
> Than comprehend.
>
> (4.3.103–7)

Like the unfortunate Captain Pollard of the whaleship *Essex*, Agath survives only to suffer again. And like Rolfe's oblique description of the unlucky captain in "A Sketch" (1.37), Agath's description of the Galapagos is called a "sketch" (4.3.102), and both titles recall the word used to name the ten sections of "The Encantadas."

Agath's final encounter is with a scorpion, an "unblest, small, evil thing" (4.4.15). Derwent is surprised at the panic displayed by such a witness of the "wonders of the deep" (4.4.33); Rolfe's defense of tried sailors starting at a spider initiates the transition from Agath's post-traumatic stress to that of the Civil War expatriate Ungar. No longer useful to the poem once this transition to a more extreme character type takes place, Agath departs from the pilgrims with a "work-day, passive face": "schooled by the inhuman sea," Agath refuses to engage humanity, "Recalling all the sailing crews / Destined to sleep in ocean sand" (4.13.4, 7, 10–11). A sadder man if only ironically described as wiser for his misfortunes, Melville's ancient mariner is not so socially acquisitive as Coleridge's; the guest-stopping eye is transferred to Derwent, a character associated by name and nature with that other Lake Poet, Wordsworth.

Melville had been a sailor. But at the time he wrote *Moby-Dick* he was a gentleman farmer, and by the time he wrote *Clarel* he was a customs inspector. Melville's various careers caution us against biographical association on the basis of the maritime vocation of a literary character: in a work like *Clarel*, minor characters like Agath and major ones like Rolfe and Clarel – even Vine, a character usually closely associated with Hawthorne – still represent internal aspects of Melville's psyche. These are different from characters who embody the external extremes of what Melville may represent: extreme skepticism, figured temporarily in the poem by the Hawthornean caricature of the geologist Margoth (who must carry a few samples of Berkshire marble left over from "Ethan Brand") but later by the more fully and bitterly developed Ungar, or extreme optimism, represented throughout the poem by Derwent. (Earlier versions of these traits, in the doubter Mortmain and the believer Nehemiah, are killed off by Melville with a mercilessness worthy of a stray bullet from James Fenimore Cooper.) Ironically, a study of maritime character in the poem may have led us circuitously to the conclusion that the character of most persistent interest to Melville is not Vine or Rolfe or the titular Clarel, but the literally gripping Derwent. Melville was never merely a sailor author.

To Hawthorne goes the credit for making the most astute comment by one author on another since Ben Jonson wrote that Shakespeare was "not of an age, but for all time" (vi): of Melville, Hawthorne famously wrote, "He can neither believe, nor be comfortable in his unbelief; and he is too honest and courageous not to try to do one or the other." (quoted in Parker 2: 300). In its mixture of sea and desert imagery, *Clarel* reminds us that, in the words of Sir Humphrey Gilbert, "We are as neere to heaven by sea as by land" (quoted in Hakluyt 8: 74). Or as far away.

REFERENCES AND FURTHER READING

Bercaw, Mary K. *Melville's Sources*. Chicago: Northwestern University Press, 1987.

Blackmore, Richard D. *Bugle of the Black Sea, or, The British in the East*. London: R. Hardwicke, 1855.

Brownell, Henry Howard. *War-Lyrics and Other Poems*. Boston: Ticknor and Fields, 1866.

Byron, Lord George Gordon. *The Poetical Works of Lord Byron*. 10 vols. London: John Murray, 1854.

Cooper, James Fenimore. *The Pilot*. 1849 Rpt. Albany: SUNY Press, 1986.

Garner, Stanton. *The Civil War World of Herman Melville*. Lawrence: University Press of Kansas, 1993.

Gidmark, Jill B. *Encyclopedia of American Literature of the Sea and Great Lakes*. Westport, CT: Greenwood Press, 2001.

Hakluyt, Richard. *The Principal Navigations, Voyages, Traffiques, and Discoveries of the English Nation*. 12 vols. Glasgow: James MacLehose, and New York: Macmillan, 1903–5.

Hayford, Harrison. *Melville's Prisoners*. Evanston, IL: Northwestern University Press, 2003.

Heffernan, Thomas F. *Stove by a Whale: Owen Chase and the* Essex. Middletown, CT: Wesleyan University Press, 1981.

Jonson, Ben. In *Mr. William Shakespeares Comedies, Histories, & Tragedies*. London: Jaggard, 1623.

Madison, R. D. "Melville's Haglets." *Leviathan* 5.2 (2003): 79–83.

—— "The Strange Fowl of 'Benito Cereno.' " *Extracts* 70 (1987): 15–16.

Mickle, William Julius. *The Lusiad; Or, The Discovery of India. An Epic Poem. Translated from* the Original Portuguese of Luis de Camoëns (Oxford: Jackson and Lister, 1776).

Milton, John. *The Poetical Works of John Milton*. 2 vols. Boston: Hilliard, Gray, and Company, 1834.

Murphy, Robert Cushman. *Oceanic Birds of South America*. New York: American Museum of Natural History, 1936.

Philbrick, Thomas. *James Fenimore Cooper and the Development of American Sea Fiction*. Cambridge, MA: Harvard University Press, 1961.

Pommer, Henry. F. *Milton and Melville*. Pittsburgh, PA: University of Pittsburgh Press, 1950.

Porter, David. *Journal of a Cruise*. Annapolis, MD: Naval Institute Press, 1986.

Scott, Sir Walter. *Critical and Miscellaneous Essays*. 3 vols. Philadelphia: Carey and Hart, 1841.

Sealts, Merton. M. *Melville's Reading: Revised and Enlarged Edition*. Columbia: University of South Carolina Press, 1988.

Smyth, W. H. *The Sailor's Word-Book*. London: Blackie and Son, 1867.

Springer, Haskell, ed. *America and the Sea: A Literary History*. Athens: University of Georgia Press, 1995.

Tennyson, Lord Alfred. *Ballads and Other Poems*. London: C. Kegan Paul, 1880.

Tuckerman, Henry T. *Characteristics of Literature*. Philadelphia, PA: Lindsay and Blakiston, 1849.

Vincent, Howard. *The Trying-Out of* Moby-Dick. Boston: Houghton Mifflin, 1949.

19

Death and Literature: Melville and the Epitaph

Edgar A. Dryden

And after all came Life, and lastly Death;
Death with most grim and griesly visage seene,
Yet he is nought but parting of the breath;
Ne ought to see, but like a shade to weene,
Unbodied, unsoul'd, unheard, unseene ....

Spenser, *Faerie Queen* 404

In what census of living creatures, the dead of mankind are included; why is it that a universal proverb says of them, that they tell no tales, though containing more secrets than the Goodwin Sands; how it is that to his name who yesterday departed for the other world, we prefix so significant and infidel a word, and yet do not thus entitle him, if he but embarks for the remotest Indies of this living earth; why the Life Insurance Companies pay death-forfeitures upon immortals; in what eternal, unstirring paralysis, and deadly, hopeless trance, yet lies antique Adam who died sixty round centuries ago; how it is that we still refuse to be comforted for those who we nevertheless maintain are dwelling in unspeakable bliss; why all the living so strive to hush all the dead; wherefore but the rumor of a knocking in a tomb will terrify a whole city. All these things are not without their meanings. (*Moby-Dick*: 36–7)

For Herman Melville writing and death are indissolubly related. He shares with Wordsworth a perception that places the fact of mortality at the origin of language and makes the epitaph emblematic of the literary. For both writers memorializing the dead is the primary theme of the surviving narrator or poet, who not only mourns and tells the dead person's story but also through a process of substitution reflects on his or her own death as if it were an event in the past. I intend here to trace this pattern as it appears in Melville's fiction and poetry and in the process suggest some of the ways Melville's imagination was enabled by his lifelong engagement with the great poets of the past who, as Hershel Parker has shown (2: 402–53), were important to him from the time of his youth and early manhood.

In the first of his "Essays upon Epitaphs" Wordsworth writes that an "Epitaph presupposes a monument upon which it is to be engraven," and goes on to add that tombs without inscriptions, "rude stones placed near the graves, or by mounds of earth raised over them," are the signs of "savage tribes unacquainted with letters." But "as soon as nations had learned the use of letters, epitaphs were inscribed upon these monuments; in order that their intention might be more surely and adequately fulfilled" (*Prose* 2: 49–50). These "engraven record[s]" (59) inscribed on the monument by a "slow and laborious hand" (60) call attention to the double sense of the act of engraving – the burying of a corpse and the making of a mark – and thereby associate death and writing, a process that Wordsworth envisions as giving to the "language of senseless stone a voice enforced and endeared by the benignity of that nature with which it was in unison" (54). This "tender fiction", as he calls it, "harmoniously unites the two worlds of the living and the dead ... " (60).

From its beginning Ishmael's narrative considers the relation between these same two worlds. However, the "frigid inscriptions" that he reads on the "bleak tablets" (*MD* 36) "masoned on the walls" (34) of the Whalemen's Chapel do not offer the "pious admonition to the living, and a humble expression of Christian confidence in immortality" (56) that Wordsworth associates with funerary monuments. Here death is not "disarmed of its sting, and affliction unsubstancialised," for these are not "tranquillising object[s] that lead to a resignation in the course of time" (Wordsworth *Prose* 2: 60). Instead their "immovable inscriptions" seem to "refuse resurrections to the beings who have placelessly perished without a grave" (*MD* 36). Of course, as Bainard Cowan has pointed out, these tablets are cenotaphs because they commemorate persons whose remains are elsewhere (78). And it is the absence of the remains that alerts Ishmael to the uncertainty inherent in the idea of death and leads him briefly proleptically to read his own fate into "the fate of the whalemen who had gone before me. Yes, Ishmael, the same fate may be thine." But soon he grows "merry again," charmed by the "delightful inducements to embark" (37). He reaffirms his decision to take to the sea as a "substitute for pistol and ball" (3), hoping perhaps through the plenitude of action in the "wild and distant seas" among the "undeliverable, nameless perils of the whale" (7) to free death from its inhuman quality. Here in the "wonder-world" (7), "which has for its furthest horizon the freedom to die" (Blanchot 104), Ishmael may be able to demonstrate his capacity to take mortal risks and in so doing triumph over death by making it an object of will.

And indeed in "The Hyena" his response to the "extreme tribulation" (226) that follows his "first lowering" into the "charmed, churned circle of the hunted sperm whale" (224) suggests that his strategy has been successful. He develops a "free and easy sort of genial desperado philosophy" that makes "death itself" seem simply "a part of the general joke" (226), and he gives written expression to this new point of view by producing a rough draft of his will.

This was the fourth time in my nautical life that I had done the same thing. After the ceremony was concluded on the present occasion, I felt all the easier; a stone was rolled away from my heart. Besides, all the days I should now live would be as good as the days Lazarus lived after his resurrection; a supplementary clean gain of so many months or weeks as the case might be. I survived myself; my death and burial were locked up in my chest. I looked round me tranquilly and contentedly, like a quiet ghost with a clean conscience sitting inside the bars of a snug family vault. (227–8)

There is a sense in which Ishmael's will, as he conceives it, is an early inauthentic version of his narrative of self-restoration. But here, as he attempts to establish a fixed boundary between his own life and its contingent surroundings, he imagines himself within a "snug family vault," a structure which, as Jacques Derrida notes, "consecrates the disappearance of life by attesting to the perseverance of life" (82). Death is provided a site that at once is a statement of Ishmael's situation and a figure that seems to contain it, apparently transforming the space of his orphaned existence into the comfortable confines of a family monument. But the duplicity involved in this trick of rhetorical substitution that leaves one's trace in writing is suggested by the figurative stone that replaces the actual one in the biblical account of Lazarus's resurrection (John 11: 41–4) as well as the obvious puns on "will" and "chest." Moreover, in *Mardi* Melville had had Babbalanja observe that after his resurrection Lazarus "rubbed . . . his eyes, and stared . . . most vacantly. Not one revelation did he make" (237). In short, the death Ishmael speaks of here, to use Maurice Blanchot's formulation, is the one "which circulates in the language of possibility, of liberty, which has for its furthest horizon the freedom to die and the capacity to take mortal risks," not that of its "double, which is ungraspable. It is what I cannot grasp, what is not linked to *me* by any relation of any sort. It is that which never comes and toward which I do not direct myself" (104). As Blanchot goes on to suggest, to contemplate suicide is to mistake one death for another, to engage in a "sort of bizarre play on words" (104), for the second has nothing to do with me, and I can know nothing of it. When death is there I am not, and when I am there death is not. Or, as Melville puts the point in *Clarel*: "Alive thou know' st not death; and, dead, / Death thou' lt not know" (2.18.122–3).

As Paul de Man has pointed out, "it is always possible to anticipate one's own epitaph, even to give it the size of the entire Prelude [or *Moby-Dick*], but never possible to be both the one who wrote it and the one who reads it in the proper setting, that is confronting one's grave as an event of the past" (9). As the concluding lines of *Moby-Dick* suggest, the finality and self-sufficient independence of the tomb is absolute: "Now small fowls flew screaming over the yet yawning gulf; a sullen white surf beat against its steep sides; then all collapsed, and the great shroud of the sea rolled on as it rolled five thousand years ago" (572). But as is often the case in literature, there remains some chance survivor to continue the story by providing the dead with voices. In *Moby-Dick* one of Ahab's unnamed oarsmen, hurled from the boat during the final encounter with the whale, remains "still afloat and swimming" (569) "*on the margin of the ensuing scene*" and reappears in the "Epilogue" as Ishmael "*another orphan*," " 'escaped alone to tell thee.' " "*The drama's done. Why then here does any one step forth? – Because one did survive the wreck*" (573). And the survivor's account of his ordeal is a memoir or memorial, an act of mourning that epitaphically at once restores the voices of the departed and in the process exposes the "tender fiction" that supports the strategy.

The "Epilogue" is not presented unambiguously as the proper ending or exemplary conclusion, the endpoint toward which the story has been moving and that will provide a retrospective unity for the whole. Rather, as Ishmael suggests in the final paragraph of "The Castaway," the "Epilogue" stands outside the narrative proper and is an imperfect and mutilated supplement to it. "For the rest, blame not Stubb too hardly. The thing is common in that fishery; and in the sequel of the narrative, it will then be seen what like abandonment befell myself" (414). This proleptic mention of the "Epilogue" in the body of the text is a formal anticipation of that which will violate its symmetry of form, an inscription within the narrative of that which will mark an exit from it. For the sequel succeeds or follows the narrative proper in the form of residue or flotsam.

Without a proper place or name Ishmael survives as one of those "queer castaway creatures found tossing about the open sea on planks, bits of wreck, oars, whale-boats, canoes, blown-off Japanese junks, and what not" (230–1); and it is he who will tell the tale of destruction and death and speak the terrible truth of his own abandonment. His shipmates are dead, and he survives that death to mourn and to narrate their story. But his narration is not an unambiguous form of recollection, as his account of Pip's experience once again suggests:

> It was but some few days after encountering the Frenchman, that a most significant event befell the most insignificant of the Pequod's crew; an event most lamentable; and which ended in providing the sometimes madly merry and predestinated craft with a living and ever accompanying prophecy of whatever shattered sequel might prove her own. (411)

This passage, the first paragraph of "The Castaway," anticipates the chapter's final one (cited above) where Ishmael associates Pip's abandonment with his own. Pip's experience here seems anticipatory or prefigurative – it provides a living prophecy – but that is a quality that it gains retrospectively when read in the light of the narrative's "shattered sequel." This is to say that in *Moby-Dick* the trope of prolepsis seems to exceed its aesthetic function of foreshadowing and to assume the formidable power of the prophetic. Indeed one of the distinguishing features of the novel (as of Melville's work in general) is the way a biblical vocabulary and the worldview it involves is put in the service of the literary.

"The Castaway," like the William Cowper poem it echoes, is an extended epitaph which not only memorializes Pip but anticipates Ishmael's own mortality. Cowper's remarkable poem begins as a description of the memorial account in *A Voyage Round the World* (1748) of one of Admiral George Anson's lost crewmen whose fate seems to the poet to prefigure the poet's own.

> Obscurest night involved the sky,
> Th' Atlantic billows roar'd,
> When such a destin'd wretch as I,

> Wash'd headlong from on board,
> Of friends, of hope, of all bereft,
> His floating home for ever left.
>
> (214, ll. 1–6)

The poet then describes the struggles of the deserted outcast – "In ocean, self-upheld" (l. 38) – as he desperately but hopelessly tries to survive, not, as it turns out, in order to memorialize the "destin'd wretch" but because his situation is a prefiguration of the poet's own death.

> No poet wept him; but the page
>   Of narrative sincere,
> That tells his name, his worth, his age,
>   Is wet with Anson's tear;
> And tears by bards or heroes shed
> Alike immortalize the Dead.
>
> I, therefore, purpose not, or dream,
>   Descanting on his fate,
> To give the melancholy theme
>   A more enduring date;
> But Mis'ry still delights to trace
> Its semblance in another's case.
>
> No voice divine the storm allay'd
>   No light propitious shone,
> When, snatch'd from all effectual aid,
>   We perish'd, each, alone:
> But I, beneath a rougher sea,
> And whelm'd in deeper gulphs than he.
>
> (ll. 49–66)

The relation between the survivor and the dead, traditional focus of the epitaph, is complicated in fascinating and suggestive ways in these admirable lines. Like the whalemen memorialized by the "bleak tablets" in the Whalemen's Chapel, Cowper's "outcast" "placelessly perish[es] without a grave" (36), and yet Anson's textual tears immortalize him, provide him with a monument in the form of the written book. For the poet, however, the memorializing narrative does not produce the "tender similitudes" that Wordsworth imagines passing through the mind of the weary pilgrim halting "in compliance with the invitation, 'Pause, Traveller!' so often found upon the monuments" (54). Indeed, when he traces his face in that of the dead sailor he offers us an account of someone who no longer lives, an account written by someone who is himself speaking from beyond the grave. In other words, he seems to describe that which is in fact unimaginable. Of course, we understand that the poet is reflecting on his current spiritual despair by representing his death as something that happened to the unnamed sailor. And Melville uses this strategy as a model for his account of Pip's significance in Ishmael's narrative.

Pip's abandonment at once results in the death of his conscious self, signified by the disappearance of the personal pronoun "I" – " 'Pip? whom call ye Pip?' " he asks Ahab. " 'Pip jumped from the whale-boat. Pip's missing' " (522) – and offers a living prophecy or prefiguration of the "shattered sequel" that takes the form of Ishmael's Epilogue. To be sure the substitution of the living "he" for the dead "I" does not give us access to the blank of the "endless end" (476) into which "Pip" has vanished, that "only an author from the dead could adequately tell" (477). But it prefigures Ishmael's later awareness of the sense in which his own abandonment repeats Pip's and allows him imaginatively to reconstitute Pip's experience long after the boy's death. For just as Pip's experiences in the "middle of such a heartless immensity" result in the substitution of a third person subject for a first person subject, Ishmael's exposure to that same "awful lonesomeness" (414) leads him to put Pip in the place of "I."

Sharon Cameron writes that "Ishmael is the lone character who does not lose his body to death. But he does become pure voice, relinquishing his life as a character" (66). This is to say that he survives in the form of the voice of the text, that personifying figure that unfreezes pure inscription and resuscitates the natural breath of language in the form of a cacophony of voices and in so doing enacts a fusion of genres – epic, dramatic, lyric, epitaphic – that blurs the boundaries between literature, philosophy, history, and politics. This romantic quality of *Moby-Dick* is nowhere more apparent than in the figure of Pip, who characteristically embodies the fusions and confusions that constitute the novel. "Oh, Pip!" Ishmael writes, "thy wretched laugh, thy idle but unresting eye; all thy strange mummeries not unmeaningly blended with the black tragedy of the melancholy ship, and mocked it!" That "light, unnatural, half-bantering, yet most piteous sound" (490) from beyond the grave resonates throughout the novel, interrupting and ironizing the prophetic and proleptic patterns that order and energize the narrative. Like John Brown of "The Portent," Pip will not rest in peace beneath the "great shroud of the sea" (566). His fears of the white whale and the "big white God" (178) it suggests are also Ishmael's even as is his abandonment. In this sense he exemplifies the critical commonplace that asserts that a successful literary character acquires a life of its own, escaping or exceeding not only the intentions of the author but the finality of death itself. Hence Pip's voice echoes in Ishmael's, an intrusion that precludes the possibility of any formal reconciliation of the novel's tensions.

Nevertheless the tension between the impulse to close and the felt need to tell is an enabling one and suggests that Melville has found a way to integrate a poetics and a hermeneutics of literature. *"The drama's done. Why then here does anyone step forth? – Because one did survive the wreck"* (573). And this survivor is Ishmael, who will tell the story of those now dead, a process emblematized by the coffin lifebuoy covered with the same "hieroglyphic marks" that on Queequeg had seemed "destined in the end to moulder away with the living parchment whereon they were inscribed" (481). As it rises from the center of the vortex to serve as a lifebuoy for Ishmael as well as a written record of his bosom friend, we are reminded that Ishmael will return to write the book in which Queequeg is resurrected epitaphically in the form of a written character.

This emblematic object at once figures the creative tensions of *Moby-Dick* and prefigures the many other forms of inscription – monuments, stones, memorial plaques, ruins and cenotaphs – that mark Melville's later work and point to his continuing concern with the relation between death and writing. As I argue in *Monumental Melville*, this concern is central to *Pierre*, the short fiction, *Israel Potter*, and *The Confidence-Man*, as Melville's negative way leads him to confront and to challenge the Wordsworthian claim for restoration in the face of death, a claim that he comes to see as implicit in the nature of the literary as such. A fine example is Melville's remarkable description in "The Encantadas" of the death of the husband and brother of Hunilla, the Chola widow.

> Before Hunilla's eyes they sank. The real woe of this event passed before her sight as some sham tragedy on the stage. She was seated on a rude bower among the withered thickets, crowning a lofty cliff, a little back from the beach. The thickets were so disposed, that in looking upon the sea at large she peered out from among the branches as from the lattice of a high balcony. But upon the day we speak of here, the better to watch the adventure of those two hearts she loved, Hunilla had withdrawn the branches to one side, and held them so. They formed an oval frame, through which the bluely boundless sea rolled like a painted one. And there, the invisible painter painted to her view the wave-tossed and disjointed raft, its once level logs slantingly upheaved, as raking masts, and the four struggling arms undistinguishable among them; and then all subsided into smooth-flowing creamy waters, slowly drifting the splintered wreck; while first and last, no sound of any sort was heard. Death in a silent picture; a dream of the eye; such vanishing shapes as the mirage shows. (*PT* 154)

In this remarkable passage the real appears as figure, perception as a form of representation. The present, that appears in front of Hunilla's eyes, is already represented. The simple acts of selecting a seat and withdrawing some branches transform the natural into the artificial. She experiences the death of her loved ones as if they were painted figures in a Salvator Rosa sea piece, or a work such as J. M. W. Turner's *The Slave Ship* or Théodore Géricault's *The Raft of the Medusa*. Melville's point seems to be that we can experience death only indirectly at a figurative distance from it. Death appears here as a picture, dream, or mirage, and its truth or reality is rendered only in Hunilla's mute, signless, and senseless response. She "gazed and gazed, nor raised a finger or a wail. But as good to sit thus dumb, in stupor staring on that dumb show" (154).

Some further implications of Hunilla's "nameless misery" (155) appear when we notice that the passage cited above echoes Wordsworth's memorial description in "The Excursion" of a "gentle Dalesman," a deaf mute whose "living ear" hears nothing.

> When stormy winds
> Were working the broad bosom of the lake
> Into a thousand thousand sparkling waves,

Rocking the trees, or driving cloud on cloud
Along the sharp edge of yon lofty crags,
The agitated scene before his eye
Was silent as a picture . . . .
                              (*Poetical Works* VII: ll. 409–15)

Wordsworth goes on to describe the solace that the Dalesman takes in books, "ready comrades" (l. 440) whose "familiar voice, / Even to old age, with unabated charm / Beguiled his leisure hours" (ll. 442–4); and after his death this voice is replaced by that of the "monumental stone" that "preserves / His name, and unambitiously relates / How long, and by what kindly outward aids, / And in what pure contendedness of mind, / The sad privation was by him endured" (ll. 472–6). The Dalesman's deprivation is partially compensated for by means of books, which have a voice that he can hear. But the nature of that voice is suggested by Wordsworth's focus on their role as "ready comrades" for a deaf-mute. As Cynthia Chase puts the point, "books do not have a voice themselves; they provide a substitute 'voice,' once they have been personified (as 'ready comrades' in the phrase of 'The Excursion' " (59). And if the voice of the books that beguile the deaf-mute is figurative or fictive, that of the monumental stone that "unambitiously relates" his "sad privation" is doubly so, for in speaking to its readers as books spoke to the deaf-mute, it offers them in their muteness "death in a silent picture."

What, then, is at stake in Melville's borrowing from Wordsworth? Does he, for example, like Wordsworth and Keats, who turn to Milton when their own voices are threatened, or like the Dalesman himself, seek a compensatory voice in the "ready comrades" of books (Chase 61)? My discussion, I hope, suggests that the answer is no. Indeed, Melville's turn to poetry after *The Confidence-Man* is one indication of his growing suspicion of Wordsworth's assumption that written language is a copy of living speech, of the idea that the text has a voice, one that in a novel takes the form of literary character. As Elizabeth Renker has shown, Melville's relation to his writing from the beginning of his career was a material one that has the effect of distancing him from the experience that he describes by focusing his attention on the act of writing itself. Of course, Wordsworth is also fascinated by written language, as his interest in the epitaph and other forms of inscriptive poetry suggests. But as the "Essays upon Epitaphs" make clear, he insists on maintaining a connection between the engraved marks on stone and living speech, a tie that Melville systematically puts into question.

The formal and generic implications of Melville's critique of Wordsworth become even more apparent when he turns, in mid-life, from fiction to poetry. His "Verses Inscriptive and Memorial" in *Battle-Pieces* (itself an epitaphic collection) violate the generic expectations of the epitaph as Wordsworth defines them by putting into question Wordsworth's assertion that "a sepulchral monument is a tribute to man as a human being; and . . . an epitaph . . . is a record to preserve the memory of the dead, as a tribute due to his individual worth, for a satisfaction to the sorrowing hearts of the survivors, and for the common benefit of the living" (*Prose* 53). Almost all of

Melville's verses memorialize the anonymous dead, and several focus on the unmarked mound and uninscribed stone that Wordsworth associates with "savage tribes." "An Uninscribed Monument," memorializing those who had died in the battles Melville describes in "The Armies of the Wilderness," offers an illuminating example.

> Silence and Solitude may hint
>   (Whose home is in yon piney wood)
> What I, though tableted, could never tell —
> The din which here befell,
>   The striving of the multitude.
> The iron cones and spheres of death
>   Set round me in their rust,
>   These, too, if just,
> Shall speak with more than animated breath.
>   Thou who beholdest, if thy thought,
> Not narrowed down to personal cheer,
> Take in the import of the quiet here —
>   The after-quiet — the calm full fraught;
> Thou too wilt silent stand —
> Silent as I, and lonesome as the land.
>
> *(Poems* 126)

In "The Armies of the Wilderness" the poet is unable to "narrate that strife in the pines" because the dead are "Sole solvers" of the "riddle of death," and his poem is contaminated by the scandal of the unburied corpse, the *"shroudless dead"* (75). "In glades they meet skull after skull / Where pine-cones lay — the rusted gun, / Green shoes full of bones, the mouldering coat / And cuddled-up skeleton" (73). And since *"No priest with book and band / Shall come to the secret place / Of the corpse in the foeman's land,"* only silence, solitude, and the poet's "obscure" and "entangled rhyme" (75) are left to hint at the din and death. In "An Uninscribed Monument" this hinting seems to follow Wordsworth's strategy of "giving to the language of senseless stone a voice" (*Prose* 54), but the voice in this case is not that of the traditional epitaph that "so often personate[s] and represent[s] him [the deceased] as speaking from his own tomb-stone." This "tender fiction" (60) is replaced here with one that exposes the secret absurdity underlying such strategies. The "I" of this poem is not that of the inscribed or "tableted" monument that in traditional inscriptive poetry is the natural or material element presupposed by the text, whose existence depends upon the particular fact that the poem is relating. The text here is not as in Wordsworth understood either as a reproduction of the letters "engraven" with "slow and laborious hand" (60), as a monument figured as speaking, or as the representation of the situation of the weary traveler who "in compliance with the invitation, 'Pause Traveller!' " (54), stops to repose and read. In the case of Melville's poem there seems to be no explanation for how the lines came to be there on the page, for the voice here is that of an uninscribed monument, a logical and thematic impossibility; and "it," in turn, asserts that the rusted guns and cannon-balls, the lone remnants of the "din which here befell . . . if just, / Shall speak with more than animated breath." This line is a strange one for several reasons. To begin with, the word "just" seems used here in the sense of being in accordance with reason, truth, or fact, and this meaning of the word seems to disqualify without erasing its sense of combat or joust suggested by the military context; and the rest of the line seems to allude to the traditional figure of the gun that speaks death but in a way that violates poetic logic. The rusted cones and spheres obviously can no longer speak in the sense intended by the conventional trope but are now said to speak with "more than animated breath," a strikingly difficult and ambiguous phrasing. The poem not only attempts to give life and voice to those inanimate and now useless instruments of death but to endow them with a power that exceeds that of both animated nature, which is said to be the home of "Silence and Solitude," and the poetic "I," which is also silent. What needs to be said here, apparently, lies beyond the power of figure as conventionally conceived and hence must be hinted at rather than spoken.

The form and nature of this hinting are the subjects of the poem's final six lines, which employ and put into question the epitaphic convention of the address to the reader, an address traditionally based either on the fiction of the dead speaking or the figures of the survivors who celebrate the lives of the dead and lament their passing. But here there is nothing to read, no "tender fiction" of a voice from the grave, no inscription representing the grief of the survivors who "speak in their own persons" (*Prose* 60, 61), only a mute scene of looking at an unlettered stone. There is no trope to supply a "tongue to muteness," and the reader ("Thou who beholdest") in the face of universal absence takes on the mute fixity of stone, caught, it would appear, in the "after-quiet" world of the dead, a world capable of being represented only by a text that speaks silence.

At issue here is Melville's response to the familiar Romantic problem of the relation between nature and the imagination, one standard version of which appears in the "Prospectus" to "The Excursion."

> Would I arouse the sensual from their sleep
> Of Death, and win the vacant and the vain
> To noble raptures; while my voice proclaims
> How exquisitely the individual Mind
> (And the progressive powers perhaps no less
> Of the whole species) to the external World
> Is fitted: – and how exquisitely, too –
> Theme this but little heard of among men –
> The external World is fitted to the Mind;
> And the creation (by no lower name
> Can it be called) which they with blended might
> Accomplish: – this is our high argument.
>
> (*Poetical Works* ll. 60–71)

Present here is the system of thought that underlies the poet's famous discussion of books and reading in Book Five of "The Prelude," where the "speaking face of earth and heaven" (l. 13) appears as that "bodily image" (l.16) informed with a "deathless spirit" (l. 18) by the "sovereign Intellect" (l. 15), and the human mind, in turn, "stamp[s]" (l. 46) its image on books. As Wordsworth goes on to suggest, however, this analogy between Mind and Nature is not completely symmetrical. The "living Presence" would "subsist" (l.34) in Nature even in the face of apocalyptic fire and earthquake, whereas the products of the mind "must perish" (l. 22).

> Oh! Why hath not the Mind
> Some element to stamp her image on
> In nature somewhat nearer to her own?
> Why, gifted with such powers to send abroad
> Her spirit, must it lodge in shrines so frail?
> (ll. 45–9)

Books become for Wordsworth "Poor earthly casket[s]" (l. 164): as engraven objects, they at once remind the poet of death and protect him from it by giving him a way to stamp his image on matter. For Melville, however, the analogy between mind and nature, books and nature does not hold, as the following passage from one of the Dead Sea cantos in *Clarel* makes clear.

> Some fed upon the natural scene,
> Deriving many a wandering hint
> Such as will oftimes intervene
> When on the slab ye view the print
> Of perished species. – Judge Rolfe's start
> And quick revulsion, when, apart,
> Derwent he saw at ease reclined,
> With page before him, page refined
> And appetizing, which threw ope
> New parks, fresh walks for Signor Hope
> To saunter in.
>   "And read you here?
> Scarce suits the ground with bookish cheer.
> Escaped from forms, enlarged at last,
> Pupils we be of wave and waste –
> Not books; nay, nay!"
>   "Book comment, though," –
> Smiled Derwent – "were it ill to know?"
>   "But how if nature vetoes all
> Her commentators? Disenthrall
> Thy Heart. Look round. Are not here met
> Books and that truth no type shall set?" –
> . . .

> "Were it a paradox to confess
> A book's a man? If this be so,
> Books be but part of nature. Oh,
> 'Tis studying nature, reading books:
> And 'tis through Nature each heart looks
> Up to a God, or whatsoe'er
> One images beyond our sphere.
> Moreover, Siddim's not the world:
> There's Naples."
>
> (*C* 2.32.44–63, 75–83)

Juxtaposed in this interesting passage are two conflicting views of the natural world. Derwent's perspective is the result of an anthropomorphism whereby human traits are unthinkingly projected onto the landscape. "Through nature," he says, each heart looks up to a higher being "beyond our sphere," echoing Wordsworth's description (cited above) of the relation between mind and nature in the early lines of "The Prelude." The normally bookish Rolfe, on the other hand, finds that the "wave and waste" of the desolate landscape disenthralls the magic of the book's measured forms and hints at a "truth no type shall set." That truth, apparently, is the unnamed otherness inhabiting but hidden by the figurations supporting our comfortable conviction that "Books be but part of nature" and hinted at here by the fossilized "print of perished species" that is juxtaposed to Derwent's printed text. This fossilized print of death undermines the Wordsworthian assumption that the stamping of the mind's image in a book ("Prelude" V, ll. 45–6) or the minting of a literary character is analogous to the process by which the deathless spirit stamps its image on nature. The "print of perished species" is the sign of that which has no name and puts an end to writing and reading.

Melville, however, continues to write, although after *Clarel* his poetry is privately published in editions of twenty-five copies. And he continues sardonically to invoke and reject the possibility of any spiritualization of nature. Indeed, as the sign of death, nature is the realm of the absolute Other and the absolute end. In *John Marr and Other Sailors*, for example, he invokes the tradition of romantic nature poetry, in particular that of the elegy and epitaph, but he does so in order to mark his distance from it. The world of *John Marr* is one marked by the "vague reserve of heaven" (*Poems* "The Haglets" 225) and "the apathy of Nature" ("John Marr" 199), a world where the poet's voice is returned neither by an echoing landscape nor by the voices of his fellow creatures. John Marr, like Wordsworth in "The Mountain Echo," seeks "Answers, and we know not whence; / Echoes from beyond the grave, / Recognised intelligence" (*Poetical Works* 166, ll. 14–16) but hears only the sound of his own words. For in Melville's sea world, nature and consciousness, imagination and perception are completely distinct realms, the world's being an absolute Other.

> In hollows of the liquid hills
>   Where the long Blue Ridges run,
> The flattery of no echo thrills,

> For echo the seas have none;
>   Nor aught that gives man back man's strain –
> The hope of his heart, the dream in his brain.
>   (*Poems* "Pebbles" 243)

Echoes for Melville are not, as they are for Wordsworth, figures of representation pointing to a direct connection between the human and natural worlds. The poetic tradition evoked by the poet's figuring the waves as mountains, a tradition where echoes are understood as "Images of voice," as they are in Wordsworth's "On the Power of Sound" (185, l. 34), and nature is represented as sending an "Unsolicited reply / To a babbling wanderer" ("Mountain Echo," ll. 5–6), works only to emphasize the distance that separates it from the poet's sea world. In the same way, Melville's "wailing" (232) Aeolian harp is not the voice of Coleridge's "one life within us or abroad" (*Coleridge* 28, l. 26). Here is "less a strain ideal / Than Ariel's rendering of the Real" ("The Aeolian Harp" 232). And that "Real" is a tale of sea sorrow suggested by "a picture stamped in memory's mint" (232), that of a wrecked lumberman. "Dismasted and adrift," "oozy as the oyster-bank," "waterlogged," "by trailing weeds beclogged," the wreck drifts "pilotless on pathless way" (232–3). This tranformation of an object that once belonged to the human world results in something more deadly than the "sunken reef," for it drifts "waylayingly," now "fatal only to the *other*" (233).

For the poet the "wail" of the wind-harp generates a picture that hints at change that can never be remembered or narrated because it can never be present, the change that is death: "Well the harp of Ariel wails / Thoughts that tongue can tell no word of!" (233). As the Other of consciousness and language, the blank that inhabits human life, death is never experienced as an event. As J. Hillis Miller has said, it "is an area in the mind that cannot be humanized" (250) – that is to say faced and named directly – and as such it is a reminder of the inhuman, of physical nature, represented in *John Marr* by the "implacable Sea."

> Implacable I, the old implacable Sea
>   Implacable most when most I smile serene –
> Pleased, not appeased, by myriad wrecks in me.
>   (*Poems* "Pebbles" 244)

Here we see most clearly the distance that separates Melville's poetics from those of Wordsworth. No less imaginary than the I AM of the Old Testament, the "Implacable I" is a figure that silences even as it seems to confer a voice, for it suggests the linguistic artifice by which the trope of personification operates. That process here takes the form of the uncovering of the natural or material veiled by the trope, the "myriad wrecks," "fatal only to the *other*" (233) that give evidence of the shapeless materiality behind human forms.

Melville, then, employs the conventional tropes of Romantic poetry, unwinds them from their conventional meanings, and in doing so exposes the truth that literature, poetry in a more obvious way than fiction, is an attempt to fill the silence and blankness of death with a form and a voice. For Melville, even more than for Wordsworth, the epitaph becomes a model for literature, not because it restores and preserves the writer's voice but because it exposes that concept as the fiction that it is.

References and Further Reading

Blanchot, Maurice. *The Space of Literature*. Trans. Ann Smock. Lincoln: University of Nebraska Press, 1989.

Cameron, Sharon. *The Corporeal Self: Allegories of the Body in Melville and Hawthorne*. Baltimore: Johns Hopkins University Press, 1988.

Chase, Cynthia. *Decomposing Figures: Rhetorical Readings in the Romantic Tradition*. Baltimore: Johns Hopkins University Press, 1988.

Coleridge, Samuel Taylor. *Samuel Taylor Coleridge*. Ed. H. J. Jackson. New York: Oxford University Press, 1985.

Cowan, Bainard. *Exiled Waters: Moby-Dick and the Crisis of Allegory*. Baton Rouge: Louisiana State University Press, 1982.

Cowper, William. *The Poems of William Cowper*. Ed. John D. Baird and Charles Ryskamp. 3 vols. Oxford: Clarendon Press, 1995.

de Man, Paul. "Time and History in Wordsworth." *Diacritics* 17 (1989): 4–17.

Derrida, Jacques. *Margins of Philosophy*. Trans. Alan Bass. Chicago: University of Chicago Press, 1982.

Dryden, Edgar A. *Monumental Melville: The Formation of a Literary Career*. Stanford, CA: Stanford University Press, 2004.

Melville, Herman. *Poems*. Vol. 16 of *The Works of Herman Melville*. Standard Edition, 16 vols. London: Constable, 1924.

Miller, J. Hillis. *Ariadne's Thread: Story Lines*. New Haven: Yale University Press, 1992.

Renker, Elizabeth. *Strike Through the Mask: Herman Melville and the Scene of Writing*. Baltimore: Johns Hopkins University Press, 1996.

Spenser, Edmund. *Faerie Queene*. Ed. J. C. Smith and E. de Selincourt. Oxford: Oxford University Press, 1977.

Wordsworth, William. *Poetical Works*. Ed. Thomas Hutchinson. Rev. ed. by Ernest de Selincourt. Oxford: Oxford University Press, 1988.

——— . *The Prose Works of William Wordsworth*. Ed. W. J. B. Owen and Jane Worthington Smyser. 3 vols. Oxford: Clarendon Press, 1974.

20

The Company of Women Authors

Charlene Avallone

Just what do we know about women authors and Melville? Remarkably little. In a 1987 catalogue of more than seven hundred inquiries into Melville's reading and source use undertaken since 1928 (Bercaw), fewer than twenty-five works written by women make an appearance. Into the 1990s even respected scholarly journals published claims that Melville lacked any interest in women writers, a view supported by much biographical interpretation of the author before Laurie Robertson-Lorant's *Melville* (1996). The models of authorship and of the literary marketplace that critics have applied in efforts to understand the context in which Melville and women wrote have reinforced the divide. As feminist studies and a revival of historical studies make their impact on how we think about literature, however, scholars have begun to expand the list of Melville's possible sources and analogues among women's texts or to give some sense of the ways that Melville and some women writers addressed similar concerns, worked within the same literary culture, or responded to the same set of historical conditions. The more we study women writers, the more aware we become of their influence on Melville's writing and on the world he inhabited. And we recognize in that world the coincidence of Melville's career, and the careers of the first critical mass of (white and black) women authors in the United States, with the emergence of cultural nationalism and industrial capitalism, marked by expanding education, new practices of creative writing and criticism that we would recognize as professional, the rise of a mass audience and a new genre hierarchy privileging fiction and journalism, and the escalation of racial and ethnic conflicts, all of which history invites interest in Melville and women writers together. Still, the relations between women and Melville remain understudied, "exasperatingly" so in the view of some scholars (Bryant 79).

So what do we know? We know that the texts of women writers were in libraries accessible to Melville from the beginning. His mother's collection contained books by women that later passed into his own library, along with others signed by his sisters. The *London Carcanet*, the anthology that Melville won as a schoolboy prize at the Albany Academy (Sealts no. 331), includes extracts from the writing of Joanna Baillie, Caroline Bowles, Charlotte Smith, and Jane Porter. The Albany Young Men's Association, which Melville joined as a teenager, appears to have offered titles by women in biography, history, and travels, as well as in the forms that we now classify as literature. Aboard Melville's first whaling ship were texts by Lydia Maria Child, Mary Howitt, Eliza Leslie, and probably Catharine Sedgwick and others, and the volumes of Harper's Family Library aboard the *United States* may have included some by Anna Jameson (Heflin 11–15). Letters and journals tell us that certain women writers' texts made their way into Melville's own library or into loud readings in the family circle (see Sealts; Kelley " 'Literary Thirst' ").

We know from Melville's journal that he held a high opinion of Caroline Kirkland and from his marginalia that he held in even higher esteem Germaine de Staël and Elizabeth Barrett Browning (*J* 8; Cowen 11: 114). Indeed, he turned to Barrett Browning in teaching himself to write poetry (Freibert). He thought enough of Anna Jameson's criticism to give to his daughter Bessie her *Characteristics of Women*, with its combined analyses of Shakespeare's female characters and the condition of nineteenth-century British women (Sealts no. 295). Allusions in Melville's own publications tell us that he likely read more texts by female authors than those that have survived in the remnants of his library or, at the least, he knew a good deal about them through intermediary sources. Parallels of theme, style, and structure in his writings and women's suggest additional links with contemporaries, as well as with later women writers (see, for example, Davis, Brown, Weinauer, Otter, Cahir). We know Melville dined with Catharine Sedgwick, argued by many to be the first American female writer of substantial international standing, and that her fiction was the subject of conversation at other social functions he attended in the Berkshires (Robertson-Lorant 289; Parker 1: 747–8). We know as well that Melville occasionally attended the celebrated Saturdays hosted by poet and teacher Ann Lynch; and while we do not know precisely which writers he may have met at these literary receptions, we do know that journalists who published responses to Melville's work – Margaret Fuller, Grace Greenwood, Caroline Kirkland, and Elizabeth Oakes Smith, in addition to Lynch herself – circulated there (see Leyda 1: 266; Kelley " 'Literary Thirst' " 50; Robertson-Lorant 175–6, 178; Parker 1: 585). Later reports, around the time he was writing *Battle-Pieces*, notice Melville in attendance at the Sunday evening receptions of Alice and Phoebe Cary (Leyda 2: 676–7), where writers including Oakes Smith, Elizabeth Stoddard, Anna Dickinson, Jennie June (Jane Cunningham Croly), Elizabeth Cady Stanton, and Mary E. Dodge appeared from time to time. Reviews and other publications show that Melville's writings made their way into the libraries of his American female contemporaries, who exhibit a broad range of reactions to them. From evidence currently available, however, we can suspect Melville's own greater appreciation of the writing of English and French women than that of Americans.

If we know all this, then why the complaint of a vexing deficiency in studies of Melville and women authors? Criticism largely has not adjusted its paradigms to accommodate such information. Literary history has been organized by nationalist and gender divisions that lead to discussing Melville as a representative American author in the company of other American men whose writing is presumed to be superior to that of women authors. Even when critics have placed Melville in the company of women writers, instead of analyzing their texts on the bases of internal or external evidence of their affiliations, studies have generally preferred to suppose analogues that correspond to critical paradigms of inferior female authorship, particularly analogues categorized as sentimental fiction or bestsellers, categories that have been used to depreciate the writing of "Mrs. [Susannah] Rowson and her imitators" (Charvat 251–2; and see 276), "Mrs. Sigourney's tales," and "bestsellers cranked out by women like Mrs. E. D. E. N. Southworth" or Susan Warner (Douglas 312). How did this come about?

Contemporary reviews might lead you to expect that you would have found the publications of Melville and women writers alike in private and circulating libraries of the day, and some evidence indicates that this was indeed the case (see Zboray 156–79; Post-Lauria, e.g. 3, 128, 153–4, 156–63). One popular magazine enthused at mid-century, "Our most brilliant and popular authors are sailors and women," such as Melville and Caroline Chesebro' (*Holden's Dollar Magazine* January 1850, 61 and see 55). Indeed, the similar popularity of these two writers was cited as demonstrating the success of American literature, the intimate character of literary relations between the US and Britain, and the need for international copyright law (*Holden's Dollar Magazine* May 1850, 316–17). Another journal placed Melville and Harriet Beecher Stowe side by side as exemplars of American literary artistry (*Putnam's Monthly Magazine* January 1853, 102). But at the same time, reading practices that appreciated both men and women writers came into tension with the dominant gender ideology that pre-scribed separate spheres for the sexes. Literary criticism brought notions of self-evident male superiority to explain the resulting contradictions. In the process, even women writers who were selected to remain in libraries across generations as "classic authors" were sorted by gender-specific categories of literary production and assessed as inferior to men. William A. Jones, for example, a colleague of Melville in publisher Evert Duyckink's literary circle and argued by some to be America's first professional literary critic, made one such case in an essay he wrote in the mid-1840s and frequently republished, "The Ladies' Library."

Jones, reviewing the previous century of women in England and the US as both producers and consumers of literature, would turn male bias and assumptions of ascendancy into matters of common sense and literary judgment. "We believe the question as to the relative sexual distinctions of intellectual character is now generally considered as settled," he asserts. "There is allowed to be a species of genius essentially feminine," but even "[t]he most limited observation ... must effectually demonstrate the superior capacity of man" (Jones 137). Jones concedes women may possess talent sufficient to merit a place on "a list of classic authors" for their writing (140), which he categorizes as

> easy narrative, ... lively descriptions of natural beauty or artificial manners, ... airy, comic ridicule ... the novel of sentiment and the novel of manners, [letters], moral tales for children, books of travels, [and] gossipping [*sic*] memoirs. (138, 140)

Yet women lack the genius to influence male writers ("become instructors of men") or themselves to write epics, tragedies, comedies, wit or humor, poetry, history, oratory, political economy, or novels of genius (140). Had questions of gender and intellect been settled, of course, Jones would not have needed to argue them for the length of his essay. Indeed, they remained the subject of vigorous contemporary debate. The notion of male superiority that Jones presents as so self-evident an index of men's writerly excellence appeared to others rather as an erroneous belief that demanded correction.

Notably, Margaret Fuller interpreted the notion of male supremacy as a sign of the need to reform ideas about gender for the welfare of both women and men, who, she believed, alike embodied and expressed mixtures of what was designated "masculine" and "feminine" creative energy (Fuller *Woman* 161–2, and see 96–101). Like Fuller, Fanny Fern would satirize the presumption of male superiority, figuring it in a pompous professor who opines that "the *female* mind is incapable of producing anything which may be strictly termed *literature*" (Fern 166, emphasis in original). Even among women writers who might express more agreement with the dominant theory of difference, some in practice challenged the limitations and debasement of its categorizations. Ann Stephens, for instance, who once wrote that "women of genius" composed something called "female literature" that was compatible with domesticity and no threat to compete with men (*Hesperian*, August 1839, 244), built her own reputation on "highly-wrought fiction" that was rated as overly ambitious and encroaching on male territory, but that nevertheless earned her a success finally greater than even bestselling novels of more approved sentiment (Baym "Novels" 208). The more that flourishing female writers and the nascent woman's movement challenged stereotypes of male incomparability, however, the more reactionary critics reiterated the self-evident "fact," even in venues with a reputation for being intellectually and politically progressive: "Woman is by nature inferior to man ... in intellect ... by the absolute decree of nature" (*Putnam's*, March 1853, 285).

Melville apparently shared in some sense of the era's widespread gendering of qualities such as understanding and emotion, although not in the worst of its reactionary male defensiveness, for his marginalia registered wonder and delight at discovering a mix of the two – "such penetration of understanding" combined with "so feminine & emotional a nature" – in Germaine de Staël's *Germany* (in Cowen 11: 114). Further, a line that he drew in the margin of that text, apparently seconding the editor's comment that "we agree with Sir James Mackintosh in regarding [*Germany*] as the greatest production of feminine genius," could, with equal probability, join in relegating Staël to the secondary rank accorded women authors as a class or join in the defense of her against hostile public opinion, such as Talleyrand's attacks on her femininity (in Cowen 11: 2). While Melville also valued Mary Shelley sufficiently to seek out a copy of *Frankenstein* and keep it in his library for more than four decades, he drew a line by a passage in one of her letters wherein she expressed her "belief" that "whether there be sex in souls or not – that the sex of [women's] material mechanism makes us quite different creatures; better, though weaker, but wanting in the higher grades of intellect" (in Cowen 10: 97).

When Melville, like Fuller and Jones earlier, wrote under the patronage of Evert Duyckinck promoting American literary nationalism, the writers his *Mosses* essay named as of a "calibre" that merited the nation "take [them] to her bosom" and "lavish her embraces" upon them like a mother were all male (*PT* 247). Expressing his disinclination to join "those, who ... 'exalt the reputation of some, in order to depress that of others' " (245), Melville in promoting American men nonetheless diminishes the place that women enjoyed in the national literature in the estimation of both general readers and many critics. Melville includes in his representative American library a range of men's production – the sentimental prose and poetry of Irving and Willis along with the transcendental idealism of Emerson and Hawthorne's Calvinistic short fiction, as well as the varied work of Whittier, Bryant, Dana, and Cooper – (although he believes none equals Shakespeare), while he excludes the women writers that Fuller and even Jones, for example, recognize – Lydia Maria Child, Caroline Kirkland, Ann Stephens, and the one American Jones counts among "classic authors" in his international "ladies' library," Catharine Sedgwick (Jones 140; see Fuller, "American Literature"). Whether Melville would find women writers among the unnamed "others of like calibre among us" toward whom his essay gestures or among the "mediocrity" that he defends for nationalistic if not literary value is uncertain (247). Unlike the case of Hawthorne and other male contemporaries with whom he is often grouped as an antagonist of female contemporaries (Gilmore; Romero 12–17), however, with Melville no evidence suggests that he protested against women as rivals for cultural leadership and audience, damned them as mere scribblers, or fantasized that women who aspired to authorship be punished with facial mutilation.

Gender assumptions continued to demote women when nineteenth-century writers began to be incorporated into academic libraries. With the emergence of the collegiate study of American literature in the latter part of the century, neither the popular nor the critical regard of contemporary or later audiences sufficed to guarantee enduring recognition to writers of either sex. Herman Melville is not to be found with the "masters" of fiction (Cooper, Hawthorne, and Poe) nor indeed anywhere in Charles Richardson's *American Literature* (1886, 1888), regarded as the first history of the topic; and the bestselling authors Maria Cummins, Harriet Beecher Stowe, and Susan Warner (labeled sentimental and pious) warrant inclusion with Catharine Sedgwick (labeled a writer for children) only among "lesser novelists," with Stowe's story collections admitted as "additions to our rich library of folk-sketches" (Richardson

1: 409–10). By the turn into the next century, the influential *Literary History of America* (1900) by Barrett Wendell would write both Melville and women (excepting only Stowe) out of the nation's literary past.

> There are certain names which we might have mentioned; Mrs. Kirkland ... wrote some sketches ... which are still vivid .... Hermann [*sic*] Melville, with his books about the South Seas, which Robert Louis Stevenson is said to have declared the best ever written, and with his novels of maritime adventure, began a career of literary promise, which never came to fruition. (229)

Women authors, like Melville, nonetheless continued to be kept alive in private libraries and an occasional critical notice. Yet the modernists' recovery of his work that would solidly enshrine it in academic libraries by the 1930s served only to bury women authors more deeply in obscurity and to reinforce the equation of female authorship with sentimentality and lesser worth. Scholarship of the Melville revival in the 1920s, as part of the agenda of "masculinizing American culture," construed Melville as the premier classic writer in American literature (Lauter 216). Over subsequent decades, the elaborating of the romance and Renaissance theses of American literature, which both exploited and further enhanced that stature, continued to oppose Melville's greatness to women's absence from the field.

The study of Melville's library in those early decades of his revival – his reading, allusions, sources, analogues, and influences – supposed the unique significance of male writers as it contributed to amplifying his pre-eminence. Most of this scholarship focused on the stimulus that Melville found in earlier men's writing and on his creative responses to those texts, building his stature through association with such literary masters as Shakespeare and Milton. Scholars who shared little of Melville's reluctance to depress the reputation of some in order to exalt that of others reinforced his greatness through comparisons that devalued women's writing in studies that sustained claims for his superiority by actively dissociating him from female writers and cheapening their achievements. The case of Ann Radcliffe suggests some of the strategies as well as the critical energy that were invested in combating the very idea of a woman's influence on a classic male author, as much anathema to some modernist critics as it had been to nineteenth-century reactionaries like Jones.

Internal evidence signifying that Radcliffe epitomized discourses of the mysterious and the horrible in Melville's imagination recurs often enough in his writings to exert some claim on scholarly attention. Anne Elwood's *Memoirs of the Literary Ladies of England* (1843), which survived into Melville's library from his sister Augusta's collection, testified to Radcliffe's celebrity in these genres, as well as to her literary "genius," originality, and "intellectual power," on no lesser authority than that of Walter Scott (Elwood 2: 159, 172). Yet the critic who took up the question of the relationship between Melville and Radcliffe framed it as a joke. He insisted that any "first response" to Melville's allusions to her "is bound to" trivialize the very thought of a significant connection:

Billy Budd and the *Mysteries of Udolpho*! ... Herman Melville and Mrs. Ann Radcliffe! Surely these are little better than laughable juxtapositions, and nothing could be idler or more pedantic than to look [at them] closely and seriously. (Arvin "Melville and the Gothic" 33)

Given such presuppositions, only the assumption of Melville's superiority could justify any serious comparison.

[He] would not be the first writer of great power to owe a certain debt to one of his small predecessors.... [O]f course, ... his mind was a very complex one.... [and] every element in the sensibility of a writer like Melville has its interest and meaning for us. (33)

At issue is the relative power of the male and female writers, not any investigation of the kind of power that Radcliffe's writing held in Melville's perception or in their literary era, and for a modernist critic the relative power of the male writer could be as self-evident and yet as needful of contention as it had been to the forerunners who defended male supremacy in the previous century. "It is, of course, Melville's own ... powers that are really important in these passages" (38). The "deeper meaning" requiring attention resides in Melville's text alone, not in Radcliffe's writing or in any intertextuality: "one speaks of these connections only for what they are, no more" (44). Although Radcliffe's writing may afford precedents for the landscape writing, symbolism, characterization, and gothic genre features and thematics in several of Melville's works (*Typee*, *White-Jacket*, *Moby-Dick*, *Pierre*, "The Encantadas," "Benito Cereno," and *Clarel*, in addition to *Billy Budd*), none of these has significance for criticism in terms of Radcliffe's own work, or of literary or contextual history, or even, finally, the workings of Melville's imagination and techniques of composition; the only thing that signifies is the superiority, in this case the "[p]rofoundly romantic" sensibility, that can be uniquely attributed to Melville and (despite Melville's own categorization of Radcliffe as a romantic in his story "The Apple-Tree Table") invoked to render the woman writer – self-evidently – inconsequential. The critic "need hardly add that the center of [Melville's] mind, in any case, lay elsewhere, or that the effect upon him even of a minor master, such as Mrs. Radcliffe certainly was, could never have been a vital one" (47). Such criticism as this, significant in marginalizing the relationship between Melville and one female influence, is even more important for its open exposure of assumptions that operated more broadly to mute the discussion of women writers in criticism of Melville.

Even when serious, respectful study presented a case that women's writing afforded a significant analogue for understanding Melville's work, as Merrell Davis did for Frances Osgood's *The Poetry of Flowers and the Flowers of Poetry*, later criticism was quick to diminish that writing as "less worthy" than men's (Arvin *Herman Melville* 90). Scholarship attempted to displace to a female relative Melville's interest in the analogue; to consign it to merely "backdrop," "largely ornament," despite acknowledging that it provided Melville's text with an important structural frame (Hillway 9); and to class it in a strain of writing by or for women that some "freak of taste" kept "[s]omewhere on the circumference of his mind" and resurfacing in his work as "languors, ... limp passages, ... insipidities" (Arvin *Herman Melville* 125).

Less strenuous means also served to marginalize women authors in Melville studies. Later criticism could rest in assumptions that a male writer of such supremacy as has been claimed for Melville would approach an American woman author only to satirize her limitations, as was premised of Melville's relation to Catharine Sedgwick, obviating the need to speculate about the possibilities of other, more positive connections with her, and thus setting a precedent that endures in scholarship (see Bickley 81–2; Douglas 300; see also, for example, Colatrella 184). Internal and external evidence of Melville's interest in women authors often is simply ignored. Of the two women whose greatness he most admired, there was no study of Elizabeth Barrett Browning until Lucy Freibert's in 1981, and there still is no significant study of Melville with the woman he rated most highly, Germaine de Staël. Studies that investigate evidence of Melville's interest are likewise ignored. Established parallels with such writers as Barrett Browning or Emily Brontë and Mary Shelley do not become assimilated into general critical assessment of Melville and his work (see, for example, Nelson, especially 251–3). Even affirmative associations of Melville's writing with female novelists and journalists that situate them in the same literary fields struggle to escape a narrow focus on Melville that prohibits discussing women writers in detail (see, for example, Post-Lauria 51, 153–4).

The most invidious and extensive division of women authors from Melville, however, follows from academic criticism that repeatedly positions his writing in the context of an American literary study that has been organized around separate-sphere gender paradigms. Because much criticism approaches Melville out of American studies, he is most often situated in the company of other great American writers, a company that the predominant paradigms construe as almost exclusively male. Whether critics follow the chief models of F. O. Matthiessen, Richard Chase, or Ann Douglas (who have theorized great American literature respectively as an original "renaissance" of culture on the pattern of Europe's earlier Renaissance, as a romance tradition defined against the novel, and as an intellectual tradition, largely Calvinist, posited against the debilitating "feminization" of middle-brow culture), they reproduce the value categories established long ago by Charles Richardson, that is, categories that classify the best of men's writing as works of intrinsic literary and intellectual merit and depreciate women's best production as lesser, mostly sentimental in character (see Baym "Melodramas"; Avallone "American Renaissance?"). Whereas modern criticism effected the recovery of Melville's writing from the obscurity it suffered in Richardson's and other foundational academic literary histories, no equivalent recuperation has redressed the eclipse of the women authors who were erased, falsely categorized, or otherwise underestimated. Even approaches that attempt to re-evaluate women's work often maintain the early categories that divided the literary world into separate spheres of enterprise, thereby continuing to eliminate from consideration women's writing that resists classification as sentimental or domestic and reinforcing the notion that women authors were a homogeneous class, while approaches that attempt to reclassify women's work, such as Nina Baym's study of the American female *Bildungsroman*, make no claims for literary valuation or affiliation that would invite study with the men of American renaissance, romance, or intellectual tradition (see Baym *Woman's Fiction*). In this system, not only do Melville and women authors end up largely estranged, often defined in opposing terms, but women who wrote in other traditions that might afford interesting comparisons to his work, for example, the stylistically ambitious and emotionally intense work that was called "highly wrought," the philosophical and psychological fiction that was labeled transcendental or metaphysical, or the serious strain of writing that critics labeled the morbid school, go undiscussed, as do women writing in traditions marked as ethnic.

The reigning paradigms have long precluded study of some of the strongest, most complex, original writers in the nineteenth century who happen to be women, writers who produced narratives, essays, and verse of psychological, social, or stylistic complexity that invite discussion with Melville's work. These paradigms also have discouraged study of shared generic traditions or comparative reception history. The predominance of the American separate spheres approach to Melville mutes as well connections between his work and that of women writers in other cultures, including such obvious but neglected topics as the intertextuality of *Pierre* and Staël's *Corinne*, a book he purchased in 1849 after hearing it discussed aboard his ship to London, and of "Benito Cereno" and Harriet Martineau's earlier historical romance of slave revolt, *The Hour and the Man*, a book he welcomed enthusiastically as a gift from a neighbor in 1851.

The separate-spheres paradigm has also structured views of the literary marketplace as a field of competition for sales and values between alienated, intellectual men on the one hand, and, on the other, complying yet controlling, conventional women. In this application as well, the paradigm again offers small grounds for discussing Melville in the company of women authors with anything like parity (see Charvat; Douglas; Gilmore). The scarcity of historical evidence brought to sustain the model of a marketplace divided into separate literary spheres has not diminished its critical predominance (see Post-Lauria 151; Romero 12–14; Zboray 157–79). Indeed, the bulk of Melville studies still operates out of the old, asymmetric assumptions about women and men.

A more balanced study of Melville with women authors requires relinquishing the old critical paradigms and assumptions of American literary history in favor of approaches that better comprehend the writing of men and women together. Appreciation of women's texts requires the sort of close textual analyses that have invested value in Melville's writing and the equitable application of standards capacious enough to consider women and Melville with parity. This does not mean that readings of women's writing should be completely sympathetic and uncritical, but rather that they be made not so asymmetrically unsympathetic and completely critical as in the past. The new approaches that aim to put Melville in postnationalist literary studies, whether transnational, postcolonial, or critical global approaches, have yet to adopt this standard. Global studies do not necessarily offer a more progressive way to study Melville, certainly not if nineteenth-century conservative American notions of separate spheres or Old-World notions of literary value admit no women, or at best only an exceptional woman author, into the discussion. The new approach, for instance, brings us no closer to reading the writings of actual factory "girls" in the *Lowell Offering* and the *Voice of Industry*, which commanded international attention, in dialogue with Melville's story of New England female mill workers, "The Tartarus of Maids," in any transnational framework if the model for study continues to follow that established early on in helping to initiate Melville's position in an international field. For Professor Philarète Chasles dismissed the writing of the "working-women, all of which [he] would unhesitatingly give for a pair of well-darned stockings, or a nicely-hemmed handkerchief. What is the use of it?" It lacks the "value" that the male author might add (218). And yet insofar as a critical transnationalism that proposes "[t]o reinscribe classic American literature in a transnational framework" and explore its "negotiation with questions of global power" continues to select its texts exclusively from those predetermined by earlier criticism to be "classic American literature," that is, "elaborate, multifaceted works that need to be read in a more expansive transnational framework," it continues to leave the study of mid-century writers as exclusively male as earlier approaches and leaves unexamined many issues of how gender enters into those questions of global power, whether literary, political, or economic (Giles 72–3). Studies that seek to recast Melville in global or transnational critical frameworks might be better informed by attending to what has worked best to achieve more parity in studies of Melville with American female contemporaries.

The resurgence of historicism in literary studies, along with the application of feminist theory, has, in the past two decades, inspired new attention to women in scholarship dealing with Melville. Some recovery work, such as Janet Gabler-Hover's study of rewritings of the scriptural story of Hagar, redresses the earlier lack of critical attention to women by elaborating a compensatory literary history focused on their writing, attending to Melville only to correct critical misperceptions about his work that have followed from the absence of this context. New attention to questions of influence and shared genre traditions has enabled the study of Melville with women authors of recognized stature, such as Linda Cahir's linking of Edith Wharton. Some recent studies of Melville and models of authorship, such as the work of Gillian Brown, Samuel Otter, and John Evelev do well in evoking selected women writers, including Fanny Fern and Margaret Fuller, as his peers in talent, acumen, and professionalism, yet these tend to strike an uneven balance in discussions that are committed to a much greater investment in Melville. Brown's analysis, linking the nineteenth-century theoretical removals of the individual, the woman, and the writer from the American marketplace, nonetheless mounts an important challenge to the longstanding division of women's writing, stereotyped as sentimental and domestic, from that of men, presented as interested solely in individual questing and achievement.

Other studies that center more on women's writing and the opportunities that doing so affords for new readings of Melville's texts achieve greater balance while they also suggest even greater revision of literary history. Priscilla Wald analyzes Harriet Wilson's anti-racism novel, *Our Nig*, with Melville's *Pierre* to show ways that the two, "companion 'thought-diver[s],' " confronted the limitations in prevailing narratives of what it meant to be an American and an author. Both alienated contemporary audiences with cultural criticism that now compels attention, as questions about who is included in stories of American identity again engage cultural discussion (Wald 156). Ellen Weinauer invites us to reimagine a more complex, divergent marketplace for literature in the mid-century US as she contrasts Elizabeth Stoddard's model of the literary market as a space of affective relations between the writer of genius and readers with Melville's model, long privileged by literary history, of the alienated genius opposed to market consumption, valuing, and recognition. Carolyn Karcher's considered comparison of Melville's writing on the Civil War and Reconstruction with that of Lydia Maria Child not only provides new readings of both writers' texts and illuminates their implication in a shared historical context, but also importantly countervails assumptions underlying the marginalization of women writers in Melville studies, particularly the notion that women writers necessarily represent more conventional thought and values, that they are incapable of the progressive thought that is now too often automatically attributed to Melville.

Essays in the collection *Melville and Women*, edited by Elizabeth Schultz and Haskell Springer, address the title topic through a number of critical approaches that put Melville variously in the company of women. Charlene Avallone synthesizes evidence of an appreciative audience for his work among female readers, including authors, while she also makes a case for the likelihood that Melville was an appreciative, if sometimes critical, audience for women writers, arguing that Elizabeth Elkins Sanders expanded his thinking about Hawaiian sovereignty and that the precedent of Catharine Sedgwick factored in his reconceiving his career with *Pierre* and his short fiction of the 1850s. Peter Balaam sets Melville with his neighbor Sedgwick in the historical context of the picturesque mode of writing about the Berkshires, showing how her *A New England Tale* (1821) elaborated the picturesque to critique the limits of Calvinist religion and how Melville, decades later in "The Piazza" (1856), in turn criticized the limits of picturesque morality and rural domesticity as he perceived them in her novel. Wyn Kelley argues the probability that Gail Hamilton's writing, particularly "The Murder of Philip Spencer," served as a catalyst for the growing complexity of Captain Vere's characterization and deepening questions about the limitations of masculine justice in *Billy Budd*; in doing so she not only elucidates the possible influence of yet another woman writer obscured when earlier critics dismissed Hamilton's writing – unread – as mere melodrama, but also extends the discussion of ethics around Melvilie's final fiction. Elizabeth Schultz examines Alice Cary's "Uncle Christopher's" and Melville's "Bartleby" as parallel responses in fiction to the abusive employment and personal relations the two writers alike saw following from economic changes at mid-century.

Recent scholarship thus promises a richer understanding of both women writers and Melville, along with a more capacious cultural history and more cogent models of gender. Although the older paradigm of devaluing women's writing remains all too prevalent in Melville studies, critics in the past decade and a half have begun to imagine alternatives to misogynist separate-spheres assumptions. Criticism is just now effectively opening the question of Melville's relations with women authors. It's an exciting time to be investigating this question.

References and Further Reading

Arvin, Newton. *Herman Melville*. The American Men of Letters Series. New York: William Sloane Associates, 1950.

———. "Melville and the Gothic Novel." *New England Quarterly* 22 (1949): 33–48.

Avallone, Charlene. "What American Renaissance? The Gendered Genealogy of a Critical Discourse." *PMLA* 112 (1997): 1102–20.

———. "Women Reading Melville / Melville Reading Women." In *Melville and Women*. Eds. Elizabeth Schultz and Haskell Springer. Kent, OH: Kent State University Press, 2006.

Balaam, Peter. " 'Piazza to the North': Melville Reading Sedgwick." In *Melville and Women*. Eds. Elizabeth Schultz and Haskell Springer. Kent, OH: Kent State University Press, 2006.

Baym, Nina. "Melodramas of Beset Manhood: How Theories of American Fiction Exclude Women Authors." *American Quarterly* 33 (1981): 123–39.

———. *Novels, Readers, and Reviewers: Responses to Fiction in Antebellum America*. Ithaca, NY, and London: Cornell University Press, 1984.

———. *Woman's Fiction: A Guide to Novels by and about Women in America, 1820–70*. 1978. 2nd. ed. Urbana: University of Illinois Press, 1993.

Bickley, R. Bruce, Jr. *The Method of Melville's Short Fiction*. Durham, NC: Duke University Press, 1975.

Braswell, William. "The Satirical Temper of Melville's *Pierre*." *American Literature* 7 (1936): 424–38.

Brown, Gillian. "Anti-sentimentalism and Authorship in *Pierre*." In *Domestic Individualism:*

Imagining Self in Nineteenth-Century America. Berkeley: University of California Press, 1990. 135–69.

Bryant, John. "Herman Melville." In *Prospects for the Study of American Literature: A Guide for Scholars and Students*. Ed. Richard Kopley. New York: New York University Press, 1997. 58–90.

Cahir, Linda Costanzo. *Solitude and Society in the Works of Herman Melville and Edith Wharton*. Contributions to the Study of American Literature, No. 3. Westport, CT, and London: Greenwood Press, 1999.

Charvat, William. *The Profession of Authorship in America, 1800–1870: The Papers of William Charvat*. Ed. Matthew J. Bruccoli. Columbus: Ohio State University Press, 1968.

Chase, Richard Volney. *The American Novel and Its Tradition*. Garden City, NY: Doubleday, 1957.

Chasles, Philarète. *Anglo-American Literature and Manners*. New York: Charles Scribner, 1852.

Colatrella, Carol. *Literature and Moral Reform: Melville and the Discipline of Reading*. Gainesville: University Press of Florida, 2002.

Cowen, Walker. "Melville's Marginalia." 11 vols. Ph.D. dissertation, Harvard, 1965.

Davis, Merrell R. "The Flower Symbolism in *Mardi*." *Modern Language Quarterly* 2 (1941): 625–38.

Douglas, Ann. *The Feminization of American Culture*. 1977. Rpt. New York: Anchor/Doubleday, 1988.

Elwood, Anne Katherine Curteis. *Memoirs of the Literary Ladies of England, from the Commencement of the Last Century.* 1843. Rpt. New York: AMS Press, 1973.

Evelev, John. " 'Every One to His Trade': *Mardi*, Literary Form, and Professional Ideology." *American Literature* 75 (2003): 305–33.

Fern, Fanny. *Ruth Hall: A Domestic Tale of the Present Time.* 1855. Rpt. in *Ruth Hall and Other Writings.* Ed. Joyce W. Warren. American Women Writers Series. Series eds. Joanne Dobson, Judith Fetterley, and Elaine Showalter. New Brunswick, NJ: Rutgers University Press, 1986.

Freibert, Lucy M. "The Influence of Elizabeth Barrett Browning on the Poetry of Herman Melville." *Studies in Browning and His Circle* 9 (1981): 69–78.

Fuller, Margaret. "American Literature: Its Position in the Present Time and Prospects for the Future." 1846. Rpt. in *Margaret Fuller: Essays on American Life and Letters.* Ed. Joel Myerson. New Haven, CT: College and University Press, 1978. 381–400.

———. *Woman in the Nineteenth Century.* 1845. Rpt. in *Margaret Fuller: Essays on American Life and Letters.* Ed. Joel Myerson. New Haven, CT: College and University Press, 1978. 82–239.

Gabler-Hover, Janet. *Dreaming Black / Writing White: The Hagar Myth in American Cultural History.* Lexington: University Press of Kentucky, 2000.

Giles, Paul. "Transnationalism and Classic American Literature." *PMLA* 118 (2003): 62–77.

Gilmore, Michael T. *American Romanticism and the Marketplace.* Chicago and London: University of Chicago Press, 1985.

Heflin, Wilson L. "New Light on the Cruise of Herman Melville in the Charles and Henry." *Historic Nantucket* 22 (1974): 26–7.

Hillway, Tyrus. Introduction. *Mardi: And a Voyage Thither.* Lanham, MD: Rowman and Littlefield, 1963.

Jones, William Alfred. "The Ladies' Library." *Literary Studies.* 1847. Rpt. *Characters and Criticisms*, vol. 1. New York: L. Y. Westervelt, 1857. 135–43.

Karcher, Carolyn. "The Moderate and the Radical: Melville and Child on the Civil War and Reconstruction." *ESQ* 45 (1999): 187–257.

Kelley, Wyn. " 'My Literary Thirst': Augusta Melville and the Melville Family Correspond-

ence." *Resources for American Literary Study* 25 (1999): 46–56.

———. " 'Tender Kinswoman': Gendered Justice in *Billy Budd, Sailor.*" In *Melville and Women.* Eds. Elizabeth Schultz and Haskell Springer. Kent, OH: Kent State University Press, 2006.

Lauter, Paul. "Melville Climbs the Canon." Rpt. in *From Walden Pond to Jurassic Park: Activism, Culture, & American Studies.* New Americanists. Ed. Donald E. Pease. Durham, NC and London: Duke University Press, 2001. 199–220.

Matthiessen, F. O. *American Renaissance: Art and Expression in the Age of Emerson and Whitman.* London: Oxford University Press, 1941.

Nelson, Lowry. "Night Thoughts on the Gothic Novel." *Yale Review* 52 (1962): 236–57.

Olsen-Smith, Steven. "A Fourth Supplementary Note to *Melville's Reading.*" *Leviathan: A Journal of Melville Studies* 2 (2000): 105–11.

Otter, Samuel. "Inscribed Hearts in *Pierre.*" In *Melville's Anatomies.* Berkeley: University of California Press, 1999. 208–54.

Post-Lauria, Sheila. *Correspondent Colorings: Melville in the Marketplace.* Amherst: University of Massachusetts Press, 1996.

Richardson, Charles F. *American Literature, 1607–1885.* 2 vols. 1886, 1888. Popular Edition. New York: Putnam's Sons, 1895.

Romero, Lora. "A Society Controlled by Women: An Overview." In *Home Fronts: Domesticity and Its Critics in the Antebellum United States.* New Americanists. Ed. Donald E. Pease. Durham, NC, and London: Duke University Press, 1997. 11–34.

Sealts, Merton M., Jr. "A Second Supplementary Note to *Melville's Reading.*" Melville Society *Extracts* 100 (1995): 2–3.

———. "A Supplementary Note to *Melville's Reading.*" Melville Society *Extracts* 80 (1990): 5–10.

———. "A Third Supplementary Note to *Melville's Reading.*" Melville Society *Extracts* 112 (1998): 12–14.

Schultz, Elizabeth. "Wall Street and Clovernook in 'Bartleby, the Scrivener' and 'Uncle Christopher's': Sites of Wage Slavery and Domestic Abuse." In *Melville and Women.* Ed. Elizabeth Schultz and Haskell Springer. Kent, OH: Kent State University Press, 2005.

Wald, Priscilla. *Constituting Americans: Cultural Anxiety and Narrative Form*. New Americanists. Ed Donald E. Pease. Durham, NC, and London: Duke University Press, 1995.

Weinauer, Ellen. "Alternative Economies: Authorship and Ownership in Elizabeth Stoddard's 'Collected by a Valetudinarian.'" *Studies in American Fiction* 25 (1997): 167–82.

Wendell, Barrett. *A Literary History of America*. Library of Literary History Series. New York: Scribner's Sons, 1900.

Zboray, Ronald J. *A Fictive People: Antebellum Economic Development and the American Reading Public*. New York and Oxford: Oxford University Press, 1993.

21

Hawthorne and Race

Ellen Weinauer

Hawthorne, Melville, and the Critics

A great deal of ink has been used to answer one of the most elusive questions of antebellum American literary history: what exactly did Nathaniel Hawthorne mean to Herman Melville? These two literary men – Hawthorne one of the period's most eminent literary figures, Melville emerging as one of the most promising and popular – first met on August 5, 1850, on a picnic at Monument Mountain, in western Massachusetts. The meeting has taken on the status of literary myth, largely because of its fervid aftermath. A week after the picnic, Melville published the first install-ment of "Hawthorne and His Mosses," an effusive two-part critical "review" of Hawthorne's *Mosses from an Old Manse* that appeared in the influential *Literary World* and that prompted grateful responses from both Hawthorne and his wife, Sophia. For the next fifteen months, Melville and Hawthorne maintained a fruitful relationship that is captured perhaps most famously in the eleven impassioned letters that Melville wrote to Hawthorne.

The import of those letters, with their hot-blooded treatment of matters emotional, metaphysical, and literary, is rendered both more intriguing and more evasive by the fact that most of Hawthorne's letters to Melville no longer survive. To add additional mystery, after Hawthorne's departure from Lenox, Massachusetts, where he was a near-neighbor of Melville, the correspondence diminished dramatically and soon came to an abrupt end; Melville wrote his last known letter sometime in early December of 1852. The two men, moreover, appeared to have seen each other only a few times in the fourteen years before Hawthorne died, in May of 1864.

The seemingly precipitate ending to what had been, by all accounts, a mutually satisfying friendship has led some critics to argue for a monumental break-up, initiated perhaps, Edwin Havilland Miller suggests, by a sexual overture on Melville's part. Others have attempted to excavate the psychological, literary, and sexual toll that Hawthorne's departure took on Melville, whose emotional investment in the friendship was, as the letters document, intense. In any event, regardless of how they read the sexual content of the relationship or the meaning of its diminution, both early and more recent biographers of both men devote considerable attention to the Hawthorne–Melville friendship.

Scholars have also been interested, of course, in the literary influences that the writers exerted on one another. Critics have identified fictional and poetic avatars of Hawthorne throughout Melville's career, including, perhaps most notably, such figures as Plotinus Plinlimmon from *Pierre* (1852), and the reserved Vine, from Melville's long poetic work, *Clarel* (1876). Along with *Clarel*, shorter poems such as "Monody" and "After the Pleasure Party" (both from *Timoleon*, 1891) are often read as reflections on Melville's friendship with Hawthorne. One can also identify less biographically explicit forms of influence across the corpus of both writers. Perhaps the most famous detail in this regard is Melville's dedication of his 1851 *Moby-Dick* to Hawthorne, "in token of my admiration for his genius"; but Hawthorne's influence on Melville extends well beyond that text. Critics have not only traced isolated references to Hawthorne's work in a variety of post-1851 texts by Melville, but also argued for more significant textual borrowings. Melville's "I and My Chimney" (1856), for example, has been shown to revisit Hawthorne's "The Old Manse," "Fire-Worship," and "Peter Goldthwaite's Treasure" (Rosenberry; Jones; Allison). "The Apple-Tree Table" (1856) has been read in terms of Hawthorne's "The Artist of the Beautiful" (Harshbarger), "Bartleby" in terms of "The Old Apple Dealer" (Levy), *The Confidence-Man* (1857) in terms of "The Celestial Rail-road," "Benito Cereno" in terms of "My Kinsman, Major Molineux," and the posthumous *Billy Budd* in terms of "The Birth-Mark." More recently, critics have situated *Pierre* as rescripting fundamental elements of *The House of the Seven Gables* (domesticity for Wyn Kelley, race and genealogy for Robert S. Levine); and "Bartleby" and "The Encantadas" as offering commentary on the "model of democratic poetics" that Hawthorne envisions in *The Scarlet Letter* (Hewitt 298).

In this essay, I propose yet another, certainly less widely investigated angle of approach to the literary link between the two writers: race. F. O. Matthiessen was among the earliest critics to note the centrality of what he called the "problem of democracy" in the work of Hawthorne, Melville, and other "American Renaissance" writers. Since his formative *American Renaissance* (1941), scholars have devoted themselves to understanding how Melville and Hawthorne mutually engage the conflicts posed by the democratic system to which they are both committed: the pull between the needs of the individual and those of the community, the perilous twinning of self-sovereignty and tyranny, the desire to write for a democratic audience and the attendant fear that to do so necessitates a sort of crass pandering that compromises genuine artistry. Additionally, critics have explored how Hawthorne and Melville examine (or, as is often argued in the case of Hawthorne, fail to examine) the pressures placed upon democratic ideals by the institution of American slavery and the racist structures of belief that underwrite it. Yet rarely have Hawthorne and Melville been understood to be in conversation with one another with regard to issues of race, or to be mutually concerned with the "problems" that race and slavery might pose for the larger "problem of democracy" that absorbs both writers. Perhaps most significantly, although Melville's engagement with the problematics of race is evident from his first novel, *Typee* (1846), critics have not explored the ways in which Melville might have read Hawthorne through the lens of race.

This essay seeks to fill in that gap by exploring the racial dynamics of one of Melville's most often discussed "discoveries" about Hawthorne: his "blackness." Famously, in "Hawthorne and His Mosses" Melville claims that "the world is mistaken in this Nathaniel Hawthorne" (*PT* 243–4), "deem[ing]" him to be merely a "pleasant writer, with a pleasant style, – a sequestered, harmless man, from whom any deep and weighty thing would hardly be anticipated" (242). Melville attempts in "Mosses" to rectify this mistake by delineating what he calls the "hither side of Hawthorne's soul, the other side" that is, he claims, "shrouded in a blackness, ten times black" (243). Following Melville's own lead – he links Hawthorne's "blackness" to a "Calvinistic sense of Innate Depravity and Original Sin" and a possible "touch of Puritanic gloom" (243) – critics have long read the "darkness" that Melville seeks to excavate from Hawthorne's work in a moral or metaphysical framework. Without undermining or denying such readings, I want to explore how we might read Melville's treatment of Hawthorne's "blackness" in the context of Melville's own concern with the meanings of race in the antebellum US. In a 1977 essay that explores Melville's "growing awareness of the profound differences between his own outlook and that of his older friend," Hyatt Waggoner offers a formulation that is remarkably apt to the present study: as Melville moved through writing the tales and sketches that draw on Hawthorne, Waggoner writes, "it must have seemed" to him that "the man he had once praised for seeing the Blackness had not seen it well enough, not as well, at least, or as unflinchingly, as *he* could" (78). Although reading "Blackness" in a different frame, I will argue, like Waggoner, that Hawthorne did not see the "blackness of darkness" "well enough" for Melville. Indeed, even as early as "Mosses," Melville registers racial anxieties operative in Hawthorne's work – anxieties that he tries, but finally fails, to transcend.

The "Blackness of Darkness" and "Hawthorne and His Mosses"

"Hawthorne and His Mosses" has become a landmark text, a touchstone both for the critical understanding of Hawthorne's work and of Hawthorne's role in Melville's evolving sense of authorship. Richard Brodhead makes what has become a representative claim when he writes that "When they met in 1850, Hawthorne moved into the highly charged field of Melville's authorial anxieties and ambitions. Projecting these concerns out onto Hawthorne, Melville seemed to see *in* Hawthorne the kind of writer he aspired to be" (29). "The action of 'Hawthorne and His Mosses,' " Brodhead goes on to declare, "is of Melville first thinking a new idea of authorship, then, on the basis of that thought, emboldening himself to assert his own literary-prophetical vocation. And when we know this, we know Hawthorne's power for Melville" (29). This argument adds resonance to Melville's claim that in writing "Mosses" "I have more served and honored myself, than him" (249). Hawthorne's "power" for Melville thus seems to have a great deal to do with what the more established writer allows him to understand not only about American authorship in general, but of his own authorship in particular. As James R. Mellow asserts, "In praising Hawthorne, [Melville] was also laying claim to his own admittance to the 'brotherhood of the arts,' and to his own election to the 'new and far better generation' of American writers that he was promoting" (336).

Melville is indeed "promoting" American authorship in "Mosses." His two-part piece was published in the *Literary World*, an influential weekly founded in 1847 by brothers Evert and George Duyckinck, who, as key members of the emerging "Young America" movement, used the magazine aggressively to promote American letters and a new national literary tradition. Not surprisingly, Melville's essay falls quite neatly into the Young American framework. "Let America then prize and cherish her writers; yea, let her glorify them," he commands, noting that "It is for the nation's sake, and not for her authors' sake, that I would have America be heedful of the increasing greatness among her writers" (247). While acknowledging the "greatness" of Shakespeare, Melville criticizes, much as Ralph Waldo Emerson did in "The American Scholar" (1837), the nation's obsession with non-native writers generally and its hero worship of "William of Avon" in particular (246). "[T]his absolute and unconditional adoration of Shakespeare has grown to be a part of our Anglo Saxon superstitions," he complains; "You must believe in Shakespeare's unapproachability, or quit the country. But what sort of a belief is this for an American, a man who is bound to carry republican progressiveness into Literature, as well as into Life?" (245).

It is Nathaniel Hawthorne, Melville asserts, who can hold his own against Shakespeare: "I do not say that Nathaniel of Salem is a greater than William of Avon, or as great. But the difference between the two men is by no means immeasurable. Not a very great deal more, and Nathaniel were verily William" (246). And it is thus Hawthorne who can and should take pride of place in a new, native literary tradition: "And now, my countrymen, as an excellent author, of your own flesh and blood, – an unimitating, and perhaps, in his way, an inimitable man – whom better can I commend to you, in the first place, than Nathaniel Hawthorne. He is one of the new, and far better generation of your writers" (248–9). Following a line of thought that had, even by Melville's time, become conventional, Melville establishes Hawthorne's Americanness in part by associating him with the purity of American nature: "The smell of your beeches and hemlocks is upon him," he proclaims; "your own broad prairies are in his soul; and if you travel away inland into his deep and noble nature, you will hear the far roar of his Niagara" (249).

Melville's reference to Hawthorne's "deep and noble nature" is of a piece with another of his review's aims: to offer an interpretation of Hawthorne's work that will demonstrate Hawthorne's particular "genius" and, thus, legitimize his place at the head of an emergent and uniquely American pantheon. And that interpretation – one that shapes not only how critics read Hawthorne but also, and perhaps even more so, how they read Melville himself – centers on the difference between "surface" and "depth." On the superficial level at which most will read, Melville suggests, Hawthorne "means no meanings" (242). But the discerning reader will more "fully fathom" what is at play in Hawthorne's work: a "depth of meaning" the very limited accessibility of which makes it all the more valuable (243). It is, after all, "the least part of genius that attracts admiration," Melville twice declares (242, 244).

It is to this "mystical depth of meaning" (243) that Melville devotes much of "Mosses," excavating for the readers of *The Literary World* a different "Nathaniel Hawthorne," one "immeasurably deeper" than most have known or suspected (243–4). This process of excavation leads Melville to Hawthorne's "blackness." In short order, Melville remarks on Hawthorne's "mystical blackness," his "great power of blackness," the "black conceit" which "pervades him," the "blackness of darkness" that lies beyond his bewitching "sunlight," and the "blackness" that "furnishes the infinite obscure of [Hawthorne's] back-ground" (243–4). It is evident, in short, that the "blackness in Hawthorne" "fixes and fascinates" him (244).

Importantly, "Mosses" provides but few racial referents for these meditations on Hawthorne's "blackness." Indeed, Melville himself gives that blackness a moral, even metaphysical inflection rather than a racial one. Although he admits to being unsure as to "whether there really lurks in [Hawthorne], perhaps unknown to himself, a touch of Puritanic gloom" (243), he declares it "certain" that the "great power of blackness in him derives its force from its appeals to that Calvinistic sense of Innate Depravity and Original Sin, from whose visitations, in some shape or other, no deeply thinking mind is always and wholly free" (243). It is clear, of course, that the writer who, while he wrote these words, was busy "weigh[ing] this world" on the massive scale that was *Moby-Dick* found the "terrific thought" of "something, somehow like Original Sin" deeply compelling, even enabling for his own art. Yet, racist rhetoric often connected racial "blackness" to innate depravity, suggesting that the racial and the metaphysical dimensions of the "blackness" that Melville associates with Hawthorne are not mutually exclusive.

When read in the context of such racial inflections, some of the text's more curious elements – Melville's authorial persona, for example – become more legible. Melville writes "Hawthorne and His Mosses" not as himself, or even as a fellow New Englander, but rather as "a Virginian Spending July in Vermont" (239). In keeping with the masquerade, the review makes reference to the author's "hot-headed Carolina cousin" (247, 248), remarks on his "quiet plantation life" (249), and depicts Hawthorne's effect on him in terms of a merger between "strong New-England roots" and "the hot soil of my Southern soul" (250). By the time Melville adopted this curious persona, along with its regionalized associations, of course, his interest in issues of race and slavery was already well established. Depicting the relatively idyllic four-month stay of a white American sailor among a tribe of Polynesian "cannibals," his first novel, *Typee* (1846), offers a preliminary investigation into the complexities of interracial contact and cross-cultural (mis)understanding that Melville would extend into much of his later work. Indeed, in the brief span between the publication of *Typee* and his meeting with Hawthorne in 1850, Melville wrote four novels – *Omoo* (1847), *Mardi* (1849), *Redburn* (1849), and *White-Jacket* (1850) – all of which take up, directly and often forcefully, race relations, racial identity, and/or slavery. In *Redburn*, Melville describes his eponymous hero's obsession with a statue of Nelson that depicts "four naked figures in chains … seated in various attitudes of humiliation and despair" (222). Although "These woe-begone figures of captives are emblematic of Nelson's principal victories," Redburn remarks that he "never could look at their swarthy limbs and manacles, without being involuntarily reminded of four African slaves in the market-place" (222). The statue is deeply affecting to Redburn: "I never went through Chapel-street without going through the little arch to look at it again," he admits (223). Redburn's repeated returns to the statue, and the thoughts of "Virginia and Carolina," the "African slave-trade," and abolitionism that it conjures up (222–3), are mirrored in Melville's own repeated returns, in his fiction, to the site of slavery and the structures of belief about race and racial meanings that make the institution possible.

When a writer of such fictional commitments comments on Hawthorne's unrecognized "blackness," when he makes reference to North–South union, to "Carolina" cousins and "plantation life," it is hard to conceive that race is not, in some fashion, on Melville's mind. To what extent, for example, might the alert and "deep reading" Melville recognize an only recently acknowledged racial undercurrent in some of the stories included in *Mosses from an Old Manse*? Might Melville have registered the ways in which "The Birth-Mark," with its depiction of Aylmer's fatal effort to eradicate the "flaw" on his wife's otherwise perfectly white cheek, can be read as commentary on white America's increasing and dangerous obsession with race purity? Might he have read "Young Goodman Brown," a story he singles out as a "strong positive illustration of that blackness in Hawthorne" (*PT* 251), in counterpoint to "The Birth-Mark"? For with its representation of a Satanic "dark figure," a "sable form" who presides over this story's black Sabbath and the ostensible corruption of a "pale wife" (Hawthorne *Mosses* 86, 87, 88), "Young Goodman Brown" can be read not only as a story about sin, faith, and redemption, but also as a story that frets over the threatening power of "blackness."

Of course, if "Mosses" is indeed a statement of Melville's own "literary-prophetical vocation" (Brodhead 29) and a declaration of his membership in the American literary "brotherhood," then the text's "fascination" with "that blackness in Hawthorne" might be said to indicate as much about his own fictional commitments to the nation's complex and troubling racial legacies as Hawthorne's. In this context, Melville's meditations on Hawthorne's dark side can be seen to point not so much to the racial meanings that the "superficial skimmer of pages" (251) is likely to miss as to a blackness that is not, finally, black enough. Paradoxically, by repeatedly directing readers to Hawthorne's "blackness, ten times black," Melville could well be underscoring the racial matters that Hawthorne (at once a mentor and, it must be admitted, a rival) fails explicitly or adequately to address – matters that Melville had long engaged and that he would continue to engage throughout his literary career, in such diverse texts as *Moby-Dick* (1851), *Pierre* (1852), "The Paradise of Bachelors and the Tartarus of Maids" (1855), "Benito Cereno" (1855), "The 'Gees" (1856), *The Confidence-Man* (1857), and his 1866 collection of poems, *Battle-Pieces and Aspects of the War*. "Hawthorne and His Mosses" has long been read as a homage to an enabling precursor who provided Melville with a model for his own authorial ambitions. But it may also be that, even as he bears witness to Hawthorne's "genius," the "Virginian" uses his "review" to pry open new space for his own work, to reveal, however subtly, gaps left by "Nathaniel of Salem" that "Herman of Pittsfield" may well be able to fill.

"Hawthorne: A Problem": Blackness and *The House of the Seven Gables*

When Melville met Hawthorne and published his "Mosses" in August of 1850, the older writer was in the flush of *The Scarlet Letter*'s success and, partly in response to the calculated urgings of James T. Fields, trying to make progress on his next novel – the book that would become *The House of the Seven Gables*. Published in the spring of 1851, just a year after *The Scarlet Letter* appeared, *House* provoked a quick and revealing response from Melville. In a letter to Hawthorne, Melville playfully adopts the tone and manner of a book review, writing that "With great enjoyment we spent almost an hour in each separate gable. This book is like a fine old chamber, abundantly, but still judiciously, furnished with precisely that sort of furniture best fitted to furnish it" (*L* 185). "Lingering," as Wyn Kelley has noted, with an almost "sensual pleasure" over the "household images the novel inspired" (91), Melville elaborates on the "sort of furniture" and appointments he finds in Hawthorne's *House*: "rich hangings," "old china with rare devices," "long and indolent lounges to throw yourself upon," "an admirable sideboard," well stocked with "good viands"; and "finally," he notes, "in one corner, . . . a dark little black-letter volume in golden clasps, entitled 'Hawthorne: A Problem' " (185). Melville does not go on to identify with any explicitness the nature of this "problem," moving instead from this delighted and, at the end, rather bemused contemplation of domestic interiority to declarations of Hawthorne's authorial power that are reminiscent of those from "Hawthorne and His Mosses." He celebrates Hawthorne as a "man who, like Russia or the British Empire, declares himself a sovereign nature (in himself) amid the powers of heaven, hell, and earth," and returns to what he called, in "Mosses," the "hither side" of Hawthorne's soul: "There is the grand truth about Nathaniel Hawthorne. He says NO! in thunder; but the Devil himself cannot make him say *yes*. For all men who say *yes*, lie; and all men who say *no*, – why, they are in the happy condition of judicious, unencumbered travelers" (186).

As in "Mosses," Melville seems to be contemplating his own work as much as he is Hawthorne's here. Kelley notes, for example, that Melville's detailed inventory of domestic details indicates that, "even as he was writing the ocean-going *Moby-Dick*, he contemplated house and home" (91) – a subject to which he would turn in his next and, at least in terms of critical response, probably most disastrous novel, *Pierre* (1852). For Kelley, the "problem" that Melville identifies in Hawthorne thus has to do with what Melville saw as a kind of failed "renovat[ion]" of the "middle-class household" in *House* – a failure to which he responds in *Pierre* (92). Like Kelley, Brenda Wineapple notes a tension in Melville's response to Hawthorne's novel, an awareness of what might be missing in the latter's work. In his "review" of *The House of the Seven Gables*, Melville praises Clifford, poised to throw himself from his window in the Pyncheon mansion into the street below, as the incarnation of an "awful truth" (185). But, as Wineapple notes, "Clifford does not jump. Hawthorne will not let him" – and the "awful truth" that Clifford might be said to incarnate is thus occluded. For Melville, then, Hawthorne may well be "like Solomon," a man who (as Melville himself would claim in another letter to Hawthorne just a few weeks later), " '*managed the truth*' " (quoted in Wineapple 82). His celebration of Hawthorne's refusal to "lie" notwithstanding, Melville hints at a belief that Hawthorne may fall short in his confrontation with the truth. "There is something lacking – a good deal lacking – to the plump sphericity of the man," Melville had already insisted in a letter to Evert Duyckinck written in February of 1851, a month before *House* appeared (*L* 181).

Melville's praise in his "review," then, might be seen to function in part as a veil for a subtextual critique of the limitations and hesitations of *The House of the Seven Gables* – limitations and hesitations, I suggest, that can also be traced to the terrain of race. At the end of the letter, after all, Melville depicts himself (not Hawthorne) as the truly "unencumbered traveler," situating himself in the continent most explicitly associated with blackness: "You see, I began with a little criticism extracted for your benefit from the 'Pittsfield Secret Review,' " he remarks, and "here I have landed in Africa" (187). Just a sentence or so later, Melville offers a more explicit remark on race. Recalling the earliest acts of commercial exchange in which Hepzibah Pyncheon engages in her shop – her "first customer" is a "sturdy little urchin" who seeks to buy a ginger cookie in the shape of "the renowned Jim Crow" (*House* 50) – Melville makes a final request to Hawthorne: "If you pass Hepzibah's cent-shop, buy me a Jim Crow (fresh) and send it to me by Ned Higgins" (187). Albeit playful and indeed participatory, this moment may point back to Melville's sense of "a problem" in Hawthorne's *House*: the novel's treatment of, and indeed its arguable participation in, the racist discourse and racial anxieties of the period.

An explicit treatment of race and slavery is, notably, largely absent from *The House of the Seven Gables*. The novel is set in Salem, a port long associated with the slave trade and, in the Jacksonian period with which *House* is concerned, the trade in West Africa. As former Surveyor of the Salem Custom-House, Hawthorne would have been well aware of Salem's past and present economic connections to Africa. Indeed, as Teresa Goddu has noted, both "The Custom-House" and the *Journal of an African Cruiser*, an 1845 text that Hawthorne edited for his friend Horatio Bridge, draw attention to those connections: "Naming the key merchants of Salem's West African trade," Goddu writes, " 'The Custom-House' underscores the *Journal*'s claim that '[m]ore vessels come to the coast of Africa than from any other port in the United States' [110] and signals Salem's imbrication within a broader trade tied to slavery" (61). Hawthorne's awareness of this "imbrication" and the novel's setting in contemporary Salem notwithstanding, *The House of the Seven Gables* eschews overt references to slavery or the "broader trade" with Africa that is tied to slavery. Yet, as Goddu and other recent critics, such as David Anthony and Paul Gilmore, have noted, Hawthorne on more than one occasion connects "blackness" to "commerce" – the Jim Crow gingerbread man, the black monkey that accompanies an Italian organ-grinder through the streets of Salem – both drawing on racial stereotypes popularized in antebellum mass culture and alluding to the market in slaves. It should thus come as no surprise that he also ties blackness to ontological dispossession, to the loss of identity that is, throughout Hawthorne's work, always terrifying.

This connection between blackness and dispossession is best illustrated in the tale of "Alice Pyncheon" that Holgrave, a Jacksonian jack-of-all-trades, writer, mesmerist, and general reformist, reads to Phoebe in the Pyncheon garden. Holgrave's tale involves what is, in essence, the "sale" of the young Alice Pyncheon to Matthew Maule, a carpenter – and an alleged wizard – from whom Alice's father seeks to obtain knowledge of a missing deed of ownership. In order to gain the desired knowledge, Maule puts Alice in a mesmeric trance, after which she becomes his

> slave, in a bondage more humiliating, a thousand-fold, than that which binds its chain around the body. Seated by his humble fireside, Maule had but to wave his hand; and, wherever the proud lady chanced to be – whether in her chamber, or entertaining her father's stately guests, or worshipping at church – whatever her place or occupation, her spirit passed from beneath her own control, and bowed itself to Maule. (208–9)

After she is sold by her father for what Maule calls a "mere hope of getting a sheet of yellow parchment into [his] clutch" (206), Alice exists in a condition akin to that of the slave, her body and spirit bearing the marks of her unfreedom. Like the slave, Alice performs meanings and actions imposed on her from without. Her selfhood violated and her interiority vacated, Alice Pyncheon bears witness to Hawthorne's awareness of the perilous vulnerability of the "inmost Me" that he sought, in both his life and his fiction, to protect. As Clark Davis has noted, "The complete collapse of one self into another is seldom if ever permitted in Hawthorne's writing, and when it does occur it is an unmistakeable evil" (42). That "evil" is certainly made manifest in this scene, which seems to offer a critique of the appropriative dynamics of slavery, the theft of self and soul that the peculiar institution entailed.

But while on the one hand the description of Alice Pyncheon points to Hawthorne's sense of the destructive power of the master–slave relation, on the other hand it points to racial anxieties that Alice's "possession" by Maule can be seen to provoke. For the violated self that Hawthorne describes in this scene is, fundamentally, a racially amalgamated, miscegenated one – Alice's "enslavement" to Maule involves her susceptibility to a kind of stereotyped blackness. Hawthorne suggests that Alice's enslavement is spiritual; hers is not an enslavement that "binds its chain round the body." Yet it is precisely Alice's body that acts according to her "master's" will: when Maule commands her to laugh, "Alice must break into wild laughter"; when he commands her to "be sad!," "down would come her tears"; and when he wills her to "dance," then "dance she would, not in such court-like measures as she had learned abroad, but some high-paced jig, or hop-skip rigadoon" (209). Recalling the gingerbread Jim Crow consumed by Ned Higgins, the "fair" Alice Pyncheon becomes, in essence, a minstrel figure, performing not the "measures" appropriate to her class but the "high-paced" and "hop-skip" routines becoming familiar on the minstrel stage. In this context, it is significant that Maule too is repeatedly linked to "blackness" and "darkness." When he first arrives at the Pyncheon mansion, he is identified with "Black Scipio," the Pyncheon family "servant," who wonders why Maule "look[s] so black at me." "No matter, darkey!" Maule replies; "Do you think nobody is to look black but yourself?" (188). And part of what motivates Maule to destroy Alice is her objectification of him. When she first lays eyes on him, Alice makes "no attempt to conceal" her admiration of the "remarkable comeliness, strength, and energy of Maule's figure" (201). Maule is aware – and resentful – of her gaze: "Does the girl look at me as if I were a brute beast!" (201), he mutters to himself in language that recalls the auction block and chattel slavery.

Reversing not only class but also racial dynamics by imposing his will on Alice, Maule thus transfuses his "black" self into Alice's "fair" one. Importantly, it is not "Black Scipio," or even the "black," objectified Maule, whose humiliations are staged for our disapproval here. Rather, it is the humiliation inflicted on the white woman become black. It is the once fair Alice, now enslaved and minstrelized, whom we look upon and pity. What disturbs the text, in this episode, is not only that the ostensibly "inviolate" interior self is opened to dangerous incursions of power, but also that those incursions involve a more specific danger: the transgression of racial boundaries where, with a (literal) pass of the hand, "white" can become "black."

Elsewhere in *The House of the Seven Gables*, Hawthorne offers arguments against efforts to police racial lines and preserve racial "purity," embracing by extension a sort of miscegenated social vision. Most notable in this regard are the Pyncheon chickens, a diminished, nearly sterile "race" which "had degenerated, like many a noble race besides, in consequence of too strict a watchfulness to keep it pure" (89). In this instance, Hawthorne offers a critique of legislative and scientific efforts to maintain a "pure" whiteness. But in the "Alice Pyncheon" chapter, that critique breaks down amidst anxiety about the ease with which the white interior can be penetrated and violated, just as is the black interior under slavery. As self becomes other, white becomes black – and it is that miscegenated self to which, one might suggest, Hawthorne's text seems to say "NO! in thunder." What *House* resists, ultimately, is the very "blackness" with which Melville has associated its author in "Hawthorne and His Mosses."

Moby-Dick, *Pierre*, and Miscegenated Selfhood

A brief look at *Moby-Dick* suggests the extent to which Melville might have read the "dark little black-letter volume" tucked away in the "corner" of *The House of the Seven Gables* in terms of race. Early on, *Moby-Dick* depicts scenes of racial anxiety that both revisit, and then revise, the kinds of anxieties about "blackness" that appear in *House*. In the first pages of the text, Ishmael describes his search, through the "dreary streets" of New Bedford, for cheap rooms. In the course of his wanderings, he comes upon a "low wide building, the door of which stood invitingly open" (9). Dubbing it "The Trap" after he stumbles over and upsets an ash-box in the front entry, he opens "a second, interior door" and comes upon a sight that causes him great distress:

> It seemed the great Black Parliament sitting in Tophet. A hundred black faces turned round in their rows to peer; and beyond, a black Angel of Doom was beating a book in a pulpit. It was a negro church; and the preacher's text was about the blackness of darkness, and the weeping and wailing and teeth-gnashing there. Ha, Ishmael, muttered I, backing out, Wretched entertainment at the sign of "The Trap!" (9–10)

The spatial movement of this scene is intriguing, staging as it does Ishmael's progression further inside, through an "interior door" that compels him to confront an inner "blackness." Discussing the episode at The Trap, Robert S. Levine notes that Ishmael's hasty retreat indicates both his fear of blackness and his concomitant "determination to hold onto his whiteness": "The white man," Levine asserts, "does not want to be trapped by 'The Trap' " ("Trappe[d]" 276). When, just a short while later, Ishmael sleeps with Queequeg, he indicates his liberation from white anxieties about race purity and the taint of racial otherness. Importantly, both Ishmael and Queequeg view their friendship as a kind of marriage. Upon awakening from his first night as Queequeg's bedfellow, Ishmael notes that "You had almost thought I had been his wife" (25); Queequeg declares that the two are married (51); and Ishmael describes how they lie in bed, "in our hearts' honeymoon . . . a cosy, loving pair" (52). Recalling the merging of husband and wife under antebellum laws of coverture (the "very being" of the woman is "incorporated and consolidated into that of her husband," explains William Blackstone in his commentary on such laws [I: 430]), the marriage between Ishmael and Queequeg involves a consolidation of identity, a merging of self and other across the lines of white and black, "Christian" and "cannibal."

This compelling, even mysterious marital merger across lines of race will come up again in "The Monkey-Rope," a chapter that describes the mechanism by which Ishmael and Queequeg are joined together during the "perilous business" of "cutting-in" to the whale (320). Recognizing the "metaphysical" implications of their union via the monkey-rope ("for better or for worse, we two, for the time, were wedded"), Ishmael remarks that "my own individuality was now merged in a joint stock company of two" (320). Insofar as it involves a dissolution of the self's boundaries –

insofar, indeed, as it involves the merging of whiteness and blackness – such a merger would certainly appear to be a "perilous business." Yet ultimately it is not a business from which Ishmael, or the text of which he is the putative author, retreats. Like the "Virginian" in "Mosses," "fixed," "fascinated," and ultimately penetrated by Hawthorne's "blackness," Ishmael is "mysteriously drawn" toward a union with Queequeg and the racial fluidity that such a union signifies. Indeed, he admits, "those same things that would have repelled most others, they were the very magnets that drew me" (51).

The language of magnetism that we encounter here suggests Melville's interest in the same sorts of occult transfusions between self and other, white and black, that engage Hawthorne in *The House of the Seven Gables* (Hawthorne will revisit these issues in his 1852 novel, *The Blithedale Romance*). That language is also instrumental in *Pierre*, a text that can be read as a more extended, and more vexed, answer to the racial anxieties that circulate through Hawthorne's *House*. In *Pierre*, too, we have a white man (Pierre) drawn "magnetically" to a dark other (Pierre's half-sister Isabel), who exerts over him a kind of mesmeric force and power. Although Isabel is never identified as "black," she is associated with a variety of racial signifiers: her face, with its "dark, olive cheek" (46), compels, dispossesses, and "unmans" Pierre (49) when he first sees it; Isabel is an "olive girl" (51) possessed of a "long dark shower of curls" (126); she is a "dark, regal being" (152), a woman of "ebon tresses" and "ebon eyes" (314); in the novel's final scene, we see Pierre's body "arbored" in the "ebon vines" of Isabel's hair (362). And just as Ishmael does in *Moby-Dick*, Pierre "marries" his dark other, allying himself with her in a relationship that has sexual, moral, and ideological ramifications. When Pierre "crosses the Rubicon" – rejecting the conventional morality and false piety of his mother and the "white-browed and white-handed" Reverend Falsgrave (99) and casting his lot with Isabel and Delly Ulver, a village girl who has borne a child out of wedlock – he chooses to "embrace his 'black shadow' " (Levine, "Blackened Hand" 37–8).

Even as the text renders this as Pierre's choice, it also returns to the ground of occult compulsion that Hawthorne visited in *The House of the Seven Gables*. During his second meeting with Isabel, Pierre becomes aware of what "he could not help believing was an extraordinary physical magnetism in Isabel": "To Pierre's dilated senses Isabel seemed to swim in an electric fluid; the vivid buckler of her brow seemed as a magnetic plate." She exerts a "marvelous power" over both "himself and his most interior thoughts and motions"; that power seems "irresistibly to draw him toward Isabel" and "away from another quarter" (151) – the fair-haired, fair-skinned, snow-white Lucy Glendinning. Just as it is in *House*, in *Pierre* the occult (and specifically mesmeric) power that one individual can exert over another is figured as a penetration of that which is "most interior" to the self, as a merging of self and other. And as in *House*, in *Pierre* that power is rendered in terms of race: in both texts, the "white" self is amalgamated with the "black" other. But whereas *House* retreats from that vision of amalgamation, rendering it as a scene of humiliating enslavement, *Pierre* suggests that the marital merger between the "white" self and its "black shadow" can be, as it is in

Moby-Dick, an empowering one. Liberated from his false past and from the effort to preserve racial purity that, he can now recognize, such a past entails, Pierre can embark on a new authorial career, one through which he intends "to deliver what he thought to be new, or at least miserably neglected Truth to the world" (283). Or so the novel seems to want to suggest.

In recounting the first part of her story, Isabel tells Pierre that she finds "no perfect peace in individualness. Therefore I hope one day to feel myself drank up into the pervading spirit animating all things" (119). With her rejection of "individualness," Isabel echoes the "miscegenated," maritally merged Ishmael in "The Monkey-Rope." But whereas in *Moby-Dick* neither Ishmael nor Melville, writing behind him, appears to recoil from the fusion of white self and black "other," *Pierre* seems unable, finally, to sustain its vision of miscegenated selfhood. Although the novel reaches toward the suggestion that Pierre's authorship is liberating and liberated, ultimately, and indeed tragically, that authorship in fact serves a reactionary function. Pierre writes not so much to purvey "new" or "miserably neglected" truths as to reclaim both his self-sovereignty and its corollary: his inviolable whiteness. Drawing on the notion of double-writing that he began to develop in "Hawthorne and his Mosses," Melville describes the text on which Pierre labors in terms of doubleness: in addition to the text the "world" will "read in a very few hours," Pierre is writing another, completely interior text, one "writ down in his soul" for his "own private shelf" (304). He is writing a text, in short, that is his own private property and that testifies, as such, to his inalienable interiority. "I fight a duel in which all seconds are forbid," he proclaims when Isabel and Lucy offer to help him in his work (349). Through Vivia, his narrative *alter ego*, Pierre reclaims himself in what can be seen as an act of racial recoil: "I am what I am," Pierre declares, as the novels (Melville's and Pierre's own) are coming to an end (325).

What Pierre "is," however, cannot be separated from the blackness that he has heretofore embraced, as the final image of the novel makes plain. Having taken the vial of poison that she has lodged between her breasts, Isabel "fell upon Pierre's heart, and her long hair ran over him, and arbored him in ebon vines" (362). In many respects, we can read the tragic elements of this final scene – like the stage at the end of a Shakespearean tragedy, the final scene of *Pierre* is littered with bodies – as indicating Melville's awareness of the destructive dangers of the sort of sovereignty that Pierre seeks. Yet the terror that is invoked by this image – Isabel "sloped sideways," her "ebon" hair running over him like living things – suggests that Melville himself may not be free of the sort of racial anxieties – anxieties about the threatening inescapability of "blackness" – in which Hawthorne participated in *House*. If *Pierre* can be read, as Wyn Kelley has suggested, as an extended answer to *House*, it can also be read as a text in which the "student" fails, finally, to surpass the "teacher."

From the moment that he begins writing to and about Nathaniel Hawthorne, I have been arguing here, Melville engages Hawthorne in part through the racial legacies that he believed were central components of an American authorial project. In the two stimulating years between their meeting and the publishing of *Pierre*,

Melville engaged Hawthorne in a conversation about racial identity and the precarious boundaries between whiteness and blackness, identifying the problematic racial anxieties that circulated through Hawthorne's "dark little black-letter volumes" – and, at times, perhaps not surprisingly, participating in those same anxieties. Nor would the conversation cease with *Pierre*. Scholars have long struggled with the prevarications over race and slavery involved in Hawthorne's 1852 campaign biography of Franklin Pierce and his controversial "Chiefly about War Matters" (1862): Hawthorne's assertion in the *Life of Franklin Pierce* that slavery is an "evil" that cannot be "remedied by human contrivances" but rather must disappear in "its own good time" (351), for example, or his deeply disturbing renditions of fugitive slaves in "Chiefly about War Matters" ("They were unlike the specimens of their race whom we are accustomed to see at the North," he writes, "wearing" as they do "such a crust of primeval simplicity" that they "seemed a kind of creature by themselves, not altogether human" [318–19]). Understandably, given such efforts to challenge the ideology and epistemology of antebellum racism as "The 'Gees" (1856) and, more significantly, "Benito Cereno" (1855), Melville has long been viewed as surpassing Hawthorne in this regard. Yet Melville's "Supplement" to his 1866 poetic collection *Battle-Pieces* evidences disturbing echoes of Hawthorne's thinking. Here, Melville redraws the very racial lines that he has, in his earlier work, sought to undercut, at one point arguing that, in the spirit of reconciliation, white northerners should not forget to extend "kindliness" to white southerners, who stand "nearer to us in nature" (*CP* 465). More than fifteen years after their initial meeting, then, Melville continues to consider – sometimes challenging, sometimes accepting – the legacy left to him by Hawthorne. As we are trying to make sense of what that legacy meant to Melville, we need to recognize the extent to which Melville could see what it has taken contemporary critics a long time to recognize: the racial "blackness" that circulates through the work of "Nathaniel of Salem."

References and Further Reading

Allison, John. "Conservative Architecture: Hawthorne in Melville's 'I and My Chimney.'" *South Central Review* 13 (1996): 17–25.

Anthony, David. "Class, Culture, and the Trouble with White Skin in Hawthorne's *The House of the Seven Gables*." *The Yale Journal of Criticism* 12 (1999): 249–68.

Blackstone, William. *Commentaries on the Laws of England. 1765–1769*. 4 vols. Ed. Stanley N. Katz. Vol. 1. Chicago: University of Chicago Press, 1979.

Brodhead, Richard. *The School of Hawthorne*. New York: Oxford University Press, 1986.

Davis, Clark. "Hawthorne's Shyness: Romance and the Forms of Truth." *ESQ* 45 (1999): 33–65.

Gilmore, Paul. *The Genuine Article: Race, Mass Culture, and American Literary Manhood*. Durham, NC, and London: Duke University Press, 2001.

Goddu, Teresa A. "Letters Turned to Gold: Hawthorne, Authorship, and Slavery." *Studies in American Fiction* 29 (2001): 49–76.

Harshbarger, Scott. "Bugs and Butterflies: Conflict and Transcendence in 'The Artist of the Beautiful' and 'The Apple-Tree Table.'" *Studies in Short Fiction* 26 (1989): 186–9.

Hawthorne, Nathaniel. "Chiefly About War Matters." *Tales, Sketches, and Other Papers*. Boston and New York: Houghton Mifflin Company, 1883. 299–345.

——. *The House of the Seven Gables*. Vol. 2 of *The Centenary Edition of the Works of Nathaniel Hawthorne*. Ed. William Charvat, Roy Harvey Pearce, and Claude Simpson. Columbus: Ohio State University Press, 1965.

——. *The Life of Franklin Pierce*. Vol 28 of *The Centenary Edition of the Works of Nathaniel Hawthorne*. Ed. William Charvat, Roy Harvey Pearce, and Claude Simpson. Columbus: Ohio State University Press, 1994.

——. *Mosses from an Old Manse*. Vol. 10 of *The Centenary Edition of the Works of Nathaniel Hawthorne*. Ed. William Charvat, Roy Harvey Pearce, and Claude Simpson. Columbus: Ohio State University Press, 1974.

Hewitt, Elizabeth. "Scarlet Letters, Dead Letters: Correspondence and the Poetics of Democracy in Melville and Hawthorne." *Yale Journal of Criticism* 12 (1999): 295–319.

Jones, Buford. *Some "Mosses" from the* Literary World: *Critical and Bibliographical Survey of the Hawthorne–Melville Relationship*. In *Ruined Eden of the Present: Hawthorne, Melville, Poe*. Ed. G. R. Thompson and Virgil L. Lokke. West Lafayette, IN: Purdue University Press, 1981. 173–203.

Karcher, Carolyn. *Shadow over the Promised Land: Slavery, Race, and Violence in Melville's America*. Baton Rouge and London: Louisiana State University Press, 1980.

Kelley, Wyn. "*Pierre*'s Domestic Ambiguities." In *The Cambridge Companion to Herman Melville*. Ed. Robert S. Levine. Cambridge and New York: Cambridge University Press, 1998.

Levine, Robert S. "*Pierre*'s Blackened Hand." *Leviathan* 1 (1999): 23–44.

——. "Trappe(d): Race and Genealogical Haunting in *The Bondwoman's Narrative*." In *In Search of Hannah Crafts: Critical Essays on* The Bondwoman's Narrative. Ed. Henry Louis Gates and Hollis Robbins. New York: Basic Civitas Books, 2004. 276–94.

Levy, Leo. "Hawthorne and the Idea of 'Bartleby.' " *ESQ* 47 (1967): 66–9.

Martin, Robert K. and Leland Person. "Missing Letters: Hawthorne, Melville, and Scholarly Desire." *ESQ* 46 (2000): 99–122.

Matthiessen, F. O. *American Renaissance: Art and Expression in the Age of Emerson and Whitman*. London: Oxford University Press, 1941.

Mellow, James R. *Nathaniel Hawthorne in his Times*. Baltimore and London: Johns Hopkins University Press, 1980.

Milder, Robert. " 'The Ugly Socrates': Melville, Hawthorne, and Homoeroticism." *ESQ* 46 (2000): 1–49.

Miller, Edwin Haviland. *Melville*. New York: Venture Books, 1975.

——. *Salem is My Dwelling Place: A Life of Nathaniel Hawthorne*. Iowa City: University of Iowa Press, 1991.

Mitchell, Thomas R. "In the Whale's Wake: Melville and *The Blithedale Romance*." *ESQ* 46 (2000): 51–73.

Rosenberry, Edward. "Melville and His *Mosses*." *ATQ* 7 (1970): 51–5.

Waggoner, Hyatt H. "Hawthorne's Presence in *Moby-Dick* and in Melville's Tales and Sketches." *Nathaniel Hawthorne Journal* (1977): 73–9.

Wald, Priscilla. *Constituting Americans: Cultural Anxiety and Narrative Form*. Durham, NC, and London: Duke University Press, 1995.

Wineapple, Brenda. "Hawthorne and Melville; or, The Ambiguities." *ESQ* 46 (2000): 75–97.

22

"Unlike Things Must Meet and Mate": Melville and the Visual Arts

Robert K. Wallace

Melville's interest in the visual arts began in the family home in New York City in the 1820s, grew as he became a reader of illustrated books in Albany in the 1830s, diversified on his voyages to Liverpool and the South Seas in 1839 and the early 1840s, found expression in his novels of the later 1840s, reached an epiphany during his voyage to London and the Continent in 1849, and achieved artistic and psychological integration in *Moby-Dick* in 1851, at the age of thirty-two. During the remaining forty years of Melville's life – in spite of vicissitudes that took him from being a famous fiction writer to a writer of unread poetry, from a professional author to a customs inspector, and from a sociable youth to a reclusive elderly man – his interest in the visual arts continued to grow. This was particularly so after the voyage to the Mediterranean in 1856–7 that introduced him to artistic monuments ranging from the pyramids of Egypt to the minarets of Istanbul, the temples of Greece, and the paintings and sculpture of Italy. The extended epiphanies of this extensive voyage, coinciding with the winding down of his career as a writer of fiction, opened two new areas of artistic satisfaction for the rest of his life – as a writer of poetry and as a collector of art.

Melville's use of visual art in his poetry from *Battle-Pieces* in 1866 to *Clarel* in 1876 to *Timoleon* in 1891 is increasingly overt, intentional, masterful, and subtle. The print collection that continued to grow as he wrote these poems in his own New York house was a work of art itself. More than four hundred prints have now been discovered and documented from his personal collection of art. Their geographical, temporal, and stylistic range – including Italian, French, Dutch, German, English, and American artists from the early Renaissance up through the modern painters of his own day – reflects the catholicity of his taste and the acuity of his eye as fully as any of the books he wrote. In the art work he had collected by the end of his life he found some of the companionship he had cultivated through more social endeavors earlier in life. One of his favorite writers on art was the English essayist William Hazlitt. In the 1824 essay on the "Marquis of Stafford's Gallery" reprinted in Hazlitt's *Criticisms on Art*, Melville drew three marginal lines next to Hazlitt's declaration that "there are only three pleasures in life pure and lasting, and all are derived from inanimate objects – books, pictures, and the face of nature" (Hazlitt 40–1).

Throughout Melville's life his interest in the visual arts reanimated Hazlitt's inanimate trinity in endlessly imaginative and satisfying ways. 'Melville and the visual arts' is still quite a recent area of study. Whereas Merton M. Sealts, Jr. began his documentation of Melville's library in the 1940s and had published the first edition of *Melville's Reading* in 1966, study of Melville's art collection did not get seriously underway until the 1980s (Wallace "Berkshire Athenaeum"). Christopher Sten provided the first biographical overview of Melville's life in the visual arts in *Savage Eye* in 1991, Douglass Robillard the first aesthetic overview in *Melville and the Visual Arts* in 1997.

1

Melville's depiction of Redburn's childhood home in *Redburn* includes a number of art objects likely to have had real-life counterparts in Melville's childhood home. "We had several oil paintings and rare old engravings of my father's, which he had himself bought in Paris, hanging up in the dining room" (6). Two "sea-pieces" specifically mentioned in Redburn's fictional home – a group of fishermen attending to a boat on shore, a ship off a lee shore in a storm – resemble in subject and style engravings after paintings by Claude Joseph Vernet and Willem van de Velde the Younger in Melville's art collection, possibly inherited from his father (Wallace *Melville and Turner*, figs. 3, 4).

In addition to the sea-pieces in the dining room, Redburn and his siblings had "two large green French portfolios of colored prints" that they would look at "every Saturday morning." In addition to "rural scenes, full of fine skies" above "pensive cows," they saw a "picture of a great whale, big as a ship, stuck full of harpoons, and three boats sailing after it as fast as they could fly." Yet another art object in Redburn's childhood home is the glass sailing ship whose "figure-head" was "a gallant warrior in a cocked hat" who "fell from his perch the very day I left home to go to sea in this my first voyage" (6–9). This portentous event has a psychological as well as pictorial function in the novel, suggesting the economic fall and fatal illness that took the life of Redburn's father, sending Redburn to sea when only a boy (as was the case with Herman). Hershel Parker has traced the original of this fictional object to "a glass ship, fully rigged, modeled after the features of some celebrated French vessel" in the home of Herman's paternal grandfather Thomas Melvill in Boston (Parker 1: 44).

It is hard to know how many of the elegant objects in the Melvill family home survived the bankruptcy of Allan Melvill in New York in 1830 or the severe impoverishment suffered by his widow Maria and her eight children after his death in Albany in 1832. If some of the family's art objects disappeared, Herman's memories of them would remain, augmented by new impressions of visual art from his teenage life in Albany. The 1830s was the first full decade of the state-of-the-art steel engravings in illustrated books that artists like J. M. W. Turner and Clarkston Stanfield were now producing in England. One such book that young Herman was certain to see was the 1836 edition of Captain Marryat's *The Pirate and The Three Cutters* illustrated with nineteen steel engravings after designs by Stanfield. Later in life Melville collected twelve of these nineteen engravings, eleven of them from *The Pirate*, a story about slavery as well as piracy. In addition to a frontispiece of *The Mast-Headed Midshipman* certain to appeal to teenage readers (figure 22.1), these engravings depicted such striking scenes as *Cutting away the Masts*, *Abandoning the Circassian*, *The Capture*, *The Destruction of the Indiaman*, *Escape on the Raft*, *The Ship on Fire*, and *Rescuing the Crew from the Burning Vessel* (Wallace *Maritime Prints*, nos. 21–32). Young Melville had access to *The Pirate and the Three Cutters* at the Young Men's Association of Albany – to which he and Gansevoort both belonged in 1836 (Wallace *Melville and Turner* 58–9). In *Typee*, Melville wrote of those "long-haired, bare-necked youths" who are sent to sea "by the united influences of Captain Marryat and hard times" (21).

When Melville went to Liverpool as a sailor on the *St. Lawrence* in 1839 his young eyes received many new impressions. Not all of them were artistic. The "dingy warehouses" in this city looked quite like those in New York. As he wrote about this voyage in *Redburn*, however, Melville turned a prosaic Liverpool guidebook into an object of art (see Robillard). Equally impressive is the power with which he transformed the chained figures at the foot of the Lord Nelson monument he had seen in 1839 (ostensibly "emblematic of Nelson's principal victories") into a meditation on the condition of slaves in the American South (155).

When Melville sailed from New Bedford to the South Seas in January 1841, he was opening his eyes to new dimensions of visual art as well as of human ecology and natural topography. The most striking example of this was the art of tattooing, to which separate chapters are devoted in both *Typee* and *Omoo*. Tommo in *Typee* describes the work of Karky, the tattooer, with all the literary bravura of one of Hazlitt's familiar essays, elevating him into "A Professor of Fine Arts." When Karky wants to tattoo Tommo's own face, however, he shudders in horror and vows to escape from the island (217–19). This prospect of "losing face," as Sam Otter has shown, provokes a crisis more intense than that of the "cannibalism" in the story (Otter 10–11). In *Omoo*, however, Melville's narrator does encounter an Englishman who has allowed "a broad blue band" to be tattooed "across his face from ear to ear" (27).

In addition to the visual art worn on the "living canvas" of the Polynesian body, Melville is attentive to the sculptural remains that have been left behind by ancient ancestors. The latter inspire this passage on "Remarkable Monumental Ruins" in *Typee*: "As I gazed upon this monument, doubtless the work of an extinct and forgotten race,

Figure 22.1 J.C. Edwards after Clarkson Stanfield. Title vignette for the 1836 edition of *The Pirate and the Three Cutters* by Captain Frederick Marryat (London: Longman & Company, and Philadelphia: Desilba, Thomas & Company). $3\frac{1}{2} \times 4\frac{1}{4}$ in. Melville Memorial Room, Berkshire Athenaeum, Pittsfield, MA.

thus buried in the green nook of an island at the ends of the earth, the existence of which was yesterday unknown, a stronger feeling of awe came over me than if I had stood musing at the mighty base of the Pyramid of Cheops" (155). That "awe" would expand exponentially in the chapter on "Time and Temples" in *Mardi* that Melville wrote a few years later amidst the libraries of New York City. Here his imagination ranges over those ancient temples whose ruins survive all over the globe. "Nero's House of Gold was not raised in a day; nor the Mexican House of the Sun; nor the Alhambra; nor the Escurial; nor Titus's Amphitheater; nor the Illinois Mound; nor Diana's great column at Ephesus; nor Pompey's proud Pillar; nor the Parthenon; nor the Altar of Belus; nor Stonehenge; nor Solomon's Temple; nor Tadmoor's towers; nor Susa's bastions; nor Persepolis' pediments" (228–9). Melville is not only cataloguing art objects here. He is documenting a universal drive by ancient cultures across the globe for monumental self-expression.

2

Melville returned from the South Seas as a sailor on the U.S. *United States*, landing in Boston in October 1844. After rejoining his mother and siblings in Lansingburgh, across the river from Albany, he wrote *Typee*. Here initiated the six-year period of growth that Melville summed up in his 1851 letter to Hawthorne: "Until I was twenty-five, I had no development at all. From my twenty-fifth year I date my life. Three weeks have scarcely passed, at any time between then and now, that I have not unfolded within myself" (*L* 193). In that six-year unfolding the visual arts played an important role. From *Typee* through *White-Jacket* Melville incorporates the visual arts in ways we have already seen – from tattooing in *Typee* and *Omoo*, to temples in *Typee* and *Mardi*, to paintings, engravings, and glass ships in *Redburn*. In *White-Jacket* the jacket itself becomes a work of art of a distinctly Melvillean kind. Approaching Cape Horn without either a "grego" or a "pea-jacket" to protect him, White-Jacket "employed myself, for several days, in manufacturing an outlandish garment of my own devising" (3). Beyond providing shelter, this "bedarned and bequilted" artifact performs a variety of functions throughout the book. Superstitiously, White-Jacket's shipmates take it for the carpenter's ghost; sociologically, the jacket separates him from the rest of the crew; psychologically, he literally cuts himself out of it after his plunge from the mast; sportively, his shipmates mistake it for the white of a shark and sink it in a shower of harpoons.

At the same time that Melville is incorporating a diverse range of visual art objects into his first five novels, he also employs his visual art knowledge in two additional ways. First, he drops the kind of allusions to famous painters or artwork that would be expected from an educated author. Thus we have decorative references to Teniers and Stonehenge in *Typee*; to Hogarth in *Omoo*; to Wouvermans and Claude in *Mardi*; to Guido and Salvatore Rosa in *Redburn*; and to Hogarth, Cruikshank, and Wilke in *White-Jacket*. Some of these allusions become quite ambitious, as when Taji declares that the attack of a right whale by some "Killers and Thrashers" would have been a fine subject for "old Wouvermans, who once painted a bull bait.... And Gudin or Isabey might have thrown the blue rolling sea into the picture. Lastly, one of Claude's setting summer suns would have glorified the whole. Oh, believe me, God's creatures fighting fin for fin, a thousand miles from land, and with the round horizon for an arena, is no ignoble subject for a masterpiece" (*Mardi*, 42).

A stronger and more subtle contribution of the visual arts to the first five novels is the degree to which Melville's literary style was influenced by his reading in the fine arts. The jaunty, familiar tone we have already noted in parts of *Typee* and *Omoo* corresponds to that in Hazlitt's art criticism that Melville read in *Table Talk* and other early collections (whose American editions were edited by Herman's friend Evert Duyckinck in the mid-1840s). The more sublime and ambitious aesthetic of *Mardi* reflects Melville's interest in John Ruskin's *Modern Painters 1*, brought out by Duyckinck in its first American edition in 1847 just as Melville was beginning to write *Mardi*. Similarly, the technical sophistication about painterly matters that Melville shows in *White-Jacket* and "The Whiteness of the Whale" in *Moby-Dick* can be traced to Charles L. Eastlake's *Materials for a History of Oil Painting* (1847), a book to which Melville had access when visiting his Shaw in-laws in Boston in 1848 (Sealts no. 198). For a detailed account of Melville's reading about the fine arts in the late 1840s, see "Swimming Through the Art Libraries of Young America" in *Melville and Turner* (Wallace).

As soon as he signed a contract for *White-Jacket* with Harper and Brothers in New York in September 1849, Melville sailed to London to negotiate a sale with an English publisher. If this had gone smoothly, he had hoped to extend his journey not only across the English Channel but all the way to the Mediterranean. As it turned out, the book took longer to sell than he thought; arriving in London on November 6, he did not come to terms with Richard Bentley until December 17, after returning from a short excursion to France and Germany. In the interim, Melville got acquainted first-hand with Old Master and modern painters he had been reading about in books by Hazlitt, Ruskin, Eastlake, and others. That it was an extremely stimulating period is shown in the journal he kept in London from November 6 to December 24, in the increased aesthetic sophistication he showed in *Moby-Dick*, and in the continuous and comprehensive interest he showed in Old Master and modern painters for the rest of his life.

Melville's London journal records visits to the National Gallery (twice), the Vernon Gallery, Hampton Court, the Painted Hall at Greenwich, the Dulwich Gallery, and the gallery at Windsor Castle. He recorded the names of artists who impressed him (Lely, Titian, Rembrandt, Claude, Salvator, Wouvermans, West, Cellini) amidst more general comments showing the development of his own critical faculty (the gallery at Windsor Castle was "cheerlessly, damnatory fine"). Melville also visited the private art collection of Samuel Rogers, perhaps the finest in London. He visited its "superb paintings" twice, alone with Rogers for a conversational "breakfast" on December 20, with other guests on December 22 (*J* 24, 45, 46). The paintings in Rogers's collection included first-rate works by Titian, Claude, Rubens, Giorgione, and Raphael. Rogers also owned original paintings and first-state engravings by J. M. W. Turner, the English seascape artist whose illustrations for the poems in Rogers's *Italy* in 1830 set the standard for stainless-steel book engraving for the rest of the decade. Rogers was a close friend of Turner (who was still alive, but not well, in London; he died in 1851). He was very familiar with Turner's entire career as an artist, as well as with the painter's celebrated private gallery, which currently held at least three of the four whaling oils that Turner had exhibited at London's Royal Academy in 1845 and 1846.

Melville's journal does not record any meeting with Turner himself, or any visit to the private gallery, but he could have learned a great deal about both the man and his work during his two visits to Rogers's collection. He also met another of Turner's closest friends, the American-born painter C. R. Leslie, at the "Paradise of Bachelors" dinner parties he attended on December 19 and 22. Leslie was the only man in London who had his own key to Turner's private gallery and could visit it at will. He invited Melville to spend Christmas at his home in St. John's Wood, but Herman had promised his wife Elizabeth he would be coming home, so he left London for Portsmouth as scheduled on December 24.

To be in the inner sanctum of English art appreciation during the breakfasts with Rogers and the dinners with Leslie, after having visited nearly all of the "Principal Galleries of England" that Hazlitt had written about in the 1820s, gave Melville a wonderful store of information that he could draw upon not only for his more immediate writing projects but for his lifelong growth as a connoisseur of visual expression. Melville continued to assimilate new impressions during his brief trip across the Channel. After visiting Versailles and the Louvre in France ("heaps of treasures of art of all sorts"), he visited both the Museum and the Cathedral in Cologne ("the city in which Rubens was born & Mary De Medici died") (31, 35). From Cologne he sailed up the Rhine to Ehrenbreitstein and Coblenz before reversing his course for home. He sailed back down the Rhine to Ostend, across to London for his meetings with Bentley, Leslie, and Rogers, and then home to his wife and son Malcolm, not yet two years old, in New York.

We know that Melville's exposure to visual art during his 1849 voyage was an extended epiphany because of the resourcefulness, range, and sophistication with which he employs visual art materials in *Moby-Dick*. Melville's use of paintings within the fictional world of the novel ranges from the painting in the Spouter-Inn, to its counterpart in Father Mapple's Chapel, to the painting being held by the London *kedger*, depicting the scene in which he lost a leg to a whale. Allusions to Old Master artists are no longer decorative. The comparison of Ahab's chest to "Cellini's cast Perseus" (123); or of a skrimshander's carving to the "barbarian spirit" of "that fine old Dutch savage, Albert Durer" (270); or of the white whale to "the white bull Jupiter swimming away with ravished Europa clinging to his graceful horns" (548) — all such allusions to the Old Master painters or their traditional subjects ring true because they are used not to showcase the author's knowledge but rather to stimulate new shocks of recognition about the maritime story of this adventuresome book. Nor is Melville averse to debunking the Old Masters when appropriate. He begins the first of three chapters specifically devoted to visual depiction ("Of the Monstrous Pictures of Whales") by chastising Guido and Hogarth. He concludes these chapters by elevating the artistic attributes of the London *kedger* and the lowly skrimshander (see Frank for illustrations of many of the visual subjects in these chapters).

One of the most striking visual art images in the entire book is that of "the Great Cathedral of Cologne…with the crane still standing upon the top of the uncompleted tower." This arises in a place where one would not expect it – at the end of the chapter on the science of "Cetology." The image itself is merely descriptive; its power comes from its application to the book Ishmael is writing: "Small erections may be finished by their first architects; grand ones, true ones, ever leave the copestone to posterity" (145). Ishmael's appropriation of the unfinished Cologne Cathedral to represent his own effort as a writer is one way in which Melville has integrated his growing aesthetic awareness into his own psychological development. Another is Ishmael's encounter with the painting in the Spouter-Inn. Ishmael devotes three paragraphs to this "boggy, soggy, squitchy picture" – even though he is not absolutely sure what it actually represents. The painting looks like "chaos bewitched" yet he can't get it out of his mind. What "most puzzled and confounded you was a long, limber, portentous, black mass of something hovering in the centre of the picture over three blue, dim, perpendicular lines floating in a nameless yeast." Once Ishmael senses that the "black mass" might be an "exasperated whale," he is able discern narrative as well as representational elements within the seeming chaos of the "artist's design" (12–13). Ishmael sees in the Spouter-Inn the fictional equivalent of the seascapes of J. M. W. Turner, whose powerful aesthetic of the indistinct had become increasingly unsettling to viewers at the Royal Academy during the 1840s. Melville's painting reads like a cross between Turner's *Snow Storm – Steam-Boat* of 1842 (figure 22.2) and *The Whale Ship* of 1845.

Melville had seen original paintings by Turner at the National Gallery and the Vernon Gallery as well as in Samuel Rogers's private gallery. An annotation he wrote on the title page of Beale's *Natural History of the Sperm Whale* in July 1850 recorded his knowledge that "Turner's pictures of whalers were suggested by this book." Of thirty-three engravings after Turner that have now surfaced from Melville's collection, an impressive number of them convey the powerful indistinctness of Turner's late style. Among them are *Ancient Rome*, *Regulus Leaving Carthage*, *Snow Storm – Steam-Boat*; *Peace – Burial at Sea; Venice – the Dogana*; *Rain, Steam, and Speed*; and *Whalers – "The Erebus"* (see Wallace *Melville and Turner* chapter 1).

Biographical details about gallery visits in London, the annotation in Beale, and the collection of Turner engravings provide some of the factual ingredients that made the creation of the painting in the Spouter-Inn possible. But none of these can account for how the epistemological instability of this painting contrasts with the theological uplift of its counterpart in Father Mapple's pulpit. Or for how the catastrophe eventually shadowed forth in Ishmael's response to the painting anticipates the

Figure 22.2 R. Brandard after J.M.W. Turner. *Snow Storm – Steam-Boat*. Engraved for *The Turner Gallery*. 1859. $7\frac{7}{8}$ × 10 in. Melville Memorial Room, Berkshire Athenaeum, Pittsfield, MA.

catastrophe that will conclude the book. Or for how Ishmael's persistent engagement with the bewildering painting, even to the point of asking other people what they think about it, initiates the dynamic of his truth-seeking quest throughout the novel. Or for how the process of perceiving the painting becomes a metaphor for the process of reading the novel. After the American Abstract Expressionists of the 1950s, the art world has become more and more used to the kind of struggle for meaning that Ishmael here embodies. As Elizabeth Schultz has shown, visual artists in the twentieth century have responded to *Moby-Dick* in every possible medium and style. Many of their greatest creations oscillate between abstraction and representation with the uncanny allure of the Spouter-Inn painting.

3

After *Moby-Dick*, visual art continued to be a strong presence in Melville's novels and stories of the 1850s. In *Pierre* in 1852 John Flaxman's engravings after Dante's *Divine Comedy* play a major role in Pierre's courtship of Lucy, herself an aspiring visual artist (Melville's own art collection included twenty-three engravings from Flaxman's Dante published in Paris in 1833). *Pierre* also contains a scathing critique of the "picturesque" versus the "povertiresque" in art. "Bartleby, the Scrivener" in 1853 locates its protagonist in a decidedly anti-picturesque work environment. "At one end" the lawyer's chambers "looked upon the white wall of the interior of a spacious sky-light shaft . . . This view might have been considered rather tame than otherwise, deficient in what landscape painters call 'life.' " For contrast, "the view from the other end of my chambers . . . commanded an unobstructed brick wall, black by age and everlasting shade" (*PT* 14). In "The Encantadas" in 1854 Melville used the pseudonym Salvator R. Tarnmoor, alluding to the Italian painter Salvator Rosa. His most seamless use of a visual art viewpoint is the fictional tableau in which he frames the death of Hunilla's beloved husband and brother through a picturesque oval of foliage in which Hunilla sees the tragedy happen.

Melville in "The Bell Tower" in 1854 harnesses his growing knowledge of Renaissance architecture to recreate the soaring imagination and searing inhumanity that enable Belladonna to erect the commanding Campanile whose clockwork mechanism kills the man who had created it at the expense of other human lives. The most striking examples of visual art in "Benito Cereno" in 1855 are revealed in a sequence of three images toward the end of the story: the "human skeleton" of the slaveholder Aranda as "the figure-head" of the ship; the conceptual art of its having supplanted "the image of Christopher Colon, the discoverer of the New World," as "the ship's proper figure-head"; and the visual personification by which the decapitated head of Babo, "that hive of subtlety, fixed on a pole in the Plaza, met, unabashed, the gaze of the whites" (*PT* 99, 107, 116).

All four of the above stories were gathered into *The Piazza Tales* in 1856 from their previous appearances in *Putnam's Monthly Magazine*. Each of the visual images cited above takes us directly into the psychosocial heart of the story in which it appears. "The Piazza," written in 1856 to introduce *The Piazza Tales*, opens in the world of the Hudson River School of American landscape: "a very paradise of painters," in which "no boy climbs hill or crosses vale without coming upon easels planted in every nook, and sun-burnt painters painting there." What they are painting is the surpassing beauty of the mountain as seen from afar, so that these "limestone hills" resemble nothing so much as "galleries hung, month after month anew, with pictures ever fading into pictures ever fresh" (*PT* 1–2). From the comfort of his own piazza, Melville's narrator registers an exquisite sequence of impressionistic atmospheric effects "painted" on the "canvas" of the distant mountain. Drawn by its magical allure, he ascends the mountain to experience its beauties first-hand. What he finds is a dilapidated mountain cottage inhabited by an impoverished, dispirited young woman. He and Marianna are unable to find common ground emotionally in spite of their similarities of picturesque perception (she has imagined his house down in the valley as the home of a "King Charming" whose life would surely be exempt from any of her own cares). This seemingly modest story, in addition to using the mountain itself as a living canvas, presents a devastating critique of the picturesque credo of the Hudson River School – and of "Mountain Beauty" in Ruskin's *Modern Painters 4* – as presented during 1855 and 1856 in the pages of *The Crayon*, America's leading art journal (see Wallace "Melville After Turner").

The Piazza Tales was Melville's ninth book of fiction in ten years. He had also completed the manuscript of the tenth, *The Confidence-Man*, which went into publication as Melville embarked on a restorative trip to the Mediterranean financed by his father-in-law Lemuel Shaw. The pressure of non-stop writing since disembarking from the U.S. *United States* in 1844 had been intense. More troubling was the fact that Melville's novels, in spite of his extremely promising debut with *Typee*, did not bring in enough money to support his growing family. Whether or not Melville had an actual breakdown at this time (testimony is divided), he did need a break. After sailing from New York for Liverpool in October 1856, his Mediterranean voyage took him to Algiers, Smyrna, Constantinople, Cairo, Jerusalem, Athens, Naples, Rome, Pisa, Florence, Venice, Genoa, and Como before heading north to Heidelberg, Amsterdam, Rotterdam, London, and Oxford, arriving home in May 1857. Not only did Melville get relief from a dozen years of "unfolding" within himself at the writing desk; he also found a new source of psychosocial stability in the perception of ancient, Renaissance, and nineteenth-century art.

The journal Melville kept of his Mediterranean voyages, like the one he kept on the voyage to England and the Continent seven years earlier, provides us with a rare and revealing record of his perceiving eye and mind. In Constantinople he was intrigued not only by the sanctity of St. Sophia but by the water taxis to the Scutari. In Egypt he was attracted not only to the Pyramids but to the "donkey boys" who resourcefully plied the tourist trade. In Jerusalem he examined pioneering Zionists as well as the sites called Holy. He found some of his deepest inspiration high above the gorge called Kedron. Sailing through the Sporades on the way to Athens, he saw the sea abstracting itself into Flaxmanesque outline engravings. "A fine sail upon the whole. But the scenery is all outline. No filling up. Seem to be sailing upon gigantic outline engravings" (*J* 97).

Once Melville arrived in Greece, his mind and heart were drawn to "The Attic Landscape" he would celebrate thirty-four years later in *Timoleon*: "No flushful tint the sense to warm – / Pure outline pale, a linear charm. / The clear-cut hills carved temples face, / Respond, and share their sculptural grace" (*CP* 245). In Athens, he perceived "The Parthenon" in such a way that thirty-three years later he could structure his poem of that title as if it were a sequence of four engravings in diminishing distance from their subject. "SEEN ALOFT FROM AFAR," the Parthenon is "Estranged in site, / Aerial gleaming, warmly white." "NEARER VIEWED" reveals that "In subtlety your form's defined – / The cornice carved, each shaft inclined." Zooming in on a detail of "THE FRIEZE," the poet celebrates the chiseled animation "Of horses gay – their riders grave – / Contrasting so in action brave / With virgins meekly bright." This appreciation of the sculptor's hand leads to an imagined whisper in the silence immediately after "THE LAST TILE" has been laid: "Hist! Art's meridian, Pericles!" (*CP* 246–7).

In Italy, Melville's eye for ancient sculpture took in the forms of Apollo, David, Antinous, Venus, Minerva, and the Dying Gladiator. In Rome the monumental architecture of the Colosseum, the Arch of Constantine, St. Peter's, and the Roman walls overwhelmed him, as did the paintings of the Old Masters in one museum after another: Raphael and the Sistine Chapel at the Vatican; Guido's Cenci and the Galatea at the Palazzo Barberino; Holbein and Dolce and Salvator at the Corsini Palace; Raphael and Correggio at the Borghese Gallery; Claude and Caravaggio and Dürer and Titian at the Sciarra Gallery; Guido and Raphael at the Quirinale Palace; Raphael and Perugino at the Vatican again; Raphael and Titian at the Doria Pamfili. This appreciation of art objects of all kinds continued throughout the rest of his Italian journey – with the difference that in Venice most impressions were wedded, in meditation, with water. One day, returning from the Lido, Melville noted the "Mirage-like effect of fine day – floating in air of ships in the Malamocco Passage, and the islands" (119).

Melville's return home over the Alps, down the Rhine, and across to England provided opportunities to record impressions both old and new. New vistas included, in a diligence from Bern to Basel, "Supurb [*sic*] views of the Bernese Alps and Jura ranges all morning" (125). In Strasbourg, his first view of the famed Cathedral provoked him to concoct an image that might seem more appropriate for an erection by Gaudí or Gehry in a later century: "Pointed – pinnacles – All sprouting together like a bed of what you call it? asparagus" (125). As an organic image for an unmoving form, this is a fine complement to his description of St. Sophia as "Suspended from above like fully blossomed tulip from its stem" (158).

In Amsterdam and Rotterdam Melville got his first hometown exposure to many of the sixteenth-century Dutch artists who were to play a significant role in his subsequent poetry and art collecting (see Berthold). Arriving in London during the last week of April 1857, he was much changed from the younger and more gregarious self who had visited the city eight years earlier. Perhaps exhausted in the seventh month of his present voyage, he records no social occasions or human companions during five days in London. One of his few substantive entries records a visit to the "Vernon and Turner galleries." Now, six years after Turner's death in 1851, Melville could see in the newly created Turner Gallery many of the late, great paintings that had been unsold in the painter's private gallery at the time of his earlier visit in 1849. Among these works, he took note of the "Sunset scenes" in general and of *The Fighting Temeraire* and *Peace – Burial at Sea* in particular (128). Swinging up to Oxford and over to Stratford and down to see Hawthorne at Liverpool, Melville sailed home on the steamship *City of Manchester*, arriving in New York on May 19.

4

Melville returned from the Mediterranean in 1857 with retinal impressions of monuments, museums, churches, sculptures, and paintings that he would retain for the rest of his life. Some of these impressions would inspire poetry in *Clarel* (1876) or in *Timoleon* (1891). Others would inspire Melville to collect engravings of places seen. In addition to journal entries and retinal impressions, he returned from his trip with a Persian tile in the Qajar style (figure 22.3). Its prince rides his white horse through a flowering landscape under the protecting feathers of the mythological bird known as the *huma*. Decades later this Persian tile was joined in Melville's collection by the wide range of Persian subjects drawn by the American artist Elihu Vedder in a deluxe edition of the *Rubaiyát of Omar Khayyám* published in 1886 (Wallace "Metcalf's Prints"). Perhaps the most charming Persian subject in Melville's collection was the German engraving of a *Persian Head* from a French etching by the Italian artist Stefano della Bella – a double portrait of a camel and a camel boy, etched in Paris in 1648 (Wallace "Melville Chapin" fig. 8).

With his writing career at an impasse, Melville after returning from Europe tried his hand at the Lyceum lecture circuit. He got bookings in sixteen different cities for the 1857–8 season, but he disappointed those who were hoping for adventures among the cannibals or hunting after whales by delivering a lecture on "The Statues of Rome." His bookings dropped sharply in the next two years as the nation moved closer to its Civil War. Shortly before leaving on a voyage to San Francisco in a ship commanded by his brother Thomas Melville in 1860, Melville completed a book of poetry to be submitted to New York publishers in his absence. This proposed book was not accepted for publication, but in 1866, at the end of the Civil War, he did publish his first book of poetry, *Battle-Pieces and Aspects of the War*. Three poems in this collection were directly inspired by individual paintings that Melville identified for his reader.

"The Temeraire" was inspired by *The Fighting Temeraire* that Melville had seen at the Turner Gallery in London in 1857. Melville contrasts the poignant sight of the

Figure 22.3 Rectangular Persian tile with figure of horseman and *huma*. Composite body, molded and underglaze painted. Qajar period, mid-19th century. $13\frac{1}{2} \times 10\frac{3}{4}$ in. Berkshire Historical Society at Arrowhead, Pittsfield, MA. Photo: Robert Nicoll.

once glorious ship as "a pygmy steam tug tows [it], / Gigantic, to the shore," with the "deadlier lore" of a Civil War in which "the rivets clinch the iron-clads" (*CP* 39). "The Coming Storm" and "Formerly a Slave" were both inspired by paintings Melville saw at an exhibition at the National Academy of Design in New York in April 1865. "The

Coming Storm" responds to a painting by S. R. Gifford owned by Edwin Booth, brother of Abraham Lincoln's assassin. The poet sees the painted storm as suggesting not only the "demon cloud" of the nation's fratricidal war but also its owner's brother's parricide against the nation itself (94). In "Formerly a Slave" Melville sees the aged subject of Elihu Vedder's portrait as a woman whose "deliverance" has come "too late" for herself. Yet she still has positive faith for her "children's children," as her prophetic "face is lit with sober light, / Sibylline, yet benign" (101). (See Cohen for reproductions of these and other visual sources that influenced Melville's Civil War poems.)

Melville and his family had moved from Pittsfield, Massachusetts to New York City in 1863. They occupied a brownstone at 104 East 26th Street in which Herman would live for the rest of his life. In December 1866 he took a job as a customs inspector for the port of New York from which he retired in December 1885. During those nearly twenty years, his activities as a poet and as a connoisseur of art developed hand in hand, as twin avocations for his evening and weekend hours. During the ten years before he published *Clarel: A Poem and Pilgrimage in the Holy Land* in 1876, Melville was making significant additions to his library of books about art. He had acquired Valery's *Historical, Literary, and Artistical Travel in Italy* in 1857 and Vasari's five-volume *Lives of the Most Eminent Painters* in 1862 (Sealts nos. 534, 534a). Now he acquired the five-volume edition of Ruskin's *Modern Painters* in 1865, the two-volume edition of Hazlitt's *Criticisms on Art* in 1870, the two-volume *Works of Eminent Masters* in 1871, and Duplessis's *Wonders of Engraving* in 1875 (Sealts nos. 531, 263a, 564, and 195; for a list of "Books on the Visual Arts Owned or Borrowed by Herman Melville," see Sten). In addition to these books primarily about visual art, Melville also acquired the celebrated sixteen-volume edition of the *Life and Works of Lord Byron* with illustrations by Turner (Sealts nos. 112 and 369). All of these books greatly enriched not only *Clarel* and *Timoleon* but "At the Hostelry," an eight-part meditation on the "picturesque" via conversations among Old Master painters, unpublished in Melville's lifetime but thought to have been written in the early 1870s (*CP* 313–38).

Melville's use of visual art in *Clarel* is an extremely rich subject still in need of comprehensive study. Many of his allusions to specific painters or artworks are explicit, evident on the surface of the poem. Two of these appear in canto 12 of Book 2 in which "The Banker" is characterized with the aid of "Holbein's Dance of Death / Sly slipped among his prints from Claude" (2.12.30–2). "Prelusive" begins with an extended allusion to "Piranesi's rarer prints," whose "Interiors measurelessly strange" reveal an "inventor" who "miraged all the maze, / Obscured it with a prudential haze" (2.35.29–30). Not quite so explicit, but sufficiently clear in the context of Melville's print collection, is the allusion to Turner's *The Golden Bough* in the lines that conclude the characterization of Vine in "The Recluse": "No monk was he, allow; / But gleamed the richer for the shade / About him, as in somber glade / Of Virgil's wood the Sibyl's Golden Bough" (1.29.55–8). One might take this simply as an allusion to the "Sibyl's Golden Bough" in Virgil's *Aeneid* were it not for two separate black-and-white engravings that Melville owned of Turner's *The Golden Bough*, whose Sibyl offers the bough to Aeneas in a "sombre glade" whose "shade" matches the literary chiaroscuro of Melville's poem (reproduced in Wallace "Berkshire Athenaeum" and Wallace "Barton Chapin").

More subtle but equally interesting are three visual art allusions that one would be unlikely to recognize without a specific knowledge of Melville's print collection. In "Tomb and Fountain," immediately before "The Recluse" in Book 1, Nehemiah and Clarel walk outside Jerusalem to visit "the rifled Sepulcher of Kings" whose "sculptured frieze above a tomb" reveals "Palm leaves, pine apples, grapes" in "bloom" (1.28.24–8). Melville's verbal imagery can be directly traced to the pictorial imagery in Melville's copy of *Monument Sépulcral des Rois de Juda* after L. F. Casas, published in Paris in 1799. At the end of the same canto, when Clarel and Nehemiah descend from the "Tomb" to the "Fountain," we read that "Aslant they come / Where, hid in shadow of the rock, / Stone steps descend unto Siloam" (1.28.94–6). This image corresponds in topography, mood, and chiaroscuro with Melville's copy of *The Pool of Siloam* by the American engraver James D. Smillie (Wallace "Barton Chapin" figs. 12, 13). A more obscure and surprising image occurs in the canto on "The Arch," where Melville introduces Jerusalem's Ecce Homo arch with a seemingly unrelated maritime image: "Blue lights sent up by ship forlorn / Are answered oft but by the glare / Of rockets, from another, torn / In the same gale's inclusive snare" (1.13.1–4). Tell-tale words in this passage identify it as an allusion to Turner's 1840 Royal Academy painting *Rockets and Blue Lights (Close at Hand) to Warn Steamboats of Shoal Water,* now at the Clark Institute in Williamstown, Massachusetts, seven miles from Melville's former home in Pittsfield.

Melville was probably alluding to his own activity as a print collector when he wrote "Sly slipped among his prints from Claude" in *Clarel* (2.12.31). Our first documented evidence of this activity is the 1869 letter he wrote to Elias Dexter, a New York picture framer, in which he thanks Dexter "for the little print after Murillo" (*L* 409). It seems likely that most of the more than four hundred engravings that have now been documented from his collection were acquired in the final decades of his life, and perhaps especially after 1884 when his wife Elizabeth received a legacy which allowed her to give him $25 a month "to spend on books and prints" (Leyda 2: 787). Some of the prints that surrounded him late in life on East 26th Street may also have been a legacy from his father, including one or more "rare engravings" alluded to in the opening chapter of *Redburn*. Unfortunately, Melville left no record of the prints that he owned, so we have no way of knowing what percentage the four hundred prints that began to surface in 1986 represent of the whole. In the collection as currently known, Old Master painters from the Italian, French, Dutch, German, and English schools are well represented, but comparatively few works are by American artists. Turner, Flaxman, Claude, and Rubens are prominent among the individual painters and engravers, but each of the Old Master schools specified above is represented by an impressive range of artists.

Melville stored most of his prints unframed in unbound portfolios, but a number of works have come down to us in the frame in which he displayed them in the privacy of his New York brownstone. Among these are *The Enchanted Castle* and *Landscape with*

Figure 22.4 F. Vivares and William Woollett after Claude Lorrain. *The Enchanted Castle*. Published by Susanna Vivares, March 12, 1782. $16\frac{1}{2} \times 22\frac{3}{8}$ in. Private collection. Photo: Courtesy of the Fogg Art Museum, Harvard Art Museums.

Cephalus and Procris Reunited by Diana after Claude Lorrain, *The Shepherds of Arcadia* and *Landscape with a Man Washing his Feet at a Fountain* after Nicolas Poussin, *A Brisk Gale* after Willem Van de Velde the Younger, *Satan Exalted Sat* by John Martin, *The Golden Bough* after J. M. W. Turner, and a color print of the *Bay of Naples*. In addition to the hundreds of prints, framed and unframed, that Melville collected on his own initiative, he was also the recipient of three watercolors that artist Peter Toft created in response to Melville's literary art: *Flamboro Head*, *Mar Saba*, and *Redondo*, inspired by *Israel Potter*, *Clarel*, and "The Encantadas," respectively (Wallace "Berkshire Athenaeum").

Soon after Herman retired from the Customs House in 1885, his wife Elizabeth wrote that "he has a great deal of unfinished work at his desk" (Leyda 2: 797). Among the results of that work are the poems of *Timoleon*, the prose of *Billy Budd*, and the remains of his print collection to the extent that it can be reconstructed today. In *Timoleon*, as in *Clarel*, the relation between Melville's poetry and his visual art is rich, provocative, and seamless. We have already seen the explicit use he made of "The Parthenon" and other elements of "The Attic Landscape" among the Greek portion of his "Fruit of Travel Long Ago." In another Greek poem, "Off Cape Colonna," Melville draws upon contrasting images that Turner had created of *The Temple of Minerva Sunias, Cape Colonna* (Wallace " 'Aloof,' " figs. 11 and 12). Among the Italian subjects in "Fruit of Travel Long Ago," "Venice," "Milan Cathedral," and "Pisa's Leaning Tower" make obvious use of architectural images from the 1857 tour. The most sophisticated use of fine art knowledge in this section, however, comes in "Pausi-lippo," where the landscape tradition of Melville's Italianate landscapes after Claude, Turner, and Richard Wilson is brought to life in a waterside encounter whose contemporary pain is in sharp contrast to that ancient "dream of years serene" (*CP* 244). Subtle psychological probing of this kind also distinguishes "After the Pleasure Party" in *Timoleon*, a narrative poem in which Melville creates, in the psyche of a female astronomer, a world in which the yearning seen in Melville's prints of *The Enchanted Castle* after Claude Lorrain (figure 22.4) and *The Enchanted Isle* after Antoine Watteau is internalized in a contemporary setting. *Timoleon* ends with "The Great Pyramid," a poem returning to some of Melville's earliest musings over ancient temples and monumental ruins in *Typee* and *Mardi*. In its closing stanza, "Craftsmen, in dateless quarries dim, / Stones formless with form did trim, / Usurped on Nature's self with Art, / And bade this dumb I AM to start, / Imposing him" (255).

Ages after those "dateless" craftsmen of the Pyramids, Greek and Roman sculptors shaped other "formless stones" into the form of Antinous, the beloved of Emperor Hadrian. Melville was deeply struck by the monumental statue of this figure in Rome's Capitoline Museum – as well as by the delicate head in bas-relief at the Villa Albani ("like moss rose with curls & buds"). Later in life he "acquired a more than life-sized copy of the bust of the boy," which his granddaughter Frances Osborne remembered standing "on a tall white pedestal in the corner of the front parlor" at 104 East 26th Street (*J* 106, 107, 465). Frances Cuthbert Osborne was one of four daughters of Melville's daughter Frances Melville Thomas. She and her three sisters, Jeanette Ogden Chapin, Kathleen Gansevoort Binnian, and Eleanor Melville Metcalf, have, with their many descendents, preserved almost all of Melville's surviving prints until such time as scholars have shown interest. A landmark in the public preservation of this legacy was Eleanor Melville Metcalf's donation of nearly three hundred prints from her grandfather's collection to the Berkshire Athenaeum in 1952 (see Wallace "Berkshire Athenaeum"). The bust of Antinous, unfortunately, is currently untraced.

The last vestiges of visual art in Melville's prose came in *Billy Budd, Sailor,* the manuscript he left unpublished at his death. This work, too, contains numerous explicit allusions to specific works of art or their subjects. One is a reference to Haden's etching of the wreck of the ship *Agamemnon.* Another is Captain Vere's reference to "the divine judgment on Ananias!" immediately after Billy delivers a "convulsed" blow to Claggart's high forehead (a double allusion to Raphael's tapestry of the *Death of Ananias* and to Hazlitt's commentary on it in his essay on Hampton Court). In contrast to the technical sophistication of such allusions to the visual arts is the emotional satisfaction with which the form and spirit of the ancient Antinous pervade the spirit and body of Billy himself (see Coffler). Invisible on the skin of the story, Antinous is woven through the fiber of its heart.

The title of my essay is from Melville's eleven-line poem "Art" in *Timoleon.* What must "meet and mate" are five contrasting categories: "A flame to melt – a wind to freeze; / Sad patience – joyous energies; / Instinct and study; love and hate; / Audacity – reverence." Melville, throughout his life, explored such contraries in the visual as well as the literary art of disparate ages and nations. The shock of recognition that Melville so often felt when word and image intersected had much to do with the realization that his own deepest contrarieties must "mate, / And fuse with Jacob's mystic heart, / To wrestle with the angel – Art" (*CP* 231).

REFERENCES AND FURTHER READING

Berthold, Dennis. "Melville and Dutch Genre Painting." In Sten, 218–45.

Coffler, Gail. "Classical Iconography in the Aesthetics of *Billy Budd, Sailor.*" In Sten, 257–76.

Cohen, Hennig. *The Battle-Pieces of Herman Melville.* New York: Thomas Yoseloff, 1963.

Frank, Stuart M. *Herman Melville's Picture Gallery: Sources and Types of the "Pictorial" Chapters of Moby-Dick.* Fairhaven, MA: Edward J. Lefkowicz, 1986.

Hazlitt, William. *Criticisms on Art, and Sketches of the Picture Galleries of England.* 2 vols. London: J. Templeton, 1843, 1844.

Otter, Samuel. *Melville's Anatomies.* Berkeley: University of California Press, 1999.

Robillard, Douglass. *Melville and the Visual Arts: Ionian Form, Venetian Tint.* Kent, OH: Kent State University Press, 1997.

Schultz, Elizabeth A. *Unpainted to the Last.* Lawrence: University Press of Kansas, 1995.

Sten, Christopher. *Savage Eye: Melville and the Visual Arts.* Kent, OH: Kent State University Press, 1991.

Wallace, Robert K. " 'Aloof' and 'Aloft': Cape Colonna in Melville's Poem and Turner's Engravings." In *Melville 'Among the Nations': Proceedings of an International Conference, Volos, Greece, July 2–6, 1997.* Ed. Sanford E. Marovitz and A. C. Christodoulou. Kent, OH: Kent State University Press, 2001. 463–71.

———. *Maritime Prints from Herman Melville's Collection of Art*. New Bedford, MA: New Bedford Whaling Museum, 1999.

———. "Melville after Turner: 'The Piazza,' *The Crayon*, and Ruskin." *Nineteenth-Century Contexts* 19 (1996): 285–303.

———. *Melville and Turner: Spheres of Love and Fright*. Athens: University of Georgia Press, 1992.

———. "Melville's Prints and Engravings at the Berkshire Athenaeum." *Essays in Arts and Sciences* 15 (1986): 59–90.

———. "Melville's Prints: David Metcalf's Prints and Tile." *Harvard Library Bulletin* n.s. 9 (1997): 3–33.

———. "Melville's Prints: The E. Barton Chapin, Jr., Family Collection. *Leviathan* 2 (2000): 5–65.

———. "Melville's Prints: The Melville Chapin Collection." *Harvard Library Bulletin* n.s. 11 (2000): 5–54.

Part V
Texts

23
The Motive for Metaphor: *Typee, Omoo,* and *Mardi*

Geoffrey Sanborn

In the early summer of 1840, not long before his twenty-first birthday, Herman Melville left home for Galena, Illinois. Like thousands of other unattached or displaced white men, he and his companion, Eli Fly, were hoping to find on the Western frontier the work they could not find at home. But after a trip that took them from Albany to Buffalo via canal boat, from Buffalo to Chicago via steamboat, and from Chicago to Galena via coach, Melville and Fly appear to have received none of the help they had expected from their connection in Galena, Melville's uncle Thomas. By that fall they were back in New York, and before the year was out Melville had signed on to the whaler *Acushnet*, bound for the Pacific Ocean (Parker 1: 166–79).

Because Melville didn't turn the journey to Galena into a loosely autobiographical narrative like *Typee, Omoo, Redburn,* or *White-Jacket,* it usually doesn't receive much attention. But it's worth thinking about what he must have experienced on this trip. For one thing, he must have discovered what it was like to be in the company of a large number of reckless and opportunistic white American men. A few of those men must have been something like Steelkilt, the fictionalized Midwesterner in "The Town-Ho's Story": "vengeful and full of social quarrel," the pure products of the "latitudes of buck-horn handled Bowie knives" (*MD* 244). And a great many of them must have been hunters, in the broadest sense, like the passengers on board the Mississippi riverboat in *The Confidence-Man*: "farm-hunters and fame-hunters; heiress-hunters, gold-hunters, buffalo-hunters, bee-hunters, happiness-hunters, truth-hunters, and still keener hunters after all these hunters" (9). There must have been, in other words, more than a few representatives of what he calls in *Typee* the "Anglo-Saxon hive," that swarm of freebooting white men who were in the process of opening up "the greater part of the North American continent," and, in doing so, wiping out "the greater portion of the Red race" (195).

For someone of Melville's sensibility and standards – he would later express his disapproval of racism in the American West by saying that "Xavier and Eliot despised not the savages; and had Newton or Milton dwelt among them, they would not have done so" ("Mr. Parkman's Tour," *PT* 231) – this must have been a somewhat uncomfortable introduction to the social experience of white men in America. It must have led him to wonder if there was a world elsewhere for someone like him, a world where he could enjoy his freedom and pursue his happiness without feeling complicit in a collective crime. It must have been at least a part of what drove him first to sign on to the *Acushnet* and then, a year and a half later, to jump ship on the Marquesan island of Nukuheva. When he escaped into the mountains in the center of the island and began his second experience of a colonial frontier, he must have been looking for an alternative not only to conventional domestic experience, but also to the Galenas of the world, all those places that promised freedom and opportunity in exchange for a willingness to participate in a massive expansion of white male power.

In what follows, I will argue that the desire for an alternative to the white male identity that was associated with the American frontier is one of the most powerful shaping forces in Melville's first three books. It energizes and haunts *Typee*; it lurks, frustrated, in the sailor-world of *Omoo*; it turns in the direction of literature in *Mardi*. In a letter to his publisher, Melville famously described the career change he made in *Mardi* as the consequence of feeling "irked, cramped & fettered" by the genre of the travel narrative (*L* 106). But it was, as well, the consequence of feeling "fettered" by the increasingly standard identification of white American men with aggressiveness, acquisitiveness, and practicality (Nelson; Rotundo; Saxton). Turning toward the "world of mind" didn't set him free, but it did open up a gap between himself and the stereotypical white American man, a gap that he would struggle to maintain, and to widen, for the rest of his writing life.

"The Most Ferocious Animal on the Face of the Earth"

For the first quarter of *Typee*, Melville's main project is to separate himself from the social environment of white sailors.[1] Even though he has spent six months on the *Dolly* when the book begins, and even though another three weeks then elapse before the ship anchors at Nukuheva, we learn almost nothing about the thirty other men on board. We are told the names of the ship's rooster (Pedro) and the ship's dog (Boatswain), but with the exception of four men – Jack, Ned, Toby, and Mungo, the black cook – the crew is an anonymous mass. Not a very nice mass, either; it is composed of "dastardly and mean-spirited wretches, divided among themselves, and only united in enduring without resistance the unmitigated tyranny of the captain" (21). Most of them are "coarse in person [and] in mind"; when the girls from Nukuheva arrive, there is no barrier between "the unholy passions of the crew and their unlimited gratification" (32, 15). Hence the tremendous appeal of Toby, who, like Melville, "had evidently moved in a different sphere of life," and who spends his time "gazing wistfully upon the shore, when the remainder of the crew would be rioting below" (32). Toby is the only crew member who becomes a memorable character in *Typee* – and that is because he is not, in Melville's eyes, a crew member at all.

It seems clear that Melville's self-segregation from the crew is motivated by something more than a refined distaste. He asserts that sailors in general are guilty of "enormities" that "wellnigh pass belief"; there is "many a petty trader that has navigated the Pacific whose course from island to island might be traced by a series of cold-blooded robberies, kidnappings, and murders, the iniquity of which might be considered almost sufficient to sink her guilty timbers to the bottom of the sea" (27). Sailors representing the US government do not appear to be much better; the forces of the American naval captain David Porter "[set] fire to every house and temple in their route" after being beaten back from the Taipi valley, and the men of the US Exploring Expedition flattened a Fijian village, killing everyone they met, and then "call[ed] upon all Christendom to applaud their courage and their justice" (26, 27). The issue for Melville is not their lack of cultivation but their lack of principles, which makes it easy for capitalists and politicians with global ambitions to get them to do their dirty work. Up close, the typical sailor, like the typical frontiersman, looks like the author of his own private story. If you take a few steps back, he starts to look like a minor character in someone else's epic narrative of conquest.

When Melville and Toby slip past the troops of Rear Admiral Abel du Petit Thouars, then in the process of claiming the Marquesas for France, and begin a journey that will take them into the valley of the Taipi, the weight of their association with the unwitting agents of empire is at least temporarily lifted. The sufferings they experience during that journey seem to provide Melville with a kind of masochistic pleasure; you can't be a bad white man if, while wading in a ravine, you and your companion repeatedly "fall sprawling amongst flinty fragments, cutting and bruising ourselves, whilst the unpitying waters flowed over our prostrate bodies" (59). You *really* can't be a bad white man if your leg swells up so much that you can't move and your companion abandons you in a valley of cannibals. And if your physical and psychic pain becomes almost unbearable, if your miseries deepen into an absolute despair and you begin to feel as though you no longer have any kind of recognizable context for your identity – well, you might actually start to feel pretty good.

Which is what happens. His "limb suddenly heal[s]" and he begins "to experience an elasticity of mind which placed me beyond the reach of those dismal forebodings to which I had so lately been a prey" (123). Between Chapter 17, when his mind becomes elastic, and Chapter 32, when it shrinks and hardens in response to the threat of being tattooed, he becomes an old-fashioned eighteenth-century primitivist, singing the praises of the Taipi – or Typee, as he spells it – and showering curses on "civilization," that monstrous compound of affectation and avidity.

It might appear that what is at stake in these chapters is the question of whether "nature" is superior to "culture." From the 1920s through the 1970s, critics of *Typee* almost uniformly assumed that that was indeed the issue, and assumed as well that Melville was equating the Taipi with "nature." Most of them then argued that the point of the book was to show that while "nature" might be appealing, intelligent and creative white men required more out of life than the pleasures and comforts of a "bovine world" (Ruland 322). Between the 1980s and the present, the argument shifted; critics began to say that what arrests the primitivist dream is the discovery that the Taipi are in fact equivalent to "culture," that their existence is not unstructured – "spontaneous, unplanned, childlike, and inconsequential" (Stern 45) – but *differently* structured. According to these critics, when Melville backpedals away from tattooing, *tapu*, and the appearance of cannibalism, he is backpedaling away from a network of signs upholding a social hierarchy, a "culture" that is full of resemblances to the "culture" of mid-nineteenth century America (Harvey; Otter; Sanborn).

There's a lot of truth to the latter argument, but it's not the whole truth. In addition to exposing the rigid, artificial aspects of Taipi culture, the ending of the book exposes the intensity of Melville's commitment to white "civilization," a commitment he can neither explain nor justify. After his climactic discovery of "the disordered members of a human skeleton," he decides that "[o]ne only hope remained to me. The French could not long defer a visit to the bay, and if they should permanently locate any of their troops in the valley, the savages could not for any length of time conceal my existence from them" (239). Quite suddenly, we are in the midst of an already age-old American narrative, in which military force and occupation are justified by the needs of a white person who is trapped beyond some frontier. Fortunately for the Taipi, Melville doesn't have to wait around for the French cavalry, because sailors from an Australian whaler unexpectedly row into the bay to negotiate for his release. The negotiations split the tribe into two warring factions, enabling him to escape into the whaleboat. As the sailors pull toward the ship, he sees a chief in the water alongside the boat, close enough to seize an oar. "Even at the moment I felt horror at the act I was about to commit," he says, "but it was no time for pity or compunction, and with a true aim, and exerting all my strength, I dashed the boat-hook at him. It struck him just below the throat, and forced him downwards. I had no time to repeat my blow, but I saw him rise to the surface in the wake of the boat, and never shall I forget the ferocious expression of his countenance" (252).

With that, the air goes out of the project of escaping the fraternity of white men on the margins of "civilization." Earlier, Melville had been able to speak of that fraternity in ways that suggested that he himself was not a member; when he says, "The fiend-like skill we display in the invention of all manner of death-dealing engines, the vindictiveness with which we carry on our wars, and the misery and desolation that follow in their train, are enough of themselves to distinguish the white civilized man as the most ferocious animal on the face of the earth" (125), the implication is that he is not contained in the "we." Now, however, he is. There is a difference, of course, between shoving a boathook into someone's neck and participating in the invasion of a sovereign nation, but it is a difference of degree, not a difference of kind.

"One Is Judged by the Company He Keeps"

The transition from *Typee* to *Omoo* is in one sense quite smooth. The second book begins exactly where the first one leaves off, with Melville being rowed out to the Australian whaler. The narrative voice is not much different, and there is once again an almost rhythmic alternation between particular and general descriptions, between the things that happen and the thoughts they suggest.

But *Omoo* is a fundamentally different book. The first sign of that difference is that for most of his first full day on the *Julia*, Melville spends his time "chatting freely with the men," learning "the history of the voyage thus far, and every thing respecting the ship and its present condition" (8). The chapters that follow – "Some Account of the Ship," "Further Account of the Julia," and "A Scene in the Forecastle" – place us squarely where we never really were in *Typee*: in the social environment of a Pacific whaler, among named and particularized sailors.

It's not that Melville's attitude toward his fellow sailors has changed. Soon after getting on board, he tells us that "[t]he crews manning vessels like these are for the most part villains of all nations and dyes; picked up in the lawless ports of the Spanish Main, and among the savages of the islands. Like galley-slaves, they are only to be governed by scourges and chains" (14). The officers are no better; after watching the captain of the *Julia* fire on a party of Marquesan islanders, he says, "it is almost incredible, the light in which many sailors regard these naked heathens. They hardly consider them human. But it is a curious fact, that the more ignorant and degraded men are, the more contemptuously they look upon those whom they deem their inferiors" (25). What has changed is his understanding of his relation to his shipmates. In *Typee*, he seemed to believe that he could live and move and have his being among sailors while remaining essentially uncontained by the category of "sailor"; he seemed to believe he could separate who he was from what he did and who he did it with. In *Omoo*, the persistent feeling of being inwardly different from those around him simply doesn't count for as much as it did before. We find him occupying, with enormous ambivalence, the situation he once avoided even describing.

It's worth noting, in this context, that the word "situation" and its variants appear fourteen times in *Omoo*, more frequently than in any other work by Melville. On the night following the brawl between Sydney Ben and Bembo, the Maori harpooner, he says, "[m]ore than ever did I now lament my situation – but it was useless to repine, and I could not upbraid myself. So at last, becoming drowsy, I made a bed with my jacket under the windlass, and tried to forget myself" (89). Earlier, when talk of mutiny is in the air, he regrets being "so situated, that I must necessarily link myself, however guardedly, with such a desperate company.... But any thing like neutrality was out of the question; and unconditional submission was equally so" (83–4). Later, in a chapter called "One Is Judged by the Company He Keeps," he fantasizes about introducing himself to a respectable white family that he sees on the road in Tahiti before reminding himself that "situated as I was, this was out of the question" (167). Being situated in the social role of "sailor" is like being in the stocks of the Tahitian jail, where he is constantly and acutely troubled by the "consciousness of having [his] foot *pinned*; and the impossibility of getting it anywhere else than just where it was" (117–18).

Whenever he feels that way, he tries to forget himself, either by going to sleep – and there is an awful lot of sleeping in *Omoo* – or by moving around. After he and Doctor Long Ghost leave the Tahitian jail, they are mostly in motion, hunting for food, drink, sex, and above all for distraction. As D. H. Lawrence correctly observes, there is an uneasiness and unhappiness beneath all this entertainment; they appear to be "knocking about in a sort of despair" (Lawrence 149). Lawrence ascribes their "rudderless" mood to the infectious rudderlessness of Pacific islanders, who, he says, have "been turning over in the same sleep, with varying dreams," for thousands of years (141). As I have suggested, however, it makes more sense to ascribe it to the cycle of alienation, dejection, resignation, and recklessness that they experience in the company of white sailors. It's not Pacific islanders who make Melville and Doctor Long Ghost feel the impossibility of being anywhere other than just where they are; it's the society of beachcombers, a "reckless, rollicking set, wedded to the Pacific, and never dreaming of ever doubling Cape Horn again on a homeward-bound passage" (*O* 81).

If Melville's mood is connected to the Tahitians at all, it is by virtue of the fact that he consistently acts like a typical white sailor when he is around them. For instance, after observing that hunger is "ever present" among the Tahitians because "the demands of the shipping exhaust the uncultivated resources of the island," he tells us that he and the other sailors in the unguarded Tahitian jail engaged in a "systematic foraging upon the country" (132). The local islanders soon encourage them to leave, for "we were obliged to live upon their benevolence, when they had little enough for themselves. Besides, we were sometimes driven to acts of marauding: such as kidnapping pigs, and cooking them in the groves; at which their proprietors were by no means pleased" (197). Later, he and Doctor Long Ghost use islanders as colonial-style "bearers of burdens" during a game hunt; at one point, he stands by while Doctor Long Ghost senselessly fires a shot over the head of his "trembling squire" (218, 220). Finally, throughout their time on Eimeo, he and Doctor Long Ghost doggedly search out young women who are not "vitiated by recent changes" so that they themselves can vitiate them (265). Under these circumstances, the denunciations of everything that contributes to "denationalizing the Tahitians" (183) have a distinctly hollow ring.

Several reviewers of *Omoo* called attention to these inconsistencies. One quotes the description of sailors in the Pacific as "villains of all nations and dyes" and expresses surprise that

> after such an account of the morals of this gang, Mr. Melville should go on to indicate, by all that he tells us of his *acts*, his co-operation with them – though sometimes but of a passive sort; his sympathy with their lawless deeds aboard and on shore, though sometimes related as if he condemned them. He really makes himself out to be very little better than them, except in point of education and intelligence. Why it has

pleased Mr. Melville to paint himself in a semblance so bad and (as it must be) so untrue, we are totally unable to imagine. The elegance of his mind, the grace, beauty, sweetness of his fancy, bespeak refinement of the sentiments, cultivated affections, and every thing of morals and feeling that would harmonize the least with such brutal society; and yet, for some inconceivable reason, he chooses to represent himself as participating in a mutiny, as almost one of its ringleaders. (Quoted in Higgins and Parker 115)

The reviewer has clearly been convinced that Melville is indeed what he advertises himself as being: a "soul of sensibility" (166). But a soul of sensibility is, for this reviewer, definitionally incapable of performing actions that bespeak a coarse or brutal soul. The only explanation he can come up with is that Melville has perversely chosen to represent himself as doing things that he didn't – *couldn't* – actually do.

Too often, the same kind of attitude finds its way into modern Melville criticism. When a Melville narrator does or says something that seems coarse or brutal to modern sensibilities – something racist, say, or triumphantly nationalistic – critics frequently assume that Melville is being ironic, as though he couldn't, by definition, be guilty of such things (Gerlach; Duban; Samson). But as *Omoo* goes to show, it is, practically speaking, impossible to separate intention from action, consciousness from behavior, identity from external associations. To acknowledge that Melville occasionally says or does things that are incompatible with our idea of him, or with his idea of himself, is merely to acknowledge that his books were written by someone as human as we are. Melville is not someone who transcends his time and place; he is someone who, in works like *Omoo*, dramatizes the *difficulty* of transcending time and place – the difficulty of resolving the basic human conflict between immaterial potential and material situation.

The final chapter – entitled, blankly, "Which Ends the Book" – extends that difficulty into the indefinite future. After coming across an American whaler that is scheduled to round Cape Horn for home within a year or so, Melville chooses to sign up for the coming cruise only, thereby "leaving my subsequent movements, unrestrained; for, there was no knowing that I might not change my mind, and prefer journeying home by short and easy stages" (315). Rather than answering the call of "Home" and "Mother," as in *Typee*, he answers the call of the "free and easy Pacific" (235); rather than gesturing toward a state of being in which his true self will be isolated from his contingent position, he ends the book as he began it, in the situation of what he calls, in the preface, an "omoo": "a rover, or rather, a person wandering from one island to another" (xiv). He is a sailor in a world where sailors casually exploit the people around them, casually part from one another, and casually die: a pair of them step "tranquilly over the side" of a ship and go "plumb to the bottom; under the erroneous impression, that they were stepping upon an imaginary wharf, to get at their work better" (292). He is more than that, too; there is something in him that yearns for a more stable, humane, and creative existence, something that will ultimately help to make him the author of this book. But the book isn't very far removed from the kind of life it describes; it too is a parade of events that comes to an unceremonious end. Its final image is both a promise of possibility and a revelation of vacancy: "By noon, the island had gone down in the horizon; and all before us was the wide Pacific" (316).

"Something in Me That Could Not Be Hidden"

The first sentence of *Mardi*, which begins on a ship in the mid-Pacific, sounds a very different note: "We are off!" Rather than tell us where we are off to, the speaker goes into a rhapsody of description:

> The courses and topsails are set: the coral-hung anchor swings from the bow: and together, the three royals are given to the breeze, that follows us out to sea like the baying of a hound. Out spreads the canvas – alow, aloft – boom-stretched, on both sides, with many a stun' sail; till like a hawk, with pinions poised, we shadow the sea with our sails, and reelingly cleave the brine. (3)

Melville had written literary-sounding passages before, but there had almost always been something stylistically conventional about them. Here's one from *Omoo*:

> In every direction, the scenery was enchanting. There was a low, rustling breeze; and below, in the vale, the leaves were quivering; the sea lay, blue and serene, in the distance; and inland the surface swelled up, ridge after ridge, and peak upon peak, all bathed in the Indian haze of the Tropics, and dreamy to look upon. Still valleys, leagues away, reposed in the deep shadows of the mountains; and here and there, water-falls lifted up their voices in the solitude. High above all, and central, the 'Marling-spike' lifted its finger. Upon the hillsides, small groups of bullocks were seen; some quietly browsing; others slowly winding into the valleys. (212)

It's the literary equivalent of a massage. He addresses himself to one thing at a time, caresses it with slowly cadenced modifiers, and slides to the next: no strange juxtapositions, no startling figures of speech.

The passage from *Mardi* is something else entirely. The anchor is "coral-hung"; the canvas is "boom-stretched"; the ship, in imagination, "reelingly cleave[s] the brine." The rhythm has become syncopated and unpredictable, the figurative language has become almost archly extravagant, and there is, throughout, an evident joy in verbal creation. This is where we are *really* off to in *Mardi*: the world of experimentally literary language.

As I noted above, the reason usually cited for that departure is his frustration with the limitations of the "narrative of *facts*." He told his British publisher, who wanted nothing but narratives of facts from him, that after beginning to write another travel narrative, he "began to feel an incurible [*sic*] distaste for the same; & a longing to plume my pinions for a flight." Accordingly, he left off "plodding along with dull common places," claimed "the play of freedom and invention accorded only to the Romancer & poet," and wrote a book that would be "original if nothing more," a book that opens "like a true narrative – like Omoo for example, on ship board" before becoming "a story wild enough I assure you and with a meaning too" (*L* 106).

Although there can be no doubt that Melville felt stifled by the requirements of the travel narrative, they are not the only things he is trying to escape in *Mardi*. He is also trying, once again, to escape the coordinates of his social position. Rather than resign himself to the inevitability of his identification with sailors, sailor-memoirists, and white American men, he strikes out in a new direction, toward the seemingly international and transhistorical position of the "Romancer & poet." He thinks of this position as being infinitely remote from the positions of sailor and sailor-memoirist; he later instructs his publisher not to put him down on the title page of *Mardi* as "the author of Typee and Omoo" and worries about the possibility that he will be remembered as just another "man who lived among the cannibals" (*L* 114–15, 193). He is not just reacting against the genre of the travel narrative in these instances; he is reacting, quite powerfully, against the prospect of being typecast in an unwanted social role.

The intensity of that reaction is dramatically evident in the opening of *Mardi*. In the first chapter, after alluding to the "bitter impatience of our monotonous craft, which ultimately led to the adventures here recounted," the narrator says, "But hold you! Not a word against that rare old ship, nor its crew. The sailors were good fellows all, the half-score of pagans we had shipped at the islands included" (4). The captain, too, is a "trump" (5). According to the narrator, the only problem with life on the *Arcturion* is that it's boring: "Bill Marvel's stories were told over and over again, till the beginning and end dovetailed into each other, and were united for aye. Ned Ballad's songs were sung till the echoes lurked in the very tops, and nested in the bunts of the sails. My poor patience was clean gone" (5).

The imaginary archipelago of Mardi is still many chapters away, but we are already in a startlingly unreal world. In place of sharply etched sailors like Bembo and John Jermin, we have the fanciful Bill Marvel and Ned Ballad; in place of the authoritarian Captain Vangs and the ineffectual Captain Guy, we have an unnamed "trump." The narrator's issues with his shipmates are now not moral but aesthetic, and evading them is as simple as stealing a boat and paddling away, accompanied by a pleasantly deferential and mostly silent "chummy." As if that didn't establish enough distance from the actual social environment of sailors in the Pacific, we are told that the ship subsequently sinks in a storm, killing everyone on board. It's as though Melville has to reimagine and ritually annihilate the world of white sailors before he can truly take off into the empyrean of invention.

To the critic Wai-chee Dimock, there is something ominous about that clearing of the decks. The destruction of the *Arcturion* is, as she notes, only the beginning of a massive killing spree: "by the end of *Mardi*, all the characters from the first fifty chapters, with the exception of the narrator, die or disappear in one way or another" (Dimock 51). For her, the repeated invention, naming, and obliteration of characters bears witness to Melville's desire for an absolute freedom, a freedom that is dependent on the continual creation of subordinate beings. That makes the logic of *Mardi* identical to the logic of American empire; each is a radically free invention of a radically subordinate world.

But freedom and subordination are not so easily separated from one another in *Mardi*. It's true that Melville gives voice to a fantasy of perfect freedom; he frequently suggests that he, like his narrator, has something in him that exceeds his social role – a "something in me that could not be hidden" (14) – and that the free expression of that "something" will enable him to escape his social role. In the end, however, his excess and expression don't add up to escape. For one thing, excess is more complex and ambiguous than it initially appears to be; we always feel and think more than we are aware of feeling and thinking, and there are some strange, unlovely things flitting through our murky inner worlds. For another, expression is less free and transparent than it initially appears to be; we didn't invent the language that enables us to write and be read, and we are both confined by its historical shape and adrift in its ultimate shapelessness. For both of those reasons, the escape into the space of the literary artist is necessarily incomplete; it can never be anything more than what Melville calls, in the subtitle of *Mardi*, a *"Voyage Thither."* Because Melville recognizes that fact, *Mardi* is ultimately not a narcissistic act of aggrandizement. It is, instead, an exploration of what situates, limits, and determines us, a meditation on the factor in human experience that Wallace Stevens refers to, in "The Motive for Metaphor," as the "vital, arrogant, fatal, dominant X."

The plot of *Mardi*, such as it is, hinges on exposure of the sexual and aggressive components of that X. At the pivotal moment in the book, the narrator impulsively stabs to death an old man who is holding captive a virginal woman named Yillah. In the aftermath of the murder, the narrator asks himself "whether the death-deed I had done was sprung of a virtuous motive, the rescuing a captive from thrall; or whether beneath that pretense, I had engaged in this fatal affray for some other, and selfish purpose; the companionship of a beautiful maid" (135). His immediate repression of that question – "throttling the thought, I swore to be gay" – is only temporarily successful; within a few pages, he is again brooding over the fact that his secret motives to the deed "had been covered with a gracious pretense; concealing myself from myself." Again he "beat[s] down the thought"; again the beating down is followed by a bubbling up (140). Soon Yillah, the icon of proper, authorized, connubial sex, has disappeared, and the narrator, now called Taji, is trailed everywhere he goes by Hautia, the icon of improper, unauthorized, guilt- and shame-ridden sex.

The metaphysical implications of this little drama are indirectly indicated by the philosopher Babbalanja. "Our souls belong to our bodies, not our bodies to our souls," he declares. "Without bodies . . . [we] would be minus our strongest motive-passions, those which, in some way or other, root under our every action. Hence, without bodies, we must be something else than we essentially are" (505). "I keep an eye on myself, as I would on a stranger," he says elsewhere. "There is something going on in me, that is independent of me . . . . I am a blind man pushed from behind; in vain, I turn about to see what propels me" (456). Taji's dream of purity and possibility beyond the horizon of the social — neatly captured by his early vision of cloud-archways "leading to worlds beyond" (8) — accounts neither for the insistence of the body nor for the vagaries of Babbalanja's "mysterious indweller" (458). Hunger, thirst, sexual desire, jealousy, anger, guilt, shame, grief: Taji experiences all of these things as pursuers that he must outdistance in order to recover his lost ideal. Because he can't escape what's already in him and can't find what never existed, he winds up in a hellish limbo, sailing "over an endless sea," chased eternally by "fixed specters" (654).

He's obviously in no condition to write a novel. Unless we are to imagine that he had a change of heart and sailed home, like Ahab in the 1930 movie version of *Moby-Dick*, he can't be the same person as the writer who occasionally interrupts the story to tell us how things are going for him. What this means is that at some point Melville recognized "that [*Mardi*'s] true action is not his characters' adventures but his own creative process; that its real voyage is the imaginative one he has undertaken in conceiving Mardi; that the real object of its quest is nothing his characters seek but the mental world he himself discloses through the act of creating his book" (Brodhead 39). That's the message of "Sailing On," in which the writer, whom we might as well call "Melville," says, "Oh, reader, list! I've chartless voyaged." At first, he says, he simply went where he felt inspired to go, impelled by a "blast resistless." Soon, however, he began to be attracted to a specific goal: the discovery and representation of "the world of mind, wherein the wanderer may gaze round, with more of wonder than Balboa's band roving through the golden Aztec glades." He may not have achieved that goal, for "fiery yearnings their own phantom-future make, and deem it present," but if so, so be it: "better to sink in boundless deeps, than float on vulgar shoals; and give me, ye gods, an utter wreck, if wreck I do" (556–7).

This is less an egotistic expression of sovereignty than an indication of a parallel between Melville's efforts to write *Mardi* and his narrator's efforts to find Yillah. Like his narrator, Melville is "subject to contrary impulses, over which he [has] not the faintest control" (203); like his narrator, he is madly attracted to an ideal; like his narrator, he pursues that ideal into "boundless deeps." It is not a flattering parallel, if we think of how the narrator ends up. But Melville is in fact far more self-critical than his narrator, far more aware of the fundamental gap between intention and outcome. When Lombardo, a barely disguised Melville figure, looks at his *Mardi*-like book "objectively, as a thing out of him," he considers it "but a poor scrawled copy of something within, which, do what he would, he could not completely transfer" (600, 601). There is no language fitted to the "something within" and no natural end to the process of trying to find the best substitute for the perfect word; the book is, accordingly, "wild, unconnected, all episode" (597). Its actual endpoint is not an ideal state but a process; instead of creating a perfect work, he has "created the creative" (595).

We might say, then, that just as there is an X in the self, an ungraspable, ineradicable bit of amoral being, so is there an X in language, something that makes it impossible for us to become present to others — or to ourselves — by means of what we say. By dwelling on these impediments to our purity and freedom,

Melville implicitly extends and deepens his treatment of situational limitation in *Typee* and *Omoo*. He may scribble over the X of his socially defined position in the opening chapters of *Mardi*, but as soon as he tries to write himself into the new role of literary artist, new versions of the X begin to appear on the page. In the chapter called "Dreams," after suggesting that he is an inspired prophet, he writes, "My cheek blanches white while I write; I start at the scratch of my pen; my own mad brood of eagles devours me; fain would I unsay this audacity; but an iron-mailed hand clenches mine in a vice, and prints down every letter in my spite" (368). Writing is for him not a turning-outward of inwardness, but a self-interrupting enterprise that he never entirely controls. Moreover, as he will soon discover, the situation of the writer is as subject to social definition as any other. Psyche, language, and situation: all are stamped with the same mark. But this is not a matter of regret. It is the truth, the motive for metaphor, and it would have been hard to come by in Galena.

NOTE

1   To keep their readers from confusing the narrator with the author, most twentieth-century critics called the narrator "Tommo." But I don't see any reason to continue that practice. "Tommo" is nothing more than the Marquesan pronunciation of "Tom," and "Tom" is nothing more than the name the narrator decides to use while in the Taipi valley. Before he arrives in the valley, he is never addressed by name; in *Omoo*, he is called at various points "Typee," "Paul," and "The Bashaw with Two Tails." Given that *Typee* and *Omoo* are not novels but loosely autobiographical narratives with "Herman Melville" on the title page, the most logical thing to do is what the original reviewers did: treat those aliases and nicknames as the temporary appellations of someone whose name is "Herman Melville." That "someone," the narrator, is different from the real Herman Melville, but not so different that we must come up with a new name for him. We refer to the narrator of the *Narrative of the Life of Frederick Douglass* as "Douglass" and to the narrator of *Walden* as "Thoreau" without losing sight of the fact that they are literary personae; there's no reason why we can't do the same thing with *Typee* and *Omoo*.

REFERENCES AND FURTHER READING

Brodhead, Richard. "*Mardi*: Creating the Creative." In *New Perspectives on Melville*. Ed. Faith Pullin. Kent, OH: Kent State University Press, 1978. 29–53.

Bryant, John. *Melville and Repose: The Rhetoric of Humor in the American Renaissance*. New York: Oxford University Press, 1993.

Calder, Alex. " 'The Thrice-Mysterious Taboo': Melville's *Typee* and the Perception of Culture." *Representations* 67 (1999): 27–43.

Dimock, Wai-chee. *Empire for Liberty: Melville and the Poetics of Individualism*. Princeton, NJ: Princeton University Press, 1989.

Duban, James. "Chipping with a Chisel: The Ideology of Melville's Narrators." *Texas Studies in Language and Literature* 31 (1989): 341–85.

Ellis, Juniper. "Melville's Literary Cartographies of the South Seas." *Massachusetts Review* 38 (1997): 9–29.

Evelev, John. " 'Every One to His Trade': *Mardi*, Literary Form, and Professional Ideology." *American Literature* 75 (2003): 305–33.

Gerlach, John. "Messianic Nationalism in the Early Works of Herman Melville: Against Perry Miller." *Arizona Quarterly* 28 (1972): 5–26.

Harvey, Bruce A. *American Geographics: U.S. National Narratives and the Representation of the Non-European World, 1830–1865.* Stanford, CA: Stanford University Press, 2001.

Herbert, T. Walter. *Marquesan Encounters: Melville and the Meaning of Civilization.* Cambridge, MA: Harvard University Press, 1980.

Higgins, Brian and Hershel Parker. *Herman Melville: The Contemporary Reviews.* Cambridge: Cambridge University Press, 1995.

Lawrence, D. H. *Studies in Classic American Literature.* New York: Penguin, 1997.

Martin, Robert K. *Hero, Captain, and Stranger: Male Friendship, Social Critique, and Literary Form in the Sea Novels of Herman Melville.* Chapel Hill: University of North Carolina Press, 1986.

Nelson, Dana. *National Manhood: Capitalist Citizenship and the Imagined Fraternity of White Men.* Durham, NC: Duke University Press, 1998.

Otter, Samuel. *Melville's Anatomies.* Berkeley and Los Angeles: University of California Press, 1999.

Rotundo, E. Anthony. *American Manhood: Transformations in Masculinity from the Revolution to the Modern Era.* New York: Basic Books, 1993.

Rowe, John Carlos. "Melville's *Typee*: U.S. Imperialism at Home and Abroad." In *National Identities and Post-Americanist Narratives.* Ed. Donald E. Pease. Durham, NC: Duke University Press, 1994. 255–78.

Ruland, Richard. "Melville and the Fortunate Fall: *Typee* as Eden." *Nineteenth Century Fiction* 23 (1968): 312–23.

Samson, John. *White Lies: Melville's Narratives of Facts.* Ithaca, NY: Cornell University Press, 1989.

Sanborn, Geoffrey. *The Sign of the Cannibal: Melville and the Making of a Postcolonial Reader.* Durham, NC: Duke University Press, 1998.

Saxton, Alexander. *The Rise and Fall of the White Republic: Class Politics and Mass Culture in Nineteenth-Century America.* London: Verso, 1990.

Stern, Milton R. *The Fine Hammered Steel of Herman Melville.* Urbana: University of Illinois Press, 1957.

Stevens, Wallace. *The Palm at the End of the Mind.* New York: Vintage, 1972.

Weinstein, Cindy. *The Literature of Labor and the Labors of Literature.* New York: Cambridge University Press, 1995.

24

Artist at Work: *Redburn*, *White-Jacket*, *Moby-Dick*, and *Pierre*

Cindy Weinstein

One of Herman Melville's most famous letters was written on October 6, 1849 to his father-in-law and Chief Justice of the Massachusetts Supreme Court, Lemuel Shaw, upon the completion of *Redburn* and *White-Jacket*. The two novels together took Melville approximately five months to finish, and he writes about them contemptuously: "no reputation that is gratifying to me can possibly be achieved by either of these books. They are two *jobs*, which I have done for money – being forced to it, as other men are to sawing wood . . . . So far as I am individually concerned, & independent of my pocket, it is my earnest desire to write those sort of books which are said to 'fail' " (*L* 138–9). This is quite an extraordinary letter to send to one's father-in-law, whose daughter had that year given birth to her first child, Malcolm. Melville, a new father, was in no position to consider himself only "individually concerned" or "independent of pocket," and the desire for failure surely would not be considered a positive attribute in a son-in-law. Even Melville seems to realize that his words might alarm Shaw and concludes the letter with the words, "pardon this egotism." This letter illustrates just how misguided Melville's sense of his audience could be. His correspondence often reveals in miniature the economic and psychic tensions that Melville experienced in the act of writing, whether a novel of many pages or a short missive to a relative or friend. Melville's attitude toward writing is, broadly speaking, the subject of this essay. More specifically, though, Melville inserts into his novels the narrative of their own composition, or in the cases of *Redburn*, *White-Jacket*, and *Pierre*, their decomposition. Pervading Melville's texts are images of books being destroyed (as in thrown overboard), books conveying truths and yet being misunderstood, books being vapid and yet praised, books claiming to be true yet patently false, and books being failures. With the notable exception of *Moby-Dick*, Melville's narrative of writing is repeatedly a self-destructive one that tears at the very fabric of the plot itself.

Redburn: "A narrative like mine"

Melville would, indeed, write books that failed, thereby securing the artistic "success" for which he was striving; *Pierre* would be the most famous example. But before getting to *Pierre*, it is worth considering exactly why Melville had such disdain for *Redburn* and *White-Jacket*. After all, in the letter to Shaw, Melville concedes that "in writing these two books, I have not repressed myself much – so far as *they* are concerned; but have spoken pretty much as I feel" (316). The problem, then, is less the product than the process. This point is supported by the fact that Melville articulates his dissatisfaction with the novels not in terms of inadequate character development or narrative technique, but rather in the language of labor. For Melville, in other words, it is not a matter of literary merit, although it may be for contemporary critics, but rather a question of the conditions in which he wrote the novel. They are *jobs*, and authorship is supposed to be neither a job nor a profession one undertakes in order to make money. Given that he felt continually hounded by monetary concerns, however, Melville's letter to his friend, Evert Duyckinck, in which he refers to *Redburn* as "beggarly" (347), makes perfect sense. To the extent that Melville regards himself as a beggar, and his debts to Shaw (and many others) give him good reason to feel this way, *Redburn* is too.

Melville, quite simply, did not want to write *Redburn*, and his resistance to it comes through in any number of ways. Perhaps the most obvious is the critique of textuality itself that gets thematized, oftentimes comically, throughout the novel. Such an antagonism toward books finds one of its clearest articulations in the middle chapter, "Redburn Grows Intolerably Flat and Stupid over Some Outlandish Old Guide-Books," in which the main character journeys through Liverpool and its environs with his father's books in hand. Virtually all of the books that Redburn possesses are misguided. That they are guidebooks makes their errors all the more problematic. The narrator makes the point that not only are these books utterly inaccurate, and therefore useless, within the context of Redburn's own adventures in England, but that they were, perhaps, also inauthentic representations of the English landscape, and therefore questionable even in Redburn's father's own time. Such a realization is devastating because the care and love with which Redburn treats his father's guidebooks registers the son's unquestioning adulation of his father. As the authority of the books goes, however, so goes the word of the father.

In this chapter about guidebooks, the older Redburn-narrator conducts a reading of the younger Redburn-character's reading and finds it laughably naïve. History has intervened to change the landscape and its monuments, leaving Redburn dizzyingly lost as he tries to navigate his way through Liverpool with his father's guidebooks as his guide. At first, he remembers "reverentially" folding a map of London that had been used by his father, and recalling "the many fond associations connected" with the volume entitled, " 'THE PICTURE OF LIVERPOOL' " (*R* 142). And yet, this reverence soon dissipates under the light of harsh reality. He remarks upon the frontispiece of a volume "bringing together at one view the towers and turrets of King's College and the magnificent Cathedral of Ely, though geographically sixteen miles apart" (142). Redburn, furthermore, casts doubt on the motives of the authors of such guidebooks by suggesting that when one of them inserts "nine thickly printed pages of a neglected poem by a neglected Liverpool poet" amidst the volume called " '*Survey of the Town,*' " the poet is, in fact, the "author of the Guide-Book" (147). The narrator also ironically presents himself as defender of the volume that he has just eviscerated in deciding not to quote from "the chapter of antiquarian researches" (149) because the citation would not convey "all the pleasant associations which the original carries to me!" (149). He also insists that the chapter would be grist for the mill of "shallow-minded readers" (150) who would not only "skip and dishonor" the text but would accuse Redburn of "swelling out my volume by plagiarizing from a guide-book." Lest we forget, Melville has just done exactly that, having quoted from various guidebooks, dishonored them in the process, and committed in the self-consciously overblown words of Redburn, "the most vulgar and ignominious of thefts!" (150).

If Melville is here having some fun describing his aggressive relation to the text that he would have preferred not to have written (he could not skip writing *Redburn*, so he dishonored it instead), the early chapters of the novel allegorize the desire to be done with it, if it must be done at all. Although Redburn claims that he wants to go abroad, the fact is that he is also deeply resistant to leaving. One might say that the wish to go on a voyage represents the youthful, naïve Redburn, who imagines "with what reverence and wonder people would regard me, if I had just returned from the coast of Africa or New Zealand" (5), whereas the desire to remain reflects the Redburn who knows what lies ahead, including the labors, humiliations, and shocks to his youthful self's romantic sensibilities. That we, as readers, would be able to separate Redburn's "original" intentions from their retrospective narration is, however, as naïve as Redburn imagining that his father's earlier maps of Liverpool could be legible texts for the son. No "original relation to the universe" to quote Emerson's essay, "Nature," is to be had (*Selected Writings* 3). Although Redburn is the narrator of his own experience, even he does not have an original relation to it, because, as the chapter about reading his father's guidebooks demonstrates, history has happened, experience has intervened, and, perhaps most importantly, Melville has decided that this is a text he would rather skip. As a result of this last, Redburn's journey functions as a vehicle for Melville to write a narrative about not wanting to write this particular narrative.

To be sure, like their creator, many of Melville's protagonists want to jump ship at some point (one thinks of *Typee*'s Tommo and *Mardi*'s Taji), but it is not clear that Redburn wants to board it in the first place. He lives in "a pleasant village on the Hudson River" (3) and is forced out of his relatively comfortable domicile by the twinned circumstances of "the necessity of doing something for myself" and "sad disappointments in several plans" (3). Although excited by the prospect of romantic travels, he seems even more interested in fantasizing about his return and the new-found admiration he will garner when he recounts his adventures. Like Henry Fleming in Stephen Crane's *The Red Badge of Courage*, Redburn imagines less the going out than the coming home: "how dark and romantic my sunburnt cheeks would look" (5) and how "I would hereafter be telling my own adventures to an eager auditory" (7). Redburn's experience of travel is completely textualized, as scripted by his father's books; even before he sets foot on the *Highlander*, Redburn believes that when it comes to telling his lived experience, that narration will jive with his father's. But if the experiences are the same – the written and the lived – perhaps Redburn need not go through the trouble of having the experience.

Thus, he imagines his return at precisely the moment that his ship leaves home. "As the steamer carried us further and further down the bay ... I would have given any thing if instead of sailing *out* of the bay, we were only coming *into* it; if we had crossed the ocean and returned, gone over and come back; and my heart leaped up in me like something alive when I thought of really entering that bay at the end of the voyage" (33). That Redburn desires not to leave, or, more precisely, to compress the temporality of the experience by anticipating it and dispensing with it, as if it had already happened (which it has, to the older Redburn-narrator), has interesting thematic as well as narrative consequences. Given his reluctance to leave New York, Redburn often experiences new lands as mirror images of what he has left behind. Turning new scenes into images of old ones is, of course, a way of not leaving home. Upon first seeing Wales, for instance, he writes, "the general effect of these mountains was mortifyingly like the general effect of the Kaatskill Mountains on the Hudson River" (126). Elsewhere, Redburn observes that "Liverpool, away from the docks, was very much such a place as New York" (202). His desire to conclude the voyage before it begins gets transformed into a story about a journey that does not take one anywhere.

On another level, it signifies Melville's wish not to launch into the narrative that is *Redburn*. This resistance to or impatience with his subject gets figured throughout the text. At the beginning of Chapter 24, for example, the narrator writes that "the Highlander may as well make sail and get there as soon as possible" (114). Furthermore, that many chapters need not be in the order in which they appear suggests the flexibility, to spin the point positively, or purposeful carelessness, to put it more critically, of the account. Like many of Melville's texts, the story meanders in the vein of Washington Irving's Geoffrey Crayon, although, in the case of *Redburn*, there is a kind of aggressiveness, what Wai-chee Dimock describes as "orchestrated literary offenses" (90) with which the narrator calls attention to the fact that he is not paying attention to the story. In the space of four paragraphs, he writes, "As I shall not make mention of the Grand Banks on our homeward-bound passage, I may as well here relate" (97), and then notes, "I had almost forgotten to make mention of the Gulf Stream" (97). Chapters are often connected by metonymy as one incident "reminds" (92, 180, 207) Redburn of another, suggesting a casual and jaunty narrative style. This is Tommo's style in *Typee*, as well as Ishmael's in *Moby-Dick*, and yet unlike those novels, the overt and frequent carelessness of Redburn's story has less friendly intimations: "My adventure in the News-Room in the Exchange, which I have related in a previous chapter, reminds me of another, at the Lyceum, some days after, which may as well be put down here, before I forget it. I was strolling down Bold-street, I think it was, when I was struck by the sight of a brown stone building" (207). It is difficult to imagine a narrator less invested in his subject. If he might forget it, is it worth putting down? And was it Bold-street, or not?

The abrupt ending of the novel confirms not only that having never psychically left, Redburn need not narrate his return, but also that Melville need not give the text a coherent conclusion. Harry Bolton's disappearance at the novel's end offers compelling evidence of Melville's impatience with the text. He's finished it. Redburn is home, and nothing more needs to be said. One need not read the letters to Duyckinck or Shaw to know how Melville felt about *Redburn*. It is in the text itself. In one particularly self-conscious attack on his own work, as if Melville could tear it apart before his critics could (and, indeed, he was surprised, but not especially pleasantly, when they liked it), he describes the process by which sailors make "a clumsy sort of twine, called *spun-yarn*" (114). "For material, they use odds and ends of old rigging called '*junk*,' the yarns of which are picked to pieces, and then twisted into new combinations, something as most books are manufactured" (114–15). For Melville, *Redburn* fit into the category of "most books," and consequently was, like them, junk. For the reader, however, the manufacturing of *Redburn* is crucial. We see Melville's artistry at work, specifically how his irony, humor, and self-conscious meditation on literature and the world find their way onto the pages of a book against which he harbored such ill-will.

White-Jacket: "To return to the gig."

Melville wrote *White-Jacket* immediately after completing *Redburn*. If *Redburn* represents, in its own contorted way, the journey away from home, *White-Jacket* is the return. In fact, on two occasions, when the narrator strays too far from the subject at hand, he checks himself by the phrase, "to return" (272, 351). Getting home, though, is no easy or enjoyable task, especially when one's vehicle is a man-of-war. The prospect of flogging, the constant labors aboard the ship, and the lack of physical space, all combine to make the journey "Homeward-Bound" (the title of Chapter 2) as tough as the outward-bound one, both corporeally and psychically. Furthermore, that the man-of-war ship, the *Neversink*, and the destination to which it is returning, the United States, become images of each other makes the return home an anxious one. As with *Redburn*, in which the structural opposition governing the plot (home and England) disintegrates, so too with *White-Jacket*, in which the key poles of the narrative – the man-of-war ship as guided by the Articles of War and the land as governed by the Constitution – become indistinguishable. This collapse is complete in Chapter 91, where the narrator meditates upon previous chapters and concludes that "we have seen that a man-of-war is but this old-fashioned world of ours afloat" (390). If home is no different from what is not home, if the world is now a "man-of-war world" (229), why return?

As if that were not complicated enough, the text that images these intricate relations is one about which Melville has profoundly mixed feelings. Although somewhat less antagonistic toward *White-Jacket* than *Redburn*, he famously writes to Richard Henry Dana, author of *Two Years Before the Mast*, as if they were one, and in none too complimentary terms at that: "did I not write these books of mine almost entirely for 'lucre' – by the job, as a woodsawyer saws wood – I almost think I should hereafter – in the case of a sea book – get my M.S.S. neatly & legibly copied by a scrivener – send you that one copy – & deem such a procedure the best publication" (*L* 160). Melville reprises his objections to his two novels in the language that he had used with his father-in-law. That he wrote them for money, and that they were jobs, sullies his experience of them, even if it does not for the reading public. In fact, Dana wrote Melville in order to praise both books. Melville claims that "this is indeed delightful to me," but his response is more ambiguous than straightforward delight might suggest, because if he has written these books "as a woodsawyer saws wood," then is not Dana's appreciation of them undercut and even misguided? From Melville's perspective, Dana's validation would invalidate Dana as a judge of what is good literature.

It is as if Melville just cannot restrain himself from either attacking those who attack his books or attacking those who like them. This lose/lose situation finds its way into the narrative of *White-Jacket*, which repeatedly stages its own destruction in order both to beat the critics to it and to vent Melville's own dissatisfaction with it. His reluctance to narrate the journey home replays his resistance to the voyage out in *Redburn*. The tensions in the narrative are profound. At one point, for example, the narrator goes ashore and is compelled not to write "a few good chapters" about his "dashing adventures," because "in this book I have nothing to do with the shore further than to glance at it, now and then, from the water; my man-of-war world alone must supply me with the staple of my matter; I have taken an oath to keep afloat to the last letter of my narrative" (226). He might keep his oath here, but he breaks it throughout because as his journey proceeds, the distinctions between the shore and the ocean break down, and the indictment of the man-of-war world *is* an indictment of the world. That the narrator of *White-Jacket* speaks in far more congenial and seemingly confident tones than the narrator of *Redburn* does not conceal the fact that Melville, once again, is not happy about writing this book and inscribes that discontent into the text. The question that logically follows, then, is why write it?

Two answers come to mind. The first is money. He needed to write a book that would sell and, as Willard Thorp explains in the historical note to the Northwestern–Newberry edition of the text, Melville modestly succeeded in this respect. He secured a $500 advance from the American publishers Harper & Brothers, and sales in the first year garnered Melville approximately $600.00 in profits (*WJ* 407–8). The second is to right a wrong, which in this case is the brutal treatment of sailors in the navy. To put on display the arbitrary usages of power and to reform them is presented as the novel's *raison d'être*. Although the two motives of reform and money seem unrelated, they may have been connected. Dimock reminds us that some critics accused Melville of specifically choosing the topic of naval reform in order to make money, and that "not much was controversial about such a critique" (99), other than that the critique was, perhaps, generated more by questions of personal economy rather than by a sincere concern for social improvement.

However one wishes to parse the ambiguity of Melville's motives, it is clear that an ambivalence about writing the text is written into its very fabric. It is the narrative pull of *Redburn* in reverse, but it is also *Redburn* redux. It is as if having finally overcome the psychic inability to leave home, Redburn has to return to it all too quickly, and in order to do so must repeat the work of disconnection (only this time from the fact of *not* being home) and launch, once more, into narrative. If this description of the relation between *Redburn* and *White-Jacket* sounds an awful lot like Melville's experience of composing these novels, and we do well to recall that the books were written one right after the other in a space of less than five months, it is meant to. No sooner has Melville managed to contain his disinclination toward the writing of *Redburn* long enough to write it than Melville has to embark upon another novel that he considers beneath him.

Melville's most overtly self-conscious reflections upon the writing of *White-Jacket* occur in those chapters where he discusses the white jacket itself (clearly a sartorial relative of Redburn's shooting jacket). That the white jacket is not only an object in the novel or, better, *the* object of the novel, but also the name of the protagonist, the narrator, and the title of the book makes for some very complicated and tormented reflections. Before moving on to a discussion of this dominant metaphor in and of the text, however, I want to analyze a few less obvious places where we see the author's troubled hand at work. As in its predecessor, *Redburn*, several passages of *White-Jacket* attack texts, especially those like *White-Jacket*. In describing a book being written aboard the *Neversink*, White-Jacket explains that since it "contained reflections some-what derogatory to the dignity of the officers, the volume was seized by the master-at-arms, armed with a warrant from the Captain. A few days after, a large nail was driven straight through the two covers, and clinched on the other side, and, thus everlastingly sealed, the book was committed to the deep" (43). Here, Melville represents the reception of the novel as an occasion for its certain demise and martyrdom to the cause of naval reform. He predicts that *White-Jacket*, like the sailors whom the text depicts, will be victimized and suppressed by an unfair use of authority.

Another example occurs in a chapter that initially seems not to be a self-conscious reflection on much of anything, but instead an occasion to describe the ship's daily goings-on. As we know from *Moby-Dick*, though, descriptions of shipboard routines tend to expand in a variety of rhetorical directions, often dilating upon the writing process itself. In this particular instance, we witness the character, White-Jacket, attempting to make duff, a type of pudding composed of flour, raisins, and beef fat. He fails miserably, makes an atrocious duff, "grew desperate; despised popularity; [and] returned scorn for scorn" (61). The scene about the duff clearly becomes an opportunity for Melville to rail against his critics, although, interestingly, he admits that his duff (*White-Jacket*'s version of *Redburn*'s junk?) is lousy. As with the earlier chapter that has *White-Jacket* being thrown overboard, this scene contains an image of something (and someone) being committed to the deep; in this case, it is the character, White-Jacket. He reports that a particularly acrimonious member of the mess suggests that "the fatal pudding should be tied round my neck, like a mill-stone, and myself pushed overboard" (61). Author and duff (book) are chucked overboard, not because the authorities are suppressing the book, as Melville suggested in the first instance, but because the book is bad (bad duff) or the readers of the book "nourished a prejudice against my white-jacket" (61).

Here, Melville seems to blame others for not understanding his work. That *White-Jacket* is not any good is a judgment that comes not from Melville himself but rather from the outside. Other moments in the text, however, strongly indicate that Melville himself felt it to be inadequate, and that having "nourished a prejudice against my white-jacket" wished "the book was committed to the deep." In one description of the making of his white-jacket, White-Jacket speculates that his mess-mates think of it "as a cloak to cover pilferings of tit-bits from the mess" (61). He explains the manufacturing of the jacket, which becomes, as with the duff, a representation of Melville writing the novel. Like White-Jacket, who "sew[s] a sort of canvass ruffle round the skirts, by way of a continuation or supplement to the original work" (100) Melville, according to Thorp, "appropriated passages from other writers ... [for] his extensive pillages in *White-Jacket*" (Thorp 417). Unlike with *Moby-Dick*, he has comparatively little regard for this "original work," and so Melville continually represents its demise.

Indeed, White-Jacket's antagonism toward the garment bearing his name (and Melville's toward the novel bearing that same name) reaches comic proportions when he tries to get it auctioned off. An earlier chapter has White-Jacket being mistaken for a ghost, thanks to the jacket, and nearly dying as a result. Because the jacket is killing him, he desperately wants to be rid of it. At auction time, White-Jacket conceals himself and witnesses his own humiliation at the hands of "the discriminating public" (201) that wants nothing to do with the jacket. He finds himself once more in possession of it, as well as of fantasies of destroying it: "If I sink my jacket, thought I, it will be sure to spread itself into a bed at the bottom of the sea, upon which I shall sooner or later recline, a dead man" (203). The penultimate chapter entitled "The Last of the Jacket" makes this fantasy come true, at least for the character if not for its creator. White-Jacket violently separating himself from his white-jacket points to Melville's fantasy of disconnecting himself from *White-Jacket*. Author and book will not go down together, and Melville chooses to destroy the book in an ending reminiscent of *Typee*'s. "I whipped out my knife, that was tucked at my belt, and ripped my jacket straight up and down, as if I were ripping open myself. With a violent struggle I then burst out of it, and was free" (394).

Moby-Dick: "Out of the trunk, the branches grow; out of them, the twigs. So, in productive subjects, grow the chapters."

With *Moby-Dick*, Melville seems to have finally found "plenty of room to swing in" (*WJ* 79). He is free; free to "speak the sane madness of vital truth," ("Mosses," *PT*

244), free to write the way he wants, free to tell Hawthorne, in a letter written in June of 1851, only a few months before completing *Moby-Dick*, that "from my twenty-fifth year I date my life. Three weeks have scarcely passed, at any time between then and now, that I have not unfolded within myself" (*L* 193). Melville senses, as he writes *Moby-Dick*, that he is "coming to the inmost leaf of the bulb, and that shortly the flower must fall to the mould" (*L* 193). The organic imagery with which he describes his own development, as well as his text's, contrasts dramatically with the writing process as indicated in the earlier texts. Metonymy, not metaphor, is their governing principle, and the arbitrariness with which chapters follow one another has little in common with the expansiveness and connectedness described here. Chapters in *Moby-Dick* are intricately related, especially the ones explaining how a whaler works and the many tools required to hunt and kill whales. For example, in order to understand "the whale scene shortly to be described" (278), Ishmael explains that "I have here to speak of the magical, sometimes horrible whale-line." After Stubb kills the whale, a chapter, "The Dart," follows in order to clarify "an incident in the last chapter" (278). The tightly knit quality of the chapters might suggest the opposite of narrative freedom, and yet one might speculate that if Melville has at last "come to the inmost leaf of the bulb" and is writing the book that he wants to write, then he does not want to be careless about it, as with *Redburn*, or self-destructive, as with *White-Jacket*.

That Melville was not as free as he had hoped is evident in the reception accorded to *Moby-Dick*, as well as in that very letter to Hawthorne where we see, yet again, a familiar lament: "Dollars damn me . . . . What I feel most moved to write, that is banned, – it will not pay. Yet, altogether, write the *other* way I cannot. So the product is a final hash, and all my books are botches. I'm rather sore, perhaps, in this letter; but see my hand! – four blisters on this palm, made by hoes and hammers within the last few days" (*L* 191). Melville's heady sense of his interior expansion quickly comes up against the hard fact of earning a living. With good reason. Only three days after the British publication of *The Whale* (Allan Melville's note telling Bentley of Melville's decision to change the title to *Moby-Dick,* "a better *selling* title" [*C* 205] didn't reach the British publisher in time), Elizabeth gave birth to Stanwix, their second child.

Yet as sore and frustrated as Melville might have felt at certain points during the composition of *Moby-Dick*, especially in those months when he was trying to "finish him up in some fashion or other" (*L* 192), the difference between his relation to this novel as opposed to his earlier texts is considerable. Upon receiving a letter from Hawthorne, in which he praises *Moby-Dick*, Melville basks in the glow of Hawthorne's validation, going so far as to say, "I am content and can be happy" (*L* 213). It is as if Melville has found a way to protect his narrative from his penchant for destroying it by finding a safe place to put his self-destructiveness, and that is in the character of Ahab. Ahab, not Melville, tries to destroy Moby-Dick, but *Moby-Dick* is safe. Thus, unlike the complicated delight with which he received Dana's praise, here is true delight, as Melville reads Hawthorne's "joy-giving and exultation-breeding letter" (*L* 212). In the months to follow, as reviews came in that applauded it, but failed to comprehend what Melville was trying to do, or criticized the novel mercilessly

(Parker and Hayford 5–18), Melville would need to lean on Hawthorne's singular understanding of the novel in order to maintain some modicum of perspective regarding the tremendous literary accomplishment that was *Moby-Dick*.

Unlike the narratives of *Redburn* and *White-Jacket*, in which Melville's discontent with their very existence is on display, I am suggesting that the complexity of Melville's relation to *Moby-Dick* has more to do with its reception than its composition. Although it is true that as pressure mounted to finish the book and to support his growing family, he experienced the writing process as "work" and "slave[ry]" (*L* 191), we need only look at moments in the text where Melville reflects upon writing to see how his relation to it bears little resemblance to his earlier works. These reflections begin right at the start with "Etymology" and "Extracts," as Melville outlines the grand, some might say imperial, ambitions of the project (Dimock, Rogin, Franchot). Together, these origins of *Moby-Dick*, "Etymology" in a compact way and "Extracts" in an expansive sense, reveal several things. First and most obviously, the whale will comprise the text's subject matter. Second will be the ways in which various nations and cultures have defined and understood the whale. This embrace of cultural and linguistic diversity will be registered by an attentiveness to language and its signifying capabilities. The list of languages, from Hebrew to Swedish to Dutch, and the different symbolic structures used to designate the whale indicate that the subject matter of *Moby-Dick* is as much the language(s) used to represent the whale as the whale. Third, and related to the first two points, is the inextricable relation between the whale as nature and the whale as text. To compose the history of the whale is to read the previous histories of the whale's composition, and the "Extracts" section makes the reader keenly aware of Melville's knowledge of virtually every writer who has attempted to tell the story of the whale. Melville may not be the first writer to take on this topic, even though he writes to Bentley about the "great novelty" of his new work (presumably in an effort to get his British publisher interested in the project and secure a sizeable advance), and observes, "I do not know that the subject treated of has ever been worked up by a romancer; or, indeed by any writer, in any adequate manner" (*L* 163), but he will do it better than anyone else. Given what we have already seen in *Redburn* and *White-Jacket*, it should come as no surprise that the story of Moby Dick, or the whale, will also be the story of *Moby-Dick, or the Whale*.

There is, however, this fundamental difference. In the earlier novels, Melville all but tells his audience that his books are no better, and perhaps worse, than anyone else's, whereas with *Moby-Dick*, he communicates his sense that he is writing something better, truer, grander than what has come before. Many aspects of the text convey this point. One might look at the novel's generic expansiveness, bringing together poetry, song, drama, and sermon. Or, one might note the range of discourses, as Melville folds in the scientific with the religious, the legal with the ethnological, the philosophical with the Shakespearean. The humor, as well, comprises a key tonal aspect of the novel, which also has an ideological purpose, as Ahab's narcissistic and deadly account of Moby Dick comes up against Ishmael's more capacious and comic understanding of the whale. Unlike in his earlier narratives, here Melville seems neither careless nor rushed, neither impatient nor reluctant, and although he claims in "The Affadavit," "I care not to perform this part of my task methodically" (203), the fact is that *Moby-Dick* explicitly takes up the issue of its own method, and in a methodical way at that.

At times, Melville seems to perform his novelistic task according to the logic of the organic metaphor as described in the letter to Hawthorne and the citation in the heading of this section. Elsewhere, however, Melville is conscious of the fact that the principle upon which his text is organized is profoundly artificial and anything but organic. Many chapters begin with a scientific inquiry into, for example, the material that comes out of the whale's spout or the texture of the whale's skin, only to conclude with a statement of complete bewilderment. "Cetology" is, perhaps, Melville's most self-conscious expression of the unknowability of natural phenomena, even when one has experienced them first-hand, but rather than lament his inability to have a transparent relation to nature (à la Emerson), Melville, through the voice of Ishmael, celebrates the freedom that comes with this acknowledgment of the arbitrariness of representation and finds humor in it. He authoritatively states, "I divide the whales into three primary BOOKS (subdivisible into CHAPTERS)" (137) and then proceeds to demonstrate how the boundaries between the books are so porous as to make those boundaries ridiculous and the subdivisions within chapters highly questionable as well. Thus, although he claims otherwise at the start of the chapter, this classificatory system is not meant to provide the reader with "some sort of popular comprehensive classification" (136) or "hit the right classification" (140), but rather to undo classification itself by parodying its methods and aims (Porter). After offering up and then thoroughly undermining his own statement of methodology by demonstrating its reliance on arbitrary and false assumptions, Ishmael confesses that "this whole book is but a draught – nay, but the draught of a draught" (145).

But this draft of *Moby-Dick* has an enormous pay-off for Melville, which differentiates it from *Redburn* and *White-Jacket*. When Ishmael throws up his hands in mock despair at his inability to figure out what comes out of the whale's spout, or where the skin ends and the blubber begins, or even what a whale is, that is not the final word. Steeped in doubt about any conclusions he might draw regarding the content of what he sees, Ishmael transforms those doubts into meditations on philosophy, religion, and literature. That "vast, mild head overhung by a canopy of vapor" leaves Ishmael with "divine intuitions [which] now and then shoot, enkindling my fog with a heavenly ray ... doubts of all things earthly, and intuitions of some things heavenly; this combination makes neither believer nor infidel, but makes a man who regards them both with equal eye" (374). The doubts, in other words, do not arrest the development of Ishmael's speculations. They act as a spur to the narrative. This is quite different from the earlier texts in which the challenges to the narrative called attention to its failure and registered Melville's internal struggle against the book he was writing; in the case of *Moby-Dick,* Ishmael's narrative of inconclusiveness and doubt wins the day. There is no junk, no duff, only sperm, that complex, rich symbol of brotherly love, purity, sex, and creativity.

Pierre: "I write precisely as I please"

Melville began writing *Pierre* immediately after finishing *Moby-Dick*, and like *Redburn* and *White-Jacket*, the two novels of the early 1850s are intricately connected. Once reviews of *Moby-Dick* began to appear, and it was quickly apparent that the novel would not make him the money (or the reputation) that he had anticipated, Melville was already writing to Bentley about his new book, hawking its "unquestionable novelty," "treating of utterly new scenes & characters," and "much more calculated for popularity than anything you have yet published of mine" (*L* 226). For Melville, *Pierre* both was and wasn't new. The story takes place on terra firma. Female characters, such as Lucy, Isabel, and Mrs. Glendinning, play a significant role. And Pierre is, notoriously, in love with all three.

Yet *Pierre* also follows the path of *Redburn* and *White-Jacket*. Their self-destructiveness and Melville's self-loathing are taken to new heights (or depths) in *Pierre*. We have seen it before, though: the narrative that virtually grinds to a halt; the narrator, who looks a lot like Melville, lodging a critique of the book and lashing out at those who would critique it; and the text that continually stages its own destruction. That Melville would be so utterly wrong about *Pierre*'s popularity registers two things. The first is his desperate desire to write a popular book, given his dire financial straits (Parker and Hayford 844), and the second is his dire psychic state, given the reception of *Moby-Dick*. Even, and especially, his good friends, George and Evert Duyckinck, did not understand what Melville had accomplished. In the second installment of Evert's *Literary World* review, he writes: "we do not like to see what, under my view, must be to the world the most sacred associations of life violated and defaced" (Branch, 267). With friends like this, it is no wonder that Melville tells Bentley: "let bygones be bygones; let those previous books, for the present, take care of themselves. For here now we have a *new book*, and what shall we say about *this*? If nothing has been made on the old books, may not something be made out of the new?" (*L* 226–7) Here, Melville groups *Moby-Dick* with his earlier books, a devastating acknowledgment of its financial failure and a brave, though impossible, attempt to move forward. To invoke his letter to Shaw, Melville had written the kind of book that would fail (*pace* Hawthorne), and instead of feeling like success, it felt like failure.

Moby-Dick would not be a bygone. If it failed, if it were just like the beggarly *Redburn* and *White-Jacket*, what could Melville write that would be popular and profitable? Perhaps by leaving the man-of-war world and writing "a regular romance ... representing a new & elevated aspect of American life" (*L* 226), Melville would finally make some money. That he thought *Pierre*, with its well-developed theme of incest, would accomplish this, that it was in any sense of the term "regular" or "elevated," is as misguided as thinking that *Moby-Dick* could be relegated to one of "those previous books." Melville simply could not and would not let that happen, which is one of the reasons why the narrative of *Pierre* is so tortured, so strange, and so bloody. As with the earlier texts, he does not want to write it, which is why there is so much foreshadowing in the early parts of the book. He is projecting the novel's conclusion when the book is barely underway because that is when Melville will have successfully killed off Pierre, killed off the book Pierre is writing, and ensured that *Pierre* itself would self-destruct, which, according to reviews of the period, it admirably did.

The texture of the narrative can, perhaps, be most clearly described by focusing on the novel's beginning or, more precisely, beginnings. There is the novel's bizarre opening, the story of Isabel's origins, the history of Pierre's friendship with his cousin, Glendinning Stanly, the account of Pierre's authorship, and Plinlimmon's pamphlet. Both the plot and language of *Pierre* can be said to begin "but beginningly as it were" (117). Words pile up without accreting meaning, and prose has difficulty getting out of its own way. We read the dialogue and inner thoughts of characters who use the same words over and over again, such as Lucy's initial greeting to Pierre, " 'Pierre; – bright Pierre! – Pierre!' " (4), or Mrs. Glendinning's soliloquy in which she refers to the docility of Pierre and Lucy no less than eight times in one paragraph. The characters' penchant (or compulsion) for repetition is also reflected in the narrative voice. The narrator refers to Pierre's grandfather as "grand old Pierre" five times in a single paragraph, repeating the name and its epithets as if "he" were an insufficient mode of designation: " 'I keep Christmas with my horses,' said grand old Pierre. This grand old Pierre always rose at sunrise" (30). Such verbal excess signals not only the grandiosity of Pierre's grandfather but Pierre's diminishment. The more room taken up by the grandfather – on the page, in the psyche, in Saddle Meadows – the less room for Pierre. Words and their variants are repeated, such as "descended" (7, 9, 17) "endless descendedness" (9), "blood-descent" (10), "far-descended" (11), "descending" (12), and "double-revolutionary descent" (20), or the title of Book IX, "More Light, and the Gloom of That Light. More Gloom, and the Light of That Gloom" (165). The words that are *Pierre*, like the novel's characters, are incapable of doing much more than repeating, mirroring, or descending from themselves. There will be no room for *Pierre* either.

Just as individual words get in each other's way, so too the narrative of *Pierre* is constantly bumping into itself. The narrator repeats descriptions, ideas, and passages while calling attention to those repetitions, as if he were unable to find a stable temporal rhythm through which to tell the story. As early as section 3 of the opening chapter, the narrator repeats himself: "it has been said that the beautiful country round about Pierre appealed to very proud memories" (8). At the start of section 4, he asserts, "we poetically establish the richly aristocratic condition of Master Pierre Glendinning, for whom we have before claimed some special family distinction" (12). He then alludes to Pierre's grandfather as "the same grandfather several times herein-before mentioned" (13) and concludes the section with a phrase from its second paragraph, "we shall yet see again, I say, whether Fate hath not just a little bit of a word or two to say in this world" (14). The narrative is made up of obstructions to itself, as evidenced in this quotation from section four: "In conclusion, do not blame me if I here make repetition, and do verbally quote my own words in saying that *it had been the choice fate of Pierre to have been born and bred in the country*" (13). This passage offers itself as a conclusion – as if the narrative has progressed from point a to point b – when the passage is a citation from section 2, indicating that the narrative has circled back upon itself. But the narrator is not hiding that fact, because this "conclusion" refers to its status as a moment in an earlier part of the text. The sentence acknowledges itself *as* an act of tautology, or citationality, through italics and with the phrase "do verbally quote my own words in saying." The sentence is a conclusion only insofar as it occurs last in a series of repetitions. It is the origin repeated a bit later.

This narrative blockage is registered at the level of character as well. Just as words cannot get out of each other's way, by virtue of their philological relatedness, Pierre cannot escape the fact of his own relatedness, try as he might. For every "blood relation" (218) spurned by Pierre, another one takes its place. Blood permeates the text, whether it be the "too much generous blood in [Pierre's] heart" (222) or the "blood-red" (92) sunrise of Saddle Meadows or the "the blood-shedding times" (75) of the French Revolution. Pierre's mother, upon suspecting him of leaving Lucy, declares, "I feel my blood chemically changing in me" (131), and Pierre, in thinking about the "unproven fact of Isabel's sisterhood," notes that "his very blood seemed to flow through all his arteries with unwonted subtileness, when he thought that the same tide flowed through the mystic veins of Isabel" (139). Isabel's fateful letter to Pierre, in which she declares their relatedness, is blotted with tears that "assume a strange and reddish hue – as if blood and not tears had dropped upon the sheet" (64–5). The novel appropriately concludes by staging its own destruction as the "black vein in this Glendinning" (358) opens up and "the dark vein's burst" (362).

The creativity of *Moby-Dick*'s sperm has been replaced by blood and tears, the new registers of Melville's rage, sadness, and attitude toward his text. Blood is at once a metaphor for the consanguineous relations that Pierre cannot escape, and for Melville's self-destructiveness, in the wake of *Moby-Dick*'s failure, which bleeds onto the pages of *Pierre*. When Pierre is at work on his masterpiece, which is continually being undercut and jeered at, the narrator, in an unusual moment of sympathy, observes that two books are being written: "the larger book ... whose unfathomable cravings drink his blood; the other only demands his ink" (304). Although Redburn, White-Jacket, and Ishmael share many of Melville's literary interests, it is in *Pierre* that Melville at last makes his protagonist an author. As a result, the distance between narrator and author, which Melville has a great deal of difficulty maintaining even when his narrators are not authors, collapses, and we see the author at work. It is not a pretty picture. In one especially self-reflexive passage, the narrator remarks upon Pierre's desire to "hurl his deep book out of the window, and fall to on some shallow nothing of a novel, composable in a month at the longest, [and] then could he reasonably hope for both appreciation and cash" (305).

That Melville would imagine hurling *Pierre* out the window is not especially surprising given similar images in his earlier texts. That he would suggest that the answer to Pierre's suffering is the composition of a "shallow nothing of a novel," like *Redburn* or *White-Jacket*, speaks to Melville's tortured realization that writing is as much about "appreciation and cash" (even if that appreciation or the cash that comes with it is a result of critics who misunderstand the text) as it is about metaphysical speculation, political commentary, or literary originality. Writing, from Melville's perspective, was not supposed to be a job like a woodcutter's. That it virtually always was made the process of writing a deeply conflicted one. The results are not "botches," but rather narratives that record their own making and unmaking, and in the process of doing so construct a reader at work, a reader whose interpretive job is to understand the ways in which Melville, while hating to do it, wrote great books.

NOTE

This essay is dedicated to Michael T. Gilmore.

REFERENCES AND FURTHER READING

Branch, Watson G., ed. *Melville: The Critical Heritage*. London: Routledge & Kegan Paul, 1974.

Dimock, Wai-chee. *Empire for Liberty: Melville and the Poetics of Individualism*. Princeton, NJ: Princeton University Press, 1989.

Emerson, Ralph Waldo. "Nature." In *Selected Writings of Emerson*. New York: The Modern Library, 1940.

Franchot, Jenny. "Melville's Traveling God." In *The Cambridge Companion to Herman Melville*. Ed. Robert S. Levine. Cambridge: Cambridge University Press, 1998. 157–85.

Gilmore, Michael. *American Romanticism and the Marketplace*. Chicago: University of Chicago Press, 1982.

Otter, Samuel. *Melville's Anatomies*. Berkeley: University of California Press, 1999.

Parker, Hershel and Harrison Hayford, eds. Moby-Dick *as Doubloon: Essays and Extracts (1851–1970)*. New York: W. W. Norton, 1970.

Porter, Carolyn. "Call Me Ishmael, or How to Make Double-Talk Speak." In *New Essays on* Moby-Dick. Ed. Richard Brodhead. Cambridge: Cambridge University Press, 1986. 73–108.

Rogin, Michael Paul. *Subversive Genealogy: The Politics and Art of Herman Melville*. New York: Knopf, 1983.

Weinstein, Cindy. *Family, Kinship, and Sympathy in Nineteenth-Century American Literature*. Cambridge: Cambridge University Press, 2004.

——. "Melville, Labor, and the Discourses of Reception." In *The Cambridge Companion to Herman Melville*. Ed. Robert S. Levine. Cambridge: Cambridge University Press, 1998. 202–23.

25

The Language of *Moby-Dick*: "Read It If You Can"

Maurice S. Lee

Language is everywhere in *Moby-Dick* (1851), not simply because writing is Melville's chosen medium, but also because the book is about (among other things) the power and limitations of words. Ishmael ponders the prospects of language in a famous chapter, "The Whiteness of the Whale," where he tries to define the "nameless" and "ineffable" quality of Moby Dick, even as he "almost despair[s] of putting it in a comprehensible form" (188). "Comprehensible" indicates the duty of language to make itself understood, but it also hints at Ishmael's desire to give a comprehensive account of whales and the world. In this sense, Melville in *Moby-Dick* is ambitious to the point of hubris. As an allusive and wildly experimental author at the peak of his imaginative force, he draws variously on literary histories, social idioms, and linguistic theories while striving to achieve what he called in 1850 "real originality" ("Hawthorne and His Mosses," *PT* 246). This is one reason why *Moby-Dick* can be so challenging. It is simultaneously traditional and inventive, simultaneously a part and ahead of its time. And while the book tells its story, it also examines the ways in which stories are told, making the language of Melville's most celebrated novel intensely self-referential. Like Ishmael's attempt to systematize whales, explaining the language of *Moby-Dick* remains an unending project. Yet as Ishmael says when contemplating the inexplicable meaning of whiteness, "[I]n some dim, random way, explain myself I must, else all these chapters might be naught" (188).

Literary History ("By Way of Variety")

Early reviews of *Moby-Dick* called the book a "chowder," a "salmagundi," and a "dish" "flung together salad-wise" (Parker and Hayford 49, 53, 7). But while some readers did not mind that it was "impossible to submit such books to a distinct classification," more often than not they objected to the "queer mixture" of Melville's work (Parker and Hayford 49, 46). Like the *Pequod* itself, *Moby-Dick* is composed of disparate and not always harmonious parts; and just as Melville describes the beams and oakum that hold the *Pequod* together, he takes a kind of rebellious pleasure in displaying the incongruities of his book. Sexual puns sit alongside serious researches into the natural sciences. Descriptions of the day-to-day life of a whaling ship turn suddenly into metaphysical rhapsodies over perception and God. The largely self-educated Melville read widely, and in *Moby-Dick* his interests take multiple forms, demonstrating both an affinity for and a resistance to literary precursors.

Moby-Dick is primarily a novel, but it incorporates many genres and subgenres. Like Melville's earlier and more popular works, the book is a sea-adventure in the tradition of Sir Walter Scott's *The Pirate* (1822) and James Fenimore Cooper's *The Pilot* (1823). There are also gothic trappings described in lurid language – dark prophecies, a madman, a supernatural monster, the mystery of Fedallah and his crew – so much so that some reviewers likened *Moby-Dick* to the writings of Monk Lewis, while later readers hear echoes of American gothic authors such as Charles Brockden Brown, George Lippard, and Poe. *Moby-Dick* can also resemble a frontier tall-tale full of humor, violence, self-conscious hyperbole, racial difference, and man's battle with nature. But while Melville paints larger-than-life romantic figures and recounts breathless scenes of carnage and courage, he also follows Richard Henry Dana's *Two Years before the Mast* (1840) by narrating in journalistic detail the trials of a first-time sailor. Sections of *Moby-Dick* are as informative as a logbook and as technical as a whaling manual; and Melville does not exclude impolite topics such as the butchering of whales. Considering Melville's attention to laborers struggling within an industrial system, and given the book's frequent suspicion that humans live in a deterministic world, *Moby-Dick* can seem as much a realist novel as a romantic one. It even becomes something more than a novel when it shifts into other genres. The dense musicality of *Moby-Dick*'s language has prompted some to call the book a prose-poem. Most strikingly, as early critics such as F. O. Matthiessen and Charles Olson note, *Moby-Dick* is also committed to dramatic forms, obviously in the book's scenes and soliloquies replete with stage directions but also (as Alan Ackerman, Jr. has argued) in its foregrounding of spectacle within the public sphere. Many novels, of course, are omnivorous in their literary samplings, but *Moby-Dick* remains an extreme example that cuts across generic lines.

Melville's transgression of boundaries is also evident in the style of *Moby-Dick*, which reflects a largesse of literary influences from the United States and abroad. Like classical mythology and the Bible, the novel's intensely symbolic language invites allegorical interpretation, particularly given Melville's tendency to echo the diction and rhythms of scripture. *Moby-Dick* is also indebted to sixteenth- and seventeenth-century British literature. When Ahab cries, "I am madness maddened!" or when Pip gibbers with the wisdom of a fool, it is difficult not to think of Shakespeare, whose plays Melville read and attended in the months leading up to *Moby-Dick* (168; Chapter 37). As indicated by Melville's marginalia – and as Robin Grey and Christopher Sten have shown – Spenser, Milton, and William D'Avenant also left their marks, helping to shape *Moby-Dick*'s epic eloquence and sometimes tangled syntax. Elsewhere, Melville's learned rambles resemble those of the polymath Thomas Browne, and his playful digressions recall *Tristram Shandy* (1761), which Melville read in 1849. More contemporary influences include Coleridge and Carlyle, both of whom scale metaphysical heights but, like Melville, subvert their own claims with a romantic irony that ranges from parody to prophecy.

In addition to American forerunners such as Brown, Cooper, and Poe, two very different romantics, Washington Irving and Emerson, also resonate with *Moby-Dick*. Irving's Knickerbocker histories lightly mock pedants such as the sub-sub-librarian, while Emerson's penchant for mystic pronouncement is satirized – and to some degree, shared – by *Moby-Dick*. More than any American writer, however, Hawthorne had an impact on the novel. In 1850, Melville wrote "Hawthorne and His Mosses," a rapturous review of the author to whom Melville would dedicate *Moby-Dick*. Melville famously praised Hawthorne's "power of blackness" while also lauding his gentle and melancholy tones, even as Melville himself embarked on a project that would largely lack the quiet blasphemies and balanced structures of Hawthorne's works (*PT* 243). Ishmael does have peaceful moments rendered in an "enchanted mood," but much of *Moby-Dick*, like many of Melville's sources, indulges a style that almost gleefully violates conventions of decorum, symmetry, and order (159; chapter 35).

All of which suggests that Melville in *Moby-Dick* was trying to do something outlandish, something new that yet retained by way of reference the traditions it would leave behind and revisit. An indication of his ambition is what one review called Melville's inveterate "wordmongering," for *Moby-Dick* uses extraordinary language that is simultaneously archaic and fresh (Parker and Hayford 11). Characters are "predestinated," "befooled," and ruled by "sympathetical" feelings (171, 568, 179; chapters 39, 134, 41). And when the white whale "heaps," "tasks," and "swerve[s]" Ahab, Melville does not so much coin new words as use old ones in new ways (164, 168; chapters 36, 37). "Fossiliferous" is one of many abstruse terms that Melville lifts from specialized fields, while "Leviathanism" is a monstrosity of Melville's own creation (455, 145; chapters 104, 32). Such reworking of language is writ large in *Moby-Dick*'s relation to literary history, as if Melville suffered some anxiety of influence when seeking what he called "an aspect of newness" (*PT* "Mosses" 246). Fittingly, the most powerful literary models for *Moby-Dick* are themselves iconoclastic. And in a later story, "The Happy Failure" (1854), Melville creates a frustrated inventor who complains that "there's not much left in an old world for an old man to invent" (*PT* 260), a problem related to a larger concern: How successful is Melville in making *Moby-Dick* a compellingly original work?

Even twentieth- and twenty-first-century readers accustomed to postmodern pastiche can, like early reviewers of *Moby-Dick*, find its heterogeneity confusing or laborious. This may be why some readers abandon the book one-third of the way through when Ishmael's first-person, plot-driven story becomes increasingly fragmented. The lack of unity is further complicated by multiple and not always distinguishable narrative voices: an authorial perspective often associated with Melville, the intrepid sub-sub-librarian, Ishmael (for some critics, both a younger and an older version), and Ahab, who so dominates sections of the book as to pull the story into his orbit. Some early scholars have attempted to identify and track these various voices; and even recent poststructuralist readers who point to the indeterminate nature of language tend to view the novel as a dialectical struggle between Ishmael and Ahab. The difference between these two protagonists is not only ideological (classically, Ishmael's democratic plural-ism versus Ahab's despotic absolutism). It is also one of dialect – of linguistic variation – insofar as Ishmael's ironic musings are drowned out by Ahab's bellicose rants only to resurface suddenly at the conclusion of the book. Binary approaches remain the dom-inant way of understanding *Moby-Dick*, yet Pip's "crazy-witty" ravings can also repre-sent the challenge of the novel's narrative instability (435; chapter 99). When Pip chants in "The Doubloon" chapter, "I look, you look, he looks; we look, ye look, they look," he indicates the tangle of perspectives that form the frolic architecture of *Moby-Dick* (434). Even further, when Stubb overhears Pip and surmises that he has been reading "Murray's Grammar," Melville suggests that the problem of perspective is manifest at the most basic levels of language and that efforts to impose systematic control cannot quell Pip's babbling subjectivism (434). The narrative of *Moby-Dick* may be finally too protean for all but the loosest of formulations, for the novel tempts but finally frustrates any critical rage for order.

Moby-Dick can even be so wild as to seem downright careless. Characters such as Bulkington get lost in the shuffle, and the story's chronology is sometimes haphazard. No one accuses the book of being tightly plotted, particularly when sub-plots are introduced and abandoned. Moreover, Melville's style, for all its magnificent expan-siveness, can feel occasionally self-indulgent. Is he being ironic or simply bathetic when Ahab cries like "a heart-stricken moose" (163; chapter 36)? Was an early reviewer entirely wrong to say that "[e]xtravagance is the bane of the book" (Parker and Hayford 13)? Writing under financial pressures, Melville hurried to complete *Moby-Dick*; and he complained to Hawthorne in 1851 that his books were all "botches" and a "hash" (L 191). Yet for all the excesses and unevenness that have bothered some readers from Melville's day to our own, *Moby-Dick* offers not only a provocative multiplicity but also a governing logic of sorts. Just as Melville compares his book to a sprawling, whale-like production, Ishmael says of his cetological studies, "There are some enterprises in which a careful disorderliness is the true method" (361; chapter 82).

Indeed, the wildness of *Moby-Dick* seems very much a self-conscious and even calculated achievement. To some degree, the reviews comparing *Moby-Dick* to a chowder or stew are persuasive, yet Melville refuses to be limited by even so inclusive a metaphor. In Nantucket, Ishmael is initially asked to choose between clam or cod chowder, but by the end of his meal he is demanding both, as well as smoked herring "by way of variety" (67; chapter 15). Similarly, Melville in *Moby-Dick* takes in a diversity of forms, which he fails – or more accurately it seems, refuses – to blend together smoothly. Such resistance may be a romantic reaction against the genteel

continuities of neoclassicism. But while Melville instantiates the splintered epistemologies and aesthetics of romanticism, the latent possibility for unity remains, if
only because so many disparate elements are gathered in one book. Rough-hewn,
fractured, heterogeneous, and yet connected by proximity and careful disorderliness –
Moby-Dick's multiple voices and styles are unmistakably Melville's. They may even be
a convincing representation of human experience. Such diversity is not only a
distinctive feature of the language of *Moby-Dick*; it is an aesthetic that the novel
names, if only implicitly.

In the chapter, "Of Whales in Paint; in Teeth; in Wood; in Sheet-iron; in Stones; in
Mountains; in Stars," Ishmael surveys a range of artistic expressions – verbal and
visual, high and low, European and what he ironically calls "savage" (270). The
chapter also praises "skrimshander articles," those "numerous little ingenious
contrivances" that sailors carve from "rough material" (269). These pieces can stand
for the many components that make up *Moby-Dick*; and for Ishmael they share the
"maziness of design" found in Hawaiian war-clubs, whose "full multiplicity and
elaboration of carving, is as great a trophy of human perseverance as a Latin lexicon"
(270). Here Melville pays tribute to the grammatical structures and intellectual
foundations of his language and culture, but he does not privilege scholarly lexicons
over more extravagant artistic forms such as Hawaiian war-clubs. Language, of course,
remains Melville's medium and literary history matters in his work, but he will not be
bound by the conventions of either in the pages of *Moby-Dick*.

Culture ("Parts of the Times")

As if to simultaneously claim and renounce the authority of canonical learning, the
opening "Extracts" of *Moby-Dick* come not from a traditional scholar but instead are
provided by the sub-sub-librarian, a "painstaking burrower and grubworm" who has
"gone through the long Vaticans and street-stalls of the earth" picking up "any book
whatsoever, sacred or profane" (xvii). Particularly within the last few decades, critics
have interpreted *Moby-Dick* as a cultural artifact that registers a host of practices and
discourses. It is not simply that Melville discusses current events in the argot of his
day. Rather, the language at Melville's disposal structures and is structured by social
forms and conditions of the period. In this sense, the language of *Moby-Dick* is not
transparent or transcendent, nor can we ascribe to Melville's text an unmediated
authorial voice. In "Hawthorne and His Mosses," Melville to some extent agrees that
literature is historically embedded: "[G]reat geniuses are parts of the times; they
themselves are the times; and possess a correspondent coloring" (*PT* 246). *Moby-Dick*
is indeed affected by antebellum American culture, even if the correspondence
between Melville and his times is not stable or over-determined.

In addition to the sub-sub-librarian's quotations from Spenser, Montaigne, and
Dryden are sources that indicate Melville's broad interest in popular print culture.
These include an array of travel narratives, an excerpt from a political speech, and an

unnamed document that Melville calls " '[s]omething' unpublished" (xxvii; "Extracts"). Elsewhere *Moby-Dick* also incorporates newspaper headlines, lading lists, coin imprints, and gravestone inscriptions; and even the wrinkles on the white whale's brow resemble a kind of script. Such examples suggest that written words are for Melville more than abstract symbols; they themselves are material objects that have presence and use in the world. This is especially evident in a scene where Ishmael and Queequeg look through a book. Queequeg leafs attentively through its pages, but he cannot read the text, nor can Ishmael describe in his companion's language the contents of the book. Nonetheless, these obstacles do not stop the men from becoming "Bosom Friends." Ishmael writes:

> We then turned over the book together, and I endeavored to explain to him the purpose of the printing, and the meaning of the few pictures that were in it. Thus I soon engaged his interest; and from that we went to jabbering the best we could about the various outer sights to be seen in [New Bedford]. Soon I proposed a social smoke; and, producing his pouch and tomahawk, he quietly offered me a puff. (51)

What matters at this moment is not the book's words so much as its social function, for Ishmael and Queequeg move from handling the book, to discussing real world "outer sights," to finally enjoying together the physical comforts of a pipe. Thus the book-as-material-object facilitates a shared experience in a way that the book-as-symbolic-system cannot, suggesting that the wide-ranging functions of literature are not restricted to abstractions.

A more complicated instance of Melville's interest in the materiality of writing is *Moby-Dick*'s conflation of whales and texts. The "Cetology" chapter classifies whales as folios, duodecimos, and octavos; and in "The Blanket" Ishmael uses a translucent piece of whale-skin as a bookmark in his book about whales. Here *Moby-Dick* challenges the distinction between whales and written accounts of whales, particularly when Ishmael fancies that the skin has "a magnifying influence" on the text, as if the physical product of butchering whales furthers scholarly efforts to dissect them in print (306). Yet what seems like a conflation can be equally a juxtaposition, for Melville points out some crucial differences between the writing and the reality of whales. The scrap of whale-skin implies what is everywhere demonstrated by Ishmael's unfinished cetology – namely, that no book howsoever comprehensive can contain the entirety of whales (no more than can the so-called "blanket sheets" of the antebellum popular press). Moreover, Ishmael goes on in "The Blanket" to discuss "the visible surface of the Sperm Whale," which is covered by markings that resemble "the finest Italian line engravings" (306). Importantly, such marks do not penetrate to the inner layer of the whale-skin, suggesting a problem that lies at the heart of Ahab's fury and Ishmael's doubt: Can the physical signs of language be trusted? Do they represent or mask deeper truths, if such truths even exist? Questions like these are not only, as we will see, an issue for philosophers of language. They are also, as Samuel Otter has shown, embodied in antebellum cultural discourses of race, tattooing, and phrenology. Skin color, inking, skull bumps, whales – all can be a kind of material language, a discursive system of "visible objects" that Ahab hopes to "strike through" (164; chapter 36). By this he explicitly means thrust through or get beyond physical appearances in order to discover ideal truths. At the same time, as Elizabeth Renker has argued, "strike through" can also refer to an editor's lineout, implying that the best one can do with writing is pile more writing upon it, thus further obscuring any effort to see beyond the physical textuality of the object world. *Moby-Dick*'s diversity of print forms and attention to the materiality of language calls forth a range of interpretive possibilities, though whether one can accurately decipher the universe is a mystery that Melville does not answer, except to show that culture and hermeneutics are tightly intertwined.

Just as language in *Moby-Dick* can trick the eye, so too can it fool the ear, a matter of concern for antebellum Americans who valued the practice of oratory. As James Perrin Warren details, the antebellum era's "culture of eloquence" was founded on the belief that powerful speech could move democratic citizens toward moral and social perfection. Conversely, Kenneth Cmiel has emphasized how Americans feared that artful speech could be abused by smooth aristocrats and rabble-rousing demagogues alike, mystifying and enraging the People on whose judgment the nation relied. The uncertain prospects of antebellum oratory played out in a variety of contexts – at camp meetings and established churches, in the Senate and on the stump, at lyceums that aimed at the middle classes but occasioned promiscuous mixing. In *Moby-Dick*, Melville mimics high and low, sacred and profane oratorical practices, all the while continuing to wage his quarrel with official forms of language.

The main speechmaker in *Moby-Dick* is obviously Ahab, whose magnetic voice issues commands from the cabin before he ever appears on deck. When he does, his performances echo Shakespeare's characters, most notably King Lear, and to a lesser degree classical orators who were models for antebellum rhetoricians. As Alan Heimert, Donald Pease, and Wai-chee Dimock have argued, Ahab can also represent political oratory of the time, particularly if he stands for antebellum figures such as Daniel Webster, William Lloyd Garrison, Andrew Jackson, and American Indian speakers. Ahab's oratory is a catastrophic success. In "The Quarter-Deck," he assembles his crew and inspires them to hunt the white whale, even as the mass of sailors marvel "how it was that they themselves became so excited" by Ahab's fiery speech (161). Nor (we learn later) can the reflective, skeptical Ishmael resist the pull of his captain: "I, Ishmael, was one of that crew; my shouts had gone up with the rest. . . . A wild, mystical, sympathetical feeling was in me; Ahab's quenchless feud seemed mine" (179; chapter 41). Like some dark version of a sentimental hero, Ahab's bursting heart and boiling blood cast an affective spell on his audience. Part mesmerist, part actor, part preacher, part tyrant, the eloquent Ahab speeds the *Pequod* to its doom, overmastering Ishmael, the crew, and Starbuck's middle-management objections, so much so that in *Moby-Dick* the lungs are mentioned almost as much as the heart and the head.

While Ahab offers a cautionary example of grandiloquence, other characters speak in lower frequencies – from the jargon of the garrulous sailors, to the pidgin of Queequeg and Tashtego, to displays of African-American dialect such as Fleece's sermon to the sharks in "Stubb's Supper." That scene is reminiscent of blackface minstrelsy, a popular tradition of the antebellum era wherein authors and actors, predominantly white, caricatured African-Americans even while admitting common fears and desires by way of psychological projection. In many ways, the broken grammar and absurd solemnity of Fleece's sermon are demeaning ("Dough you is all sharks, and by natur wery woracious ... 'top dat dam slappin' ob de tail!" [295]). Still, the content of the speech is thoughtful and for the most part benevolent; and Melville carefully shows that Fleece's sermon comes at the order of the humorist Stubb, suggesting that Melville recognizes not only the inequities of blackface minstrelsy, but also the possibility that everyone is in some way a performer and slave. Disagreements over Melville's political views often hinge on the question of whether his irony can escape the oppressive ideologies of his time. *Moby-Dick*'s use of racialized dialect fuels this controversy, for Melville exposes the racist vernacular of minstrelsy even while exploiting its comedic potential. David Reynolds has argued that Melville also employs related cultural forms of humor including nautical and frontier hi-jinks, urban burlesques associated with the showman P. T. Barnum, and transgressive race- and class-based jokes that Reynolds labels "radical-democrat" (Reynolds 541). Reynolds helps to explain some of *Moby-Dick*'s more idiomatic moments such as Stubb's fanciful sallies and Ishmael's sly puns, though whether or not such humor serves egalitarian purposes is open to debate.

One way to think about the relationship between language and politics in *Moby-Dick* is as a contest between official written documents and subversive oral forms. The subject of *Moby-Dick* can be traced to Owen Chase's *The Wreck of the Whaleship Essex* (1821), which Ishmael refers to in "The Affidavit," a chapter that attempts to validate his story by citing textual sources. At the same time, Melville also relies not on written authority but on nautical folklore, including the legend of Mocha Dick that circulated among sailors. In *Moby-Dick* itself, stories of the white whale are ubiquitous and untraceable, so much so that the monster seemingly appears "in opposite latitudes at one and the same instant of time" (182; Chapter 41). The *Pequod*'s harpooners and Starbuck all know Moby Dick by different signs; and Father Mapple's sermon discusses Leviathan by retelling the story of Jonah and the Whale as a wonderfully vernacular "yarn" (42; Chapter 9). These tales, rendered in diverse idioms, imply that the history of Moby Dick cannot be contained in books or affidavits; and perhaps the most remarkable rumor of the whale is related in "The Town-Ho's Story," an inset chapter that explores the subversive potential of speech.

The central narrative, Steelkilt's failed mutiny and successful disappearance into regions unknown, shows that authoritarian systems are resilient and yet can be challenged and eluded. Equally important is that the tale is communicated through a series of oral performances. Ishmael relates the story to the reader by describing how he told it to some Spanish friends in Lima. By allowing this audience to interrupt with questions, digressions, and (much) wine, Melville shows how knowledge circulates in unofficial, oral, cosmopolitan, and even carnivalesque channels, not unlike the way that goods are moved by the "Canallers" described in the chapter (248). When Ishmael's listeners doubt his story, he swears its veracity on the Bible: "So help me Heaven, and on my honor, the story I have told ye, gentlemen, is in substance and its great items, true.... I trod the ship; I knew the crew; I have seen and talked with Steelkilt" (259). Ishmael carefully qualifies his claims ("in substance and its great items, true"). But the main irony is that his authority comes, not from scripture or first-hand knowledge of the mutiny, but rather from the fact that he walked the *Town-Ho* and talked with Steelkilt and other participants. Here Melville hints that the Bible, the most authoritative text in his culture, is actually — like the story of the *Town-Ho* — a compilation of oral testimonies that are impossible precisely to verify. Unlike the Bible, however, the *Town-Ho's* story is not an official narrative, for it contains a "secret part" that "never reached the ears of Captain Ahab or his mates" and "was unknown to the captain of the Town-Ho himself" (242). These secret parts are told to Ishmael by "three confederate white seamen," suggesting an underground society of laborers who communicate, not through printed forms, but through the spoken word. In "The Town-Ho's Story," these words emphasize the need for sailor solidarity in the face of tyrannical leaders; and in a novel that equates nations and ships, the chapter implicitly defends the right to violent revolution.

In this way, *Moby-Dick* imagines an oral alternative to dominant narratives, though for Melville the possibility of liberating speech remains a tenuous one. As Wyn Kelley emphasizes, the secret part of "The Town-Ho's Story" is transmitted by sailors described as "white," a reminder that class-consciousness in the antebellum era could not rid itself of racial divisions any more than the crew of the *Pequod* can escape the racism that boils over in "Midnight, Forecastle." Furthermore, the underground tale of the *Town-Ho* is told to Ishmael in "The Gam," a chapter that registers Melville's concerns about the capacity of ideology to co-opt dissent. According to the *Oxford English Dictionary*, Melville in *Moby-Dick* first used the word "gam" to describe what he calls a "social meeting" of whaling ships at sea. Ishmael even lays claim to the coinage, bragging that "Dr. Johnson" did not know the word and that "Noah Webster's ark does not hold it" (240). Thus Melville seems to lift the vernacular of sailors over official written forms, if only because during a gam stories circulate beyond the surveillance of captains. As a new word and a subversive way of communicating, "gam" offers the potential for original freedoms. Yet just when Melville appears to reject traditional linguistic and political structures, Ishmael recommends that his new usage "be incorporated into the Lexicon" (240). Whether "incorporated" implies a conservative appropriation or a more radical restructuring is unclear; but as Melville suggests in *Israel Potter* (1855) and "Benito Cereno" (1855), revolutions and revolutionary speech have a way of reverting to tyrannical patterns. After declaring his independence from the owners of the *Pequod*, Ahab has little difficulty dominating his crew, who do not follow the radical model offered by the *Town-Ho* dissidents. Which is to say that Melville's skepticism about the potential for political reformation parallels his doubts about a continuously free and original language. Because words in *Moby-Dick* are culturally embedded, whether in written or oral forms, they can never be separated from the oppressive and liberating possibilities of power.

Theory ("Which Language Cannot Paint")

In its "Extracts" section, *Moby-Dick* quotes from a James Montgomery poem that refers to "Fishes of every color, form, and kind; / Which language cannot paint" (xxiv). We have seen how Melville strains against the conventions of literary history; and we have seen how the language of *Moby-Dick* struggles to escape dominant social discourses. Another challenge that language poses in the novel is one of representation: Can words sufficiently illustrate the multitudinous depths of experience or does the problem of defining the whiteness of the whale extend to every aspect of life? Many serious writers come in some way to interrogate the operations of their medium, yet Melville in *Moby-Dick* is especially committed to exploring theories of language. He does not do so in a vacuum, nor do we when we study his study of words. Just as Melville responds to philosophies of language that were available during his time, modern accounts of *Moby-Dick* often follow the lead of twentieth-century theorists, some of whom Melville appears to anticipate in practice and design.

Moby-Dick's provocative thoughts on language can be understood in contrast to prevailing views of the antebellum period, most notably the Scottish Enlightenment philosophy of Thomas Reid, Dugald Stewart, and the rhetorician Hugh Blair who advanced a "common sense" theory of language based in Lockean principles. Locke held that words reflect a subject's ideas that, in turn, point back to nature; and by positing the representational fidelity of language, common-sense thinkers argued that everyone could share accurate perceptions of the object world. In certain instances, *Moby-Dick* voices a similar confidence. By reading Ahab's doubloon as nothing more than "a round thing made of gold," Flask offers a literal reading of the coin that delimits its symbolic implications (433; Chapter 99). Along these lines, Starbuck insists that the white whale is only a "dumb brute," resisting Ahab's transcendental idealism and suggesting that the safest interpretation of signs comes from a realist, empirical point of view (163; Chapter 36).

Yet howsoever much *Moby-Dick* acknowledges the prudence of conventional epistemologies, and no matter how minutely Melville describes the material reality of whaling, more often than not his novel subverts common-sense theories of language. "The Whiteness of the Whale" is one striking example, but there are many others. Pip, who saw the workings of the universe and "spoke it," seems insane to the uncomprehending crew, a problem suggesting that language cannot communicate deep truths or bridge the distance between other minds (414; Chapter 93). Also – Flask's literalism notwithstanding – the doubloon shows how interpretations can proliferate until signs become so laden with subjective referents as to preclude any shared understanding. Much that *Moby-Dick* tries to say appears to be just beyond reach; and in this Melville shows that language is slippery, partial, approximate, subjective, and contingent – a modern (and postmodern) sense of representation that has precedents in the antebellum period.

In the realm of politics, Americans worried that words were forever fallible and hence that democracy was always in danger of misprision, corruption, and collapse. Hume and, more powerfully for Melville, Hobbes provided a basis for such fears. They argued that words do not always point to nature but rather are susceptible to self-interested manipulation, an anxiety that Thomas Gustafson has traced from classical rhetoric and early modern philosophy to *The Federalist Papers*, Cooper, and Melville. The threat of an unmoored, biased language is particularly evident with Ahab, not simply because he is an eloquent despot, but also because he comes to mediate nature, the referent that according to Scottish common sense was equally and directly available to all. After thunder turns the ship's compass in "The Needle," Ahab declares himself "lord of the level loadstone," spectacularly "magnetizing" a steel splinter in part "to augment the awe of the crew" (518–19). Ahab still abides by the earth's magnetic laws, but his performance convinces the men that his subjectivity alone can read nature and that the steering of the ship rests entirely on him. As with Hobbes, language in *Moby-Dick* never achieves representational fidelity and can at most enforce consensus, for better or for worse.

Another linguistic worry that Melville exploits is the conflict over biblical interpretation. As Philip Gura has shown, most theologians of the era studied the Bible in philological terms, assuming that primary scriptural sources represented God's true will. However, the German higher criticism of Johann Herder and J. G. Eichhorn was coming to antebellum America through Unitarian and (later) Transcendentalist channels. The higher critics argued that scripture was shaped by fallible testimony, history, and translation, so much so that biblical language was more metaphoric than precisely representative and thus was open to individual interpretation, a point emphasized by Horace Bushnell. For Gura, Melville suggests as much in "Jonah Historically Considered" and "The Prairie"; and "A Bower in the Arsacides" further satirizes the desire for exegetical certainty. Here Ishmael describes the skeleton of a whale "worshipped" by a group of Arsacidean "priests" who refuse to let Ishmael measure their "god" and wind up hitting each other with their own "yard-sticks" (449–50). Ironically, the sectarian fracas allows Ishmael to make his own "admeasurements" whose "accuracy" he guarantees (451). The deeper joke, however, is that he cuts his own yardstick according to no authoritative standard, recalling his earlier warning to himself, "A veritable witness have you hitherto been, Ishmael; but have a care how you seize the privilege" (448). Ishmael knows that testimony can be unreliable, and so he turns to more empirical tools. Yet Melville hints that even these facts can be doubted, particularly if they are calibrated by a recently cut "green measuring-rod" (450). As any carpenter or sailor knows, and as Melville points out in "The Life-Buoy," fresh boards shrink over time, a reality implying that holy texts – in this case, the whale skeleton – are always open to interpretation because there is no unchanging standard in yardsticks or in hermeneutics.

Politically and theologically, Melville subverts the claims of Lockean empiricism, but he also quarrels with romantic theories of language that in New England were challenging the common-sense orthodoxy. It is a complicated story, in part because Melville shares doubts with the romantics he critiques. In general, American transcendentalists sympathized with German higher critics and British romantics such as Coleridge, if only because they also considered Scottish realist traditions stultifying. Transcendentalists preferred instead an unfettered symbolic language in which the natural world came to stand for higher subjective truths. At the same time, as Michael West has shown, romantics continued to ground language in nature. Indeed, they complained that in the Lockean system ideas muddied the relationship between signs and things. Drawing on the philological work of Charles Kraitsir and Guillaume Oegger, transcendentalists sought a more immediate, more transparent, more rooted correspondence between words and nature, a possibility that *Moby-Dick* entertains in "The Mark" when Queequeg signs a contract with Peleg. Once again, standard written forms try to contain vernacular others, but the official language of the *Pequod*'s owner is not up to the task. He makes the "obstinate mistake" of calling Queequeg "Quohog" (a variant of quahog), suggesting that while Peleg may think that he is linking words to natural facts, in reality his ideas are so faulty as to mistake a man for a clam (89). Queequeg corrects Peleg by signing the contract with a symbol that is tattooed on his body; but even if the unspoiled harpooner explicitly attaches language to things, he does so within a contractual framework that subordinates nature to commerce.

Moby-Dick thus registers a subcultural shift from common sense to natural theories of language, but Melville remains an equal-opportunity skeptic who subscribes to neither system. One helpful indication of such skepticism is the novel's use of hieroglyphics that, for John T. Irwin, invokes another theoretical background for Melville's indeterminate language. Ishmael repeatedly refers to hieroglyphics when discussing the unknowability of whales; and in "The Prairie" he describes the sperm whale's brow – as well as every other physiognomy – as a living hieroglyphic that has "no Champollion to decipher" (347). Jean-François Champollion decoded the Rosetta Stone in the 1820s, arguing that its signs worked on three levels: literal, phonetic, and symbolic. The literal level can correspond, not only to natural theories of language, but also to Melville's interest in print culture and the physical textuality of the world. The phonetic level points to *Moby-Dick*'s commitment to oral and vernacular forms, while the symbolic is more representative of transcendent, abstract truths. These categories offer just one schema for the many antebellum conceptions of language, but importantly Melville finds no Champollion to coordinate the different orders of meaning. *Moby-Dick* does not structure but instead opens up the multitudinous prospects of language; and so "The Prairie" ends its rumination on the sperm whale's brow with an invitation and a challenge: "Read it if you can" (347).

That critics still respond to Melville's summons evinces among other things *Moby-Dick*'s uncanny ability to anticipate subsequent theories of language. Paul Brodtkorb offers an early account of the novel's indeterminacy; and in later studies

Ahab operates under a metaphysics of presence, while even Ishmael on occasion tries to pin down the "identity" of Moby Dick (183; Chapter 41). Ahab's destruction and Ishmael's failure reveal the futility of ontological definitions; and in this way *Moby-Dick* offers a kind of proto-deconstructionist critique – one in which intertextuality, self-reference, and parody turn language on itself; and one that shuns the false certainty of the land in favor of a "shoreless," "indefinite," "infinite" ocean of linguistic indeterminacy (107; Chapter 23). How successfully the book deconstructs dualisms is a related question. "A Squeeze of the Hand" breaks down boundaries that separate subject and object; and "The Sperm Whale's Head" imagines what it might be like to synthesize dialectical visions. Such chapters can reflect a romantic desire for unity or an anti-dualistic poststructural urge; but whatever the case, *Moby-Dick* is wary of leaving dualities entirely behind. Ahab's madness comes from a body and soul that "bled into one another"; and Ishmael warns that those who lose their "identity" and become "diffused through time and space" risk plummeting from their masthead reveries into "Descartian vortices" (185, 159; Chapters 41, 35). Perhaps the best indication of *Moby-Dick*'s ambivalence is modern critical readings that, despite post-structural methodologies, often struggle to escape the Ahab/Ishmael binary, suggesting that this dualism remains a fundamental element of the book.

A frequent criticism of poststructuralism in general and deconstruction in particular is that they evade political and moral meanings by tending toward relativism and subsuming any world outside the text. Whether such charges are fair or not, some post-metaphysical work on *Moby-Dick* relates Melville's indeterminate language to social and ethical concerns. Writing from a Heideggerian perspective, William Spanos reads *Moby-Dick* and its scholarship as rejecting nationalistic and imperialist formulations of American literature. For Spanos, Ishmael's refusal to name the whiteness of the whale and to name himself in any ontological sense suggests how a post-humanist language and politics might resist Ahabian power. Eyal Peretz is also interested in justice and power after metaphysics; and for him Ishmael's uncertain testimony and witness remain possible moral responses to Ahab's language of dominance. Scholars usually associate Ishmael with playfulness, skepticism, and ambiguity, while Ahab typically seems locked in a losing struggle for metaphysical certainty. For K. L. Evans, however, Ahab illustrates the ordinary-language philosophy of Wittgenstein; and it is Ahab who strives to find a connective, redemptive use of language in a world without absolutes.

What is striking about these and other readings of *Moby-Dick* is that the novel comes not only to instantiate the claims of some modern and postmodern theorists, but it also seems to predict with shocking recognition advances in twentieth-century philosophies of language. This sense of prolepsis pays tribute to the explanatory power of recent theory; but it also demonstrates that *Moby-Dick* is a book about writing and language and, as such, wrestles with longstanding questions of subjectivity and representation. Perhaps most poignantly, *Moby-Dick* celebrates Melville's indulgence of language, even as the novel insists that words are never entirely sufficient – that some truths cannot be spoken, either because language is itself inadequate or because readers and cultures do not (or cannot) listen closely enough. In recognizing the quandary of representation, Melville seems to have recognized the passing of metaphysics, perhaps because he was a genius ahead of his time, or perhaps because he participated in vanguard intellectual projects such as romanticism's challenge to the Enlightenment and transcendentalism's prologue to pragmatism. Attuned to the limits of language and reason, *Moby-Dick* seems prophetic because Melville's interests remain in many ways our own.

As Samuel Otter suggests, when reading *Moby-Dick*'s allusion to Narcissus, "the key to it all" may be that readers will always find themselves in the book (5; Chapter 1). This can be true, of course, for any text but especially for Melville's novel. "Moby Dick," "The Whiteness of the Whale," "The Doubloon," allusions to Narcissus and monomania – all suggest that Melville realizes that subjectivity is self-fulfilling, particularly when indeterminate signs offer so many interpretive possibilities. The possibilities of *Moby-Dick* do not seem to me as carefully structured as the puzzles of Melville's short fiction, for *Moby-Dick* is too immense, diverse, and interconnected for that kind of skrimshander work. More powerful than any individual chapter expostulating on solipsistic subjectivity is the accrued experience of reading and giving meaning to the hyperallusive density of the book. The process can feel like surfing the internet. There is so much there that one is bound to find whatever one seeks, just as the *Pequod* is a kind of search engine directed by the key term "Moby Dick." But even if the connected, non-linear paths of the novel can work like a hypertext, *Moby-Dick*'s encyclopedic energy fits within a historicist framework, for the antebellum explosion of print culture and language placed Melville squarely within an information age.

A Final Word ("Slobgollion")

The language of *Moby-Dick* cannot be shut down, but "slobgollion" can serve as a kind of conclusion (417). The word appears in "A Squeeze of the Hand" and refers to the residue left in a tub after sperm oil is broken up and decanted. In accordance with his desire for "real originality," Melville – as cited in the *OED* – was the first to use "slobgollion" in print. Ishmael, however, offers the term as "an appellation original with the whalemen," thus reinforcing Melville's link to oral and vernacular traditions (417). The *OED* has no definite etymology for the word, except for "slobber" (late Middle English) and "gullion" (meaning drunkard, origins unknown). But the onomatopoeic quality of slobgollion would surely please natural-language theorists insofar as the sound of the word seems rooted in the nature of the thing. Ishmael describes slobgollion as "an ineffably oozy, stringy affair" that he takes to be "the wondrously thin, ruptured membranes of the [spermaceti] case, coalescing" (417). The language of *Moby-Dick* shares the oozy and alien richness of slobgollion; and though nothing is thin about Melville's prose, it contains the residues of variously ruptured literary forms that, despite an uneven stringiness, do indeed coalesce. Or rather are in the process of coalescing, for slobgollion suggests how language and literature are never stable or completely representative. As happens in "A Squeeze of the Hand," a whale or a tale can be captured and barreled through loving and intersubjective labor, but some ineffable residue is always left behind, some part of nature or experience escapes the rendering process. Enough, then, of this language on language. Emphasizing that words are made comprehensible through open and risky community participation, Ishmael says of slobgollion (as well as "Gurry" and "Nippers"), "But to learn all about these recondite matters, your best way is at once to descend into the blubber-room, and have a long talk with its inmates" (417).

REFERENCES AND FURTHER READING

Ackerman, Alan L., Jr. *The Portable Theater: American Literature and the Nineteenth-Century Stage*. Baltimore: Johns Hopkins University Press, 1999.

Brodtkorb, Paul. *Ishmael's White World: A Phenomenological Reading of* Moby-Dick. New Haven, CT: Yale University Press, 1965.

Cmiel, Kenneth. *Democratic Eloquence: The Fight over Popular Speech in Nineteenth-Century America*. New York: William Morrow, 1990.

Dimock, Wai-chee. *Empire for Liberty: Melville and the Poetics of Individualism*. Princeton, NJ: Princeton University Press, 1989.

Evans, K. L. *Whale!* Minneapolis: University of Minnesota Press, 2003.

Grey, Robin. *The Complicity of Imagination: The American Renaissance, Contests of Authority, and Seventeenth-Century English Culture*. Cambridge: Cambridge University Press, 1997.

Gura, Philip. *The Wisdom of Words: Language, Theology, and Literature in the New England Renaissance*. Middletown, CT: Wesleyan University Press, 1981.

Gustafson, Thomas. *Representative Words: Politics, Literature, and the American Language, 1776–1865*. Cambridge: Cambridge University Press, 1992.

Heimert, Alan. "*Moby-Dick* and American Political Symbolism." *American Quarterly* 15 (1963): 498–534.

Irwin, John T. *American Hieroglyphics: The Symbol of Egyptian Hieroglyphics in the American Renaissance*. New Haven, CT: Yale University Press, 1980.

Kelley, Wyn. *Melville's City: Literary and Urban Form in Nineteenth-Century New York*. Cambridge: Cambridge University Press, 1996.

Matthiessen, F. O. *American Renaissance: Art and Expression in the Age of Emerson and Whitman*. New York: Oxford University Press, 1941.

Olson, Charles. *Call Me Ishmael*. New York: Reynal and Hitchcock, 1947.

Otter, Samuel. *Melville's Anatomies*. Berkeley: University of California Press, 1999.

——— ."Blue Proteus: *Moby-Dick* and the World We Live In." Unpublished manuscript.

Parker, Hershel and Harrison Hayford, eds. Moby-Dick *as Doubloon: Essays and Extracts (1851–1970)*. New York: W. W. Norton, 1970.

Pease, Donald. *Visionary Compacts: American Renaissance Writings in Cultural Contexts*. Madison: University of Wisconsin Press, 1987.

Peretz, Eyal. *Literature, Disaster, and the Enigma of Power: A Reading of* Moby-Dick. Stanford, CA: Stanford University Press, 2003.

Renker, Elizabeth. *Strike Through the Mask: Herman Melville and the Scene of Writing*. Baltimore: Johns Hopkins University Press, 1998.

Reynolds, David. *Beneath the American Renaissance: The Subversive Imagination in the Age of Emerson and Melville*. New York: Knopf, 1988.

Spanos, William. *The Errant Art of* Moby-Dick: *The Canon, the Cold War, and the Struggle for American Studies*. Durham, NC: Duke University Press, 1995.

Sten, Christopher. *The Weaver-God, He Weaves: Melville and the Poetics of the Novel*. Kent, OH: Kent State University Press, 1996.

Warren, James Perrin. *Culture of Eloquence: Oratory and Reform in Antebellum America*. University Park: Pennsylvania State University Press, 1999.

West, Michael. *Transcendental Wordplay: America's Romantic Punsters and the Search for the Language of Nature*. Athens: Ohio University Press, 2000.

26

Threading the Labyrinth:
Moby-Dick as Hybrid Epic

Christopher Sten

An epic is the most ambitious of genres. Yet in composing *Moby-Dick*, Melville undertook a doubly ambitious plan, bringing together the two main traditions in the form, the ancient national epic of combat, as exemplified by the *Iliad* or *Beowulf*, and the modern epic of spiritual quest, as exemplified by the *Divine Comedy* or *Paradise Lost*. The ancient epics, too, of course had a spiritual dimension in that they were intended to explain the intrusions of the gods into the affairs of humankind; they are, as Arthur Hutson and Patricia McCoy, among others, have said, concerned in a fundamental way with mythology. But, beginning with Dante, the epic became essentially inward, and not simply psychological but spiritual, centering on the search for the soul or the soul's salvation. As an epic of the universal story of mankind, therefore, *Moby-Dick* is more than a local instance of mythmaking or nation-building, comparable to the *Odyssey* of ancient Greece or the *Aeneid* of early Rome. It is also Melville's attempt to show that the powers behind the great spiritual epics of the world are the same ones that propelled its major religious mythologies – Judeo-Christian, Hindu, Egyptian, among others Melville knew (Franklin) – and that they were as alive in his own day as in earlier times.

My understanding of Melville's conception of epic writing has been informed by several searching studies of the epic poem, especially work by Lascelles Abercrombie, Albert Cook, and John Kevin Newman. But my understanding of Melville's rendering of the spiritual epic, with its focus on a journey or quest, is indebted primarily to modern students of psychology, religion, and myth, particularly C. G. Jung, Mircea Eliade, and Joseph Campbell, who define life in terms of individuation or spiritual awakening and explore, from a psychological point of view, the gap between the seen and the unseen, the conscious and the unconscious worlds. Campbell offers a well-known formulation, in *The Hero with a Thousand Faces*, though he in no way limits his discussion to the epic, when he says the hero's journey is structured like the "monomyth" found in rites of passage, with a three-part structure of separation, initiation or trial, and return: "A hero ventures forth from the world of common day into a region of supernatural wonder:

fabulous forces are there encountered and a decisive victory is won: the hero comes back from this mysterious adventure with the power to bestow boons on his fellow man" (30). The Greek legends of Prometheus and Jason, the biblical narratives of Moses and Christ, the legend of the Buddha, even the ancient epic stories of Odysseus and Aeneas all contain versions of this basic pattern, typically represented in terms of the hero's being swallowed by a monster and then being reborn.

When seen in relation to *Moby-Dick*, such a scheme, with its emphasis on transformation and the turning toward spiritual self-knowledge, naturally points to Ishmael as the true hero of the book; he alone completes an initiatory test and returns to tell about it. By contrast, Ahab, the representative of the ancient epic with its emphasis on personal courage, resists such a test, even as he resists all reminders of his mortality. In Eliade's terms, Ahab clings to his existence as a "natural" man and is never "born to the spirit" (*Quest* 115). However, there are larger social and political consequences to such resistance. Entrusted with the power to rule, Ahab is an instance of the ruler turned tyrant, a dangerous figure who sacrifices the public good for his own benefit (see Campbell 15). Unredeemed and un-reborn, Ahab is incapable of seeing beyond the needs of his ego; he thus brings not benefit or knowledge but ruin and death to his people and himself. While much of the discussion that follows will focus on the modern, spiritual epic and Melville's intricate tracing out of Ishmael's awakening to the soul, in fact Ahab's quest is virtually always present in the narrative, as a reminder of the older, national epic that highlights Ishmael's development. And at the end of my discussion, the fate of the national epic will come back to the fore explicitly, as Ahab takes center stage in the late chapters of *The Whale* for a final reckoning.

Like the *Divine Comedy* and other spiritual epics, *Moby-Dick* opens with its hero in a fallen state of emotional torpor and confusion. Ishmael is a spiritually dead man in a dead land, seeking the relief of the condemned everywhere. He has grown weary of existence, as one does when his youth is spent and he finds himself, as Dante said at the start of his story, "In the middle of the journey of our life." Like Ahab, he suffers from a malaise or schism in the soul, an aggression so intense as to prove deadly. As Ishmael confesses, only by holding to "a strong moral principle" can he keep from "deliberately stepping into the street, and methodically knocking people's hats off." Whenever he finds himself overtaken by such an urge, he figures it is "high time to get to sea as soon as I can." But whether this is just another way to realize a death wish or a means of regaining health, Ishmael himself seems unclear. Going to sea, he says equivocally, "is my substitute for pistol and ball" (3). Yet even if he is unsure, his unconscious seems to know there must be a dying to the world before there can be a rebirth. That is the only way one can ever hope to overcome the death of the spirit. Ahab's example attests to that fact by his failure, as Ishmael's does by his success. For the hero to come back as one reborn, filled with creative energy, he must first give up the world and everything in it.

Ishmael is not alone in his suffering or his hunger for release and relief. Like other heroes of epic, he is a representative or exemplary figure, one meant to point the way to his fellow "Manhattoes." On a dreamy Sunday afternoon, he sees "crowds of water-gazers," thirsting for adventure (3–4). What distinguishes Ishmael from these more timid islanders is simply that he accepts the call to the sea. He does so without full understanding of what he is doing, but he lives intuitively and trusts his inner promptings. Because the episodes in his journey represent trials of the spirit, psychological trials, his passage is inward as much as it is across water – "into depths where obscure resistances are overcome," as Campbell explains, "and long lost, forgotten powers are revivified, to be made available for the transfiguration of the world" (29).[1]

In *Moby-Dick* this inner realm is represented by the sea, a universal image of the unconscious, where all the monsters and helping figures of childhood are found, along with the talents and other powers that lie dormant in us. Chief among these, for Ishmael, is the "overwhelming idea of the great whale himself." But that he is responding as much to a lure from within the self as from without is suggested when, after examining his motives, he asserts that "the great flood-gates of the wonder-world swung open, and into the wild conceits that swayed me to my purpose, two and two there floated in my inmost soul, endless processions of the whale, and, midmost of them all, one grand hooded phantom, like a snow hill in the air" (7). For Ishmael, this phantom whale is the beginning and the end, and represents all the instinctual vitality locked within the self.

Because the way of the hero is through a strange realm filled with danger and hardship, he requires the help of a guide, or master of the world beyond, who can instruct him in the rules of the game and point out "the way." While the guide is sometimes a woman, like Beatrice in Dante's vision, more typically it is a man, as in the *Divine Comedy* again, where Virgil assumes the role in the early stages. In *Moby-Dick* Ishmael is led through the early episodes by the master harpooneer, Queequeg, an alleged cannibal with strange tattoos, a hideous scalp-knot, and a tomahawk. Queequeg seems an unlikely candidate for a mentor when Ishmael first encounters him in his darkened room at the Spouter-Inn. The "abominable savage" (22), just returned from peddling shrunken heads in the streets of New Bedford, nearly scares Ishmael out of his wits. As it turns out, Queequeg is not a cannibal; but in the logic of the book, his reputation as a man-eater makes him a fit guide for one whose initiation will require him to be swallowed, as it were, by a whale. Though Ishmael "aint insured" (24), he could hardly do better than to trust himself to this implausible guide whose coffin will one day save him from the wrath of the White Whale.

After making peace and spending the night together in the landlord's marriage bed, Ishmael wakes to find Queequeg's arm – "tattooed all over with an interminable Cretan labyrinth of a figure" – thrown over him in a loving, protective embrace (25). Ishmael is too green to recognize that the harpooneer's tattoo represents a map of the path in and out of the maze of the Minotaur, the beast he must slay, or defeat, to gain its treasure. He can hardly be expected to know that he himself will become an American Theseus, though later he will turn up with a tattoo on his own arm bearing the dimensions of a huge beached whale, whose labyrinthine skeleton Ishmael wanders into and out of, in "A Bower in the Arsacides" (Chapter 102). An experienced whaler himself by this time, Ishmael is then ready to lead his readers into the belly of the whale and out again. In the end, he becomes their guide, the epic hero who shows his readers the way.

However, if Ishmael is to convince his readers to take up the contest themselves, he must do more than explain how it is played. He must portray the men who are its champions and capture the spirit of their peculiar activity. He must engage the interest of his readers in the lives of exemplary heroes who are caught up in a quintessential contest, and he must raise the stature and importance of their under-taking to a universal symbol. That, more than anything else, according to Abercrom-bie, is the principal task of the epic poet, something Ishmael attempts to do in Chapter 24 and the chapters that follow (Abercrombie 16–17).

Thus, in rich, irony-filled example after example, Ishmael builds a hyperbolic case for the nobility of the whale, the dignity of whaling, and the royalty of the whale-man's lineage, as in the "Knights and Squires" chapters. As the mocking tone of "Postscript" (Chapter 25), suggests, however, and as Ishmael asserts at the end of Chapter 26, the concern with nobility in the epic genre, the preoccupation with titles, bloodlines, and pomp, is a concern merely with the trappings, rather than the essence, of the epic story. Anticipating his portrayal of the sorrowful "fall of valor in the soul" of Starbuck, who tries but fails to stand up to Ahab, Ishmael states that "this august dignity I treat of, is not the dignity of kings and robes, but that abounding dignity which has no robed investiture." In oxymoronic language typical of the epic, Ishmael describes his subject as "that democratic dignity which, on all hands, radiates without end from God; Himself!" – as exemplified in such "champions" from "the kingly commons" as John Bunyan and Andrew Jackson. Repeatedly, it is natural, self-made courage – the kind found in the ancient epics – and not inherited rank or station, that forms the basis of such dignity, in Ishmael's view, and that makes even the "meanest mariners, and renegades and castaways" who serve the whaling industry worthy of epic treatment (117). Starbuck possesses such courage to a degree, though for him it is "a thing simply useful" in hunting whales (116). And Stubb and Flask do as well, though on a lower plane, the one being simply "indifferent" and the other "dead" to any sense of danger in whaling (118–19). The higher forms of courage, on the other hand, simple daring and coolness under pressure, are represented in the harpooneers, Queequeg, Tashtego, and Daggoo, and in Ahab, who is first seen staring out over the ship's bow with "an infinity of firmest fortitude, a determinate, unsurrenderable wilfulness" in search of Moby Dick (124).

All of these examples are early signs that Melville was working self-consciously in the epic tradition, a tradition that has proved self-consciously imitative, as Tom Winnifrith has argued, or parodic, as John Kevin Newman has said. In all the traditional epics, whether oral or literary, the most conspicuous value is courage. These works remind us, as Abercrombie explains, that while courage may not be the only significant attitude one can hold toward life, "Man can achieve nothing until he has first achieved courage." Given the precariousness of life, particularly in the time of the oral epics, it follows that courage is "the absolutely necessary foundation for any subsequent valuation of life," and so it proved to be, even in the development of the spiritual epic, though there what is needed is a courage of the spirit – a courage of faith (68–9).

More than any other character, Ahab dominates the early sea-going chapters of *Moby-Dick*. As "supreme lord and dictator" of the *Pequod* and the protagonist in Melville's story, he is also, of course, the book's central character (122). However, he remains Melville's version of the traditional epic hero – traditional and failed. He is not the redemptive figure of the spiritual epic but its opposite, the worldly tyrant who forsakes his public duty for his private need, as Melville explains in "The Specksynder" (Chapter 33). And in the process, he brings his whole world to ruin. Ahab is a man who repeatedly refuses the call to the soul's awakening and who, instead of submitting to God's will, holds desperately to the bit of mortality allotted to him. On his first entrance, he is described as one who has somehow escaped a trial by fire – "like a man cut away from the stake, when the fire has overrunningly wasted all the limbs without consuming them." Of the rod-like mark running down his face, Ishmael says it resembles the seam in a great tree trunk after a lightning bolt (symbol of Zeus) has ripped through it, "leaving the tree still greenly alive, but branded" (123). Only after scrutinizing these sinister details does Ishmael even notice Ahab's "barbaric white leg," the book's chief symbol of mortality. Only then does he observe that the "moody stricken" Ahab carries the look of a "crucifixion" in his face, sign of the redeemer but one who feels forsaken (124).

In the last paragraphs of this chapter Ishmael underscores the fact that Ahab has been near death, not only from his recent wound but also from the ravages of age and winter. As the *Pequod* sails south, into spring and the whale's feeding grounds, Ahab comes up on deck more and more, his face each time more alive, like a "thunder-cloven old oak" that at last sends forth "some few green sprouts" (125). Summoned back for one last encounter with the Father, Ahab believes he is on a mission of destruction that will guarantee his immortality. Only later does he admit his fear that he is the one who will be destroyed. As in the spiritual epics of Dante, Milton, and others the world over, Ahab's refusal of the invitation to come home to God is a refusal to give up his narrow, earthly conception of what constitutes his self-interest. He looks at the future not in terms of dying and rebirth, but as a relentless threat to his vitality, his identity. Fearful of death, sensitive to insult, resistant to loss or change, Ahab is incapable of taking even a step into the unknown. So rigid is he that he contests to the death any will that challenges his own. To a man like Ahab who lives in time, locked in the grasp of the ego, even the divinity becomes an enemy. " 'Talk not to me of blasphemy, man,' " he exclaims, when Starbuck questions his motives in pursuing Moby Dick; " 'I'd strike the sun if it insulted me' " (164). He refuses to see that life perpetually enacts the mystery of dismemberment, even as it enacts the mystery of renewal.

Despite his fear and blasphemy, Ahab is a glorious figure, the representative man of his time, the American at mid-century. As the book's epic hero manqué, dependent on brute courage and force rather than faith or spirit to sustain him, he contains within him not only the common, universal values of his type but Melville's summation of the cultural values of the US at the time – pride, independence, manly determination, pragmatism. These are not the highest values, and they are not the only ones found in America at the time, but they are the predominant ones. So, too, Ahab's greatness is a "mortal greatness," a "disease," and not the immortal kind that Ishmael comes to exemplify (74). Though Ahab is a powerfully sympathetic figure, it seems clear Melville did not subscribe to the values he embodies. If anything, he saw them as leading to America's doom. What he perceived, in looking at the young nation, was a culture trapped, as Emerson said, in the temporal realm; incapable of throwing off the childish ego; sensitive to threats, big or small; quick to defend its sovereignty and honor; lacking faith in the spirit world of the soul, to support life and give it transcendent meaning.

For Ishmael, the crucial question is not whether he can, unlike Ahab, contain his anger and vengefulness, but whether he can resist Ahab and the temptation to make Ahab's feud his own. If he is to have a chance at the epic experience of being swallowed by the whale, he must keep from being swallowed up in Ahab's rage, like the others on the *Pequod*. For a time, Ishmael does succumb. As he says at the opening of chapter 41, after the quarterdeck ceremony when Ahab impels the men to join in the hunt for the White Whale, "I, Ishmael, was one of that crew; my shouts had gone up with the rest; my oath had been welded with theirs.... Ahab's quenchless feud seemed mine." The "dread" he admits to feeling "in my soul" during the ceremony, therefore, is caused by his unconscious fear of Ahab, not by fear of Moby Dick (179). He will spend much of the rest of the book, up through "A Squeeze of the Hand," "The Cassock," and "The Try-Works" (Chapters 94–6), struggling to free himself from Ahab, his domineering "double." The real question is: where will he find the force, the self-mastery, to do so?

In the early days of the hunt, Ishmael cannot know that the White Whale will be his salvation. He cannot know that Moby Dick will empower him, by the force of its example and its vitalizing effect on his imagination, to break the stranglehold Ahab has over his ego, to throw off Ahab's rage, and resume the course of his personal adventure. Melville has constructed his Whale in such a way that practically everything about it is "moral" or symbolic of some fundamental human trait or truth. In every feature, it is fraught with human meaning, even as the entire Whale is supercharged with profound significance – the significance of epic rendering.

Though he claimed not to "oscillate in Emerson's rainbow" (*L* 121), Melville agreed with Emerson's famous dictum that "the whole of nature is a metaphor of the human mind." He too believed, as Emerson proclaimed in *Nature* (1837), that "the laws of moral nature answer to those of matter as face to face in a glass" (35). The process of "cutting in," or stripping away the whale's flesh, for example, is presented as a metaphor for the fleshly discipline that one must practice to attain spiritual concentration. Similarly, the chapters devoted to this process, going back to "Stubb kills a Whale," shadow forth the process of life's unfolding, from birth to death, as one of dismemberment and dying. While in the beginning Ishmael sees the whale's body as something holy, glistening in the sun, by the time it has been gouged by sharks, cut into by the crew and stripped of its "blanket," it lies at its funeral, colossal but "desecrated" (309). However, as the novel's central metaphor for the power of the soul, the whale is more than a symbol. It is the hero's ultimate guide or authority in the journey to self-understanding. While earlier Ishmael had more than hinted there is something valuable to be learned from the whale, it is not until the first of the anatomy chapters – particularly "The Blanket," together with "Cutting In" – that he makes explicit the idea that mankind should actually model itself after the whale. In this sense the whale can be said to embody, like the figure of the Goddess of the World, the totality of what can be known. It is a metonym for nature and the laws of creation.

In the anatomy chapters, the trials of the hero in his encounters with the whale can be seen as instructive, and his willingness to imperil his life in this bloody business can be understood to pay off handsomely. For only with the first-hand experience of whaling can one gain the wisdom the whale embodies. In Chapter 68, after deciding that the whale's skin is constituted not of the thin isinglass coating on the surface of the beast but the whole enveloping layer of blubber, Ishmael points out that this thick mass is like a "blanket or counterpane," an image that recalls the counterpane he shared with Queequeg in the Spouter-Inn. Like that counterpane, the whale's "blanket" permits its inhabitant "to keep himself comfortable" in any weather or climate. "[Herein] we see," Ishmael observes, "... the rare virtue of thick walls.... Oh, man! admire and model thyself after the whale! Do thou, too, remain warm among ice. Do thou, too, live in this world without being of it" (307). In a similar fashion, later, when viewing the sperm whale's head as it hangs from the ship's side, Ishmael proclaims the wisdom of patterning the growth of one's mind after the whale's, which is clearly more "comprehensive" and "subtle" than man's, since it is capable of taking in two opposed views at once. ("Why then do you try to 'enlarge' your mind?" he asks. "Subtilize it" instead [331].)

In "The Great Heidelburgh Tun" (Chapter 77) and the following "Cistern and Buckets," where Queequeg rescues Tashtego from the whale's head after it breaks loose and sinks, Melville begins to introduce language that involves a vast conceit according to which the sperm oil stands for the vital "fluid" of the human soul. Repeatedly described as "precious" or "invaluable" and "pure," the sperm is contained in the "secret inner chamber and sanctum sanctorum" of the whale. This curiously holy, sexually charged, life-giving substance is Melville's version of the object of the epic quest in its essential form, the "unalloyed" oil that requires a "marvelous," if sometimes "fatal," operation to tap it (339–40, 344).

In fact, these and the next twenty-eight chapters, up through "Ahab's Leg," focus on the whale's interior. All the world seems rushing to gain entrance there, to search for its riches and experience its transforming power, to *know* the beast from inside. Opening with Tashtego's accidental entombment in the sperm whale's tun, this section closes with Ishmael's deliberate venture inside a whale's skeleton, in "A

Bower in the Arsacides," where he has gone to gather measurements for his study of the monster. Half the chapters in this section are concerned with methods of gaining access to the whale's interior and the treasures to be found there. Still others examine the containers used for processing or holding oil and other prizes, once collected. These include chapters on the ship's hold; the hand; the try-works; the lamp; the decanter; and the doubloon. Melville's preoccupation with themes of containment is symptomatic of his interest in the vitalizing boon or treasure, the thing contained that is the object of the hero's quest. But it is also symptomatic of his interest in the process of the hero himself being contained or imprisoned, tried and transformed inside the whale, as Jonah and Tashtego, Pip, Captain Boomer (his arm, at least), and even Ishmael are.

In these chapters, then, Melville also develops themes of death and resurrection, of the awakening of the self to new life. Death by land is the common death. But there is also a death by water, which is initiated by an escape from convention and ends in a dying to the world, as in baptism. This death ends in rebirth, or in a saving glimpse of the world beyond this one. However, as Pip's example testifies, unless the break-through occurs within the ritual of the hunt, the experience can be so overwhelming as to drive the initiate "mad" (414). He may return from his journey a changed man, but he will lack the sanity and self-command required to function in the world.

In developing the themes of transformation, of the hero's dying and renewal, Melville continues with the "anatomy" of the whale begun earlier. But in keeping with these themes, he emphasizes the whale's masculinity and godlike power. If one is to perform the equivalent of miracles and raise the living from the dead, and bring oneself to life as if after a long sleep, one must possess the strength and regenerative power exemplified in the whale. In "The Prairie," for instance, Ishmael sings praises to the "mighty," "sublime" character of the sperm whale's brow, gazing on which "you feel the Deity and the dread powers more forcibly than in beholding any other object in living nature" (346). And in "The Fountain," "A Squeeze of the Hand," and "The Cassock," he celebrates the procreative powers of the whale, its sexual potency. Such efforts at suggesting the masculinity of the whale are in keeping with Melville's development of the penultimate stage in the hero's adventure, represented in traditional religions and mythical stories as the reconciliation with the Father. Though cast in confrontational terms, this encounter typically leads to resolution, for the hero must recognize that he will never achieve atonement by aggression or force of will. The Father, the ruling power of the world, is simply too mighty to be overcome by such means. Atonement results only from the hero's trust in the Father's mercy and his abandonment of all egoistic urges.

Most people, however, are cut off from the source of all truth, the Father. Trapped in their ego, they have no memory of God and no aptitude for seeing Him in the present, no capacity for wonder and worship. In what Melville, in "The Prairie" (Chapter 79), called "the now egotistical sky" of his own century, there was no evidence of the "gods of old." They all seemed to have vanished, to be lured back again only by a "highly cultured, poetical nation," such as Melville was trying to create in writing his epic (247). But as Ishmael asserts in this chapter on the whale's forehead, the image of God can be recollected in the "imposing" frontal view of the sperm whale. The "high and mighty god-like dignity inherent in the brow" of other creatures is so greatly amplified in the brow of the sperm whale that "gazing on it . . . you feel the Deity and the dread powers more forcibly than in beholding any other object in living nature" (346). Seeing the Father face to face represents the ultimate revelation in the epic hero's journey of spiritual recovery, the supreme test of his readiness and character.

To gain this "sublime" view, one must put one's life in jeopardy (346). But there are less dangerous ways of glimpsing the whale's mysterious face, Melville's symbol of the face of the Father. "The Grand Armada" tells the story, on a grand scale and in miniature, of the whole epic hunt. What it reveals about the whale's face — here imaginatively portrayed as the collective expression of a whole pod — is its moody doubleness, its capacity to be both excited and calm, even at the same time. Ishmael tells of this episode when the *Pequod* is making its way through the Straits of Sunda into the China seas, the favored haunt of Moby Dick. Passing through these straits, he says, one has the sense of entering "the central gateway opening into some vast walled empire" — the fabled East, with its "inexhaustible wealth of spices, and silks, and jewels, and gold" (380). The wealth that awaits the crew at this point is not, however, a material treasure but "a spectacle of singular magnificence" — a great "host of vapory [whale] spouts" all spread across the horizon "up-playing and sparkling in the noon-day air" (382).

Following a lengthy chase in which the crew is made to earn its reward, they suddenly catch up to the herd of gallied whales, now seemingly "going mad with consternation." After Queequeg harpoons a lone whale on the edge of the caravan, the wounded beast throws a "blinding spray" in their faces, and "then running away with [them] like light, steered straight for the heart of the herd" (385). Dragged deeper into the "frantic shoal," they come upon a great calm or "sleek" at the "innermost heart" of the immense herd. "Yes," Ishmael exclaims, "we were now in that enchanted calm which they say lurks at the heart of every commotion." Within moments, these simple whalers experience the two sides of the Spirit of God that in the opening of Genesis is said to move on the face of the waters. Now hemmed in by the "living wall" that shuts out their fellow sailors, they are "visited by small tame cows and calves; the women and children of this routed host" (385–7). In this magic circle, inside not a single whale but a whole pod, they witness leviathan versions of the same domestic scenes they left behind on land: the swelling forms of expectant mother whales, the motionless forms of nursing mothers, even a newborn, and "young Leviathan amours in the deep." "Some of the subtlest secrets of the seas," Ishmael exclaims, "seemed divulged to us in this enchanted pond." Most importantly, amid the turmoil on the face of these waters, he discovers an objective correlative for the "eternal mildness of joy" deep within his own soul (388–9).

"The Try-Works" culminates the process of breaking down the whale's flesh into light-bringing, life-giving oil, the final step in the transfer of power that will end in the initiate's triumph over darkness, temporality, and death. Here, a wonderful transformation occurs: all the impurities are burned off in a "horrible" smoke, leaving sweet oil that only whalemen can know in its "unvitiated state" (422, 426). Not coincidentally, this fiery scene is the turning point in Ishmael's own trial, the moment when he comes to understand why he must renounce Ahab's mad plan. Waking from a "brief standing sleep" while tending the ship's helm, Ishmael explains, "I was horribly conscious of something fatally wrong": the *Pequod* is headed in the wrong direction and about to be destroyed. Later, he realizes that, like Ahab, he has been looking "too long in the face of the fire" of the try-works, has in fact become "inverted" and "deadened" by it. Warning his readers to "believe not the artificial fire, when its redness makes all things look ghastly," he goes on to explain that "the glorious, golden, glad sun" – image of the Father – is "the only true lamp – all others but liars!" (424–5).

The great challenge for the spiritual hero like Ishmael, however, is to learn to recognize the Father by his absence as well as by his light. Unlike Starbuck, who admits to not believing in the sun at midnight, he must have faith during the dark times as well as the bright. And he must come to see that the two are but parts of one whole. The god of the sundoor, as Campbell says, is "the fountainhead of all the pairs of opposites." "In him are contained and from him proceed the contradictions, good and evil, death and life, pain and pleasure, boons and deprivation" (145). To the person who accepts this complexity, life is not a trial but a blessing. If, like a good whaleman, he stays the course and seeks only what Ishmael, in "The Lamp," calls "the food of light," he will meet with such success as to "live in light" perpetually, such an abundance of oil will be his (426).

Given the proximity to Ishmael's discussion of the sun as "the only true lamp" in "The Try-Works," the next chapter, "The Lamp," clearly correlates the light from the sun with the light from whale oil. These images in turn are related to the light that pours forth from the soul, as suggested first in Father Mapple's sermon, where the lamp in Jonah's ship-cabin is said to symbolize the future prophet's conscience, the inner source of light available to all. *This* is the ultimate boon, the discovery that the light of the soul, of truth, is within oneself, that the hero and the Father are one. Sun, whale oil, soul, and God – all are variations of the same principle of light and life.

By contrast, the doubloon, a graven image of the sun, is a false version of the true light. A circle of gold that Ahab has affixed to the mainmast as a reward for the first sailor to sight Moby Dick, the doubloon competes with the sun for the crew's attention and homage. Rather than generating light, however, it reflects it, whatever the source, true or false. It is a mirror, not a lamp, to borrow M. H. Abrams's terms, reflecting back the subjective state of the observer who looks at it, as it reflects back Ahab's egotism: "'There's something ever egotistical in mountain-tops and towers,'" he soliloquizes, "'and all other grand and lofty things . . . three peaks as proud as Lucifer'" (431).

Still, the doubloon, too, is double. As the White Whale's "talisman," it is also a magical vehicle for raising Moby Dick and achieving the highest form of spiritual illumination. Minted in Ecuador, a country named for its proximity to the sun, and bearing in its inscription a segment of the zodiac, with the "keystone sun" entering Libra, or the scales (sign of judgment), the gold coin is presented as having powerful affinities with the sun. It is what Ishmael terms a "medal of the sun," a symbol of the source of all life (431). Pip reveals his unconscious understanding of this when he calls it the "ship's navel," a common mythological image of the magical spot or "door" through which the vivifying energies of the spirit life pour into the world. The last to make his entrance in the doubloon chapter, Pip speaks for the entire crew when he observes that the men "are all on fire to unscrew it" (435). They all yearn to set free the flow of life into the body of the world, to restore vitality and meaning to their lives.

For Ishmael, Melville's lone epic hero, this will be the life-saving consequence of his finally gaining a complete, unobstructed view of Moby Dick on the last day of the chase. All the power in the navel of the world, in the whale, will pour into him, in the form of spiritual energy or grace, and buoy him up in the face of death. For, beneath the spot represented as the navel of the world, as Campbell explains this universal image, is "the earth-supporting head of the cosmic serpent, the dragon, symbolical of the waters of the abyss, which are the divine life-creative energy and substance of the demiurge, the world-generative aspect of immortal being" (40–1). As the successful spiritual hero, then, Ishmael is himself the umbilical point through which life's energies enter into the creation. On one level, the doubloon is nothing more than a gold coin. But, as a symbol, it reveals that any object, no matter how small or insignificant, is open to the spirit and can be a place of special knowledge and power.

At this point, then, Ishmael has sounded his soul; he has mastered his ego and thereby achieved mastery of life. As he shows in "A Bower in the Arsacides," where he speaks of making a visit, later in life, to a temple formed of the skeleton of a great sperm whale on an imaginary island, he is able, finally, to go in and out of the "belly of the whale" without fear, at will. Following the wise example of Theseus, the ancient hero who used a string to find his way out of the Cretan labyrinth after venturing inside to kill the Minotaur, Ishmael employs a "ball of Arsacidean twine" (the "ball of free will" that dropped from his hand earlier in "The Mat-Maker" [215]?), wandering through the convoluted interior of the skeleton until his line runs out, and then retracing his steps out again (450).

Like the hero of the spiritual epic, what Ishmael confronts, in the course of his descent into the whale, is his own mortality, the naked fact of death. Emerging from the same opening where he had entered, then, he says simply, "I saw no living thing within; naught was there but bones" (450). There is irony (and wry humor) here, but the fact remains that in the metaphoric sense, he has reached the end of his line. His quest is virtually finished; all that remains is for him to see Moby Dick, to glimpse a vision of God, and make his return. By this point, he has defeated his hypos and seen beyond his death; and he is prepared to do something worthy with the life that remains to him. Now he can repeat the cycle, guiding others along the path of trials to the same sort of life-transforming spot where he achieved his triumph, the triumph of life over death.

"Ahab's Leg" (Chapter 106), the book's central symbol of human mortality, marks a sharp shift from the matter of Ishmael's spiritual development to Ahab's earlier dismemberment by the White Whale, the event that precipitated the quest, and his inconsolable grief at his loss. From this point on, the narrative belongs to this "grand, ungodly, god-like man" (79), as in the beginning it belonged to Ishmael. The previous chapter, "Does the Whale's Magnitude Diminish? – Will He Perish?," had made an explicit case for the whale's immortality, confirming one last time its aptness as a symbol for the soul. But "Ahab's Leg" emphasizes human mortality and the insufficiency of pride or ego as a "standpoint." As Thomas Greene has argued, the epic hero must be made to see that, in spite of his tremendous energy and effort at control, "his inescapable limitations await him"; he is human (16). Repeatedly in these last chapters we are told of the destruction and mutability that attend the *Pequod*'s voyage. Ahab's leg breaks again and again; the barrels of oil in the hold start leaking; Queequeg takes sick and almost dies; other crew members die from accidents; whaleboats are stove and, once repaired, stove again; the log line deteriorates and snaps; the lifebuoy dries out and sinks. Under the misguided command of "Old Thunder" (92, 505), everything on ship runs to decay and disorder. Unlike the ageless thunder that speaks in the typhoon, Ahab is dying; his power inexorably "leaks" away (474).

Because Ahab is committed to the life of the ego and not of the soul, his every move, from this point on, as his purpose intensifies, is seen to contribute to his destruction. In the remaining chapters, Melville, using epic motifs and tropes, dramatizes his version of the classic argument concerning the causes of the tragic hero's downfall. In "The Blacksmith" and "The Forge" (Chapters 112–13), where Ahab oversees the manufacture of the harpoon he imagines as infallible, he stakes his whole enterprise on the capacity of the "artificial fire" to lead him to his prey. Baptizing the finished weapon in the name of the devil, he underscores his determination to defy his Maker rather than admit his dependence on Him. Yet in "The Dying Whale" (Chapter 116), the implication is clear that Ahab should instead follow the example of reverence and trust displayed by the last of several whales they hunt down and slay, when it turns "his homage rendering and invoking brow" toward the sun. Ahab's suspicion, however, soon overcomes him and he concludes it is vain for the dying whale to "seek intercedings with yon all-quickening sun," for it "only calls forth life, but gives it not again." From here on, he commits himself to a "prouder, if a darker faith," or nihilism, as he smashes the quadrant and turns away from the sun (496–7). Toward the evening of that day, a Typhoon, "the direst of all storms," bursts on the Japan Sea, stripping the ship of her sails and leaving the men helpless before its wrath (503). It is as though Ahab's sacrilege, his rejection of the sun and his declaration of independence, have so angered the gods as to cause them to lash out with a tempest, one that serves also to warn him to turn back.

Still, in "The Candles" (Chapter 119), and in several midnight scenes that follow, when thunder roars and the *Pequod*'s masts mysteriously burst into flame, Ahab maintains a stance of bold defiance. The burning masts suggest to Ishmael that

"God's burning finger has been laid on the ship" (506), but Ahab stands in the flashing light and proudly swears to the inviolability of his ego: "In the midst of the personified impersonal, a personality stands here . . . . while I earthly live, the queenly personality lives in me, and feels her royal rights." While gleefully owning the flashing flame as his "fiery father," he vows to worship his "sire" not with reverence but "defyingly" (507–8). His feud is beyond all reason now. What we learn in *Moby-Dick* is what the great religious mythologies of the world – of Zeus, Yahweh, or the Supreme Buddha – have always taught: those who come to the Father in pride will be struck down, while those who come in humility will see the Father and recognize Him to be at one with the soul.

Death is the great subject of *Moby-Dick*, death and immortality. Nowhere is this more apparent than in the final chapters, where to read of Ahab's quickening pursuit of the White Whale is to witness a man rushing uncontrollably into the jaws of destruction. More and more as the *Pequod* moves toward its fateful confrontation with Moby Dick, it is as though it travels in a realm of death, a wasteland, where men disappear or perish without a trace. As they near the outskirts of the equatorial fishing grounds, on the line closest to the sun, the crew hear cries, before dawn, that sound like the voices of "newly drowned men" (523). At sunrise the next morning, the ship loses one of its own men when he falls from aloft, a premonition of the many sacrifices to come. And on the next day, they meet the *Rachel*, whose captain has lost a son, while hunting the White Whale.

The waters inhabited by the White Whale are the waters of life as well as of death. But to a man such as Ahab, whose pride corrodes all faith, they will never bring renewal. As symbolized by the loss of his hat, or crown, Ahab is a dying king who is fast losing his power to rule, a type of the Fisher King for whom the living waters will never flow. Only when he sheds a single tear as he stands gazing into the sea and muses over all he has missed on shore over forty years of striving – human sympathy, friendship and family life, the green world – is it clear he understands the sacrifice he has made. And only then is it clear he is worthy of our attention and sympathy, and capable of common, human feeling. "[Nor] did all the Pacific contain such wealth as that one wee drop," Ishmael explains, for that one drop symbolizes a human soul lost (543–4).

Whether Ishmael, more than any of the rest of the *Pequod*'s crew, deserves to live – more than Queequeg, say, or little Pip – is the book's crowning mystery. Ahab's fate is predictable. Even the destruction of all the ship's crew comes as no surprise. The great mystery for Melville, in the end, is not death but life, the unfathomable gratuitousness of it. The "Epilogue," a little treasure that radically alters the meaning of all the rest of the book, conveys nothing so strongly as Ishmael's own wonder at his survival of the wrath of the avenging God. Ishmael makes little attempt to explain his escape. All he says is that "the Fates ordained" (573) he would be the one called to take Fedallah's place in Ahab's boat on the third day of the chase, after the Parsee had gone down with the Whale. From there, it just so happened that, of the oarsmen tossed out of the boat on the next collision with Moby Dick, Ishmael was the one left a castaway, floating beyond the Whale's frenzy. Otherwise, the fact that he alone was specially chosen is presented as a matter beyond understanding. A lone man somehow persisting in a hostile universe, with sharks and sea-hawks all around, buoyed up on a miniature version of the world – part lifebuoy, part coffin – Ishmael in the end is an image of us all, gifted with life and miraculously surviving, moment by moment.

An everyman figure, Ishmael is also, paradoxically, the specially chosen. He alone is the universal epic hero of *Moby-Dick*. Though an orphan and outcast, lacking family, wealth, and other common forms of legitimacy, he is the one man on the ill-fated *Pequod* whose cry God hears. Indeed, his name means "God shall hear." "Ishmael," of course, is not his given name, but the name he gives himself because it captures his experience as a castaway who finds the Father after all. Like other spiritual epics, therefore, Ishmael's story climaxes with the discovery of the outcast hero's true nobility and ends with his return to the community of his birth to bear witness to his experience. His retelling of that story, in turn, begins with the famous line that announces his new identity: "Call me Ishmael." It is the vitalizing declaration of a man who knows from experience that God and the soul of the redeemed hero are one.

His identity revealed in the moment of his soul's greatest triumph, Ishmael returns to share the wealth of his discovery with those Sunday "water-gazers" who long for the adventure that will liberate the soul. This wealth or treasure is contained within the pages of *Moby-Dick*, the book that records its hero's experience on the *Pequod* and bodies forth the wisdom Ishmael has gained from the events leading up to the fateful encounter with the Whale. Ishmael does not capture the beast with a harpoon, as Ahab tries to do. Being divine, Moby Dick can never be taken that way. But Ishmael can be said to capture him with his pen in the book called *The Whale* – with potentially life-changing consequences for his readers.

NOTE

1   To be sure, the epic is historically a masculine form, which Melville does nothing to universalize in a way that would explicitly include the female quester. All of Melville's female characters – Ishmael's stepmother, Mrs. Hussey, Ahab's and Starbuck's wives – are landlocked, at best playing supporting roles, like Aunt Charity, "a most determined and indefatigable spirit" who leads the effort at provisioning the *Pequod* in "All Astir" (96). However, femaleness is represented in the novel in the androgynous nature of the whale and the more pervasive androgyny of the natural world, as Melville portrays it, in "The Symphony," for example, where the firmaments of air and sea come together in a moment of gentle harmony before the final hunt: "the pensive air was transparently pure and soft, with a woman's look, and the robust and man-like sea heaved with long, strong, lingering swells, as Samson's chest in his sleep." As seen here, male and female were complementary principles for Melville, parts of the same whole, divided but equally alive and necessary: "those two seemed one; it was only the sex, as it were, that distinguished them" (542).

References and Further Reading

Abercrombie, Lascelles. *The Epic*. 1914. Rpt. Freeport, NY: Books for Libraries Press, 1969.

Abrams, M. H. *The Mirror and the Lamp: Romantic Theory and the Critical Tradition*. 1953. Rpt. New York: Norton, 1958.

Campbell, Joseph. *The Hero With a Thousand Faces.* 1949. Rpt. Princeton, NJ: Princeton University Press, 1986.

Cook, Albert. *The Classic Line: A Study of Epic Poetry.* Bloomington: Indiana University Press, 1966.

Eliade, Mircea. *The Quest: History and Meaning in Religion*. Chicago: University of Chicago Press, 1969.

——— . *The Sacred and the Profane: The Nature of Religion*. Trans. Willard R. Trask. New York: Harcourt, 1959.

Emerson, Ralph Waldo. "Nature." In *Selections from Ralph Waldo Emerson*. Ed. Stephen E. Whicher. Boston: Houghton Mifflin, 1957. 21–56.

Franklin, H. Bruce. *The Wake of the Gods: Melville's Mythology*. Stanford, CA: Stanford University Press, 1963.

Greene, Thomas. *The Descent from Heaven: A Study in Epic Continuity*. New Haven, CT: Yale University Press, 1963.

Hutson, Arthur E. and Patricia McCoy. *Epics of the Western World*. Philadelphia, PA: Lippincott, 1954.

McWilliams, John P., Jr. *The American Epic: Transforming a Genre, 1770–1860*. Cambridge: Cambridge University Press, 1989.

Miller, Dean A. *The Epic Hero*. Baltimore: Johns Hopkins University Press, 2000.

Mori, Masaki. *Epic Grandeur: Toward a Comparative Poetics of the Epic*. Albany, NY: State University of New York Press, 1997.

Newman, John Kevin. *The Classical Epic Tradition*. Madison: University of Wisconsin Press, 1986.

Quint, David. *Epic and Empire: Politics and Generic Form from Virgil to Milton*. Princeton, NJ: Princeton University Press, 1993.

Tillyard, E. M. W. *The Epic Strain in the English Novel*. London: Chatto and Windus, 1958.

Weston, Jessie L. *From Ritual to Romance*. 1920. Rpt. New York: Peter Smith, 1941.

Winnifrith, Tom, Penelope Murray, and K. W. Grandsden, eds. *Aspects of the Epic*. London: Macmillan, 1983.

27

The Female Subject in *Pierre* and *The Piazza Tales*

Caroline Levander

Given the paucity of women in his writing, one might initially think that Herman Melville was supremely uninterested in the female subject. In fact, writers as well as readers who have contemplated the question of women in Melville's writing have attempted to fill in the glaring gaps that Melville leaves – on the rare occasions when he mentions women at all. Much as Jean Rhys takes the forgotten madwoman in the attic of *Jane Eyre* as her subject in *Wide Sargasso Sea*, so have some writers attempted to depict the lives of the women that Melville and his male characters leave behind on shore. In novels like *Ahab's Wife*, for example, Sena Jeter Naslund takes the very female subjects that Melville ignores as her focus in a novel aiming to be as long, intricate, and psychologically complex as Melville's *Moby-Dick*. Relegating Captain Ahab to the sidelines of her story much as Melville did Ahab's wife, Naslund depicts a woman who creates an adventurous, daring life that takes her from the domestic sphere, to which women were traditionally confined in antebellum America, to the high seas and back.

Yet whether women are physically present or not in Melville's most popular fiction, scholars such as Robyn Wiegman, Gillian Silverman, Wyn Kelley, Gillian Brown, and myself have recently suggested that women act as an important, if often absent, feature of Melville's all-male worlds. If Melville, more than any other nineteenth-century writer, has been widely perceived by scholars such as Sacvan Bercovitch, Michael Rogin, and Eve Kosofsky Sedgwick among others as the American master of male bonding narratives, a stable feature of that male bond is the idea of gender difference – represented either by the rare image of a woman or the evocation of the feminine space of otherness. Thus the sailor communities which are the subject of much of Melville's writing, even though comprised entirely of men, recreate the very gender structures they seem to have temporarily escaped, with some men occupying relatively feminized, domestic roles and others assuming positions of masculine dominance and command. At the same time that male characters reproduce gender differences within the seafaring community they create, the female subject is projected outward onto both the men's prey and the native peoples the sailors encounter. Thus do Melville's men often enact what Nina Baym has termed "melodramas of beset manhood" in which male characters seek to escape from female influence only to recreate it among themselves in diverse and varied ways.

What then about those few Melville texts that do feature women and concern themselves directly with domestic matters? The most notable – or notorious in the minds of many contemporary reviewers – was *Pierre; or, the Ambiguities*. With a book review entitled "Herman Melville Crazy," the *New York Day Book* declared that *Pierre* represented "the ravings and reveries of a madman" (Higgins and Parker *Reviews* 419). Stating that Melville's 1852 novel demonstrated that "he can commit more and wilder follies on land than on water," the Charleston, South Carolina *Mercury* concurred that the author "was really supposed to be deranged," but the review went on to assure readers that Melville's "friends were taking measures to place him under treatment." In attempting to write a novel directly concerned with women and domestic matters, then, the novelist had written what Boston newspapers uniformly agreed was "the craziest fiction extant." Asking "were there no mad doctors in that part of the country where [the characters] lived? Were the asylums all full?," *Boston Daily Times* reviewer Charles Creighton Hazewell concluded that both writer and characters were a "collection of lunatics" (Higgins and Parker *Reviews* 419).

Current scholars no longer dismiss the novel as the ravings of a madman, but they have tended to read Melville's exploration of female characters and the domestic arena as a critical commentary on (some would argue parody of) the primarily woman-authored sentimental novels that were popular with nineteenth-century reading audiences (see for example Gillian Brown, Samuel Otter, and Gavin Jones). Concerned directly with women's development within the circumscribed world of home and family, sentimental novels – and what Nathaniel Hawthorne famously termed "that damned mob of scribbling women" who wrote them – tended to be more widely read than their male counterparts, a fact that concerned writers like Melville and Hawthorne. Sentimental novels tended to emphasize the affective and emotional bonds that women forged, to portray heroines who conformed to the stereotypical "angel in the house" ideal of pure womanhood, and to depict the true woman's power of moral suasion over others. Thus by portraying the concerns and lives of women circumscribed within the private sphere, bestselling mid-century novels like Maria Cummins's *The Lamplighter* (1854) and Susan Warner's *Wide, Wide World* (1851) not only directly competed with what was still a predominantly male literary market but also enjoyed wide sales that often eclipsed those of their male counterparts.

It is easy to see why scholars might consider *Pierre* to be a critique of such a woman-authored sentimental literary tradition. Not only had Melville failed to gain the same popular renown as many of his female counterparts, but also his depiction of domestic life and women characters employs many of the classic strategies of sentimental fiction with a frequency and intensity that suggests at times irony toward rather than endorsement of the sentimental genre. Indeed some critics have concluded from the novel's overblown prose and hyperbolic depiction of domestic life that *Pierre*, among other things, expresses Melville's disdain for women writers and their subject matter (see, for example, Robert S. Forsythe and Ann Douglas). Such readings, as Gillian Silverman has recently pointed out, work to emphasize Melville's difference from (and imply his superiority to) the many women writing sentimental fiction at the time. In so doing, readings that distinguish Melville's novel from sentimental fiction tend to sustain a longstanding hierarchy between woman-authored "popular" novels and male-authored "great" fiction – a hierarchy that, as we will see, obscures the very real and significant interests that Melville shared with the women writers of his time.

Indeed in writing *Pierre*, Melville attested to his kinship with women writers and expressed his shared interest in domesticity, family structures, and women's social place. Just as many women wrote out of financial exigency, so too did Melville hope, especially after the relative financial failure of *Moby Dick*, that the subject matter of *Pierre* would prove popular and therefore profitable. Without the higher education that might credential him for more remunerative pursuits, Melville, like the vast majority of women who wrote at mid-century, had fewer genteel career options than many men and was acutely aware of his relative socioeconomic vulnerability. Indeed at the time that he began to write *Pierre* Melville found himself in precisely the same socioeconomic situation as the women writers with whom he was competing. Thus did Melville assure Sophia Hawthorne, after he wrote *Moby-Dick*, that his next book would not be "a bowl of salt water" but rather "a rural bowl of milk" meant to appeal to the literary preferences of women readers (Melville to Sophia Hawthorne, January 8, 1852, *L* 146). Disproportionately shouldering the burdens of domestic want in antebellum America even as they found themselves most economically vulnerable (due to married women's inability to hold property independently), women often found themselves in the position of needing to produce pages and pages of prose to keep hunger and indigence at bay. The drive of the author writing for bread rather than fame is represented in painful detail in the novel as Pierre's attempt to write a great work of literature is gradually destroyed by his family's material need. Like the many women writers who expeditiously turned out a proliferation of novels in order to put food on the table, Pierre – as did Melville – finds his literary career increasingly shaped by market forces over which he has no control. Thus acutely aware of the socioeconomic similarity between himself and many popular women writers of the era, Melville charts within his novel how an aspiring male writer finds himself susceptible to the same socioeconomic forces that shaped the literary efforts of women writers such as Harriet Beecher Stowe, E. D. E. N. Southworth, Sarah Josepha Hale, Frances Hodgson Burnett, and Susan Warner, to name only a few.

Melville explores the female literary tradition not only in his depiction of the male writer's similarity to prominent women writers of the day but in the major themes and interests of *Pierre* as well. Taking domestic concerns as his broad focus, Melville analyzes the nature of the emotional bonds that shape the family circle – bonds between mother and son, brother and sister, and finally absent father and each of the family's members. Melville in short is concerned with what Pierre repeatedly terms the "heart of a man," but his domestic novel is not so much a criticism of the world of the heart as an exploration of its underlying shape and texture (289). Thus the potentially incestuous relationship between Pierre and his alleged sister Isabel is not so much a parody of domestic fiction's repeated interest in love relations between young women and the men who act as surrogate brother or father figures to them as a consideration of its logical outcomes. Just as Willie Sullivan finally marries his surrogate "sister" Gerty Flint in Cummins's *The Lamplighter*, so too does Pierre feel a responsibility for Isabel's wellbeing that is most successfully expressed by a form of marriage between the two. The similarities between Cummins's and Melville's domestic plots do not end there, as both novels depict in detail how an orphaned woman's discovery of her biological father alters a series of primary and secondary relationships between family members. However, if Cummins's novel imagines the claiming of such bonds as a necessary step for all individuals finally to find happiness, Melville shows the potential of such family alliances to permanently foreclose the possibility of a happy ending. Thus unlike Cummins's novel which ends with mother, father, brother and sister reunited joyfully within the domestic sphere, *Pierre* ends with an account of how all individuals can be gradually destroyed by the family ties that should protect them.

In his exploration of the family formations with which domestic fiction is primarily concerned, Melville considers the "natural," as well as contractual, bonds that family members forge with one another. In Pierre's relationship to his newly discovered sister, for example, Melville not only represents but calls into question the "natural" love between siblings, when he describes how that love produces rather than proceeds from Isabel as sister: "so perfect to Pierre had long seemed the illuminated scroll of his life thus far, that only one hiatus was discoverable by him in that sweetly-writ manuscript. A sister had been omitted from the text. He mourned that so delicious a feeling as fraternal love had been denied him" (7). Producing the very sister of which he bemoans the lack, these lines suggest a narrative reversal of cause and effect: it is not that Pierre loves his sister because he has one but rather that Pierre's love of the idea of a sister produces her. The unique causality of Pierre's family formations not only constitutes, but also undermines these seemingly natural, if newly discovered, family relations. Although the narrator insists that Pierre feels only brotherly love for Isabel, this assurance is undercut by Pierre's attention not to Isabel's recounting of her genealogy but to the intimate details of her body – to her "wonderfully beautiful ear, which chancing to peep from among her abundant tresses, nestled in that blackness like a transparent sea-shell" (119). Thus assertions that Pierre would "never . . . be able to embrace Isabel with the mere brotherly embrace; while the thought of any other caress . . . was entirely vacant from his uncontaminated soul" (142) register the insufficiency of family nomenclature to encompass the full range of feelings that proximal relations, once discovered, can produce. It is this "nameless awfulness of [Pierre's] still imperfectly conscious, incipient, new-mingled emotion" (206) toward his sister Isabel which Melville endeavors to explore and finally give a "name" in writing *Pierre*.

Like his feeling for Isabel, Pierre's relations with other women within his family – namely his mother and his fiancée Lucy – are similarly infused with a complex, often difficult-to-describe emotional energy that works to denaturalize as well as to sustain the family relations between mother and son, and husband and wife, with which sentimental fiction is primarily concerned. Pierre's relationship with his mother dominates the novel in that, even after she disowns him and then dies, Mrs. Glendinning wields a powerful influence over her son. Maternal influence over male as well as female children was a conceptual mainstay of sentimental narration. Cummins's Willie Sullivan, for example, recounts to Gerty Flint how he experienced maternal visions that kept his dead mother's influence clearly before him while he traveled the world. Enabling him to remain true to the family values with which he was raised, this posthumous apparition suggests a mother's capacity to wield moral suasion from beyond the grave and to maintain the domestic structures created while alive, regardless of how far male offspring may travel from home. Mrs. Glendinning exerts a similar influence on Pierre, but whereas Mrs. Sullivan's influence ensures that her son will rise to wealth, prominence, and happiness, Mrs. Glendinning's enduring authority causes Pierre to slowly self-destruct. Guilt-ridden over his mother's death and disownment, Pierre cannot subordinate Mrs. Glendinning's maternal power to his own ethical choice to reconfigure his new family to accommodate the unrecognized as well as canonical relations that families inevitably include and produce. Therefore the choice to acknowledge his illegitimate sister Isabel through a pretended marriage that confers on her the Glendinning family name on the one hand represents Pierre's attempt to radically reconstitute the idea of family to legitimize all its "nameless" members, and on the other hand verifies the ultimate impossibility of such an undertaking.

Pierre, however, not only explores the often unacknowledged intricacies and complexities of the domestic life with which woman-authored sentimental fiction was primarily concerned, but in addition the novel offers an extended commentary on the series of powerful women who shape the male protagonist's worldview. Mrs. Glendinning's affection for Pierre, for example, causes her to plan a marriage for him that will reinforce rather than erode her emotional primacy in her son's life. Thus she rejoices to learn that Pierre's intended "little wife, that is to be, will not estrange" (20) mother and son, but will rather work to maintain the mother's centrality to her son's emotional and psychological world. Not only does the knowledge of an illegitimate daughter, then, confuse the licit family relations that sentimental fictions takes as its focus, but, as importantly, Melville suggests, such knowledge has the potential to cause immense pain to the wives of such men. Mrs. Glendinning's desire to maintain the loyalty of her son at all costs can then be seen as a desire born, at least in part, of her husband's unacknowledged disloyalty. Pierre's memory jogged by Isabel's account of her origins, he suddenly recalls incidents from his childhood that shed "another twinkling light upon her history," and these "mystical corroborations in his own mind" help to substantiate Isabel's claims (137). Thus even though Mrs. Glendinning insists that her husband was "profoundly in love" with her, Pierre suddenly remembers his aunt's account of the impassioned relationship with a foreign woman of unknown class that preceded his father's more "suitable and excellent" match with his mother (19, 76). Despite his increasing conviction that his father sired an illegitimate child before marrying Mrs. Glendinning, Pierre's final inability to renounce his mother's idealized image of his father – even in the face of such persuasive evidence to the contrary – suggests her irresistible power as a maternal figure and his deepseated need to protect her from the pain that such a disclosure would produce. Thus it becomes possible to see Pierre's refusal to marry his mother's choice, Lucy, as both an act of protection of the women in his family and a refutation of maternal control.

While Lucy initially seems to be the least psychologically dynamic woman in the novel, she elicits and admits strong desires that work to complicate her conformity to the traditional, pure womanhood with which much sentimental fiction was interested. As the prototypical angel of the house Lucy is largely seen but not heard, remaining "noiseless" except for the "panting hush" (35) she produces when with Pierre. Indeed Melville insists on Lucy's traditional brand of femininity by equating it with the pastoral landscape of Pierre's domestic estate. Thus when Pierre looks at Lucy "all the waves in Lucy's eyes seemed waves of infinite glee to him … in Lucy's eyes there seemed to shine all the glory of the general day, and all the sweet inscrutableness of the sky" (25, 35). Yet as the following lines of text suggest, her presence, in the form of her feminine accoutrements, produces powerful sexual longings in Pierre – longings which Lucy does not deny as her passionless sentimental sisters would, but enthusiastically reciprocates:

> Now, crossing the magic silence of the empty chamber, he caught the snow-white bed reflected in the toilet-glass.... So he advanced, and with a fond and gentle joyfulness, his eye now fell upon the spotless bed itself, and fastened on a snow-white roll that lay beside the pillow. Now he started; Lucy seemed coming in upon him; but no – 'tis only the foot of one of her little slippers, just peeping into view from under the narrow nether curtains of the bed. Then again his glance fixed itself upon the slender, snow-white, ruffled roll; and he stood as one enchanted. Never precious parchment of the Greek was half so precious in his eyes. Never trembling scholar longed more to unroll the mystic vellum, than Pierre longed to unroll the sacred secrets of that snow-white, ruffled thing. (39)

Even as the repetition of 'snow-white' insists upon Lucy's purity, objects such as her slippers produce not only Pierre's sexual longing but the object of it – Lucy herself. Entering the room as Pierre fingers her writings, Lucy conflates sexual and textual favors when she tells Pierre that he can "read me through and through. I am entirely thine" (40). It is to this same bedroom – now with Lucy sleeping in it – that Pierre returns once he has declared himself married to Isabel. "Advanc[ing] slowly and deliberately toward her" in order "to pronounce to her her fate" (183), Pierre confronts only to resist the sexual desire that Lucy elicits and admits. Yet unlike other sentimental heroines, Lucy instead of retreating from her frustrated desire for Pierre finally chooses to join the alternative domestic sphere that Isabel and Pierre create in the city.

If Mrs. Glendinning and Lucy represent Melville's explorations of the mother and domestic angel at the center of the sentimental tradition, Isabel is Melville's version of the genre's stock abandoned woman and dark temptress. And in this role she excels. Asking Pierre for "pity, pity" as she "freeze[s] in the wide, wide, world" (64), Isabel describes her abandonment with the words that in the 1850s most powerfully signify young women's experience of psychological disorientation and crisis because of family dissolution. In the tradition of Susan Warner's famous novel *Wide, Wide World*, popular women writers such as E. D. E. N. Southworth consistently describe the plight of their female protagonists as that of being without "friend or companion in the wide, wide world" (*Fatal Marriage* 62). Just as the heroine of Southworth's immensely successful *The Fatal Marriage* finds herself calling upon the aid of an affluent young man who then lures her into a clandestine marriage, so too does Isabel's request for help lead to a secret and fatal marriage. And just as Southworth's heroine Lionne enlists the help of Orville with "tones [that] have power to thrill [his] whole nature" (72), it is the "low melodies of [Isabel's] far interior voice" (118) that overpower Pierre.

As this attention to the sound of women's speech suggests, Melville's exploration of the abandoned woman engages with contemporary debates about women's voices. Indeed, public discussion regarding women's circumscribed speech goes far toward explaining one of the most unusual elements of Melville's novel – the "incidentally embodied" (48) sounds Isabel produces in concert with her magical guitar. When Isabel "in low, sweet, and changefully modulated notes . . . breathed the word *mother, mother, mother*! There was profound silence for a time; when suddenly . . . the magical untouched guitar responded with a quick spark of melody." The guitar produces "low, sweet, and changefully modulated notes" and "breathe[s] the word *mother*" (149) without being touched, lending magical credence to Isabel's claim that "I never knew a mortal mother" (114). As Isabel, in unison with her guitar, reveals the "inmost tones of [her] heart's deepest melodies to [Pierre]" (113), he finds himself "bewitched" and "enchanted" by "first the enigmatical story of the girl . . . [the] haziness, obscurity and almost miraculousness of it . . . and then, the inexplicable spell of the guitar, and the subtleness of the melodious appealings of the few brief words from Isabel sung in the conclusion of the melody" (128). Such a sensational scene seems at odds with sentimental fiction, which by and large reinforced political commentators' arguments for the purity and appropriateness of women's speech. Women's conversation was considered by social and political commentators from Daniel Webster to Henry James to be the direct manifestation of women's own physical and mental purity, chastity, and unaffectedness. Yet even as prominent men of letters from Webster to William Dean Howells argued that the slovenly and uncouth utterance of American women must be avoided at all costs, others contended that the passion-less female speech so valued by some was destroying the nation's rugged, physical identity. Thus when Isabel reveals the taboo story of her illegitimate origins she is giving voice to the "sex, womanhood, maternity, desires, lusty animations, organs and acts unmentionable," that, according to Walt Whitman's 1850s *The Primer of Words*, are too often forced to "skulk out of literature with whatever belongs to them" (737). The subversive story of illicit origins that Isabel's speech and guitar describe to Pierre finally reorders rather than reinforces the middle-class culture that sentimental fiction depicts. Deciding to "write such things … to gospelize the world anew, and show them deeper secrets than the Apocalypse!" (273), Pierre is not only inspired by Isabel's tale, but he also takes inspiration from the unique means through which she communicates it by having Isabel play "her mystic guitar till [he feels] chapter after chapter born of its wondrous suggestiveness" (282).

As we have seen, Melville's *Pierre* offers an extended engagement with the woman-authored sentimental tradition, the female-dominated domestic sphere, and finally the female subjects who inhabit it. Far from decrying such topics, Melville explores their power over male characters and their socially subversive dimensions. These interests, which are at work implicitly in Melville's earlier male-dominated stories, become the exclusive focus of Melville's one domestic novel, but what then happens to them in Melville's subsequent writing? *The Piazza Tales* signal Melville's recovery of the literary reputation that *Pierre* jeopardized. As the Richmond *Southern Literary Messenger* declared: "For some time the literary world has lost sight of Herman Melville, whose last appearance as an author, in *Pierre or the Ambiguities* was rather an unfortunate one, but he turns up once more in *The Piazza Tales*, with much of his former freshness and vivacity" (Higgins and Parker *Reviews* 472). The Boston *Evening Traveler* concurs that *The Piazza Tales* "is in the real *Omoo* and *Typee* vein. One reads them with delight and with rejoicing that the author has laid his rhapsodizing aside" (473). It is certainly true that the stories that make up the collection return to Melville's earlier themes of seafaring in the case of "Benito Cereno" and "The Encantadas; or, Enchanted Islands," male power relations in "Bartleby, the Scrivener" and "The Lightning-Rod Man," and men's often obsessive drive for originality, creativity, and meaning in "The Bell-Tower." Yet as the introductory tale makes clear, such concerns are not divorced from women, but integrally bound up with them. Thomas Powell of the *New York News* draws our attention to such issues when he renames "The Piazza" "Marianna of the Piazza" in recognition of the importance of the story's one female character to the collection as a whole (Higgins and Parker *Reviews* 471). Pondering the significance of what Melville describes as "a lonely girl, sewing at a lonely window. The pale-cheeked girl, and fly-specked window" (*PT* 8) – a female subject who, the narrator admits, "haunts" him – this reviewer recognizes her profound importance as a listener not only to the stories that the male protagonist tells her but to those that follow "The Piazza." Indeed Marianna's desire to traverse the physical distance that separates her from the home of her male visitor and in so doing to escape from the "dull woman's work – sitting, sitting, restless sitting" (12) that traps her in her mountain home structures not only the introductory story of *The Piazza Tales*, but can be seen to be at work even in those that do not boast a single female character.

If we turn to "Bartleby, the Scrivener" with such concerns in mind, for example, we can see how the male protagonist's repeated and now notorious declaration that "I prefer not to" acknowledges a system of preference explicable within the context of the gendered separate spheres that structured nineteenth-century middle-class life. Although the public arena of the law office in which Bartleby is hired as a scrivener is peopled entirely by men, Bartleby's entry unsettles the office's capacity to function despite its recognition of the private preferences and domestic habits of its male members. The scriveners' desks – filled with foodstuffs and personal articles – represent at once their domestic needs and the subordination of those domestic needs to their public pursuits. Separated from their employer's office by "ground-glass folding-doors" that, according to the narrator, "divided my premises into two parts, one of which was occupied by my scriveners, the other by myself," the scriveners' desks represent both the incontrovertibility of male workers' private, domestic need and the strict subordination of such need within the marketplace. While the narrator admits that he upholds or traverses this boundary as suits him – "[a]ccording to my humor I threw open these doors, or closed them" – Bartleby permanently unsettles this delicate balance by occupying a desk on his employer's side of the glass, and thus "privacy and society were conjoined" (*PT* 19). His employer initially embraces this transgression of public and private functions, admitting, "I never feel so private as when I know you are here" (37). Occupying an unstable position between the two worlds the office contains, Bartleby, however, exploits his position by making his workplace into his home, and his desk into his house. Pressured by clients' negative comments about Bartleby's position and preferences, his employer tries to exorcise the public sphere of the domestic taint that Bartleby represents by inviting Bartleby to live with him. Yet the threat that Bartleby's refusal to comply with his employer poses to the market leads to Bartleby's forced expulsion from the workplace, his incarceration, and finally his death.

Just as *Pierre* explored the possibility of creating a radical and radicalized domesticity that would acknowledge illegitimate as well as legitimate family members and that would be recognized and economically supported by the literary marketplace, so too does "Bartleby, the Scrivener" tease out the possibility of the marketplace accommodating itself to the radical domesticity of male workers such as Bartleby. A marketplace that is flexible enough to recognize and accommodate the needs, dependencies, and preferences of its workers just like a private sphere that can acknowledge the full range of illicit as well as licit human relationships that market forces often help to produce – these are the interlocking concerns that Melville uses the female subject to explore, whether she is or is not physically present in the text. Melville's use of the female subject to interrogate the possibility of achieving more socially just private and public worlds had much in common with the endeavors of women reformers of his day. Whether they were fighting for dress reform, abolition, or labor reforms, nineteenth-century women activists consistently described the impact of unjust social conditions by depicting their effects on women.

Melville's interest in questions of social justice – questions that nineteenth-century women addressed in the antebellum era through pro- and anti-slavery activism – leads him explicitly to address the topics of race and slavery in "Benito Cereno." Yet the interest in women subjects and female subjectivity does not evaporate once Melville locates his narrative on water rather than on land. Indeed the ship with which Captain Delano becomes fascinated – a ship distinctly unlike the *Bachelor's Delight* with which he is familiar – operates much like a woman on Delano's imagination: "With no small interest, Captain Delano continued to watch her – a proceeding not much facilitated by the vapors partly mantling the hull, through which the far matin light from her cabin streamed equivocally enough" (*PT* 47). "Her maneuvers" appear strange to the Captain's practiced eye, and as Eric Wertheimer suggests, "Delano launches into his investigation of the historical come-on: Is this ship playing sinister, perhaps flirtatious?" (142). Yet the story that Captain Delano learns to read is a story not so much about gender as about racial and national difference. Committed to reading Don Benito's passivity and reserve as lack of authority over his men, Captain Delano only very belatedly comes to understand that Cereno's passivity is not due to a history of conflict with his men that has jeopardized his masculine authority but rather to a history of racial conflict that makes him the captive of his former captives. Thus does the education that Captain Delano receives through his involvement with Benito Cereno require that he expand his interpretive framework to include not only gendered but also racialized strategies of reading.

Such a reading strategy is paramount to understanding Melville's haunting depiction in "The Encantadas" of Hunilla, the Chola widow. A remnant of and testimony to the plethora of postcolonial victims and ignominious patterns of history that make up the Galápagos, Hunilla represents the silences and mutations produced in the wake of modern exploration. Hunilla the Chola widow, as Wertheimer suggests, embodies in her feminine presence the historical narratives that can never speak their own stories fully. Melville inscribes a female, part-Indian presence among the social world of North American explorers in order to point out that history which can no longer be spoken because it has been destroyed. In shunning the queries of the Americans with the words "Señor, ask me not" (*PT* 157) her feminized muteness operates as a dignified refusal to comply with their demand for information. Hunilla, in other words, haunts the crew with her ability to humanize nature and to embody in her muteness the devastation that imperial cultures produce on the natural and social worlds with which they are interested.

Representing the last remains of conquest history in her refusal to comply with the crew's desire to know her story, Hunilla offers us a revealing point of comparison with Isabel's seemingly magical power to vocalize her hidden past. In each case, the female subject represents through her speech or denial of it a past hidden from but produced by the exploitative systems of desire in which male characters engage. Be it the nuclear family struggling to uphold its social hegemony or the national family committed to worldwide dominance, the female subject interrupts, resists, and complicates the stories these groups tell themselves and each other in order to normalize their power. In so doing, Melville's women characters hold the key to understanding his career-long commitment to critiquing the systems of social justice from which his sailors seem to be trying to escape when they set sail, only seeming to leave the womenfolk behind on land.

REFERENCES AND FURTHER READING

Baym, Nina. "Melodramas of Beset Manhood: How Theories of American Fiction Exclude Women Authors." *American Quarterly* 33.2 (1981): 123–39.

Bercovitch, Sacvan. "How to Read Melville's *Pierre.*" In *Herman Melville: A Collection of Critical Essays.* Ed. Myra Jehlen and Edgar Dryden. Englewood Cliffs, NJ: Prentice Hall, 1994. 116–26.

Brown, Gillian. "Anti-Sentimentalism and Authorship in *Pierre.*" In *Domestic Individualism: Imagining Self in Nineteenth-Century America.* Berkeley: University of California Press, 1990. 135–70.

Douglas, Ann. *The Feminization of American Culture.* New York: Knopf, 1977.

Dryden, Edgar. "The Entangled Text: Melville's *Pierre* and the Problem of Reading." In *Herman Melville: A Collection of Critical Essays.* Ed. Myra Jehlen and Edgar Dryden. Englewood Cliffs, NJ: Prentice Hall, 1994. 101–16.

Forsythe, Robert S. "Melville in Honolulu." *New England Quarterly* 8.1 (1935): 99–105.

Higgins, Brian and Parker, Hershel. "The Flawed Grandeur of Melville's *Pierre.*" In *Herman Melville: A Collection of Critical Essays.* Ed. Myra Jehlen and Edgar Dryden. Englewood Cliffs, NJ: Prentice Hall, 1994. 126–39.

——— . *Herman Melville: The Contemporary Reviews.* New York: Cambridge University Press, 1995.

Jones, Gavin. "Poverty and the Limits of Literary Criticism." *American Literary History,* 15.4 (2003): 765–92.

Kelley, Wyn. "Pierre in a Labyrinth: The Mysteries and Miseries of New York." In *Melville's Evermoving Dawn: Centennial Essays.* Ed. John Bryant and Robert Milder. Kent, OH: Kent State University Press, 1997. 393–406.

——— . "Pierre's Domestic Ambiguities." In *The Cambridge Companion to Herman Melville.* Ed. Robert S. Levine. Cambridge: Cambridge University Press, 1998. 91–114.

Levander, Caroline. "Foul-Mouthed Women: Disembodiment and Public Discourse in Herman Mel-

ville's *Pierre* and E. D. E. N. Southworth's *The Fatal Marriage.* In *Voices of the Nation: Women and Public Speech in Nineteenth-Century American Literature and Culture.* New York: Cambridge University Press, 1998. 35–57.

Levine, Robert S. "Pierre's Blackened Hand." *Leviathan: A Journal of Melville Studies* 1.1 (1999): 23–44.

Miles, Robert. " 'Tranced Griefs': Melville's *Pierre* and the Origins of the Gothic." *ELH* 66 (1999): 157–77.

Otter, Samuel. *Melville's Anatomies.* Berkeley: University of California Press, 1999.

——— . "The Overwrought Landscape of *Pierre.*" In *Melville's Evermoving Dawn: Centennial Essays.* Ed. John Bryant and Robert Milder. Kent, OH: Kent State University Press, 1997. 349–75.

Penry, Tara. "Sentimental and Romantic Masculinities in *Moby-Dick* and *Pierre.*" In *Sentimental Men: Masculinity and the Politics of Affect in American Culture.* Ed. Mary Chapman and Glenn Hendler. Berkeley: University of California Press, 1999. 226–44.

Rogin, Michael. *Subversive Genealogy: The Politics and Art of Herman Melville.* New York: Knopf, 1983.

Sedgwick, Eve Kosofsky. *Between Men: English Literature and Male Homosocial Desire.* New York: Columbia University Press, 1985.

Silverman, Gillian. "Textual Sentimentalism: Incest and Authorship in Melville's *Pierre.*" *American Literature* 74.2 (2002): 345–72.

Southworth, E. D. E. N. *The Fatal Marriage.* Philadelphia, PA: T. B. Peterson, 1863.

Spanos, William. "Pierre's Extraordinary Emergency: Melville and 'The Voice of Silence.' Part 1." *Boundary 2: An International Journal of Literature and Culture* 28.2 (2001): 105–31.

Tolchin, Neal. *Mourning, Gender, and Creativity in the Art of Herman Melville.* New Haven, CT: Yale University Press 1988.

Toner, Jennifer. "The Accustomed Signs of the Family: Rereading Genealogy in Meville's *Pierre*." *American Literature* 70.2 (1998): 237–63.

Wertheimer, Eric. *Imagined Empires: Incas, Aztecs, and the New World of American Literature, 1771–1876*. New York: Cambridge University Press, 1999.

Whitman, Walt. *The Primer of Words*. In *Daybooks and Notebooks*. Ed. William White. Vol. 3. New York: New York University Press, 1978.

Wiegman, Robyn. "Melville's Geography of Gender." In *Herman Melville: A Collection of Critical Essays*. Ed. Myra Jehlen and Edgar Dryden. Englewood Cliffs, NJ: Prentice Hall, 1994. 187–99.

28

Narrative Shock in "Bartleby, the Scrivener," "The Paradise of Bachelors and the Tartarus of Maids," and "Benito Cereno"

Marvin Fisher

Between 1853 and 1856 Melville wrote fifteen short stories, most of which appeared in monthly magazines named for publishing firms: *Harper's* or *Putnam's*. For most of the century following their initial publication, these stories drew scant critical attention, the consensus being that they marked the period of Melville's growing disappointment and the decline of his talent and reputation. By 1960 this evaluation began to change, and in the 1970s three critical studies focused exclusively on the short fiction as examples of advanced or experimental narrative, attempts at innovative symbolism, and frequently penetrating efforts to define and evaluate American manners, institutions, and ways of thought. Now, in the twenty-first century, Melville's short stories seem to speak urgently to a world unaware of its own moral, social, and political failings. The one hope, Melville's stories suggest, lies in their narrators' limited capacities for empathy and spiritual evolution.

Initially, Melville seemed not to have intended any of these stories to form a collection such as Irving, Poe, and Hawthorne had done; but when that possibility developed he gathered five of his published tales and composed an introductory story, which provided his title for *The Piazza Tales* (1856), named for the covered porch or verandah that he had recently added to his house in western Massachusetts. The term "piazza" supplies a unifying metaphor for the collection and his other stories as well. Physically, Melville's piazza offers his narrator a vantage point from which he can view the surrounding world; indeed the narrator's literal perspective provides most of the plot for a simple sketch concerning perception, exploration, and revising misperception. In a literary sense, however, his "piazza" is an instructive site for the reader, an announcement that where one stands, one's point of view, controls what one sees, thinks, and does. Thus the concept of point of view is technique as well as theme in these stories and constitutes much of Melville's modernity.

Indeed, although lacking the specific focus of James Joyce's *Dubliners* or Sherwood Anderson's *Winesburg, Ohio*, Melville's fifteen stories (*The Piazza Tales* and those remaining uncollected) share pressing concerns with these twentieth-century collections. Melville, no less than Joyce, was preoccupied with the moral and spiritual paralysis of his time, and Melville's short fiction, like the stories of *Dubliners*, explores a series of social, intellectual, and spiritual crises. In the three stories examined here, Melville considers grave and distinctly American cultural dilemmas – capitalism, wage labor, slavery. Speaking from his "piazza" as a dismayed witness, Melville's typical narrator registers the shock of his encounter with America's moral and social failures. Even now, a century and a half later, his words continue to resonate, and his vision seems remarkably relevant to a new age.

"Bartleby, the Scrivener"

"Bartleby, the Scrivener. A Story of Wall Street," as Melville's first published story was entitled, appeared in the November and December, 1853, issues of *Putnam's Monthly Magazine*. The subtitle announces that the law office, its employer and employees, its interior arrangements and procedures epitomize the American financial world, with its power structure, division of labor, and distribution of profits, all contributing to a hardening system of class and caste relationships. For some literary critics of the past fifty years, "Bartleby" has appeared as a pessimistic view of the fate of the writer in America, forced to abandon the originality of his own expression and made to copy what his employer (or publisher) commands; other readers, moving from focus on artistic creativity to spiritual fulfillment, emphasize the ethical incompatibility of Christian doctrine and the way of Wall Street. Melville might not have objected to any of these interpretations; for him the story was one of several he would write to illustrate how mid-nineteenth-century America had failed to maintain its youthful promise and come to exhibit faults associated with older societies. But the story also stresses the importance of point of view, perception, and interpretation of character and event in determining the "truth" or meaning of a story. The reader sees nothing from Bartleby's point of view and must learn what ails him with the help and hindrance of the lawyer-narrator's interpretation of his clerk's behavior. As the lawyer tells us in the opening paragraph: "Bartleby was one of those beings of whom nothing is ascertainable, except from the original sources, and in his case, those are very small" (*PT* 13). Yet despite the scarcity of sources, the narrator provides a detailed account of Bartleby's last days, becoming an unlikely, unwilling, and unwitting evangelist in the process. His account has its inherent limitations, but it is the only gospel we have.

Melville's handling of the point of view in this story is a conscious and sustained artistic achievement unprecedented in American literature, and his development of the narrator's character and values displays a deft dependence on ironic self-revelation without self-realization. With an air of genial ease, the lawyer proudly conveys his sense of success and self-satisfaction. As a narrator, he is reliable at times and unreliable at others, revealing and obscuring the meaning of his troubling experiences. A representative of conservative business interests, he is eager to profit greatly without laboring unduly, has little genuine philanthropy or piety, but in his own way is considerate of his employees and able to overlook their faults if he can make use of them at predictable times. Despite his limitations, he proves to be capable of considerable moral growth, even though he has to convince himself that his charity will also have some practical benefits. Melville's most telling tactic, much like that of Mark Twain in *Adventures of Huckleberry Finn*, is to make the narrator's language suggest far more than the character consciously realizes. When his words suggest meaning (or double meanings) beyond his understanding, we sense the author's point of view. Thus the narrator's attitudes, actions and reactions, and most importantly his vocabulary reveal the meanings that his mind cannot reach. For Melville, the sustained irony of a narrator unaware of his own verbal duplicity provides the strategy by which he unfolds his moral project: to show the collapse of democratic principles and the breakdown of community, communication, and communion.

Within the physical and social divisions of the Wall Street office, however, all three have failed. Again the narrator's words reveal a truth he would prefer to suppress: the possessive pronoun forms the core of his value system, as he informs us of "myself, my *employés*, my business, my chambers," adding in the next sentence that "some such description is indispensable to an adequate understanding of the chief character about to be presented" (13). By these means, Melville means to tell us to watch the narrator. He introduces himself before he introduces Bartleby, and the author's managed meta-narration suggests that this is the lawyer's story, even more than it is Bartleby's. Bartleby is the pitiable instrument by which the lawyer is made to realize his moral deficiency.

Like the complacent lawyers in "The Paradise of Bachelors," men insulated from the trials of life who use the law to right no wrongs, the narrator has sought "the cool tranquility of a snug retreat" where he can "do a snug business among rich men's bonds, and mortgages, and title-deeds" (14). Known as a "safe" man possessing such virtues as "prudence" and method, he omits morality, justice, passion, or compassion from his value system. Money is his goal, and "the late John Jacob Astor" is his god (14). He serves in a priesthood of profit, and his proprietary attitude includes not only his business office but also the men he employs. They can be inventoried like the inanimate furnishings of his office, for they have value only as means to serve his financial ends.

Some readers might object to so harsh a judgment, citing the lawyer's tolerance of human weakness or eccentricity in his clerks, Turkey and Nippers. He can put up with Turkey's drinking, irritability, and carelessness, however, only if it is confined to a limited part of the day and as long as his elderly clerk remains useful and productive during a predictable remainder of the day (an affordable kindness, since he pays his copyists on a piecework rate rather than a salary or an hourly rate). Turkey is unreliable in the afternoon, but Nippers, the other copyist, is at his best then. Between them, they produce a day's work – a situation acceptable to the narrator as "a good natural arrangement" (15–18). Since the narrator proudly fills "the Master's office," and accepts the deference and servility of his aides, whose remarks are customarily prefaced by a phrase like "With submission, sir," this "good natural arrangement" suggests Melville's more cynical observations on the lack of democracy in the workplace. The narrator offers no encouragement or direction to his younger, more ambitious clerk. Instead of admiring Nippers for his enterprise, he resents "his diseased ambition," and feels no obligation to lessen the authority of his office by raising a subordinate to greater responsibility.

"The Master's office" refers to the position of Master in Chancery, to which the narrator has been appointed. The holder of such office exercised considerable quasi-judicial power, rendering decisions in matters of equity, which common law did not cover and the courts were not constituted to settle. "Equity" can and does refer to what is fair, just, and impartial, yet it also refers to financial holdings, mortgages, bonds, and shares of stock – in short the business in securities and equities associated with Wall Street. Needless to say, the partiality and self-interest of the narrator are never in doubt, and his conscience through most of the story evinces the internalized values of Wall Street.

Against this value system, Bartleby's refusal to aid in proofreading, repeatedly saying "I would prefer not to" when asked, is far more than the complaint of an employee who feels that the request lies outside the requirements of his job description. It is an assertion of autonomy that threatens a carefully controlled network of assumptions, expectations, and relationships. The next stage of his peculiar insurrection moves from insubordination to appropriation of private property for personal use. Sleeping in the office strikes the narrator where he lives, threatening his property, his status, even his masculine power. He first feels "disarmed" (21) by Bartleby's rebellious behavior and ultimately "unmanned" (27) by the threat to his authority.

Feeling weak and impotent after every attempt to cajole, persuade, entice, command, or bribe Bartleby to provide even a semblance of what he was hired to do, the narrator finds his will stiffened by the Wall Street society that has served him so well. The attitude of benign accommodation that has so often enabled him to manage difficult circumstances to his own benefit fails repeatedly when confronted by Bartleby's bland, unreasoning refusal. Turning to the forms and phrases of Wall Street business communication, he offers a helping hand while denying any real sense of community, or at best mocking it: "If, hereafter, in your new place of abode, I can be of any service to you, do not fail to advise me by letter" (33). With this speech, he rids himself of Bartleby (or so he thinks) in brilliant fashion. Reveling in what he has achieved without bullying, bravado, or even raising his voice, he boasts of a mission accomplished without violence, "Masterly I called it," and again, "I could not but highly plume myself on my masterly management in getting rid of Bartleby" (33). The key adjective "masterly" (unintentionally, in the narrator's mind) refers to the narrator's title, his position in the office hierarchy, his masterly use of authority, and quite possibly the masterly defense of slavery in the South in contrast to the condition of "wage-slaves" in the industrial and commercial North.

Thus far Melville has established a system of class and caste antithetical to American political promise. But beyond the obstacles to community and the barriers to communication, there lies another level of indictment that widens the gap between the all-powerful and the powerless: the impossibility of communion between one human being and another. When Bartleby will not be moved by his employer's various modes of "masterly management," the narrator offers a series of blunt rhetorical questions: "What earthly right have you to stay here?" (not realizing that something more than "earthly right" might be involved). "Do you pay any rent? Do you pay my taxes? Or is this property yours?" As his anger mounts, reaching a crescendo of self-righteousness, he is beset by a wave of liberal sympathies that erode his hard-headed Wall Street creed and soften his hard-hearted masterly ways. Tenderly he wonders whether "the circumstances of being alone in a solitary office . . . entirely unhallowed by humanizing domestic associations" could cause Bartleby's insidious eccentricities (35–6). Under the influence of this new perception, and as true as he tries to remain to his Wall Street principles, the narrator moves toward redemption as he confronts his radically unsettling humanizing association with Bartleby. His progress is limited, however. Thrust Bartleby into the street he cannot, so he takes the unlikely course of moving his offices to another location. By separating himself from Bartleby, leaving Bartleby for others to deal with, and denying any further responsibility, the narrator decisively fails the test of Christian gospel.

Yet as failed as it is, this transformation in the lawyer is really the crux of the story. Bartleby is the agent, the instrument, the defeated victim powerless to save himself, yet strong enough to save another. Through Bartleby's influence, the lawyer, whose efforts at charity are at first so prudent and pragmatic, becomes increasingly suffused with a sense of humanity and compassion. Never completely free of his Wall Street proprieties, he gradually shows less need to rationalize his actions or find a utilitarian justification for them. His private reflections reveal not only the growth of tolerance and sympathy, but also the greater profundity of a spiritual conversion:

> For the first time in my life a feeling of overpowering stinging melancholy seized me. Before, I had never experienced aught but a not unpleasing sadness. The bond of a common humanity now drew me irresistibly to gloom. A fraternal melancholy! For both I and Bartleby were sons of Adam. (28).

"The bond of a common humanity," a deepened sense of a shared susceptibility to the human condition – these form the foundation for an ideal of community, a concept of communion, and they penetrate the narrator's conscience, though only so far. In an ironic reversal of Christ driving the money-men from the Temple, Wall

Street landlords and city authorities, with considerable difficulty, remove Bartleby from the office, arrest him as a vagrant, and lock him in the Tombs prison. In Matthew 25, Jesus says, "I was sick, and ye visited me; I was in prison, and ye came unto me." The narrator plays his part but can stimulate in Bartleby no will to live. Bartleby's last words to his repentant former employer, who has tried to stress that signs of encouragement exist even in this environment, are "I know where I am" (43), and indeed this place of total enclosure is familiar – the same encircling walls, the same repressive and punitive normality, and the same stony embodiment of anti-human institutions.

Appended to the story is an unconfirmed rumor about Bartleby's previous employment as "a subordinate clerk in the Dead Letter Office at Washington" (45). Its position and its content providing the only information about Bartleby's past, it compels the reader to look more carefully than does the narrator, who sees only a possible source for Bartleby's negativism and depression: "Dead letters! does it not sound like dead men? Conceive a man by nature prone to pallid hopelessness, can any business seem more fitted to heighten it than that of continually handling these letters, and assorting them for the flames" (45). Yet, considering those undeliverable letters, he sees a little more: "For by the cartload they are annually burned. Sometimes from out the folded paper the pale clerk takes a ring – the finger it was meant for perhaps, moulders in the grave, a bank-note sent in swiftest charity – he whom it would relieve, nor eats nor hungers any more; pardon for those who died despairing, hope for those who died unhoping; good tidings for those who died stifled by unrelieved calamities. On errands of life, these letters speed to death. Ah, Bartleby! Ah, humanity!" (45). Although the lawyer's words seem sentimental and melodramatic, they are not banal. He has come far in his account of Bartleby and what it means to him, letting himself be drawn into a human problem for which there is no neat legal solution.

To consider the lawyer's moral evolution, then, enables us to estimate how a man who embodies Wall Street greed could come to express tragic insight. For although Bartleby does not rise from the Tombs, his story does, and the story is evidence that the narrator has accomplished in his record of mind, memory, and conscience the only immortality Bartleby is to have. Without the encounter with Bartleby, the narrative would not exist, and we would not have witnessed the transformation by which this man is saved. In Melville's dimly lit theater of hope, life is often a surrealistic allegory, and art, which can counter the conventional view of the world and invert the more typical judgments of society, is the only feeble means of enlightenment and redemption.

"The Paradise of Bachelors and The Tartarus of Maids"

Although Melville wrote and published nearly all of his short stories between 1854 and 1856, one of them, "The Two Temples," was not published in his lifetime. It was rejected, with regret, in separate letters from the editor and the publisher of *Putnam's*

Monthly Magazine, because they feared it would offend "religious sensibilities" and arouse "the whole power of the pulpit" (*PT* "Editorial Appendix" 700–2). That story, like "The Paradise of Bachelors and the Tartarus of Maids," had two parts, one exploring an American scene and the other a contrasting British scene. The American "temple" describes the narrator's experience in the newly opened, ostentatious Grace Church where he encounters outright class discrimination in a setting of conspicuous consumption, religious hypocrisy, and spiritual sham. The British panel of the diptych, however, is set in a London theater where the impoverished American visitor is given a free ticket, enjoys generous hospitality amid strangers, and witnesses a superb merger of art and artistry in a "temple" of imaginative expression. Apparently the theme of grace ironically linking the two panels was too subversive a challenge to the sanctimonious and the powerful.

How, then, did "The Paradise of Bachelors and the Tartarus of Maids," with its hints of perversion, its unflattering portrayal of the legal profession, the subjugation and exploitation of women in "the land of the free," the gynecological features of the landscape, and its extended metaphorical parody of insemination, gestation, and birth, escape the censorship that befell "The Two Temples"? Perhaps the majority of readers remained unaware of the story's complexities of narrative perspective and point of view. Only Melville's more careful readers recognized that there was more irony than envy in "Paradise," his depiction of the life of London's bachelor lawyers, or in "Tartarus," his "pained homage to [the] pale virginity" of silent mill girls (*PT* 334). His bachelors, the modern Templars, unlike the supposedly heroic Knights Templars of yore, are impotent, effete caricatures pursuing their own pleasure and self-indulgence. For their part, his New England maids, subjected to an obsessive paternalism and Puritanism, remain physically chaste while exposed to a system of technological exploitation that violates their wills, perverts their sexuality, and transforms the New World garden into a metaphorical hell.

Melville had gathered many of the impressions recorded in the London part of the story during a four-day period in December 1849, when he visited, dined, and break-fasted at Elm Court, Lincoln's Inn, and the Erectheum Club. The experiences recorded in his *Journal* seem to have been pleasant; the dinners were "glorious," the company "fine fellows," and even in midweek these gatherings lasted "till noon of night" (*J* 44). It was the first of these occasions that he termed in his *Journal* "The Paradise of Bachelors," but his entries also make clear that his mind was elsewhere. Two days before his first visit to the Temple, he mentioned buying a silver fork for his infant son Malcolm and then working on the manuscript of *White-Jacket*, for which he had received an advance payment and which he felt pressed to send to his waiting publisher (43). And just before the first of his "glorious" dinners, he recorded that "a letter was left for me – from home! All well and Barney [Malcolm] more bouncing than ever, thank heaven" (45). These entries make clear that he had more in common with the "Benedick tradesmen" the narrator of "Paradise" passes on the street, whose furrowed brows reflect their worry about the "rise of bread and the fall of babies," than with the "banded bachelors" whose unclouded company he was about to enjoy (*PT* 316).

The experience that led to "The Tartarus of Maids" occurred much closer to home in Melville's visit to a paper mill about five miles from Pittsfield in late January, 1851. His only recorded mention of this visit appears in a letter to Evert A. Duyckinck about two weeks later on a sheet which was one of a "sleigh-load of this paper" from Carson's Old Red Mill. In *The Melville Log* Jay Leyda suggests that Elizabeth Melville's second pregnancy, occurring at the same general time, probably sparked the fantastic conceit linking aggressive technology and submissive femininity (1: 403–4). If true, it recalls the reference to the "rise of bread and the fall of babies."

Whether or not we accept Leyda's conjecture concerning the germ of the story, it is safe to say that the first half of the diptych is characterized by suppressed eroticism, even homoeroticism, and the second by sexual guilt when the narrator is confronted by the suppression of Eros. It would not be in error to suggest too that Melville's "Tartarus" supports Karl Marx's bleak view of how repetitive mechanized production impinges on the worker or Freud's emphasis on sexuality and its effect on psychology and human behavior. It also anticipates contemporary feminist criticism that focuses on the social, political, and religious subjugation of women.

The opening pages of each half of this two-part story underscore the contrasts central to Melville's strategy. In the first tale the narrator is simply an American ostensibly admiring the ease, tradition, and gentility of England and rather proud of his historical knowledge, establishing the disjunction between the twelfth-century Knights Templars (part of the Western European coalition's attempt to regain Holy Land sites in Muslim lands in an extended series of crusades) and a luxury-loving fraternity of London lawyers who have gained possession of former Templar property in the Inns of Court. In the second tale the narrator identifies himself as a "seedsman" seeking to purchase envelopes for his business. Given that the "Paradise" draws upon details from Melville's *Journal*, critics have assumed that the narrator is no mere tourist but an American writer in London on literary business. Indeed in the earlier-mentioned letter to Evert Duyckinck in February 1851, Melville refers to his visit to the paper mill to purchase writing-paper for his craft and his correspondence. The metaphor suggests, then, that the narrator's "seeds," his stories, will take root and develop in his readers' minds. The narrator speaks for the author, softening his criticism in the first half but reacting with horror and shock in the second.

With the narrator's access to the central scene of each story, Melville announces the stratagem of parallel contrasts. To get to the Paradise of Bachelors from the Strand "is like stealing from a heated plain into some cool, deep glen, shady among harboring hills." Past Temple Bar, which then separated the busy city from the pastoral sanctuary of the Inner Temple, the topography is like "Eden's primal garden," sweeter than "the oasis in Sahara." There are parks and flower beds with "the Thames flowing by," as once "flowed the mild Euphrates." Inside this protective cocoon, bachelor barristers invite the reader to enter the "soft reclusion of this serene encampment" and "in mild meditation pace the cloisters, take your pleasure, sip your leisure ... linger in the ancient library ... worship in the sculptured chapel ... dine among the banded Bachelors … Not dine in bustling commons … but tranquilly, by private hint, at a private table" (316–17).

The protection of this Old World retreat is without parallel in "Tartarus," where the warmth, comfort, insulation, and indolent luxury of the bachelors contrasts with the exposure of New England maids to petrifying cold, a barren landscape, and the rigid discipline and punitive sterility of their lives and labors. Here the narrator also penetrates a narrow gateway to reach his destination. But the path is less defined semantically, and the landscape lies dense with symbolic, gothic imagery. Echoing the sentence pattern that began the first tale, he writes, "It lies not far from Woedolor Mountain in New England. Turning … east … from among bright farms and sunny meadows, … you enter ascendingly among bleak hills" (323). From this point on, the approach to the mill (which the narrator discovers in a frigid hollow after passing through "a Dantean gateway" into the hollow, known locally as "the Devil's Dungeon" [324]) is marked with increasing imputations of horror. Forewarned by these references that some form of Hell lies beyond and that it holds inmates in some semblance of penal confinement, the reader encounters descriptions so frankly physiological that their appearance in a mid-nineteenth-century issue of a mainstream American periodical signals not only Melville's audacity but also the unsuspecting innocence and complacency of editor and audience.

For, to this audience, the benign view of female workers in New England mills, whether they produced paper or textiles, was that they worked in safe, chaste, closely regulated, morally protected circumstances. In dormitories and dining-halls, they were protected from sinful encounters. The hours were long, but their wages strengthened important family values – helping pay off a family mortgage, sending a brother through college, or amassing a dowry that provided a stronger financial foundation for a delayed marriage. Parents were reassured by compulsory attendance at church services and in many cases the availability of a properly selected library.

Melville's "seedsman" sees things very differently. His efforts to speak to several of the girls are frustrated by their lack of protection from the paralyzing and petrifying chill of this American gulag. Blue with cold, pale from exhaustion and dietary deficiency, and fearful of the wrath of their "dark-complexioned well-wrapped" supervisor, known as "Old Bach" (327, 330), they remain silent, forbidden to speak even as the machinery hums incessantly. The narrator sees no benign example of the Protestant Ethic reinforced by protective paternalistic constraints. Like the bachelor barristers whose brotherhood of celibacy still maintains hints of their monkish origins, the maids form a sisterhood of sterility, whose white habit marks their new order. The mill owner or the corporation formulates the vows by which the maids (girls, not women) renounce all joys, comforts, and vanity. The narrator, seeing the naked truth of this technological totalitarianism, compares himself to Actaeon, who has watched Artemis bathing in a stream. To silence him, she turns him into a stag and his own hounds tear him apart – punishment for his prurience. The author/narrator has indeed viewed an obscenity, but it stems from the theocratic, paternalist brand of technological efficiency abetted by faith in capitalism.

Intuitively Melville must have felt that the maids' encounter with the machine at the center of this early mass production process seemed to foreshadow the end of humanity, a view shared by some of his literary contemporaries. Through much of *Walden*, also published in 1854, Thoreau articulated a similar despair over the impact of technology, asserting that "we do not ride on the railroad; it rides upon us" (83), but he ultimately finds spiritual renewal in the regenerative power of nature – a position Melville rejected in "Bartleby." Nevertheless, in a Melvillean mood, Thoreau names the locomotive "Atropos," after that one of the Greek Fates who snips the cord marked off to indicate the preordained measure of a person's life (107). When Atropos cuts the thread at its allotted length, that soul descends to Tartarus. In Melville's story the narrator writes the name of his guide on a bit of paper which Cupid drops into the mass of pulp. In precisely nine minutes it emerges: "a scissory sound smote my ear, as of some cord being snapped; and down dropped an unfolded sheet of perfect foolscap, with my 'Cupid' half faded out of it, and still moist and warm ... For a moment a curious emotion filled, me, not wholly unlike [what] one might experience at the fulfillment of some mysterious prophecy" (332). Even as the narrator tries to assure himself that he has watched "a mere machine," the author suggests that it is a good deal more: "struck ... by the inevitability [and] the evolvement power in all its motions ... Something of awe now stole over me" (333). Less frightened by the machine's ponderous size, he is terrified by "the metallic necessity," "the unbridging fatality," and "the autocratic cunning." As he "stood spell-bound and wandering in my soul" before the supreme power of the mechanized Atropos that will brook no appeal, he experiences another Actaeon-like forbidden vision, a funeral parade of female victims carried to a Tartarean underworld on the moving conveyor belt of technological ingenuity: "Before my eyes – there, passing in slow procession along the wheeling cylinders, I seemed to see, glued to the pallid incipience of the pulp, the yet more pallid faces of all the pallid girls I had eyed that heavy day. Slowly, mournfully, beseechingly, yet unresistingly, they gleamed along, their agony dimly outlined on the imperfect paper, like the print of the tormented face on the hand-kerchief of Saint Veronica" (333–4). Sharing Thoreau's recognition of the mechaniza-tion of mid-nineteenth-century America, and the rapid social change it brought, Melville's imagination also outraced Thoreau's locomotive in its metaphysical daring: his image shows mankind (significantly represented by voiceless and voteless women) carried to its collective Golgotha by an inscrutable, godlike machine that mimics human reproduction, ultimately frustrating and replacing it by mass production methods. Together technology and capitalism efficiently combine the *locus* and *modus* of creation and destruction, the birth of a new age and the end of an older.

Melville's vision underscores not only the obscenity of biomechanical mimicry but also the ultimate horror of what the ideal worker had to become. In his explanation of his hiring practices the bachelor owner reveals biases that exist even a century and a half after Melville's "Tartarus" first appeared: "We want none but steady workers: twelve hours to the day, day after day, through the three hundred and sixty-five days, excepting, Sundays, Thanksgiving, and Fast-days – and so, having no married women, what females we have are rightly enough called girls." The narrator has one more question before his exposé is complete. In phrasing his question, he conveys knowledge of its answer: "Then these are all maids," followed by the corroboration "All maids." Involuntarily paying "homage to their pale virginity" (334), he acts the part of Actaeon for the third time: first having perceived the silent white slaves of this New England mill; secondly, witnessing the cruel authority of the new technological master; and thirdly, seeing the naked hypocrisy of protecting the sexual innocence of the girls while draining their procreative power and compelling their robotic transformation and submissive efficiency. He has seen the future, and it works all too well – but at appalling cost.

It is unlikely that Henry Adams had any knowledge of Melville's story, yet his chapter on "The Dynamo and the Virgin" is permeated by a similar sense that technology (as he observed it in the Hall of Machines in Chicago's Columbian Exposition, a World's Fair marking the 500th anniversary of Columbus's transatlantic voyage) has irrevocably severed the continuity of culture and obviated the function and dissipated the power of religion, love, and femininity. With feelings of shock and dismay, he describes his sense of crawling along a knife-edge of history that "divided two kingdoms of force," asserting that "in America neither Venus nor Virgin had any value" (383). Recognizing that in past centuries "the Woman had once been supreme" and that "in France she still seemed potent, not merely as a sentiment but as a force," he asks, "Why was she unknown in America?" (384). The Puritan sense of sin and the repression of sex were part of the answer; the eager acceptance and rapid multiplication of the means of material progress provided the rest. "An American virgin would never dare command; an American Venus would never dare exist" (385). The spiritual and creative power of sex in Adams's America was supplanted by the machine, and he, like Melville decades earlier, pursued the track of frightening new forces.

One panel of Melville's literary diptych depicts the repression of Eros in the decadent Old World of morally detached, tradition-shielded bachelors, and the second suggests it even more starkly in the aggressive New World of regimented maids. To convey his vision, Melville allegorizes the clash of two principal images of value: one evoked by associations of nature and female fertility, and another evoked by industrial technology – the coldness of increased efficiency and greater reliance on mechanized production procedures. The collision of these images produces an intense sense of danger and dislocation in the shocked and sympathetic narrator, who sees in each part of the story a series of ironic epiphanies, disclosing a darkening future.

"Benito Cereno"

"Benito Cereno" is the only one of Melville's short stories based on an existing narrative describing the actual experience of a non-literary author. In rewriting one episode from Amasa Delano's *A Narrative of Voyages and Travels in the Northern and Southern Hemispheres* (1817), Melville created a remarkable study in the problems of perception. Delano's *Narrative* does have an apparent clarity and focus that "Benito Cereno" lacks; and in all likelihood the reader who dislikes the ambiguity in Melville's story might actually prefer the more assured style of the original. Delano's account obscures almost as much as it reveals, however, and Melville's exploration of individual perception and misperception creates problems that Delano never recognized. In raising these issues, Melville subjects his reader to the perceptual and conceptual difficulties that beset his protagonists. Like the Spanish sailor whose many-ended intricate knot totally confounds Captain Delano, Melville knots character, setting, symbol, and incident into a cultural puzzle, defying solution. When questioned about the purpose of the knot, the old sailor answers, "For someone else to undo" (76). This answer constitutes Melville's challenge to readers of "Benito Cereno."

Whereas the narrators of "Bartleby" and "Paradise and Tartarus" eventually register the shock of their encounters with the unknown, the narrative voice of "Benito Cereno" stays close to characters who cannot or do not articulate that something is deeply wrong. For the greatest part of its length, the third-person narrative is limited and controlled by the consciousness, values, preconceptions, and outlook of Amasa Delano, a generous, tolerant, assuredly practical man. It is his voice we hear, whether speaking to the Spanish captain Benito Cereno or to his devoted African servant Babo. But when Melville describes Delano as "a person of a singularly undistrustful good-nature, not liable . . . to indulge in personal alarms, any way involving the interpretation of malign evil in man," he raises a warning flag, made more obvious in a line of awkwardly ironic exposition: "Whether in view of what humanity is capable, such a trait implies, along with a benevolent heart, more than ordinary quickness and accuracy of intellectual perception, may be left to the wise to determine" (47). Melville had good reason to doubt that such wise readers existed in sufficient numbers to support the kind of story he aspired to write in 1855. More than any other of Melville's tales, "Benito Cereno" requires a reader willing to reread the story, ready to re-examine the circumstances and reconsider their meaning – a reader who can abandon comfortable social assumptions, relinquish the security of conventional wisdom, loosen the confines of his culture, and hear the voices of silent speakers with differing points of view.

Melville suggests, on the surface, at least, that the story concerns a benevolent American captain, Delano, coming to the aid of a weak, capricious, and inefficient Spanish captain, Benito Cereno, whose ship, the *San Dominick*, carries a cargo of African men, women, and children destined for slavery on South American plantations and led by their captain Babo. All perceptions of the truth, however, are shaded by the characters' biases. Captain Delano perceives the situation on the *San Dominick* in terms of cultural and political stereotypes drawn in part from his preference for Anglo over Hispanic colonial policy, a contrast strongly favoring Protestant America for its work ethic and Enlightenment legacy over Catholic Spain with its Inquisition legacy of superstition and intolerance. These stereotypes were probably shared by a majority of mid-nineteenth-century Americans, but when imposed on a situation artfully contrived like that of the concealed rebellion on the *San Dominick*, the stereotypes become instruments of error rather than of analysis.

Complicating these problems of perception is the story's historical framework. From the ship's figure-head, honoring Christopher Columbus, the agent of Spain who opened the New World to colonialization and exploitation, to Benito Cereno's unhappy retreat and death in the monastery of Mount Agonia in Lima, to the legalized barbarism of Babo's execution, the drama on the *San Dominick* telescopes centuries of Spanish history. The discovery of the New World and the promise of an age of Spanish glory coincided in 1492 with the crest of the Inquisition, a woefully misguided attempt to strengthen national unity and honor the Catholic faith by forced removal of the Moors and all vestiges of Islam. It aimed to demonstrate the love of Christ and his Holy Mother by forced conversion of the Jews, using an adept technology of torture. In pursuit of purity of blood, this policy of ethnic cleansing and Sephardic diaspora drove out Spain's cultural capital and helped revive commerce and the learned professions elsewhere in the lands rimming the Mediterranean – Southern Europe, Turkey, the Middle East, and North Africa. Raising empty symbols of national pride and depriving the nation of human, cultural, and economic resources, Spain defeated itself by following a course designed to protect against the diseases of modernity. It became, however, a course leading to decadence, degeneracy, withdrawal, and isolation.

Melville's readers were no doubt more familiar with this image of Spain so closed off to the influence of Renaissance, Reformation, and Enlightenment than are many modern readers. Thus even this brief summary of Spanish decline should help explain the significance of numerous otherwise unconnected details, such as the appearance of the *San Dominick* in the Chilean harbor of Santa Maria "like a whitewashed monastery" with "Black Friars" pacing the cloisters (the Dominicans, or Black Friars, were prominent sponsors of the Inquisition). Other details in the early pages refer to the ship's "slovenly neglect" as if "launched from Ezekiel's Valley of Dry Bones," its "hearse-like" aspect with the state-cabin windows "hermetically closed and calked" (48–9), the infirm "unstrung" (52) appearance of its captain, all marking the deterioration of a once imperial state and the decline of its aristocratic leaders. The fading grandeur and structural rot of this floating microcosm contrasts with the power and pride once conveyed by its heraldic castle and lion, and Don Benito is an exhausted relic, the handle of his sword projecting from an empty, artificially stiffened scabbard.

Delano's misperceptions of the true story of the *San Dominick* derive as much from persistent racial stereotypes as from national prejudices. Delano thinks he knows blacks and holds no bias; rather he admires Babo for being such a devoted and uncomplicated servant, like a dog capable of returning love and loyalty to a hard-hearted master. Fulfilling Delano's expectations, Babo projects an image of fidelity that reinforces the American's confidence. In truth, Babo plays two roles simultaneously – the one perceived by Delano and the other by Cereno, to whom he seems a heartless savage, an amoral monster inspired by pure evil. Neither the fawning dog nor the fiendish devil is the true Babo, a resourceful Third World leader. Like Bartleby and the maids of "Tartarus," Babo never speaks for himself; but unlike them, he creates a complex deception in pursuit of an ever greater strategy: employing artful cunning and purposeful violence against Old and New World oppressors. Delano and Cereno, however, are too blind to see the art of this African artifice.

With two profoundly flawed captains in apparent control of the two ships, the one individual actually in command for most of the story pretends to be a mere servant. But Babo is also the author of the phrase written in Spanish on the bowsprit beneath the bleached bones of Aranda, nominally the owner of the ship's cargo: "Follow your leader" (29). These simple words recalling a childish game warn anyone who dares to resist the insurgents that he could share the fate of Alexandro Aranda, the murdered owner of the slaves. They can also apply to Columbus, whose likeness as figurehead is replaced by Aranda's skeleton and whose Christian name ironically identifies him as the bearer of Christ's message to the New World. They are also the battle cry of the American sailors who retake the *San Dominick* from the insurgents. But most tellingly those three little words apply to their author Babo, leader of the rebellion, resourceful in life, stubbornly silent at his trial, unabashed even in death. Possessing ingenuity and insight, art and artifice, ready to die for freedom rather than live as a slave, Babo is far better equipped to lead than the two captains who for reasons of character, intelligence, courage, and experience are so conspicuously unfit.

Many readers and several critics have construed Benito Cereno's physical and psychological trauma, his tortured recognition of evil, as the central meaning of the story, and some even go so far as to identify Cereno with Melville, who they feel was similarly appalled by the immediacy and horror of evil. This identification further assumes the author's approbation of Cereno's outlook and ignores his effeteness, impotence, and inability to confront the consequences of his participation in the slave trade. His monastic withdrawal is no more adequate or admirable a way of dealing with culpability than is the carefree bachelor approach of Amasa Delano. The two men are as opposed to each other in their conceptions of the world as the two sides of a Galapagos tortoise, and their confrontation leads only to glancing communication and no real cultural understanding. Neither benefits from the other's strength or insight; they remain morally and psychologically crippled. If Amasa Delano, unscarred by pain, misery, or tragedy, lives in an ambiance of benign expectation, Benito Cereno lives with the agony of his existence and the ceaseless nightmare of memory. The American is a historical amnesiac untroubled by the past; the Spaniard is forever the victim of unforgettable trauma, stemming not only from the recent events on the *San Dominick* but also from the way the ship epitomizes the burdens of history.

The symbolism of the story points, however, to the wave of the future. The enigmatic sternpiece of the *San Dominick* bears "a dark satyr in a mask, holding his foot on the prostrate neck of a writhing figure likewise masked" (49). To Delano it conveys the image of Spanish ascendancy; to Cereno it conveys the image of the African insurgency. To the attentive reader, however, it reveals a new role for nineteenth-century America when Delano saves the terrified Spaniard with his left hand while "his right foot … ground the prostrate Negro" into the bottom of the small boat – a heraldic representation of America triumphant over decadent Europe and backward Africa (98–9).

Differing greatly in language and tone from the first two-thirds of the narrative, which is limited to the consciousness of Amasa Delano, the concluding depositions, the presumptive timeline, and the judgments that follow promise to clarify the ambiguities of the preceding text but instead add another layer of deception and rationalization. The seeming objectivity of the deposition is actually permeated by the values of the Spanish colonial establishment, unconcerned about Spanish injustice and protective of the *status quo*. Read against the undercurrent of Melville's text, it seems more like a contrived cover-up than a revelation of the truth, glossing over the civilized savagery of the Spanish and condemning black barbarities. Even the American sailors, inspired by their leader's quick suppression of Babo, follow with a pre-emptive strike resulting in an indiscriminate massacre of blacks and Spaniards, tactically similar to an urban SWAT force in our time, or to the action of an imperial power in Melville's time. ("Nearly a score of negroes were killed" (102), none of the Americans.) Thus the legalistic expression of the establishment view, in its intent to reveal the "true history of the *San Dominick's* voyage" (103), provides a socially acceptable fiction – a device Melville also employs at the end of *Billy Budd*, where the historical record leaves an account of how the mutinous foreigner Budd stabbed the patriotic Claggart and was duly executed for his crime.

The depositions follow the narrative as if to unlock its mysteries, clarify its deceptions, and offer reassurance about the system of justice. But the more attentive reader knows that the complexities of the knot have not been resolved, even though Melville has provided a key to fit the padlocked narrative. Like Atufal's shackles, the locked-up truth of the narrative remains enchained only as long as the victim, or the victimized reader, participates in the deception. The legal procedures serve to wrap the reader in new coils of deception as they seem to unwrap the old. The key in this narrative, as in life, might seem to be that no person should be merely a spectator or a follower; significant art or a meaningful life compels participation and engagement before it yields enlightenment.

In the largest and smallest of conflicts questions of leadership are bound to arise. Melville does not advocate on behalf of any of the three "leaders" in this story; instead each seems flawed congenitally or fatally. "Follow your leader," however, seems the worst and most dangerous sort of advice, words of warning turned into a national rallying cry; for to do so could mean "Never question authority," and we know Melville would have resisted that option. Deeply aware of Spain's decline from the sixteenth through the eighteenth century, and just as deeply concerned about what in the case of Amasa Delano is clearly a glaring deficiency in analytical intelligence, Melville seems to have cast a "no confidence" vote for the quality of American leadership, as he knew it; and his story leaves us wondering whether Americans today, living in what through much of the twentieth century was called the last of the "great powers," have the knowledge, experience, and will to undo the knot that Melville's contemporaries were unequipped to handle.

With sustained horror, the narrators of "Bartleby, the Scrivener," "The Paradise of Bachelors and the Tartarus of Maids," and "Benito Cereno" envision morally repellent but distinctive and recurrent aspects of American experience. The meaning of this vision – compounded of shock and (generally misguided) sympathy – is crucial to our understanding of contemporary American culture as well as the forces that have shaped it. The relevance of Melville's thought and the resonance of his art are sometimes better conveyed in the best of his short fiction than in his better-known longer works.

References and Further Reading

Adams, Henry. *The Education of Henry Adams*. Boston: Houghton Mifflin, 1974.

Bickley, R. Bruce, Jr. *The Method of Melville's Short Fiction*. Durham, NC: Duke University Press, 1975.

Dillingham, William B. *Melville's Short Fiction, 1853–1856*. Athens: University of Georgia Press, 1977.

Fisher, Marvin. *Going Under: Melville's Short Fiction and the American 1850s*. Baton Rouge: Louisiana University Press, 1977.

Fogle, Richard H. *Melville's Shorter Tales*. Norman: University of Oklahoma Press, 1960.

Gross, Seymour L., ed. *A "Benito Cereno" Handbook*. Belmont, CA: Wadsworth Publishing. 1965.

Thoreau, Henry David. *Walden*. New York: Random House (The Modern Library), 1950.

29

Fluid Identity in *Israel Potter* and *The Confidence-Man*

Gale Temple

Introduction: Nature and the Nation

In the decades between the American Revolution and the Civil War, the dynamics of social interaction in the United States changed in significant ways. What was once predominantly an agricultural, craft economy, by the mid-nineteenth century had undergone what historian Charles Sellers calls a "market revolution," a transition that "establish[ed] capitalist hegemony over economy, politics, and culture" (5). One of the most significant consequences of this shift was that citizens conceptualized themselves, and related to each other, differently. To generalize considerably, one might say that an erstwhile spirit of communal cooperation and reciprocal exchange gave way to the ideal of competitive individualism. New technologies sent mass-produced commodities such as clothing, cosmetics, home decorating items, novels, and magazines to ever-expanding markets, inspiring common citizens to adorn themselves and their parlors in ways that had previously been available only to members of the leisured class. As Richard Bushman argues, this predominantly middle-class quest for gentility configured public life as a running display, a "continuous performance, perpetually subject to criticism" (xiv). And the development of industry fueled phenomena such as urbanization, immigration, and the systemization and division of labor. In the midst of these changes, concerned citizens and social critics anxiously questioned the direction the nation seemed to be heading. To what extent, for example, should money and material goods be regarded as keys to self-actualization, or as reliable indicators of personal character? And with so many commodities available on the market for self-adornment, what exactly constituted a "true" self? Finally, how would it be possible to trust other citizens in a society where the financial transaction was rapidly becoming the primary mediator of personal interaction?

Two related developments were inspired by a desire to mitigate the greed, materialism, and superficiality that many felt grew out of market capitalism in the early nineteenth century. One was a fervent patriotic nationalism. Inspired by their victory over the British in the 1812 War, Americans wanted to believe that they and their national project were invested with providential significance. Patriotic enthusiasm gave rise to associated commodities and discourses such as fictionalized biographies of famous Americans, historical accounts of America's ostensibly divine origins, and a host of paintings and poems that tied American progress to the aesthetics of the developing landscape.[1]

The other development was Transcendentalism, a philosophy that stressed self-trust, hope in the future, and submission to what Emerson and his circle sometimes called the "Oversoul," a kind of divine poem in the sky that ideally connected individuals to each other, to nature, to their imaginations, and ultimately to their own "true" selves. To view America's past and future as underwritten by a divinely guided "nature" represented a powerful and reassuring antidote to developing anxiety about the commercialism and materialism of the age. In his essay, "Man the Reformer," for example, Emerson writes:

> What is a man born for but to be a Re-former, a Re-maker of what has been made; a renouncer of lies; a restorer of truth and good, imitating that great Nature which embosoms us all, and which sleeps no moment on an old past, but every hour repairs herself, yielding us every morning a new day, and with every pulsation a new life? (147)

Emerson believed that Americans should invest the future with new forms of hope and promise, continually "re-forming" themselves through a sort of ever-evolving ecstatic idealism. Frustrated with the mass-market ideology that seemed increasingly on the ascendant and with the mental lassitude that accompanied reliance on systems rather than the individual self, the Transcendentalists desperately wanted to believe that there was something more to America, a redemptive "truth" that could be attained if only citizens could get themselves right with the natural world.

In his novels *Israel Potter* (1855) and *The Confidence-Man* (1857), Herman Melville trenchantly critiques the notion that either patriotism or Transcendentalism might redeem the developing market. In *Israel Potter*, Melville's protagonist is a common soldier who, through a series of improbable events, interacts with American Revolutionary War heroes such as Benjamin Franklin and John Paul Jones on the most intimate of levels. Much like that of a consumer of patriotic biography or historical fiction, Israel's life is made meaningful through his fragmentary interactions with these men. Rather than finding a sense of stable, "natural" identity, however, Israel is continually set adrift once his relationships end, to find yet another meaningful engagement to give his core self meaning and legibility. Israel becomes like a consumer of the various forms of identity available in the patriotic marketplace, in a sense mirroring the ways citizens in antebellum America experienced various incarnations of what a true American could be. Through this portrayal, Melville suggests that patriotism is less a unified, organically underwritten reality than a market-mediated patchwork, a pastiche of sketches and impossible ideals that benefit the overall economy far more than the common citizens who so devotedly imbibe those ideals.

The plot of *The Confidence-Man*, like that of *Israel Potter*, is driven by the quest for a sense of integrated selfhood. The Confidence Man senses the anxieties and hopes that drive his victims, and he alters his message – his very identity – to draw those tendencies out. He wants his victims to believe that they can be fulfilled in specific ways if only they buy what he is selling, whether it is an herbal treatment for consumption, a boy for hire, or simply a buoyed sense of self-esteem. Significantly, the messages peddled by the Confidence Man are consistent with the most prominent and respected values, discourses, and institutions of nineteenth-century American life: Christian charity; the sense of hope and promise that has sustained the vision of America since the time of the Puritans; the disciplined and self-interested individualism championed by Scottish philosophers such as Adam Smith and put into practice by American icons such as Benjamin Franklin; and the sense that America itself was oriented to and guided by a benevolent nature, a logic that was central to the tenets of mid-nineteenth-century American Transcendentalism.

One might well ask why it would be such a bad thing to foster and nurture beliefs that were (and continue to be) sacrosanct to American life. For Melville, the answer to this question is that these ideals are not realizable under capitalism, at least not in any lasting sense. Rather, they open up in individuals a psychological divide between what is and what "should" be, inspiring citizens with a perpetual desire to bridge that gap in order to fulfill their mythical, ostensibly immanent potentials as Americans. The desires the Confidence Man inspires symbolize the impossible yet systemically necessary hopes that cycle individuals through new and ever evolving models of selfhood, while simultaneously directing them away from the pursuit of actual, materially recognizable forms of justice and equality.

Israel Potter: Fluid Identifications in the Patriotic Market

During a visit to London in 1849, Melville came across a small chapbook called *The Life and Remarkable Adventures of Israel Potter*. Published in 1824, the work Melville found was an account of an enlisted man who fought in the American Revolution, was taken to England as a prisoner of war, and lived most of his life there as a relative pauper, only to return to America in the twilight of his years, forgotten, penniless, and seeking a pension that he probably never received from the United States government. *The Life and Remarkable Adventures* was ghostwritten by Henry Trumbull, a popular hack writer of his day who apparently intended his work to appeal to the rising patriotic sentiment that was sweeping America in the decades after the War of 1812 (Bezanson 174–86). Trumbull's book was not alone in its portrayal of the heroic life of a Revolutionary War soldier. According to Richard Dorson, over two hundred of these works are catalogued in the United States Library of Congress, and they both appealed to and inspired a sense of national identity, patriotic allegiance, and reverence for the common men who fought for America's independence from Britain. As Dorson states, "[i]n writing their memoirs for a rising market, the patriots were catering to the new nationalism that spread throughout the land following the War of 1812. American character types had begun to emerge in newspapers, almanacs, farces, and public-house stories, the frontier boaster and the cunning Yankee, and the Revolutionary chronicles amplified these homespun heroes, giving them actual dimensions and proven triumphs" (4). The Revolutionary War veteran's narrative was part of a movement to glorify and give substance to the common man – the plucky, clever, virulently independent Yankee soldier – and to establish him as the foundation for a national patriotic identity, one in which citizens could ground their sense of the past and take pride as the cornerstone for a future based on liberty and equality not just for a select elite, but for all Americans.

Despite his best efforts, however, Trumbull's Israel seems less like a heroic Yankee soldier than a pathetic victim who somehow found himself lost in the currents of global historical change, a simple man who, although he lived most of his life in England, still fought in the Revolution and lived to tell about it and could therefore serve as a focal point for what Trumbull saw as a marketable tale. Melville must have sensed the gap between what Israel was and what his story represented him to be and decided to exploit that incongruity as a metaphor for how citizens continually seek after, but ultimately fail to realize, the patriotic ideals that the market dangles before them.

In an obviously ironic parody of the American myth of self-making, then, Melville portrays the initial stages of Israel's life as profoundly influenced by the legacy of Benjamin Franklin. Throughout his youth, Israel's enterprising spirit leads him into a series of self-interested projects aimed at elevating himself in the social hierarchy, a process that Franklin enshrined in his *Autobiography* as axiomatic to ideal citizenship for young American men. Israel is portrayed as continually aspiring to "rise up," to cultivate himself diligently in the present so that he will be able to capitalize on any favorable eventuality that might arise in the future. One sees this formula throughout Franklin's *Autobiography*. For example, because of Franklin's early interest in books, he finds that his company is more sought after than that of his boss, a slovenly man named Keimer. As he says, "My Mind having been much more improv'd by Reading than Keimer's, I suppose it was for that Reason my Conversation seem'd to be more valu'd" (57). Franklin portrays virtually every event in his life as structured according to this formula; he cultivates various aspects of himself in the present with the confidence that eventually those traits will pay dividends in the world market.

In Melville's reworking of this formula, however, Israel's preparations seem more like hollow clichés than meaningful forms of self-improvement, for they provide him with little actual material reward. When he decides to try his hand at hunting and trapping, for example, Israel is described as "qualifying himself for a marksman of men ... at Bunker's Hill." When he takes a job on a whaler, he is "still, unwittingly, preparing himself for the Bunker Hill rifle" (*IP* 9, 10). It seems that the highlight of

Israel's life will be the relatively minor role he will play in a battle that signifies in the national imagination more as a symbol than an actual wellspring for popular empowerment. Unlike Franklin, who prepares himself for a major part on the world stage, Israel's experiences all lead him to a moment that is, if nothing else, anticlimactic, for it represents the beginning of the end of his life in America. After the battle, he enrolls in the fledgling United States Navy, is promptly captured and taken back to England as a prisoner of war, and begins his life as an exile.

After making his escape from the British while in England, Israel is hired as a courier by American sympathizers there. His first mission is to carry secret documents to Franklin himself, who is at that time staying in Paris. In the face of Franklin's sage-like pronouncements and directives, Israel becomes a naïve initiate, like a schoolboy or bumpkin who implicitly and deferentially accepts Franklin's wisdom and advice. However, along with his learned and authoritative edicts, Melville's Franklin is also a petty tyrant, a self-serving, bombastic epicure masquerading as prudence incarnate, taking advantage of Israel in various ways while simultaneously providing him with abstract advice and lessons for disciplined self-abnegation. When Israel asks for wine at dinner, Franklin provides him with a lengthy lecture on how wine is a waste of time and money. Meanwhile, he pilfers Israel's cognac. When Israel expresses a wish to see the sights of Paris, Franklin instead banishes him to his room along with a dry guidebook and a copy of *Poor Richard's Almanac*. Israel momentarily feels the sting of Franklin's sententious and condescending rhetoric. When he opens the *Almanac* Franklin gives him, he stumbles upon a famous passage about social mobility: " 'So what signifies wishing and hoping for better times? We may make these times better, if we bestir ourselves. Industry need not wish, and he that lives upon hopes will die fasting, as Poor Richard says. There are no gains, without pains. Then help, hands, for I have no lands, as Poor Richard says.' " "Oh confound all this wisdom!" Israel declares. "It's a sort of insulting to talk wisdom to a man like me. It's wisdom that's cheap, and it's fortune that's dear. That ain't in Poor Richard, but it ought to be" (53–4).

Israel's dissatisfaction with Franklin's "wisdom," which represents a substitute for actual material wellbeing, epitomizes the frustration citizens often feel with the dynamics of the market. The plausible fiction behind Franklin's *Autobiography* is that Franklin's enormous fame, wealth, and success result from the humble ideals he committed himself to early in life. Franklin "speculates" in himself, and eventually that self pays dividends. For Israel, conversely, those Franklinesque ideals lead nowhere. Instead of finding significant forms of payoff, as Franklin does, for his early self-speculation, Israel continually finds himself back where he began, with the hope promised by the nationalist icons with whom he associates resolutely foreclosed. He becomes an abstract cipher, waiting for yet another ideal or icon to fill him with some form of intelligible, habitable identity. Israel's plight is a trenchant metaphor for how self-knowledge in antebellum America was increasingly animated by discourses available in the marketplace. In order to keep the market functioning smoothly, however, those ideals could not, by their very nature, provide for any sense of fulfillment, for capitalism depends on its subjects forever feeling that their current selves are inadequate and incomplete, and that their "true" selves can at some indeterminate (and perpetually deferred) stage be realized through judicious practices of commodity consumption. What is more, through this portrayal Melville subtly yet forcefully illustrates how many of the most sacrosanct middle-class ideals – forbearance, self-abnegation, thrift – are perfectly suited to maintaining the existing social hierarchy, for they encourage citizens to believe that poverty and inequality are faults of their own, even necessary prerequisites for idealized citizenship, rather than systemic flaws that benefit the wealthy at the expense of the poor.

Throughout his exile, Israel seems on a continual search for a habitable identity, a "self" in which he can feel secure and comfortable and that will belong in significant ways to the collectivity that is the nation. He impersonates, at various times, a ghost, a scarecrow, a cripple, a British sailor, but it seems he is never able just to "be himself," to arrive finally at a place either psychologically or materially where he can finally say "this is who I am." Melville implies that the notions of a divinely inspired patriotic identity that citizens could find refuge in once the detritus of social convention was shed, and of a Transcendent "true self" that could be accessed through a benign nature, are myths that generate new, market-friendly imperatives for self- and social fashioning. Israel's quest for a true self leads merely to further representational surfaces, to an infinite regress of textualized and commodified identity forms like those available in popular and patriotic historical accounts, and in fictionalized reworkings of America's past like those epitomized in the Revolutionary War veteran's narrative.

Israel's remarkable tendency to take on an identity that complements those whom he encounters is epitomized in his interaction with John Paul Jones. While in the presence of Franklin Israel seems to be a countrified simpleton, but with Jones he becomes a waggish, swashbuckling punster. In response to Israel's claim that he despises the British, Paul enthusiastically exclaims, "By heaven, you hate so well, I love ye. You shall be my confidential man; stand sentry at my cabin door; sleep in the cabin; steer my boat; keep by my side whenever I land. What do you say?" Israel's response seems totally out of keeping with the personality he manifests with Franklin:

> "I shall be a vice to your plans, Captain Paul. I will receive, but I won't let go, unless you alone loose the screw."
> "Well said. To bed now; you ought to. I go on deck. Good-night, ace-of-hearts."
> "That is fitter for yourself, Captain Paul; lonely leader of the suit."
> "Lonely? Aye, but number one cannot but be lonely, my trump."
> "Again I give it back. Ace-of-trumps may it prove to you, Captain Paul; may it be impossible for you ever to be taken. But for me – poor deuce, a trey, that comes in your wake – any king or knave may take me, as before now the knaves have."
> "Tut, tut, lad; never be more cheery for another than for yourself. But a fagged body fags the soul. To hammock, to hammock! while I go on deck to clap on more sail to your cradle."
> And they separated for that night. (92–3)

Israel's identity shifts in accordance with the character or discourse with whom he interacts. Jones's swashbuckling rhetoric inspires Israel with a similar sense of patriotic fervor. However, Israel never really benefits from his patriotism, at least not in the same way Jones does. After a significant naval victory, for example, Melville's narrator wryly says, "This cruise made loud fame for Paul, especially at the court of France, whose king sent Paul a sword and a medal. But poor Israel, who also had conquered a craft, and all unaided too – what had he?" (113). Patriotism itself, the novel suggests, enlists common citizens in the prosecution of the larger demands of the nation and its economy, while simultaneously redirecting their energies away from profound forms of injustice and inequality throughout the socio-economic system. What is more, the extreme acts of violence that Israel commits while under Jones's aegis – in the battle between the *Richard* and the *Serapis*, for example, Israel drops a grenade down the hatchway of the *Serapis*, "instantly" killing "more than twenty men" and wounding "nearly forty" more (127) – illustrate how patriotism is often a justification for overt acts of aggression, receiving its sanction from the ostensible interests of the nation. The fictions that drive the patriotic market, then, are not merely empty commodities, but powerful ideological weapons that encourage the Israel Potters of the world to fight for ideals that never significantly propel them up the socioeconomic ladder, but rather enable the continuing revolutions of self and nation that drive the market and benefit those who already possess wealth and power.

If Melville's novel suggests that patriotism is a construct that drives the capitalist market while simultaneously taking advantage of the poor and benefiting the wealthy, what model for citizenship and national belonging should be offered in its stead? And if the notion of a "true" self is a market-mediated construct, how should individuals begin to forge more ethically responsible and empowering identities for themselves and their communities in the absence of patriotic master narratives? At one of the lowest points in his life as an exile, Israel seems to find at least a semblance of a response to this dilemma. He is forced to take a job as a brick-maker, standing in a pit of mud all day filling molds with clay. Instead of actively furthering the interests of his nation, Israel finds himself, ironically, "helping, with all his strength, to extend the walls of the Thebes of the oppressor." In the midst of this environment, standing knee-deep in the soil, Israel thinks to himself, "What signifies who we be, or where we are, or what we do? . . . Kings as clowns are codgers – who ain't a nobody? . . . All is vanity and clay" (157). For Melville, humanity itself holds an innate dignity. National allegiance is not a matter of concern for men like Israel, just as it matters little for his fellow brick-makers in the pit. They are united by their common membership in a class for whom patriotic allegiance is less a form of empowerment than a shunt, an ideological ruse that focuses their energies and their hopes on impossibly commodified ideals rather than on their more legitimate interests, which might be, for example, finding a way to achieve a greater sense of equality in the here and now than in the oft-glamorized future.

In the end, however, Melville's novel suggests that market fictions are far more appealing than the reality of plebeian veterans such as Israel, who finally returns to his native home after a life of exile in England, arriving on the day of the fiftieth anniversary of the battle of Bunker Hill. Israel is nearly killed by a "patriotic triumphal car ... flying a broidered banner, inscribed with gilt letters" that reads: "BUNKER HILL. 1775. GLORY TO THE HEROES THAT FOUGHT!" (167). The "actual" hero, in this case Israel, is not particularly heroic, and as such does not have significant market appeal. The market representation, however, *is* appealing, and symbolically leaves Israel in its wake. Melville's novel suggests that appealing fictions overwhelm the stories of common men and women whose lives do not often mirror prevailing stereotypes, and even more often do not support the prevailing trajectories of the patriotic marketplace.

Confidence, Commerce, and Contingent Identity

If *Israel Potter* is about the futile search for an intelligible patriotic identity, *The Confidence-Man* is about its titular character's ability to shift his identity in order to make dupes of those with whom he interacts. *The Confidence-Man* is an unusual novel, even by Melville's standards. The plot has no significant rising action, no identifiable climax; no actions are undertaken either to create or resolve major crises. It is often difficult to tell just exactly who is speaking, for characters are usually identified not by name or by degrees of heroism or villainy, but merely by flat, seemingly mundane descriptions: the "man with the weed," the "cosmopolitan," the "sophomore," the "man with the brass plate," the "good merchant," and so on. Part of this difficulty can be explained by considering the setting of the story, which is a paddle-wheeled steamboat called the *Fidèle*, traveling from St. Louis to New Orleans. The *Fidèle* symbolizes a fluid world, not just of climate and geography, but of the very selves that inhabit that world. One might think of the *Fidèle* as a community where individuals relate to each other not on the basis of genealogy or shared ties to a specific locale, but by virtue of their common linkage to the economic framework that was coming to dominate virtually all aspects of life in the mid-nineteenth century, that is, market capitalism. Melville describes passengers on the *Fidèle* as "[m]erchants on 'change' " who "buzz" the decks. "Auctioneer or coiner, with equal ease, might somewhere here drive his trade" (*CM* 8). Modern community and modern market are virtually synonymous on the *Fidèle*, for interpersonal action is mediated by the commercial transaction, a contractual form of engagement that symbolizes the shifting nature of public relationships in nineteenth-century America. The passengers, too, are remarkably variegated:

> Natives of all sorts, and foreigners; men of business and men of pleasure; parlor men
> and backwoodsmen; farm-hunters and fame-hunters; heiress-hunters, gold-hunters,
> buffalo-hunters, bee-hunters, happiness-hunters, truth-hunters, and still keener

hunters after all these hunters . . . . Dives and Lazarus; jesters and mourners, teetotalers
and convivialists, deacons and blacklegs; hard-shell Baptists and clay-eaters; grinning
negroes, and Sioux chiefs solemn as high-priests. In short, a piebald parliament, an
Anacharsis Cloots congress of all kinds of that multiform pilgrim species, man. (9)

The passengers on the *Fidèle* are not linked in any sort of natural way; instead, they
are connected through their common membership in a globally oriented socioeconomic field distinguished by what the narrator calls "hunting" – after profits, after
each other, after various forms of social distinction or ascendancy. They epitomize
what C. B. Macpherson describes as a "possessive market model" of society, for as
participants in a perpetually pan-competitive network they are forever seeking
advantage in various forms, while at the same time protecting themselves from the
incursions of others into their own right to "pursue." According to Macpherson, in a
society linked through market exchange no citizen is ever exempt from the spirit of
competition:

> Since the market is continually competitive, those who would be content with the level
> of satisfactions they have are compelled to fresh exertions by every attempt of others to
> increase theirs. Those who would be content with the level they have cannot keep it
> without seeking more power, that is, without seeking to transfer more powers of others
> to themselves, to compensate for the increasing amount that the competitive efforts of
> others are transferring from them. (59)

Much like the participants in Macpherson's possessive market model, the figures on
Melville's steamboat each have an agenda – whether it is proselytizing for a religion,
seeking after a husband, or finding a gullible victim for their own profit-making
ventures – and this phenomenon creates an environment both of anticipation and
paranoia, for the nature of the transaction configures all others in the social milieu
always as either potential victims or potential victimizers.

In the midst of this environment of competitive paranoia, even charity itself is
thrown into question. Melville suggests that to be charitable is often less an act of
disinterested Christian selflessness than a way of reinforcing social hierarchy in a
society that, while championing egalitarianism, nevertheless makes resolute distinctions between social classes and races. Early in the novel, the Confidence Man
disguises himself as a crippled Negro called "Black Guinea" who performs for the
passengers on the *Fidèle* in exchange for alms. Guinea "shuffles" about on the deck,
"throwing back his head and opening his mouth like an elephant for tossed apples at a
menagerie; when, making a space before him, people would have a bout at a strange
sort of pitch-penny game, the cripple's mouth being at once target and purse, and he
hailing each expertly-caught copper with a cracked bravura from his tambourine"
(11). The passengers are charitable toward Guinea, offering him money ostensibly
because he is doubly disenfranchised as a black man and a cripple. But perhaps more
significantly, their charity is also a form of entertainment, one that is based on

viewing blacks as minstrel figures. Black Guinea shuffles about Jim Crow-style, "hailing" each of the coins tossed into his mouth by shaking his tambourine, sycophantically appealing to the whites' desire for commodified racial stereotypes. Charity is palatable for the *Fidèle*'s passengers because it involves a contractual give and take; they give Black Guinea money and take from him a good show and a reassuring sense of racial superiority.

All at once, however, at the prompting of an apparently skeptical malefactor, the crowd begins to mistrust the "authenticity" of Guinea's minstrel-show act. "Is he, or is he not, what he seems to be?" – asks the Episcopal minister about Guinea later in the voyage (29). This question is not so simple to answer, for it points to the difficulty of making clear distinctions between "seeming" and "being" in mid-nineteenth-century American life. On the one hand, Black Guinea is obviously *not* what he seems, for he is "actually" the Confidence Man in blackface, playing the role of Jim Crow in order to fleece the *Fidèle*'s passengers of their money. On the other hand, however, he is exactly what he seems, a performer, with behavioral characteristics that were certainly no less real than those manifested by slaves in their relationships to white masters who demanded what Frederick Douglass called "crouching servility" from their underlings (46), or "real" African Americans who performed on minstrel stages throughout the country, or even Harriet Beecher Stowe's Jim Crow figures. One could argue that the distinction the passengers demand between "seeming" and "being" is impossible to make, a false binary invoked in order to help them concep-tualize learned racial characteristics, as well as the hierarchies those characteristics enable, as natural. "Nature," Melville implies, is often a market fiction generated to appeal to a consuming public hungry for non-threatening, entertaining stereotypes that confirm existing visions of the social status quo.

Black Guinea's disguise opens up the possibility that all forms of identity are based on what Judith Butler calls "performativity," on "acting" in accordance with the various cues, assumptions, and norms of a given social milieu (12). Melville's novel suggests that in a society based on market exchange, citizens temporarily take on identities in the moment of the financial transaction. For example, when the Confi-dence Man, disguised as the "man with the weed," encounters a merchant whose card he has acquired while in his previous disguise as Black Guinea, he pretends to be an old acquaintance. The man with the weed says to the merchant: " 'Are you not, sir, Henry Roberts, forwarding merchant, of Wheeling, Pennsylvania? Pray, now, if you use the advertisement of business cards, and happen to have one with you, just look at it, and see whether or not you are the man I take you for' " (19). The identity of "Henry Roberts, forwarding merchant" is not, in this case, a providentially inspired, predestined thing. Instead, it is inseparable from how he functions within the relationships established by the market. When his identity is briefly thrown into doubt by the Confidence Man's masquerade, he refers to his business card, a two-dimensional textual representation rather than an organically determined reality. What is more, the man with the weed does not ask if his interlocutor "is" Henry Roberts; he instead asks if he is the "man I take you for," indicating that for both characters, the nature of identity itself is fluid and transitory, a thing that comes into being as a way of mediating contractual personal engagements in a society based on perpetual exchange.

The Confidence Man does not so much coerce his victims as draw out their latent tendencies, opening them up to the trust that is necessary to involve them in a commercial transaction. Confidence is necessary for the aspirations that inspire citizen-consumers to seek after new and ostensibly improved versions of themselves, and the Confidence Man agitates to keep those aspirations active, for without them, the capitalist economy would eventually stagnate. As the Philosophical Intelligence Officer says to the shaggy Missouri misanthrope, "Confidence is the indispensable basis of all sorts of business transactions. Without it, commerce between man and man, as between country and country, would, like a watch, run down and stop" (128). The Confidence Man reassures his victims, providing them with a solid footing for what they want and how they might obtain it. He offers them a temporary mooring point for their otherwise fluid identities, a temporarily stable "self" that will then serve as the site of a commodity engagement. Perhaps the most significant of these mooring points is the ideal of nature, which the Confidence Man repeatedly deploys as a way to lend authority and authenticity to his products and messages. For example, the "omni-balsamic reinvigorator" ointment that he peddles is so potent because it comes from nature, he says, rather than from the more invidious "science," which he calls "atheistical," and "occult," "scarce compatible with reverential dependence upon the power above" (79). The effectiveness of the nature invested in the omni-balsamic reinvigorator depends upon the consumer's ability to trust that it will work in his or her favor. As the Confidence Man says to the invalid, " 'Hope is proportioned to confidence. How much confidence you give me, so much hope do I give you. For this,' lifting the box, 'if all depended upon this, I should rest. It is nature's own' " (81). Nature, in this case, is less a concrete phenomenon than an abstract sense of imaginative speculation, dependent upon one's ability to become, as Emerson might have said, childlike, reverential, and willing to trust in his or her inevitable progression.

The ideal of a benevolent nature that would serve as the ethical and foundational backdrop for American progress was axiomatic to all sorts of institutions and discourses in the mid-nineteenth century. For Emerson and the Transcendentalists, faith in nature was inseparable from faith in the human imagination to continually remystify existence, to reinvest everyday life with drama, wonder, and reverence. Emerson encourages his followers to restore to their lives "truth and good, imitating that great Nature which embosoms us all, and which sleeps no moment on an old past, but every hour repairs herself, yielding us every morning a new day, and with every pulsation a new life." The important thing about Emerson's directive is not so much the final success of the endeavor, but the process itself. As he writes, "it would be like dying of perfumes to sink in the effort to reattach the deeds of every day to the holy and mysterious recesses of life" (156). To invoke nature, then, is akin to invoking the spirit of confidence, a sense of imaginative reinvestment that encourages citizens to strive for new incarnations of self, each of which requires new commodities and new forms of self-adornment that help to keep the market viable and active. As such, nature plays a vital role in nineteenth-century justifications for a market logic, for it is foundational in that one can invest in it one's product claims, one's self, one's notion of final truth, but at the same time it shifts, mutates, and develops in keeping with the revolutions (or, in Emerson's parlance, "reformations") of self that the marketplace requires.

Just as the Transcendentalists promised imaginative rebirth for those who would reacquaint themselves with the soil, the Confidence Man sells "promise" as intrinsic to nature. In the exchange between the PIO man and the shaggy, misanthropic Missouri bachelor, the Confidence Man gently insinuates that despite whatever current behavioral shortcomings his boys-for-hire might manifest, they contain within themselves the "seed" of something far better. In the words of the PIO man:

> Suppose a boy evince no noble quality. Then generously give him credit for his prospective one. Don't you see? So we say to our patrons when they would fain return a boy upon us as unworthy. "Madam, or sir, (as the case may be) has this boy a beard?" "No." "Has he, we respectfully ask, as yet, evinced any noble quality?" "No, indeed." "Then, madam, or sir, take him back, we humbly beseech; and keep him till that same noble quality sprouts; for, have confidence, it, like the beard, is in him." (122)

The PIO man's logic is replete with similar analogies. He identifies a trait currently lacking in the boys he hires out, then compares it to a similar phenomenon in nature, where the wanting quality inevitably metamorphoses into something better and higher. If a boy is a rascal, says the PIO man, he tells the patron to "wait till, in the now swift course of nature, dropping those transient moral blemishes you complain of, [the boy] replacingly buds forth in the sound, even, beautiful, and permanent virtues" (123).

In one sense, the PIO man's argument is generous and optimistic, characteristic of the forward-looking rhetoric of the time about the progress of the young nation and the citizens who comprised it. As Thomas Jefferson argued in 1816, for example, "laws and institutions must go hand in hand with the progress of the human mind. As that becomes more developed, more enlightened, as new discoveries are made, new truths disclosed, and manners and opinions change with the circumstances, institutions must advance also, and keep pace with the times. We might as well require a man to wear still the coat which fitted him when a boy, as civilized society to remain ever under the regimen of their barbarous ancestors" (1401). Jefferson imagines an inevitable and immanent progression in the American character, an abiding faith that each successive stage will represent an improvement over its predecessor. At the same time, however, as evidenced by the PIO man's logic, this sort of forward-looking optimism is also an ideal sales pitch, ideal because sanctioned by nature itself. The inevitable "natural" progress of the boy is always oriented to the desires of the "patron." The hope and promise inherent in the boy, then, are ripe for exploitation via the market in that they allow for the infinite *potential* fulfillment of the future, but at the same time depend upon an incomplete, undeveloped, inadequate present. As Wai-chee Dimock effectively puts it, this dynamic represents "the commodification of time, the incorporation of the future into the structure of the commodity" (196). In other words, "confidence" as it is represented in Melville's novel is tantamount to belief in what Dimock calls the "promising self" (196), a notion of identity that is under-pinned by belief in the *future* fulfillment perpetually dangled by the commodity form.

In *Israel Potter*, patriotism represents a set of ideals that encourage citizens to imbibe new imperatives for self-fashioning, all the while holding back any final, definitive fulfillment or self-actualization. Similarly, in *The Confidence-Man*, nature helps to justify the myriad new incarnations of self required by the market as further represen-tations, or further stages, in the ostensibly natural development of the "true" self. For Melville, however, nature, at least as invoked by the Transcendentalists, was less a mystical, timeless ideal than it was an unreflective, solipsistic form of self-justifying logic. John Moredock, the "Indian Hater Par Excellence," merely acts according to his nature when he kills Native Americans, just as the "savages" he so despises are apparently acting in accordance with the nature that lies within them, either dormant or expressed, when they act as scoundrels. Mark Winsome, Melville's fictionalized Emerson, so admires the viper, a "perfectly instinctive, unscrupulous, and irresponsible creature" (190), because it is perfectly self-absorbed, a world unto itself, seeking only after gratification according to its nature, and in no way accountable to other creatures. In fact, according to Winsome, it is the duty of other creatures to give the rattlesnake a wide berth, for nature "marks" creatures in accordance with their core essence. "[W]hoever is destroyed by a rattle-snake," says Winsome/Emerson, "it is his own fault. He should have respected the label" (191). Nature, for Winsome, is an ideal that justifies a logic of self-protection and personal freedom without accountability. Winsome's philosophy envisions a universally competitive social milieu in which the primary imperatives are allegiance to self, vigilant policing of the boundaries of one's own personal sovereignty, and an active faculty for "reading" the signs of other citizens' natures.

Winsome's philosophy, despite its airy and mystical trappings, is based in a profound sense of social paranoia, for it calls for the promotion of one's own best interest while simultaneously protecting oneself against the self-interested exertions of others. Not surprisingly, the market both fosters and thrives on this dynamic, for an atmosphere of anxiety and alienation prevents any sense of self or social stability while inspiring a running desire for commodities that promise safety and protection. This process is dramatized in the novel's final scene, when the cosmopolitan converses late at night with a snowy-haired and distinguished man in the gentleman's cabin. As the two discuss the biblical Apocrypha, a sort of gypsy boy, "a juvenile peddler" in motley array, approaches them. The items the boy sells are intended to help protect travelers from petty criminals: "the traveler's patent lock," which fastens to one's cabin door to prevent burglaries; a money belt, which conceals one's money from pickpock-ets; and finally, as a bonus for the two previous purchases, a "Counterfeit Detector," which is a paper detailing how one can tell true from counterfeit bills (245, 246). The self-protective paranoia that Mark Winsome lauds – one should be on the lookout for signs, or markings, of potential victimizers, for nature "marks" confidence men just as it marks the rattlesnake – helps to keep the market fresh, for it inspires in citizens a continuing desire to protect themselves. That self-protection takes the form of judicious buying; one consumes one's way to a safe space, just as the snowy-haired gentleman attempts to do by purchasing trinkets from the gypsy boy, who more than anything else is selling fear. Paradoxically, then, the gypsy inspires fear and paranoia – a lack of confidence – only then to suggest that the products he sells, such as the "counterfeit detector," will bring confidence that the fear of others (like himself) can be overcome.

Conclusion: Market Resistance

Israel Potter dies, significantly, on "the same day that the oldest oak on his native hills was blown down" (169). To a degree, then, Israel is connected with the nature of his homeland, his death symbolically linked with that of the landscape. There exists, in this sense, an actual geographical home for Israel to which he finally returns, and although he never fully regains the sense of belonging and identity stability promised by his early life, he does find a semblance of a resting place after his exile in England. Melville's novel also attempts to redeem the memory of Israel, a common man whom the narrator calls a "plebeian Lear or Oedipus," by entering his work into the literary marketplace (161). The market will paradoxically serve as a site of redemption for a man whose story was in many ways co-opted by that same literary marketplace. But rather than telling a stirring, jingoistic tale about a triumphant Revolutionary hero, as Trumbull attempts to do, Melville redeploys Israel's story to represent his struggles in the face of a society that cares more for saleable clichés than for the often disagreeable implications of lived histories. Israel Potter, both as man and as novel, disrupts the complacency of a society inextricably wedded to the logic of the market.

The Confidence-Man, however, is a very different work. One gets the sense that by the time Melville wrote it, he saw no way out of the dynamics of the market, for all forms of desire and rebellion, the novel implies, can be absorbed by the logic of capitalism. By the end of the novel, the principal villain (if such a villain even exists) has not been arrested and brought to justice, nor have the conflicts raised in the work run their course so that life can return to some semblance of normalcy. Instead, the snowy-haired old man retires to his cabin, carrying a chamber-pot that he mistakenly thinks is a life-preserver. "Something further may follow of this masquerade," the narrator intones (251). The old man's desire for self-protection is less a form of justifiable prudence than yet another in an endless succession of gullings. The processes represented in the book have a cyclical quality; new victims will pop up for the Confidence Man like a series of ducks at a carnival game on a mechanical loop, and he will continue to alter his identity in keeping with their ever-novel hopes and desires. The "masquerade" that serves as a metaphor for America's nineteenth-century socioeconomic milieu has no endpoint, no foundational reality that can be unearthed once the accretions of social forms and institutions have been stripped away. Instead, one finds only further layers of fictionalized representation in the continuing revolutions and re-formations of the market, and the fluid identities that inhabit it.

And yet perhaps it is this very fluidity that allows Melville's final novel a space for resistance amidst an all-devouring market, for in its liberating, even exhilarating, deployment of irony and narrative free play, *The Confidence-Man* evades readerly attempts at definitive classification or comprehension. Much like the character of the Confidence Man, Melville seems to take a perverse pleasure in thwarting his readers' expectations, denying them any sense of closure to the conflicts generated by the narrative, and effectively thumbing his nose at the imperatives of the literary marketplace. Perhaps for Melville, humor – albeit a sort of reckless, desperate humor – represents the most viable way to achieve a space for personal sovereignty in a society that takes itself, and its desire for material gain, far too seriously.

NOTE

1 For more on American optimism surrounding the ideal of progress after the War of 1812, see Feller, *The Jacksonian Promise*. For more on the significance of nature to antebellum American art, politics, economic institutions and so on, see Horwitz, *By the Law of Nature*.

ACKNOWLEDGMENT

For their help and suggestions with various incarnations of this essay, I would like to thank Chris Castiglia, Danny Siegel, Cheryl Temple, and particularly Wyn Kelley. This essay is dedicated to Samuel Charles Temple, who occasionally slept while his father wrote.

REFERENCES AND FURTHER READING

Bellis, Peter. "Autobiography as History as Fiction." *American Literary History* 2 (1990): 607–26.

Bezanson, Walter. "Historical Note to *Israel Potter*." In *Israel Potter: His Fifty Years of Exile*. By Herman Melville. Ed. Harrison Hayford, Hershel Parker, and G. Thomas Tanselle. Evanston and Chicago: Northwestern University Press and the Newberry Library, 1982. 173–235.

Bushman, Richard. *The Refinement of America: Persons, Houses, Cities*. New York: Knopf, 1992.

Butler, Judith. *Bodies that Matter: On the Discursive Limits of "Sex."* New York: Routledge, 1993.

Castronovo, Russ. *Fathering the Nation: American Genealogies of Slavery and Freedom*. Berkeley: University Press of California, 1995.

Chacko, David and Alexander Kulcsar. "Israel Potter: Genesis of a Legend." *William and Mary Quarterly* 41 (1984): 365–89.

Christophersen, Bill. "Israel Potter: Melville's 'Citizen of the Universe.'" *Studies in American Fiction* 21 (1993): 21–35.

Dimock, Wai-chee. *Empire for Liberty: Melville and the Poetics of Individualism*. Princeton, NJ: Princeton University Press, 1989.

Dorson, Richard. *American Rebels: Narratives of the Patriots*. New York: Pantheon Books, 1953.

Douglass, Frederick. *Narrative of the Life of Frederick Douglass*. 1845. In *Frederick Douglass: The Narrative and Selected Writings*. Ed. Michael Meyer. New York: Modern Library, 1984. 3–127.

Emerson, Ralph Waldo. "Man the Reformer." 1841. In *The Collected Works of Ralph Waldo Emerson*. Ed. Alfred R. Ferguson, Joseph Slater et al. Vol. 1. Cambridge, MA: Harvard University Press, 1971. 141–60.

Feller, Daniel. *The Jacksonian Promise: America, 1815–1840*. Baltimore: Johns Hopkins University Press, 1995.

Franklin, Benjamin. *The Autobiography of Benjamin Franklin: A Genetic Text*. Ed. J. A. Leo LeMay and P. M. Zall. Knoxville: University Press of Tennessee, 1981.

Horwitz, Howard. *By the Law of Nature*. Oxford: Oxford University Press, 1991.

Jefferson, Thomas. "Letter to Samuel Kercheval on Reform of the Virginia Constitution." 1816. In *Thomas Jefferson: Writings*. Ed. Merill D. Peterson. New York: Library of America, 1984. 395–403.

Karcher, Carolyn. *Shadow Over the Promised Land: Slavery, Race, and Violence in Melville's America*. Baton Rouge: Louisiana State University Press, 1980.

Lackey, Kris. "The Two Handles of Israel Potter." *College Literature* 21 (1994): 32–45.

Macpherson, C. B. *The Political Theory of Possessive Individualism*. London: Oxford University Press, 1962.

Rampersad, Arnold. *Melville's* Israel Potter*: A Pilgrimage and Progress*. Bowling Green, OH: Bowling Green University Press, 1969.

Reagan, Daniel. "Melville's *Israel Potter* and the Nature of Biography." *ATQ* 3 (1989): 257–76.

Reising, Russell. *Loose Ends: Crisis and Closure in the American Social Text*. Durham, NC: Duke University Press, 1996.

Rogin, Michael. *Subversive Genealogy: The Politics and Art of Herman Melville*. Berkeley: University Press of California, 1979.

Samson, John. *White Lies: Melville's Narratives of Facts*. Ithaca, NY: Cornell University Press, 1989.

Sellers, Charles. *The Market Revolution: Jacksonian America 1815–1846*. New York: Oxford University Press, 1991.

30

How *Clarel* Works

Samuel Otter

In a review of Melville's *Clarel: A Poem and Pilgrimage in the Holy Land*, which appeared in the Chicago *Tribune* on July 1, 1876, shortly after Melville's book was published, the writer offers a curious, accurate observation. After criticizing the meter and syntax of the poem, the "very hard, eight-syllable verse" and "the strange jumbling of the language" (complaints that continue to be made by many readers), the reviewer suggests that "the manufacture of the poem must have been a work of love. It bears internal evidence of having been labored over as a blacksmith hammers at his forge, and only a mastering passion for the severest task-work could have sustained the author through it all" (Higgins and Parker 534).

Although the reviewer is frustrated by Melville's poetic choices, he acknowledges the strenuous effort and artistic devotion involved in the "manufacture of the poem." Melville's recent biographer, Hershel Parker, reminds us that *Clarel* was indeed a labor of love. The book had its sources in Melville's experience on a trip to Europe and the Levant in 1856–7, the journal he kept during his travels, his study of poetry (especially British poetry) and poetics, and his reading about the "Holy Land". Melville toiled on *Clarel* for longer than on any other book he wrote. It was a work of love and also a work about love: the love (and fear of and longing) for God, the love of learning and artistic craft, the love of man for woman and man for man. Like *Mardi*, *Moby-Dick*, and *The Confidence-Man*, *Clarel* aspires to be encyclopedic. Melville writes about a variety of topics: Protestantism, Catholicism, Judaism, comparative world religions, settler colonialism in Palestine and the United States, the meanings of "America" (one character, Ungar, a scarred Confederate veteran of the Civil War, delivers a blistering indictment of moral hypocrisy and "civic barbarism" in the "New World"; see Part 4, canto 21), European revolution, democracy, selfhood, psychology, sexuality, manliness, tourism, landscape (urban, desert, ocean, Palestinian, Pacific, American), speech, and silence. *Clarel* is a Victorian poem of faith and doubt articulated on a global scale. It is a remarkable, puzzling book. For the student, it offers relatively uncharted literary terrain.

In four parts, 150 cantos, and nearly 18,000 lines of mostly iambic tetrameter (with inverted syntax, frequent enjambment, and many irregular end rhymes), Melville describes the journey of the impressionable young Clarel, a Protestant American theology student who has come to Jerusalem in search of God, history, and self. Prevented from seeing Ruth, the Jewish American woman with whom he has fallen in love, now confined in mourning for her murdered father Nathan, Clarel accompanies several others on a journey through the desert to Jericho, the Jordan River, the Dead Sea, the Mar Saba monastery in the Judah Mountains, Bethlehem, and then back to Jerusalem. The poem's narrator contrasts these diminished pilgrims to those who set out from the Tabard Inn in Chaucer's *Canterbury Tales* (C 2.1). Among those whom Clarel encounters during his sojourn in Palestine are Celio, a young Italian who doubts his Catholic faith and church; Derwent, a facile Anglican priest; Mortmain, a Swedish exile from revolutionary Paris; Nehemiah, an American millennialist; Rolfe, an American sailor who is a quester and world traveler (and whom some critics identify with Melville himself); Vine, an elusive American artist of the beautiful and the moral (whom some critics identify with Nathaniel Hawthorne); Margoth, a German Jewish geologist and materialist; Salvaterra, a Franciscan ascetic; and the Lyonese, a young French Jew whose prodigality and sensuality tempt Clarel. When he returns to Jerusalem, Clarel learns that Ruth has died in his absence. During Easter week, he mourns and broods. On Whitsuntide, after joining the procession on the Via Dolorosa, he meditates on access and silence: "From slopes whence even Echo's gone, / Wending, he murmurs in a low tone: / 'They wire the world – far under sea / They talk; but never comes to me / A message from beneath the stone' " (4.34.49–53). Then Clarel vanishes into obscurity.

The pivotal figure in criticism of the book is Walter E. Bezanson. In the long introduction and extensive notes to his 1960 edition (reprinted as a "Historical and Critical Note" in the 1991 Northwestern University and the Newberry Press *Clarel*), Bezanson made the case for the poem as a major nineteenth-century work of art, theology, psychology, and history. (For surveys of the criticism on *Clarel*, see Bezanson, "Historical and Critical Note," 542–52; Kenny 52–69; and Parker, "Historical Supplement," 665–8.) Bezanson analyzed *Clarel* as a literary response to the disconcerting impact on Western religion of science, particularly geology, the higher criticism of the Bible, and evolution. He linked Melville's long poem with contemporary poems similar in theme written by James Russell Lowell, Emily Dickinson, Alfred Tennyson, Arthur Hugh Clough, and especially Matthew Arnold, whose work Melville knew and appreciated. Rather than seeing Melville's choice of a four-beat meter for his long poem as misguided in conception or flawed in practice, Bezanson argued that this tetrameter represented an expressive strategy: not a decline from the lyricism of his prose but "a wholly new mode of contracted discourse" whose limits imitated his thematic concern with the constrictions of modernity (507). He also noted the metrical variety provided by the many short poems that are sung, spoken, or read by the characters. Bezanson described the ways in which *Clarel* was structured in mythological and epic patterns of descent and return. He emphasized Melville's complicated character analyses and the role played by the poem's narrator. He suggested a personal register for the poem as well, speculating that Rolfe was a self-projection for the author and that, in representing Clarel's interest in Vine, Melville was replaying his own intense, frustrating relationship with the reserved Hawthorne.

Since Bezanson's edition, critics have paid more attention to *Clarel*. William H. Shurr has described the poet's inconclusiveness and the symbolic structure of the poem. Nina Baym has analyzed Clarel's sexual dilemmas, especially the tension between his heterosexual desires and his Christian ideals. Joseph G. Knapp, Vincent Kenny, and Stan Goldman have explicated the spiritual crisis in the poem, the nineteenth-century struggle between faith and doubt. For Knapp and Kenny, the poet represents, thematically and metrically, a dissonance in search of harmony, and he ultimately counsels a heroic endurance. For Goldman, who provides the most cogent theological interpretation, Melville, steeped in biblical metaphors, idioms, genres, and issues, presents an intricate dialogue among a range of voices. Responding especially to *Job*, *Ecclesiastes*, *Jeremiah*, and *Psalms*, Melville chronicles both a persistent objection and a loving submission to a hidden God. Hilton Obenzinger has shifted attention to the American and international political contexts of the poem. Focusing on characters such as the Civil War veteran Ungar and the American farmer Nathan, whose spiritual wanderings take him from the Puritanism of his ancestors to deism, pantheism, Judaism, and Zionism, Obenzinger shows how Melville criticizes providential narratives that impel colonial expansion in the New World, as well as the Old. Edgar A. Dryden has returned to questions of character in *Clarel* with a literary and philosophical emphasis. He describes a "poetics of double dealing" in which Melville uses his verbal resources to construct unstable illusions of character and to circle around issues of absence and death (147). Most recently, William Potter has expanded the religious discussion of the poem beyond Protestantism, Catholicism, and Judaism. Analyzing *Clarel* as a study of comparative religion and mythology, Potter sees Melville indicting Protestant (and especially American) individualism and materialism and searching for beliefs that transcend doctrine, sect, and nation.

Although interest in *Clarel* has grown over the past forty years, critics still tend to avoid confronting the complex "manufacture of the poem": the four-beat lines, twisted syntax, and contrived rhymes on which Melville labored. As Jenny Franchot has suggested, the "exacting trial" of Melville's poetics in *Clarel* may require a readerly perseverance, even a faith, that can be seen as imitating or extending the theological discipline in the book (182). Other critics, following Bezanson, have interpreted the meter as appropriate to the theme of the poem, deliberately reinforcing the confinements of antithesis (Knapp 23) or the truncated qualities of thought (Kenny 98). Varying this approach, Bryan C. Short has described a contest between the metrical regularity of Clarel's tetrameter and the imaginative freedom of its lyrics and its pentameter Epilogue. Impatient with the obstacles presented by Melville's rhetorical choices, Stan Goldman has suggested that *Clarel* should be read primarily as narrative, akin to prose fiction, rather than as poetry (6). Yet these approaches tend to restrict (or, in the case of Goldman, ignore) the variety and reach of Melville's poetics. Looking at what happens in Melville's lines might move our understanding beyond dismissal, abstraction, or apology. Such scrutiny might unsettle the received wisdom about how *Clarel* works and open up our sense of the poem. If we attend to the manufacture of *Clarel* – *how* it means – we might deepen our appreciation of *what* it means. In the pages that follow, I will focus on three aspects of Melville's technique – diction, meter, and rhyme – in an effort to approach the "heart" of the poem.

Words and Stones

At the level of the word, *Clarel* is stranger, more intense (and more fun) than critics have acknowledged. Melville uses the resources of poetry – line, syntax, trope, rhythm, meter, rhyme – to stress and weigh his words with a peculiar precision unavailable in prose. Take, for example, the word "stones." A hard, simple noun. Yet in the lines of *Clarel*, the word is turned and twisted until it comes to serve as a synecdoche for the poem.

In the canto "A Halt" (2.10), the narrator provides an ode to stones. This poetic interlude precedes a narrative pause in which the travelers stop for some wine, biscuits, and talk. (Melville's speaker often supplies a poetic counterpoint to the narrative rhythms of the poem.) Cataloguing the varied appearances of stones in the landscape and the Bible, the narrator extends their significance:

> Stones rolled from well-mouths, altar stones,
> Idols of stone, memorial ones,
> Sling-stones, stone tables; Bethel high
> Saw Jacob, under starry sky,
> On stones his head lay – desert bones;
> Stones sealed the sepulchers – huge cones
> Heaved there in bulk; death too by stones
> The law decreed for crime . . .
> (2.10.3–10)

Melville disrupts the meter here. In tension with the expected iambic tetrameter (four measures of unstressed then stressed syllables), some lines have six beats. The compound words, such as "well-mouths" and "Sling-stones," imply spondees (two successive stressed syllables), rather than iambs. Several of the lines begin with stresses, the first and the sixth above emphasizing the word "stones."

These irregularities diverge from the relative symmetry of the 1856–7 journal passage describing the "Stones of Judea," on which Melville based the opening lines of "A Halt": "Stony mountains & stony plains; stony torrents & stony roads; stony walls and stony feilds [*sic*], stony houses & stony tombs; stony eyes & stony hearts. Before you, & behind you are stones. Stones to right & stones to left" (*J* 90). In revising this passage, in moving from prose to poetry, in thinking across the years that separated the journal from *Clarel*, Melville has altered the rhythm. He fragments it and makes it rougher, as though the words themselves were stones, slowing the movement across the lines. Like the "bells" in Poe's famous poem "The Bells," first published in 1849, the "stones" in "A Halt" are used rhythmically to imitate their objects. Melville also specifies his stones, tying them to biblical events. Later in "A Halt" he alludes to the stones placed over Absalom in 2 Samuel 18: 6–17, the stoning of Naboth in 1 Kings 21: 1–14 and Stephen in Acts 7: 57–60, and the stones with which Christ was threatened in John 8: 59.

With repetition, as the stones accumulate over the course of the poem, they take on the aspect of characters. The nature of stones – their origin, substance, resistance, structure, use, and fate – becomes key to the meanings of *Clarel*. Are stones altars? Idols? Memorials? Weapons? Bones? Graves? Who has broken, rolled, gathered, and heaved them? Who wields them? In the passage quoted above, the narrator invokes the biblical story of Jacob, who rested his head on a stone, dreamed of a ladder from earth to heaven, and then set up the stone to mark the house of God (Genesis 28: 10–22). Are stones pillows? Pillars? How are stones turned into parables? The narrator observes that stones in Palestine are "profuse" and "suggestive," "Attesting here the Holy Writ": "Behold the stones! And never one / A lichen greens; and, turn them o'er – / No worm – no life; but, all the more, / Good witnesses" (2.10.23, 24, 27, 30–3). Yet what have the stones seen? What kind of witnesses are they? Are we? What do we learn when we behold stones?

Later in the canto "A Halt," the millennialist Nehemiah tries to remove stones to prepare the way for God, but his efforts only expose more stones. Are stones the proper object for theology? Geology? (This is the approach of the character Margoth.) Arid and omnipresent, what do stones signify? Of what totality are they the part? Are they remnant, ruin, fossil, surplus, refuse, token, omen? Are they the vestiges of some great structure, like the small vertebrae of the whale in Chapter 103 of *Moby-Dick* ("Measurement of the Whale's Skeleton"), which, detached from their spine, have become the playthings of children? Or is there no whole? Or no whole that we can know? In the last part of the poem, when the travelers see Jerusalem from a distance on their way to Bethlehem, the narrator describes the city, holy to Christianity, Judaism, and Islam, as a "Stony metropolis of stones" (4.2.12). The opening and closing repetition in this line and the tautological linking of adjective and noun emphasize both the prominence and the recalcitrance of stones.

What, the poet asks across the lines of *Clarel*, is a stone? This is a deceptively simple question, resembling the child's query – "What is the grass?" – in Whitman's "Song of Myself" (first published without a title in the 1855 edition of *Leaves of Grass*) Like "grass," the word "stone" in *Clarel* gathers significance and becomes a trope. The stones in *Clarel* invite us to reflect on how language makes its references. Melville takes the word "stone," the most literal of nouns, and turns it into a meditation on the relationship between literal and figurative meanings and between parts and wholes. The Russian theorist Victor Shklovsky helps us to understand (with a surprising echo) how and why words become tropes in Melville's *Clarel*. In the early twentieth century, Shklovsky argued for the power of art to unsettle habit and renew perception:

> And art exists that one may recover the sensation of life; it exists to make one feel things, to make the stone *stony*. The purpose of art is to impart the sensation of things as they are perceived and not as they are known. The technique of art is to make objects "unfamiliar," to make forms difficult, to increase the difficulty and length of perception because the process of perception is an aesthetic end in itself and must be prolonged. *Art is a way of experiencing the artfulness of an object; the object is not important.* (741)

Without accepting the aesthetic insulation (an "end in itself") or perceptual indulgence ("*the object is not important*") or the distinction Shklovsky makes elsewhere in the essay between poetry and prose (impeded versus smooth, opaque versus transparent), we can see the relevance of his ideas for understanding *Clarel*. Melville strives, and sometimes strains, to make beliefs, landscapes, and words "unfamiliar." Practicing what Elizabeth Renker has called a "poetics of difficulty" (13, 30), he slows down perception and insists that his readers savor the roughness. Rather than dividing perception and knowledge, as Shklovsky suggests, Melville in *Clarel* tells the story of the gap between the two and the search for their coincidence.

In *Clarel*, things happen to words, and words are felt as things. That which has been taken for granted, the stone – the emblem of the actual for both Shklovsky and Melville – is revealed as alien and resistant. To write that a stone must be made *stony*, or that Jerusalem is a "Stony metropolis of stones," is not simply redundant. The repetition reveals or regenerates the qualities of the noun, makes it vivid to perception. Such a vividness, not only as an end in itself but also as a means to comprehend the nouns, proper and improper, at the center of the poem – Palestine, America, democracy, revolution, science, God, Christ, the Jew, sin, sexuality – is one of the aims of Melville's repetitive poetics in *Clarel*. The poet seeks clarity, even in the face of obscurity or calamity.

Meter, Rhyme, and Division

While several critics have argued for Melville's tetrameter as a strategy, they tend to limit its expressive range. In such views, his four-beat line is about constraint and impediment, compared with the pliant iambic pentameter of Shakespeare or Milton. (A notable exception is Helen Vendler, who has described Melville in *Clarel* as "the most robust of the major American poets" [42].) Yet constriction is not the inevitable effect in the tetrameter poems that have been regarded as possible models for Melville, such as Samuel Butler's *Hudibras*, Byron's *Giaour*, Matthew Arnold's "Stanzas from the

Grande Chartreuse," or John Greenleaf Whittier's "Snowbound" (Bezanson, "Historical and Critical Note," 568; Parker 2: 686). Instead of treating Melville's meter as the cage for his thought, we might consider it as the structure in relation to which the poet articulates and deviates his lines. Melville describes such a relationship in Chapter 47 of *Moby-Dick*, "The Mat-Maker," when Ishmael is assisting Queequeg with his weaving:

> There lay the fixed threads of the warp subject to but one single, ever returning, unchanging vibration, and that vibration merely enough to admit of the crosswise interblending of other threads with its own. This warp seemed necessity; and here, thought I, with my own hand I ply my own shuttle and weave my own destiny into these unalterable threads. Meantime, Queequeg's impulsive, indifferent sword, sometimes hitting the woof slantingly, or crookedly, or strongly, or weakly, as the case might be; and by this difference in the concluding blow producing a corresponding contrast in the final aspect of the completed fabric; this savage's sword, thought I, which thus finally shapes and fashions both warp and woof; this easy, indifferent sword must be chance – aye, chance, free will, and necessity – no wise incompatible – all interweavingly working together. (214–15)

In *Clarel*, this play of necessity (the fixed warp of meter), free will (the poet's shuttle plying its own rhythms), and chance (the blows of a distant God) produces a remarkably varied poetic and intellectual texture.

Across the poem, and especially in the frequent debates among characters, in cantos such as "The Priest and Rolfe" (2.21), "Derwent and Ungar" (4.20), "Ungar and Rolfe" (4.21), "Derwent and Rolfe" (4.23), and in the absent dialogue of "Vine and Clarel" (2.27), Melville uses tetrameter to divide and multiply positions. As Tim Wood argues, Melville often combines a four-beat alliterative meter (almost Anglo-Saxon in its sequence of two beats, followed by a caesura or pause, and then two beats) with end rhyme to forge a poetic line particularly suited to generating binaries and juxtaposing contradictions between and within characters. For Wood, the prosody ultimately contains the contradictions, suturing what it severs. Yet Melville stresses the divisions. In the second part of *Clarel*, a Dominican friar, debating with the Anglican Derwent, blames the Protestant Reformation: "This riot of reason quite set free: / Sects – sects bisected – sects disbanded / Into plain deists underhanded" (2.25.102–4). According to the Dominican, the revolt against the one true church, the Catholic Church, has led to splitting, anarchy, and the descent from faith to reason. This disorder is reflected in his lines, with their nine syllables exceeding the expected meter. The second quoted line is cut by alliteration, caesurae, sharp stresses, and the repetition of the plosive "sect," as though it were a curse. While the narrator does not endorse the Dominican's story of origin (he is surprisingly sympathetic, though), the poem diagnoses a similar modern predicament. The meter and syntax often convey a divided spiritual, political, and sexual condition.

The landscape of Palestine, too, is sundered, not only in its profusion of stones but also in the image of the Kedron, brook and gorge, that recurs throughout the poem.

The Kedron connects three major symbolic locations, Jerusalem, the Mar Saba monastery, and the Dead Sea:

> Profoundly cloven through the scene
> Winds Kedron – word (the scholar saith)
> Importing anguish hard on death.
> And aptly may such named ravine
> Conduct unto Lot's mortal Sea
> In cleavage from Gethsemane
> Where it begins.
> (2.11.72–8)

> . . . All the mountain-land
> Disclosed through Kedron far withdrawn
> Cloven and shattered, hushed and banned,
> Seemed poised as in a chaos true,
> Or throe-lock of transitional earth
> When old forms are annulled, and new
> Rebel, and pangs suspend the birth.
> (3.21.13–19)

These two passages, the first describing the desert wilderness and the second an early-morning view from the Mar Saba heights, portray the fissure opened by the Kedron. Linking the scene of Jesus's betrayal in the garden of Gethsemane to the doomed cities of Sodom and Gomorrah near the Dead Sea, the Kedron in *Clarel* joins agony and catastrophe and marks an ending that is also a beginning, as the last enjambed half-line in the first quotation and the final image in the second imply. In the inverted chronology of the first passage, the Kedron moves from Gethsemane to the Dead Sea, from "New" to "Old" Testament. In the second passage, only the effects of the Kedron are visible: the mute rock cut and exposed. The scene, like the monastery and the pilgrims, is suspended uncomfortably between sky and earth, old and new, annulment and resistance. Something may emerge, but what? Why is birth conjoined with rebellion? In the poem, the Kedron is repeatedly associated with forms of the verb "to cleave." The verb itself is poised between transitive and intransitive meanings, between breach and intimacy: "to cleave to" and "to cleave through." On the levels of word, syntax, meter, image, and landscape, the poetry of *Clarel* often explores the spaces between positions and possibilities. (For other striking landscapes, see the cantos "Of Deserts," "Of Petra," "By the Marge," "Sodom," "The High Desert," and the Emily Dickinson-like image at the end of "The Night Ride": " . . . The valley slept – / Obscure, in monitory dream / Oppressive, roofed with awful skies / Whose stars like silver nail-heads gleam / Which stud some lid over lifeless eyes" [4.29.148–52].)

Melville the poet is fascinated with rhyme and the questions it raises. How is the space between rhymes filled? How are expectations for reappearance generated, satisfied, thwarted? In what ways do end rhymes connect different lines? When do sound and sense converge and diverge? These are questions of form in *Clarel* and also of substance. In the canto "The Recoil" (3.31), the narrator explicitly addresses the meanings of rhyme. In the preceding canto, Clarel has met a monk and pondered the life of celibacy with its allure of calm but also its troubling absence of women. His thoughts then turn to Vine, who has rejected his desires for intimacy, and then back to his betrothed Ruth, and then to the bond between the biblical David and Jonathan. Rhyme here imparts a psychological cadence. It indicates Clarel's shifting between desires for women and for men and his questioning of the relationship between flesh and spirit. At the beginning of "The Recoil" (and here again, as in "A Halt," Melville joins topic, scene, and rhythm), Clarel wonders how to reconcile the Virgin Mary's immaculacy and humanity. And then his doubts produce a response:

> But came ere long profound relapse:
> The Rhyme recurred, made voids or gaps
> In dear relations; while anew,
> From chambers of his mind's review,
> Emerged the saint, who with the Palm
> Shared heaven on earth in gracious calm,
> Even as his robe partook the hue.
> (3.31.13–19)

During this interval, Clarel is comforted by the apparent balance achieved by the blue-robed celibate and the Mar Saba Palm, which grows over the precipice. Both seem to partake of heaven on earth. (The Palm is a crucial symbol in the third part of the poem, interpreted by the major characters. See 3.25–32.) In *Clarel*, though, the equilibrium is always temporary. When the rhyme "recurs" in this canto, it brings an unexpected fit: not congruity but revulsion – a "recoil." Clarel's calm is unsettled by further questions: "Love feminine! Can Eve be riven / From sex, and disengaged retain / Its charm?" (3.31.38–40). If Eve's attraction is partly of the flesh, then is love for her impure?

Clarel is filled with end rhymes that aspire to perfection but often are partial or proliferate into larger, less regular designs. In the passage quoted above, the steady tetrameter heightens the final rhymes. "Palm" is linked with "calm," but "relapse" is also tied to "gaps." In "The Recoil," Melville joins a meditation on rhyme with an exposure of Clarel's longings and anxieties about "dear relations." Clarel's desires for Ruth are entwined with and complicated by his desires for Celio, Vine, and the Lyonese. Characters, as well as words, are arranged in patterns that link and skew. Rhyme in the poem raises larger questions about identity and correspondence. Clarel attempts to think beyond "Eve," outside of the male/female dichotomy and the constraints of standard rhyme, and to imagine a love without gender: "That *other* love!" (3.31.53). Ultimately, he responds according to convention, returning to Ruth and then assuming the role of her mourner.

The "Heart" of *Clarel*

Halfway through the long poem, in the reflexive, vertiginous canto "Prelusive" (2.35), Melville brings together theology, sexuality, psychology, and landscape, and he considers his own poetic practice in *Clarel* and artistic creativity more generally. Just before the descent into "Sodom" (the next canto), when the pilgrims will encounter the agitated waters of the Dead Sea ("Whose bubbling air-beads mount and break / As charged with breath of things alive" [2.36.8–9]) and when they will brood on what sins could have prompted the city's devastation by God, the narrator pauses and warns. He offers an extended metaphor, one of the most prolonged figures in the entire poem, in which he compares the human heart to a labyrinthine prison. The images in "Prelusive" are based on the *Carceri*, eighteenth-century etchings of imaginary prisons by the Italian artist Giovanni Battista Piranesi:

> In Piranesi's rarer prints,
> Interiors measurelessly strange,
> Where the distrustful thought may range
> Misgiving still – what mean the hints?
> Stairs upon stairs which dim ascend
> In series from plunged Bastiles drear –
> Pit under pit; long tier on tier
> Of shadowed galleries which impend
> Over cloisters, cloisters without end;
> The hight, the depth – the far, the near;
> Ring-bolts to pillars in vaulted lanes,
> And dragging Rhadamanthine chains;
> These less of wizard influence lend
> Than some allusive chambers closed.
> (2.35.1–14)

In the late 1740s, Piranesi etched on copper plates a series of fourteen designs for prints, all of which depicted confined spaces. These "Prisons" were decorated with stairs, galleries, arches, cloisters, and chains. In the early 1760s, Piranesi reworked his *Carceri*. He further etched his original designs, producing darker and more disorienting images, and he added two new prints. The second edition of the *Carceri* depicts wrenching perpendiculars, broken and jutting forms, more elaborate instruments of torture, and passages that lead into the shadows, or nowhere.

The struggle outlined at the beginning of the "Prelusive" canto – the effort to ascend through darkness, to discern what is hidden, to penetrate recesses – describes the prison, the pilgrimage, and the characters' elusive interiors. (Thomas De Quincey, the British Romantic writer, also connected Piranesi's prisons with human psychology in his *Confessions of an English Opium Eater*, which Melville had read.) Melville uses his meter and syntax to, as he puts it later in the canto, "mirage the maze." Caesurae, alliteration, and repetition split and double many of the lines: "Stairs upon stairs,"

Figure 30.1 This image, the title plate in the second edition of Piranesi's *Carceri*, is reproduced from a volume that probably was part of the nineteenth-century Astor Library, whose reference collections were open to the public during the years Melville lived in New York and worked on *Clarel*. Photo: Art & Architecture Collections, Miriam and Ira D. Wallach Division of Art, Prints and Photographs, The New York Public Library, Astor, Lenox and Tilden Foundations.

"Pit under pit; long tier on tier," "Over cloisters, cloisters without end; / The hight, the depth – the far, the near." After the first four introductory lines, whose rhymes are syntactically suspended in an abba pattern, the next eight descriptive lines repeat but also unsettle the design, presenting rhymes that unfold in a shifting array: cddccdee, with the ee syllables partially rhyming with the bb in the first quatrain. And (of course) Melville adds an extra syllable to the already polysyllabic and hard-to-scan second line about strange measures. The final line, ending with the word "closed," does not rhyme with any other, but, instead, is hinged with the first line of the next stanza.

The trick and the joke of these first fourteen lines of "Prelusive" is that this gothic space is less alarming and also less intriguing than "some allusive chambers closed" and one recess in particular:

> Those wards of hush are not disposed
> In gibe of goblin fantasy –
> Grimace – unclean diablery:
> Thy wings, Imagination, span
> Ideal truth in fable's seat:
> The thing implied is one with man,
> His penetralia of retreat –
> The heart, with labyrinths replete:
> (2.35.15–22)

"Ward" is an intricate word here. It means a specific area, but "ward" also names the divisions of space in a prison, thus reinforcing the metaphor of this canto. "Ward" also refers to the ridges projecting from the metal fitting inside a lock that oppose the turning of any key that is not of the proper form or, conversely, to the incisions in the bit of a key that permit it to pass along this fitting. That is, the word can refer both to the obstacle to opening a lock and to the structure that enables entry. This one little word, then, epitomizes the fascination of the poem and the prints: will the movement through space and time provide or balk access?

In the next lines, the allusions further etch the chambers of the heart:

> In freaks of intimation see
> Paul's "mystery of iniquity:"
> Involved indeed, a blur of dream;
> As, awed by scruple and restricted
> In first design, or interdicted
> By fate and warnings as might seem;
> The inventor miraged all the maze,
> Obscured it with prudential haze;
> Nor less, if subject unto question,
> The egg left, egg of the suggestion.
>   Dwell on those etchings in the night,
> Those touches bitten in the steel

By aqua-fortis, till ye feel
The Pauline text in gray of light;
Turn hither then and read aright.
(2.35.23–37)

In the "Prelusive" canto, we enter the "Prisons," climb up and down the stairs, go back and forth across the tiers, drag our chains, use our key, enter the sanctum, and find . . . a heart. This heart is not inscribed with the Spirit of the living God, as Paul writes in his second letter to the Corinthians 3: 3. Instead, its surface, like "steel" (which Melville substitutes for Piranesi's copper), has been "bitten . . . by aqua-fortis," cut by acid like Piranesi's prints. At the end of our metaphorical journey in this canto, we find a scarred heart, and an egg. What is an egg doing in this prison? As in the phrase "very milk and sperm of kindness" in the chapter "A squeeze of the Hand" of *Moby-Dick* (416), Melville here unconventionally female and male, confounding categories.

The phrase "mystery of iniquity," from Paul's second letter to the Thessalonians 2: 7, appears again later in Melville's career. The narrator of *Billy Budd* uses it while trying to account for the character of the malevolent master-at-arms John Claggart, who falsely charges the young Billy with mutiny and is killed by his impulsive blow (76). In both *Clarel* and *Billy Budd*, the "mystery of iniquity" is associated with the promptings of the heart and particularly with the stigmatizing of male desire for other men. The phrases "heart, with labyrinths replete" and "mystery of iniquity" echo earlier and later passages concerning Clarel and Vine, human recesses, and "the negatives of flesh" (see 2.27, 3.7, 3.30). These phrases also point to the next canto, "Sodom," treating the infamous city whose sins, including sexual transgressions, were punished in a rain of brimstone and fire, according to Genesis 18 and 19. The scored heart, the "touches" compared to the bites of acid, the "penetralia of retreat," the prison bristling with hints, and the "freaks of intimation" all suggest the poet's intense and conflicted representation of male desire. Conflicted, but not condemnatory. The poet sounds the depths of such yearnings and struggles to understand them in the contexts of what the narrator of Billy Budd will describe as "fate and ban" (88).

While the heart is figured as a space of incarceration and as a surface burned by acid, both prisons and prints are also coupled with artistic creation. We can read the "inventor" who feels "restricted in first design" and who revises to "mirage all the mazes" as either a writer or a printmaker. The two activities are repeatedly linked in *Clarel*. How are impressions made? What is the character of the lines? How long do they last? How is the illusion of depth created? What do copies in a series signify? Stasis? Progress? Intensification? Disintegration? Infinity?

What are the meanings of repetition? This is one of the crucial questions in the poem. For the tourist, what does it mean to see sights in the "Holy Land" centuries after the events described in Scripture? For those who seek belief, do shrines, rituals, and sacred texts still signify an original divine presence? For the lover, does desire diminish with each new object? Is love corrupted by flesh? For the poet, and especially the poet who writes in tetrameter, do the series of twos and fours confine or redeem? For Melville in *Clarel*, what does it mean to revisit his career, his biography, and the themes, settings, and characters of his earlier books? The perversity of *Clarel* is evident in the injunction to "read aright" that climaxes the Piranesi canto, in whose designs there are no proper angles, at the center of a poem in which there are no right or final answers. The "manufacture" of *Clarel*, to once again quote the reviewer in the Chicago *Tribune*, involved the painstaking creation of spaces like the human heart that turns out to be a fantastic prison. To read *Clarel* is to wind through these labyrinths, to develop a sense of their forms, rhythms, and recesses. In the mazes of *Clarel*, God, Palestine, America, faith, science, sex, and doubt all become strange. It is a notoriously dense, yet surprisingly spacious poem – a work of complex pleasures.

References and Further Reading

Arvin, Newton. *Herman Melville*. New York: William Sloane Associates, 1950.

Baym, Nina. "The Erotic Motif in Melville's *Clarel*." *Texas Studies in Language and Literature* 16.2 (Summer 1974): 315–28.

Bezanson, Walter E. "Historical and Critical Note." *Clarel: A Poem and Pilgrimage in the Holy Land*. 1876. Vol. 12 of *The Writings of Herman Melville*. Ed. Harrison Hayford, Alma A. MacDougall, Hershel Parker, and G. Thomas Tanselle. Evanston and Chicago: Northwestern University Press and the Newberry Library, 1991. 505–637.

——. "Melville's Reading of Arnold's Poetry." *PMLA* 69.3 (June 1954): 365–91.

Cannon, Agnes Dicken. "On Translating *Clarel*." *Essays in Arts and Sciences* 5.2 (1976): 160–80.

Dryden, Edgar A. *Monumental Melville: The Formation of a Literary Career*. Stanford, CA: Stanford University Press, 2004.

Franchot, Jenny. "Melville's Traveling God." *The Cambridge Companion to Herman Melville*. Ed. Robert S. Levine. New York: Cambridge University Press, 1998. 157–85.

Goldman, Stan. *Melville's Protest Theism: The Hidden and the Silent God in* Clarel. DeKalb: Northern Illinois University Press, 1993.

Higgins, Brian and Hershel Parker, eds. *Herman Melville: The Contemporary Reviews*. New York: Cambridge University Press, 1995.

Kenny, Vincent. *Herman Melville's* Clarel: *A Spiritual Autobiography*. Hamden, CT: Archon Books, 1973.

Knapp, Joseph G. *Tortured Synthesis: The Meaning of Melville's* Clarel. New York: Philosophical Library, 1971.

Obenzinger, Hilton. *American Palestine: Melville, Twain, and the Holy Land Mania*. Princeton, NJ: Princeton University Press, 1999.

Parker, Hershel. "Historical Supplement." *Clarel: A Poem and Pilgrimage in the Holy Land*. 1876. Vol. 12 of *The Writings of Herman Melville*. Ed. Harrison Hayford, Alma A. MacDougall, Hershel Parker, and G. Thomas Tanselle. Evanston and Chicago: Northwestern University Press and the Newberry Library, 1991. 639–73.

Piranesi, Giovanni Battista. *The Prisons (Le Carceri): The Complete First and Second States*. Intro. Philip Hofer. New York: Dover Publications, 1973.

Potter, William. *Melville's* Clarel *and the Intersympathy of Creeds*. Kent, OH: Kent State University Press, 2004.

Renker, Elizabeth. "Melville's Poetic Singe." *Leviathan: A Journal of Melville Studies* 2.2 (October 2000): 13–31.

Robillard, Douglas. Introduction. In *The Poems of Herman Melville*. Ed. Douglas Robillard. Kent, OH: Kent State University Press, 2000. 1–49.

Rosenberg, Warren. "Melville's Turn to Poetry: A Genre Approach to *Clarel*." Dissertation, City University of New York, 1981.

Rosenthal, Bernard. "Herman Melville's Wandering Jews." In *Puritan Influences in American Literature*. Ed. Emory Elliott. Urbana: University of Illinois Press, 1979. 167–92.

Shklovsky, Victor. "Art as Technique." 1917. Trans. Lee T. Lemon and Marion Reis. In *The Critical Tradition: Classic Texts and Contemporary Trends*. Ed. David H. Richter. New York: St. Martin's Press, 1989. 737–48.

Short, Bryan C. "Form as Vision in Herman Melville's *Clarel*." *American Literature* 50.4 (January 1979): 553–69.

Shurr, William H. *The Mystery of Iniquity: Melville as Poet, 1857–1891*. Lexington: University Press of Kentucky, 1972.

Spengemann, William C. "Melville the Poet." *American Literary History* 11.4 (Winter 1999): 569–609.

Vendler, Helen. "Desert Storm." *The New Republic* (December 7, 1992): 39–42.

Warren, Robert Penn. Introduction. In *Selected Poems of Herman Melville: A Reader's Edition*. Ed. Robert Penn Warren. New York: Random House, 1970. 3–88.

Wood, Tim. " 'Unsearched by the Prose Critic Keen': The Versification of *Clarel*." Unpublished essay. 2000.

31

Melville the Realist Poet

Elizabeth Renker

Most serious readers are surprised to learn that Herman Melville was a poet. Once they learn how much poetry he wrote with how deep a dedication, they are doubly surprised that this part of his career was ignored when they studied Melville in college. In the world of literary criticism, where his poetry is more familiar but still not widely known, the most common account of his poetic career has been that it was a failure. This narrative explains why the poems typically do not make it into the curriculum, or from there into our culture's broader vision of Melville as an American writer.

The narrative of Melville the Failed Poet has become so entrenched in histories of American literature that the small corps of scholars trying to bring the poetry to broader attention has met with a tepid and skeptical reception. This essay will propose a new way of thinking about Melville the poet, one that I integrate with a larger challenge to the standard accounts of postbellum poetry more generally. The standard narrative of Melville's failure misconstrues both the nature of his poetry and its tense but engaged relation to its literary age. I suggest that we merely toss into the dustbin of history the phrase, "Melville the poet was a failure." The one-sentence account of his poetic career with which I want to replace that tired formulation is the following: Melville was a realist poet writing in an age of realist prose.

My proposition distills into one sentence the crux of Melville's difficulties as a poet. In an era in which poetry was often based in idealist, romantic illusions, Melville wrote poetry – but he wrote poetry of realism. In an age in which realism electrified fiction and created a lively marketplace for it, Melville abandoned fiction – and wrote poetry. He came at his poetic craft and at the literary marketplace antagonistically. Melville the realist poet thus shares with Melville the writer of fiction a brilliantly embattled engagement with genre, which Melville scholars have long recognized as one of the thorniest and most interesting aspects of his relation to art (Baym "Quarrel"). Indeed, it seems no accident that his first collection of published poems was called *Battle-Pieces*.

My case about Melville the poet challenges not only the standard account of his poetic failure. It also challenges another traditional – but equally erroneous – account about American literary history after the Civil War. As recorded by countless textbooks, anthologies, and works of scholarship, this narrative holds that American poetry between the Civil War and about 1910 was moribund; that while the classic poetic innovators, Walt Whitman and Emily Dickinson, pushed the art of poetry in radical new directions, it fell into a long quietus thereafter; and that it was only rescued by the advent of modernism in the nineteen-teens.

I use the phrase "long quietus" in this narrative of American poetic history deliberately. Melville scholars will recognize it as the phrase famously coined by Raymond Weaver in one of the first works of scholarship ever produced about Melville, the 1921 *Herman Melville: Mariner and Mystic*, a work that would inaugurate the reclamation of Melville's reputation as a great writer (an era that scholars now refer to as the Melville Revival). When Weaver conceptualized the long quietus, he envisioned Melville's three decades of prolific poetic production as an extended period of failing artistic power that amounted to nothing more than silence. I use Weaver's coinage against itself, in part to challenge his narrative of Melville's failure as poet; but I also borrow it strategically, to stress the fact that the routine story about Melville's failed postbellum poetry is very similar to the routine story told about American poetry more generally: another long period that produced negligible poems not worth a second look.

It is not accidental that these two narratives so closely resemble one another; rather, both are tied up in fundamental misconceptions about postbellum American poetry. Let me begin with the formulation that Melville was a failed poet. In greater detail, this story typically takes the following form: after the failure of his masterwork *Moby-Dick* in the literary marketplace of 1851, Melville wrote increasingly bitter and incomprehensible fiction, culminating in his last novel, *The Confidence-Man*, published in 1857; by 1866, when he turned almost exclusively to writing poetry, his career as a novelist was over and his artistic powers had been mostly extinguished. The career as a poet to which he then turned produced mostly disappointing poems that reveal how burned out he was. His genius flowered again once, in his final great work of fiction, *Billy Budd*, which he began in his last years of life and left unfinished when he died in 1891. In sum, Melville was a great writer of fiction who, having left that genre behind in 1857, fortunately returned to it in order to produce one last masterpiece.

One of the many aspects of Melville's career that this tale ignores is that, although Melville wrote and published novels for only a little more than a decade (1846–57), he wrote and published poems for more than thirty years. He published four volumes, left one volume in manuscript, and produced a substantial body of other unpublished poems. Nevertheless, standard accounts construe the three decades during which he wrote poetry as an unfortunate dark period during which he misguidedly lost touch with his real talent: writing fiction.

This account of Melville's poetic failure is bolstered by the narrative that postbellum American poetry was a period of failure. The single person most responsible for this "long quietus" narrative about American postbellum poetry is Edmund Clarence Stedman: poet, anthologist, and influential man of letters. Stedman published an anthology of American poetry in 1900 in which he refers to the period as a "twilight interval" (Stedman *Anthology* xxviii). He meant the phrase to indicate both that the greater poetic lights of earlier in the century had flickered out (he particularly loved Emerson, Poe, and the Fireside Poets) and that no major lights had yet replaced them. But American writers were producing a great quantity of published verse at late century. In fact, as Carlin T. Kindilien points out, more books of verse were published in the US between 1880 and 1900 than ever before. This marketplace was one in which romantic, realist, decadent, symbolist, and other poetic strains coexisted, a lively climate indeed (Kindilien 5). While Stedman was waiting for new poetic greats, he was blind to the changing voice of American poets ringing through his own era. He believed that genius in poetry expressed itself in an idealist, romantic, and sentimental aesthetic. Literary historians identify him as the leading voice of what they call "the genteel tradition." His ideology of the "twilight interval" is a function of his own genteel conception of poetry; by definition, it minimizes or obscures poems that do not conform to genteel standards.

It is within this framework of minimization that we must situate Stedman's assessment of Melville the poet. Stedman did not reject or condemn Melville's poetry; indeed, his 1889 *A Library of American Literature* and his 1900 *An American Anthology 1787–1900* both featured selections from Melville. (And Stedman's son Arthur, a young admirer of Melville's writing, became Melville's literary executor [Sealts *Early Lives* 47]). But Stedman's definition of the entire era as one of minor, "twilight" poetic voices gave Melville a paradoxical imprimatur as a minor poet in a landscape of similarly negligible voices. Given Stedman's ideology of poetry, we must thoroughly challenge the lukewarm way in which he approves of Melville and instead explore the ways in which Stedman and the generations of literary histories that adopted a similar narrative fundamentally misconstrued Melville's poetic project. Nancy Ruttenburg argues that *Billy Budd* is Melville's "retrospective account of his own professional failure" (348). She proposes that the metaphorics of speech in *Billy Budd* rejects both Emerson's and Whitman's visions of the national poet as essentially voiceless, a voicelessness they associate with purity and innocence.

Stedman's melancholy assessment of poetry's twilight status is based not only in what he sees as its aesthetic sluggishness. He also thinks poetry is facing a new downturn: it is losing market share as a literary product. He believes that fiction (which he calls "imaginative prose") has overtaken poetry in two crucial senses: both in popular taste (what readers most want to buy and read) and as the art form most attracting literary talent (what talented artists are most inclined to write). From the vantage of 1900, Stedman locates this shift in literary taste around 1875. In his view, prose not only overtook poetry as a popular art; prose also cultivated what he calls a "distaste for poetic illusion." In this sense, prose actively hurt the cultural position of poetry (Stedman *Anthology* xxviii). Stedman's cultural shorthand requires unpacking lest it remain remote to today's readers. When he talks about the anti-illusory, late-century developments in prose that have changed the literary terrain, he is talking specifically about the rise of realism.

The term "realism" is a complex one with a variety of definitions in philosophy, art, and literature. Generally speaking, realist projects engage the questions of what constitutes the "real," how our minds could recognize it, and how to represent it. American literary realism as a specific phenomenon in the history of art surged in the US after the Civil War for an array of social and historical reasons. Cataclysmic social changes during and after the war – a national transition from a primarily rural farm-based economy to an increasingly urban, industrial order; new large-scale systems of communication and transportation, such as the transcontinental railroad, that radic-ally changed not only the conduct of business but the routines of daily life; the growth of monopoly capital; increasing labor strife; and other equally massive transitions – changed the culture that gave rise to American art as well as the expectations and responses of its audience (Wiebe 3–4).

Like Stedman's assessment that fiction was fundamentally at odds with poetry, a long tradition of scholarship on American realism locates realism in the genre of fiction and ignores poetry entirely. Most American literature anthologies, for ex-ample, routinely address fiction by a relatively standard group of authors (such as Howells, Twain, James, the local colorists, Dreiser, and Crane), but rarely address poetry at all. Like the anthologies, conventional scholarly accounts of American realism also fail to engage poetry. Even recent articles about expanding the canon of American realism neglect poetry entirely. Cheryl Walker has pointed out that the neglect of poetry's place in American realism is a product of history, since as late as the 1930s poetry was still considered part of the realist tradition (Walker 25, 39). In this sense, contemporary scholarship on American realism reiterates the claims of Sted-man, that realist fiction so dominated the literary scene as to leave poetry a generic casualty. Stedman thought that the massive bloodshed of the war had changed poetry and diminished its cultural role because it killed so many of the young men who might have been poets (Stedman *Anthology* xvii). What he did not grasp was that it was not poetry itself but, rather, his own definition of poetry, that was the real casualty.

The two narratives of failure with which I began influence and sustain one another. When American literary histories do discuss Melville the poet, they often hold him up as an exemplar of the era's typically bad poetry. To cite only one among many such examples, Roy Harvey Pearce's influential 1961 *The Continuity of American Poetry* entirely dismisses Melville's poetry as "not of sufficient body and strength, nor of sufficient influence, to have a place in this narrative." He also derides late-century poetry in general as "uncertain and confused" (Pearce 205, 253). Melville the poet thus holds a dubious distinction. He has been most instrumental to American literary history as the consummate bad poet of an age in which the bad poet was all too familiar a figure. It is time to rewrite both of these narratives, and Melville provides an excellent case for doing so.

When I describe Melville as a "realist poet," I mean to suggest that the "distaste for poetic illusion" that Stedman saw in late-century fiction does not emerge exclusively within the genre of fiction. In Melville's case, the "distaste for" poetic illusion emerged within poetry itself. Melville's realist poetry eschews traditional poetic illusion and attempts to offer a new mode of poetic vision, one that is compatible with (although surely not identical to) the realist projects of his age. Scholars of realism such as Michael Davitt Bell and Eric J. Sundquist have pointed out correctly that the practice of realism contains tremendous variation and modes that are sometimes at odds with one another. Realism does not always look the same just because it's realism. What links various realist projects is the attempt to represent the real, with all the attendant complications, both literary and ontological, that such a project entails. Melville's realist poetry participates in this realist project; simultaneously, he engages, invokes, and rejects in lively ways the poetic conventions of the romantic and the sentimental against which realism tended to situate itself as an artistic movement. Once we see Melville the poet in such terms, as a poet specifically engaging the context of American realism, it is no longer necessary to defend him in the terms scholars sometimes use to reclaim Melville's poetry from the charges of failure: that he was a modernist ahead of his time (for example, Shetley). This argument, while conceptually appealing, is flawed by anachronism. Melville was not a modernist ahead of his time: he was a realist poet writing in an age of realist prose.

My claim that Melville was a realist poet has at least two important implications, one for American literary history more generally and one for Melville studies more specifically. First: realism as a mode in American writing was not limited to fiction, nor was it in its major forms limited to fiction. Major scholars of American realism have sensibly explored its importance to fiction; Donald Pizer, for example, points out that "realism as a literary mode was sited in the most popular literary form of the day, the novel" (Pizer 6). But while the scholarship on realist fiction is certainly compelling, necessary, and historically grounded, the shadow into which it has cast poetry of the era of realism is not. Melville's realist experiments challenge the dominant genre-bound definition of realism and call us to reassess our narrative not only of American poetic history but of American literary history more broadly.

Second: Melville's conventional designation as primarily a writer of prose working in the antebellum era of American romanticism distorts the actual shape of his career. (The term "American romanticism" has long been used in American literature scholarship to designate a broad array of literary, political, and philosophical impulses, mostly centered in celebrations of individuality and idealism. Transcendentalism is often interpreted to be its fullest flowering and, like transcendentalism, American romanticism is usually described as tapering off after 1860. It is the romanticism of the antebellum period that literary histories aptly juxtapose with the realism that becomes increasingly central in the latter half of the century.) The focus in literary scholarship on Melville the antebellum writer of fiction has elided the phenomenon of Melville the postbellum poet. The "long quietus" narrative in which Melville was not only allegedly silent but also hermetic and out of touch has sustained a surprising blindness to the fact that he lived, wrote, and published during the era of high realism. Sanford E. Marovitz has aptly pointed out that *Billy Budd* was composed during this time and is shaped by that context (Marovitz 29). Marovitz's refreshing argument is surely correct. *Billy Budd* shows throughout that it is a direct response to the confrontation between realism and romance that animated the period's debates about art. When Melville's narrator tells us in that text that Billy's stutter indicates that the story is "no romance," he is staking literary ground for *Billy Budd* as a realist work (*BB* 53).

Melville began composing what would become the novella *Billy Budd* by writing a poem, "Billy in the Darbies," which eventually ended the tale. *Billy Budd* is a meditation on realism; it is also a meditation on genre relationships between poetry and prose. The realist *Billy Budd* is thus also, in this sense, of a seamless piece with the alleged long quietus: Melville had for years been experimenting extensively with mixed prose–verse formats, in works such as "John Marr," "Tom Deadlight," and "Rip Van Winkle's Lilac," in all of which he challenges and dismantles generic boundaries. Melville's combinations of prose and verse provide an additional challenge to standard accounts of poetic history holding that modernists like Ezra Pound were the first to pursue such innovations. This modernocentric claim has in turn encouraged the anachronistic attempt to recuperate Melville the poet as a proto-modern, as if modernism provided the essential criterion of poetic value and therefore retroactively justified Melville's poetic practice. We might rather consider that the moderns inherited the work of prior generations of innovators – a concept they themselves wanted to reject in their mantra to "make it new." Pound's defensive acknowledgment, in his poem "A Pact," of his debt to Whitman provides merely one example of modernist sensitivity on this point. *Billy Budd* was not Melville's sudden, final work of fiction after decades of writing poetry. It was yet another of his challenges to boundaries between poetry and prose after having pursued such innovative work for decades.

Even apart from "Billy in the Darbies," the language of the novella is steeped in poetic terms: Captain Vere's nickname "Starry Vere" finds its origin in a poem by Andrew Marvell; the narrative interpolates a couplet (53); a current of poetic terms subtly flavors the narrative throughout. For example, the narrator describes Admiral Nelson's ship as "a poetic reproach ... to the *Monitors* and yet mightier hulls" (57). Indeed, Billy is himself a poet: "He was illiterate; he could not read, but he could sing, and like the illiterate nightingale was sometimes the composer of his own song" (52). Here the narrator uses two of the nineteenth century's most vivid terms – "nightingale" and "song" – commonly understood to denote poets and poetry. *Billy Budd*'s extended meditation on poetry exemplifies the motivated connections between this final work and Melville's decades-long poetic project.

Once we see that, like *Billy Budd*, Melville's poems too are realist works, Melville as a writer becomes fully integrated both in his own career and in American literary history more generally. It is important to note that Melville was not the only postbellum poet to explore realist strategies. Although he is my sole focus in this essay, he is one among a number of poets constituting this lost tradition in postbellum poetry (Renker forthcoming). The other major American realist poet to have emerged in recent scholarship is Sarah Piatt, whose extensive career Paula Bernat Bennett has traced in her superb edition. The phenomenon of realist poetry, although it reached a cusp in the 1890s along with realist fiction, began much earlier, a genealogy whose exact lines scholarship has not yet traced. Indeed, a great deal of scholarly work remains to be done in postbellum poetics.[1]

Whether in prose or verse, American realist texts often imagine, at the meta-artistic level, their own romantic antitheses. (When literary critics talk about the meta-artistic, they mean the level at which a work of art reflects upon its own artistic practice in addition to its more overt engagements with plot or characters or content.) In other words, these realist texts simultaneously present the romantic versions of their own stories in order to show the inadequacy of their counterparts. Thus in Charles Chesnutt's "The Passing of Grandison" (1899), Grandison's false, plantation-romance performance as the loyal slave is played against the real self he so shrewdly hides. In William Dean Howells's *The Rise of Silas Lapham* (1885), the main characters debate how real human behavior compares to the (silly) romantic behavior of characters in novels. In Mark Twain's *Adventures of Huckleberry Finn* (1884), Tom's engrossment in romantic visions of heroic escape like those he has read about obscures the real and efficient means of releasing Jim from his imprisonment. Piatt's "The First Party" (1882) quietly juxtaposes a daughter's excited chatter about her first flush of romance with her mother's dark and almost entirely unspoken knowledge about the real pain of love, marriage, and loss. Edwin Arlington Robinson's "Richard Cory" (1897) ends by revealing the utter falsity of the romantic image with which the townspeople invest the title character. Such exposés are a common realist practice.

Melville the realist poet exemplifies this tradition of staging a romantic counterpoint, and presents it as a poetic manifesto, in "The Aeolian Harp," published in *John Marr and Other Sailors* (1888). The poem offers ample evidence that Melville was engaged with the literary-historical context of romantic poetry; it also shows that he invoked that romantic tradition in order to imagine what an alternative poetry, a realist poetry, might look like. When Melville published "The Aeolian Harp," realism as a fictional mode was at its height. This poem addresses both the realist practice of his age and the romantic poetic tradition and meditates on Melville's ties to both.

The Aeolian harp was of course a common trope for inspiration in romantic poetry. Coleridge's poem by the same title figures the mind as a harp traversed by "wild and various" thoughts that will give rise to poems. Melville was a deep student of the poetic tradition and surely had Coleridge in mind. Whereas in Coleridge's poem "that simplest Lute" is caressed by a "desultory breeze," "Like some coy maid half yielding to her lover," with the "stilly murmur of the distant Sea" in the background, in Melville's poem the scene alters: the Sea is brought from the distance to the foreground and rendered violent, so that the lute no longer plays the sound of what Coleridge calls the "delicious surges" of lovers. For Melville, the harp's sound is "Stirred by fitful gales from sea." Coleridge's "delicious surges" become not those of Eros but of Thanatos: "Shrieking up in mad crescendo – / Dying down in plaintive key!" (Melville *Poems* 290).

The second stanza of Melville's poem continues the dialogue with romanticism. Here, Melville explicitly rejects what he calls the "strain ideal" and offers instead "Ariel's rendering of the Real" (290). "The Aeolian Harp" offers Melville's explicit engagement with the project of representing the "real." It does so as overtly as any statement by Howells, the influential leader, prime defender, and major practitioner of American realism in the postbellum literary marketplace.

In his characteristic, sometimes mind-bending knottiness, Melville here offers not merely the Real as opposed to the Ideal, which would be far too simple. Instead, he offers "Ariel's rendering of the Real." Why does Ariel appear here? Shakespeare's Ariel, of course, is a sprite, so perhaps the figure least suited to be an agent of realism. This apparent self-negation is a classic Melvillean formulation, given his predilection for phrases built around multiple negatives and other forms of self-cancellation. But the apparent self-cancellation in the figure of Ariel is apparent only. Ariel is also a creator of shipwrecks, as is Melville in this poem, and Ariel is a figure for Shakespeare, master poet much beloved of Melville. Melville loved Shakespeare for his "quick probings at the very axis of reality" and, simultaneously, for the way he only told the truth "covertly" ("Mosses" *PT* 244). In invoking Ariel as realist, Melville, I contend, explicitly sets out what is for him part of his poetic agenda: to create an art of poetry that is simultaneously an art of realism.

Here I imagine Melville taking on the claims of transparency in realism articulated by Howells, who construed realism as "nothing more and nothing less than the truthful treatment of material" (Howells *Criticism* 38). For Howells, realism was an art of transparency and democracy, democratic in the sense that art needn't be created by genius but was within the capability of ordinary folk (Marovitz 35). In Melville's account, on the other hand, realism is not transparent but an art, and an art in which the artist figure is pivotal. On both counts Melville is much closer to another major realist, Henry James, than to Howells. For Melville as for James, art must struggle to represent truth. The struggle is a debilitating one that requires the vision and force of the artist, not the mere reporting of the Howellsian craftsman. Melville's poem "Art" figures writing by way of metaphors of physical as well as spiritual strenuousness: according to the conclusion of the poem, to produce art is "To wrestle with the angel" (Melville *Poems* 322). James meditates on how art rather than mere reportage best represents the real in "The Real Thing," in which pictorial images are most "real" when art has processed and transformed them through the powers of the artist, rather than merely recording them transparently. (Bell has ably explored the differences between the realisms of Howells and James.)

In the last stanza of "The Aeolian Harp" we find the poem's essential paradox: "Well the harp of Ariel wails / Thoughts that tongue can tell no word of!" (291). In other words, despite the fact that he's just devoted the substance of a poem to it, Melville concludes with the observation that the horror the harp "wails" cannot be put into words. The domain of "the Real" that this poem wants to record is beyond language as well as beyond conventional poetry. Melville's realism was nowhere more caustic than in its unwillingness to offer up consolation and satisfaction, whether for the lover of conventional poems or for the seeker after the essential truth of human existence. Melville's realist project eventuated not in Howells's lucid prose and capable omniscient narrators but in the wordless wailing of his Aeolian harp and in the ragged edges of *Billy Budd*.

In 1890, Howells admiringly quoted a British critic who praised the American realist novel as "the real Realism" whose success inhered in its "faithful, almost photographic delineation of actual life, with its motives, its impulses, its springs of action laid bare to the eye, but with no unnatural straining after the intenser and coarser emotions ... " (Howells *Study* 266). Contra the Howellsian model of realist transparency, in which realist writing simply lays life bare as does a photograph, "The Aeolian Harp" is essentially concerned with epistemological opacity. Is reading a realist text more like looking at a photograph or like hearing music or like recalling memories? My rhetorical question points at exactly the kind of ontological disagreement between Howells and Melville about what constitutes truth, how one might know it, and how one might engage it in a literature of realism. For Melville, texts easily read, those which "laid bare" the delineations of life, would betray truths not easily apprehended – or, to use the language of Melville's poem, "Thoughts that tongue can tell no word of!" That paradoxical knot, that "rendering of the Real," is at the heart of Melville's realist poetics.

Realist texts not only chronically imagine their romantic antitheses, as I noted above; they also chronically imagine such juxtapositions through motifs of vision. Howells's "photographic" realism lays phenomena "bare to the eye"; James viewed the artist's eye as the conduit of "the real thing" to those who would view his sketches. Melville too explores a thematics of vision as a meta-artistic corollary to the larger issues of representation that animate and divide the discourse of realism. Melville was in fact deeply interested in the visual arts; he dedicated *Timoleon* to the American painter Elihu Vedder, for example. His interest in visual arts is related to his interest in his own poems as visual objects encountered by readers. The conflation between these levels of visual art for Melville is well attested by his poetic focus on art objects, in *Timoleon* (1891) in particular.

I want to conclude this essay by exploring one visual motif in the late poems through which Melville engages what he sees as the marketplace predicament for his realist poems. (Indeed and alas, from the standpoint of sales, the poetry was undoubtedly a "failure." But given that he published his last two volumes privately in editions of only twenty-five copies – which means they were not sold at all – sales figures are an inaccurate metric for talking about Melville's later career. See Giordano for a new analysis of Melville's conception of his own place in the postbellum marketplace, as outsider to the economy of literary publishing houses.) In *Weeds and Wildings with a Rose or Two*, the volume of poems Melville left unpublished at his death, he includes numerous poems focused on scenarios of vision: literally, they describe scenes in which viewers confront various kinds of plants that fall within the botanical categories in the volume's title. Melville uses these botanical tropes of vision as a meta-poetic device to imagine readers reading his realist poems.

Nineteenth-century culture was replete with literal and metaphorical flora, ranging from the century's fascination with amateur and expert botany (Baym *American Women*) to a lively common practice of floral symbolism called the "language of flowers." Countless manuals codified the language of flowers, explaining which particular blooms stood for particular attributes (for example, rose for love, white lily for purity, narcissus for egotism, daffodil for regard, and bell flower for gratitude) and allowing people to send messages with flowers rather than words. Even today, handbooks, pamphlets, and advertisements continue to map out a semiotic of floral messages in this tradition (Ohrbach).

The title of Melville's volume indicates that he conceives of these poems in metaphorically botanical terms. A wilding is a wild plant or flower, while a weed is a wild plant that is useless, troublesome, or valueless. The difference between them is one of what Marxists would call use-value: if the rover or gardener can use or otherwise value the plant (say, use it for medicinal applications or value its scent or beauty), it is a wilding; if the rover or gardener judges the plant negatively, it becomes a weed. One rover's weed is, of course, another's wilding. Melville's title thus overtly flags the issue of how we value poems. In addition, his volume gives us not only weeds and wildings but also "A Rose or Two." The weeds and wildings stand in implicit contrast to the highly cultivated rose, widely prized by nineteenth-century gardeners. Poetic value is the subtle subject encoded in the volume's language of weeds, wildings, and roses.

In using such floral tropes, Melville also alludes to a long tradition in English poetry of punning on the word "posy," which means both a type of flower and a type of "poesy" or poetry. Roses were a particularly standard trope for idealized beauty and love throughout the history of poetry written in English and also in genteel post-bellum poetry in particular. Here it is important to introduce some biographical context into Melville's personal investment in the idealized poetry of love. Literary criticism has long recognized that language, by its very nature, generates multiple levels of meaning; for example, the language in a work of literature (or any other kind of language, for that matter) works literally as well as figuratively; it is also in touch with the cultural associations prevalent at the time it was written; it frequently engages the history of literature's other uses of similar tropes; it resonates with the author's biography and his individual associations with words; and so on. In the case of Melville's aggressive critique of the romantic poetry of beauty and love, we find both his engagement with poetic history and a reflection of the far more painful subject of his own life. His marriage and family dynamics were extremely unhappy for himself, his wife (Elizabeth Shaw Melville, usually called "Lizzie"), and his four children, the eldest of whom committed suicide at the age of eighteen. I have explored this wrenching history in precise detail elsewhere (Renker "Melville").

A number of critics have argued that the rose poems are love poems to Lizzie (for example, Bryant; Robertson-Lorant). But Vernon Shetley's remark about the love-poem reading of one of the rose poems, "Amoroso," with its predominant imagery of iciness ("To feel your cheek like ice"), indeed applies to the volume as a whole: "it would be a surprised and puzzled woman, one suspects, who found herself courted by a love-poem like this" (Shetley 202). Lizzie suffered severely each summer from what she called her "rose-cold," a form of seasonal allergy. For her, roses did not signify love, but suffering: her rose-cold was so severe that she had to keep a wet towel over her face in order to breathe. Often she left town entirely in order to get a change of air (Robertson-Lorant 452, 272). Critics have tried hard to redeem the Melville marriage as a good one by reading Melville's rose poems as love poems to Lizzie, but neither the rose poems nor the biographical facts of the marriage sustain such a case (Renker "Melville").

In fact, Melville's experiment with the idea of writing romantic rose poems was a two-fold challenge: first, it was a challenge to literary-historical tradition; second, it was a passive-aggressive expression of personal disappointment about the actualities of marriage. These two registers of meaning are of course related, since Melville's disappointment in the daily realities of marriage was related to the ridiculously idealized and false images of marriage purveyed by poems and by American culture more generally in the nineteenth century. Bennett has recovered a nascent tradition of American women's poetry after 1858 "keenly aware of the oppressive potential within nineteenth-century marriage" and pitched against romantic images of marriage as ethereal paradise ("Descent" 593). Melville was thus not alone in challenging idealized views of marriage; given his oft-noted status as a writer whose work features few women characters, he is in paradoxically excellent company with a group of female poets in his own era.

The longstanding association in poetic history between roses in particular and the poetry of romantic idealization explains why Melville juxtaposes this botanical emblem of cultivation with weeds and wildings that represent alternative orders of aesthetic value. The later realist poet Edwin Arlington Robinson showed how rebarbative a poet's response might be to the dominance of idealized poetry when he commented,

> When it comes to "nightingales and roses" I am not "in it" nor have I the smallest desire to be. I sing, in my own particular manner, of heaven & hell and now and then of natural things (supposing they exist) or a more prosy connotation than those generally admitted into the domain of metre. (13)

Moving backward to the 1860s, Emily Dickinson's "This was a Poet – It is That" engages in a similar estrangement from the poetic cliché of the rose. Her poem does not even name the flower but refers to it only as "the familiar species / That perished by the Door –" (5–6).

Melville participates in this meta-poetic dialogue about roses as emblems of kinds of poems. His use of floral tropes foregrounds not the use value and aesthetic value of literal flora but the use value and aesthetic value of the poems in which we find such imagery. Melville's floral poems pose scenarios in which readers participate in judging poetic worth. He typically presents viewers who cannot see the meaning or value of the real plants they are confronting, trapped as they are in an aesthetic of ideal roses. They either fail to notice the alternative flora entirely or more deliberately reject them as inferior. The viewers in these poems stand in for the readers of poems, who are, in Melville's view, specifically looking for the wrong kinds of flowers.

In "The American Aloe on Exhibition," another mixed prose and verse format, Melville opens with a prose discussion of "floral superstition" about the aloe's reputed inability to bloom more than once per century. The poem depicts viewer-readers who are interested only in looking at the aloe when it flowers: that is, who usually ignore it. The prose section has already told us that these viewers are thoroughly wrong about everything. They finally look at the flowering aloe only because they believe it to be a once-in-a-century phenomenon, but the narrator has already explained that "When in any instance the flowering is for decades delayed beyond the normal period (eight or ten years at furthest), it is owing to something retarding in the environment or soil" – in other words, the viewers themselves are what stultify the aloe's development. "Few" (1) come to see the aloe even in flower; before that nobody at all would look.

This poem is in fact characterized by a visual standoff between the viewers (readers) and the aloe, a figure for the poet who writes poetry with an alternative kind of aesthetic value; hence the poem's insistent visual imagery: "came to see" (1), "stare" (7), "to view" (8). When the viewers at last pay attention, both they and the aloe stare at one another in mutual incomprehension: "In strange inert blank unconcern / Of wild things at the Zoo, / The patriarch let the sight-seers stare – / Nor recked who came to view" (5–8). The ambiguous grammar allows the opening clause about "blank unconcern" to modify both "the patriarch" and "the sight-seers" as they look at one another. In the aloe's final lament, he challenges the poetry of ideal values: "But, ah, ye Roses that have passed / Accounting me a weed!" (15–16). These "roses," with their romantic associations in the history of poetry as well as their connection to the genteel poetry rampant in the marketplace of Melville's own time, stand opposed to his poetic text, the "weed" (16) that recalls the title of the volume.

The aesthetic system of accounting ("Accounting me a weed!" [16]) that would value roses over weeds, or define weeds as weeds only because of the aesthetic of roses, is the system that Melville's poetry of realism challenges in *Weeds and Wildings*. In "A Way-Side Weed," a "charioteer from villa fine" (2) (thus a character dressed in romantic trappings) fails to understand the value of "A way-side Weed divine" (4) and cuts it with his lash, thus flouting "October's god" (6). Like the inert reader-viewers of "The American Aloe on Exhibition," the charioteer does not understand his own actions, nor the value of the weed (divinity) whose aesthetic is remote from him. In "Field Asters," we find another visual standoff. Here, too, the poem associates the title flower ("Wild ones," 3) with the wild poems that Melville has branded as his own. The poem first describes these common real flowers as "every autumn seen – / Seen of all, arresting few" (3–4). In this initial formulation, the field asters resemble the aloe whom "few" come to see; they also resemble the way-side weed, who does not arrest the charioteer as he "whisks along" (1) with his "passing lash" (3). Yet the second stanza of "Field Asters" challenges the formulation with which its first stanza seemed to rest. It opens: "Seen indeed." In the poem's realist predicament, the viewer/readers who so quickly judge the wild asters have actually not really looked at them at all; they are unable to see what is real. This theme in Melville's late poems provides an excellent example of how his ontology of realism differs from that of Howells, for whom the realist "photographic" image is self-evident to all.

Melville's unpublished manuscript is divided in two sections, a three-part section called *Weeds and Wildings* and a two-part section called *A Rose or Two*. The correspondence in *A Rose or Two* between the number of its parts and the number of roses thematized by its title is another indication of Melville's motivated association between roses and text. Melville's presentation of his own poems as weeds and wildings that operate in an aesthetic of the real rather than the ideal renders it intriguing as well as necessary to ask why and how he handles the figure of the rose in his own poems. As Shetley has pointed out, Melville's rose poems engage in an extended critique of the rose as a stable symbol (Shetley 197). They do so by pursuing extended forms of word play with the word "rose" and with associated words and sounds (Rosamond, Rosicrucians, rose window, rosary beads, amoroso, roseate, hearth-roses). This linguistic enterprise empties the rose of its stable ideal content since it shows the rose to represent nothing so well as instability and transitory value.

In the poem "Rosary Beads" – a title that evokes the material form of the poem with its three short sections following one another like beads on a rosary – Melville experiments with the word-root, "rose," and with how many ways he can use it in how many forms (rosary, roses, rose-fane, rose-priests, rose-bed, and so on). This celebratory word association resists conventional idealized poetic associations with the rose as a stable and easily readable symbol of natural beauty or love. *A Rose or Two* challenges the very notion of the symbol itself, by exploring all the contingencies of association that Melville teases out of the word (Shetley 196–7).

Just as the title of Melville's volume imagines a juxtaposition of kinds of value by way of realist poetic weeds and wildings versus idealized roses, "Rosary Beads" ends with Melville's realist obliteration of the ideal garden: "Grain by grain the Desert drifts / Against the Garden-Land; / Hedge well thy Roses, heed the stealth / Of ever-creeping Sand" (12–15). Realist and romantic strains in American literary culture would continue to battle for artistic territory, marketplace popularity, and cultural importance, then as today. Melville the realist poet, far from being a failure disconnected from his age, was and is an integral part of American literary history and its conflicts. Like the wildings in his poems, he remains right in front of us but still unseen.

NOTE

1   Cheryl Walker has identified a realist trend in American women's poetry including Alice and Phoebe Cary and Maria White Lowell at mid-century; Paula Bennett describes Sarah Piatt as a poetic realist. See also Giordano on postbellum poetry more generally. I am working on a book on American realist poetry, *The Lost Era in American Poetry, 1865–1910*.

References and Further Reading

Baym, Nina. *American Women of Letters and the Nineteenth-Century Sciences: Styles of Affiliation.* New Brunswick, NJ: Rutgers University Press, 2002.

——. "Melville's Quarrel with Fiction." *PMLA* 94 (1979): 909–23.

Bell, Michael Davitt. *The Problem of American Realism: Studies in the Cultural History of a Literary Idea.* Chicago: University of Chicago Press, 1993.

Bennett, Paula Bernat. " 'The Descent of the Angel': Interrogating Domestic Ideology in American Women's Poetry, 1858–1890." *American Literary History* 7 (1995): 591–610.

——, ed. *Palace-Burner: The Selected Poetry of Sarah Piatt.* Urbana and Chicago: University of Illinois Press, 2001.

——. *Poets in the Public Sphere: The Emancipatory Project of American Women's Poetry, 1800–1900.* Princeton, NJ, and Oxford: Princeton University Press, 2003.

Bryant, John. "Melville's Rose Poems: As They Fell." *Arizona Quarterly* (1996) 52: 49–84.

Coleridge, Samuel Taylor. "The Eolian Harp." (1796, 1817). In *Coleridge: Poetical Works.* Ed. Ernest Hartley Coleridge. 1912. Oxford: Oxford University Press, 1969. 101.

Dickinson, Emily. "This was a Poet – It is That." In *The Complete Poems of Emily Dickinson.* Ed. Thomas H. Johnson. Boston: Little, Brown, 1955. 215.

Giordano, Matthew. "Dramatic Poetics and American Poetic Culture, 1865–1904." Ph.D. dissertation, Ohio State University, 2004.

Howells, W. D. *Criticism and Fiction and Other Essays.* Ed. C. M. Kirk and R. Kirk. New York: New York University Press, 1959.

——. *Editor's Study by William Dean Howells.* Ed. J. W. Simpson. Troy, NY: Whitston Publishing Company, 1983.

James, Henry. "The Real Thing." 1892. In *The Norton Anthology of American Literature.* Ed. Nina Baym. New York: Norton, 2003. Vol. C: 506–24

Kindilien, Carlin T. *American Poetry in the Eighteen Nineties.* Providence, RI: Brown University Press, 1956.

Marovitz, Sanford E. "Melville Among the Realists: W. D. Howells and the Writing of *Billy Budd.*" *American Literary Realism* 34 (2001): 29–46.

Melville, Herman. *The Poems of Herman Melville.* Ed. Douglas Robillard. 1976. Kent, OH: Kent State University Press, 2000.

——. *Weeds and Wildings Chiefly: with a Rose or Two.* In *'Weeds and Wildings Chiefly: with a Rose or Two.* By Herman Melville. Reading Text and Genetic Text, Edited from the Manuscripts, with Introduction and Notes.'* Ed. Robert C. Ryan. Dissertation, Northwestern University, 1967.

Ohrbach, Barbara Milo. *A Bouquet of Flowers: Sweet Thoughts, Recipes, and Gifts from the Garden with "The Language of Flowers."* New York: Clarkson N. Potter, 1990.

Pearce, Roy Harvey. *The Continuity of American Poetry.* Princeton, NJ: Princeton University Press, 1961.

Pizer, Donald, ed. *Documents of American Realism and Naturalism.* Carbondale: Southern Illinois University Press, 1998.

Renker, Elizabeth. "Herman Melville, Wife Beating, and the Written Page." *American Literature* 66 (1994): 123–50.

——. " 'I Looked Again and Saw': Teaching Postbellum Realist Poetry." In *Teaching Nineteenth-Century American Poetry.* Ed. Paula Bernat Bennett and Karen L. Kilcup. New York: MLA, forthcoming.

Robinson, Edwin Arlington. *Selected Letters of Edwin Arlington Robinson.* New York: Macmillan, 1940.

Ruttenburg, Nancy. *Democratic Personality: Popular Voice and the Trial of American Authorship.* Stanford, CA: Stanford University Press, 1998

Sealts, Merton M., Jr. *The Early Lives of Melville: Nineteenth-Century Biographical Sketches and Their Authors.* Madison: University of Wisconsin Press, 1974.

Shetley, Vernon Lionel. "A Private Art: Melville's Poetry of Negation." Ph.D. dissertation, Columbia University, 1986.

Stedman, Edmund Clarence, ed. *An American Anthology 1787–1900: Selections Illustrating the*

Editor's Critical Review of American Poetry in the Nineteenth Century. Boston: Houghton Mifflin, 1900.

——— . *Poets of America.* Boston: Houghton Mifflin, 1885.

Stedman, Edmund Clarence and Ellen Mackay Hutchinson. *A Library of American Literature from the Earliest Settlement to the Present Time.* Vol. VII. New York: Charles L. Webster, 1889.

Sundquist, Eric J., ed. *American Realism: New Essays.* Baltimore: Johns Hopkins University Press, 1982.

Walker, Cheryl. "Nineteenth-Century Women Poets and Realism." *American Literary Realism* 23 (1991): 24–41.

Weaver, Raymond. M. *Herman Melville: Mariner and Mystic.* New York: George H. Doran, 1921.

Wiebe, Robert H. *The Search for Order 1877–1920.* New York: Hill and Wang, 1967.

32

Melville's Transhistorical Voice: *Billy Budd, Sailor* and the Fragmentation of Forms

John Wenke

From "Billy in the Darbies" to the Handsome Sailor

Following the monumental achievement of *Clarel* (1876) and its resounding commercial failure Herman Melville found himself in the late 1870s forced by some combination of weariness and demoralization into a fitful state of creative intermittence. The sustained rigor of composing, polishing, and publishing the 18,000-line masterwork of theological and philosophical dialectic – his last grand attempt to contain the world in a book – gave way to an insular form of self-talking. As William B. Dillingham suggests, "An aging and nostalgic Herman Melville ... indulge[d] himself by creating imaginary playmates, as it were, to recapture some of the pleasure of the past" (11). His work on the "Burgundy Club" materials helped fill the void left by *Clarel*'s consignment to unpopularity. This tinkering with the interrelationship of new prose sketches and old, newly revised poems allowed Melville to think of himself as a writer, albeit on a reduced scale. The path of his wrecked and re-wrecked career had finally led him to lower, or at least shift, his conceit of attainable artistic felicity. In the wake of *Clarel*'s failure and in grudging opposition to the gravitational pull of increasing age Melville had settled into what Hershel Parker describes as "puttering with unambitious literary endeavors" (2: 834). Until his retirement from the New York Custom House on December 31, 1885 Melville must have continued spinning new strands and dabbling with loose ends, writing and reading in the evenings, on weekends, and at other fugitive moments. How he managed his creative life during his last Custom House years remains a matter of speculation: the documentary record from 1880 to 1885 is unusually scant. Indeed, in his biography Parker explores the implications of Melville's odd disappearance from much of the family correspondence (2: 845–77). The aging man was there – somewhere – although he is hardly mentioned. But in a 10 January 1886 letter to Catherine Lansing, Elizabeth Shaw Melville enlarges on her husband's recently concluded Custom House career and his literary prospects:

> This month was a good turning-point, completing 19 years of faithful service, during which there has not been a single complaint against him – So he retires honorably of his own accord – He has a great deal of unfinished work at his desk which will give him occupation, which together with his love of books will prevent time from hanging heavy on his hands – and I hope he will get into a more quiet frame of mind, exempt from the daily invitation of over work. (Leyda 2: 796)

Sometime in the next months Melville wrote a ballad in the voice of a sailor on the eve of his execution for complicity in a mutinous plot. The old salt possesses a wry, even sardonic, attitude toward the exposed conspiracy and his impending death: "O, 'tis me, not the sentence they'll suspend. / Ay, ay, all is up; and I must up too" (*BB* 132: leaf 349).[1] Without question this poem would have found its place with the retrospective sea-verse that became *John Marr and Other Sailors* (1888) had not Melville's intentions undergone a momentous sea-change. "Billy in the Darbies" initiated a compositional process that engaged Melville until his death. Under Melville's hand, the old Billy Budd was radically transformed into the heroic Handsome Sailor – a figure of brimming youthfulness, spiritual purity, and physical power. But the poem's speaker evokes young Billy only by contrast. Whereas the original Billy is guilty of mutiny, young Billy is absolutely innocent of the charges levied against him by John Claggart, the depraved master-at-arms. Whereas old Billy possesses a wily duplicity of utterance, an appreciation for double entendre, the Handsome Sailor lacks the "sinister dexterity" required for "double meanings and insinuations of any sort" (49, leaf 30). In fact, there is only one imagistic anticipation of Baby Budd's untimely doom in the poem. The speaker wistfully recalls the sea-burial of "Taff the Welshman when he sank. / And his cheek it was like the budding pink" (132, leaf 350), a harbinger, perhaps, of "the rose-tan of [Billy's] cheek" (98: leaf 222). (For significant discussions of the relationship between Melville's late poetry and *Billy Budd*, see Stern, *Billy Budd* xxv–xxxiv; Milder, "Melville's Late Poetry" and "Old Man Melville.")

Over five slow years Melville pondered and recast and pondered some more the tortuous implications and violent consequences of young Billy's impressment from a merchant vessel *The Rights of Man* into a battle-ready, outward-bound warship named first the *Indomitable* and later the *Bellipotent*. At an early stage Melville used the ships' names to evoke the narrative's encompassing political context, one that includes Edmund Burke's conservative critique of revolutionary forms in *Reflections on the Revolution in France* (1790) and Thomas Paine's reply affirming the right to revolution in *The Rights of Man* (1791). (For discussions of the politics of revolution see Scorza;

Reynolds, *Revolutions* and "Unrest.") Billy, however, is completely unaware of political contexts. He takes his impressment with a light heart and loves his work in the foretop: "He was soon at home in the service, not at all disliked for his unpretentious good looks and a sort of genial happy-go-lucky air. No merrier man in his mess" (49, leaf 32). But he incurs the seemingly unprovoked ire of John Claggart, who devises a series of "mantraps" that snaffle and baffle Billy (70, leaf 111). Seeking counsel regarding this "petty trouble" (68, leaf 106), the Handsome Sailor is incredulous when the cynical, old Dansker cryptically informs him that the Master-at-Arms "is down on" him (71, leaf 114). Claggart's hatred of Billy leads him to approach Captain Vere and make false accusations regarding Billy's role in fomenting a mutiny. Suspicious of Claggart, Vere tests the allegations with his customary "directness" (63, leaf 87). After the captain positions Claggart and Billy face to face, the young sailor is so shocked by Claggart's assertions that he can utter no word. From out of Billy's self-strangling perplexity comes a powerful fist that strikes Claggart in the forehead. In this instant Melville has staged one of the great anomalous moments of world literature: a nearly perfect, seemingly prelapsarian young man has just committed homicide. Following a hastily assembled and legally dubious drumhead court Captain Vere plays the role of sole witness and judge. He leads the court to convict Billy of murdering a superior officer. Billy is hanged the following dawn. In an ironic twist "Billy in the Darbies," the poem with which Melville began, concludes *Billy Budd, Sailor.* The poem stands as a rueful coda, a misapprehending legend spun by an unnamed sea bard.

During the long process of composition Melville dramatized and complicated the problem of how to read the narrative and what to make of the horrifying collision between primal, nearly perfect, innocence and absolute, though deferential, evil. As he proceeded, Melville made startling innovations in his use of first-person narrative form, especially as he developed the voice of his elusive and problematic transhistorical narrator. The narrator not only tells Billy's story, but he positions himself as a vexed and self-conscious reader of this "Inside Narrative," frequently using dramatic incidents to propel the reader toward an engagement with encompassing transnational and transhistorical contexts. Melville's narrative innovations are largely responsible for infusing the tale of an individual "nipped in the vice of fate" (119, leaf 303) with an astonishing array of dialectically charged social, political, historical, and mythic figurations.

Genesis: Making "Ragged Edges"

Throughout the multiple stages of revision Melville retained the basic plot, though as Hayford and Sealts note in the "Editors' Introduction" to their landmark edition of *Billy Budd, Sailor (An Inside Narrative)*, each major revision created resonances among retained material from earlier inscriptions:

> In three main phases [Melville] had introduced in turn the three main characters: first Billy, then Claggart, and finally Vere. As the focus of his attention shifted from one to another of these three principals, the plot and thematic emphasis of the expanding novel underwent consequent modifications within each main phase. Just where the emphasis finally lay in the not altogether finished story as he left it is, in essence, the issue that has engaged and divided the critics of *Billy Budd*. (3)

Until the months preceding his death, Melville was still, in pencil, making decisive changes that alter the narrative's hermeneutical implications, especially regarding Vere's character and his decision to hang Billy. In the Hayford and Sealts genetic text of *Billy Budd*, the reader of this unfinished novel can trace the textual manifestations of Melville's evolving choices. The genetic text is not to be confused with a facsimile reproduction of the manuscript. Instead, it is a scholarly construct, an encoded transcription depicting successive fair-copy stages with accompanying emendations, each fair copy begun with the printer's eye in mind, each fair copy leading Melville into further revision. Whereas the words and symbols inscribed in the genetic text do not necessarily constitute or reveal intention, they do provide primary evidence on which arguments regarding intention can be based. It is, perhaps, ironic that the main lines of *Billy Budd* criticism were firmly entrenched well before the publication of the Hayford and Sealts volume and with few exceptions – the most notable being Milton R. Stern's 1975 edition of *Billy Budd* – very little criticism or scholarship prior to Hershel Parker's *Reading* Billy Budd (1990) paid close attention to the genetic text and the illuminating, though problematic, materials available therein.

Thus much of *Billy Budd* criticism flows from the premise that the narrative contains the artistic expression of an animating – usually ideological – intention. As Parker makes clear in *Reading* Billy Budd, the novel's rapid canonization following its 1924 publication was partly a consequence of the need among a handful of influential writers in England to see a *completed final work* as a last artistic will and testament, a conclusive message from the departed master (53–71). As early as 1933 E. L. Grant Watson proclaimed *Billy Budd, Foretopman* – the superseded title appearing in all editions prior to 1962 – a textual monument to Christian acceptance of life's God-given, ineluctable tragedies. In his "Introduction" to *Critical Essays on Melville's "Billy Budd, Sailor,"* Robert Milder deftly summarizes the history of "acceptance theories" and positions them in opposition to various "ironist" readings that become, in Milder's words, "social or antireligious in content, and rebellious in posture" (4–5). The critical history replays the question of whether Vere was right or wrong to hang Billy – as though one might find in the embrace of categorical certainty a skeleton key to unlock the complexities of Melville's mind. These arguments – so called "pro-Vere" and "anti-Vere" – usually lead critics to assess Melville's intentions as reflecting conservative or liberal affiliations. To the conservative Melville, Vere has no choice but to hang Billy and thereby uphold the efficacy of "lasting institutions" (63, leaf 84). (The fullest and most persuasive pro-Vere arguments can be found in Stern, *Fine Hammered Steel* 206–39 and *Billy Budd*, "Introduction.") To the liberal Melville, however, Vere does little more than slaughter the Innocent in a wrongheaded and vicious display of power-mongering oppression. (Major ironist arguments can be found in Schiffman, Withim, Widmer, and Garner.)

But in treating any reading text of *Billy Budd* as a cohesive reflection of Melville's final intention, by approaching any reading text without as least some recourse to the genetic text, one proceeds without reference to the undeniable tendency of Melville's revisions and the very essence of what continues to make *Billy Budd, Sailor* such a critical "boggy ground" (57, leaf 65). As Hayford and Sealts point out, "in making the revision Melville was doing what he had consistently done in the whole course of composition: he was *dramatizing* the situation (and its implications) which he had previously *reported*" (35, italics in original). Early in the composition, the story of innocence destroyed had a determinate conclusion. At Stage B, well before the expansive development of Vere at draft stage X, Billy Budd kills Claggart and he is hanged for it. The narrative abruptly concludes on a starkly worded note of ironic reversal: "Here ends a story not unwarranted by what sometimes happens in this [*word undeciphered*] world of ours – Innocence and infamy, spiritual depravity and fair repute" (422, leaf 344, italics in original). The primary context is political and allegorical rather than personal and idiosyncratic: the forces of history steamroll Billy Budd. The transposition of categories takes precedence over the death of a man: "Innocence" becomes perceived as "infamy" and "spiritual depravity" masquerades as "fair repute." This position becomes more fully developed in the next draft stage (C) where the narrator indicts a civilization that permits, or perhaps requires, such a reversal of values and such a sacrifice. The narrator juxtaposes the sailor's "frankness" and the landsman's "finesse. Life is not a game with the sailor, demanding the long head – no intricate game of chess where few moves are made in straightforwardness and ends are attained by indirection, an oblique, tedious, barren game hardly worth that poor candle burnt out in playing it" (86–7, leaf 172). In assessing the larger picture the narrator considers the conflict between a natural state of primeval innocence and the involutions that reinforce the shabby constructs of a failed civilization.

At this early point in the composition Melville had yet to develop the inscrutable contours of Claggart's mania; nor had he brought forward Captain Vere's direct involvement and his problematic responses to Claggart's death. As he reworked and expanded the manuscript Melville moved away from this determinate summary conclusion toward writing the sort of story that never really ends, away from closure toward openness, away from a fiction that contrives the high finish associated with "an architectural finial" toward the "ragged edges" that are a consequence of "[t]ruth uncompromisingly told" (128, leaf 335) – images inscribed late in the process at the F/G stage. Indeed as *Billy Budd* grew Melville found himself writing the kind of book he favored in *Mardi* (1849), *Moby-Dick* (1851), *The Confidence-Man* (1857), and *Clarel* – a fiction, whether in prose or verse, characterized by a conscious commitment to an aesthetics of incompletion. For all its prolixity *Mardi* concludes with open-ended irresolution: Taji is being chased over an "endless sea" (654). As Ishmael proclaims in the "Cetology" chapter of *Moby-Dick*, "God keep me from ever completing anything. This whole book is but a draught – nay, but the draught of a draught" (145). In the aftermath of *The Confidence-Man*'s conclusion, we are still waiting for the "something further [that] may follow of this Masquerade" (251). In *Clarel*, Rolfe – one of Melville's projected *alter egos* – is beleaguered by his "hollow, Manysidedness!" (3.16.263). By the end of the long poem the speaker can do little more than embrace knowledge as a means of enlarging ignorance: "Degrees we know, unknown in days before; / The light is greater, hence the shadow more" (4.35.18–19). What seems crucial, and what should animate one's attempt to engage the critical contexts of *Billy Budd*, is that Melville himself was reading and remaking a text that intrigued, haunted and even baffled him. He was seemingly unable to recopy his manuscript without reconceiving parts of it. (For extended discussion of the critical and scholarly implications of the genetic text see Parker *Reading* Billy Budd 97–162; Wenke "Complicating Vere" and "Melville's Indirection.")

"A Quizzing Sort of Look": The Dynamics of Reading

The narrative's hermeneutical openness is a direct consequence of Billy's status as a kind of text to be read and deciphered. Billy, however, never analyzes himself. When he speaks he offers flat, denotative statements: "And good-bye to you too, old *Rights of Man*" (49, leaf 29, italics in original) is not Billy's "satiric sally," as Vere assumes (95, leaf 208). Billy means nothing by this loaded statement: he calls goodbye to a ship that might have had any other name. Similarly he ingenuously expresses his ignorance. When asked about his birth and parentage he replies, "God knows, sir" (51, leaf 40). His lack of self-consciousness evokes Adamic innocence and noble primitivism. He has no "trace of the wisdom of the serpent . . . . Of self-consciousness he seemed to have little or none, or about as much as we may reasonably impute to a dog of Saint Bernard's breed" (52, leaf 42). It is this strange anomaly of character that turns Billy into the object of many a pondering gaze. (For an extended discussion of Billy as natural primitive, see Scorza 19–35.)

Within the text, three characters – the Dansker, Claggart, and Vere – possess the psychological acuity to explore the disjunctive implications stirred by Billy's very presence aboard the *Bellipotent*. The Dansker, for example, looks at Billy as an engrossing subject of private study. At first, the "unsentimental" Dansker finds Billy comically at odds with "the warship's environment." Later,

> the old Merlin's equivocal merriment was modified; for now when the twain would meet, it would start in his face a quizzing sort of look, but it would be but momentary and sometimes replaced by an expression of speculative query as to what might eventually befall a nature like that, dropped into a world not without some mantraps and against whose subtleties simple courage lacking experience and address, and without any touch of defensive ugliness, is of little avail; and where such innocence as

man is capable of does yet in a moral emergency not always sharpen the faculties or enlighten the will. (70, leaves 110–11)

Unlike the Dansker, Claggart does not interpret Billy's presence with any trace of "patriarchal irony" (70, leaf 112). Instead Billy sets off a roiling sense of dis-ease. Claggart cannot stand the presumption that Billy has somehow been exempt from the consequences of the Fall. He looks "askance" at Billy's "frank enjoyment of young life" and feels "magnetically" averse to the ontological implications of Billy's innocence: "[I]n its simplicity [Billy's nature] never willed malice or experienced the reactionary bite of that serpent" (78, leaf 140). It irritates Claggart that "Handsome is as handsome does" (77, leaf 137) – that is, Billy's pure ontological condition achieves direct expression in his behavior without the masking or duplicity characteristic of life in "Cain's city" (53, leaf 45). Captain Vere also reads Billy with acute powers of discernment. Shortly after Billy strikes and kills the Master-at-Arms, Vere interprets Claggart's death as divinely ordained and, by implication, Billy as an instrument of divinely sanctioned justice: "Struck dead by an angel of God!" Vere's next pronouncement – "Yet the angel must hang!" – reflects the summary conclusion with which all readers must contend (101, leaf 232).

At the center of *Billy Budd* – and indeed the primary consequence of the narrative's long genesis and its arrested, rather than finished, condition – is Melville's creation of an unfolding drama of conflicting imperatives. Far from upholding a distinct ideological bias or fixed political position, Melville writes himself away from determinate conclusions in favor of enmeshing the reader within an argumentative domain of dialectically charged possibilities, a "boggy ground" of competing critical interpretations. Here, reasonable arguments exist for a multitude of seemingly valid, though sometimes contradictory, conclusions. Indeed, one can find weighty reasons to condone *and* condemn Vere – a circumstance that manifests itself within the revisions. For example, Melville's revisions of six superseded leaves complicate the surgeon's role (376–8, leaves 229a–f). The surgeon is the first person on the murder scene, the first to assess the shocking situation, and the first to respond to Vere's erratic behavior. In an earlier draft the surgeon reacts with sympathy to Vere's calm statement that he needs "yet a few moments to mature the line of conduct I shall adopt" in this "trying" situation. The surgeon concurs: "Too well the thoughtful officer knew what his superior meant." He considers "how more than futile the utmost discretion sometimes proves in this human sphere subject as it is to unforeseeable fatalities" (376–7, leaves 229b, c). Following revision, the "thoughtful" surgeon becomes the "prudent" surgeon – an ambiguous, if not pejorative, term in Melville's lexicon, evoking as it does the Dansker's self-protective, self-regarding aspect. In the latest draft the surgeon perceives Vere's now agitated outbursts as "mere incoherences" (101, leaf 232). But to make the surgeon the locus of interpretive authority would be to dismiss other possibilities. It would explicitly give undue credit to the surgeon's lack of antecedent information, celebrate his penchant for rushing to judgment, and disregard, as Chapter 26 dramatizes, the surgeon's inane capacity for pedantry. While the surgeon believes that Vere may be "unhinged," the narrator refuses to specify what he thinks (102, leaf 235). In an early version, the narrator regards the notion that Vere might be "the victim of aberration" and declares, "I for one, decline to determine" (382, leaf 237). After revision the narrator invites readers to decide for themselves and thereby create the meaning of the text: "Whether Captain Vere, as the surgeon professionally and privately surmised, was really the sudden victim of any degree of aberration, every one must determine for himself by such light as this narrative may afford" (102, leaf 237). At stake is not a futile admission of indeterminacy but a recognition of how the novel achieves its power: it dramatizes the seemingly irresolvable interplay of conflicting possibilities, especially the difficulty of establishing responses that reconcile pragmatic and ideal imperatives. Thus reading *Billy Budd* becomes less a matter of blaming or exonerating Vere and more a process of engaging the proliferating host of terrible complexities.

The dramatic activity of the Dansker, Claggart, and Vere attempting to read Billy Budd becomes extended and complicated via the narrator's own engagement with the dynamics of reading, especially insofar as the narrator is both expressive and retentive, determinate and indeterminate. He tells what he purports to know in relation to what he purports not to know. He judges and he resists, or evades, judgment. To articulate the shifting terms of these multiple possibilities is to engage the purposeful ambiguity toward which Melville aspired. (For extended discussions of the narrative's intrinsic uncertainty see Brodtkorb; Johnson.) Throughout *Billy Budd*, therefore, Melville makes reading, or one's attempt to fathom the meaning of Billy's nature, Claggart's character, or Vere's choice, not simply a trope but the novel's primary epistemological activity. Given the centrality of reading as a dramatic activity within the text and as a hermeneutical consequence of this activity, one must examine the narrator as Melville's most elusive creation. In fact, the text that becomes *Billy Budd, Sailor* probably had its origin when Melville took the words out of the mouth of the sailor in "Billy in the Darbies" and gave them to the enigmatic transhistorical narrator. Within the "inside narrative" the insular affairs of one ship invite a host of global associations.

The Narrator's Transhistorical Reach

Melville's narrator creates a transhistorical arena in which his language crosses the divide between then and now, between "the time before steamships" and his compositional present (43, leaf 2). The narrator is intermittently a self-referential presence, an "I" who calls attention to specific events in his own past, which on at least two occasions correspond directly to documented events in Melville's life. For example, in describing the unsettled state of the British Navy in 1797 and the government's nefarious means of filling a ship's muster, especially by kidnapping men and emptying jails, the narrator refers to a hearsay account of an incident that Melville mentions in his journal entry of November 21, 1849 (*J* 23). In an early version the narrator refers to "a strange thing which I heard in my youth from an old American Negro who had years before served in the British navy" (319–20, leaf 97). Under revision the passage becomes more specific in identifying place and time, a more distinct adaptation of an autobiographical moment in Melville's life to the life of this narrator:

> Such sanctioned irregularities, which for obvious reasons the government would hardly think to parade at the time and which consequently, and as affecting the least influential class of mankind, have all but dropped into oblivion, lend color to something for the truth whereof I do not vouch, and hence have some scruple in stating; something I remember having seen in print though the book I cannot recall; but the same thing was personally communicated to me now more than forty years ago by an old pensioner in a cocked hat with whom I had a most interesting talk on the terrace at Greenwich, a Baltimore Negro, a Trafalgar man. (66, leaf 97)

Melville's use of his own experience may, or may not, signal his identification with all, some, or none of the narrator's conceptions, suppositions, or arguments. Where Melville stands in relation to this narrator has inspired an extensive, divided, sometimes acrimonious critical and scholarly debate. These readings often generate from the premise that the text contains a knowable, authorially endorsed point of view – a narrator who functions as a projection of Melville's attitude, whether conservatively or liberally inclined; or a narrator who functions as an ironic foil for a Melville who could not possibly mean what the narrator seems to be saying, especially when justifying, even obliquely, Vere's decision to hang Billy. At the very least, these autobiographical moments have the effect of bringing the narrator before the reader *as* a person, or more precisely as a fictional version of a person, a self-conscious presence within the text – one who reaches back through his own life toward the story's historical moment and thereby accentuates the limited, provisional, contextual nature of his own narrative authority. His attempt to write this historical narrative is part of the historical narrative itself. He *pursues* the truth rather than conveys a Truth. The extent, if any, of Melville's identification with this narrator remains open to conjecture: indeed, in considering this matter, "[E]very one must determine for himself by such light as this narrative may afford" (102, leaf 237). However one comes to interpret the voice that presents the "inside narrative" and its relationship with Melville, one might first consider a few elements that describe the narrator's expansive and problematic presence. One might argue, in fact, that criticism of the novel must proceed from a working assessment of the narrator's activity, his very engagement with the dynamics of telling this story.

The narrator's transhistorical status – his oscillation between then and now over a range of about one hundred years – finds him operating not only as a self-referential presence but also as one who expands the conventional province of first-person narration. Melville's narrator combines the attributes of first- and third-person voices. Though occasionally referring to events in his own past – which were events in

Melville's own past – the narrator more frequently leaves behind the subjective limitations usually coincident with first-person voice and embraces an expansive mode of rendering psychological access and historical consciousness. When describing Claggart's response to Billy's spilled soup, the narrator speaks in a determinate manner: "But, at heart and not for nothing, as the late chance encounter may indicate to the discerning, down on him, secretly down on him, [the Master-at-Arms] assuredly was" (73, leaf 123). When operating as a third-person voice he takes a stand well beyond the limits of his own personal experience. He assumes a privileged, but by no means complete, access to most but not all events. Nor does he provide a fully articulated account of each character. At another moment the narrator declares his inability to render Claggart's "portrait" in language: "His portrait I essay, but shall never hit it" (64, leaf 88). On occasion he has little or nothing to report about critical events or issues. Vere's closeted interview with Billy never achieves dramatic representation, though the narrator does offer a number of conjectures regarding what might have taken place during the meeting. The narrator can seem to champion Vere as a conservative mindful of discipline and selflessly concerned with "the peace of the world and the true welfare of mankind" (63, leaf 84). Or Melville, in his revisions, can give the narrator an arresting qualification of Vere. In a late pencil addition, patched to the leaf, regarding the captain's nickname, Starry Vere, Melville changed "How such a designation happened to fall to him was in this wise" (311, leaf 79) to read "How such a designation happened to fall upon one who whatever his sterling qualities was without any brilliant ones, was in this wise" (61, leaf 79). These revisions were made after Melville restored (at G) the material on Admiral Nelson that had been removed earlier. This particular version, coming in Chapter 6 shortly after the Chapter 4 Nelson material, clearly has the narrator undermining Vere's stature, though the narrator goes on to make numerous subsequent affirmations of Vere's "exceptional character" (62, leaf 81). Insistently, the narrator offers a conflicted, even contradictory, delineation – one that invites debate and warns latter-day critics against glib historical or hermeneutical reductionism. As he does elsewhere, the narrator quotes an invented source, perhaps as a means of bolstering his own authority:

> Says a writer whom few know, "Forty years after a battle it is easy for a noncombatant to reason about how it ought to have been fought. It is another thing personally and under fire to have to direct the fighting while involved in the obscuring smoke of it. Much so with respect to other emergencies involving considerations both practical and moral, and when it is imperative promptly to act." (114, leaves 282–3)

There seems to be no "writer" as such, no material being quoted from an original source, only Melville making perhaps a mordant reference to his own unpopularity. Nevertheless this passage becomes a text-within-the-text that informs one's reading of Vere's decision. By concentrating on the "obscuring smoke" the narrator focuses the reader's critical attention on the exigencies complicating Vere's choice – issues that are intrinsically tangled and, perhaps, irresolvable. These issues include the importance of Melville's historical sources, especially the mutinies at the Nore and Spithead and even the relation to the *Somers* case of 1842, as well as the original presence of the Admiral Nelson material, its removal from the manuscript, and its late reinsertion with expanded commentary. Vere's decision also needs to be understood in relation to the possible appearance of the enemy at any time as well as to his more encompassing belief that he is upholding the forms of Christian order in opposition to the ostensibly atheistic mayhem incited by the French Revolution and Napoleon. (Extensive, authoritative discussions of issues related to the impingement of Melville's sources on the narrative can be found in Hayford and Sealts 24–39; Stern *Billy Budd* vii–xl; Sealts)

Significantly, however, Melville's revisions at every point compound the complexity of Vere's choice and thereby accentuate this skein of tangled irresolution. In combining the possibilities of first- and third-person voices, the narrator consciously builds a story in which determinate and indeterminate formulations exist in a dialectical relationship – the effect of which is to encourage the protean activity of hermeneutical pursuit but also to undermine, if not obviate, the prospect of argumentative closure. Such colliding views, Melville seems to be suggesting, bring one as close as possible to the insurmountable complexities of achieving full historical access. *Billy Budd* pays homage to, because it depicts, the root uncertainty inherent in any pursuit of "[t]ruth uncompromisingly told." Once again, the involutions of this widely ranging narrator reveal Melville's preference for "ragged edges" over contrived finish (128, leaf 335). Central to this process is Melville's continuing displacement or qualification of the narrator's authority. Variously expressive and retentive, the narrator presents what he knows in relation to what he does not know. In his speculations, in his retentiveness, in his admissions of ignorance, in his presentation of other interpreters and other texts within his text, the narrator frustrates the possibility of forging an official, unambiguous reading and celebrates instead the contextual validity – and indeed the epistemological necessity – of provisional formulations.

Along with oscillating between first- and third-person narrative perspectives, the narrator frequently uses imagery that unsettles conventional categories of containment, complementing and extending the narrator's transhistorical approach to storytelling. At the beginning of the novel, the narrator introduces the figure of the Handsome Sailor, even as he dramatizes how such a figuration transcends narrow boundaries of representation. The Handsome Sailor moves among common sailors "like Aldebaran among the lesser lights of his constellation" (43, leaf 3). This astronomical image creates a rippling effect of multiple associations. The brightest star in the constellation Taurus, Aldebaran serves as the eye of the bull. This image rises above terrestrial boundaries and forms an archetypal figure that anticipates the luster and oddity, if not otherworldliness, of Billy's personal attributes. The association with Taurus also prefigures Billy's ontological connection with various animal images, with primitivism, and with mythic innocence. In seeking to extend the range of such exotic associations the narrator evokes his compositional moment and in so doing he connects the reader to a time from his distant past, another moment from Melville's own experience, this one from his first voyage in 1839 on a merchant vessel, the very circumstances that Melville fictionalized in *Redburn* (1849):

> A somewhat remarkable instance recurs to me. In Liverpool, now half a century ago, I saw under the shadow of the great dingy street-wall of Prince's Dock (an obstruction long since removed) a common sailor so intensely black that he must needs have been a native African of the unadulterate blood of Ham – a symmetric figure much above the average height. (43, leaves 3–4)

The narrator describes this Handsome Sailor as a "black pagod of a fellow" who "beamed with barbaric good humor" (43, leaves 4–5) – a prefiguration of Billy as "a sort of upright barbarian" (52, leaf 44). But here the narrator elides racial difference to assert ontological identification. By first meeting the black Handsome Sailor we are introduced to the white Handsome Sailor. The erasure of racial difference coincides with the erasure of national and cultural difference. The Handsome Sailor might come from Africa or England or anywhere. When Lt. Ratcliffe perceives Billy as "Apollo with his portmanteau" (48, leaf 26) he associates Billy with a mythic figure and reinforces the transhistorical connotations evoked by Billy's unique attributes. (For an extensive account of Billy's mythic and archetypal status see Scorza 19–35; Coffler.)

The narrator accentuates the transnational presence – the archetypal form – of the Handsome Sailor by associating the surrounding sailors with Anacharsis Cloots and the rag-tag deputation he culled from the Paris slums. At the very least, the Cloots reference links Billy with France and with Cloots's attempt to inspire the French Assembly to disregard national boundaries. The black Handsome Sailor travels with a multicultural and multiracial "company of . . . shipmates. These were made up of such an assortment of tribes and complexions as would have well fitted them to be marched up by Anacharsis Cloots before the bar of the first French Assembly as Representatives of the Human Race" (43, leaf 5). The narrator anticipates the anomalous nature of Billy Budd by locating the Handsome Sailor outside conventional categories of representation. In fact, the novel dramatizes how inimical Billy Budd is to the involutions of time and history. The range of the narrator's Cloots reference has even a more striking connection with Billy Budd and points to an arresting erasure of national and historical difference. The self-proclaimed champion of human federation, Cloots was himself guillotined during the Reign of Terror. Possibly, Cloots's political murder parallels Vere's execution of Billy. As a matter of practical policy, Vere's attempt to sustain "lasting institutions" (63, leaf 84) is essentially indistinguishable from France's "red meteor of unbridled and unbounded revolt" (54, leaf 52). Neither the idealist nor the innocent has much chance to flourish, or even survive, within the vise grip of historical forces.

The narrator's primary representational mode is to proceed by way of "indirection" (74, leaf 126), first through the dialectical intersection of determinate and indeterminate formulations and, second, through unsettling conventional categories of narrative containment. In the same way that Ishmael's protean fusion of narrative voices in *Moby-Dick* allows him to respond to circumstantial exigencies in a host of seemingly contradictory or inconsistent ways, so too does the narrator of *Billy Budd* evade narrow reductionism in favor of orchestrating an expansive range of interpretive methods and a shifting range of hermeneutical possibilities. Like Ishmael, the narrator of *Billy Budd* responds to the exigencies of the moment in ways that flout the limits of conventional narrative representation. These forms seem to be disjunctive strategies on Melville's part rather than accidental effects of a narrative proliferating out of the author's control. At a late point in the composition (at G), in preparing to present materials on Admiral Nelson, the narrator invites the reader to follow him into a "bypath," a digressive foray promising "that pleasure which is wickedly said to be in sinning, for a literary sin the divergence will be" (56, leaf 58). In reading *Billy Budd*, one can do little more than follow the narrator's wavering, divergent, indirect path.

Vere's "Directness": The Fragmentation of "Measured Forms"

Vere's approach to reality diametrically opposes the narrator's expansive orchestration of ambiguous possibilities. If the narrator is characterized by a multiplicity of techniques, Vere is characterized by "directness" (63, leaf 87). This trait leads Vere to turn himself into a functionary. Vere believes that his position as captain and his duty to the Crown demand that he reject actions that derive from the free play of dialectical inquiry. Vere sees himself as wedged in by historical forces, especially by disciplinarian imperatives foisted upon him by the Spithead and Nore mutinies:

> That the unhappy event ... could not have happened at a worse juncture was but too true. For it was close on the heel of the suppressed insurrections, an aftertime very critical to naval authority, demanding from every English sea commander two qualities not readily interfusable – prudence and rigor .... The essential right and wrong involved in the matter, the clearer that might be, so much the worse for the responsibility of a loyal sea commander, inasmuch as he was not authorized to determine the matter on that primitive basis. (102–3, leaves 238–40)

Shortly after Billy kills Claggart, Captain Vere's appearance assumes "quite another aspect .... The father in him, manifested towards Billy thus far in the scene, was replaced by the military disciplinarian" (100, leaf 228). To impose the full rigor of the law is for Vere to displace his human emotions: "But a true military officer is in one particular like a true monk. Not with more of self-abnegation will the latter keep his vows of monastic obedience than the former his vows of allegiance to martial duty" (104, leaf 243). And "martial duty" militates against the dialectical possibilities associated with the narrator's tactical indirection. During the trial Vere lays out the issue with unstinting "directness." Private conscience and the qualifying contingencies of moral casuistry are inimical to the demands of monolithic law. Vere "strive[s] against scruples that may tend to enervate decision" (110, leaf 266). Such scruples generate from the relationship between Billy's primal innocence and his homicidal act, the very nuances that the narrator invites the reader to consider. Moving within Vere and the members of the court is "Nature" and, standing in opposition to "Nature," the "private conscience" (111, leaf 271) and the "heart, sometimes the feminine in man" (111, leaf 270) are the constructs of human society most manifested by a captain's duty to a king:

> But do these buttons that we wear attest that our allegiance is to Nature? No, to the King. Though the ocean, which is inviolate Nature primeval, though this be the element where we move and have our being as sailors, yet as the King's officers lies our duty in a sphere correspondingly natural? So little is that true, that in receiving our commissions we in the most important regards ceased to be natural free agents. (110, leaves 267–8)

In the cause of saving "lasting institutions" Vere believes he must reject the vagaries of free will, emotional flux, and moral ambiguity – the elements that most characterize the tortured and tangled domain of human agency. By rejecting the "bypaths" (56, leaf 58) and involutions of hermeneutical "indirection" (74, leaf 126), Vere remains true to his character. He upholds what seems a reductive maxim: " 'With mankind,' he would say, 'forms, measured forms, are everything; and that is the import couched in the story of Orpheus with his lyre spellbinding the wild denizens of the wood' " (128, leaf 333). His axiom is actually a highly determinate aesthetic theory. The artificer, rather than liberating the world, must use his power to quell "the disruption of forms" (128, leaf 333). Vere sees the great enemy as the French Directory and not, certainly, his own possible misapplication of authority. But rather than overtly critiquing Vere, the narrator evokes Peter the Barbarian and thereby creates a complex transnational image that complicates the implications of Vere's affiliation with the King's England. In commenting on Vere's wish to maintain secrecy regarding his handling of Claggart's murder, the narrator equivocally writes:

> Here [Vere] may or may not have erred . . . . Some imaginative ground for invidious comment there was. The maintenance of secrecy in the matter, the confining all knowledge of it for a time to the place where the homicide occurred, the quarter-deck cabin; in these particulars lurked some resemblance to the policy adopted in those tragedies of the palace which have occurred more than once in the capital founded by Peter the Barbarian. (103, leaves 241–2)

The narrator displaces Vere's nationality, associating his actions with a more encompassing and sinister figure of absolute despotism. Vere's embrace of "forms, measured forms" allows him to use the notion of a mythic artist's power – here the "spellbinding" power of Orpheus – as a way to serve the state and as a justification of hegemonic imperatives (128, leaf 333).

But Captain Vere's decision and his subsequent "agony of the strong" (115, leaf 289) have little or no effect on the unfolding historical circumstances. Not only does Vere die shortly after Billy's death, but the official version, as supplied by "News from the Mediterranean," turns Billy into a mutinous "ringleader" possessing "extreme depravity" and "patriotic" Claggart into a man "respectable and discreet" (130, leaves 341–3). And an unidentified poet later transfigures the young Handsome Sailor into the conspiratorial sailor of "Billy in the Darbies." At the end of *Billy Budd* Melville returned to the beginning, though the narrative's final words by no means mark its conclusion. Had he lived longer and regained better health Melville would have come back to the manuscript and, perhaps, embarked on making another final fair-copy version. In the process he would no doubt have continued to violate "[t]he symmetry of form attainable in pure fiction" in favor of exploring how "truth uncompromisingly told" demands the fragmentation of symmetrical forms (128, leaf 335). But left as it was, in its still unfinished state, *Billy Budd, Sailor (An Inside Narrative)* remains a text wherein readers and rereaders find not a final statement emanating from the pen, the pencil, or the crayon markers of a self-assured master, but a cryptic tale that seemed to be telling Herman Melville many things at the same time, a haunting story that he could not, or would not, bring to any kind of peaceful ease.

NOTE

1 References to *Billy Budd, Sailor (An Inside Narrative)*, ed. Harrison Hayford and Merton M. Sealts, Jr. are cited parenthetically by page number and leaf. The Hayford and Sealts text prints in succession the reading text and the genetic text. A citation to the reading text by way of page number and leaf number can be cross-referenced to the genetic text by way of leaf number. I also make some citations of superseded materials that appear only in the genetic text. These citations are also made parenthetically through page and leaf numbers. These citations can likewise be cross-referenced to the reading text by way of leaf number.

REFERENCES AND FURTHER READING

Brodtkorb, Paul, Jr. "The Definitive *Billy Budd*: 'But Aren't It All Sham?' " *PMLA* 82 (1967): 600–12.

Coffler, Gail. "Religion, Myth, and Meaning in the Art of *Billy Budd, Sailor*." In *New Essays on* Billy Budd. Ed. Donald Yannella. Cambridge: Cambridge University Press, 2002. 49–82.

Dillingham, William B. *Melville and His Circle: The Last Years*. Athens: University of Georgia Press, 1996.

Garner, Stanton A. "Fraud as Fact in Herman Melville's *Billy Budd*." *San Jose Studies* 4 (1978): 82–105.

Johnson, Barbara. "Melville's Fist: The Execution of 'Billy Budd.' " *Studies in Romanticism* 18 (1979): 567–99.

Milder, Robert, ed. *Critical Essays on Melville's "Billy Budd, Sailor."* Boston: G. K. Hall, 1989.

——. "Melville's Late Poetry and *Billy Budd*: From Nostalgia to Transcendence." *Philological Quarterly* 66 (1987): 493–507.

———. "Old Man Melville: The Rose and the Cross." In *New Essays on "Billy Budd."* Ed. Donald Yannella. Cambridge: Cambridge University Press, 2002. 83–113.

Parker, Hershel. *Reading* Billy Budd. Evanston, IL: Northwestern University Press, 1990.

Reynolds, Larry J. *"Billy Budd* and American Labor Unrest: The Case for Striking Back." In *New Essays on "Billy Budd."* Ed. Donald Yannella. Cambridge: Cambridge University Press, 2002. 21–48.

———. *European Revolutions and the American Literary Renaissance.* New Haven, CT: Yale University Press, 1988.

Schiffman, Joseph. "Melville's Final Stage, Irony: A Reexamination of *Billy Budd* Criticism." *American Literature* 22 (1950): 128–36.

Scorza, Thomas J. *In the Time Before Steamships: "Billy Budd," The Limits of Politics, and Modernity.* De Kalb: Northern Illinois University Press, 1979.

Sealts, Merton M., Jr. "Innocence and Infamy: *Billy Budd, Sailor.*" In *A Companion to Melville Studies.* Ed. John Bryant. New York: Greenwood Press, 1986. 407–30.

Stern, Milton R., ed. *Billy Budd, Sailor: An Inside Narrative.* By Herman Melville. Indianapolis: Bobbs-Merrill, 1975.

———. *The Fine Hammered Steel of Herman Melville.* Urbana: University of Illinois Press, 1957.

Watson, E. L. Grant. "Melville's Testament of Acceptance." *New England Quarterly* 6 (June 1933): 319–27.

Wenke, John. "Complicating Vere: Melville's Practice of Revision in *Billy Budd.*" *Leviathan: A Journal of Melville Studies* 1 (1999): 83–8.

———. "Melville's Indirection: *Billy Budd,* the Genetic Text, and 'The Deadly Space Between.' " In *New Essays on "Billy Budd."* Ed. Donald Yannella. Cambridge: Cambridge University Press, 2002. 114–44.

Widmer, Kingsley. *The Ways of Nihilism: A Study of Herman Melville's Short Novels.* Los Angeles: Ward-Ritchie Press, 1970.

Withim, Phil. *"Billy Budd:* Testament of Resistance." *Modern Language Quarterly* 22 (1959): 115–27.

Part VI
Meanings

33

The Melville Revival

Sanford E. Marovitz

Melville studies remain confused and misinformed as to the basic facts of the Melville Revival. (Clare Spark, *Hunting Captain Ahab.*)

The "Melville Revival," widely said to have commenced early in the past century, has become a critical commonplace, but its exact meaning remains unclear. Indeed, most general readers simply assume that Melville's writing has remained alive in the public eye since first published. When and where did this revival begin, who or what initiated it, and how long did it last? How might contemporary social issues have affected the revival's evolution? And what might be said about its long-term effects? Throughout a history that spans seven decades, from the first hint of its advent in 1883 through the publication of the Moby-Dick *Centennial Essays* in 1953, Melville became one of America's most highly esteemed authors.

Avant-garde

In 1963 Michael P. Zimmerman maintained that two limited Melville revivals preceded the primary one that began with his centennial in 1919. The first started in 1891, he said, the year of Melville's death, and lasted into the early 1900s, when the second commenced and continued until the major one began. Although Melville's re-emergence as a leading American author did gather force around 1919, the revival actually began at least thirty-six years earlier, when W[illiam] Clark Russell praised *Redburn* in 1883 as "one of Herman Merivale's delightful sea tales" (Higgins *Bibliography* 198). Russell had the surname misspelled, but that would not have mattered to Melville, who admired the distinguished English author of *The Wreck of the* Grosvenor (1877) and other maritime fiction. On July 21, 1886, Melville opened a correspondence with Russell, and in reply Russell praised his "admirable genius" (L 731–2). Two years later Melville dedicated *John Marr and Other Sailors* (1888) to the English novelist, asserting that *"The Wreck of the* Grosvenor entitles the author to the naval crown in current literature"* (Vincent *CP* Introduction 469n). Russell then dedicated his own forthcoming novel, *An Ocean Tragedy* (1889), to Melville as "that magnificent American sea-novelist." As early as 1899, one "T. B. F." reported to the *New York Times* from London that Russell's praise had stimulated a "conspicuous revival of interest in America's sea author" (Higgins *Bibliography* 235).

In addition to Russell, H. S. Salt, also in England, showed a decided interest in Melville's writing in the 1880s. Salt, a prominent literary figure and socialist with connections among British artists and writers, published two articles on Melville (1889 and 1892) in which he gave special praise to *Typee* and *Moby-Dick*. To be sure, *Typee* had been the book of choice for most readers of Melville since mid-century with only *White-Jacket* achieving similar popularity, and it remained so into the 1880s and 1890s, although by 1900 *Moby-Dick* had begun to achieve greater tributes as admiration for Melville's work spread among the English literati.

Salt also reprinted in 1901 an essay by Archibald MacMechan, "The Greatest Sea Story Ever Written," brought out originally two years earlier in an obscure Nova Scotia journal, the *Queen's Quarterly* (Parker *Recognition* 137–45). MacMechan joined the faculty at Dalhousie as a Carlyle scholar and remained there throughout his career; admired as both a teacher and a scholar, he also taught summer programs at Columbia and Harvard. Wherever he taught, he praised *Moby-Dick* and its author, whom he had aspired to meet but never did. MacMechan gained countless readers for Melville's classic novel well before 1919 and for several years after (Kennedy and Kennedy).

No less eager in his early support of Melville was Arthur Stedman, son of Edmund Clarence Stedman, a notable American poet and critic in the late nineteenth century who included six of Melville's poems in his *American Anthology: 1787–1899* (1900). Young Stedman visited Melville periodically during the ailing author's final years. On Melville's death, his widow, Elizabeth, appointed Stedman as his literary executor. Keen on helping to restore Melville's tarnished reputation, and knowing that most of his writings were no longer in print, Stedman edited *Typee, Omoo, White-Jacket*, and *Moby-Dick* for the United States Book Company in 1892. His bio-critical "Introduction to the Edition" appeared in the first of these; despite its critical limitations, Merton M. Sealts, Jr., assessed it as "the best short Life written in the nineteenth century" (*Early Lives* 154–66). In it, Stedman described Melville as "independent" of mind and "trust[ing] to the verdict of the future" for a just assessment of his work (*Early Lives* 166). Another early biography – "Herman Melville" – was written by J. E. A. Smith and published serially in the Pittsfield *Evening Journal* in 1891. An acquaintance of Melville in the Berkshires, Smith provided a sympathetic overview of Melville's life but gave only minimal attention to the writings after *Omoo*, although he did reprint two poems from *Battle-Pieces* (Sealts, *Early Lives* 140–2). The next year, John Murray, the original British publisher of *Typee* and *Omoo*, brought out reprints of both early editions in 1896 with new prefaces by H. S. Salt.

Although such advocates as Russell, MacMechan, the Stedmans, Salt, and others attempted to restore Melville's diminished literary stature around the end of the century, they probably had no conception of making him a truly popular author however much they felt he deserved such status. After all, even when Melville was at the peak of his lifetime fame between 1846 and 1850, neither *Typee* nor *White-Jacket* became a bestseller. Only about 10,000 copies of *Typee* were printed and sold in the US by the end of the century and fewer still in Britain. *The Whale* and *Moby-Dick* fared much worse, with a total of at best around 4,000 copies printed in both countries, and of them not more than a few hundred were sold in Britain. Compare these figures with those of Melville's contemporaries, Sarah Payson Willis, Maria Susanna Cummins, and especially Harriet Beecher Stowe, whose early sales often were in the tens of thousands; *Uncle Tom's Cabin* sold 75,000 copies in the first three months off the press in spring 1852. That was the dreadful year that Melville published *Pierre*, a financial disaster.

Grand Recognition

Due to the efforts of his early advocates, however, Melville began to receive more and greater praise from other literati. From 1883 the seeds of the revival were being planted, then tended until germination occurred. That may have commenced with the publication of Carl Van Doren's short chapter on Melville in *The Cambridge History of American Literature* (1917), edited by W. P. Trent, whom the zealous Archibald MacMechan had introduced to *Moby-Dick* several years earlier. Van Doren, then on the Columbia University faculty, called *Moby-Dick* "one of the greatest sea romances in the whole history of the world," although at that time he still valued *Typee* more highly (quoted in Kennedy and Kennedy 64).

With the centennial the seeds of the revival began to sprout and, two years after that, to flower. Percy H. Boynton's *History of American Literature* (1919) referred to "[t]he present 'Melville revival,' " which he attributed partly to the current appeal of South Seas literature and partly to prevailing skepticism during the postwar period, but mainly to the recognition that "in Melville has been rediscovered one of the immensely energetic and original personalities of the last hundred years" (Higgins *Bibliography* 265). Early in August 1919, Raymond M. Weaver followed a suggestion by his senior colleague at Columbia, Carl Van Doren, and published "The Centennial of Herman Melville" in the *Nation*, of which Van Doren was literary editor. Weaver was then new to Melville scholarship; he wrote admiringly of *Moby-Dick* but denigrated or disregarded the later writing and characterized the author as suffering from increasing despair after returning from the South Pacific. A week later, Frank Jewett Mather, Jr., renowned professor of art and archeology at Princeton, also published an excellent essay on Melville in the New York *Review*; there he surveyed Melville's writings, lavished praise on *Moby-Dick*, and wrote favorably even of works that had typically been dismissed, such as *Mardi*, *Pierre*, and the poetry – including *Clarel*. "No ordinary person loves Melville," he perspicaciously declared (Parker *Recognition* 156). The following year brought imaginative essays from London by E. L. Grant Watson and Viola Meynell, including her introduction to the widely distributed Oxford World Classics Edition of *Moby-Dick*.

Two years after publishing his initial article on Melville, Weaver gave the revival new impetus with the first full-length biography of the author, *Herman Melville: Mariner and Mystic* (1921). His research began with the centenary article. Shortly after discovering with astonishment that no substantial Life had yet been written and the published criticism was minimal, Weaver resigned from his teaching position to write one. He engaged the support of Eleanor Melville Metcalf, Melville's granddaughter, who gave him "access to all the surviving records of her grandfather: Melville manuscripts, letters, journals, annotated books, photographs, and a variety of other material." "To Mrs. and Mr. Metcalf," he wrote, "I owe one of the richest and most pleasant associations of my life" (acknowledgment page). He could not know then *how* rich that association would prove for him as Melville's first full-scale biographer.

In the opening pages of his biography Weaver characterized Melville after 1851 as repudiating the world that had scorned him for rebelling against convention on returning from the sea. This disappointment, Weaver posited, was the first of Melville's two severe disillusionments; the second was the hostility he suffered from critics after his initial success. "His whole history is the record of an attempt to escape from an inexorable and intolerable world of reality" (19). According to Weaver, Melville's three major achievements were discovering the South Seas for literature, realistically depicting a sailor's life at sea, and writing *Moby-Dick*, his "undoubted masterpiece" (25). After *Moby-Dick*, however, came "The Long Quietus" in which disillusionment reigned, leading only to the production of mostly inferior and unacceptable work, although Weaver quotes from *Battle-Pieces* and *Clarel*, admiring "passages of beauty,...vigour and daring" amid its "arid wastes" (365). The biography is often inaccurate in its details and too dependent on Melville's travel narratives for autobiographical reference and documentation. His portrait of Melville as a failure beyond the writing of *Moby-Dick* is simply wrong, and his view of him as a bitter rebel through the rest of his life is at best questionable. Yet because it was the first full-length study of Melville, Weaver's biography had enormous importance. Reviewed with great favor, it became the prime source for later biographers and critics, and not until well into the 1930s did some of them become aware of its limitations. Nor was Weaver's importance to Melville studies limited to the biography because afterwards he edited a collection of short fiction, Melville's journal of his journey to the Near East, and perhaps most important, the first edition of *Billy Budd*.

Although selected Melville titles had been issued prior to Weaver's biography, not until 1922–4 was the first collected edition published by Constable in London. Constable was the firm of Michael Sadleir, who in 1922 had brought out a descriptive bibliography of Melville first editions with a laudatory introduction. Also published in 1922 was a volume compiled by Meade Minnigerode, *Some Personal Letters of Herman Melville and a Bibliography*, in two sections; the first includes extracts of

Melville's letters (written 1846–62) within a biographical context, and the second is a substantial bibliography of first editions and later printings with selected reviews of each. To an extraordinary degree the Constable edition stimulated the rapid publication between 1922 and 1930 of Melville's individual prose narratives; all of his titles reappeared anew except *The Confidence-Man*. G. Thomas Tanselle pointed out, "There has been no other period of such intense activity in republishing so many of Melville's books" (Bryant *Companion* 809), but the revival still had a long way to go.

Two more biographies of Melville followed Weaver's before the decade was out, both indebted to their predecessor. Like Weaver, in *Herman Melville* (1926) John Freeman presented his subject caught in an ideological struggle between his ideals and reality that led to Melville's withdrawal after most of his prose was written. Yet Freeman did note things to praise in the fiction beyond *Moby-Dick*, and he gave some attention to the poetry, though, again following Weaver's lead, he found little of merit in Melville's work written after 1851. Three years later, Lewis Mumford published his *Herman Melville* (1929), which became the standard Life of the author before 1951, when the collaborative efforts of Leon Howard and Jay Leyda led to Howard's *Herman Melville* and Leyda's two-volume *Melville Log*. Mumford's biography, like those of his predecessors, depended heavily on Melville's ostensibly autobiographical revelations in his fiction, which severely limited its accuracy, but his criticism was often astute. Melville's greatness was puzzling to his contemporaries, Mumford wrote, because "they valued him for those lesser virtues in which he more clearly resembled themselves" (4); Mumford observed that Melville was being revived because he grappled with spiritual dilemmas and dove deep into himself trying to resolve them. Melville's persistent search for answers where none were forthcoming led him to "the tragic sense of life: the sense that the highest human flight is sustained over an unconquered and perhaps unconquerable abyss" (5). Mumford accurately predicted that "Each age... will find its own symbols in *Moby-Dick*" (194), and of the novel that immediately followed and failed economically, he anticipated the psychological insights of Henry A. Murray by two decades, recognizing the autobiographical truths that lay behind it: "*Pierre* itself, then, was a blow, aimed at his family with their cold pride, and at the critics, with their low standards" (221). Regarding the author himself as the first decade of the revival in full flower approached its end, Mumford accurately proposed, "The day of Herman Melville's vision is now in the beginning" (368).

Another biographical account of the 1920s is a brief but penetrating bio-critical overview by Vernon L. Parrington included in *Main Currents in American Thought* (1927). His tone is predictable, given the single word *"PESSIMIST"* beside Melville's name on the headnote. Identifying Melville as a "rebellious transcendentalist," Parrington asserted, "There is no other tragedy in American letters comparable to the tragedy of Herman Melville." Parrington's debt to Weaver is immediately apparent both in drawing what he took to be autobiographical facts from Melville's narratives and in describing Melville's alleged disillusionment and defiance; attacked as a nonconformist, "he bade the world go to the devil" and withdrew from it (2.250).

Parrington highlights the internal conflict that affected Melville for most of his life. On Nuku Hiva he loved the kind, simple existence of the natives, but as an inheritor of "Christian conscience" and as "a child of Hebraic ideals of righteousness, he could not eradicate the deep roots of ethical unrest" (2.253).

In addition to the biographies and editions published during the 1920s, of course, were a number of articles and commentaries that helped the revival to flourish. As was true of W. Clark Russell, sometimes only a few brief comments by notable people had a disproportionate effect on Melville's growing reputation. For example, in the New Orleans *Double Dealer* (January 1922), novelist Carl Van Vechten lauded Melville's later works, among which he categorized *Mardi* because he found it more sophisticated than the other narratives written before *Moby-Dick* (Higgins *Bibliography* 281). The following year, H. M. Tomlinson, a British journalist and sea-novelist, noted in the *Christian Science Monitor* (10/14/22) that the first two volumes of the Constable edition were out. He added that for a long time *Moby-Dick* was "a semi-secret wonder" used as a touchstone by the literary elect to determine the quality of other readers' taste. Late the next year, Leonard Woolf noted the correspondences in theme and structure between James Joyce's *Ulysses* and *Moby-Dick* (Higgins *Bibliography* 291–2, 302).

Probably the most important critical commentaries published on Melville in the 1920s were two chapters in D. H. Lawrence's *Studies in Classic American Literature* (1923). Lawrence's recognition of American writings as classic was highly significant, and placing Melville's work among them added thrust to the developing revival. The first of his two chapters probes *Typee* and *Omoo*, in which he assumes that Tommo is Melville and identifies the author as fundamentally a mystic and idealist yet also a savage drawn to the Eden of Nuku Hiva. In his second chapter, Lawrence examines *Moby-Dick*, which for him was the greatest sea story ever written; perhaps enchanted by it, he devotes more space to long quotations from the text than to analyses. Yet the last two pages of that chapter are stunning for the imaginative depth and breadth of comprehension they reveal in both authors – in Melville for plunging into his psyche and exposing imagistically what he found there, and in Lawrence for fathoming it in terms of psychological revelation. He depicts Moby Dick as manifesting "the deepest blood-being of the white race" (173), which Ahab must seek and kill to gain supremacy over it, but he cannot. In bringing about his own death, he causes the destruction of his white-owned ship and crew, suggesting that Melville knew the white race itself was doomed.

Another and very different reading of *Moby-Dick* appeared the following year in a limited hardbound edition of only nine pages written by A. S. W. Rosenbach, a Philadelphia bibliophile, dealer, and collector with an almost legendary reputation. His *Introduction to Herman Melville's* Moby-Dick; or, The Whale (1924) describes and extols *Moby-Dick* rhapsodically; in it, Melville created "something that will survive as long as the sea itself, an incarnation that will grow more vivid, more permanent with the roll of the years." In Rosenbach's eyes, Melville gave Moby Dick "a personality as rich in individualism as Hamlet. In fact, Moby Dick, as a tragic figure, in many respects is not unlike him" (2–3). Like Lawrence, Rosenbach perceived the White

Whale as "the theme closest to [Melville's] soul, . . . unconquerable, inviolate as the sea itself," and unattainable, "the precious Desire that can never be fully realized" (3). Beyond the rhapsody, Rosenbach praised Melville's realistic description of whales and maritime life, as well as his characterization and especially his style, which "rolls on" one page after another, never stopping and always changing; in *Moby-Dick* he gained heights undreamed of by other sea-writers, resembling "his own Catskill Eagle" (9).

Rosenbach's acuity becomes strikingly clear in the light of his early prediction that the highest values in American manuscripts would be those of writings by Melville and Eugene O'Neill (Higgins *Bibliography* 344). As a dealer and collector, Rosenbach profited from his foresight. In 1927 he recalled purchasing a first edition of *Moby-Dick* for two dollars some years earlier, but his real prize was Melville's signed presentation copy of that novel to Hawthorne, which he had bought for $150 from the poet John Drinkwater, who himself had acquired it for a few dollars at a New York bookstore (Higgins *Bibliography* 328). These memories of purchases made perhaps twenty or twenty-five years earlier (the dates are unstated) confirm the rapidly increased values of Melville's books over a relatively short period of time. In 1926 Hart Crane's now famous poem, "At Melville's Tomb," was published in *Poetry*, and on July 14, 1927, William Faulkner, then still far from achieving the recognition he would eventually gain, may also have helped move the revival a step farther when he was quoted in a Chicago daily as saying, "I think that the book which I put down with the unqualified thought 'I wish I had written that' is *Moby-Dick*" (Higgins *Bibliography* 330).

Moreover, during the second half of the twenties, Melville was popularized with the first film appearances of *Moby-Dick*: *The Sea Beast* in 1926 and *Moby-Dick* in 1930. Another enduring contribution was the series of brilliant ink-drawing illustrations created by Rockwell Kent for the spectacular three-volume Lakeside Press edition of *Moby-Dick* in an aluminum case (Schultz 28, 335). In the same year, 1930, nearly all the original illustrations were included in a Random House edition; this led in 1944 to the publication of the Modern Library Giant edition, which immediately evoked an expanded readership and remains a bargain at its modest price. An abundance of other illustrations of *Moby-Dick* appeared over the decades that followed, but none has achieved the classic status of Kent's drawings, which have accompanied translations of the novel around the world.

Critical Inquiry and Investigation

From the late nineteenth century to the centenary, Melville's relatively few advocates had been so excited over his works that they seem to have felt it a solemn duty to bring him the distinction he deserved. Those who followed in much larger numbers in the 1920s were equally ebullient, but with the opening of the 1930s, a new type of reader emerged, no less enthusiastic but more analytical. Not only did Melville's work become subject to critical analysis in the 1930s, but also his own life was exposed as significantly at variance from the way he appears to have presented it in the fiction. As a result, criticism in the 1930s and after is more eclectic, thematic, and rational, especially but not only in approaching Melville's quasi-autobiographical narratives.

In 1931 a first edition of *Moby-Dick* sold at auction for $300, and four years later a first edition of *The Whale* went for $1,575. Such sales boded well for Melville's stock in the 1930s and 1940s. The first of several short books published during that decade was Vega Curl's *Pasteboard Masks* (1931); initially an honors thesis at Radcliffe, it explored the Emersonian transcendental relation between inner and outer reality as Curl saw it in the work of Melville and Hawthorne. Stanley Geist's *Herman Melville: The Tragic Vision and the Heroic Ideal* (1939), also originally an honors thesis but at Harvard, showed how Melville's heroic ideal emerged from the tragic recognition of darkness at the core of life.

Two books published late in the decade have proved exceedingly influential: first, Willard Thorp's collection of extracts from Melville's writings: *Herman Melville: Representative Selections, with Introduction, Bibliography, and Notes* (1938); the second, Charles Roberts Anderson's *Melville in the South Seas* (1939). From a more recent perspective, Thorp's *Representative Selections* seems limited; although in his Introduction he referred briefly to some of Melville's later fiction and devoted several pages to *Pierre* in a sound discussion of the "trilogy" (with *Mardi* and *Moby-Dick*), he included no prose published after *Moby-Dick*. However, the book does contain two reviews in addition to "Hawthorne and His Mosses" and an excellent choice of letters for so limited a venue; nor did he overlook the poems, having selected examples from *Battle-Pieces*, *John Marr*, and *Timoleon*.

Anderson's contribution, too, is valuable far beyond its restrictive coverage of Melville's maritime years because it was the first book that paid close attention to historical records outside the perimeter of family, friends, and literary associates, to document what is surely one of the most important periods of his life, 1841–5. It is impossible to overestimate the value of these two books in the growth of Melville studies; whereas Thorp introduced Melville inexpensively to countless new readers, Anderson lifted Melville scholarship to a whole new level of accomplishment and revelation. A review in *Time* of *Melville in the South Seas* mentioned the hundreds of publications on Melville since 1919 to confirm he has become "one of the major figures of U.S. letters" (Higgins *Reference* 83).

In addition to the books, however, several other influential chapters and articles appeared during the 1930s. In 1931 Louis Untermeyer included a bio-critical commentary on Melville in his popular volume, *American Poetry from the Beginning to Whitman*, with extracts from *Moby-Dick* and selections from each of Melville's books of poetry, including *Clarel*. In the same year, Constance Rourke devoted several pages to *Moby-Dick* in *American Humor: A Study of the National Character* to exhibit how Melville's use of American folklore enabled him to break "through the mask of comedy to find its ultimate secret"; the Janus-like duality of humor and violence of mythic animals of American folk tales ties humanity to the gods and lifts Melville's narrative to epic heights (157). On the road to his mystical philosophy the following year, in *Texts and Pretexts*, Aldous Huxley explained Melville's allusion to the "all" feeling near the end of his letter to Hawthorne (June 1?, 1851); in fact, Huxley was already familiar with Melville's writing at least as far back as 1925, when a character in *These Barren Leaves* suggests that *Moby-Dick* lacks greatness only because of its quasi-Shakespearean style (208).

Source studies began gaining strength even before the 1930s. As early as June 1928 in *PMLA* Harold B. Scudder identified Melville's principal source for "Benito Cereno" as Amasa Delano's *Narrative of Voyages and Travels* (1817). In July 1932 Raymond Hughes compared *Moby-Dick* with Shakespeare's tragedies, pointing out numerous correspondences; his was but the first of many such studies to come. Three years later Robert Gibbings definitely pointed to Owen Chase's *Essex* narrative as a major source for *Moby-Dick*, and in autumn 1936 Frederick B. Adams, Jr., did the same with Scoresby's *Account of the Arctic Regions...[and] the Northern Whale Fishery* (1821). Earlier that year, Thomas Russell already had identified Charles S. Stewart's *A Visit to the South Seas* (1831) as a primary source for *Typee*. In November 1937 William Braswell analyzed Melville's marginalia in three volumes of Emerson's *Essays*, categorizing his comments about Emerson's views on the poet, life, and evil.

Earlier in the decade Stanley T. Williams briefly surveyed Melville in his book *American Literature* (1933); except for a mixed review of Mumford's biography, this limited commentary was his first publication on Melville, but Williams's significance to the Melville revival is not dependent on his published criticism. Instead, as a professor of English at Yale in the 1930s, he became the most consequential Melville instructor during the formative period of Melville studies. A list of his doctoral students from this period includes at least eleven of the most prominent names in Melville scholarship, all of whom published significantly on his writings within the following three decades: James Baird, Walter Bezanson, Merrell R. Davis, Charles Feidelson, Jr., Elizabeth A. Foster, William H. Gilman, Harrison Hayford, Tyrus Hillway, Henry F. Pommer, Merton M. Sealts, Jr., and Nathalia Wright.

This bare list of names cannot do justice to the historic contributions of the identified authors, whose careers as Melville scholars commenced with Williams's guidance. For example, Bezanson's superb essay, "*Moby-Dick*: Work of Art," has often been reprinted after first appearing in the Moby-Dick *Centennial Essays* (1953). In addition, Harrison Hayford's contributions to Melville studies extend beyond his invaluable editorial work with Hershel Parker and G. Thomas Tanselle on the definitive edition of Melville's *Writings* (1968–). From his seminal dissertation of 1943 relating Melville to Hawthorne, Hayford drew many letters, journal extracts, and other manuscript materials first made public in that study and included them later in several important articles. What did Williams's former students think of him as a teacher and advisor? Their opinions varied; some were pleased with his lectures, writing instruction, and advice, while others found him uncharismatic and could not grasp what made his classes and assistance so successful. Nonetheless, studying Melville with Professor Williams had a mystique that markedly affected his students (Sealts *Closing* 51; Wright 1–4).

Frank Luther Mott said in 1947 that with the revival *Moby-Dick* began selling in the hundreds of thousands, qualifying it as a bestseller at last; well over half a million copies had been sold in the US since 1921 (Mott 132). Four years later, Malcolm Cowley implied that Melville's "stock" was losing value (Higgins *Reference* 292), but Stanley T. Williams began his chapter on Melville in *Eight American Authors* (1956), a bibliographical assessment of biography, criticism, and editions of major American authors of the nineteenth century, by saying: "No complete bibliography of Melville can come into being until after the subsidence of the present wave of biographical and critical writing. The detailed eight-page record in L[*iterary*] H[*istory*] [*of the*] U[*nited*] S[*tates*] (1948) is already inadequate" (Williams 207). That was in 1956, and, of course, the wave has not ended yet, nor is there a hint of its diminishing soon.

Faith, religion, and moral issues were leading themes in criticism of the later 1930s and early 1940s. In *Maule's Curse* (1938) Yvor Winters explained Melville's symbolism in selected works, but the focus was on *Moby-Dick*, which Winters recognized more as an epic poem than a novel, and on *Pierre*, which, like its predecessor, considers the judgmental relation of perception to principle. Three years later one of the most impressive books yet written on American Romanticism was published – F. O. Matthiessen's *American Renaissance: Art and Expression in the Age of Emerson and Whitman* (1941). Melville was one of the five principal authors who shared a "devotion to the possibilities of democracy" (ix), among other common themes, especially the relation of the individual to society and the conflict between good and evil, which was related to tragedy. In his section on Melville, *Moby-Dick* received the most attention; in both it and *Pierre* Matthiessen exposed the impact of Shakespearean tragedy, especially the Elizabethan's language in *Moby-Dick* and the tortured mind of Hamlet in *Pierre*. Matthiessen's close textual readings, relations drawn among authors of different periods, and integration of interdisciplinary themes made *American Renaissance* an essential resource for many students of American Romanticism for decades.

Not long afterward, William Braswell published *Melville's Religious Thought* (1943), in which he argued that although Melville yearned for the peace that doctrinal Christianity offered he was too critical by nature to accept it. He continued to find fault with organized religion and, especially in *The Confidence-Man* and after, to maintain a pessimistic view of humanity, yet in *Billy Budd* and "Daniel Orme" he seems to have accepted "the wisdom of resigning the heart to the fate of man" (114–15, 122). The following year, in *Herman Melville: The Tragedy of Mind*, William Ellery Sedgewick also traced Melville's deep exploration of his consciousness and his unfolding awareness of the darkness within. In *Call Me Ishmael* (1947) Charles Olson included a revision of his article "*Lear* and *Moby-Dick*" (1938), in which he had examined the marginalia in Melville's edition of Shakespeare to trace its influence on the composition of *Moby-Dick*. Olson's highly stylized book also discussed the significance of natural force in that novel; according to Olson, Melville's belief that Americans desired to overcome nature more than to be free appears in his use of the *Essex* disaster as a major source. Also emphasized are the significance of (1) the Pacific to Melville as an "experience of SPACE," (2) "a comprehension of PAST, his marriage of spirit to sources" (including a search for the father), and (3) "a confirmation of FUTURE" in the West (114–19).

In February 1945, the revival advanced significantly when Tyrus Hillway, Harrison Hayford, and bibliographer John Birss established the Melville Society and a news-letter, *Melville Society Extracts,* edited by Hillway. This formal new society put the seal on Melville's status as one of America's most significant authors; it is now the oldest single-figure literary association in the US. Melville's elevated status in the American literary canon was further substantiated in 1968 when *Typee* appeared as the first volume of the definitive *Writings of Herman Melville,* published jointly by the North-western University Press and the Newberry Library of Chicago under the general editorship of Hayford, Parker, and Tanselle.

In 1947 Howard P. Vincent made another important step forward with the first American edition of *The Collected Poems of Herman Melville,* published by Hendricks House and meant to serve as the opening volume in a new annotated set of the collected works, but the set was never completed. The volumes that appeared, however, included introductions and notes by leading Melville scholars: Murray's *Pierre* (1949), Mansfield and Vincent's incomparable edition of *Moby-Dick* (1952), Foster's *The Confidence-Man* (1954), and Bezanson's invaluable *Clarel* (1960). In 1949 Jay Leyda published *The Complete Short Stories of Herman Melville* and in 1952 brought out *The Portable Melville,* an excellent selection of extracts from the letters, fiction, essays, journals, and poems. Although the journal from Melville's pilgrimage to Europe and the Near East had been edited by Raymond Weaver and published in 1935 as *Journal up the Straits,* the record of his earlier voyage, *Journal of a Visit to London and the Continent . . . 1849–1850,* did not appear until 1948, ably edited with a valuable Introduction and Notes by his granddaughter Eleanor. That year, also, F. Barron Freeman brought out a new edition of *Billy Budd.*

By the mid-1940s, publications on Melville were frequently appearing in academic journals as well as more popular venues, and the mid-century years 1947–53 consti-tuted the single most fruitful period of scholarship on Melville since the revival began. New Criticism came into vogue, encouraging close readings that found meaning in such internal devices as symbols, imagery, ambiguity, and irony rather than in external references. At this time, too, interest in Melville abroad was increasing. In Europe and Japan, his work began to attract readers again after World War II, and criticism expanded with his growing readership. In 1948 the *New York Times Book Review* borrowed the heading "Forgotten Man" from an obituary of Melville and reused it ironically to indicate that the Melville "boom" was still progressing apace (Higgins *Reference* 186). The following year, in a review of recent publications on Melville, David Daiches acknowledged that the extent of new editions and criticism verified his status as a true classic (Higgins *Reference* 214).

The next five years brought twenty more books and well over 500 additional articles, chapters, and notable references in various other publications. The books included four biographies, thirteen bio-critical and critical volumes, and three edi-tions. The most useful of the critical studies was Howard P. Vincent's *The Trying-Out of* Moby Dick (1949), a thorough investigation of Melville's whaling references that showed how Melville's experience on the *Acushnet* was transformed into Ishmael's on the *Pequod*. *The Trying-Out* is as engaging as it is informative because of Vincent's literary allusiveness as he conjoined his scrutiny of whaling sources with an account of the novel's composition and his own suggestions "concerning interpretation and meaning" (7).

In contrast to Vincent's source study, Richard Chase's *Herman Melville* (1949) separated Melville from the ideologies with which other critics had associated him and described his writings as those of a secularized "new" liberal whose thought was free, skeptical, and humanistic. Chase devised a complex scheme that integrated the Prometheus myth with figures from American folklore and reconciled symbolic polarities in Melville's fiction. Less contrived and imaginative than Chase's study, Geoffrey Stone's *Melville* (1949) offered a straightforward reading of the works; the perspective is Catholic but not restrictively so. Also published in 1949 was the Hendricks House edition of *Pierre* with Henry A. Murray's penetrating psychological Introduction to Melville's problematic novel. Unlike most earlier critics, Murray identified Pierre and the Glendinnings directly with the author and his family, explaining incidents and characters in Jungian and Freudian terms. Two years later in the *New England Quarterly* he published one of his most influential articles, "In Nomine Diaboli," a profound Freudian reading that identifies Ahab with Satan and the White Whale as an actual cetacean as well as "the projection of Ahab's Presbyterian conscience," an embodiment of the Calvinistic conception of a fearful God, and a symbol of Melville's "zealous parents" (86, 88).

A more hostile reading of *Pierre* than Murray's appeared in Newton Arvin's bio-critical study *Herman Melville* (1950), which tied the individual works to what Arvin believed was the state of Melville's mind when he composed them. Arvin offered a more thoughtful, sympathetic analysis of the early writings through *Moby-Dick* than of the later prose, most of which he denigrated as products of Melville's ailing mind. With the poetry, he said, Melville's mind regained wholeness. In *The Enchafèd Flood: The Romantic Iconography of the Sea* (1950), W. H. Auden integrated selections from *Moby-Dick* with those of other authors in an imaginative, eclectic meditation on symbols and heroes related to romantic representations of the sea.

If any single year may be taken as supreme for publications on Melville, 1951 is it. During that year three biographies and a critical study were published. The two full Lives – Leon Howard's *Herman Melville: A Biography* and Jay Leyda's *The Melville Log: A Documentary Life* in two volumes – were collaborative, complementary efforts that should be read and consulted together. Howard's biography is the first full Life of Melville since Mumford's, and with the *Log* it remained the standard before Hershel Parker's massive two-volume study appeared at the turn of the century (1996, 2002). The *Log* is a chronological listing of entries pertaining to Melville's life from birth to death; it is as inclusive as Leyda could reasonably make it to allow "each reader the opportunity to be his own biographer of Herman Melville, by providing him with the largest possible quantity of materials" (1.xi).

Also in 1951 William H. Gilman employed Anderson's methodology in *Melville in the South Seas* for his own *Melville's Early Life and* Redburn, a study of Melville's life between 1819 and 1841, when he first left home to go a-whaling. Ronald Mason's *The Spirit above the Dust: A Study of Herman Melville* (1951) effectively traced Melville's spiritual journey from a loss of innocence to experience that brought a restoration which Mason found evident in *Billy Budd*. For this British author, no small part of Melville's greatness lay in his being "the only American writer of genius effectively to sink the confining consciousness of nationalism in the wider context of the human soul" (20). Lawrance Thompson's study, *Melville's Quarrel with God*, was published the following year. According to Thompson, Melville acquired in his youth a firm belief in the angry, demanding God of Calvinism and developed an increasing hostility toward this divinity as he matured and aged. Because Melville felt certain that revealing this personal quarrel with God in his writing would create an adverse public reaction, Thompson proposed, he became deceptive in the subtle ways he exposed it.

In 1953, the final year for this selective history of the revival, three books worth special note were published, and Melville received signal attention in a fourth. Over thirty years earlier, Eleanor Melville Metcalf had made unpublished family documents available to Weaver, and in 1953 she used them with other primary materials for a personalized documentary biography of her grandfather, *Herman Melville: Cycle and Epicycle*. Her sensitive, detailed presentation as an immediate family member made this well-documented study complementary to any other Life of Melville. In 1951 a *Moby-Dick* centennial celebration produced a volume of Moby-Dick *Centennial Essays*, edited by Tyrus Hillway and Luther S. Mansfield; the range of topics was considerable and the authors all distinguished Americanists if not specifically Melvilleans. Also published in 1953 was a cynosure of the New Criticism, *Symbolism and American Literature*, by Charles Feidelson, Jr., which discusses the five authors Matthiessen examined in *American Renaissance* but in terms of their symbolic method rather than more broadly their concern with democracy. Feidelson saw symbolism as an essential component of American Romanticism, specifically as a means by which the authors could assert their literary independence.

If the thesis of *Melville's Quarrel with God* was controversial, it was no more so than C. L. R. James's *Mariners, Renegades, and Castaways: The Story of Herman Melville and the World We Live In*, privately published in 1953. James's most impressive chapters analyze *Moby-Dick* as representing a tyrant (Ahab/Hitler) ruling a crew of able workers willing to serve him however he directs them; the savage harpooners are the best of those workers; and Ishmael is an intellectual white outcast alienated from both his social class and all on the crew but Queequeg. Referring to Steelkilt's unsuccessful mutiny (revolt) aboard the *Town-Ho*, James said that Melville's "main theme [is] how the society of free individualism would give birth to totalitarianism and be unable to defend itself against it" (60). Although James's interpretation is not universally accepted, his book remains a powerful and persuasive analysis.

As in the 1920s, the increased attention Melville received in print also generated new versions of *Moby-Dick* in other media in the 1940s and early 1950s. Bernard

Herrmann's *Moby-Dick: A Cantata* was first performed in April 1940 with a text selected from the novel by W. Clark Harrington. While composing it Herrmann thought of it as "great literature set to music, rather than as a purely musical piece" (Herrmann). Four years later a recording of the novel was produced by Decca with Charles Laughton as Ahab (1944). In the program notes, Louis Untermeyer explained that *Moby-Dick* has popular appeal because its diversity and comprehensiveness are inspiring; it evokes an aura of nobility with its celebration of courage and spirit (Higgins *Reference* 134). A radio adaptation of the novel by Henry Reed was performed early in 1947, and in February 1951 a dramatic version of *Billy Budd*, by Louis O. Coxe and Robert Chapman, was successfully staged at the Biltmore Theater in New York. In December that year Benjamin Britten's operatic version of Melville's novelette, libretto by E. M. Forster and Eric Crozier, was first produced at London's Covent Garden. Since then it has been performed often by many opera companies, including the Metropolitan Opera, which has added *Billy Budd* to its repertoire.

No Trust

Before the publication of Clare Spark's recent study, *Hunting Captain Ahab: Psychological Warfare and the Melville Revival* (2001), the only substantial studies of the revival were two dissertations now forty-five and fifty years old. Spark has partly filled that gap of nearly half a century, although her book is that of an intellectual- and social-historian, not a literary critic, as she herself acknowledges. Spark paradoxically believes that the revival is "only tangentially about the author of *Moby-Dick*. It is but one telling episode in a long-standing global effort to maintain authoritarian social relations in an age of democratic aspirations" (11). From her perspective, twentieth-century progressives – including many of those instrumental in the Melville revival – were "paternalists attempting to preserve, recover, or attain class power and authority" (12). Melville was strongly concerned "with the rights of citizens and the duties of authority" (6), she observes, but the critics she identifies as instrumental in shaping interpretations of his work – including Weaver (after publishing his biography), Olson, and particularly Murray and Leyda – posited symbolic values for his characters, especially Ahab but others as well, that she believes differ vastly from Melville's intended ones.

As her book title implies, critics' interpretations and representations of Ahab, as he relates to Adolf Hitler as tyrant and especially to Melville himself, are focal. Spark sees Ahab as a strong, determined leader and seeker striving for truth wherever it may lead him, as she perceives Melville himself, too. Other critics, however, understand Ahab's fierce determination as madness, as Ahab himself acknowledges. Spark states that in the mid-1930s some American elites admired Hitler for protecting traditional "community" and opposing Communism and "international Jewry." Murray linked Hitler, Ahab, and Melville as romantic instigators of popular revolt.

Ishmael, now viewed as Melville's major persona in *Moby-Dick* as a pluralistic artist supportive of community, became the "moderate" antithesis to the "extremists" Ahab and Hitler, whose assertive individualism and defiance were no longer admissible. This switch in Ahab's symbolic value is unacceptable to Spark, who perceives in it a devious means by which Murray and Leyda especially maintained their own elite status as paternalists guiding a docile democracy represented by their portrait of a conciliatory Melville.

In "Melville Climbs the Canon" (1994), Paul Lauter also deals with "Melville's reputation and how it was constructed and deployed" rather than specifically with Melville himself or his writings (2). Lauter wrote this article after discovering that his students responded negatively to Melville's work because it was too difficult for them, and they found that experience belittling (2). His explanation begins with the 1920s, a decade that "represent[s] the ascent of the ideology we call 'modernism' and of the academy and its adjuncts in the hierarchy of cultural authority" (3). Hershel Parker had pointed out in 1967 that shortly after Weaver's biography was published young Americans started to consider Melville a caustic social critic whose fiction seemed to strike out against the postwar conventionalism in their own era as it did in his. In this sense, he became a timely ally of such contemporary satirists as Sinclair Lewis, whose *Main Street* (1920) and *Babbitt* (1922) reflected similar hostility to the limitations these young people saw in their society (Parker, *Recognition* ix).

Amid this strife in postwar America, Lauter adds, young intellectuals sought "a new champion" who could express the cynicism of their own age and "sustain certain established American values" under question (5). Melville was their choice, Lauter says, and therefore " 'Melville' was constructed in the 1920s as part of an ideological conflict which linked advocates of modernism and of traditional high cultural values – often connected to the academy – against a social and cultural 'other,' generally, if ambiguously portrayed as feminine, genteel, exotic, dark, foreign, and numerous"; that is, for these last four adjectives, read *immigrants* and black Americans. In effect, "a distinctive masculine Anglo-Saxon image of Melville was deployed as a lone and powerful artistic beacon against the dangers presented by the masses" (6), against whom the Modernist elite used the difficulty of his prose to test their literary "worthiness" as readers (15). Moreover, matters of "race, eroticism, democracy, and the like" were overlooked in their fabricated "Melville" image, he says, and "Melville's dramatization of American racism remains altogether hidden" behind it (6, 13). Lauter's students, acculturated amid different values in the 1990s from those of the 1920s, sensed the class hostility the Modernists had invested in Melville's writing and reacted accordingly. Spark and Lauter alike, then, consider Melville's reputation to be a construct created by critics for ideological and practical reasons that differed for each, and that, Lauter says, "tells us more about them than about him" (20).

Is Melville's alleged "greatness," then, a fabrication, as well? This is a question Myra Jehlen might have asked Lauter. Also in 1994 she pointed out that although current literary critics are skeptical about ideas on transcendence, "the universal and the timeless," in favor of generalized values of the prevailing culture, they continue to recognize Melville's "greatness" and take it for granted. Earlier critical icons who admired Melville have been deposed, she says but current theorists continue to regard him as a "great" author. "Thus they depict Melville and his writings always engaged in a dialogue with his particular place and time," and "his authority within that limited realm appears unlimited, as if he were locally transcendent" (1–3, 6). Indeed we have seen throughout this history that Melville's realm is not local, that it transcends most limits of time and place, so his "greatness" evidently does as well, and the revival continues to flourish.

However, *universal* and *timeless* are not necessarily *transcendent*, and sustained admiration for Melville's writing is probably attributable to worldly rather than otherworldly virtues. John Bryant has suggested that it "epitomizes the inevitability of revolution inherent in democratic culture. . . . Melville's diversity, his experimentation, his cosmopolitanism, the odd turns and shape of his career – all these have lasting relevance because they expose the perpetual needs, conflicts, and nature of self, art, and democracy in our lives. This is the key to the persistence of Melville" ("Persistence" 10). Regarding Melville and his works as manifestations of the cultural and political freedom available to artists in the US and wherever else such freedom exists confirms Bryant's sound hypothesis as far as it goes. Yet it omits reference to the integrative power of Melville's vital imagination as an enduring source of reflection and stimulation that makes his writing engaging, provocative, and profoundly moving.

REFERENCES AND FURTHER READING

Arvin, Newton. *Herman Melville*. New York: William Sloane, 1950.

Anderson, Charles Roberts. *Melville in the South Seas*. New York: Columbia University Press, 1939.

Braswell, William. *Melville's Religious Thought*. Durham, NC: Duke University Press, 1943.

Britten, Benjamin. *Billy Budd*. 1951

Bryant, John, ed. *A Companion to Melville Studies*. New York: Greenwood, 1986.

——. "The Persistence of Melville." In *Melville's Evermoving Dawn: Centennial Essays*. Ed. John Bryant and Robert Milder. Kent, OH: Kent State University Press, 1997. 3–28.

Chase, Richard. *Herman Melville: A Critical Study*. New York: Macmillan, 1949.

Freeman, John, *Herman Melville*. London: Macmillan, 1926.

Gilman, William H. *Melville's Early Life and Redburn*. New York: New York University Press, 1951.

Herrmann, Bernard. "The Music of *Moby Dick*." Record album sleeve. UNS 255. London: Unicorn Records, 1940.

Higgins, Bryan. *Herman Melville: An Annotated Bibliography. Volume I: 1846–1930*. Boston: G. K. Hall, 1979.

——. *Herman Melville: A Reference Guide, 1931–1960*. Boston: G. K. Hall, 1986.

——. "Supplement to Volume I." *Extracts* 37 (1979): 10–15.

Hillway, Tyrus and Luther S. Mansfield, eds. *Moby-Dick Centennial Essays*. Dallas, TX: Southern Methodist University Press, 1953.

Huxley, Aldous. *Those Barren Leaves*. London: Chatto & Windus, 1925.

James, C. L. R. *Mariners, Renegades and Castaways: The Story of Herman Melville and the World We Live In.* New York: C. L. R. James, 1953.

Jehlen, Myra, ed. Introduction. In *Herman Melville: A Collection of Critical Essays.* Englewood Cliffs. NJ: Prentice-Hall, 1994. 1–14.

Kennedy, Frederick James and Joyce Deveaux Kennedy. "Archibald MacMechan and the Melville Revival." *Leviathan* 1.2 (1999): 5–37.

Lauter, Paul. "Melville Climbs the Canon." *American Literature* 66.1 (1994): [1]–24.

Lawrence, D. H. *Studies in Classic American Literature.* New York: Doubleday, 1951.

Lee, A. Robert, ed. *Herman Melville: Critical Assessments.* Vols. I–IV. Robertsbridge, Sussex: Helm Information Ltd, 2001.

Mason, Ronald. *The Spirit Above the Dust.* London: John Lehman, 1951.

Mott, Frank Luther. *Golden Multitudes: The Story of Best-Sellers in the United States.* New York: Macmillan, 1947.

Mumford, Lewis. *Herman Melville.* New York: Library Guild/Harcourt Brace, 1929.

Melville, Herman. *The Works of Herman Melville.* 16 vols. London: Constable, 1922–4.

Murray, Henry A. "In Nomine Diaboli." In *Endeavors in Psychology.* Ed. Edwin S. Shneidman. New York: Harper & Row, 1981. 82–94.

Olson, Charles. *Call Me Ishmael.* New York: City Lights, 1947.

Parker, Hershel, ed. *The Recognition of Herman Melville.* Ann Arbor: University of Michigan Press, 1967.

Parker, Hershel, and Harrison Hayford, eds. *Moby-Dick as Doubloon.* New York: Norton, 1970.

Parrington, Vernon Louis. *Main Currents in American Thought. Volume 2: 1800–1860: The Romantic Revolution in America.* New York: Harcourt Brace/Harvest Book, 1954.

Rosenbach, A. S. W. *An Introduction to Herman Melville's* Moby Dick; or, The Whale. New York: Mitchell Kennerley, 1924.

Rourke, Constance. *American Humor: A Study of the National Character.* Garden City, NY: Doubleday, 1951.

Sealts, Merton M., Jr. *Closing the Books.* New York: Vantage, 1999.

——. *The Early Lives of Melville.* Madison: University of Wisconsin Press, 1974.

——. "The Flower of 'Fame': A Centennial Tribute." *ESQ* 38.2 (1992): 89–117.

Schultz, Elizabeth. *Unpainted to the Last.* Lawrence: University of Kansas Press, 1995.

Spark, Clare L. *Hunting Captain Ahab: Psychological Warfare and the Melville Revival.* Kent, OH: Kent State University Press, 2001.

Vincent, Howard P. *The Trying-Out of* Moby-Dick. Boston: Houghton Mifflin, 1949.

Weaver, Raymond M. *Herman Melville: Mariner and Mystic.* New York: George H. Doran, 1921.

Williams, Stanley T. "Melville." *Eight American Authors.* New York: Norton, 1956. 207–70.

Wright, Nathalia. "Melville and STW at Yale: Studies Under Stanley T. Williams." *Extracts* 70 (1987): 1–4.

Zimmerman, Michael P. "Herman Melville in the 1920s." Unpublished dissertation, Columbia University. DA 25 (1963): 1224.

34

Creating Icons: Melville in Visual Media and Popular Culture

Elizabeth Schultz

Circumnavigating the globe in pursuit of Moby Dick, Ahab discovers himself both pursued and pursuing. So, a student tracking allusions to *Moby-Dick* finds herself also being tracked by them. Boats, large and small, and invariably white, with the name and image of Melville's whale inscribed on their transoms or bows, ply the waters of North America's lakes and coasts, while grand yachts, similarly inscribed, sail the seven seas. Such vessels anchor in harbors in the Caribbean, Greece, Turkey, and Tonga, and friends send photos of other boats from Japan, Thailand, France, and Australia. And when the student, amazed by discovering Moby Dick wherever she goes on water, turns inland, she finds everywhere hotels, restaurants, coffee shops, bars, and souvenir stores all named for Melville's great white whale.

Among "the long Vaticans and street-stalls of the earth," picking up "whatever random allusions to whales ... sacred or profane" he could find for his compilation of "higgledy-piggledy whale statements" in "Extracts" at the beginning of *Moby-Dick*, Ishmael, too, was amazed. He claims that these whale statements are "valuable or entertaining" in the degree that they can provide "a glancing bird's eye view of what has been promiscuously said, thought, fancied, and sung of Leviathan by many nations and generations, including our own" (*MD*, xvii). Ishmael's three chapters on "Monstrous Pictures of Whales," "Less Erroneous Pictures of Whales, and the True Pictures of Whales," and "Whales in Paint; in Teeth; in Wood; in Sheet-Iron; in Stone; in Mountains; in Stars" suggest he was fascinated by visual representations of whales. A contemporary examination of the diversity and the ubiquity of visual manifestations of *Moby-Dick*, in particular, as well as of other works by Melville, notably *Typee*, "Bartleby, the Scrivener," and *Billy Budd*, indicates that though we might obtain only "a glancing bird's eye view," Melville's works resonate across "nations and generations, including our own."

Given the frequently made observation that *Moby-Dick* is the best-known and the least-read American novel, it would seem that Walter Benjamin's argument that reproductions of an original work of art depreciate the power of the original and jeopardize its authority is valid (221). Certainly, no other American literary text can rival *Moby-Dick* in having so many reproductions – in written, cinematic, musical, dramatic, and visual products – throughout the United States and the world.[1] As recently as the fall of 2004, *Moby-Dick* (with a three-minute dramatization titled "Moby Dude") was chosen as the subject for WNYC's Studio 360 as the lead program in an NEH-funded series on American icons. In the number and range of its visual manifestations, *Moby-Dick*'s only rivals among other works of literature are *Don Quixote*, *Faust*, and *Hamlet*. Countering Benjamin's argument, however, I contend that *Moby-Dick*'s visual interpretations – as well as those of other Melville works – testify not only to the enthusiasm of Melville's readers but also to the fact that Melville enthusiasts in the twentieth and twenty-first centuries have iconized Melville and *Moby-Dick*. Although "the Whale or at least vague shadows of that image have penetrated the nation's popular consciousness where deep and threatening thoughts are so handily sugar-coated for popular consumption," John Bryant proclaims that we may "have our Whale and eat him, too" (xix).

Possibly one free-standing work of art based on Melville's writing was done during his lifetime (1819–91) – a carved and painted wooden trade sign by an anonymous carver of a grim-countenanced Captain Ahab, black-coated, top-hatted, harpoon in hand. Thought to have been created in the late nineteenth or early twentieth century, it was offered for sale by Sotheby's in 1998 for between $4000 and $6000. Despite his own predilection for referring to visual images and artwork in his writings, for inserting graphic devices into them, and for creating *tableaux vivants* (Schultz "Illustrated" 3; *Unpainted* 18), Melville never saw his writing professionally illustrated. Given that the nineteenth century was a period when both British and American publishers promoted novel sales with lavishly illustrated editions, Melville's lack of success with his contemporary readers is indicated by the absence of illustrations from publications of his works. Perhaps anticipating a more open audience in the twentieth century, however, publishers in the last decade of the nineteenth century in both Britain and the US began issuing illustrated editions of *Typee*, *Omoo*, *White-Jacket*, and *Moby-Dick*, usually with a frontispiece and four full-page, captioned pictures inserted into the text. Notable among these early illustrations were John LaFarge's titillating images of a nude Fayaway spreading out her tappa cloth from the bow of her canoe (1892, 1895).

The Melville Revival of the 1920s, however, catapulted Melville into popular culture. Publishers quickly understood the value of illustrating Melville's works, and illustrators rose to the challenge of interpreting his words visually, with several distinguished illustrated editions of *Moby-Dick* appearing during the decade (and discussed at length in Schultz, "Illustrated" and *Unpainted*). In 1925, the novel was also transformed into the silent film, *The Sea Beast*, starring matinee idol John Barrymore, rapidly becoming a box-office hit. It is noteworthy that although ingenious covers have been created for paperback editions of *Mardi*, *Redburn*, and *Israel Potter* throughout the twentieth century, the only fully illustrated editions of these novels appeared during the 1920s.

In 1930, two events visually heralded *Moby-Dick* as a popular and global phenomenon: first, the publication of the Lakeside Press's three-volume edition of the novel with Rockwell Kent's 280 illustrations, and second, two new versions of *The Sea Beast*, one American, titled *Moby Dick*, the other German, titled *Das Seebiest*, both with sound and with Barrymore again in the lead (Inge 696–701). In Kent, for the first time, Melville had an artist who recognized his novel's multiple layers and nuances – its historical, mythic, mystical, comedic, dramatic, philosophical, scientific, and aesthetic possibilities, its human characters as well as its whales (Schultz *Unpainted* 27–63; "Common Continent"). Many of Kent's illustrations would become iconic. They were duplicated repeatedly in pottery produced by the Vernon Kilns and in advertisements, and William Faulkner posted Kent's powerful image of Ahab standing on the *Pequod*'s deck over his desk. Editions of *Moby-Dick* with Kent's illustrations rapidly led to translations of Melville's novel, beginning with a Czech edition in 1933. Leland Phelps lists twenty-five editions and reprints of *Moby-Dick* with Kent's illustrations, including those in Bengali, Bulgarian, Chinese, French, Hebrew, Japanese, Lithuanian, Norwegian, Portuguese, Russian, Slovakian, Swedish, and Urdu (xix). (I've also seen a Polish edition of *Moby-Dick* with Kent's illustrations.) Kent's illustrations for Soviet editions of *Moby-Dick* were especially cherished (Gilenson). The single-volume Modern Library edition of *Moby-Dick* with 270 of Kent's distinguished illustrations remains in print today.

While American and British illustrators following Kent largely held to the realistic tradition of illustration, European illustrators, such as Otto Tschumi, Will Sohl, Horst Janssen, and William Klein "deconstruct the images of men and whales in complex and entangled abstract terms" (Schultz "Seeing Globally" 411). Notable among British illustrators of Melville's works is Garrick Palmer, whose cross-hatched wood engravings for *Moby-Dick*, "Bartleby," "Benito Cereno," and *Billy Budd* reflect the treacherous bonds of society and fate. Boardman Robinson's 1943 *Moby-Dick* illustrations have been thought by some to rival Kent's with their brooding and claustrophobic scenes, and Robert Shore's smudged ink-and-oil paintings of *Typee* (1958), *Moby-Dick* (1962), "Benito Cereno," and *Billy Budd* (1965) project a gloomy, hell-fired world. During the 1970s, several illustrators of *Moby-Dick* challenged the iconicity of Kent's drawings – Ronald Keller (1974), LeRoy Neiman (1975), Warren Chappell (1976), and Barry Moser (1979) (Schultz *Unpainted* 89–122). Maurice Sendak's erotic and anguished illustrations for *Pierre*, influenced by Blake, Ingres, and Fuseli, appeared to acclaim in 1997 (Schultz "Invisible").

Beginning in the 1940s, visual interpretations of Melville's works in the US could be placed in two categories: those that were produced principally for commercial gain and appealed to popular culture, on the one hand, and those, on the other hand, that were created by individual artists and appealed to a more broadly based audience, including such elite groups as art collectors and scholars. Critically, these two interpretive planes – the commercial and the aesthetic – coexisted, intersected, and influenced each other, simultaneously appealing to both a popular and an elitist audience. A combination of factors worked to guarantee an audience for Melville's works: their canonization in university curricula and by university scholars; their aesthetically varied illustrated editions, many of which can be characterized as having crossover appeal; their re-creation as films, drama, and even opera. As a result of this simultaneous appeal, *Moby-Dick* became iconized not only nationally but also internationally. Like other icons, *Moby-Dick* – both novel and whale – looms large, embodying a complexity, a heterogeneity, and a mystifying ambiguity which puts both novel and whale up for grabs across cultures and history.

Melville and Popular Visual Culture

Commercialized, the whale appears in the names of multiple shops (Moby Jane – maternity clothes, Moby Dock – maritime supplies, Moby Disk – computer equipment, Moby Gym – exercise spa, Moby Dip – ice cream, Moby Dude – surfer shop) and multiple products (toys, cookie jars, water sprinklers, refrigerator deodorizers, caulking powder, thimbles, banks, wallpaper, sleeping bags, ornaments, ashtrays, salt-and-pepper shakers, clothing of every sort), as well as in its multiple references in films (*Star Wars*, *The Big Sleep*, *Fried Green Tomatoes*, *Zelig*, *Heathers*, *Shine*, *Ricochet*, *Before Night Falls*, *Deep Impact*), songs, editorials, advertisements, jokes, and cartoons (Schultz *Unpainted* 257–60). Reflecting *Moby-Dick*'s popular appeal was the "Moby Dick Hunt," the central attraction at the Boston-area theme park, Pleasure Island, in which a white whale rose out of the water to spritz guests with water at the end of performances. This enterprise successfully Disneyfied Melville's whale between 1959 and 1969.

Since the 1940s, the covers for Melville's works belie their complex contents, with editions of *Typee* depicting an Edenic tropical paradise, of *Moby-Dick* focusing on the final violent confrontation, and of *Billy Budd* portraying only a blond, blue-eyed sailor. From this decade on, editions of *Moby-Dick* have also contained visual aids – historical, cartographic, cetological, and nautical information – to assist readers with Melville's specialized subject matter related to nineteenth-century whaling and sailing. These editions have existed side by side with complete editions as well as with comic-book versions, children's editions, abridged editions, and adapted editions – all with illustrations and some succeeding in illuminating *Moby-Dick*'s "little lower layer[s]" (*MD* 164). In all, eleven comic-book versions of *Moby-Dick* have been published in English, most recently in 2001, with other *Moby-Dick* comics appearing in Brazil, France, Israel, Italy, Japan, Spain, and Sweden as well. At least two animated film versions of *Moby-Dick* have also been created. Over thirty editions of *Moby-Dick* in English have appeared for children as well as multiple adapted and abridged versions, most recently in 2002 (Burt, Thomas, and McCabe), with numerous children's editions also published abroad. Apart from two comic versions of *Typee*, to my knowledge, no children's editions of other Melvillean texts have been published.

Moby-Dick has also been subjected to revision in the goofy *Moby Duck* comic and the acerbic *Mad Magazine* as well as in adult comic books – "The Super-Moby Dick of Space" in *Adventure Comics* (1965); "Waters of Darkness, River of Doom" in *Ka-Zar, Lord of the Hidden Jungle* (1972); *Grimm's Ghost Stories* (1975); and to spectacular effect in the seven issues of *Abraxas and the Earthman* (1982) (Inge 713–14). *Moby-Dick* has also been parodied by Katsuhiro Otomo, Japan's well-known manga artist, and by the Italian comic-illustrator Bruno Brindisi for *Dylan Dog: Sulla Rotta di Moby Dick* (On the Course of Moby Dick, 2001). Although Melville's exultant and experimental language and layered vision are consistently diminished – if not distorted – in these revised versions of *Moby-Dick,* on occasion illustrators honor both text and vision, creating visual interpretations of Melville's works which have crossover appeal, proving of interest to both adults and children and retaining links with Melville's language. Among such revisions are Bill Sienkiewicz's 1990 comic book and Victor G. Ambrus's 1996 children's edition. Significantly, both artists reverse the racial inaccuracies and insensitivities of typical popularizing texts to reflect complex individuals among the *Pequod*'s ethnically diverse harpooners and crew (Schultz "Visualizing Race").

John Huston's 1956 film version of *Moby-Dick*, scripted by Ray Bradbury, with Gregory Peck portraying Ahab, Yul Brunner Queequeg, and Orson Welles Father Mapple, assured the novel's popularity. Globally and in the US, clips from this film provided illustrations for new editions of *Moby-Dick*, comic books, and advertise-ments, and Peck's image of Ahab came to represent the "essential" Ahab for many. Not even Patrick Stewart, *Star Wars* hero, could successfully challenge this image in his four-hour, made-for-TV 1998 version of *Moby-Dick*, and Huston's film, with its erroneous conclusion of Ahab tangled in whale lines wrapped around Moby Dick, remains readily available at supermarket video outlets. The flexibility and appeal of *Moby-Dick*'s narrative was tested by its transformation into the 1977 western, *The White Buffalo*, in which Charles Bronson assists a Native American chieftain whose daughter was killed by a monstrous white buffalo.

Film and theater continue to make Melville's works visible. M. Thomas Inge comprehensively documents the visibility of *Typee*, "Bartleby," *Billy Budd*, and, above all, *Moby-Dick* in American and British films and television through the mid-1980s (in addition to radio performances and recordings). He neglects to note, however, the staged versions of *Moby-Dick* which also reflect the novel's populariza-tion, including a successful run of an adaptation in Paris in 1949 with program notes by Albert Camus; Tyrus Hillway's drama, *Captain Ahab* (1953); Orson Welles's only play, *Moby Dick – Rehearsed* (1962); the York Theater Company's operatic *Moby-Dick* (1986); Eric Hawkins's dance performance, *Ahab* (1986); puppet-shows by Chicago's Red Show's Theater and New York's Theater for the Birds; a children's dramatic adaptation by Mark Rosenwinkel (accompanied by "The Ish-Meal" – a fund-raiser in Flint, Michigan); numerous one-man productions, most recently by Carlo Adinolfi (2001) and Christopher Moore (2003); and an engrossing 2004 German production staged with three men.

Even *Omoo* was transformed into a film in 1949, *Omoo-Omoo (The Shark God)*, and in 1958 *Typee* was renamed *Enchanted Island* for a Warner Brothers film. In 1962, *Billy Budd* was first adapted for film, based on a 1951 play script which was performed on Broadway, with Peter Ustinov playing Vere and Terence Stamp Billy, while the first cinematic version of "Bartleby" was produced by Pantheon Film in 1971 with Paul Scofield as the lawyer. There have also been numerous dramatizations of "Bartleby" – three French film versions (1957, 1978, 1993), one Australian version (2000), and a 2002 production, directed by Jonathan Parker, locating Bartleby in a dysfunctional Silicon Valley office. "Benito Cereno" was the basis for one of three plays written by Robert Lowell in 1968 under the general title, *The Old Glory*, and in 1992 Joyce Sparer Adler dramatized it, as well as *Moby-Dick* and *Billy Budd*. Benjamin Britten's superb 1951 *Billy Budd* has become part of the world's operatic repertoire. In 1999, Claire Denis recreated *Billy Budd* into *Beau Travail*, a disturbing film set in a French Foreign Legion outpost in Djibouti, and Leos Carax located a romantically excessive *Pierre* in a contemporary French setting in *Pola X*. In 2002, the Denver Center Theater took up the challenge of putting *Pierre* on stage, and in 2004 a musical version of *The Confidence-Man* was performed in the riverboat city of Cincinnati, Ohio.

If *Moby-Dick* appealed to Faulkner as well as to novelists John Gardner, John Calvin Batchelor, Henry Carlisle, Jay Cantor, Kurt Vonnegut, John Irving, Ralph Ellison, Richard Wright, Sena Jeter Nasland, and Deborah Joy Corey in her 2003 *The Skating Pond*, it also appealed to the writers of science fiction, detective fiction, police procedurals, spy novels, and romance novels (Schultz "Avatars"). *Moby-Dick*'s well-known opening line, "Call me Ishmael," has been parodied by numerous writers and cartoonists and continues to be well worn, as its surprising appearance in William Gibson's erudite *Pattern Recognitions* (2003) indicates.

Although *Typee* provides a subtext for Alice Fulton's short story, "The Real Eleanor Rigby" (2003), only Bartleby's "I would prefer not to" rivals "Call me Ishmael" as a cultural commonplace.

Melville and Fine Art

In the 1940s, as *Moby-Dick* continued to be a popular phenomenon in the United States, its powerful appeal to non-commercial artists guaranteed its iconization. "The flood-gates of [*Moby-Dick*'s] wonder-world" (*MD* 7) opened to both abstract expressionists and realistic painters to explore the possibilities of representing the novel in free-standing works of art – paintings, sculptures, and visual narratives. This "wonder-world" was initially documented in 1976 by the Schleswig-Holstein Landesmuseum exhibition of *Moby-Dick* artwork; as has often happened historically, such recognition came not in the US, where most *Moby-Dick* art has been and continues to be created, but abroad. Evan Firestone's pioneering 1980 article on "*Moby-Dick* and the Abstract Expressionists" was the first acknowledgment of *Moby-Dick*-inspired art in the US.

Karl Knaths's 1935 still-life depicting Melville's novel with a ship in a box and various geometric shapes is credited as the first abstract representation based on *Moby-Dick* (Schultz *Unpainted* 123–48). But the appearance of two paintings related to *Moby-Dick* by Jackson Pollock – *Pasiphae* and *(Blue (Moby Dick))* – in 1943 provided a catalyst for other abstract artists during the 1940s and 1950s. Paintings by Ellsworth Kelly, Robert Motherwell, Paul Jenkins, William Baziotes, Theodoros Stamos, and Sam Francis; lithographs by Norman Ives; and sculpture by Seymour Lipton, Theodore Rozak, Nick Vaccaro, Cranston Heintzelman, and Alexander Calder followed in rapid succession. During a period when these artists, most of whom stand amongst America's best-known abstractionists, were seeking radically innovative ways to respond to the horrors of World War II and to the consumer-oriented and consensus-conscious culture which emerged after the war, *Moby-Dick* provided them with a significant model. Titling their paintings most often after the white whale or Ahab, these artists plumbed the depths of *Moby-Dick* for political, philosophical, and psychological meanings. They also sought in the novel's narrative and in its evocation of space both a mythic and a specifically American identity. In addition, the novel's experimental use of language liberated them to be equally experimental in their use of paint. As Harold Rosenberg explains in a 1952 essay, "[T]he American vanguard painter took to the white expanse of canvas as Melville's Ishmael took to the sea" (31).

To my knowledge, *Moby-Dick* is the only work of American literature which has so consistently, so diversely, so strongly appealed to abstract artists. With the exception of Thorp Feidt's multiple large oil paintings of *Pierre*, which he has been working on since the early 1980s, and of Frank Stella's fourteen creations which reference *Omoo* and *Mardi*, none of Melville's other writings has prompted abstract work. Into the present day, however, abstract artists have continued to find *Moby-Dick* an inspiration. Judging from the titles of their works, Ahab remained a focus in William Kienbusch's mystical painting (1966) (Kelley), Tony Rosenthal's 1966 nearly eleven-foot bronze statue, and Carl Chiarenza's 1991 photographic print, projecting the captain of the *Pequod* in a composition of shining, dagger-shaped shards. In 1986 Richard Serra and in 1991 Aristides Demetrios created powerful sculptures titled *Call Me Ishmael*. Vaccaro's 1982 impressionistic painting of white dots, *For Herman*, continues earlier abstractionists' interest in Ishmael's description of whiteness as "the visible absence of color, and at the same time the concrete of all colors" (*MD* 195), and Marco Maggi's complex work titled *Great White Dialogue* (2000), comprised of 24,549 sheets of paper, suggests that grasping "the ungraspable phantom of life" (*MD* 5) is both impossible and absurd.

European abstract artists also responded fully and enthusiastically to *Moby-Dick*. The 1960s were distinguished by Czech Jan Koblasa's chunky wooden sculpture of *Moby Dick*, and German Carl Barth's two oil paintings, *Huldigung an Melville* (Homage to Melville) and *Stilleben mit weissen Kopf* (Still Life with White Head, 1973), both focusing on a mysterious white head. German-American Friedel Dzubas' large, fluid image of the *White Whale* (1958) in pale colors, Austrian-American Henry Koerner's symbolic and surrealistic painting (1977–8), and the assemblages of German Rebecca

Horn (1991) and Finn Juhani Harri (1994), the latter three all titled *Moby Dick*, further testify to the interest Melville's novel holds for European artists working in several non-realistic traditions (Schultz "Seeing Globally").

Without question, however, no abstract art inspired by *Moby-Dick* has had a global impact comparable to that of Frank Stella's expansive and exuberant *Moby-Dick* series. From 1985 through the next twelve years, as Robert K. Wallace details in his stunning book on the series, Stella created 266 artworks based on all of *Moby-Dick*'s 138 chapter titles with 2700 additional individual objects, including editioned prints, reliefs, collages, scarves, a tote bag, a block-long architectural mural, and an immense model for a building yet unbuilt (Wallace *Stella* 4). Excepting the small bag and scarves, Stella's *Moby-Dick* series is comprised of massive pieces; many span walls, defying boundaries; others stand free of walls, rising into space precariously; all of them suggest layers heaped upon layers; all of them allow space to open up and flow. They are provocative and vigorous, evoking the rhythms and movements of human and natural life, fusing abstraction with narrative and image, occasionally suggesting violence, occasionally tenderness. Wallace's catalogue of sightings of individual pieces from Stella's series, in exhibitions and museums around the world, demonstrates that, like Moby Dick himself, Stella's *Moby-Dick* works have become a global phenomenon (Wallace "Chasing"; Wallace *Stella* 293–313).

As abstract artists' response to *Moby-Dick* emerged and evolved, other aesthetic traditions and trends flourished simultaneously. Artists committed to realistic traditions of narrative and portraiture, in particular, were also drawn to Melville's novel for inspiration from the early 1940s on. Gilbert Wilson, one among several realistic artists who took *Moby-Dick* as a new bible, responded to the novel in various aesthetic ways. Over the course of decades – 1949 to 1972 – he created individual paintings of scenes and characters, a prize-winning film, drawings of stage sets for an operatic version of the novel titled *The White Whale*, murals for a post office, and a traveling show which brought many of these components together with music (Schultz *Unpainted* 162–85). In addition to illuminating memorable images of Ahab's suffering, of Moby Dick's might and majesty, and of Pip's position in the narrative, he was the first artist to envision Ahab's wife. Wilson perhaps remains best known for the powerful *Insanity Series* (c.1950), a sequence of six portraits of Ahab, showing the face of the *Pequod*'s captain gradually fracturing with rage as his obsession intensifies.

Anticipating Stella's *Moby-Dick* series, Norman Ives's sixteen abstract lithographs, *Illustrating Moby Dick*, which formed a sequence of intricately and iconographically linked images (Schultz *Unpainted* 186–94), and Wilson's *Insanity Series*, both done in 1950, were the first to recognize the advantages of using sequences to attempt to grasp the "ungraspable." Usually drawing on realistic scenic and portraiture traditions, these sequences often explicitly connect images under a single title. Among these are Benton Spruance's twenty-seven colored lithographs, *The Passion of Ahab* (1967–8), Leonard Baskin's eight lithographs, *The Moby Dick Suite* (1970), and Wallace Putnam's book of Zen-like pen-and-ink drawings and handwritten personal commentary on the novel, *Moby Dick Seen Again* (1975) (Schultz *Unpainted* 195–210, 228–38).

Figure 34.1   George Klauba. *The Castaway* (2004). Acrylic on panel. 18 × 14.5 in.

Mico Kaufman, Claus Hoie, John Sandlin, Catherine Kanner, and George Klauba, while also creating vivid images of the great white whale, concentrated principally on representing the individual dramatis personae of *Moby-Dick*. Despite their small size – only four inches high – Kaufman's 1976 pewter sculptures render his four figures identifiably, each in a characteristic attitude. In 1988 Hoie created glowing, foreboding watercolors of Ahab, Ishmael, each of the *Pequod*'s mates, and each of the ship's harpooners, while John Sandlin from the late 1960s through the early 1980s created stark woodcuts of Ahab, Starbuck, Pip, and "Seaman." His 1977 lithograph, *Melville Portrait: Pacific Man,* with deep-set, far-seeing eyes, might well be Ishmael. (Between 1984 and 1994, Sandlin also created thirteen lithographs of Galapagos tortoises – intrepid and whimsical – for an *Encantadas Series.*) Kanner's 1996 *Cetus: The Whale* brings together twelve black-and-white line drawings of characters from *Moby-Dick.* Placed one after another, the portraits unfold from the book into a single sheet, appearing before the viewer both as individuals and as members of a crew. In 2004, with the precision of a tattoo artist, Klauba used intricate lines and intense color to create a fantastical portrait gallery of Ahab and his crew, each conceived as a different bird (Figure 34.1).

Predictably, since the mid-nineteenth-century decline in whaling and with the rise in tourism at the end of that century, Nantucket artists have been fascinated with *Moby-Dick,* given that it was from this "ant-hill in the sea" (*MD* 64) that the *Pequod* began its circumnavigation of the globe. For the novel's sesquicentennial year in 2001, several Nantucket artists brought their *Moby-Dick* works together for an exhibition. All working out of realistic traditions, they, too, responded to the novel serially. From work done in 1960, George C. Thomas exhibited lithographs which captured scenes from the novel with sweeping, pulsating movement – *Father Mapple, Thar She Blows, Ahab's Revenge,* and *The Chase* – as well as a pencil drawing of a tall, gaunt Ahab, clutching himself and entirely self-enclosed. In 1972 Janet Ball, using diverse materials, made a dozen colorgraphic etchings, overlaid with rope and intaglio to produce a dense, layered effect. She was represented in the exhibition with *The Spouter Inn, Queequeg with Yojo, Ishmael in the Masthead,* and *Moby Dick.* John F. Lochtefeld contributed single-dimensional woodcuts in which the white whale is poised against a star-studded, midnight blue sky or swims nonchalantly beneath a whaling ship. During the exhibition, Louis Guarnaccia displayed in his studio an oil painting of the penultimate scene in *Moby-Dick*: the sea, stretching to the horizon, resembles "the great shroud ... as it rolled on five thousand years ago" (*MD* 572), while the whale disappears in the distance, and a ship with an unknown man at the masthead comes into view.

Two artists whose representations of *Moby-Dick* have shifted between realistic and abstract interpretations over the course of decades are Robert Del Tredici and Mark Milloff. Their long-term involvement with illuminating *Moby-Dick* and with the process of grasping the novel can be related to the sequential endeavors of other artists. Del Tredici, crediting *Moby-Dick* with having transformed his life, began drawing small, often cartoon-like scenes related to specific passages from the novel in 1964–5, but turned at the end of the twentieth century toward large, shimmering, multi-colored, multi-dimensional silkscreens. Milloff, who also testifies to his personal response to Melville's novel, began transferring his rough-and-tumble realistic visions of it onto immense sheets of paper with pastels in the 1980s, abandoned these for abstract work textured and thick with white oil paint in the 1990s, and recently returned to large pastels, some of which extend beyond the frame to include nautical objects as well as video projection and sound (Schultz *Unpainted* 210–28, 240–56, "Seer" 1–4; Wallace "Chasing"). Wallace's comparison of the movement from narrative and figurative illustration to abstract silkscreen in Del Tredici's work can apply equally to Stella and Milloff: "Pictorial artists who respond most deeply to Ishmael's vision often find themselves, before they are done, as did Melville himself, oscillating between the figurative and the abstract in the drift and the drive of their own expressive needs" (Wallace "Flood Tide" 15).

In addition to Del Tredici and Milloff, two European artists, A. C. Christodoulou of Greece and Charley Reuvers of the Netherlands, have each created an extended series of artworks relating to visual interpretations that challenge a linear, narrative viewing of *Moby-Dick*. Christodoulou, who translated *Moby-Dick* into Greek (1971), has illuminated *Mardi* (*c*.1995–9) with six images and *Moby-Dick* (*c*.1995–2002) with thirty-four. These are small, finely detailed images having the luminous intensity of icons. Focusing primarily on faces, Christodoulou strikes through the pasteboard masks (*MD* 164) to reveal unexpected psychological or philosophical states. Reuvers's series includes eight etchings (13″ × 10″) and eight paintings (52″ × 40″), done in the early 1990s. Palimpsestic, each of his works is a collage of subtle colors, incorporating incongruous elements reflecting his own and Melville's interest in geography, biology, theology, anthropology, and archeology as well as in art and literature and employing a range of visual symbols and puns.

Although those artists working with sequential images of *Moby-Dick* have been engaged with its visual possibilities and complexities over long periods of time, since the 1940s American and European artists have also continuously attempted to capture the novel in single paintings and sculpture. Some abstract artists, such as those listed above, created only one or two *Moby-Dick* artworks, as did realist artists. These works include George Snow Hill's oil-painting (*c*.1950) with a red-eyed and smoking Moby Dick approached by a boat filled with an abject and appalled crew and an anomalous, bonneted woman in the bow; N. Caruso's watercolor (*c*.1960), where Ahab is shown encouraging his boat forward before the white whale sounds in a misty sea; Edward Laning's 1980 sketch for a New York Public Library mural, in which Moby Dick breaches to the stars (Schultz *Unpainted* 185–6); Michael McMillen's ninety-six-inch long, mixed media construction, *Pequod II*, with a decidedly precarious, "old fashioned claw-footed look about her" (*MD* 69); Arthur Moniz's 2001 graphite and watercolor painting of *The Chase – Moby Dick* with the whale's white tail rising mystically out of a tumultuous blue sea to encircle a minute ship; and Kevin Sprague's 2001 photomontage of Moby Dick's undulating form superimposed upon the Berkshire mountains beneath a sky on which the map of the world is traced.

Intersections of Pop Culture and Fine Art: Politics, Race, Nature, Gender

In 1970, the US Post Office issued a six-cent envelope with the image of a white sperm whale embossed in a blue circle. Increasingly from this decade, *Moby-Dick* has been interpreted by single works of art, reflecting an astonishing diversity of aesthetic trends – pop art, funk art, photorealism, magic realism; in a plurality of forms – photographs, installations, bridges, architecture; with a variety of modes – comic, theoretical, "sacred and profane," and with several critical themes, focusing on politics, race, the environment, and gender. These recent artworks, however, seldom depict *Moby-Dick*'s individual scenes and characters, which were the concern of artists from the 1930s through the 1970s. They more frequently use the novel's status as an icon either to honor American identity or ideals, to comment on them, or to mock them. In some instances, it seems that as "the great American novel," *Moby-Dick* becomes the vehicle for considering the construction and deconstruction of iconization itself, for demonstrating that an icon's sustaining value in a culture is dependent upon its being not only fluid and open, but also able to endure parody and ridicule.

Sightings of *Moby-Dick* in single cartoons in the *New Yorker* and syndicated newspapers as well as in cartoon sequences, including *The Far Side*, *Peanuts*, *Shoe*, *Fox Trot*, *Calvin and Hobbes*, *Mother Goose and Grimm*, *Sherman's Lagoon*, and *Red and Rover* from the 1970s into the present signify this resilience of *Moby-Dick* in popular culture. The trend toward a self-reflective consideration of *Moby-Dick* can be seen as beginning with Robert Indiana's three *Moby-Dick*-related pieces – *Melville Triptych* (1961), *Melville* (1962), and *Ahab* (1962–92). Indiana, associated with the pop art movement, prints Melville's words on these works in bold stencils in relation to simple geometric forms, as if to create new American signage. However, the destination or the information on Indiana's signs seems incomplete, uncertain. Tom Jordan's *Moby Trick* (1971), with its sixteen interlocking parts of wood and other materials, is a playful spoof on *Moby-Dick*'s complexity (Schultz *Unpainted* 262–8).

Several single works from the 1970s simultaneously acknowledge and query *Moby-Dick*'s iconic status: Ralph Goings's 1970 *Moby Truck*, Robert Warrens's 1972 *Moby Dick*, Bob Arneson's 1975 lithograph of *Moby Brick*, and Kim Weston's 1978 photograph of *Moby-Dick Meets Mr. and Mrs. Avocado*. Doug Anderson claims his 1984 *Perfect Mom #3* originated from "a bathroom epiphany" he experienced while musing on *Moby-Dick* wallpaper; to judge from his stultified image of the white whale, his epiphany is that Melville's novel, like the idea of a perfect Mom, has been and can be duplicated in our culture an infinite number of times, rendering it culturally meaningless (Schultz *Unpainted* 266–76). Red Grooms's enormous 1992 cartoon-like sculpture (180″ × 300″ ×540″) of the New York Public Library with white whales greeting visitors at the front entrance rather than lions and scenes within of Melville writing *Moby-Dick* and Queequeg nearby quaffing beer, converts iconization to geniality and makes the great book, the great author, and the great whale seem at home in New York. In a two-page spread in the *New York Times* (June 6, 1996), Russell Connor mocked the ubiquity of the white whale as a subject for American artists by inserting its massive head into a series of Winslow Homer's iconic sea paintings, each accompanied by a satiric letter from Melville to Homer. In Tim Hawkinson's gigantic installation, *Überorgan* (2000), the "300-foot network of twelve enormous air-filled polyethylene bladders" (Insko), derived from his vision of Moby Dick, Ahab's white whale as the incarnation of evil is entirely deflated, but Melville's white whale is not demystified. While on display at the Massachusetts Museum of Contemporary Art, *Überorgan* continuously rumbled and farted, giving viewers the Jonah experience of being in the whale's belly as well as the Ishmael experience of the whale's wonder.

Parodied and ridiculed, sanitized and commercialized, *Moby-Dick* has also become the vehicle for multiple social and political ideologies. Numerous editorial cartoonists, including Bill Mauldin, Doug Marlette, and Doug Wuerker, have attached their particular issues to an obsessed Ahab and the object of his obsession, the white whale (Schultz *Unpainted* 288–90). In the wake of World War II, critics associated Ahab's tyrannical and charismatic behavior with Hitler. He has also been equated with slave masters and captains of industry who care little for their workers, and has recently been identified as a model for an effective CEO (Athitakis). In attempts to comprehend the events of September 11, 2001, writers have aligned characters in *Moby-Dick* with the players in that tragedy, with Ahab being associated with both Osama bin Laden and George W. Bush. Many commentators noted the relevance of the prophecy regarding a "BLOODY BATTLE IN AFGHANISTAN," which Ishmael claims "formed part of the grand programme of Providence" (*MD* 7). With Fedallah looking very much like bin Laden in his painting *Drawn Up Toward Heaven As If By Invisible Wires* (2002), Milloff implies that the peoples of all nations and religions are "enveloped in whale-lines" together (*MD* 281). In his forthcoming essay, "*Moby-Dick* and the World We Live In," Samuel Otter attributes the multiple post-9/11 interpretations which *Moby-Dick* has provided to the novel's protean nature.

Moby-Dick has been used to project visually concerns regarding war, imperialism, and environmental and racial injustice. Jerry Beck's elaborate 1988 installation, *In Search of Moby Dick and the Tattoo Palace*, involving multiple objects in empty spaces at Boston's City Hall, emphasized his conviction that in *Moby-Dick* whaling was synonymous with "territorial expansion and man's attempt to discipline nature," with the whale being "a rebuttal of both man's commercial greed and possessive imagination" (quoted in Schultz *Unpainted* 295). Beck's images of Ahab's lost foot implanted on the globe itself and of his hand reaching up from the seas in a grasping fist reinforce Melville's antipathy toward "the all-grasping western world" (*MD* 380). Whether categorized as hyperrealist or postmodernist, Vincent Desiderio's large triptych, *The Progress of Self-Love* (1990), relates figures from myth, history, and literature to contemporary circumstances in troubling ways. He flanks his central picture depicting a crater of dead soldiers with an interior painting of murder on the left and a cutaway painting of the sea on the right. The latter reveals a modern-day one-legged Ahab, his gunboat looming behind him, still compulsively searching on the sea's surface even though the white whale lies rotting on its bottom.

In Richard Ellis's 1984 mural at the New Bedford Whaling Museum, Moby Dick swims through turquoise waters in a pod of other sperm whales, young and old. Ellis represents the white whale not only with scientific accuracy but also as luminous and serene, despite the barbs jutting forth from his body. Half life-size, the whales appear in the loveliness of life on a museum wall, with all the deadly implements from the nineteenth-century whaling trade surrounding them, as a powerful statement on behalf of the necessity of preserving cetaceans. Vali Myers, an Australian-born artist, who has lived and painted primarily in Italy, emphasizes both the cruelty of whaling as well as the wonder of whales (and other animals) in several minutely detailed paintings – *Moby Dick* (1972–4), *The Whale* (1980–3), *The Whaler's Daughter* (1990), and *Stella Maris* (1998). Hers is an ecofeminist perspective in that she identifies whaling's cruelty with the cruelty which women have experienced in patriarchal societies, claiming that Moby Dick is female and that every harpoon which penetrates the whale's body also penetrates hers (Schultz *Unpainted* 281–3; "Seeing Globally" 414). Her paintings evoke not only the nightmarish carnage of whaling, but also tranquil relationships between humans and animals. From 1986 through the early 1990s in over fifty works, Robert McCauley used *Moby-Dick* to explore diverse aspects of the nineteenth century's legacy, including its excessive greed and its exploitation of nature (Schultz *Unpainted* 326–8). Thus a sculptural piece such as *Ahab's Leg* (1986), in which McCauley piles deer antlers high into a column, forces contemplation of the extensive loss of animal life that follows from the pursuit of personal vengeance. In her oil pastel on vellum, *Will He Perish?* (1997), Theresa Zillig puts Moby Dick's immense brow before viewers in such a way as to confront them with the possibility of the whale's demise. Given Melville's concern that like the once multitudinous herds of buffalo, "the hunted whale cannot now escape speedy extinction" (*MD* 460), Zillig depicts a minute buffalo herd traveling as if in memory across the broad and mottled white expanse of Moby Dick's brow. Although comic-books and children's versions of *Moby-Dick* have deplorably degraded the complexity of the racially and ethnically diverse crew of the *Pequod* (Schultz "Visualizing Race"), several free-standing artworks use Melville's novel explicitly to question America's racist policies. Among these are Walter Martin's installation piece, *Old Fleece Preaching to the Sharks* (1985–6), and the several images, titled *The Whiteness of the Whale*, which Tim Rollins created with KOS, a group of South Bronx teenagers, in the mid-1980s. Martin establishes an audience of a pile of white bones for a headless black dog, placed in front of a microphone, to suggest, with grim humor, that blacks in the US have had as little success communicating to whites as the black cook in *Moby-Dick* has speaking to sharks. Painting pages from the novel with thin layers of white, Rollins's works question whether American whites have succeeded in whitewashing Americans of other racial and ethnic backgrounds or if the hegemony of whiteness obscures clarity in thinking about race in the US (Schultz *Unpainted* 300–6).

Most dramatically, however, an interest in Queequeg has increasingly replaced the fascination earlier artists had with Ahab. Certainly, sequential artists, including Louis Zansky, illustrator of the first *Moby-Dick* comic book, as well as Wilson, Baskin, Hoie, and Kanner, placed Queequeg along with the other harpooners and non-white crew in their portrait galleries. Other artists such as Marc Davis and Milloff also give special attention to the Polynesian harpooner. Through his manipulation of cubistic patterns,

Figure 34.2   Mark Milloff. *Stripping the Whale* (2003). Pastel on paper. 75 × 50 in.

Davis focuses on the harpooner in *Queequeg in the Bow* (*c*.1956). Milloff explicitly named Queequeg his hero and foregrounds him dramatically in his works – *Stripping the Whale* (1985) (Figure 34.2) and *Queequeg Rescues Tashtego* (1986). Joseph Foster and Abby Schlachter have created different, but equally revisionary images of Queequeg – Foster with an imposing black-and-white woodcut presenting him as a benign androgynous figure, whose multicultural gestures and tattoos are nurturing and beneficent, and Schlachter with two white body casts of herself, each inscribed with hieroglyphs over the surfaces of their undeniably female shapes (Schultz "Common Continent" 27–9).

Since the Melville Revival of the 1920s, critics of *Moby-Dick* have found its lack of female characters and its emphasis on masculine pursuits problematic. In the last decade scholars and artists – both women and men – have reassessed this evaluation, using feminist theory and historical criticism as well as creating artworks and performance pieces specifically allowing women to participate in performative interpretations of the novel. The first known visual response to *Moby-Dick* by a woman is Ann Wilson's 1955 *Moby Dick* quilt. Convinced that women quilters were the first abstract expressionists, Wilson responds to the novel by using cloth to emphasize its layers of meaning and patchwork to emphasize its stitching together of heterogeneous materials and concepts (Schultz *Unpainted* 277). Subsequently, other women quilters and seamstresses have appropriated *Moby-Dick*: Marion Cheever Whiteside Newton's forty-eight panel, story-book quilt (*c*.1958) depicts Ishmael in the upper left-hand block starting out on his journey and in the lower right-hand block on Queequeg's coffin; Elaine Reichek's 1997 sampler, *Moby Dick: A Sailor's Yarn*, cunningly incorporates several of the novel's references to weaving and to looms into its design; Susan R. Boardman's embroidered maritime narratives (2000–1) float the white whale along amidst lively maritime events as an ineffable and inviolate presence.

Women artists, including Barbara Johnson, Celia Smith, Joyce Alexander, Margo Kren, Vali Myers, Margo LeMieux, Aimée Picard, and Kathleen Piercefield, have responded to *Moby-Dick* with artworks which counter those centered on Ahab and his pursuit. Their works focus on the whale and tend to evoke a synergistic natural world in which men and whales exist in relation to other living beings (Schultz *Unpainted* 276–88). With her extensive series of paintings and drawings inspired by *Moby-Dick* – created between 1998 and 2004 and numbering over seventy – Aileen Callahan projects a complex organic vision of the novel. Influenced by paintings by Leonardo da Vinci, Goya, El Greco, van Swanenburgh, Turner, and Ryder, Callahan's dense brush and pencil work oscillates between depth and surface, darkness and light. Although her titles suggest a commitment to narrative or realism – for example, *The Birth of Moby Dick*, *Whale Mouth*, or *Breaching Heart* – her aesthetic is abstract, with her paintings reflecting the same difficulties of perception and the felt-experience of wonder and terror as does Melville's novel (Callahan). In addition to works focused on women and whales, Piercefield has created a bold image of a powerfully masculine Queequeg, whose heart holds a photograph of Melville, suggesting the author's special affection for the compassionate Polynesian (Figure 34.3).

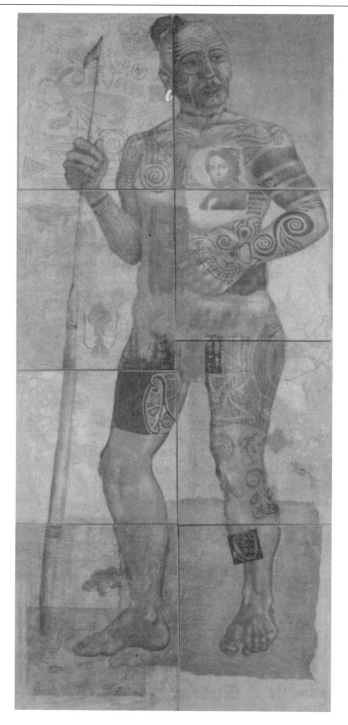

Figure 34.3   Kathleen Piercefield. *Queequeg in His Own Person* (2004). Monotype, collagraph, polymer-plate lithography, etching, and hand-coloring on canvas. 96 × 40 in.

Figure 34.4   Ellen Driscoll. From sketches for *Ahab's Wife* (1998). Ink on paper. 11 × 8.5 in.

Women's roles in interpreting *Moby-Dick* through performance, a phenomenon which started in the mid-1980s with Patty Lynch's drama, *Wreck of the Hesperus*, have evolved significantly – in music, dance, drama, opera, and multimedia extravaganza. Certainly prior to the 1990s, men, including Gilbert Wilson and Orson Welles, created a space for women in dramas based on *Moby-Dick*, and men continue to generate and to participate in *Moby-Dick*-inspired performances; however, the proliferation of women in these events postulates the novel's resilience and its exuberant vision of a pluralistic society. The 1992 British rock musical, *Moby Dick*, in which a girls' academy attempts to stage a version of Melville's novel, was initially proclaimed a flop, but the show continues to be performed for laughs, as recently as 2004 in Topeka, Kansas. Bill Peters's drama, *Hunting for Moby Dick*, which opened in San Francisco in 1996 with women in several lead roles, was critically acclaimed, and several women performed as crew in Leon Ingulsrud's successful *Moby Dick*, which was staged in the US and Japan in 2000 and 2001, and a 2004 Philadelphia production of Welles's *Moby-Dick – Rehearsed* had an all-female cast. Joanne Spies's one-woman musical entertainment, *Me & Melville*, has been a hit with audiences in the Massachusetts Berkshires since 1997.

The appearance of women in these works established a context for three compelling postmodern pieces, each of which demands that its audience accept the position of women in Melville's novel – Ellen Driscoll's poetic dance-drama, *Ahab's Wife, or the Whale* (1998) (Figure 34.4); Laurie Anderson's *Songs and Stories from Moby Dick* (1999); and Rinde Eckert's opera, *And God Created Great Whales* (2000). Combining music, drama, and dance with stunning visual effects (supplemented, in the case of Driscoll's work, by numerous artworks) and with moving, original scripts based on Melville's novel, these three works have moved visual interpretation of *Moby-Dick* into pulsating new art forms in which women's lives are given a central place.

At the end of the twentieth century, *Moby-Dick* was substantially and visibly embodied in American architecture – a house on Martha's Vineyard, bridges at Lake Washington outside of Seattle, and Douglas Darden's unbuilt spatial monument, *Melvilla* (Schultz *Unpainted* 311–21, 330; Darden). Since its first appearance in Knaths's 1935 painting, *Moby-Dick* has also repeatedly been re-embodied as a book. However, contemporary artists, in converting the book itself into an artwork with a three-dimensional validity, raise questions about its iconicity as well as its readability. Robert McCauley boxes up two editions of *Moby-Dick* for two pieces, each titled *Moby-Dick Altered* (both 1991), thereby simultaneously enshrining the novel and locking it up, making it altogether unreadable. Philip Smith's 1989–90 sculpted leather box, portraying Ahab, whose grim face is fused with a furious sea, could frighten a reader from opening its clasp and discovering within an Arion edition of *Moby-Dick* covered in the same deep blue leather – but now worked to suggest a gleaming, tranquil sea. By converting the front cover and the spine of the Barnes-Noble edition of *Moby-Dick* in 1996 into an American flag, Sharon Wysocki calls attention to "the great American novel," but she also calls this sobriquet into question by slathering the back cover with black tinged a fiery red. In 2002, Cheryl Sorg inscribed the entire text of *Moby-Dick* onto a cylinder, with an eleven-foot diameter, titling her work, "Surely All This is Not Without Meaning." For her 2003 interactive piece, *Moby Dick, Used*, Sharon Butler encouraged people to contribute copies of the novel for display on shelves in a Connecticut art gallery, with overflows going on the floor, a process which led her to compare Ahab's obsessive search with her own search for knowledge (Callis). In their emphasis upon *Moby-Dick* – the book – these artists question its iconization and imply that it inhibits the novel's being read. They also challenge viewers to read the book as does Ishmael when he addresses his readers in relation to the sperm whale's brow: "I put that brow before you. Read it if you can" (*MD* 347).

Moby-Dick's reputation as the best-known, least-read novel has generated the argument that its visual interpretations (as well as those of Melville's other works) have pre-empted reading. Critics note that an artist's personal agenda or the impact of a given cultural moment also constricts or distorts reader response. However, teachers – in graduate schools, colleges, summer seminars, high schools – increasingly are using visual media to complement their instruction of *Moby-Dick*.[2] Far from deterring students' engagement with Melville's works, these teachers report that the introduction of images into the classroom as well as student assignments to create images (including diverse individual artworks, websites, PowerPoint presentations, multimedia archives, and elaborate exhibitions) have enriched their students' reading and stimulated long-lasting interest in Melville's writings. Reading Melville's writings in relation to their ever-proliferating, diverse visual interpretations confirms that they will remain "unpainted to the last" (*MD* 264), as Ishmael says of the whale, but that like other cultural icons they will remain mysterious, resilient, and always open to new perceptions.

NOTES

1   Neither *The Scarlet Letter*, *The Adventures of Huckleberry Finn*, nor *Uncle Tom's Cabin* has generated an equivalent response from artists in the US or around the world, although each has been the catalyst for significant works of art, drama, and cinema. The only American story with a response perhaps equivalent to that of *Moby-Dick*'s in popular culture globally is *The Wonderful Wizard of Oz*.
2   In conversations with the author, Jill Barnum (University of Minnesota), Wyn Kelley (Massachusetts Institute of Technology), Laurie Robertson-Lorant (NEH Summer Seminar), Patrick Dooley (University of Kansas, Department of Design), Dan Rockhill (University of Kansas, School of Architecture), Tanya Van Hyfte (Lafayette, Indiana High School), and Robert Wallace (Northern Kentucky University) have all reported success using visual materials in teaching *Moby-Dick*.

References and Further Reading

Athitakis, Mark. *Business* 2.0 (September 2003). See Fred Koeppel, "Moby-Dick's Ahab could teach CEO's about leadership?" "Book Notes." koeppel@gomemphis.com. September 7, 2003.

Benjamin, Walter. "The Work of Art in the Age of Mechanical Reproduction." *Illuminations*. Ed. Hannah Arendt. New York: Schocken Books, 1969.

Burt, Tamia A., Joseph D. Thomas and Marsha L. McCabe. *Moby Dick*. New Bedford, MA: Spinner Publications, 2002.

Bryant, John. "Introduction: A Melville Renaissance." In *A Companion to Melville Studies*. Ed. John Bryant. Westport, CT: Greenwood Press., 1986.

Callahan, Aileen. "Eye to Eye." *Leviathan* 5.1 (March, 2003): 52–7.

Callis, Marion. E-mail to rlevine@umn.edu and sotter@socrates.berkeley.edu. March 18, 2004.

Darden, Douglas. *"Melvilla." Melville Society Extracts* 91 (1992): 1–10.

Del Tredici, Robert. *Floodgates of the Wonderworld: A* Moby-Dick *Pictorial*. Kent, Ohio: Kent State University Press, 2001.

Firestone, Evan. "Herman Melville's *Moby-Dick* and the Abstract Expressionists." *Arts Magazine* 54 (1980): 120–4.

Gilenson, Boris. *"Moby-Dick* in Russian." *Soviet Life* (November, 1969): 18–19.

Inge, M. Thomas. "Melville in Popular Culture." In *A Companion to Melville Studies*. Ed. John Bryant. Westport, CT: Greenwood Press., 1986. 695–739.

Insko, Jeffrey. "Art After Ahab: Review of *And God Created Great Whales*." http://www3.iath.-virginia.edu/pmc/text-only/issue.901/12.1.r_insko.txt.

Kelley, Wyn. "Kienbusch, Melville, and the Islands." In *Melville "Among the Nations."* Ed. Sanford E. Marovitz and A. C. Christodoulou. Kent, OH: Kent State University Press, 2001.

Kruse, Joachim, ed. *Illustrationen zu Melvilles "Moby-Dick."* Schleswig: Schleswiger Druck und Verlagshaus, 1976.

Marovitz, Sanford E. "Herman Melville: A Writer for the World." In *A Companion to Melville Studies*. Ed. John Bryant. Westport, CT: Greenwood Press., 1986.

———. "Mystical Visions of *Mardi* and *Moby-Dick*: Wondrous New Paintings of A. C. Christodoulou." *CEA Critic* 63.1 (Fall, 2000): 71–83.

Phelps, Leland R. *Herman Melville's Foreign Reputation: A Research Guide*. Boston: G. K. Hall & Co., 1983.

Rosenberg, Harold. *The Tradition of the New*. New York: McGraw-Hill, 1965.

Schultz, Elizabeth. "The Avatars of *Moby-Dick* in Contemporary Popular American Fiction." *Journal of Popular Literature* 1.2 (Fall/Winter, 1985): 2–44.

———. " 'The Common Continent of Men': Visualizing Race in *Moby-Dick*." *Artists After Moby-Dick. Leviathan* 3.2 (special issue, October, 2001): 19–34.

———. "The Illustrated Melville," *Melville Society Extracts*, 103 (December, 1995): 1–18.

———. (1997). "The Invisible Made Visible: Maurice Sendak's *Pierre* Illustrations." *Leviathan* 111 (December, 1997): 2–6, 8–9, 10–13, 17–21.

———. "Seeing *Moby-Dick* Globally." In *Melville "Among the Nations."* Ed. Sanford E. Marovitz and A. C. Christodoulou. Kent, OH: Kent State University Press, 2001.

———. "The Seer & the Scene: Robert Del Tredici's Illustrations for *Moby-Dick*." In *Floodgates of the Wonderworld: A* Moby-Dick *Pictorial*. Kent, OH: Kent State University Press, 2001. 1–4.

———. *Unpainted to the Last:* Moby-Dick *and Twentieth-Century American Art*. Lawrence: University Press of Kansas, 1995.

———. "Visualizing Race: Images of *Moby-Dick*." *Leviathan* 3.1 (March, 2001): 31–60.

Wallace, Robert K. "Chasing *Moby-Dick* across Paper and Canvas: Five Decades of Free-Floating Literary Art." *Leviathan* 3.2 (October, 2001): 5–16.

———. "Flood Tide: Del Tredici's Return to Printmaking." In *Floodgates of the Wonderworld: A* Moby-Dick *Pictorial*. Kent, OH: Kent State University Press, 2001. 11–15.

———. *Frank Stella's* Moby-Dick: *Words and Shapes*. Ann Arbor: University of Michigan Press, 2000.

35

The Melville Text

John Bryant

Whether we imagine Melville as a person who lived and wrote, or as a set of ideas that excite and challenge us, or as a presence in his time and in ours, or simply as a sequence of things written, "Melville" exists for us only as Text. That is, biography, philosophy, history, publications – these versions of Melville have no reality except in the form of texts; they have no transmission except through texts; they cannot be comprehended until they are read as texts. Even objects have no reality for us until we attach words to them. Before we can attempt to know what Melville *means* to us, we need to know what Melville *is*. Melville is a Text. But like any text, the Melville Text is elusive, for it exists invisibly in mind as well as visibly in documents – letters, journals, manuscript, and various forms of print. Because we witness texts most directly in documents, we assume that the Melville Text is the sum total of what we can see. But we also know that Melville composed in his mind, and on documents lost to us, far more words than what meets our eye in print. Furthermore, we assume that these invisible and lost texts are irretrievable, and with that false assumption, we allow ourselves to slide the slippery slope to the false conclusion that these unseen texts are meaningless. Even worse, our means of publishing, our critical approaches, and even our habits of reading conspire to support this false conclusion, for publishers, critics, and readers naturally want their Melville in clearly printed formats that reduce the fullness of the Melville Text to a set of books, or a set of ideas, or even to a single version of a single work: *Moby-Dick*. What is insidious about our current mode of the production and consumption of literary works is that it encourages readers to ignore the many versions of Melville's various works, *Moby-Dick* included. In this chapter, I want to avoid the reductions of past practice, and much of what I have to say has to do with textual editing, or the means by which we may witness unseen texts. As I hope to show, editing is our only way of making the invisible Melville visible.

By "Melville Text," I mean to stress process as well as product, that is, the labor Melville expended in writing what he wrote, as is evident in manuscripts as well as printed works. But more, I mean to include the invisible text of his revision. This revision text is not just the various versions produced by hand or press; it is also our construction of the "working" he performed to produce those versions; it is the story of how his revisions flow from version to version. If we are to tell the full story of Melville's "fluid text," we will have to consider all materials related to his creative process, including the sources Melville drew upon, borrowed or stole. As I have written elsewhere, the fluid text is not only a matter of authorial and editorial revision; it also includes "cultural revision," the versions of Melville that other artists, writers, and editors have taken *from* Melville either in adaptation of Melville or as homage to him or as speculative constructions of his intentions (*Fluid Text*, Ch. 4). But here we have space to consider only the most directly observable forms of revision that make up the Melville Text.

Text as Words and Wording

My expanded notion of the Text called "Melville" is bound to irritate separate critical camps in separate ways. Traditional literary historians who bring biography and social developments into play in the interpretation of mostly imaginative works will welcome the inclusion of sources and biographical materials but might balk at the extension of "Melville" to include adaptations of him. What relevance, they might ask, are the twentieth-century film and stage productions of *Moby-Dick* (let us say) to the social and aesthetic dynamics occurring in 1850 when Melville wrote his "whale"? And New Historicists who take text as cultural discourse and the writer as a function of culture either in compliance with or resistance to that culture would in their camp welcome the "intertextuality" implicit in this enlarged "Melville," but might at the same time question its rejuvenated focus on the individual writer writing. What relevance, they might ask, are revisions, versions, and fluid texts to our understanding of the genres and "thematics" ingrained in the cultural fabric of the published text?

These objections from historicists, traditional and new, are rooted in the assumption that "text" is limited to a fixed, material object. In fact, literary works invariably exist in multiple versions due to some form of revision, either by authors themselves, or editors, or other readers empowered to make changes. If this is true – and *Typee*, *Moby-Dick*, and *Billy Budd* are major examples of this textual phenomenon – then scholars, critics, and general readers need to broaden their awareness of textuality to embrace this reality, not deny it. The fundamental reorientation required is our coming to understand that "text" is both material and immaterial. It is fixed in tangible words, both handwritten and in print. But this fixing represents only a fraction of the intangible words, or wording, that emerge in the ongoing process of writing. The Melville Text is words and process, or rather, words and wording.

By the statement "Melville is words" I mean to equate Melville with all the words he wrote, in the order in which he wrote them, as best we can find them and determine the sequence of their composition. A "descriptive bibliography" gets us close to this ordering as it lists the many forms in which Melville's published books exist in the order of publication. (The projected descriptive bibliography in the Northwestern–Newberry edition has not emerged. Until it does, readers should consult Blanck; see also Tanselle.) But the Melville Text is far broader than such a list, and of course Melville was writing long before he began publishing. The earliest words we have in Melville's hand are as follows:

> My dear Aunt
>   You asked me to write
> you a letter but I thought tht I coul-
> d not write well enough before this. I
> now study Spelling[,] Arithmetic[,]
> Grammar[,] Geography, Reading, and
> Writing. (*L* 4)

This letter from a nine-year-old, impeccable in its penmanship, except for the chirographic oddities – the compressed "that," the hyphenated "could," and three mirror-image commas (see brackets) that curl to the right – that only a nine-year-old can concoct, is certainly not the first words that Melville wrote, as the letter itself implies. Signed "Herman, Melvill" (this time with an oddly placed comma), the letter seems to have little meaning for us beyond the charm of a schoolboy's struggle to compose his proud capitals and the relief (no doubt) of reaching an end to his letter-writing duty. We might take note that some form of the verb *to write* appears in each of the quoted clauses, and that the scribe's previous anxiety that he "could not write well enough" has long since proven ironic. The letter marks a boy's triumph over self-doubt and his sudden mastery of a skill (if not the comma). Of course, his "writing" is more penmanship than self-expression. But I would not rob this boy of the astonishing moment of recognition recorded here; it is the birth of a writer coterminous with the words "I thought tht I coul-d not write." And with this emergence of self-consciousness, its hint of self-abnegation, and its triumphant reversal, the writing process begins.

Of course, we cannot separate the process from the words, or the text from the person; they are all of the same fabric and looming. We expect the statement "Melville is words" to mean merely that "the body of written work by Melville consists of all the words he wrote." But an added meaning is the following: "our conception of Melville as a person consists entirely of words." We fancy that biography gives us the "life," but, of course, that living soul is dead; the life is gone. Biography gives us words instead of life, based on documents written by the writer (beginning with the letter to Aunt Lucy) and documents written by others – more letters, journal entries, reports, even deeds and wills or passports – all words. Thus, we have nothing but words to link us to the past; and Melville – his work and his life – exists only in the form of words. It behooves us then to find as many words as we can.

"Melville is wording." This second statement is more challenging. Thus far, the equation of Melville and words seems convincing because of the solid material nature of words themselves, and our principal obligation (apart from figuring out what the words mean) is to collect them (about which more later). But by extending the equation to include "wording," we move to the immaterial process that makes the material words, and to a set of words that we can only infer Melville wrote. This sounds dangerous, so let me proceed with caution.

"Wording" derives from the verb "to word," meaning to put an idea, thought, or feeling into words, as in "I would word your letter differently," or "he worded the Declaration more carefully." If we scratch at this verb usage, we recognize that it implies an important ontological condition: Thoughts and feelings exist in mind independently of the words used to represent them. These elusive thoughts and feelings can be variously worded, first sub-vocally in a focused and active part of our mind and then more tangibly when tentatively written on paper, and then altered again in revision. Idea and word are not the same, and an idea can be worded in different ways. Melville's most famous three words might have come to mind immediately as soon as the problem of introducing the narrator of *Moby-Dick* arose; or he might have considered other wordings: My name is Ishmael, or I am called Ishmael, or They call me Ishmael. As it happens, we have no evidence that Melville actually entertained these options; they are, in fact, the potentialities of the language itself, purely the results of letting the language operate on the energy of its own process. Wording just happens.

But we do not need to make up a history of the revision of "Call me Ishmael"; we have numerous examples of other Melville wordings and rewordings to illustrate this phenomenon, and some additional problems as well.

In 1846, Melville's first major literary work, *Typee*, was issued in three separate and different wordings, or versions, one in Britain and two in America. The first American edition was similar to the first British text, except that Melville's American publisher, John Wiley, removed a handful of (to him) unpleasant sentences of a sexual nature. Some months later, Melville issued (again with Wiley) a massively expurgated edition of *Typee* that removed even more passages of a sexual, religious, and political nature (see Howard). Melville argued in a letter to his British publisher, John Murray, that Murray, too, should adopt this heavily reworded text for the novel's continued publication in Britain; the revision, he insisted, reduces the polemical nature of his text and "imparts a unity to the book which it wanted before" (*L* 56). (Murray did not accept Melville's suggestion, and *Typee* has thus existed in these two radically different American and British versions.) In changing the print text of *Typee*, Melville did more than cut; he also revised specific words, and this fact brings us to the illustrative point I wish to make. One such revised word appears just as the book's narrator and protagonist, Tommo, is escaping from the Typees. In this scene, Tommo's native lover Fayaway is observed sobbing "indignantly" in the British version; however, in his revised American version Melville has Fayaway sob "convulsively."

Quite obviously, this differently worded scene affects us differently, and our awareness that two wordings exist affects us even more, but in a different way. To begin with, we recognize that if Fayaway is sobbing "indignantly" over Tommo's abrupt departure, she has reason to be indignant, and this has to do with her sense of Tommo's abandonment and betrayal of her and her people. On the other hand, "convulsively" suggests that she is merely sobbing out of control, with no resentment implied whatsoever: she is distraught over losing her lover. I would argue that Fayaway's indignation in the British version is a projection of Melville's own guilt over his sexual use of Fayaway and that his revision to "convulsively" is a cover-up induced by the fact that at the time Melville made this revision, he was approaching his engagement to Elizabeth Shaw and did not want his future wife's family to ponder too much on why a Polynesian girl might be so indignant over his leaving. I am sure that other interpretations can be constructed to explain this important rewording. But no matter how one interprets this text of revision, certain facts must be acknowledged: that neither version is "better" than the other, that both are "right" for their moment; that in terms of a time frame, the "indignantly" wording preceded "convulsively," and that this sequence of revision is integral to the meaning of the revision. That is to say, when it comes to interpreting a revision such as this, we are not simply interpreting the *words*; we are also assessing the intangible unworded space between the two words. More specifically, we are addressing the *direction* of their change, from "indignantly" to "convulsively" and not vice versa. Moreover, we are actually constructing a new wording – "indignantly becoming convulsively," let's call it – and this wording is a "text of revision" that represents the invisible process of revision.

Previously, I said that this *wording* phenomenon illustrates certain additional problems, and these problems relate to an earlier suggestion that the idea of "Melville as wording" leads us to the dangerous matter of allowing ourselves to infer (as we have just done) a text that Melville may have written or only thought. The problems are manifold but intriguing. For starters, the text of the "wording" just discussed does not exist in any single book; it is, as it were, unprintable. The British version prints one word, the American another; but where is the "text of revision" itself? It exists in its totality only as we write it out for Melville. The now standard, scholarly Northwestern–Newberry edition of *Typee* prints "indignantly" (250) and lists "convulsively" along with hundreds of cuts and changes in an appendix (358), but it does not, or rather will not, according to its editorial principles, interrupt the printed reading text in some way to register Melville's rewording. The dilemma has as much to do with the limitations of print as it does with scholarly editing, for two words cannot occupy the same place in a text. An editor might invent a symbol to render the revision – something like "indignantly → convulsively" – so that readers can be alerted to the fact and directionality of the change. Or an editor might develop an electronic edition of *Typee* that gives readers swifter and more direct access to this revision sequence. I have developed a form of what I call "fluid text-editing" that uses these techniques (Bryant, *Herman Melville's* Typee). But the deeper problem is that whatever editorial scheme can be devised to represent a revision, the wording of the revision, that is, the process that created it, remains unworded to the last.

The problem with determining the Melville Text – all the words and wording – is that there is more text in a text than meets the eye, and that the text of the additional invisible wording can only be made visible through our editorial construction of it. Moreover, editing cannot happen without a critical understanding of the meaning of change. Skeptics may squint, as well they should, for the construction of Melville's "invisible wordings" sounds suspiciously like our rewriting of Melville. But no writing, including Melville's, reaches print without editing, and no edition of Melville exists without a rewriting of him (a point I will demonstrate later). In this case, the editorial construction is a matter of discerning and bringing to light (witnessing and giving access to) what is most likely to have happened in the process of revision. It involves filling in the spaces between variant words rather than replacing one Melville text with another, or inventing a substitute text of our own instead of Melville's. But since wording, not just words, is the focus, and since processes like wordings are sequential, they are best rendered as narratives: people performing actions. Thus, the text of Melville's wording is best rendered in what I call a revision narrative. Fayaway's sobbing illustrates the point.

One limiting factor in our attempt to witness Melville's wording is that our evidence of revision exists in the two, British and American, print variants only. And because the two variant adverbs exist only in separate books, and because we know of the revision only by having collated (compared) these two print texts, we can witness only the endpoints of the sequence of revision. But if we were to find this revision in manuscript, we would have a fuller record of Melville's wording process. At the very least, we would see Melville's cancellation of "indignantly" in pencil or ink and his insertion of a set of alternatives, either "convulsively" by itself, or a series of other adverbs culminating with "convulsively," inscribed on whatever white space is available on the manuscript leaf. Given our limitation here to print-evidence only, we can only guess at the other adverbs Melville might have entertained when he set about revising "indignantly," in much the way we might guess at the different options Melville might have considering in his opening to *Moby-Dick*. One guess, however, is a material certainty, and that is, no adverb at all. That is, while we cannot reliably infer that Melville actually considered having Fayaway sob, let us say, "hysterically" or "soulfully," we can argue that he considered dropping an adverbial modifier from the scene altogether, thus giving us Fayaway simply "sobbing." In fact, we can make this inference on the basis of a technicality rooted in the process of handwriting, for no matter how quickly a writer revises there is a necessary time lag between the cancellation of a word and the insertion of a revision. Thus whether Melville intended it or not, the unmodified "sobbing" would have existed as part of Melville's text as his wording made its way from "sobbing indignantly" to "sobbing convulsively."

By resorting to this degree of textual technicality, I know that I invite charges of madness, for readers are bound to ask what relevance any of this has to what Melville "finally wrote" and how we read that final text. But if we want to know Melville, we must look not only to the words he finally printed but to the wordings that transpired as he wrote. Only by witnessing this process do we come closer to the life in Melville's texts. If the Melville Text, then, is fundamentally a text of revision, we must challenge our conventional notions of finality in the writing process and of reading as well. It is a truism among modern writers (and Melville was the first among moderns) that a text is never really finished but surrendered to the publisher. And our principal access to writing is through publishing. But publishing is a notoriously problematic part of the process. It is a commercial venture that converts a writer's necessarily unfinished text into print for marketing and distribution. Given that far more writing goes into a book than readers ever see, publishing is also a highly reductive process. Readers, none the wiser, have no choice but to take the market's singularized and fixed print text as the "work itself"; they have no way to witness the fuller fluid text. In an effort to establish a reliable common text for reading and analysis, scholars and critics are complicit in the reduction of fluid texts to single print texts by limiting our reading text to that version that represents only the writer's final intentions just before going to print. But as the example of Fayaway's sobbing demonstrates, Melville's intentions shifted and have no finality. Moreover, our reading of the ending of *Typee* will change depending on which intended adverb we read. More to the point, our reading changes even more when we consider the forces that made Melville's intentions shift at this point in his text. That is, because we (more than Melville's first British and American readers) know that Melville altered the way he wanted his readers to see Fayaway, we readers (more fully conscious of the writing process) must consider our modern awareness of Melville's rhetorical manipulation as part of our own reading experience. Melville's shifting from one adverb, to none, to another suggests a person expanding and restraining himself in a complex attempt to adjust his relation to his politics, to women, to family, and to the ideologies of his culture. These are not irrelevant.

Thus far, I have tried to show that whether as a person, a body of work, or a cultural icon, Melville is known to us only as text, and that to comprehend the Melville Text with any degree of fullness, we need to recognize the nature of textuality and that it encompasses not only print words but also the process of wording, or revision. In fact, this process involves a variety of materials – documents, manuscripts, sources, books, editions, and adaptations – but an essay of this scope cannot treat the full range of Melville's fluid text. Therefore, let's focus on the central problem of editing, for to *read* Melville, we must witness his texts, and we cannot witness a fluid text without editing it.

Editing Melville

Unless you are reading directly from a manuscript, it is impossible to read the Melville Text without accessing it in an edited form. Editing is not simply a convenience for the sake of legibility; it is the means by which words and wordings are transformed, in both form and content, into print and submitted to the market-place. It is also a form of revision, sometimes involving a collaboration of author and editor, but oftentimes not. Moreover, writers and their readers merge most frequently in printed texts; that is, readers enact the writer's words by reading them, most often in books. And the critical facilitator of that merging is the editor. Editing is essentially a process of rewriting in which writer, publisher, and editor participate; it is an extension of the writer's creative process. Editors suggest or insist upon changes, and therefore both assist and resist writers in performing this role; and for their part, writers resist but also submit to and comply with their editors' suggestions and impositions. This phase of composition is inherently collaborative, and no published text exists, historically or in modern scholarly format, without editorial intervention of one degree or another. It behooves us, then, to know Melville's editors, not as functionaries but as contributors to his text. Who are these editors?

Manuscript and other evidence tells us that, aside from Melville himself, the first editor for *Typee* was his brother Gansevoort, who suggested revisions in manuscript (Bryant *Melville Unfolding* Ch. 12) and was later recruited by Herman to make changes as he read in England the page proofs of the first British edition. British publisher John Murray's copy-editor, Henry Milton, and probably Murray himself required changes in *Typee* reflecting matters of taste and style. Then American publisher John Wiley and his editor (as well as Melville's friend) Evert Duyckinck made small changes once the book was accepted for American publication (Howard). Perhaps Duyckinck grudgingly assisted Melville in complying with Wiley's wishes that *Typee* be heavily expurgated. Probably with the desire to reduce the number of hands playing with his text, Melville had *Moby-Dick* (five years later) set up through a private typesetter, R. Craighead, and arranged for the American publishing firm, Harper and Brothers, to print and distribute the book unaltered (Tanselle "Historical Note"). But to have the novel published in England, Melville sent corrected and revised proof sheets to British publisher Richard Bentley, who edited the novel, expurgating numerous sexual, religious and political passages, thus creating his own version of *Moby-Dick*, entitled *The Whale*. Melville's last editor was his literary executor Arthur Stedman, who, soon after Melville's death, published new versions of *Typee* and *Moby-Dick* that included (in *Typee*) changes requested by the author.

Editing Melville invariably means rewriting Melville. This is true not only for Melville's historical editors with whom Melville actively worked but also for Melville's modern scholarly editors who strive to bring reliable editions of Melville into print for other scholars, critics, students, and general readers. As we can see, to reprint either *Typee* or *Moby-Dick* for successive generations of readers, modern editors must choose to copy from one historical version rather than the other, and choosing such a "copy-text" requires critical judgment. Most would agree that the British edition of *Typee* and the American edition of *Moby-Dick* come closer to Melville's intentions when he first went to press with each work. But each work's expurgated editions also include Melville's intended revisions, and a case can be made for *Typee* that Melville intended even the expurgations. How do editors, then, account for these variations in the edited texts they produce? Even the most cautious editor seeking only to "correct" obvious errors in the copy-text version must alter Melville's historical print text; thus, modern editors invariably create new versions of their own. More adventurous editors following the so-called Greg Bowers tradition of scholarly editing might do more than correct obvious errors. They will combine the texts of historical versions and, if necessary, create wordings of their own, along the lines of a critically determined principle of authorial intention and editorial intervention. But obviously, whether cautious or adventurous, an editor works without benefit of the deceased author's input.

The case of *Billy Budd* all the more demonstrates the power of editors to rewrite Melville. Melville never submitted his novella to a printer or even converted his still-evolving text into fair copy for printing; thus, he never collaborated with editors or publishers in squiring the work through the press. Melville's intentions exist incompletely somewhere only in the revisions found in his unpolished manuscript. This manuscript was discovered thirty years after the author's death, and to be read at all, it has to be first deciphered, then edited. But successive generations of editors do not agree on the text of *Billy Budd*. The first to edit *Billy Budd* (somewhat insufficiently) was Raymond Weaver in 1924; a significantly different but also problematic version was produced by F. Barron Freeman in 1948; and the most reliable but necessarily debatable version appeared in the Hayford and Sealts edition of 1962. Three generations of editors have produced three different *Billy Budd*s.

To read any published Melville work means reading a version of it in the form of an editor's edition of it. To the extent that editions (historical or scholarly) are versions of the work, they are also essentially revisions performed by specialized readers called editors. These scholars, reliable to be sure, nevertheless operate in the context of not only the logics, aesthetics, and politics of their day but also their own personal biases and tastes in reading the past as well as their assumptions about the needs of their own readerships. Thus, the revisions that editors make reflect their relation to text, history, and culture. To know the Melville Text, we are therefore obliged to know the strategies and dynamics of editing. Histories of the editorial versions of each Melville publication and their reprintings in the twentieth century can be found in the Textual Note of each volume of the Northwestern–Newberry (NN) edition. G. Thomas Tanselle, chief textual scholar for the NN project and author of each textual note, has also prepared a checklist of editions of *Moby-Dick* (1976). His invaluable essay, "Melville and the World of Books" in Bryant's *Companion to Melville Studies*, is a richly detailed account of the development of Melville's reputation through successive editions of his text. In addition, Elizabeth Schultz has contributed essays to *Extracts* and *Leviathan* on illustrated editions of Melville works in general and of *Moby-Dick* in particular, an important but understudied form of the editorial extension of the Melville Text.

Because of the obscurity into which Melville's reputation had fallen, a complete, standardized edition of his works – both fiction and poetry, published and in manuscript – did not appear until Michael Sadleir's Constable edition of 1922–4. This

British publication based largely on American texts remained a standard until certain volumes in the Hendricks House series (including *Omoo, Mardi, Moby-Dick, Pierre, Piazza Tales, Clarel,* and the poems) first appearing in the late 1940s began to supplant it. Textually erratic, these volumes remain valuable largely for their introductions and annotations. The current standard edition is *The Writings of Herman Melville,* edited by Harrison Hayford, Hershel Parker, and G. Thomas Tanselle, and published by Northwestern University Press and the Newberry Library. Thus far, this exemplary and indispensable editorial project has issued volumes on all of the published fiction; the serialized tales, essays, lectures, and reviews; the correspondence, the journals, and the epic poem *Clarel.* Each volume offers in its appendix an apparatus that displays the textual variants of each version of the featured work as well as a list of those variants and emendations the editors chose to adopt for their text. Still to be published in this series are the remaining published poems, soon to appear in one volume, the late manuscripts (including the rest of Melville's poetry and *Billy Budd, Sailor*), and a descriptive bibliography.

But even when these final volumes appear, the editing of Melville will not be "done," for given the nature of textuality, editing itself is an endless, critical process. Just as successive generations develop new notions of textuality, so will they find new ways to edit Melville. In fact, one announced goal of the NN edition is to make sure that its textual information is available for future editors to reconfigure into differently edited texts, organized on critical principles different from those used by the NN editors. Good editing inspires and begets re-editing. This may sound disturbing to readers who assume texts are fixed things, but as editors know and readers are coming to know, texts are fluid and cannot be fixed; they can only be managed and displayed in reliable ways.

The reliability of any modern scholarly edition, like the NN project, depends upon its adherence to announced critical and editorial principles. Its reliability is also enhanced to the degree in which it informs readers of variant versions and engages readers in its editorial decisions. In making an edition, editors invariably confront revision sites in a text in which variant words must be either adopted or put aside. In some cases, in which a text does not make sense, the editor may decide to supply language of his or her own. However a textual dilemma may be resolved, the editor is obliged to follow his or her pre-established principles of editing. Following the Greg Bowers tradition of editing, the NN edition presents a text designed to approximate the editors' conception of Melville's "final intention" for a given work. In this approach, intentionality is limited to a single stage of creative finalization independent of publishers, marketplace considerations, or reviewers; and this stage is best represented by a fair-copy manuscript submitted to an editor. But for Melville, such fair copies no longer exist, and first-edition texts must serve as the closest representation of this "final" moment of intentionality. And since works like *Typee* and *Moby-Dick* exist in variant first American and British editions, both of which contain words arguably representative of Melville's final intention, the NN editors adopt wordings from either version at certain places in the text. The result is an "eclectic edition" that essentially conflates separate historical versions into one modern version that Melville never witnessed, although theoretically might have wanted.

While in most cases the NN editors' application of the eclectic approach is astute and critically justifiable, the approach itself can be and has been challenged in a couple of ways. First, Melville surely had a plurality of intentions in writing works as structurally complex as, let us say, *Typee*, and the revisions he may have performed in moving from manuscript to the first British edition, or from his first American edition to his revised edition, certainly represent several sets of "final" intentions. Thus, his change from *indignantly* to *convulsively* (discussed at the beginning of this chapter) may be linked to shifting family conditions, so that both are equally valid, and both "final" for the moment in which they appear. However, the change from *literally interpreted* to *liberally interpreted* in the same work called *Typee* (103) may be merely a correction back to an original intention, or a change of mind with significant political ramifications. Our inability to know for certain the direction of Melville's shifting intentions severely complicates any attempt to reduce the text of *Typee* to one or the other option, or to mix in eclectic fashion the intentions of the first set of variants with the intentions of the second, which the NN edition of *Typee* does when it prints *indignantly* from the British edition and *liberally* from the American revised edition.

A second concern over the eclectic approach is that apart from the problem of intentionality, the NN edition represents a notion of the Melville Text that is allowed to transcend its own historical moment. In their days, both *Typee* and *Moby-Dick* were expurgated, and no one wants to read a censored Melville; but, in fact, the historical American readers of *Typee* and the historical British readers of *Moby-Dick* did read censored Melville texts, and those censorings tell us a great deal about Melville's readership and culture. The NN edition gives us a clear reading text (one without any editorial markings) that rightly restores all expurgations, but it is a text that purports to be freed from the coercions of historical editors, politicized reader responses, and the marketplace, a condition which Melville never experienced. If we want to read Melville with some sense of the historical fact that his texts were in fact coerced, we would have to re-edit the Melville Text to reflect, in some way, the very social pressures that the NN edition seeks to transcend.

Of course, readers seeking this kind of "Social Text," to use Jerome McGann's apt term, should know that abundant evidence of the expurgations of both *Typee* and *Moby-Dick* exists in each volume's textual apparatus located in the appendix. Unfortunately, when trade and college text publishers seek permission to reprint the NN edition texts for *Typee* and *Moby-Dick* (or any Melville work), they reprint the clear reading text but invariably drop the textual apparatus. Thus, with such truncated, popular and college text editions, readers have no way of knowing where *Typee* or *Moby-Dick* was expurgated, or where Melville might have revised a word, or where modern editors might have made up a word of their own. When marketers for such truncations claim that the text is "definitive" or "authoritative," readers are made even more vulnerable, for they also have no way of knowing that these edited texts represent a fluid and in effect indefinite textual condition and that the "author" did not "authorize" any of them. Thus, editors are made invisible, and their work – a highly sophisticated critical interpretation in the form of a modern conflation of separate historical versions – is made out in the marketplace to be something that it is not. Once again, but in unexpected ways, the marketplace conspires to deliver us *less* of the Melville Text than we hope to experience, even as it purports to give us more.

Without a doubt the NN edition is a landmark in Melville scholarship, and its clear reading texts are the recognized standard for this *Companion*, the *Companion* I have edited, and for that matter, any serious critical study involving Melville. And given the wealth of its textual apparatus, it is also the foundation for subsequent editorial projects. Hershel Parker's "Kraken Edition" of *Pierre* (illustrated by Maurice Sendak) is a case in point. Following his theory that Melville, angered by negative reviews of *Moby-Dick*, altered his writing of *Pierre* by satirizing the literary establishment and converting Pierre into a thwarted writer, Parker attempts to reconstruct a version of Melville's initial conception of the work (a gothic psychological novel) by paring away the satiric and writerly sections from the standard NN text. Given the absence of any manuscript, and given that an infinite range of possible textual stages might have occurred up to the point of Melville's angry reaction to his reviewers, there is no assurance that Parker's reduced text constitutes a version that corresponds to what Melville might have originally conceived *Pierre* to be (see *Fluid Text* Ch. 6). Nevertheless, in this case, *less* Melville can be seen as a kind of *more*, for the Kraken *Pierre* shakes us out of a certain textual complacency regarding the alleged stability of print texts. Properly speaking, Parker's version of *Pierre* is a simulacrum, a print fragment that is less an edition of what Melville's novel might have been and more a symbol of process, reminding us that Melville typically altered his intentions for a text, as he composed. It amounts, in any case, to a kind of rewriting of Melville.

But as I have noted, rewriting is what editors do. In my own editorial work, I have attempted to give presence to the revision steps that Melville most certainly had to have performed, if not directly on paper then mentally as he inhabited the language during the act of composition. In writing out these otherwise inaccessible features of Melville's fluid text, I want to show, editorially, that there is, in fact, more to the Melville Text than we have previously known. I have done this in various formats. In editing the poem "Art," based on Robert Ryan's work, for instance, in *Melville's Tales, Poems, and Other Writings*, I have laid out the growth of that poem, from an epigram to a "truncated sonnet" of varying lengths, in six discrete versions derived from the poem's multilayered manuscript. In my Random House edition of *The Confidence-Man*, I have included a lengthy revision sequence and revision narrative representing Melville's step-by-step revisions of an important paragraph on originality in Chapter 14. My Penguin edition of *Typee* includes my transcription of the *Typee* manuscript, a fraction of the electronic archive located in the University of Virginia Press's Rotunda edition of the manuscript appearing on-line. And the new Longman Critical Edition of *Moby-Dick* (2006), edited by myself and Haskell Springer, varies from the NN text in that it offers an emulation of the first American edition with the various sites of revision and expurgation marked with light gray screening over the text and with each site explained in an accompanying revision narrative.

The Melville Text in the Digital Age

The next era in the editing of Melville is the Melville Electronic Library (MEL), conceived by Bryant and Springer, and still in its conceptual stages. In this on-line site, users will have more access than ever before to the Melville Text in its entirety: it will include digitized images of letters, journals, and manuscript, with accompanying transcriptions and, where applicable, revision sequences and narratives; electronic versions of all published works, with links to first, revised, and scholarly editions; and source materials and marginalia. The idea is to create a space where readers can witness Melville's textual world. Therefore, MEL will include "rooms" where users can explore Melville's visual world: the art works he viewed in museums and lectured on, the prints he collected, and art and illustration that his works have generated in other artists. To accommodate the Melville Text to its fullest, most fluid extent, still other rooms will be opened to display adaptations of Melville works in children's books, comic books, single-panel cartoons, stage plays, radio, TV and film productions, musical performances, and opera. In a sense, such a room demonstrates a culture's insistence upon revising and rewriting Melville. The rooms of the Melville Electronic Library are places where readers can witness the heretofore unwitnessable text of revision in Melville's work and in the works Melville inspired. It is one large fluid text, still evolving.

Reading and Writing are an intimate pair: Writers read in order to write, and they read their own words when they revise what they write. Readers write the texts they read when they offer up interpretations, or so Stanley Fish tells us. But more than this, readers take Melville's text and rewrite it, physically, when they quote, and in quoting they create a version of Melville, one that fits a thesis or supports an idea or simply "says it like it is." This quoted Melville is that reader's own private Melville, and hence a rewriting of Melville. Still more, and for whatever reason, readers angered by Melville will expurgate him to make him cleaner or less offensive; and editors will strategize to display him one way or another; and readers infatuated with him will abridge him for children; and playwrights equally in love will convert him for the stage; and musical composers will transform his text into sounds or songs; sculptors will bend metal with him in mind. Each new creation is a rewriting is a revision is a version. The Melville Electronic Library will be a place on-line where readers can witness and have access to this fluid Melville Text.

Reading is a form of possession. In reading Melville, we fall into a world of texts, and, caught in this world, we are his. But in reading, we also possess him; he is ours. We remake his text in our own image when we interpret, and we rewrite him in our quotations, editions, and adaptations. Our versions of Melville extend and expand the Melville Text. And in turn: the Melville Text is a measure of ourselves.

References and Further Reading

Blanck, Jacob. "Herman Melville." In *Bibliography of American Literature*, vol. 6. New Haven, CT: Yale University Press, 1955–.

Bryant, John. *The Fluid Text: A Theory of Revision and Editing for Book and Screen*. Ann Arbor: University of Michigan Press, 2002.

——. *Melville Unfolding: Typee as Fluid Text*. Ann Arbor: University of Michigan Press, forthcoming 2007.

Fish, Stanley. "Interpreting the *Variorum*." In *Is There a Text in This Class?: The Authority of Interpretive Communities*. Cambridge, MA: Harvard University Press, 1980. 147–73.

Higgins, Brian, and Hershel Parker. "The Flawed Grandeur of Melville's *Pierre*." In *New Perspectives on Melville*. Ed. Faith Pullin. Kent, OH, and Edinburgh: Kent State University Press and Edinburgh University Press, 1978.

Howard, Leon. "Historical Note." In *Typee*. *The Writings of Herman Melville*. Vol. 1. Ed. Harrison Hayford, Hershel Parker, and G. Thomas Tanselle. Evanston and Chicago: Northwestern University Press and the Newberry Library, 1968.

McGann, Jerome. *Social Values and Poetic Acts: The Historical Judgment of Literary Work*. Cambridge, MA: Harvard University Press, 1988.

Ryan, Robert C. "Melville Revises 'Art.' " In *Melville's Evermoving Dawn: Centennial Essays*. Ed. John Bryant and Robert Milder. Kent, OH: Kent State University Press, 1997.

Schultz, Elizabeth. "Re-viewing Melville: The Illustrated Editions." *Melville Society Extracts* 103 (December 1995): 1–18.

——. "Visualizing *Moby-Dick*." *Leviathan: A Journal of Melville Studies* 3.1 (March 2001): 31–60.

Tanselle, G. Thomas. *A Checklist of Editions of Moby-Dick: 1851–1976*. Evanston and Chicago: Northwestern University Press and the Newberry Library, 1976.

——. "Historical Note, VI." In *Moby-Dick. The Writings of Herman Melville*. Vol. 6. Ed. Harrison Hayford, Hershel Parker, and G. Thomas Tanselle. Evanston and Chicago: Northwestern University Press and the Newberry Library, 1988.

——. "Melville and the World of Books." In *A Companion to Melville Studies*. Ed. John Bryant. Westport, CT: Greenwood Press, 1986.

Melville Editions (in chronological order)

Constable. *The Works of Herman Melville*. Ed. Michael Sadleir. 16 vols. London: Constable, 1922–4. Rpt. New York: Russell & Russell, 1963; Tokyo, 1983.

Hendricks House. *The Complete Works of Herman Melville*. 7 vols. to date. Ed. Howard Vincent (*Poems*), Vincent and Luther Mansfield (*Moby-Dick*), Henry A. Murray (*Pierre*), Egbert Oliver (*Piazza Tales*), Walter Bezanson (*Clarel*), Harrison Hayford and Walter Blair (*Omoo*), Nathalia Wright (*Mardi*). Chicago (later New York): Hendricks House, 1947–.

Northwestern–Newberry. *The Writings of Herman Melville*. Ed. Harrison Hayford, Hershel Parker, and G. Thomas Tanselle. 13 vols. to date. (All published books, the short prose works, journals, correspondence.) Evanston and Chicago: Northwestern University Press and the Newberry Library, 1968–.

Parker, Hershel, ed. *Pierre; Or, the Ambiguities*. Pictures by Maurice Sendak. Kraken Edition. New York: HarperCollins, 1995.

Bryant, John, ed. *Melville's Tales, Poems, and Other Writings*. Modern Library Edition. New York: Random House, 2001. *The Confidence-Man: His Masquerade*. Modern Library Edition, 2003. *Typee*. Penguin Classics Edition, 1996, 2005.

Herman Melville's Typee: *A Fluid-Text Edition*. University of Virginia: Rotunda, 2006. http://rotunda.upress.virginia.edu.

Index

Entries in bold face refer to main treatment of topics in chapter and section headings.